SELLING

Building Partnerships

SELLING

Building Partnerships

Stephen B. Castleberry
University of Minnesota Duluth

John F. Tanner Jr.
Baylor University

10

Mc Graw Hill Education

SELLING: BUILDING PARTNERSHIPS, TENTH EDITION

Published by McGraw-Hill Education, 2 Penn Plaza, New York, NY 10121.

This book is printed on acid-free paper.

1 2 3 4 5 6 7 8 9 0 LWI 22 21 20 19 18

ISBN 978-1-259-57320-0 (bound edition)
MHID 1-259-57320-6 (bound edition)
ISBN 978-1-260-14121-4 (loose-leaf edition)
MHID 1-260-14121-7 (loose-leaf edition)

Portfolio Manager: *Meredith Fossel*
Product Developer: *Laura Hurst Spell*
Marketing Manager: *Robin Lucas*
Content Project Managers: *Rick Hecker and Rachel Townsend*
Buyer: *Laura Fuller*
Design: *Jessica Cuevas*
Content Licensing Specialist: *Lori Slattery*
Cover Image: ©*Tom Merton/Getty Images RF*
Compositor: *Lumina Datamatics, Inc.*

All credits appearing on page or at the end of the book are considered to be an extension of the copyright page.

Library of Congress Cataloging-in-Publication Data

Names: Castleberry, Stephen Bryon, author. | Tanner, John F., author.
Title: Selling : building partnerships / Stephen B. Castleberry, University of Minnesota Duluth John F. Tanner, Jr., Baylor University.
Description: Tenth edition. | New York, NY : McGraw-Hill Education, [2019]
Identifiers: LCCN 2017049553 | ISBN 9781259573200 (alk. paper)
Subjects: LCSH: Selling.
Classification: LCC HF5438.25 .W2933 2018 | DDC 658.85–dc23
LC record available at https://lccn.loc.gov/2017049553

mheducation.com/highered

To Norah, Declan, Margaret, Caleb, April, Reuben, and Asher; you've brought so much joy to my life. And to my Creator, Redeemer and Friend, without whom I would be nothing.

–Steve Castleberry

To Karen–you make all the hard work worthwhile.

–Jeff Tanner

PREFACE

The 10th edition—wow! We are so grateful to you, sales faculty, sales professionals, and students, who have supported us through 10 editions. So much has changed over those editions. From written proposals to e-mails and chat, from Rolodexes to CRM systems, the field has evolved in many ways.

Still, we've remained faithful to the premises that caused us to write the first edition more than 25 years ago:

- We don't want to teach the history of selling—we want our students to know how it is done now and why, so that as the field continues to change, they will be prepared.
- Partnering skills are critical skills for all businesspeople.
- Adaptive communication skills—probing, listening, and presentation—are important in all areas of life but especially for salespeople.
- Students need to practice these skills through role playing.
- Helping people make the right decisions is not only the most ethical sales strategy but also the most effective strategy for long-term success.

At the same time, we've recognized that several factors are changing the face of selling:

- Increased use of multichannel go-to-market strategies, including inside sales.
- Changing roles for both technology and salespeople.
- Changing trends in how organizations buy, specifically the increasing use of technology, self-service, and presale search.
- Economic cycles, global political forces, and new company forms.

As we've revised the text, faithful adopters will see that we've held to the principles that made this book unique when it was launched and kept it in a leadership position. While others may have tried to copy role playing, partnering, or technology, none have truly captured the essence that makes this book the leading text.

WHAT'S NEW IN THE TENTH EDITION

- **Original examples** written specifically for this book. We have been blessed to have the support of sales faculty and salespeople around the world, many of whom took the class and used this book.
- New chapter-opening **profiles**—all chapters open with a real salesperson or sales manager's perspective on the chapter. Each profile is new and original to this edition, and we've also integrated the profiles into each chapter as a running example to increase this feature's functionality.
- All-new **"Building Partnerships"**—boxed features that provide more detailed examples of chapter material and present chapter material in a slightly different light.
- New **"Sales Technology"**—boxed features in each chapter, most new to this edition, that illustrate how technology is used and some of the challenges that technology creates. Whether it is CRM, campaign management, or GIS tools, students will be introduced to new technology here.
- All-new **"From the Buyer's Seat"**— technology, economy, politics—all of these affect buyers, too. In each chapter, we offer a boxed feature that highlights the world of the buyer, aiding future salespeople in understanding that world.
- **Feature questions**—embedded in the end-of-chapter material are discussion questions that direct students back to the profiles, "Building Partnerships," "From the Buyer's Seat," and "Sales Technology" features so these features are read and used more fully.
- New **Role Plays**—we've written a new set of role plays featuring Purina ONE SmartBlend and Gartner. Purina ONE SmartBlend is a pet food product line, and you can use this if you want to use simple role plays that span both trade sales and sales to users (kennels, animal shelters, and so on). Gartner is a consultancy that primarily serves the CIO. it is the new sponsor and product used in the National

Collegiate Sales Competition, with whom we are working so that your students can maximize their time on developing their sales skills and not learning a plethora of products for various competitions. This set of role plays can be a bit more complicated. Each set (Purina and Gartner) have 10 prospect scenarios (with two buyer information sheets each in the Instructor's Manual) at the end of the book. If you would like to sell something different, let us know by e-mailing Jeff directly: jtanner@odu.edu.

- New **minicases**—each chapter has a new or significantly revised minicase as well as favorite minicases to choose from.

IMPORTANT FEATURES OF *SELLING: BUILDING PARTNERSHIPS*

Customer loyalty, customer lifetime value, the Challenger Sales model—all are influencing the way sales is done and taught. We believe that the partnering approach continues to be the best overall way to learn how to sell, particularly in the broader context of undergraduate education. Several unique features place this book at the cutting edge of sales technology and partnering research:

1. A continued emphasis on the partnering process, with recognition that multiple sales models may be appropriate in a company's total go-to-market strategy. We focus on the partnering process as the highest level of selling because the other models of transaction—focus, problem solver, and relational partner—still need to be learned as a foundation to partnering, and the partnering process fits the value-driven sales models currently in use in the field.
2. A thorough description of the partnering and buying processes used by business firms and the changes occurring in these processes. A number of important trends affecting buyers, such as more rigorous online research and social media use, also affect sellers.
3. A discussion of methods of internal and external partnering so that the value chain delivers the right value, in recognition of the salesperson's role in relationship management and value creation. This emphasis also broadens the applicability of the course for students who may not be interested in a sales career.
4. An emphasis throughout the text on the need for salespeople to be flexible—to adapt their strategies to customer needs, buyer social styles, and relationship needs and strategies.
5. A complete discussion of how effective selling and career growth are achieved through planning and continual learning.
6. An emphasis on the growing need for salespeople in organizations to carry the voice of the customer to all parts of the organization and beyond to suppliers and facilitators. This role is reflected in new product development, supply chain management, and many other functions in a customer-centric organization.

These unique content emphases are presented in a highly readable format, supported by the following:

- **Ethics questions**—at least two questions at the end of each chapter relate the chapter material to ethics.
- **Four-color exhibits and photographs**—these support the examples highlighted in the book. Students find this book easy to read and use.
- **"Thinking It Through"**—these features embed discussion questions into the text itself; for this edition, we've also offered teaching suggestions to integrate this feature more fully. There are several of these features in each chapter.
- **Minicases**—two small cases are available at the end of each chapter. These are useful for in-class exercises or discussion or as homework. In this edition, you'll find one new or revised minicase in each chapter.
- **Ethics icon**—because we've emphasized ethical partnering since the inception of this book, we highlight the integration of ethics by noting any ethics discussion with an icon in the margin. You'll find ethics discussed in every chapter.
- **Selling Yourself**—a feature at the end of each chapter that relates the material in the chapter to the student's life *right now*. It's more than just the student's job search process, however. Selling Yourself helps students see the connections between chapter material and all aspects of their lives, such as how a student can sell an organization to new members, working with apartment managers to resolve issues, interacting with friends and family members, how to add value as a group member in a class team project, and so forth.
- **Key terms**—each key term defined in a chapter is listed at the end of the chapter, along with the page number on which the term is discussed. Key terms reflect current usage of sales jargon in the field, as well as academic terms.
- **Glossary**—key terms are also defined in a glossary at the end of the book.

FOR FACULTY

Instructor's manuals are available with any text, but the quality often varies. Because we teach the course to undergraduates and graduates, as well as presenting and participating in sales seminars in industry, we believe that we have created an Instructor's Manual (available in the Connect Instructor Resources connect.mheducation.com) that can significantly assist the teacher. We've also asked instructors what they would like to see in a manual. Based on their feedback, we include suggested course outlines, chapter outlines, lecture suggestions, and answers to questions and cases. On that site, you'll also find the slides, which are integrated into our teaching notes.

- **Slides** are available in PowerPoint, but given feedback from users (and our own experience), we've simplified their presentation. They are easily adapted to your own needs, and you can add material as you see fit.
- We also include many of the **in-class exercises** we have developed over the years. These have been subjected to student critique, and we are confident you will find them useful. You will also find a number of **additional role play scenarios.**
- Students need to practice their selling skills in a selling environment, and they need to do it in a way that is helpful. **Small group practice exercises, including role playing,** complete with instructions for student evaluations, are provided in the Instructor's Manual. These sessions can be held as part of class but are also designed for out-of-class time for teachers who want to save class time for full-length role plays.
- The **Test Bank** has been carefully and completely rewritten. Questions are directly tied to the learning goals presented at the beginning of each chapter and the material covered in the questions and problems. In addition, key terms are covered in the test questions. Application questions are available so students can demonstrate their understanding of the key concepts by applying those selling principles.

PARTNERING: FROM THE FIELD TO THE CLASSROOM

Faculty who use our book have reviewed it and offered suggestions, and we have taken their comments seriously. What is different is that sales executives and field salespeople who are locked in the daily struggle of adapting to the new realities of selling also reviewed *Selling: Building Partnerships*. They have told us what the field is like now, where it is going, and what students must do to be prepared for the challenges that will face them.

Students have also reviewed chapters. They are, after all, the ones who must learn from the book. We asked for their input prior to and during the revision process. And judging by their comments and suggestions, this book is effectively delivering the content. There are, however, several places where their comments have enabled us to clarify material and improve on its presentation.

As you can see in "About the Authors," we have spent considerable time in the field in a variety of sales positions. We continue to spend time in the field engaging in personal selling ourselves, as well as observing and serving professional salespeople. We believe the book has benefited greatly because of such a never-ending development process.

Acknowledgments

Staying current with the rapidly changing field of professional selling is a challenge. Our work has been blessed with the excellent support of reviewers, users, editors, salespeople, and students.

Reviewers include the following:

Ellen P. Daniels, Kent State University
Maria McConnell, Lorain County Community College
Vicki West, Texas State University
Susan Yarrington Young, Eastern Michigan University

Readers will become familiar with many of the salespeople who contributed to the development of the tenth edition through various selling scenarios or profiles. But other salespeople, sales executives, buyers, and sales professors contributed in less obvious, but no less important, ways. For reviewing chapters, updating cases, providing material for selling scenarios, and other support, we'd like to thank the following:

Drew Bauer, University of Minnesota Duluth
Seth Bleiler, 3M
Chareen Bogner, McKesson
Brendan Brooks
Travis Bruns, Crown Lift
Lindsey Buran
Justin Carter, Hewlett Packard Enterprise
Christian Caywood, University of Minnesota Duluth
Rebecca Clark, Hilton Garden Inn Schaumburg
Christine Cortina, Enterprise Fleet Management
Bruce Culbert, Pedowitz Group
Taylor Dixon, 3M
Kimberly Drumm, ESI
Chad Engle, GILLIG, LLC
Dr. Bob Erffmeyer, University of Wisconsin-Eau Claire
Brenda Finlayson, ESI
Sean Fulton, Oracle
Molly Gilleland, Comcast Spotlight
Zachary Goss, Tom James Company
Mary Gros, Teradata
Sheena Guzzo
Rikki Ingram, Smithfield Foods
Beth Jeanetta
Dennis Jensen, Duluth Transit Authority
Rob Keeney, Keeney Sales Training
Jim Keller, Teradata

Eric LaBelle, Vista Outdoor
Matt Leaf
Jessica Lehrer
Karl Macalincag, GDP Technologies
Eddy Patterson, Stubb's Bar-B-Q
Juan Guillermo Peredo, Technodent S.R.L.
Taylor Price, TravelClick
Mike Rausch, Fastenal
Mike Rocker, 3M
Spencer Ryan, Stryker
Camille Sandler, ACell Inc.
Kristen Scott, Oracle
Tim Simmons, Teradata
Camille Sandler, ACell Inc.
Emeritus Professor Karl Sooder, University of Central Florida
Dr. Jeff Strieter, State University of New York College-Brockport
John Tanner, Southwest Airlines
Dr. Brian Tietje, California Polytechnic State University
David Timmons, Fastenal
R.J. Zimmerman, The Aspire Group

In addition to the support of these individuals, many companies also provided us with material. We'd like to express our sincere gratitude for their support.

The McGraw-Hill team, as is the usual, was wonderful to work with. Our greatest interaction during manuscript preparation was with Jennifer Blankenship, development editor, and we appreciate her quick response and dogged determination to make sure we turn out a great product. Rick Hecker, our content project manager, is another important contributor to the physical product and the team who makes sure that what you are holding in your hands meets the standards set so high in our previous editions. Laura Hurst Spell, our associate portfolio manager, and Robin Lucas, our director of marketing manager, also make sure the product is excellent and then help us communicate that to the market. We really appreciate their efforts on our behalf.

Several people assisted in research and manuscript preparation, and we gratefully appreciate their help: Bryant Duong and W. T. Tanner. Many students and teachers have made comments that have helped us strengthen the overall package. They deserve our thanks, as do others who prefer to remain anonymous.

–Steve Castleberry

–Jeff Tanner

ABOUT THE AUTHORS

STEPHEN B. CASTLEBERRY

Courtesy of Stephen B. Castleberry

Dr. Castleberry received his PhD from the University of Alabama in 1983. He taught at the University of Georgia for six years and for three years was UARCO Professor of Sales and Marketing at Northern Illinois University. Currently he is a professor of marketing and business ethics at the University of Minnesota Duluth. He has received eight awards for teaching excellence, including the best teacher award at his university and the Morse Award, the highest recognition by the University of Minnesota system of its most distinguished scholar teachers. His commitment to teaching has resulted in a number of cases, as well as articles in the *Journal of Marketing Education, Business Case Journal, Journal of Business Ethics Education*, and *Marketing Education Review*, that describe his teaching style and methods.

Dr. Castleberry's research has been published in over 50 journals such as the *Journal of Personal Selling and Sales Management, Industrial Marketing Management, Journal of Business Ethics, Journal of Selling and Major Account Management, Journal of Business and Industrial Marketing, Journal of Business to Business Marketing, Journal of Marketing Management, Journal of Consumer Marketing, Journal of Business Research, Journal of the Academy of Marketing Science*, and *International Journal of Research in Marketing*. He has also presented his work at the National Conference in Sales Management, as well as other national and regional conferences. He is past marketing editor of the *Journal of Applied Business Research* and serves on several journal editorial boards. He has received research grants and support from entities such as the London Business School, Gillette, Quaker Oats, Kimberly-Clark, Procter & Gamble, Coca-Cola Foods Division, and the Alexander Group/JPSSM.

Dr. Castleberry appeared as an academic expert in eight segments of *The Sales Connection*, a 26-segment video production shown on national PBS TV stations. He also appeared as the special guest on several broadcasts of *Sales Talk*, a nationally broadcast call-in talk show on the Business Radio Network.

Dr. Castleberry has held various sales assignments with Burroughs Corporation (now Unisys), Nabisco, and G.C. Murphy and has worked as a consultant and sales trainer for numerous firms and groups. His interests outside academic life include outdoor activities (canoeing, hiking, bicycling, skiing, and so on) and everything related to living on his 100-acre farm in northern Wisconsin. For 19 years and still counting he has been a volunteer firefighter and for 10 years served as a medical first responder in the small township he lives in. He and his wife currently own and operate a publishing company, marketing and distributing popular press books internationally.

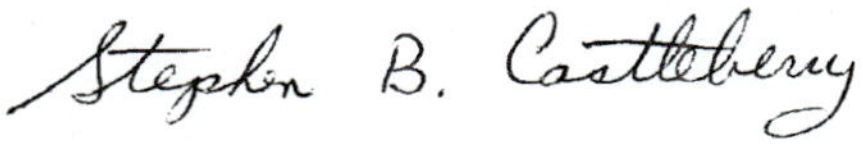

scastleb@d.umn.edu
www.d.umn.edu/˜scastleb

JOHN F. TANNER JR.

Courtesy of John Tanner

Dr. Tanner is dean, Strome College of Business, Old Dominion University. He earned his PhD from the University of Georgia. Prior to entering academia, Dr. Tanner spent eight years in industry with Rockwell International and Xerox Corporation as both salesperson and marketing manager.

Dr. Tanner has received several awards for teaching effectiveness and research, including the Distinguished Teacher award from the Society of Marketing Advances. He has also been named Reviewer of the Year and coauthor of the Paper of the Year by the *Journal of Personal Selling and Sales Management*. Dr. Tanner has authored or coauthored 15 books, including *The Hard Truth about Soft Selling* with George Dudley. His book, *Dynamic Customer Strategy: Big Profits from Big Data*, was published in 2014 and in Chinese in 2015.

Research grants from the Center for Exhibition Industry Research, the Institute for the Study of Business Markets, the University Research Council, the Walmart Foundation, and others have supported his research efforts. Dr. Tanner has published over 80 articles in the *Journal of Marketing, Journal of Business Research, Journal of Personal Selling and Sales Management,* international journals, and others. Twice, he has served as special issue editor for JPSSM and he is currently the editor of *Marketing Educators' Review*. He serves on the review boards of several journals, including *Marketing Education Review, Journal of Personal Selling and Sales Management, and Industrial Marketing Management.*

Dr. Tanner has been a featured presenter at executive workshops and conferences for organizations such as the Marketing Science Institute, National Retail Federation, Canadian Association of Exhibition Managers, and Oracle's OpenWorld. Over the past 10 years, he has taught executive and graduate programs in India, Australia, Trinidad, Colombia, Canada, France, the United Kingdom, and Mexico, and his consulting clients include IBM, Cabela's, EMC, SAP, and others. Jeff and his wife also breed and race thoroughbred horses.

jtanner@odu.edu
hsb.baylor.edu/html/tanner

Walkthrough

Selling: Building Partnerships remains the most innovative textbook in the selling course area today with its unique role plays and partnering skills which are critical skills for all businesspeople. The authors emphasize throughout the text the need for salespeople to be flexible–to adapt their strategies to customer needs, buyer social styles, and relationship needs and strategies. This is followed by a complete discussion of how effective selling and career growth are achieved through planning and continual learning. The 10th edition has been updated to continue its relevance in the selling market today just as it was more than 25 years ago.

The **chapter-opening profiles** in this edition are the product of strong selling partnerships. Faculty from around the country introduced Steve Castleberry and Jeff Tanner to their former students who had gone on to careers in sales. The results are exciting new profiles from sales professionals who were students with an earlier edition and understand the philosophy of this book. The profiles are also integrated into the chapter with additional examples involving the profiled salesperson and end-of-chapter questions. Students can easily relate to these young professionals who have benefited from wonderful faculty and *Selling: Building Partnerships.*

PROFILE

"Selling is a part of everyone's life, whether you realize it or not."

Zachary Goss, Tom James Company

PROFILE Selling is a part of everyone's life, whether you realize it or not. My name is Zachary Goss and I am a graduate of Texas State University–San Marcos with an undergraduate degree in business marketing and a masters in business administrations. In my undergraduate studies, I had the privilege of taking Mrs. Vicki West's professional selling class, where I discovered the amazing world of sales. I was a very competitive person growing up, being a triplet and playing sports all of my life, and sales seemed like the best way to stimulate my competitiveness.

Utilizing what I had learned in Mrs. West's class, I was able to sell myself to the Tom James Company and was hired as a sales professional upon graduation. This role required me to call on new prospects and maintain the relationship after the prospect became a client. The Tom James Company sells custom clothing directly to consumers. I call on new prospects and sell them on the idea to meet with me by conveying to them that I can save them time and money compared with how they are traditionally shopping for their clothing.

The interaction of the meeting is just as important, if not more, than the services and products I provide. I like to say that sales is the transfer of enthusiasm from the salesperson to the buyer. When I am enthusiastic and excited about the products and services I can provide, the buyer is more receptive and buys more often than when I'm not enthusiastic during the sales presentation. The decision maker has to trust the salesperson and realize the benefits and how they cover a need in order for an economic exchange to take place. If the buyer realizes the benefits and how they cover a need, but does not trust the salesperson, the buyer may go to another company that will offer similar benefits. If the buyer trusts the salesperson, but does not understand the benefits of the product/service or does not feel a need would be solved, then there is no value for the buyer to engage in an economic exchange.

Looking at the top sales performers in the company, I notice some similarities among them. They are excellent communicators in that they listen more than they talk, and seek to really understand the buyer's needs. They are continuously learning and enhancing their skills. They are creative in finding different ways to get in front of prospects and finding creative ways to solve problems. These traits benefit not only salespeople, but also all people in interviews, relationships, and everyday interactions.

Visit our Web site at: www.tomjames.com.

Courtesy of Zachary Goss

ETHICS PROBLEMS

1. Let's assume that as a salesperson for a logistics management company, you are a key channel manager and work with a number of supply chain vendors to help make sure your client, Home Depot, gets excellent value. While working closely with one channel member, Effective Inventory Management, Inc., you learned exactly how it completes an extensive inventory situation analysis. Given your newfound knowledge, should you suggest to your firm that it do the inventory situation analysis itself, thus negating the need to work with Effective Inventory Management, Inc. entirely? Basically, you would be using knowledge that you gained through your observations of Effective Inventory Management, Inc. You did not sign a nondisclosure agreement with that firm.
2. As a salesperson, two traits you have been trained to display are confidence and optimism. Let's say that one of your clients asked you, "I'm getting a little worried about your new model, the X15J. I thought we were going to see prototypes of it by January, and here it is late February and we've not seen anything. I'm about to hire some additional workers to help with installing those models this summer. Is it going to be released on time?" As the salesperson, you know that the X15J has hit some significant snags and there is not a definite timeline for its release at the present. But you don't want to jeopardize the verbal sales commitment from the buyer, thinking that the buyer might purchase from a competitor. So you answer, "Sure, Jason! That's what we've been promising and you know you can trust us. I have confidence in our new product development team. You should too!" What are your thoughts on this interaction?

Professional sales **ethics** have always been the hallmark of this text, and the new edition integrates ethics throughout each chapter, as well as in discussion questions devoted to this topic. Each chapter has separate ethics discussion questions, some of which were suggested by former students' experiences or current events.

Current and continued emphasis on selling examples from China, India, Europe, and all around the globe reflects the reality of the global nature of selling.

This American salesperson needs to recognize the differences between communicating in an Arab culture and an American culture.

©Image Source/ Getty Images RF

- Use common English words that a customer would learn during the first two years of studying the language. For example, use *expense* rather than *expenditure* or *stop* instead of *cease.*
- Use words that do not have multiple meanings. For example, *right* has many meanings, whereas *accurate* is more specific. When you use words that have several meanings, recognize that nonnative speakers will usually use the most common meaning to interpret what you are saying.
- Avoid slang expressions peculiar to American culture, such as *slice of life, struck out, wade through the figures,* and *run that by me again.*
- Use rules of grammar more strictly than you would in everyday speech. Make sure you express your thoughts in complete sentences, with a noun and a verb.
- Use action-specific verbs, as in *start the motor,* rather than action-general verbs, as in *get the motor going.*
- Never use vulgar expressions, tell off-color jokes, or make religious references.
- Expect that it may take longer to build trust and relationships.

SALES Technology 6.1

STREAMLINING PROSPECTING THROUGH THE USE OF BIG DATA

Given the competitive market today, sales organizations' success hinges on solutions to meet customers' needs. New technologies are helping streamline this process; analyzing large amounts of customer and prospect data, referred to as Big Data, provides specific insight into purchasing habits and needs of customers. Today, it is estimated that, on average, only 15 percent of data, that happens to be at a company's disposal, is actually analyzed.

While Big Data are not the only solution to effective prospecting, analytic tools can put salespeople on a more successful track to profitable prospecting. To effectively grow sales, research on which analytical data sources are the best to implement must still be conducted. The best strategy is to find a partner that can best offer a reliable data source to push prospecting efforts.

Traditional prospecting required cold calling, an outdated time-consuming and resource-intensive practice, and that was just to find leads who still needed qualifying. Then came the acquisition of contact lists by lead providers that sometimes resulted in wasted effort. Now, by the way of advanced technology and data analytics of customers and prospects, firms can identify potential customers who have a better chance of building a relationship and turning into a client. For example, companies in the biopharmacy industry are generating customer value analytics (CVA) using Big Data to help find the best way to approach leads and consistently meet the needs of omnichannel prospects and customers, all while lowing customer acquisition costs (CAC). Cold calling is now warm calling with the ability to build rapport to tailor a unique sales message and build long-lasting relationships.

Prospecting through Big Data develops leads in both B2C and B2B sales environments. Furthermore, Big Data help firms better know how to construct targeted messages and successfully predict how a buyer will probably respond to a sales presentation. In summary, Big Data provide a tool to help an organization become most efficient in gaining clients and achieving sales profitability.

Sources: Louis Columbus, "Ten Ways Big Data Is Revolutionizing Marketing and Sales," May 9, 2016, *Forbes.com*; Ilya Semin, Young Entrepreneur Council, "The Sales Shakeup: How Data Is Redefining Sales Prospecting," *The Huffington Post*, December 17, 2015

Many technologies, including the sales cloud (or Sales 3.0 technology), pad computers, GPS, the Internet, and CRM software, have changed how salespeople operate. The tenth edition includes all-new illustrations with its feature **"Sales Technology,"** which discusses how selling and technology interact within the context of each chapter.

"Thinking It Through" boxes (at least two per chapter) are engaging exercises that can inspire classroom dialogue or serve as a short-essay exam question to help students experience concepts as they read.

thinking it through Which do you think you would prefer: an inside sales job or a field sales job? What makes one more attractive to you than the other?

"From the Buyer's Seat" is an all-new original feature that provides students with a buyer's inside perspective. **"Building Partnerships"** boxes examine how successful salespeople build relationships. All are original to the book—many using examples provided by former students of faculty around the country. And all are discussed as part of the end-of-chapter questions so that you can fully integrate them into the class.

From the BUYER'S SEAT 4.1

CAN WE TALK?

Change is the new normal in retail; this is the main thing a sales representative needs to understand if he or she wants to grow my business and build a strong relationship with a buyer today.

I have been in purchasing for almost 10 years now. I have witnessed many sales representatives fail to navigate their business through the changing retail environment and shift in customer spending habits. The path for the few who do experience success is truly driven by strong communication skills and adaptation.

Strong communication skills in sales come down to timely, transparent, and direct two-way conversations. Conversations between parties (buyer and seller) can be through e-mail, text, in person, or phone call depending on the given circumstances. Here is an example of a strong business relationship and strong communication skills resulting in a positive sales outcome.

My business had been very turbulent, specifically in a particular shade of pink color tops. My customers were not consistently purchasing this color top and I was concerned that we had too much inventory and too much on the way in this color. Just about that same time, my vendor sent me a text to tell me he was concerned about production on a style of this color and he was going to work hard to maintain delivery for me. I asked him to call me and we discussed the current selling of the color along with his production concerns. Together we were able to work together to alleviate any risk by changing the color (a benefit for my customer) and working on an updating production timeline based on the change (a benefit for his team). It was a win-win for both.

I understand this example seems very simple. However, this is not always the route sales representatives take. Many reps will work really hard to make their customer happy and would not have reached out at the first sign of trouble ahead, instead opting to try to fix the problem. As a result of the timely and transparent communication of this sales representative we were able to collaborate to find a solution that benefited both of us and only strengthened our relationship.

Adaptation is critical in success as a sales representative in today's retail environment. In order to adapt, a sales representative must be open-minded and possess strong listening skills as well as communication skills. As retail is rapidly changing, the way a company does things and the way the customer purchases are evolving. Unfortunately, many sales representatives have a difficult time changing quickly enough to keep up with the retailer's needs or have a difficult time keeping up-to-date in communication. Here is an example of a sales representative who was one of my key representatives; now I no longer work with him as things changed:

Our customers had changed quickly. We simply were not evolving our trends fast enough to satisfy customer needs. We also found that our customers were frustrated that our product looked too similar to our competition's. The sales representative I worked with also sold to my competition and had a strong history with my company. This individual had grown familiar with looking at his own selling reports and what was selling at the competition to offer me suggestions on what to buy for my customers. I communicated to him that while that had worked for us for many years, our customers had changed, and I needed the supplier to evolve the product offering to be trendier. Our sales had slowed down and we needed to make a change. The sales rep did not want to change how he had worked with me. After each meeting I gave him the same feedback–I need to see newer product. Eventually the supplier communicated to me in a complaining manner about the decline in the sales of his product and I explained that he needed to change the way he was conducting business. He did not take this feedback seriously and continued to try to do things the way he had in the past without communicating to me and was not willing to work something out. Eventually, I had to tell the supplier that other sales representatives had been able to adapt to changing times and offer me newer product and had grown their business with us. I no longer needed to work with the original seller, as it was not offering me anything unique.

From my seat, the sales representatives that can focus on remaining open-minded and being transparent in their communication with their buyers will see their businesses grow. If a sales representative is unable to create this open dialogue relationship, it will be difficult for his or her to find success.

Sheena Guzzo personal correspondence, used with permission; other names kept confidential upon request.

BUILDING Partnerships 5.1

HOW I USED THE C LEVEL TO LEVERAGE A SALE

The highest-level executives at companies usually have titles that begin with the word *chief* (like chief executive officer, chief operating officer) resulting in a group of executives that is often simply referred to as the C-suite or C-level. Most salespeople are not comfortable selling at the C-level. There are many individual and organizational reasons for this, but my example will relate to my experience in a follow-up from an organizational meeting.

Initial stumbling blocks that I have experienced start with availability. How do I get the introduction; they won't return my call? Plus, there is the fear of creating friction with my current, lower-level contact by going around that individual. The greatest challenge I have, though, is fear or intimidation in getting the meeting and then having to present. Don't get me wrong! I'm not uncomfortable talking in front of other people, but what do I talk about, and how do I know what is important to them?

Selling a product or service to non-C-level types is fairly routine. My firm's marketing, product management, and other departments have provided all the right literature, samples, and talking points that the buyer or engineer is looking for when trying to better understand my product. I also have a myriad of additional competitive references, benchmarks, and examples of how other customers like them have gained efficiency, cost labor savings, and supply chain efficiencies. I'm confortable telling my story to lower-level buyers, and people like engineers, since I've a story to tell that I'm familiar with. I've created it and I'm comfortable telling it.

Now, what training or mentorship have I received on how to navigate the top-level executives? None, and the same is true of many other salespeople! I didn't fully realize the impact of this issue until I started joining organizations where the owners of my customers were attending. I wasn't in their office, but I was getting face time and was able to ask some informative questions. This was a dialog that was outside my typical points of discussion to a buyer or engineer. I wasn't selling these C-level people on product features, unless they specifically asked about some details. I had a colleague trying to hand out samples; it was poorly received, and I believe he was looked at only as a product information or order taker, not a partner to their business.

My approach was more fact finding on what was important to them, searching for their exact needs. I followed up by finding out who in their organization was responsible or would have the greatest impact that I should talk with.

Take this instance for reference: I attended a meeting for industrial packaging companies. Topics at the luncheon were around trends and industry conditions. I had listened and tried to make as many introductions to C-level people as I could. Weeks later I was in the lobby of my customer, Duravent, starting to walk back with my distributor and an engineer of Duravent. At that exact moment, the Duravent owner walked by, stopped to talk to me, and asked what I thought about our recent meeting. The impact was not product related, but I did have the full attention of the Duravent engineer for that next meeting! He did not ask about the relationship with the owner, but I could tell that he was influenced just by the fact that I apparently knew his bosses' boss. We were able to work through the design issues that morning and the Duravent engineer specified our product, and a sale was made!

Source: Anonymous, used with permission, names changed.

Class-tested **minicases** at the end of each chapter work well as daily assignments and as frameworks for lectures, discussion, or small group practice. Each chapter includes at least one new minicase. The cases encourage students to apply theories and skills learned in the text to solve sales situations.

case 9.2

Passport Health

Each year up to 20 percent of people suffer from the results of the flu. Thankfully there are vaccinations that can help reduce the incidence of the flu. The Centers for Disease Control and Prevention (CDC) claims, "The first and most important step in preventing flu is to get a flu vaccination each year." Yet many people claim they are just too busy to get to a clinic, or that the local drugstore that provides the vaccinations is too crowded. That's where Passport Health can help.

Passport Health will provide onsite flu clinics at your workplace. Trained nurses administer the shots, and Passport Health provides all of the coordination, administration, and any registration needed. The results should be fewer sick days and lower health care costs, which should result in a more efficient and productive workforce.

Assume you are a salesperson for Passport Health. Today you are calling on a large manufacturing plant (or service provider) in your area. You have never called on this organization before.

Questions

1. Create an effective story that can help strengthen your presentation. This story should help the buyer understand how important it is to get a flu vaccination. The story should be from your own experiences, or from experiences of others whom you personally know. In other words, don't just go to the Web and find a story. Your story might tell how someone suffered from the flu who didn't get a flu shot, or how someone avoided a common flu that was rampant because that person got the flu shot, or some other story that makes the point effectively.
2. Create a second effective story that can help strengthen your presentation. This story should help the buyer understand that clinics and storefront providers of flu shots are often crowded, or inconvenient in some way for the average "9 to 5" employee.

Students can practice their partnering skills in brand-new **role play exercises** that encourage personal growth and experiential learning. Each role play features Gartner, the company used in the National Collegiate Sales Competition. Also, new comprehensive role plays are available at the end of the book, featuring new products from Purina and Gartner, with additional role plays included in the Instructor's Manual.

ROLE PLAY CASE

At the end of each chapter, beginning just below this paragraph, you'll find a short role play exercise that focuses on Gartner. Gartner is a company that provides research and information services to other companies. To find more information on the product, view sales support materials, and more, visit www.gartner.com/ncsc. There is also additional material at the back of the book in the role play section.

Graduation is coming up soon so you've decided to get serious about interviewing. You went online to look at what's going on in your school's Career Services Center, where you saw a job posting for Gartner. Apparently it is some sort of business information and research services company, which also does consulting. You've always thought you'd enjoy consulting so you thought you'd sign up. Today is your interview. Be yourself; interview honestly as if you were truly talking with Gartner. To help you prepare for this job interview role play, you may want to take some time to find out about Gartner by visiting www.gartner.com for more information.

To the instructor: Additional information needed to complete the role play is available in the Instructor's Manual.

McGraw-Hill Connect® is a highly reliable, easy-to-use homework and learning management solution that utilizes learning science and award-winning adaptive tools to improve student results.

Homework and Adaptive Learning

- Connect's assignments help students contextualize what they've learned through application, so they can better understand the material and think critically.
- Connect will create a personalized study path customized to individual student needs through SmartBook®.
- SmartBook helps students study more efficiently by delivering an interactive reading experience through adaptive highlighting and review.

Connect's Impact on Retention Rates, Pass Rates, and Average Exam Scores

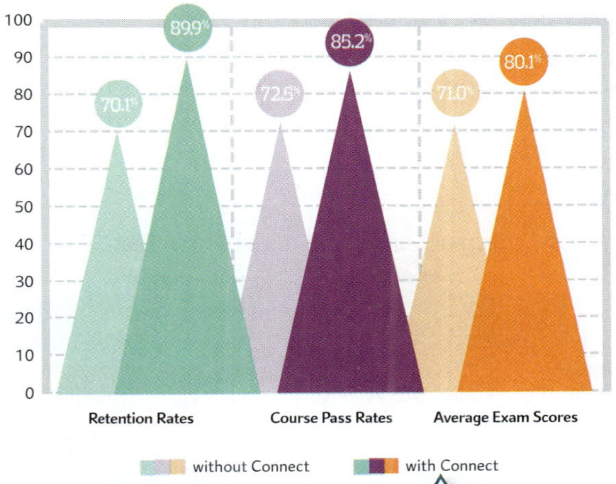

Over **7 billion questions** have been answered, making McGraw-Hill Education products more intelligent, reliable, and precise.

Using **Connect** improves retention rates by **19.8** percentage points, passing rates by **12.7** percentage points, and exam scores by **9.1** percentage points.

73% of instructors who use **Connect** require it; instructor satisfaction **increases** by 28% when **Connect** is required.

Quality Content and Learning Resources

- Connect content is authored by the world's best subject matter experts, and is available to your class through a simple and intuitive interface.
- The Connect eBook makes it easy for students to access their reading material on smartphones and tablets. They can study on the go and don't need internet access to use the eBook as a reference, with full functionality.
- Multimedia content such as videos, simulations, and games drive student engagement and critical thinking skills.

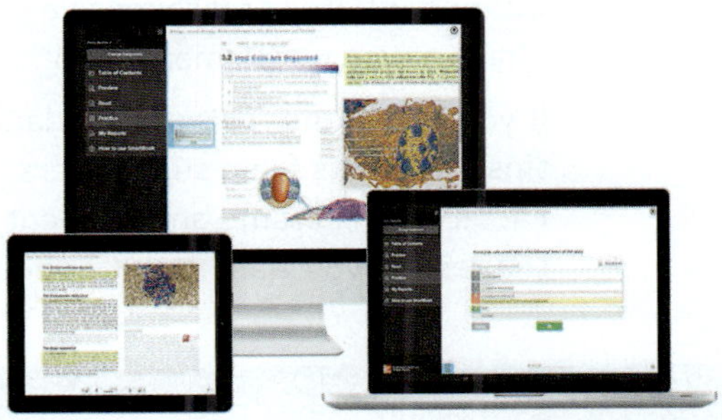

©McGraw-Hill Education

Robust Analytics and Reporting

©Hero Images/Getty Images

- Connect Insight® generates easy-to-read reports on individual students, the class as a whole, and on specific assignments.
- The Connect Insight dashboard delivers data on performance, study behavior, and effort. Instructors can quickly identify students who struggle and focus on material that the class has yet to master.
- Connect automatically grades assignments and quizzes, providing easy-to-read reports on individual and class performance.

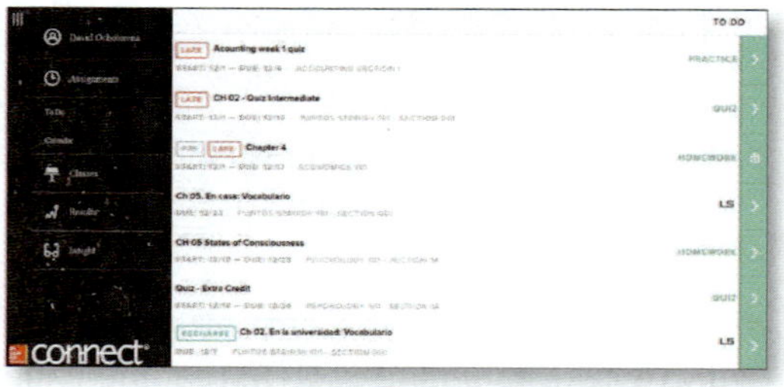

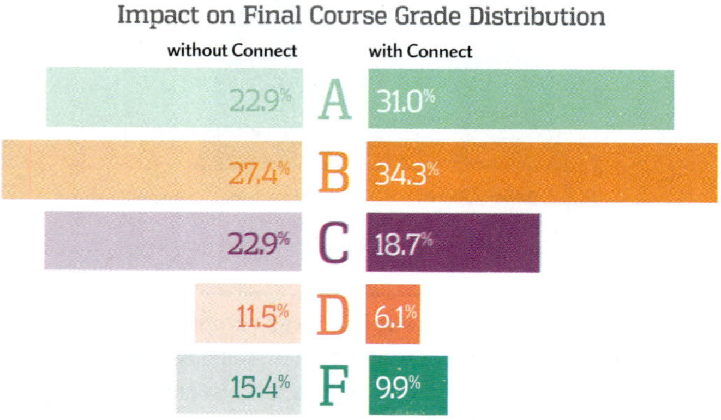

More students earn **As** and **Bs** when they use **Connect**.

Trusted Service and Support

- Connect integrates with your LMS to provide single sign-on and automatic syncing of grades. Integration with Blackboard®, D2L®, and Canvas also provides automatic syncing of the course calendar and assignment-level linking.
- Connect offers comprehensive service, support, and training throughout every phase of your implementation.
- If you're looking for some guidance on how to use Connect, or want to learn tips and tricks from super users, you can find tutorials as you work. Our Digital Faculty Consultants and Student Ambassadors offer insight into how to achieve the results you want with Connect.

CONTENTS IN BRIEF

Preface vi
Acknowledgments ix
About the Authors xi

Chapter 1
Selling and Salespeople 2

part 1

KNOWLEDGE AND SKILL REQUIREMENTS 28

Chapter 2
Ethical and Legal Issues in Selling 28

Chapter 3
Buying Behavior and the Buying Process 58

Chapter 4
Using Communication Principles to Build Relationships 92

Chapter 5
Adaptive Selling for Relationship Building 124

part 2

THE PARTNERSHIP PROCESS 146

Chapter 6
Prospecting 146

Chapter 7
Planning the Sales Call 174

Chapter 8
Making the Sales Call 198

Chapter 9
Strengthening the Presentation 228

Chapter 10
Responding to Objections 256

Chapter 11
Obtaining Commitment 286

Chapter 12
Formal Negotiating 318

Chapter 13
Building Partnering Relationships 344

Chapter 14
Building Long-Term Partnerships 370

part 3

THE SALESPERSON AS MANAGER 402

Chapter 15
Managing Your Time and Territory 402

Chapter 16
Managing within Your Company 432

Chapter 17
Managing Your Career 464

Role Play Case 1: Purina ONE SmartBlend Dog Food RP-1

Role Play Case 2: Gartner RP-6

Glossary G-1

Endnotes EN-1

Indexes I-1

CONTENTS

Preface vi
Acknowledgments ix
About the Authors xi

Chapter 1
Selling and Salespeople 2

Why Learn about Personal Selling? 4
Everyone Sells 5
Creating Value: The Role of Salespeople in a Business 6
What Do Salespeople Do? 8
Client Relationship Manager 8
Account Team Manager 10
Supply Chain Logistics and Channel Manager 10
Information Provider to Their Firm 10
Types of Salespeople 11
Selling and Distribution Channels 11
Describing Sales Jobs 14
The Sales Jobs Continuum 16
Examples of Sales Jobs 17
Characteristics of Successful Salespeople 17
Self-Motivated 18
Dependability and Trustworthiness 18
Integrity and Ethical Sales Behavior 18
Customer and Product Knowledge 18
Analytical Skills and the Ability to Use Information Technology 18
Communication Skills 19
Flexibility and Agility 19
Creativity 19
Confidence and Optimism 19
Emotional Intelligence 19
Are Salespeople Born or Made? 20
Rewards in Selling 20
Independence and Responsibility 20
Financial Rewards 20
Management Opportunities 21
The Building Partnerships Model 21
Selling Yourself 22
Summary 23
Key Terms 23
Ethics Problems 24
Questions and Problems 24
Case Problems 25
Role Play Case 27
Additional References 27

part 1

KNOWLEDGE AND SKILL REQUIREMENTS 28

Chapter 2
Ethical and Legal Issues in Selling 28

Ethics and Selling 30
The Evolution of Selling 31
Ethics and Partnering Relationships 32
Factors Influencing the Ethical Behavior of Salespeople 33
Selling Ethics and Relationships 37
Relationships with Customers 37
Relationships with the Salesperson's Company 41
Relationships with Colleagues 43
Relationships with Competitors 44
Legal Issues 44
Uniform Commercial Code 45
Misrepresentation or Sales Puffery 46
Illegal Business Practices 48
International Ethical and Legal Issues 51
Resolving Cultural Differences 51
Legal Issues 52
Selling Yourself 53
Summary 53
Key Terms 54
Questions and Problems 54
Case Problems 55
Role Play Case 57
Additional References 57

Chapter 3
Buying Behavior and the Buying Process 58
Why People Buy 60
Types of Customers 60
Manufacturers 60
Resellers 61
Government Agencies 62
Institutions 63
Consumers 63
Organizational Buying and Selling 64
Complexity of the Organizational Buying Process 64
Derived versus Direct Demand 65
How Do Organizations Make Buying Decisions? 65
Steps in the Buying Process 65
Creeping Commitment 67
Types of Organizational Buying Decisions 68
New Tasks 68
Straight Rebuys 69
Modified Rebuys 70
Who Makes the Buying Decision? 70
Users 71
Initiators 71
Influencers 71
Gatekeepers 72
Deciders 72
Supplier Evaluation and Choice 73
Organizational Needs and Criteria 74
Individual Needs of Buying Center Members 76
Supply Chain Management and Professional Purchasing 78
Supply Chain Management 79
Multiattribute Model of Product Evaluation and Choice 82
Performance Evaluation of Characteristics 82
Importance Weights 83
Overall Evaluation 84
Value Offered 84
Supplier Selection 84
Implications for Salespeople 85
Selling Yourself 86
Summary 87
Key Terms 87
Ethics Problems 88
Questions and Problems 88
Case Problems 89
Role Play Case 90
Additional References 91

Chapter 4
Using Communication Principles to Build Relationships 92
Building Relationships through Two-Way Communication 94
The Communication Process 94
Communication Breakdowns 94
Sending Verbal Messages Effectively 96
Choice of Words 96
Voice Characteristics 96
Stories 97
Keep Open Lines of Communication 98
Active Listening 98
Repeating Information 100
Restating or Rephrasing Information 101
Clarifying Information 101
Summarizing the Conversation 102
Tolerating Silences 103
Concentrating on the Ideas Being Communicated 103
Reading Nonverbal Messages from Customers 103
Body Angle 104
Face 104
Arms 104
Hands 105
Legs 105
Body Language Patterns 105
Sending Messages with Nonverbal Communication 106
Using Body Language 106
The Role of Space and Physical Contact 108
Appearance 109
Communicating via Technology 111
Telephone and Voice Mail 111
Text Messages and E-mail 112
Social Media 114
Adjusting for Cultural Differences 115
Selling Yourself 118
Summary 118
Key Terms 119
Ethics Problems 119
Questions and Problems 120
Case Problems 120
Role Play Case 122
Additional References 123

Chapter 5
Adaptive Selling for Relationship Building 124

Types of Presentations 126
Standard Memorized Presentation 126
Outlined Presentation 126
Customized Presentation 126
Adaptive Selling and Sales Success 127
Adaptive Selling: The Importance of Knowledge 130
Product and Company Knowledge 130
Knowledge about Sales Situations and Customers 130
How to Create Knowledge 131
Retrieving Knowledge from the Knowledge Management System 131
The Social Style Matrix: A Training Program for Building Adaptive Selling Skills 132
Dimensions of Social Styles 133
Categories of Social Styles 133
Identifying Customers' Social Styles 136
Social Styles and Sales Presentations 137
Versatility 139
Recap: The Role of Knowledge in Adapting 140
Systems for Developing Adaptive Selling Skills 140
Selling Yourself 141
Summary 142
Key Terms 142
Ethics Problems 142
Questions and Problems 142
Case Problems 143
Role Play Case 144
Additional References 145

part 2

THE PARTNERSHIP PROCESS 146

Chapter 6
Prospecting 146

The Importance of Prospecting 148
Characteristics of a Good Prospect 148
Does a Want or Need Exist? 149
Does the Lead Have the Ability to Pay? 149
Does the Lead Have the Authority to Buy? 149
Can the Lead Be Approached Favorably? 149
Is the Lead Eligible to Buy? 150
Other Criteria 150
How and Where to Obtain Prospects 150
Satisfied Customers 151
Endless-Chain Method 152
Networking and Center of Influence 153
Social Media 155
Other Internet Uses 156
Marketing Department 158
Shows, Fairs, and Merchandise Markets 158
Webinars and Seminars 159
Lists and Directories 159
Databases and Data Mining 160
Cold Calling 160
Spotters 161
Inside Salespeople 162
Expertise 163
Sales Letters 163
Other Sources of Leads 165
Lead Qualification and Management Systems 166
Overcoming a Reluctance to Prospect 167
Selling Yourself 168
Summary 169
Key Terms 169
Ethics Problems 170
Questions and Problems 170
Case Problems 171
Role Play Case 172
Additional References 172

Chapter 7
Planning the Sales Call 174

Why Plan the Sales Call? 176
Obtaining Precall Information 177
The Prospect/Customer as an Individual 178
The Prospect's/Customer's Organization 178
Sources of Information 180
Resources within Your Company 180
The Internet and Social Media 180
Secretaries and Receptionists 181
Noncompeting Salespeople 182
Traditional Secondary Sources 182
The Prospect 182
Other Sources 182
Setting Call Objectives 182
Criteria for Effective Objectives 183
Setting More Than One Call Objective 185
Setting Objectives for Several Calls 185
Buyers Are Setting Goals Also 187

Making an Appointment 188
The Right Person 188
The Right Time 189
The Right Place 189
Cultivating Relationships with Subordinates 189
Telephoning for Appointments 190
Additional Planning 191
Selling Yourself 192
Summary 193
Key Terms 193
Ethics Problems 193
Questions and Problems 194
Case Problems 195
Role Play Case 196
Additional References 196

Chapter 8
Making the Sales Call 198
Making a Good Impression 200
Waiting for the Prospect 200
First Impressions 201
Selecting a Seat 202
Getting the Customer's Attention 202
Developing Rapport 204
When Things Go Wrong 205
Identifying the Prospect's Needs: The Power of Asking Questions 206
Asking Open and Closed Questions 208
Spin® Technique 209
Reiterating Needs You Identified before the Meeting 212
Additional Considerations 212
Developing a Strategy for the Presentation 214
Offering Value: The Solution to the Buyer's Needs 214
Relating Features to Benefits 215
Assessing Reactions 217
Building Credibility during the Call 219
Selling to Groups 221
Selling Yourself 222
Summary 223
Key Terms 223
Ethics Problems 224
Questions and Problems 224
Case Problems 225
Role Play Case 226
Additional References 227

Chapter 9
Strengthening the Presentation 228
Characteristics of a Strong Presentation 230
Keeps the Buyer's Attention 230
Improves the Buyer's Understanding 230
Helps the Buyer Remember What Was Said 230
Offers Proof of the Salesperson's Assertions 232
Creates a Sense of Value 233
How to Strengthen the Presentation 233
Verbal Tools 233
Visual Tools 234
Product Demonstrations 240
Handouts 242
Written Proposals 243
Value Analysis: Quantifying the Solution 244
Dealing with the Jitters 251
Selling Yourself 251
Summary 252
Key Terms 252
Ethics Problems 252
Questions and Problems 253
Case Problems 254
Role Play Case 255
Additional References 255

Chapter 10
Responding to Objections 256
The Goal Is to Build Relationships and Sell Value 258
When Do Buyers Raise Objections? 258
Setting Up an Initial Appointment 259
The Presentation 259
Attempting to Obtain Commitment 259
After the Sale 259
Common Objections 261
Objections Related to Needs 261
Objections Related to the Product 262
Objections Related to the Source 262
Objections Related to the Price 263
Objections Related to Time 264
Other Objections 264
Behaviors of Successful Salespeople 265
Anticipate Objections 265
Forestall Known Concerns 265
Relax and Listen—Do Not Interrupt 267
Evaluate Objections 268
Always Tell the Truth 268

Effective Response Methods 269
Direct Denial 270
Indirect Denial 271
Compensation Method 272
Referral Method 273
Revisit Method 273
Acknowledge Method 274
Postpone Method 274
Using the Methods 275
Confirming That the Objection Has Been Answered 276
Objections When Selling to a Group of Buyers 277
The Price Objection 277
Use Up-to-Date Information 277
Establish the Value 277
Use Communication Tools Effectively 279
Dealing with Tough Customers 280
Selling Yourself 281
Summary 282
Key Terms 282
Ethics Problems 282
Questions and Problems 282
Case Problems 284
Role Play Case 285
Additional References 285

Chapter 11
Obtaining Commitment 286

Securing Commitment Today 288
Part of the Process 288
The Importance of Securing Commitment 289
Financial Terms and Conditions 290
Discounts 290
Credit Terms 291
Shipping Costs 292
Presenting Price 293
When to Attempt to Obtain Commitment 293
Buyer Comments 294
Nonverbal Cues 296
How to Successfully Obtain Commitment 296
Maintain a Positive Attitude 296
Let the Customer Set the Pace 297
Be Assertive, Not Aggressive 298
Sell the Right Item in the Right Amounts 299
Effective Methods 299
Direct Request 300
Benefit Summary 300
Balance Sheet Method 301
Probing Method 302
Alternative Choice 303
Trial Offers 303
Other Methods 304
If Commitment Is Obtained 305
No Surprises 305
Confirm the Customer's Choice 305
Get the Signature 305
Show Appreciation 306
Cultivate for Future Calls 306
Review the Actions to Be Taken 306
If Commitment Is Not Obtained 307
Some Reasons for Lost Opportunities 307
Discovering the Cause 308
Suggestions for Dealing with Rejection 309
Bringing the Sales Call to a Close 310
Selling Yourself 311
Summary 311
Key Terms 312
Ethics Problems 312
Questions and Problems 313
Case Problems 314
Role Play Case 316
Additional References 317

Chapter 12
Formal Negotiating 318

The Nature of Negotiation 320
Negotiation versus Nonnegotiation Selling 320
What Can Be Negotiated? 321
Are You a Good Negotiator? 321
Planning for the Negotiation Session 323
Location 323
Time Allotment 323
Negotiation Objectives 323
Team Selection and Management 326
Individual Behavior Patterns 327
Information Control 329
The Negotiation Meeting 329
Preliminaries 330
General Guidelines 331
Dealing with Win-Lose Negotiators 332
Making Concessions 336
Recap of a Successful Negotiation Meeting 338
Selling Yourself 338
Summary 340
Key Terms 340
Ethics Problems 340

Questions and Problems 341
Case Problems 342
Role Play Case 343
Additional References 343

Chapter 13
Building Partnering Relationships 344
The Value of Customers 346
Relationships and Selling 347
Types of Relationships 348
Market Exchanges 348
Partnerships 350
Managing Relationships and Partnering 353
Choosing the Right Relationship 354
Using Technology to Increase Efficiency 355
Phases of Relationship Development 356
Awareness 356
Exploration 356
Expansion 357
Commitment 357
Dissolution 357
Characteristics of Successful Partnerships 358
Mutual Trust 358
Open Communication 362
Common Goals 362
Commitment to Mutual Gain 363
Organizational Support 363
Selling Yourself 364
Summary 365
Key Terms 365
Ethics Problems 365
Questions and Problems 366
Case Problems 366
Role Play Case 368
Additional References 368

Chapter 14
Building Long-Term Partnerships 370
Exploration 372
Set the Right Expectations 373
Monitor Order Processing 373
Ensure Proper Initial Use of the Product or Service 374
Follow Up 375
Handle Customer Complaints 376
Expansion 380
Generating Repeat Orders 381
Upgrading 383
Full-Line Selling 383
Cross-Selling 384
Commitment 384
Securing Commitment to a Partnership 385
Commitment Must Be Complete 386
Communication 387
Corporate Culture 387
The Salesperson as Change Agent 388
Dissolution 392
Maintaining Few Personal Relationships 392
Failing to Monitor Competitor Actions 392
Failing to Monitor the Industry 393
Falling into Complacency 393
Conflict 393
Selling Yourself 395
Summary 396
Key Terms 397
Ethics Problems 397
Questions and Problems 398
Case Problems 398
Role Play Case 400
Additional References 401

part 3

THE SALESPERSON AS MANAGER 402

Chapter 15
Managing Your Time and Territory 402
The Value of Time 404
The Self-Management Process 405
Setting Goals 405
The Need for Goals 405
The Nature of Goals 406
Types of Sales Goals 407
Setting Sales Goals 409
Allocating Resources 410
Resources to Be Allocated 410
Where to Allocate Resources 410
Account Classification and Resource Allocation 410
Investing in Accounts 414
Implementing the Time Management Strategy 415
Daily Activity Planning 416
Guidelines 417
Planning Process 418

Making More Calls 419
Handling Paperwork and Reports 422
Evaluating Performance 423
Postcall Analysis 423
Activity Analysis 424
Performance Analysis 425
Productivity Analysis 425
Selling Yourself 426
Summary 427
Key Terms 427
Ethics Problems 427
Questions and Problems 428
Case Problems 428
Role Play Case 430
Additional References 431

Chapter 16
Managing within Your Company 432
Building Internal Partnerships 434
The Importance of Internal Partnerships 434
The Role of Sales 435
Selling Internally 435
Company Areas Important to Salespeople 438
Manufacturing 438
Administration 438
Shipping and Installation 439
Customer Service 439
Marketing 439
Sales 440
Partners in the Sales Organization 440
Sales Management 441
Field Sales Managers 446
Managing Ethics in Sales 447
Ethics and the Sales Executive 448
Ethics and the Field Sales Manager 449
Responding to Unethical Requests 449
Salespeople as Partners 450
Geographic Salespeople 450
Account Salespeople 450
Product Specialists 451
Inside versus Outside 452
Sales Teams 453
Selling Yourself 455
Summary 456
Key Terms 457
Ethics Problems 457
Questions and Problems 458
Case Problems 459
Role Play Case 461
Additional References 462

Chapter 17
Managing Your Career 464
Opportunities in Selling 466
Making a Good Match 467
Understanding Yourself 467
Understanding the Company 469
The Recruiting Process 472
Selecting Salespeople 472
Applicant Information Sources 472
Selling Your Capabilities 474
Preparing the Résumé 474
Gaining the Interview 475
The Interview 479
Special Types of Interviews 483
Follow-Up 484
Interviewing Never Ends 485
Managing Your Career Goals 485
Making the Transition from College to Career 485
Dual Career Path 486
Continue to Develop Your KSAs 486
Managing Stress 489
Situational Stress 490
Felt Stress 491
Selling Yourself 492
Summary 493
Key Terms 493
Ethics Problems 494
Questions and Problems 494
Case Problems 495
Role Play Case 497
Additional References 498

Role Play Case 1: Purina ONE SmartBlend Dog Food RP-1
Role Play Case 2: Gartner RP-6
Glossary G-1
Endnotes EN-1
Indexes I-1

©Tom Merton/Getty Images RF

chapter 1

SELLING AND SALESPEOPLE

SOME QUESTIONS ANSWERED IN THIS CHAPTER ARE

- What is selling?
- Why should you learn about selling even if you do not plan to be a salesperson?
- What is the role of personal selling in a firm?
- What are the different types of salespeople?
- What are the rewards of a selling career?

PROFILE

"Selling is a part of everyone's life, whether you realize it or not."

Zachary Goss, Tom James Company

PROFILE Selling is a part of everyone's life, whether you realize it or not. My name is Zachary Goss and I am a graduate of Texas State University-San Marcos with an undergraduate degree in business marketing and a masters in business administrations. In my undergraduate studies, I had the privilege of taking Mrs. Vicki West's professional selling class, where I discovered the amazing world of sales. I was a very competitive person growing up, being a triplet and playing sports all of my life, and sales seemed like the best way to stimulate my competitiveness.

Courtesy of Zachary Goss

Utilizing what I had learned in Mrs. West's class, I was able to sell myself to the Tom James Company and was hired as a sales professional upon graduation. This role required me to call on new prospects and maintain the relationship after the prospect became a client. The Tom James Company sells custom clothing directly to consumers. I call on new prospects and sell them on the idea to meet with me by conveying to them that I can save them time and money compared with how they are traditionally shopping for their clothing.

The interaction of the meeting is just as important, if not more, than the services and products I provide. I like to say that sales is the transfer of enthusiasm from the salesperson to the buyer. When I am enthusiastic and excited about the products and services I can provide, the buyer is more receptive and buys more often than when I'm not enthusiastic during the sales presentation. The decision maker has to trust the salesperson and realize the benefits and how they cover a need in order for an economic exchange to take place. If the buyer realizes the benefits and how they cover a need, but does not trust the salesperson, the buyer may go to another company that will offer similar benefits. If the buyer trusts the salesperson, but does not understand the benefits of the product/service or does not feel a need would be solved, then there is no value for the buyer to engage in an economic exchange.

Looking at the top sales performers in the company, I notice some similarities among them. They are excellent communicators in that they listen more than they talk, and seek to really understand the buyer's needs. They are continuously learning and enhancing their skills. They are creative in finding different ways to get in front of prospects and finding creative ways to solve problems. These traits benefit not only salespeople, but also all people in interviews, relationships, and everyday interactions.

Visit our Web site at: www.tomjames.com.

WHY LEARN ABOUT PERSONAL SELLING?

What's the first thing that pops into your mind when you hear the phrase "personal selling"? Do you conjure up images of fast-talking, nonlistening, pushy salespeople who won't take no for an answer? How about this definition: "Personal selling is the craft of persuading people to buy what they do not want and do not need for more than it is worth."[1]

If that is your view of selling, we encourage you to study this book carefully. You're going to learn things about selling that you never knew before. Let's start with a more accurate definition of professional selling, which is quite different from the one just mentioned. **Personal selling** is "the phenomenon of human-driven interaction between and within individuals/organizations in order to bring about economic exchange within a value-creation context."[2] Let's look at the definition more closely:

- It is more than just a set of sequential steps that a salesperson goes through with each buyer to secure an order. It's not just about what a seller does but rather the *interaction* between sellers and buyers that makes selling work today. We will talk about steps in the selling process in this book, but remember that they are not necessarily sequential or all needed for all buying situations.
- It can often involve multiple people and organizations (not just one seller and one buyer, for example).
- Selling is all about creating **value**, which is the total benefit that the seller's products and services provide to the buyer. When describing this to prospects, the seller often refers to the collection of buyer-specific benefits as the **customer value proposition (CVP)**, described more fully in Chapter 9. Just as our definition implies, this CVP is dynamic, evolving as time goes on, and depends on the context of the situation.[3] In fact, success in future business often depends on enhancements to the original CVP. Exhibit 1.1 provides examples of ways that salespeople create value.
- The goal of selling is to create economic exchange, not merely to promote the product or service. Customers today are technology savvy and search enabled and no longer rely on salespeople alone to learn about products and

Exhibit 1.1
Examples of Ways That Salespeople Can Add Value in a Selling Situation

Provide an interface between the buying and selling companies.

Identify networks of key players in both the buying and the selling companies and then help activate them to the task of co-creating value.

Encourage two-way communication and help create effective bonds between people.

Help create a climate of coleadership in the meetings rather than having the seller always take the leadership role.

Encourage both sides to learn from and understand each other.

Facilitate truly useful meetings and conversations between all parties.

Help manage any situations that arise to bring everyone back to a value-adding perspective.

Help foster conditions of trust and commitment between parties.

Be attuned to activities that increase value adding and help facilitate more of them.

Help key players understand their own perceptions of what value is to them.

Create meaning out of situations that arise and conversations that occur.

Help provide closure on solutions that provide value to all parties.

Source: Alexander Haas, Ivan Snehota, and Daniela Corsaro, "Creating Value in Business Relationships: The Role of Sales," *Industrial Marketing Management* 41, no. 1 (2012), pp. 94–105.

services. We refer to customers who use multiple channels or sources for gathering information as **omnichannel buyers**, and will provide more insights in Chapter 3 and elsewhere in the book.

This economic exchange involves what we call profit for both parties. Everyone knows that sellers sell to make a profit. Why do buyers buy? Typically a student will say, "To satisfy a need or a want," and that is a good basic answer. More helpful is to recognize that buyers also buy to make a profit. But they calculate profit differently. A seller's profit is selling price minus cost of goods sold and selling costs. A buyer's profit, or value, is the benefit received minus the selling price and costs and hassles of buying, or time and effort, as noted in this equation:

$$\text{Personal Value Equation} = \text{Benefits received} - (\text{Selling price} + \text{Time and effort to purchase})$$

For example, when someone buys a product from a salesperson, the buyer's profit may be higher than that obtained by buying on the Internet due to the benefits received (expert knowledge in determining the appropriate product to purchase, assistance with installation, resolution of concerns, creation of new offerings based on the buyer's specific needs, and so forth). We'll explain more about benefits in Chapter 8.

EVERYONE SELLS

Interestingly, it has been estimated that more than 50 percent of college students, regardless of their major, will work in sales at some point in their lives.[4] So it is not surprising that you are reading this textbook, and probably taking some sort of course in selling.

While this text focuses on personal selling as a business activity undertaken by salespeople, keep in mind that the principles of selling are useful to everyone, not just people with the title of salesperson. Developing mutually beneficial, long-term relationships is vital to all of us. In fact, the author team has taught the principles in this book to many groups of nonsalespeople. Let's look at some examples of how nonsalespeople sell ideas.

As a college student, you might use selling techniques when you ask a professor to let you enroll in a course that is closed out. When you near graduation, you will certainly confront a very important sales job: selling yourself to an employer.

To get a job after graduation, you will go through the same steps used in the sales process (discussed in Part 2, Chapters 6 through 14). First you will identify some potential employers (customers). On the basis of an analysis of each employer's needs, you will develop a presentation (as well as answers to questions you might encounter) to demonstrate your ability to satisfy those needs. During the interview you will listen to what the recruiter says, ask and answer questions, and perhaps alter your presentation based on the new information you receive during the interview. At some point you might negotiate with the employer over starting salary or other issues. Eventually you will try to secure a commitment from the employer to hire you. This process is selling at a very personal level. Chapter 17 reviews the steps you need to undertake to get a sales job.

Nonsalespeople in business use selling principles all the time. Engineers convince managers to support their R&D projects, industrial relations executives use selling approaches when negotiating with unions, and aspiring management trainees sell themselves to associates, superiors, and subordinates to get raises and promotions.

It's not just businesspeople who practice the art of selling. Presidents encourage politicians in Congress to support certain programs, charities solicit contributions and volunteers to run organizations, scientists try to convince foundations and government agencies to fund research, and doctors try to get their patients to adopt more healthful lifestyles. People skilled at selling value, influencing others, and developing long-term relationships are usually leaders in our society.

CREATING VALUE: THE ROLE OF SALESPEOPLE IN A BUSINESS

Companies exist only when their products and services are sold. It takes skill for salespeople to uncover exactly what a customer is looking for and how a potential product or service could add such value. Because this is so critical[5] this topic is covered in great detail in multiple chapters in this book.

Companies have many options in how they can approach customers as they add value, and the various methods are sometimes called **go-to-market strategies**. Strategies include selling through the Internet, field sales representatives, business partners, resellers, manufacturers' agents, franchises, telemarketers, and others. Selling firms determine which strategy to use for each customer based on such factors as the estimated value of the customer over the lifetime of the relationship, often called **customer lifetime value (CLV)**.[6] (Because this concept is so important, it is more fully discussed in Chapter 14.) Organizations whose go-to-market strategies rely heavily on salespeople are called **sales force–intensive organizations**. Naturally some firms use several strategies at the same time, and this is called **multichannel strategy**.[7] For example, Motorola uses the Internet for very small customers, inside salespeople for midsize customers, and a field sales force for large, important customers.

Another way to view the role of salespeople in business is to realize that they are one element in the company's marketing communications program, as Exhibit 1.2 indicates. Advertising uses impersonal mass media such as newspapers and TV to give information to customers, while sales promotions offer incentives to customers to purchase products during a specific period. Salespeople provide paid personal communication to customers, whereas publicity is communication through significant unpaid presentations about the firm (usually a news story). Finally, communication also occurs at no cost through word of mouth (communication among buyers about the selling firm).

Each of the communication methods in Exhibit 1.2 has strengths and weaknesses. For example, firms have more control when using paid versus unpaid methods. However, because publicity and word of mouth are communicated by independent sources, their information is usually perceived as more credible than information from paid communication sources. When using advertising, Internet sites, and sales promotions, companies can determine the message's exact content and the time of its delivery. They have less control over the communication delivered by salespeople and have very little control over the content or timing of publicity and word-of-mouth communication. Personal selling comes out on top in flexibility because salespeople can talk with each customer, discover the customer's specific needs, and develop unique presentations for that customer. Not surprisingly, personal selling is the most costly method of communication. The average cost of a sales call can be 10,000 times more expensive than exposing that single customer to a newspaper, radio, or TV ad.

Because each communication vehicle in Exhibit 1.2 has strengths and weaknesses, firms often use **integrated marketing communications**, which are communications programs that coordinate the use of various vehicles to maximize the total impact of the programs on customers.

Exhibit 1.2
Communication Methods

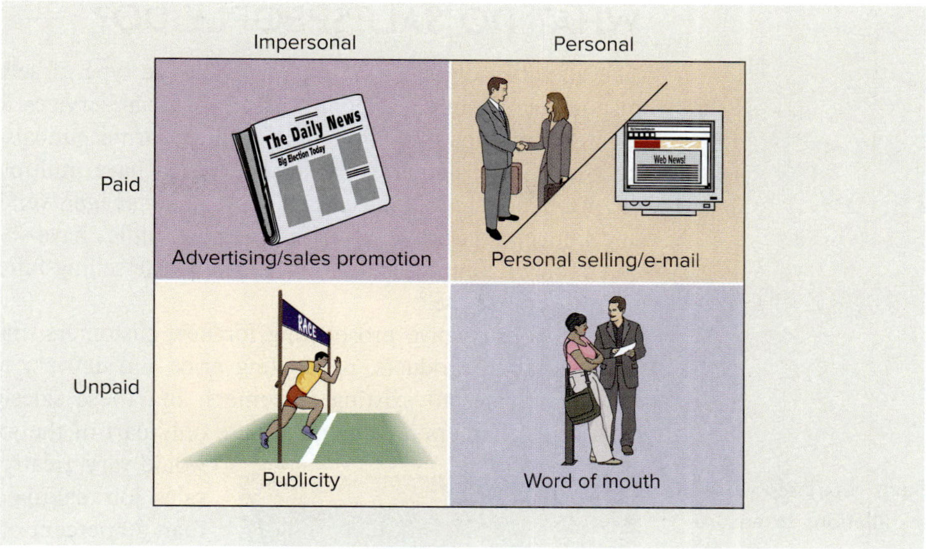

For example, when Hormel introduced its new Skippy P.B. Bites®, salespeople called on supermarkets and wholesale clubs. Advertising was created to generate awareness in consumers' minds. Coupons were offered to consumers to create interest and spur more rapid sales. Taste tests in stores were offered to build excitement and word of mouth. Publicity was generated that focused on how the Hormel founder often said that it was best to innovate (as was done with this new product), rather than to imitate. Although using salespeople in this example was an expensive part of the communication mix, it was important to do so to ensure that customers' precise needs were met.

Many students think–incorrectly–that advertising is the most important part of a firm's promotion program. However, many industrial companies place far more emphasis on personal selling than on advertising. Even in consumer product firms such as Procter & Gamble, which spends billions annually on advertising, personal selling plays a critical role.

Students sometimes also have the mistaken notion that the growing world of e-commerce and the Web as a source of information are causing the demise of salespeople. While the Web has drastically changed the life of a salesperson, salespeople are not being completely replaced by all of the new technology. However, it is critical that the salesperson actually add value in this new reality.

Let's look at this from another perspective–your own life. Have you purchased anything from the Internet? Probably every student has–travel, music, clothing, books, and more. Have you noticed that, other than Internet services, everything you purchased on the Web existed in some form before the Web? Why, then, has the Web become such a ubiquitous place for commerce? Simple. The Internet makes information as well as products and services available the way the consumer wants them. Those who sell via the Web gain competitive advantage by selling the way the buyers (or at least some buyers in some situations) want to buy.

If salespeople want to sell effectively, they have to recognize that the buyer has needs that are met not only by the product but also by the selling process itself. These needs include time savings, shopping costs such as gas if they drive around, and others. Part of the salesperson's responsibility is to sell the way the buyer wants to buy.

WHAT DO SALESPEOPLE DO?

The activities of salespeople depend on the type of selling job they choose. The responsibilities of salespeople selling financial services for General Electric differ greatly from those of salespeople selling pharmaceuticals for Merck or paper products for Georgia-Pacific. Salespeople often have multiple roles to play, including client relationship manager, account team manager, vendor and channel manager, and information provider for their firms. Studies have shown that when a salesperson's role encompasses more than simply the selling function, the seller's firm has more overall value.[8]

Sales jobs involve prospecting for new customers, making sales presentations, demonstrating products, negotiating price and delivery terms, writing orders, and increasing sales to existing customers. But these sales-generating activities (discussed in Chapters 6 through 14) are only part of the job. Although the numbers would vary greatly depending on the type of sales job, salespeople generally spend less than 50 percent of their time on-site in face-to-face meetings with customers and prospects. The rest of salespeople's time is spent in meetings, working with support people in their companies (internal selling), traveling, waiting for a sales interview, doing paperwork, and servicing customers.

Sales reps help with installations to ensure proper use.

©John Lund/Marc Romanelli/ Getty Images RF

CLIENT RELATIONSHIP MANAGER

Rather than buying from the lowest-cost suppliers, buyers often build competitive advantage by developing and maintaining close, cooperative relationships with a select set of suppliers, and salespeople play a key role in these relationships. Salespeople help customers identify problems, offering information about potential solutions and providing after-sale service to ensure long-term satisfaction. The phrase often used to describe this is **customer-centric**, which means making the customer the center of everything the salesperson does.[9] And buyers expect **24/7 service** (which means they expect a selling firm to be available for them 24 hours a day, 7 days a week). When salespeople fail in maintaining these relationships, buyers desert the firm. But when salespeople engage as effective client relationship managers, really helping buyers achieve their goals, the results are the opposite. From the Buyer's Seat 1.1 illustrates the the importance of being an effective account team manager.

The salesperson's job does not end when the customer places an order. Sales representatives must make sure customers get the benefits they expect from the product. Thus, salespeople work with other company employees to ensure that deliveries are made on time, equipment is properly installed, operators are trained to use the equipment, and questions or complaints are resolved quickly. Firms like Taylor Communications and Ortho-Clinical Diagnostics have implemented **six sigma selling programs**, which are designed to reduce errors introduced by the selling system to practically zero. This becomes increasing important, especially when one realizes how much companies are buying from salespeople. For example, Florida Power and Light spends approximately $3 billion a year on services and $3 billion a year for products.[10] Chapter 14 provides more insights on developing ongoing relationships through customer service.

From the BUYER'S SEAT 1.1

EACH SALESPERSON IS UNIQUE IN COMMUNICATION AND METHODS

No matter your age or position in life, every day you are dealing with a salesperson or being a salesperson, whether you are selling an idea to a significant other, selling yourself, or accepting a bag of groceries at the store. Each transaction you make during a day may take a different level of decision making and interaction. However, each interaction provides a learning experience.

I am a commodity manager for a large consumer products corporation where I buy the services of contract manufacturing from both large and small companies. To the companies I work with, I am the gatekeeper to attaining that first or next purchase order, helping them achieving their own goals.

My career started in research and engineering where I interacted with salespeople on a regular basis, in the capacity of an important stakeholder. Basically, they needed to make sure I was satisfied with their performance. In some cases, these salespeople tried to use me to influence the commodity manager to see their company in a favorable light. Since those days, I have moved to the procurement organization where I have purchased many types of contract manufacturing for many different platforms. During my career I have learned each salesperson is unique, as each person is his or her own individual. However, the end game is almost always the same—make the sale.

This was proven during one of my recent bids, which asked for the suppliers to bid on providing contract manufacturing in a more integrated fashion as compared to how it was performed in the past. My internal teams worked hard to guarantee the bid was unbiased and provided what the suppliers would need for a fair proposal. The bid was tens of millions of dollars in addressable spend, which certainly caught the attention of suppliers! Ten suppliers were asked to participate, and each supplier had his or her own competencies and angles to win the bid.

After the bid was initiated, I worked with one salesperson per company and gave each individual an even playing field in terms of provided content and feedback given. What I learned was that some salespeople are headstrong to stick to their bullish ways, while others learned to adapt to the rules of engagement I laid down from the onset of the process. For example, the directions instructed that no in-person meetings were allowed until the second phase of the bid, which is when we cut the supplier list to three. I did this due to resource availability and the fact that we could not successfully complete nearly 10 in-person meetings. A couple of the suppliers broke these rules as a way to gain more face time with my team to try to benefit our opinion of them. These salespersons' actions only hurt their standing in the bid process. Meanwhile, the rest of the suppliers stuck to the rules of engagement to warrant an efficient bidding process and let the content of their proposals speak to their chances of a favorable outcome.

As the bid continued I became more familiar with the salespeople I was dealing with. Additionally, I began to understand their competency as it pertains to understanding my needs and if they would be able to be my advocate within their own company, a true indication of a good salesperson. When I was talking to them I would always ask detailed, open-ended questions about their company's strategy and varied my questions from being comprehensive in nature to very "blue sky" in nature. This method gave me an understanding of how well they knew their company's vision and inner workings of their own process. This was a great way to also understand what their communication style was and let me tailor my style to get the best of them, as I would then be able to understand what incentivized these individuals on the job.

Once you understand what incentivizes people you can alter the way you act to help them benefit you. Both buyer and seller have objectives to achieve and must help each other in a mutually beneficial way to accomplish these goals.

Source: Personal correspondence, used with permission, anonymous upon request.

ACCOUNT TEAM MANAGER

Salespeople also coordinate the activities within their firms to solve customer problems. Many sales situations call for team selling, and salespeople who attempt to go it alone (sometimes called being "lone wolves") perform poorly, have lower job satisfaction, and have higher turnover intentions. An example of team selling occurred when Dick Holder, president of Reynolds Metal Company, spent five years "selling" Campbell Soup Company on using aluminum cans for its tomato juice products. He coordinated a team of graphic designers, marketing people, and engineers that educated and convinced Campbell to use a packaging material it had never used before. Approaches for improving efficiency by working closely with other functional units in the firm are fully discussed in Chapter 16.

SUPPLY CHAIN LOGISTICS AND CHANNEL MANAGER

Sometimes it is necessary to interact with other partners and vendors to meet a customer's needs, and salespeople are often the key managers of these many relationships. As one key buyer stated, "When I evaluate which salespeople I want to work with, I always ask this question, 'Can they source for things they can't provide themselves?' I'm looking to work with companies and salespeople with significant source expertise."

With regard to **supply chain logistics**, the management of the supply chain, if a customer buys a new jet from Boeing, with features that will be added by a third-party vendor, the salesperson will need to coordinate the efforts of the vendor with Boeing. Glenn Price, who sells life and disability insurance with Northwestern Mutual, realizes the importance of working with channel partners. "Today the financial services industry is very complex, as are the needs of my clients, and I can't be all things to all people. I can, however, create a team of specialists. For areas outside of my expertise, all I have to do is identify which specialists are needed and bring them in. This approach allows me to operate at maximum efficiency while providing the highest level of expertise and service to my clients."[11]

INFORMATION PROVIDER TO THEIR FIRM

Salespeople are the eyes and ears of the company in the marketplace. For example, when Bob Meyer, a salesperson at Ballard Medical Products, was demonstrating a medical device, a surgeon commented that he could not tell whether the device was working properly because the tube was opaque. Meyer relayed this information to the vice president of engineering, and the product was redesigned, substituting a clear tube for the opaque tube.

To truly have effective impact on their organization, salespeople need to be skillful at disseminating the knowledge they have acquired from customers to other people in their companies. In their reporting activities, salespeople provide information to their firms about expenses, calls made, future calls scheduled, sales forecasts, competitor activities, business conditions, and unsatisfied customer needs. It's not surprising, therefore, that the vice presidents of finance and manufacturing in most firms, for example, care greatly about the work and information provided by salespeople. Much of this information is now transmitted electronically to the company, its salespeople, and its customers and is contained in a

Salespeople share important market information with their boss and others in the firm.

©db2stock/Blend Images LLC RF

SALES Technology 1.1

SELLING AND AUTOMATION SYSTEMS

To operate an efficient business in today's society businesses are increasingly becoming more reliant on technology. Every component of business responds differently to advancements in technology. Take for example the evolution of sales techniques and processes. Obviously, making sales no longer requires walking door to door. Selling has actually been one of the industries most influenced by technology, and is used for everything from building relationships to closing a deal. New technologies continue to push the boundaries of organizations' sales productivity and efficiency.

Let us take a look at a specific technological adaptation that firms are using to further the sales process, sales force automation (SFA) systems. The art of selling from beginning to end involves numerous detailed and tedious tasks. Tasks ranging from finding leads and prospects, to the follow-up communications with customers are enhanced by SFA systems, increasing productivity and profitability. And salespeople without an SFA system will likely be more inefficient with their time management. This textbook is going to introduce you to some key SFA systems in use today.

SFA provides a valuable solution to automate tasks, freeing up time and resources for salespeople. With additional freed-up assets, an organization can concentrate more on sales activities that lead to revenue growth. An SFA system is also a strong asset for the sales managers. They allow managers to obtain up-to-the-minute access to sales data, sales employee activities, and sales figures, all key to managing selling success. With SFA systems an organization's sales employees and managers can enhance productivity, efficiency, and revenues.

customer relationship management (CRM) system. The CRM (see Sales Technology 1.1 for more insights) is updated in real time, and contains not only information needed by the firm but also extensive call information about the customer. Chapter 6 discusses the types of customer information that can be helpful for salespeople to track, while Chapters 15 and 16 discuss more fully the use of CRM systems, and the relationship between salespeople and their companies.[12]

TYPES OF SALESPEOPLE

Almost everyone is familiar with people who sell products and services to consumers in retail outlets. Behind these retail salespeople is an army of salespeople working for commercial firms. Consider a tablet computer or MP3 player you might purchase in a store. To make the player, the manufacturer bought processed material, such as plastic and electronic components, from various salespeople. In addition, it purchased capital equipment from other salespeople to mold the plastic, assemble the components, and test the player. Finally, the player manufacturer bought services such as an employment agency to hire people and an accounting firm to audit the company's financial statements. The manufacturer's salespeople then sold the players to a wholesaler. The wholesaler purchased transportation services and warehouse space from other salespeople. Then the wholesaler's salespeople sold the players to a retailer.

SELLING AND DISTRIBUTION CHANNELS

As the MP3 player example shows, salespeople work for different types of firms and call on different types of customers. These differences in sales positions come from the many roles salespeople play in a firm's distribution channel. A **distribution**

channel is a set of people and organizations responsible for the flow of products and services from the producer to the ultimate user. Exhibit 1.3 shows the principal types of distribution channels used for business-to-business and consumer products and the varied roles salespeople play.

Exhibit 1.3
Sales Jobs and the Distribution Channel

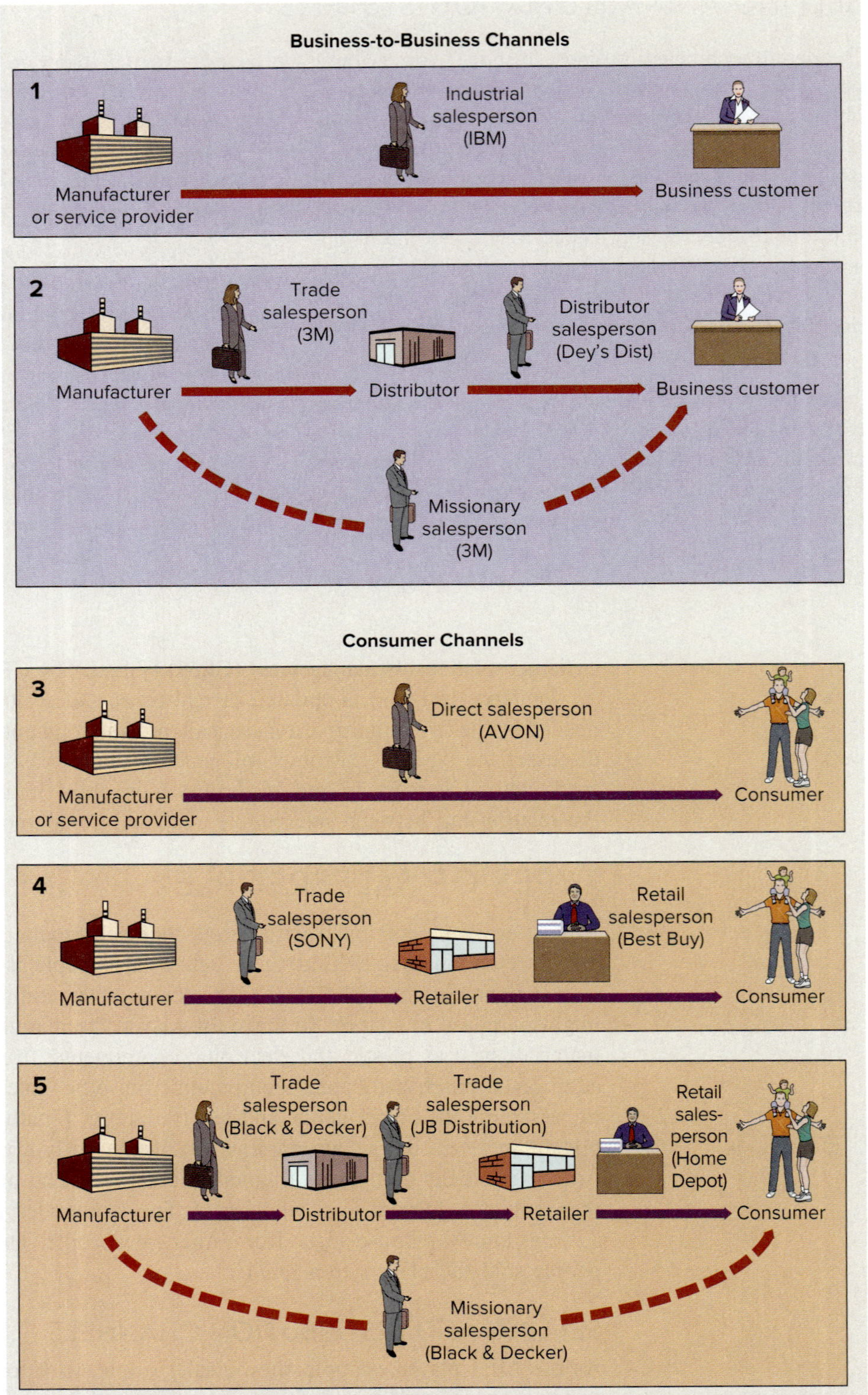

Note: Representative company names listed under each salesperson in this exhibit merely indicate the types of companies which are represented in that group.

Business-to-Business Channels

The two main channels for producers and providers of business-to-business, or industrial, products and services are (1) direct sales to a business customer and (2) sales through distributors. In the direct channel, salespeople working for the manufacturer call directly on other manufacturers. For example, U.S. Steel salespeople sell steel directly to automobile manufacturers, Dow Chemical salespeople sell plastics directly to toy manufacturers, and Nielsen salespeople sell marketing research services directly to business customers.

In the distributor channel the manufacturer employs salespeople to sell to distributors. These salespeople are referred to as **trade salespeople** because they sell to firms that resell the products (that is, they sell to the trade) rather than use them within the firm. Distributor salespeople sell products made by a number of manufacturers to businesses. For example, some Intel salespeople sell microprocessors to distributors such as Arrow Electronics, and Arrow salespeople then resell the microprocessors and other electronic components to customers such as Dell.

Many firms use more than one channel of distribution and thus employ several types of salespeople. For example, Dow Chemical has trade salespeople who call on distributors as well as direct salespeople who call on large companies.

Sales Jobs and the Distribution Channel

In the second business-to-business channel (see Exhibit 1.3), a missionary salesperson is employed. **Missionary salespeople** work for a manufacturer and promote the manufacturer's products to other firms. However, those firms buy the products from distributors or other manufacturers, not directly from the salesperson's firm. For example, sales representatives at Driltek, a manufacturer of mining equipment, call on mine owners to promote their products. The mines, however, place orders for drills with the local Driltek distributor rather than with Driltek directly. Normally missionary and local distributor salespeople work together to build relationships with customers.

Frequently missionary salespeople call on people who influence a buying decision but do not actually place the order. For example, Du Pont sales representatives call on Liz Claiborne and other clothing designers to encourage them to design garments made with Teflon, and Merck sales representatives call on physicians to encourage them to prescribe Merck pharmaceutical products.

Consumer Channels

The remaining channels shown in Exhibit 1.3 are used by producers and providers of consumer products and services. The third channel shows a firm, such as State Farm Insurance, whose salespeople sell insurance directly to consumers. The fourth and fifth channels show manufacturers that employ trade salespeople to sell to either retailers or distributors. For example, Revlon uses the fourth channel when its salespeople sell directly to Walmart. However, Revlon uses the fifth channel to sell to small, owner-operated stores through distributors. Missionary salespeople are also used in consumer channels. For example, a Black & Decker missionary salesperson may go to a Home Depot store to meet customers there and see how well Home Depot is serving its customers who purchase Black & Decker products.

Some of the salespeople shown in Exhibit 1.3 may be manufacturers' agents. **Manufacturers' agents** are independent businesspeople who are paid a commission by a manufacturer for all products or services sold. Unlike distributors and retailers, agents never own the products. They simply perform the selling activities and then transmit the orders to the manufacturers.

DESCRIBING SALES JOBS

Descriptions of sales jobs often focus on six factors:

1. The stage of the buyer–seller relationship.
2. The salesperson's role.
3. The importance of the customer's purchase decision.
4. The location of salesperson–customer contact.
5. The nature of the offering sold by the salesperson.
6. The salesperson's role in securing customer commitment.

Stage of Buyer–Seller Relationship: New or Continuing

Some sales jobs emphasize finding and selling to new customers. Selling to new prospects requires different skills than does selling to existing customers. To convince prospects to purchase a product they have never used before, salespeople need to be especially self-confident and must be able to deal with the inevitable rejections that occur when making initial contacts. On the other hand, salespeople responsible for existing customers place more emphasis on building relationships and servicing customers. For example, Lou Pritchett of Procter & Gamble, in a continuing relationship with Walmart, increased sales to Walmart from $400 million a year to over $6 billion a year by being creative and building partnerships. And the more important the buyer, the larger the group of sellers engaged in selling to that buyer. Hormel has a team of 50 who sell to Walmart in Bentonville, Arkansas.

Salesperson's Role: Taking Orders or Creating New Solutions

Some sales jobs focus primarily on taking orders. For example, most Frito-Lay salespeople go to grocery stores, check the stock, and prepare an order for the store manager to sign. However, some Frito-Lay salespeople sell only to buyers in the headquarters of supermarket chains. Headquarters selling requires a much higher level of skill and creativity. These salespeople work with buyers to develop new systems and methods and sometimes even new products to increase the retailer's sales and profits.[13]

Importance of the Purchase to the Customer

Consumers and businesses make many purchase decisions each year. Some decisions are important to them, such as purchasing a building or a computer Internet security system. Others are less crucial, such as buying candy or cleaning supplies. Sales jobs involving important decisions for customers differ greatly from sales jobs involving minor decisions. Consider a company that needs a computer-controlled drill press. Buying the drill press is a big decision. The drill press sales representative needs to be knowledgeable about the customer's needs and the features of drill presses. The salesperson will have to interact with a number of people involved in the purchase decision. Building Partnerships 1.1 describes how one salesperson learned a valuable lesson in helping a customer realize the importance of purchasing for a value-added seller.

BUILDING Partnerships 1.1

KNOWING YOUR CUSTOMER AND MARKET

I was selling recycled fibers to customers that made textbooks and three-ring binders. One of my prospects was one of the top binder manufacturers. Its finished products go into the big-box stores like OfficeMax. It also does some custom work for smaller customers. The annual potential business with this account was $4,500,000.

After several years of working my way into the organization, my company had an opportunity to test our new product. With great success in the testing we became a lead candidate for quality as well as a lead candidate due to our capabilities to meet supply demands. After being approved as a vendor, we negotiated pricing to an acceptable level, which was actually higher than some of our other customers we currently had business with. Closing in on the final signing, the customer requested that we pay $200,000 to help share in the costs it had to pay for shelf space at the big-box stores.

I presented this to my boss, thinking this was a no-brainer, as it was a one-time cost but would secure a multiyear contract. He quickly refused to comply with this request and said walk away. I was totally frustrated! Although a substantial fee up front, we were still looking to take in business at a higher margin than the other top companies we were currently working with. He drew a hard line that was difficult for me to understand at that time.

Nine months later, the competing company that the binder manufacturer signed with had quality and supply issues. The customer ended up looking for our support and wanted to switch over all the business to us. We ended up signing a new contract with the company at a slightly higher price point and did not pay the up-front shelf fee.

Looking back, my boss took a risk, but his knowledge of what the customer needed (quality, supply) and that the competition would struggle to meet the customer's expectations attributed to his decision. Sometimes you have to give up an opportunity to let the customer fully realize your value and build a viable long-term partnership.

Source: Personal correspondence, used with permission, anonymous upon request.

Even though many sales jobs do not involve building long-term partnerships, the roles of salespeople in many companies are evolving toward a partnering orientation. As you'll see in Chapter 16, partnering orientations are important within one's own organization as well as with customers. Further, salespeople are called on to build partnerships with some accounts and other types of relationships with other accounts. The partnering orientation does not prevent salespeople from developing other types of relationships; rather, people who are good partners are likely to also be good at other types of relationships. Understanding partnerships is critical to understanding the professional selling process, as will become apparent as the book unfolds.

Field salespeople go directly to the customer's place of business.

©Blend Images/Alamy Stock Photo RF

Location of Salesperson–Customer Contact: Field or Inside Sales

Field salespeople spend considerable time in the customer's place of business, communicating with the customer face-to-face. **Inside salespeople** work at their employer's location and typically communicate with customers by telephone or computer. Both types of jobs can be extremely interesting and rewarding.

thinking it through Which do you think you would prefer: an inside sales job or a field sales job? What makes one more attractive to you than the other?

The Nature of the Offering Sold by the Salesperson: Products or Services

The type of benefits provided by products and services affects the nature of the sales job. Products such as chemicals and trucks typically have tangible benefits: Customers can objectively measure a chemical's purity and a truck's payload. The benefits of services, such as business insurance or investment opportunities, are more intangible: Customers cannot easily measure the riskiness of an investment. Intangible benefits are generally harder to sell than tangible benefits.

The Salesperson's Role in Securing Customer Commitment: Information on Placing an Order

Sales jobs differ by the types of commitments sought and the manner in which they are obtained. For example, the Du Pont missionary salesperson might encourage a clothing designer to use Du Pont Teflon fibers. The salesperson might ask the designer to consider using the fiber but does not undertake the more difficult task of asking the designer to place an order. If the designer decides to use Teflon fabric in a dress, the actual order for Teflon will be secured by the fabric manufacturer salesperson, not the Du Pont salesperson.

THE SALES JOBS CONTINUUM

Exhibit 1.4 uses the factors just discussed to illustrate the continuum of sales jobs in terms of creativity. Sales jobs described by the responses in the far right column require salespeople to go into the field, call on new customers who make important buying decisions, promote products or services with intangible benefits, and seek purchase commitments. These types of sales jobs require the most creativity and skill and, consequently, offer the highest pay. It has been estimated that 20 percent (one million salespeople) of the current U.S. business-to-business sales jobs will be gone by the year 2020, while those who practice "consultant-type" selling (as opposed to merely order taking, for example) will experience growth in that same period by 10 percent.[14]

The next section examines the responsibilities of specific types of salespeople in more detail.

Exhibit 1.4
Creativity Level of Sales Jobs

Factors in Sales Jobs	Lower Creativity	Higher Creativity
1. Stage of the customer-firm relationship	Existing customer	New customer
2. The salesperson's role	Order taking	Creating new solutions
3. Importance of the customer's purchase decision	Low	High
4. Location of salesperson-customer contact	Varies, generally inside company	Field customer
5. Nature of the offering sold by the salesperson	Products	Services
6. Salesperson's role in securing customer commitment	Limited role	Significant role

EXAMPLES OF SALES JOBS

The following are brief examples of several of the thousands of sales jobs that exist today. As you read each example, notice the vast differences in the type of compensation, the number of accounts, the length of an average sales call, the length of the order cycle, the need to prospect, and so forth. All are based on real salespeople and the sales jobs they got when they first graduated from college. As you read the examples, think about which would be more attractive to you personally.

Chris is a salesperson for Cray, selling supercomputers to organizations. She has three clients, provided to her by her company, and does no prospecting for new accounts. She is paid a straight salary and travels by plane three to five days each week. Each visit to an account is roughly three hours long. For the first three years she had no sales. In her third year she made the largest sale in the company's history.

Lauree works for Taylor Communications selling digital and printed business forms and document management solutions. She has 200 clients and does a good bit of searching for new accounts. She is paid a salary plus commission and gets orders essentially every day, with no overnight travel. Each visit lasts about 45 minutes.

Scott works for Pfizer, a pharmaceutical company, calling on 100 doctors to tell them about his company's drugs. He is paid a salary plus a year-end bonus and as a missionary salesperson never gets an actual order from a doctor (the patients buy the Pfizer drugs). He does no overnight travel and never searches for new accounts, and each call is about five minutes long.

Jim sells Makita power tools and serves 75 dealers. He is paid a salary plus commission and does very limited searching for new accounts. He gets orders every day and has little overnight travel. Each call is about 30 minutes long.

Jeff works for Hormel, selling refrigerated meat products as well as pantry products like canned chili, and has about 100 accounts. He does no searching for new accounts and is paid a salary plus a year-end bonus. Each call lasts about 10 minutes, and he has no overnight travel.

Rachael works at Microsoft as a sales development specialist (an inside salesperson). She makes phone calls over Skype and sends e-mails from her office desk. The people she contacts, called leads, (see Chapter 6 for more details on prospecting) come from a system that Microsoft has created. Potential prospects for Microsoft's Office Cloud products (like Office 365, Azure, and Business Skype) are rated based on behaviors they have exhibited (like clicking through the Web site, showing a certain amount of interest in a product, etc.). The sales cycle for a prospect can be anywhere from a few days to six months or longer for bigger sales. Her job as a salesperson does not require her to leave her office. She is paid a salary and a bonus. She can be promoted to a field sales position if she desires.

Niki works for MetLife, selling life, auto, homeowners, long-term care, and disability insurance as well as investments (IRAs, mutual funds, annuities, and so forth). She has 250 clients, has no overnight travel, and is paid straight salary. She does a good bit of searching for new accounts, and her average first in-person sales call to a new account lasts about 30 minutes.

The next section reviews some of the skills required to be effective in the sales positions just discussed.

CHARACTERISTICS OF SUCCESSFUL SALESPEOPLE

The market is full of books and articles discussing why some people are successful in selling and others are not. Yet no one has identified the profile of the "perfect" salesperson because sales jobs are so different, as the examples just provided illustrated. In addition, each customer is unique. However, the following traits are generally associated with successful salespeople.

SELF-MOTIVATED

Salespeople often work without direct supervision and may be tempted to get up late, take long lunch breaks, and stop work early. But successful salespeople are self-starters who do not need the fear of an angry supervisor to get them going in the morning or to keep them working hard all day. Furthermore, successful salespeople are motivated to learn, and they work at improving their skills by analyzing their performance and using their mistakes as learning opportunities.

DEPENDABILITY AND TRUSTWORTHINESS

Customers develop long-term relationships only with salespeople who are dependable and trustworthy.[15] When salespeople say the equipment will perform in a certain way, they had better make sure the equipment performs that way! If it doesn't, the customer will not rely on them again. And dependability and trustworthiness can't just be a false front: Salespeople who are genuine and come across as authentic are better-performing salespeople.

thinking it through

Take a minute and think about yourself. How dependable are you right now? Can people count on you to do what you say you will do? Or do they have to look you up and remind you of your promises? You don't start developing dependability when you graduate from college; it is something you should be working on right now. What can you do to start improving your dependability?

ethics

INTEGRITY AND ETHICAL SALES BEHAVIOR

Honesty and integrity are critical for developing effective relationships. Over the long run, customers will find out who can be trusted and who cannot. A salesperson must exhibit complete transparency, with a willingness to share both good and bad points of a product, service, or situation. Studies show that good ethics are good business.[16] Ethical sales behavior is such an important topic that much of Chapter 2 is devoted to it.

CUSTOMER AND PRODUCT KNOWLEDGE

Effective salespeople need to know how businesses make purchase decisions and how individuals evaluate product alternatives. In addition, effective salespeople need product knowledge–how their products work and how the products' features are related to the benefits customers are seeking. Chapter 3 reviews the buying process, and Chapter 5 discusses product knowledge.

ANALYTICAL SKILLS AND THE ABILITY TO USE INFORMATION TECHNOLOGY

Salespeople need to know how to analyze data and situations and use the Internet, databases, and software to effectively sell in today's marketplace. **Selling analytics** is an attempt to gain insights into customers by using data mining and analytic techniques. Information technology will be discussed in every chapter of this book, and the use of analytical tools will be covered in Chapter 9 and other chapters.

COMMUNICATION SKILLS

The key to building strong long-term relationships is to be responsive to a customer's needs. To do that, the salesperson needs to be a good communicator. But talking is not enough; the salesperson must also listen to what the customer says, ask questions that uncover problems and needs, and pay attention to the responses.

To compete in world markets, salespeople need to learn how to communicate in international markets. Chapter 4 is devoted to developing communication skills, with discussion of communicating in other cultures.

FLEXIBILITY AND AGILITY

The successful salesperson realizes that the same sales approach does not work with all customers; it must be adapted to each selling situation. The salesperson must be sensitive to what is happening and agile enough to make those adaptations during the sales presentation.[17] Again, it is this flexibility that causes companies to spend so much money on personal selling instead of just advertising, which can't be tailored as easily or quickly to each individual.

CREATIVITY

Creativity is the trait of having imagination and inventiveness and using them to come up with new solutions and ideas. Sometimes it takes creativity to get an appointment with a prospect. It takes creativity to develop a presentation that the buyer will long remember. It takes creativity to solve a sticky installation problem after the product is sold.

CONFIDENCE AND OPTIMISM

Successful salespeople tend to be confident about themselves, their company, and their products. They optimistically believe that their efforts will lead to success. Don't confuse confidence, however, with wishful thinking. According to research, truly confident people are willing to work hard to achieve their goals. They are open to criticism, seek advice from others, and learn from their mistakes. They expect good things to happen, but they take personal responsibility for their fate. People who lack confidence, according to these same studies, are not honest about their own limits, react defensively when criticized, and set unrealistic goals.

EMOTIONAL INTELLIGENCE

Emotional intelligence (EI) is the ability to effectively understand and regulate one's own emotions and to read and respond to the emotions of others, and this is an important trait for salespeople.[18] EI has four aspects: (1) being aware of one's own feelings and emotions, (2) controlling one's emotions, (3) recognizing customers' emotions (called empathy), and (4) using one's emotions to interact effectively with customers. Bad decisions result from a lack of EI, so it is not surprising that emotional immaturity plays a large role in many employee terminations.

Salespeople need emotional intelligence to be able to recognize customers' emotions.

©Image Source RF

What are some good first steps in improving your EI? Measure your own EI (see www.EIME-research.com) to learn where you currently stand. Learn to identify and understand your own emotions as they arise and recognize the fact that it is often in your best interest to step away from emotional situations and become more reflective. Engaging in most human interactions with just a keyboard (e.g., via texting or e-mailing) can reduce one's EI.[19]

Of course, one must realize that EI can be used in negative ways as well. People with high EI can use their skills to intimidate, manipulate, and spin outcomes to their own advantage. Others have argued that emotional intelligence is less important than other traits, such as cognitive ability.[20] We discuss aspects of EI as they relate to adaptive selling and effective verbal and nonverbal intelligence in Chapters 4 and 5.

ARE SALESPEOPLE BORN OR MADE?

ethics

On the basis of the preceding discussion, you can see that most of the skills required to be a successful salesperson can be learned.[21] People can learn to work hard, plan their time, and adapt their sales approach to their customers' needs. In fact, companies show their faith in their ability to teach sales skills by spending billions of dollars each year on training programs. The next section discusses the rewards you can realize if you develop the skills required for sales success.

REWARDS IN SELLING

Personal selling offers interesting and rewarding career opportunities.[22] More than 8 million people in the United States currently work in sales positions, and the number of sales positions is growing. For the current number of salespeople in various types of sales jobs and to find average earnings, see the Occupational Outlook Handbook, created by the U.S. Department of Labor (www.bls.gov/ooh).

INDEPENDENCE AND RESPONSIBILITY

Many people do not want to spend long hours behind a desk, doing the same thing every day. They prefer to be outside, moving around, meeting people, and working on various problems. Selling ideally suits people with these interests. The typical salesperson interacts with dozens of people daily, and most of these contacts involve challenging new experiences.

Selling also offers unusual freedom and flexibility. It is not a nine-to-five job. Many salespeople decide how to spend their time; they do not have to report in. Long hours may be required on some days, and other days may bring fewer demands.

Because of this freedom, salespeople are like independent entrepreneurs. They have a territory to manage and few restrictions on how to do it. They are responsible for the sales and profits the territory generates. Thus, their success or failure rests largely on their own skills and efforts.

FINANCIAL REWARDS

Salespeople tend to earn more money the longer they sell. Occasionally the top salespeople in a firm will even earn more than the sales executives in that firm. The average amount earned by salespeople depends somewhat on the annual revenues of the firm.

The financial rewards of selling depend on the level of skill and sophistication needed to do the job. For example, salespeople who sell to businesses typically are paid more than retail salespeople. But salespeople usually don't earn overtime pay for working more than 40 hours.

MANAGEMENT OPPORTUNITIES

Selling jobs provide a firm base for launching a business career. For example, Mark Alvarez started his sales career in the Medical Systems Division at General Electric (GE) selling diagnostic imaging equipment to hospitals in central Illinois. Over the years he held positions in the firm that included district and regional sales manager and product manager; at one point he had responsibility for all Medical Systems Division business in Latin America. Sixteen years later, he was in corporate marketing and was responsible for managing the relationships between GE's 39 divisions and key customers in the southeastern United States. These include such accounts as Federal Express, Disney, and Home Depot. Some of his businesses do more than $500 million worth of business with GE annually. His entry-level job in selling provided great experience for his current assignment. Many CEOs and board chairs started their careers as salespeople.

This young manager learned the ropes as a salesperson before moving into product management at his firm.

©PhotoAlto/SuperStock RF

THE BUILDING PARTNERSHIPS MODEL

This book is divided into three parts, as illustrated in Exhibit 1.5.

The knowledge and skills needed for successful partnerships are covered in Part 1. You will learn about the legal and ethical responsibilities of salespeople, the buying process, the principles for communicating effectively, and methods for adapting to the unique styles and needs of each customer.

In Part 2 you will explore the partnership development process and the activities needed for this to occur. After completing this section, you should have enhanced skills and understanding about prospecting, planning, discovering needs, using visual aids and conducting demonstrations effectively, responding to objections, obtaining commitment, formally negotiating, and providing excellent after-sale service. Exhibit 1.6 provides a chart that summarizes the selling process.

Exhibit 1.5
The Building Partnerships Model

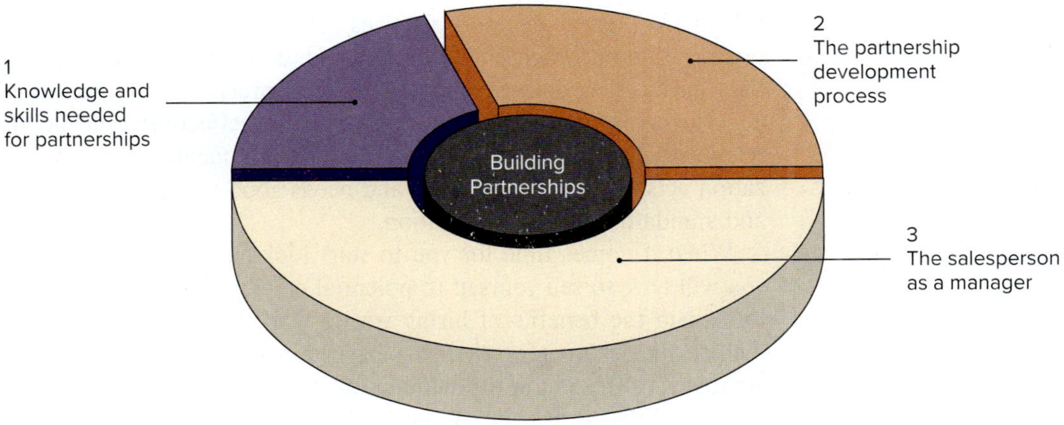

Exhibit 1.6
Steps in the Selling Process

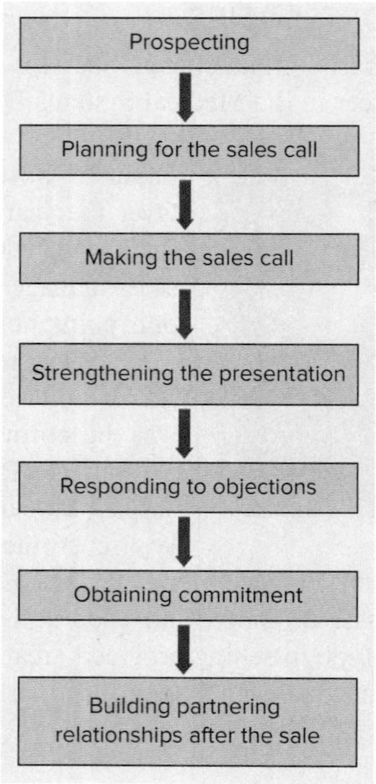

Finally, Part 3 discusses the role of the salesperson as a manager. You'll learn how you can improve your effectiveness as a salesperson by managing your time and territory and by managing the relationships within your own company. This section also discusses ways to manage your career.

SELLING YOURSELF

The "Selling Yourself" sections of this book are designed to help you see the connections of the chapter material with all aspects of your life right now. Of course we're all different, with varying interests and activities, so some of the examples might better fit you than others. But read them all and try to make a connection with something in your life. Selling is something you do all the time, and the ideas found in this book can help you now, not just after you graduate!

In many aspects of life, you engage in some aspect of personal selling. The simplest and earliest example is young children trying to convince their parents that buying them a toy will make them happy. The child will try to convey the benefits of the toy or the benefits of purchasing the toy. The kid will sometimes make a promise of good behavior as a benefit for the parent to make the purchase. The parent has to weigh the cost of the toy with the benefits the child has promised. If the parent replies with an objection, the child will use his or her creativity to come up with a solution to the parent's objection.

So, even at a young age we are naturally exposed to the concept of selling, and use different sales techniques in our lives.

A leader of a student organization also has to implement sales to be a successful leader. Most organizations need to sell their cause to students in order to recruit them to join their organization over the others. Once the organization gains new recruits, it has to convey its ideas and objectives and convince them to follow its lead. Communication, trust, and optimism are vital for the leader to hold this position and guide the organization to new heights.

Most student organizations require some form of philanthropy or fund-raising to achieve their goals and objectives. The leader has to influence the rest of the organization on which philanthropy or fund-raiser will benefit the organization and then have the organization sell its cause to prospects. The leader is typically good at influencing others through communicating effectively and building long-lasting relationships with peers, potential donors, and faculty advisors. A student organization acts like a small business and needs good salespeople to meet the objectives and standards of the organization.

When it comes time for you to start looking for employment after graduation, you will have to sell yourself to potential employers. In the interview, you will need to explain the benefits of hiring you to work for the company. Your benefits can include your character traits, past experiences, and the knowledge you possess. The company will examine the benefits of hiring you and determine if those benefits fill a need that it has. The value for both is that you will be employed and receive some form of income, and the company will gain an employee with a certain skill set that will benefit the company by increasing its profits.

So, we all have been selling in some fashion most of our lives. I wish you success as you sell in the future!

Zachary Goss, Salesperson, Tom James Company. Used with permission.

SUMMARY

You should study personal selling because we all use selling techniques. If you want to work in business, you need to know about selling because salespeople play a vital role in business activities. Finally, you might become a salesperson. Selling jobs are inherently interesting because of the variety of people encountered and activities undertaken. In addition, selling offers opportunities for financial rewards and promotions.

Salespeople engage in a wide range of activities, including providing information about products and services to customers and employees within their firms. Most of us are not aware of many of these activities because the salespeople we meet most frequently work in retail stores. However, the most exciting, rewarding, and challenging sales positions involve building partnerships: long-term, win-win relationships with customers.

The specific duties and responsibilities of salespeople depend on the type of selling position. But most salespeople engage in various tasks in addition to influencing customers. These tasks include managing customer relations, serving as the account team manager for their firm, managing the relationships with vendor and channel members, and providing information to their firm.

Sales jobs can be classified by the roles salespeople and their firms play in the channel of distribution. The nature of the selling job is affected by whom salespeople work for and whether they sell to manufacturers, distributors, or retailers. Other factors affecting the nature of selling jobs are the customer's relationship to the salesperson's firm, the salesperson's duties, the importance of the buying decision to the customer, where the selling occurs, the tangibility of the benefits considered by the customer, and the degree to which the salesperson seeks a commitment from customers.

Research on the characteristics of effective salespeople indicates that many different personality types can be successful in sales. However, successful salespeople do share some common characteristics. They are self-motivated, dependable, ethical, knowledgeable, good communicators, flexible, creative, confident, and emotionally intelligent. They also have good analytical skills and aren't afraid of technology.

KEY TERMS

creativity 19
customer-centric 8
customer lifetime value (CLV) 6
customer relationship management (CRM) 11
customer value proposition (CVP) 4
distribution channel 11
emotional intelligence (EI) 19
field salespeople 15
go-to-market strategies 6
inside salespeople 15
integrated marketing communications 6
manufacturers' agents 13
missionary salespeople 13
multichannel strategy 6
omnichannel buyer 5
personal selling 4
sales force–intensive organization 6
selling analytics 18
six sigma selling programs 8
supply chain logistics 10
trade salespeople 13
24/7 service 8
value 4

ETHICS PROBLEMS

1. Let's assume that as a salesperson for a logistics management company, you are a key channel manager and work with a number of supply chain vendors to help make sure your client, Home Depot, gets excellent value. While working closely with one channel member, Effective Inventory Management, Inc., you learned exactly how it completes an extensive inventory situation analysis. Given your newfound knowledge, should you suggest to your firm that it do the inventory situation analysis itself, thus negating the need to work with Effective Inventory Management, Inc. entirely? Basically, you would be using knowledge that you gained through your observations of Effective Inventory Management, Inc. You did not sign a nondisclosure agreement with that firm.
2. As a salesperson, two traits you have been trained to display are confidence and optimism. Let's say that one of your clients asked you, "I'm getting a little worried about your new model, the X15J. I thought we were going to see prototypes of it by January, and here it is late February and we've not seen anything. I'm about to hire some additional workers to help with installing those models this summer. Is it going to be released on time?" As the salesperson, you know that the X15J has hit some significant snags and there is not a definite timeline for its release at the present. But you don't want to jeopardize the verbal sales commitment from the buyer, thinking that the buyer might purchase from a competitor. So you answer, "Sure, Jason! That's what we've been promising and you know you can trust us. I have confidence in our new product development team. You should too!" What are your thoughts on this interaction?

QUESTIONS AND PROBLEMS

1. There are many different go-to-market strategies. For which of the following products and services do you think a sales force–intensive strategy would probably *not* be used? Why? Make any assumptions needed and list your assumptions in your answer.
   a. A local plumbing company.
   b. An office cleaning service.
   c. Warehouse alarm systems.
   d. An attorney.
2. In Building Partnerships 1.1 you read how a salesperson's sales manager helped the salesperson avoid making a mistake that would have resulted in the company making less money. Identify two key lessons you learned from reading that story.
3. Comment on each of the following statements:
   a. Salespeople are a thing of the past because buyers can learn all they need from the Internet.
   b. Salespeople should treat everyone with respect and courtesy.
   c. A successful salesperson never accepts no as the final decision by a buyer.
   d. A good salesperson can sell anything to anybody.
4. Jacob Grapentine has been working as a retail clerk at a greenhouse for three years and is considering taking a selling job with Scotts (see www.scotts.com). The job involves calling on greenhouses and retailers selling the benefits of the firm's products (mulches, bagged soils, fertilizers, weed killers, etc.). What are the similarities and differences between his retail clerk job and the selling job he is considering?
5. Declan Pederson worked his way through college by selling cable television subscriptions door to door. He has done well on the job and is one of the top salespeople at the cable company. Last week Guardianship Services offered him a job selling guard dog services to industrial warehouses. Explain the differences between selling door to door to consumers and the Guardianship Services sales job.
6. Poll at least five students who are not taking your selling course (and who, better yet, are outside the business school or program). What are their opinions about salespeople? How accurate are their opinions based on what you've read in this chapter?

7. Think about what you want in your first job out of college. Based on what you know so far from this chapter, how well does selling match your desires in a job?
8. According to the text, some sales jobs are located as inside sales instead of field sales. List five advantages that inside salespeople could experience over field salespeople.
9. Sales Technology 1.1 introduced how sales force automation (SFA) systems can help salespeople. Identify two reasons why salespeople might be reluctant to adopt new technologies like an SFA system.
10. Assume you are a sales manager and you need to recruit someone for the following sales positions. For each position, list the qualities you would want in the recruit:
    a. Salesperson selling graffiti-preventive coatings to subway operators.
    b. Salesperson calling on golf specialty retailers, selling golfing instructional videos.
    c. Salesperson selling sponsorship advertising signs at a college football stadium to businesses in the region.

CASE PROBLEMS

case 1.1

Chicago Blackhawks

Emily Hightower has been sales manager for Corporate Hospitality sales at the Chicago Blackhawks for the last three years. The Stanley Cup–winning Blackhawks are a National Hockey League franchise located in Chicago, Illinois. Blackhawks Corporate Hospitality is a unique way for businesses to entertain prospective clients or treat important customers to a special night out. The 20-person Executive Suites and 40- and 80-person Super Suites provide outstanding, panoramic views of the ice surface and can be rented on a per-game basis or a season basis. The all-inclusive packages (i.e., tickets to the event, parking passes, food and beverage, a private suite attendant, theater-style seating, easy access to elevators, multiple flat-screen televisions, and so on) make entertaining clients a breeze.

When Emily was promoted to the sales manager position, there were three full-time salespeople who called on businesses in the region. One quit right after she arrived, and Zach, a knowledgeable sports marketer with excellent connections in the business community, was hired as a replacement. Zach has been a real asset to the organization, building business in the financial and investment business community.

Emily thought everything was going smoothly until yesterday, when Chad, another salesperson, dropped a bombshell. He turned in his notice because he said he got a lucrative offer from the Chicago Bulls.

Emily sat in her office, mulling over the situation and halfheartedly working on the job description for Chad's position, when one of her most trusted administrative assistants, Amanda, walked in. After they chatted for a few minutes, the following conversation ensued:

Amanda: So why do you need a salesperson anyway? Why not just use our Web page to give prospective clients the information they need? And social media hype does a lot to help us sell our suites.

Emily: We have to have a salesperson, Amanda. I mean, there's always been three salespeople in our office.

Amanda: But I'm asking you to think outside the dots, Emily. Why do we need them? They cost the company a lot of money that we could save by just relying on Web advertising. Besides, the Chicago Blackhawks are already well known. There's no need for salespeople. The Blackhawks sell themselves!

The conversation continued in this vein for a few minutes, then Amanda left to work on some scheduling disputes. Emily sat there, thinking about what Amanda said. Who knows? Maybe Amanda had a good idea.

Questions

1. What impact would dropping one or more salespeople have on the Chicago Blackhawks Corporate Hospitality sales? You might want to review the section titled "What Do Salespeople Do?" as you answer this question.
2. Should Emily seek an inside salesperson or field salesperson for this need? Why? You might want to review the section titled "Describing Sales Jobs" as you answer this question.

case 1.2

DeSoto Hills Convention Center

Julie Hsieh is a salesperson for the DeSoto Hills Convention Center. The center is located in downtown DeSoto Hills, a small city of 25,000 people in North Dakota. The Convention Center contains approximately 230,000 square feet of meeting and event space, and is located only one block from a 650-car parking deck. The center has been successful in securing many events in the region over the 20 years it has been in existence, but lately the selling team has had trouble keeping it booked at the desired 80 percent capacity.

Julie was talking to Tyler Newton, an event planner for one of the larger manufacturers in the region. Tyler was looking for a venue to host an upcoming employee appreciation event consisting of approximately 500 attendees, with another 200 watching the event offsite at a plant in South Dakota.

Tyler: [*after taking a tour of the facilities*]: Well, it looks like you're able to accommodate anything from 25 to 6,500 people for an event. I'm impressed with the way you can arrange and partition to achieve a sense of proper scale!

Julie: Thanks, Tyler. Our clients are happy with our space and the services we provide while they're here!

Tyler: Speaking of services, I'm going to need some special equipment for the event, since we'll be having an offsite location that we want to beam the event to as well.

Julie: [*a little nervous*]: Well, we do have plenty of equipment that you can lease for the event. Do you have a list of your needs?

Tyler: [*reaching into his portfolio, and handing her a piece of paper*]: Yep, I have it right here. We always work with a convention center that can host our equipment needs in-house. We tried one conference one time where we used an outside provider to provide the equipment, and it was a nightmare. Our CEO said, "Never again! Always choose a venue that can supply everything in-house!"

Julie: [*perusing the list*]: We can certainly handle the mics, and the monitors and the audio feeds. But I'm afraid we don't have some of this cloud-based video broadcasting equipment in-house. I'm sure that Voy Entertainment, a local electronics supplier whom we have used many times, can rent some of this teleconferencing equipment to you. They will even be onsite to make sure it works correctly!

Tyler: [*disappointed*]: Hmm. Well, we'll see. Like I said before when we first started meeting, we're looking at three venues for hosting our event. Maybe one of them can offer it all to us as a 100 percent package deal.

Julie was disappointed. This was the second time in two months that DeSoto was unable to meet the equipment needs of a potential client. In the other case, DeSoto lost the business.

Questions

1. As the text says, salespeople are the eyes and ears of the company in the marketplace. Being an information provider to their firm is an important thing that salespeople do. If you were Julie, how would you do that for the DeSoto Hills Convention Center?
2. This chapter introduces the notion of customer relationship management (CRM) systems. These systems can maintain records of almost anything dealing with interactions between salespeople and prospects/clients. How might DeSoto Hills Convention Center use its CRM system to help avoid a situation like the one that occurred with Tyler?

ROLE PLAY CASE

At the end of each chapter, beginning just below this paragraph, you'll find a short role play exercise that focuses on Gartner. Gartner is a company that provides research and information services to other companies. To find more information on the product, view sales support materials, and more, visit www.gartner.com/ncsc. There is also additional material at the back of the book in the role play section.

Graduation is coming up soon so you've decided to get serious about interviewing. You went online to look at what's going on in your school's Career Services Center, where you saw a job posting for Gartner. Apparently it is some sort of business information and research services company, which also does consulting. You've always thought you'd enjoy consulting so you thought you'd sign up. Today is your interview. Be yourself; interview honestly as if you were truly talking with Gartner. To help you prepare for this job interview role play, you may want to take some time to find out about Gartner by visiting www.gartner.com for more information.

To the instructor: Additional information needed to complete the role play is available in the Instructor's Manual.

ADDITIONAL REFERENCES

Abosag, Ibrahim, and Peter Naudé. "Development of Special Forms of B2B Relationships: Examining the Role of Interpersonal Liking in Developing Guanxi and Et-Moone Relationships." *Industrial Marketing Management* 43, no. 6 (2014), pp. 887–96.

a El-Sayed Mansour, Samira. *Emotional Intelligence: The Road to Success.* Indianapolis, IN: Dog Ear, 2016.

Blount, Jeb. *Sales EQ: The Ultimate Guide to Leveraging Sales Specific Emotional Intelligence to Close Any Deal.* Hoboken, NJ: Wiley, 2017.

Brown, Linden, and Christopher Brown. *The Customer Culture Imperative: A Leader's Guide to Driving Superior Performance.* New York: McGraw-Hill Education, 2014.

Cuevas, Javier Marcos, Saara Julkunen, and Mika Gabrielsson. "Power Symmetry and the Development of Trust in Interdependent Relationships: The Mediating Role of Goal Congruence." *Industrial Marketing Management* 48 (2015), pp. 149–59.

Dowell, David, Mark Morrison, and Troy Heffernan. "The Changing Importance of Affective Trust and Cognitive Trust across the Relationship Lifecycle: A Study of Business-to-Business Relationships." *Industrial Marketing Management* 44 (2015), pp. 119–30.

Novell, Corinne, Karen A. Machleit, and Jane Ziegler Sojka. "Are Good Salespeople Born or Made? A New Perspective on an Age-Old Question: Implicit Theories of Selling Ability." *Journal of Personal Selling and Sales Management* 36, no. 4 (August 18, 2016), pp. 309–20.

Rogers, D. L. *The Digital Transformation Playbook: Rethink Your Business for the Digital Age.* New York: Columbia Business School Publications, 2016.

Stanley, Colleen. *Emotional Intelligence for Sales Success: Connect with Customers and Get Results.* New York: American Management Association, 2013.

Wakefield, Michael. *Emotional Intelligence: The Comprehensive Guide to Increasing Your EQ.* Seattle, WA: CreateSpace Independent Publishing Platform, 2016.

Walton, David. *Introducing Emotional Intelligence: A Practical Guide.* London: Icon Books, 2013.

Williams, David. *Connected CRM: Implementing a Data-Driven, Customer-Centric Business Strategy.* Hoboken, NJ: Wiley, 2014.

Yurova, Yuliya, Cindy B. Rippé, Suri Weisfeld-Spolter, Fiona Sussan, and Aaron Arndt. "Not All Adaptive Selling to Omni-Consumers Is Influential: The Moderating Effect of Product Type." *Journal of Retailing and Consumer Services* 34 (2017), pp. 271–77.

Knowledge and Skill Requirements

PART 1

©Dave and Les Jacobs/Blend Images LLC RF

chapter 2

ETHICAL AND LEGAL ISSUES IN SELLING

SOME QUESTIONS ANSWERED IN THIS CHAPTER ARE

- Why do salespeople need to develop their own codes of ethics?
- Which ethical responsibilities do salespeople have toward themselves, their firms, and their customers?
- Do ethics get in the way of being a successful salesperson?
- What guidelines should salespeople consider when confronting situations involving an ethical issue?
- Which laws apply to personal selling?

> *"Your word is your honor. If you should meet your customers socially, you can hold your head high knowing you are not just a good salesperson, you are a good person."*
>
> *Jessica Lehrer, ThyssenKrupp Elevator*

Courtesy of Jessica Lehrer

PROFILE People are people at their core and they sense when you are being dishonest. It's a simple idea but one that too often gets lost in the world of e-mails, deadlines, and sales goals. I owe much of my success in business to being approachable and treating clients as I would want to be treated.

Early in my career, I was fortunate enough to learn these lessons, sometimes the hard way but that is to be expected. No one is perfect in the beginning. My first encounter with being honest with clients happened just a couple days after I completed sales training. I had just been relocated to a branch of ThyssenKrupp Elevator and was still trying to comprehend an extremely busy construction market. My manager knew that my degree was in mechanical engineering and that I was new to sales, so he had me do a couple "ride-alongs." During one of these, he took me to lunch at an architectural firm to discuss a new (to the U.S. market) product that might be useful in the design of future buildings. The head principal of the firm, who had worked with my manager many times before, asked a fairly technical question about the safety mechanism. My manager paused a moment to think, and then attempted to answer the question. The principal cut him off, irritated, and demanded, "Stop with the games. Stop speculating; go back to your engineers and get me a real answer!" I let that statement sink in as my manager's face turned a scarlet shade of red. It came off harsh, but it was true. The principal saw right through the "runaround" answer he was given and was left feeling like his time was being wasted. Sometimes it's better to admit that you don't know something, than to be caught in a lie that may cost you both your credibility and your customer.

There were many more lessons I would learn from my short time with that manager, which greatly helped me when I was promoted to running my own territory in Memphis, Tennessee. For example, the first contract I ever received was for a small residential elevator and I was thrilled when I finally closed the deal (it took about three months, which is pretty fast in the construction world). My manager understood how happy I was and even stayed late to help me go over the contract to see what clarifications we wanted to make. Reviewing contracts can be as dry and tedious as reading the User Terms Agreement for any program you use online. As we were going through the contract, I found myself asking a lot of questions about the contractual language and why my manager kept pointing out little things I should warn the customer about when we next spoke. It was a strange concept to me that he would want the customers to know something that they might view as "bad" or "unfavorable," until my manager helped me realize that they were people too and that if I were in their shoes, having someone point out the fine print would be better than finding out the hard way. When we were done reviewing the contract he said, "At the end of day, you are in charge of your own business and will have to stand by the decisions you make." I'm happy to say that, through good guidance, I can go home every night and rest easy knowing that I did what was right for the customer.

Another problematic situation that I have encountered is accepting gifts. In my career, I've been offered everything from free hotel stays to football box tickets to ornate glass hookah sets. In general, I tend to avoid accepting any gifts as I don't want any kickback suspicion. That's not to say you can't enjoy coffee or even a fancy lunch with your clients; just make sure they are not expecting anything in return. Most companies have a corporate compliance department dedicated to helping employees navigate these areas.

After a couple of years in the business, I can speak to the importance of going the extra mile for my clients. Sometimes this particular trait feels like it goes unnoticed, but it doesn't with the right customer. I organized a customer appreciation lunch a couple weeks ago at a general contractor's facility that uses my company exclusively. We had just closed a rather large deal and I thought it be a good time to thank the firm for its continued patronage. The lunch went well with the owner and all the project managers showing up. Near the end, my branch manager was conversing and questioning the customer about an upcoming project for a different line of business. The owner of the company reassured my manager that the firm still preferred doing business with us. He then went on to say how helpful and responsive I had been on previous projects. It seems like such a small thing, but having a client recognize the effort you put in to make their lives easier is an amazing feeling.

When it's all said and done, your clients are not just e-mails in your inbox or figures on a chart. They have lives, families, and other stresses on their minds. Follow the "Golden Rule" and act in a way that is becoming to both you and your corporation. Your word is your honor. If you should meet your customers socially, you can hold your head high knowing you are not just a good salesperson, you are a good person.

Visit our Web site at: www.thyssenkrupp.com.

Jessica Lehrer, salesperson, ThyssenKrupp Elevator. Used with permission.

ETHICS AND SELLING

Wells Fargo is, perhaps, the most well-known company to hit the news media for unethical selling practices. In case you forgot, the company admitted to putting so much pressure on salespeople that they created false sales transactions, using customer names on accounts for which the customers had no knowledge. The story made major headlines in the press for two reasons: first, because the unethical practices were so pervasive at Wells Fargo and second, because salespeople are generally ethical, so when something like this happens, it is news.

Ethics are the principles governing the behavior of an individual or a group. These principles establish appropriate behavior indicating what is right and wrong. Defining the term is easy, but determining what the principles are is difficult. What one person thinks is right another may consider wrong. For example, 58 percent of sales managers in one poll report believing that sales contests between salespeople do not generate unethical behavior—such as asking customers to take unwanted orders and then returning the merchandise after the contest is over—but 42 percent do believe that unethical behaviors are a consequence of sales contests. Yet several studies suggest that it all depends on how the managers manage the contest.[1] So while feelings and experiences of sales managers are mixed when it comes to a commonly accepted practice, in the end what matters is how the individual acts.

What is ethical can vary from country to country and from industry to industry. For example, offering bribes to overcome bureaucratic roadblocks may be an accepted practice in Middle Eastern countries but is considered unethical and illegal in the United States. Further, while prevailing religions may influence ethics beliefs and practices, regional differences can occur. Egypt, Iran, and Turkey, for example, are populated almost entirely by Muslims. In Egypt the courteousness of the salesperson is an important indicator of ethical practices. Not so in Turkey, which is more like the United States in not placing so much emphasis on courtesy; rather, actual customer service is preferred. Research in Iran, though, seems to reveal a blend of the two.[2]

What is considered ethical can also vary by industry and over time. For example, in some industries giving and receiving lavish gifts were once considered ethical.

In medical sales that practice was deemed unethical in 2003 and while salespeople can still bring in a boxed lunch in exchange for a few minutes of the doctor's time, no longer can doctors expect an all-expenses-paid hunting trip or a cruise vacation from a supplier. Much of the changes in what is considered ethical are due to the evolving nature of the sales profession.

THE EVOLUTION OF SELLING

The selling function has been a part of humankind since the beginning, perhaps when one person traded meat for berries. With the arrival of the Industrial Revolution in the 1800s, companies began to make more goods more cheaply. Even so, demand outstripped supply, and for many companies, the key issue in selling was to make people aware of the product and what it could do. Forward-thinking companies such as NCR and Singer Sewing Machines hired salespeople, called drummers or peddlers, and sent them across the country to sell. Then the companies brought the most effective salespeople back into the company office and wrote down their sales pitches. These **canned sales pitches** were distributed to all salespeople, who were expected to follow the scripts every time without deviation.

Since that time things have changed greatly. The nature of business evolved, necessarily changing how people sell. Exhibit 2.1 illustrates how the role of the salesperson has evolved from taking orders through persuading customers to building partnerships.[3]

As Exhibit 2.1 shows, the orientations of salespeople emerged in different periods. However, all these selling orientations still exist in business today. For example, inbound telephone salespeople working for retailers like Lands' End and Spiegel are providers with a production orientation. They answer a toll-free number and simply take orders. Many outbound telephone, real estate, and insurance salespeople are persuaders with a sales orientation. Partnering-oriented selling is becoming more common as companies make strategic choices about the type of selling best suited to their situation, but recent research indicates that even within partnerships, there are times when the buyer needs to hear persuasive messages that might be scripted.[4]

Exhibit 2.1
The Evolution of Personal Selling

	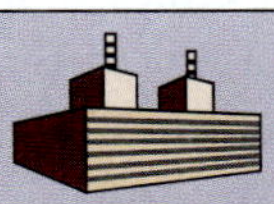 Production	 Sales	 Marketing	 Partnering
Time Period	Before 1930	1930 to 1960	1960 to 1990	After 1990
Objective	Making sales	Making sales	Satisfying customer needs	Building relationships
Orientation	Short-term seller needs	Short-term seller needs	Short-term customer needs	Long-term customer and seller needs
Role of Salesperson	Provider	Persuader	Problem solver	Value creator
Activities of Salespeople	Taking orders, delivering goods	Aggressively convincing buyers to buy products	Matching available offerings to buyer needs	Creating new alternatives, matching buyer needs with seller capabilities

From the BUYER'S SEAT 2.1

WHOM DID JIM KELLER WORK FOR?

When it came time for Jim Keller to retire, he enjoyed the usual party thrown by his friends. What's unusual is that the retirement luncheon was organized by Rob Harvey, the chief information officer at FedEx, Jim's client, rather than his colleagues at Teradata, his employer.

Not that the people at Teradata didn't value Jim; it's just that Jim worked longer with the people at FedEx. For most of his 30-year sales career, FedEx was his only account, even though he was actually employed by several companies over that time period.

So it was no surprise that Rob said, "We always knew Jim bled purple" (the FedEx color). That was the highest compliment Rob could give, and he went on to say this to Jim, "You always do the right thing for FedEx." Then he presented Jim with a wooden model Boeing 777, signed by Fred Smith, CEO. "We don't do this for everybody—this is very rare and very special."

"Life selling to FedEx wasn't always peaches and cream," notes Jim. In one instance, a FedEx manager wanted Jim escorted off the premises because he was so mad with Jim's company (not Teradata but an earlier employer). But Jim stepped in front of him and said, "I'm here to take my beating. As soon as we can get that over with, can I start fixing the problem?" Jim said the manager went on with a tirade that lasted for 90 minutes, but Jim took the punishment and immediately went back to his office and got things fixed. What the customer learned was that Jim could be counted on to do what's right.

Buyers, individually and as organizations, want relationships with ethical people and organizations. They shed those of questionable reputation and concentrate on those who are trustworthy. And when they find someone like Jim, they keep them around as long as they can.

Source: Jim Keller, personal interview.

Even so, the move from a production orientation to a partnering orientation has affected the ethical perspective of the sales profession. The marketing orientation has created a customer-focused perspective that increases awareness of the buyer's needs. This customer awareness naturally leads to a less selfish seller and increases the importance of ethics. Further, the partnering orientation of the current period means long-term relationships are the norm. Salespeople who are less than ethical get caught in long-term relationships. The era of the peddler who can leave town and dupe the citizens of the next town is over.

ETHICS AND PARTNERING RELATIONSHIPS

Ethical principles are particularly important in personal selling. Most businesses try to develop long-term, mutually beneficial relationships with their customers. Salespeople are the official representatives of their companies, responsible for developing and maintaining these relationships, which are built on trust. Partnerships between buyers and sellers cannot develop when salespeople behave unethically or illegally.[5] Further, research shows that trust deteriorates rapidly even in well-established relationships if integrity becomes questionable.[6] As noted in From the Buyer's Seat 2.1, companies and buyers seek out and maintain long-term relationships with ethical salespeople and the companies they represent because they want trustworthy partners.

Legal principles guide business transactions. The issues governing buying and selling are typically straightforward when the transaction is simple and the purchase is a one-time deal. The terms and conditions can be well defined and easily written into a traditional contract. In longer-term relationships, though, legal principles cannot cover all behaviors between buyer and seller. Buyers want relationships with sellers like Jessica Lehrer, people they can trust to do the right thing.

Ethical principles become increasingly important as firms move toward longer-term relationships. Many issues cannot be reduced to contractual terms. For example, a salesperson might make a concession for a buyer with a special problem, anticipating that the buyer will reciprocate on future orders. Yet there is no legal obligation for the buyer to do so; this type of give-and-take is exactly why trust is such an important part of relationships. Because of the high levels of investment and uncertainty, the parties in these relationships cannot accurately assess the potential benefits–the size of the pie–accruing from strategic investments in the relationships or the contributions of each party in producing those benefits. Thus, the parties in a longer-term relationship have to trust one another to divide the pie fairly. Further, many business settings require that the pie be divided among several suppliers or subcontractors, as well as with the customer.

A basic principle of ethical selling is that the customer remains free to make a choice. **Manipulation** eliminates or reduces the buyer's choice unfairly. Salespeople can persuade; with **persuasion**, one may influence the buyer's decision, but the decision remains the buyer's. Manipulation is unethical; persuasion is not. Keep that difference in mind as you read the rest of this chapter.

Here are some examples of difficult situations that salespeople face:

- Should you give an expensive Christmas gift to your biggest customer?
- If a buyer tells you it is common practice to pay off purchasing agents to get orders in his or her country, should you do it?
- Is it acceptable to use a high-pressure sales approach when you know your product is the best for the customer's needs?
- Is it OK to *not* share information about your product that could cost you a sale?
- How do you handle a customer who has been lied to about your product by one of your competitors?

thinking it through How would you respond to the situations in the preceding list? Why? How do you think your friends and your family would respond?

FACTORS INFLUENCING THE ETHICAL BEHAVIOR OF SALESPEOPLE

Exhibit 2.2 illustrates the factors that affect the ethical behavior of salespeople. The personal needs of salespeople, the needs of their companies and customers, company policies, the values of significant others, and the salesperson's personal code of ethics affect ethical choices.[7]

Personal, Company, and Customer Needs

Exhibit 2.3 shows how the personal needs of salespeople can conflict with needs of their firms and their customers. Both the salesperson's company and its customers want to make profits. But sometimes these objectives are conflicting. For example, should a salesperson tell a customer about problems his or her firm is having with a new product? Concealing this information might help make a sale, increase the company's profits, and enhance the salesperson's chances of getting a promotion and a bonus, but doing so could also decrease the customer's profits when the product does not perform adequately.

Exhibit 2.2
Factors Affecting Ethical Behavior of Salespeople

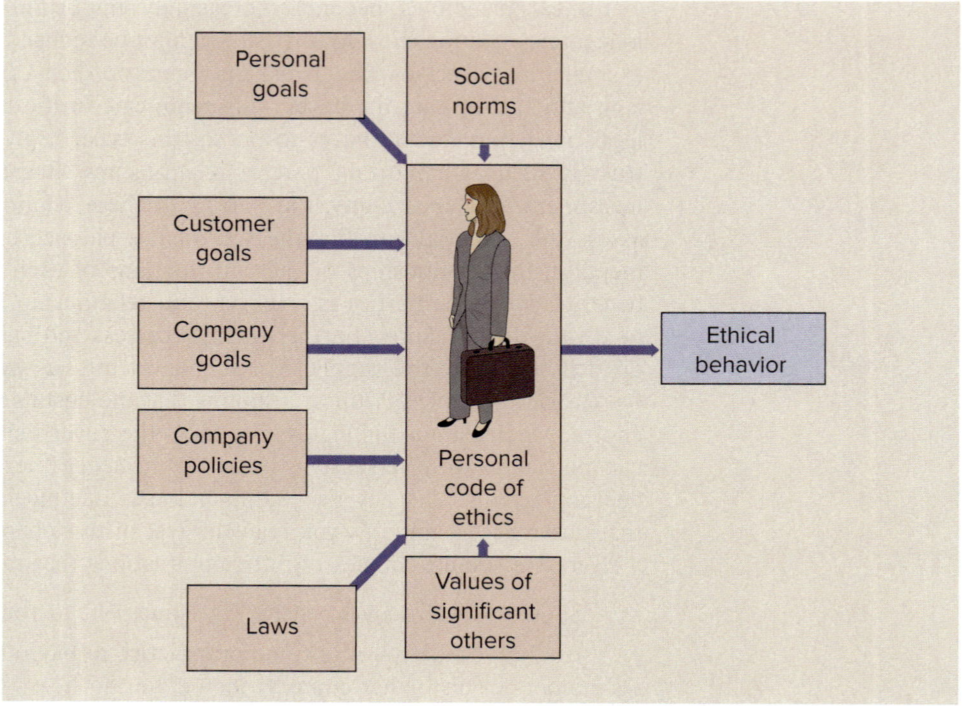

Exhibit 2.3
Conflicting Objectives

Company Objectives	Salesperson Objectives	Customer Objectives
Increase profits	Increase compensation	Increase profits
Increase sales	Receive recognition	Solve problems, satisfy needs
Reduce sales costs	Satisfy customers	Reduce costs
Build long-term customer relationships	Build long-term customer relationships	Build relationships with suppliers
Avoid legal trouble	Maintain personal code of ethics	Avoid legal trouble

Companies need to make sales, and that need can drive some unethical behavior. That seems to be what drove sales management at Wells Fargo to sign up customers for services they never authorized. Once the behavior was made public, though, new accounts not only plummeted, but so did activity with current customers.[8] Research shows that unethical behavior in banking sales has led to decreased interactions with salespeople, with customers opting for Internet-based interactions.[9] Thus, everyone in the sales profession is hurt when only one organization engages in unethical behavior.

Resolving serious ethical problems is difficult, but companies that resolve ethical issues well experience many benefits. Research shows that a positive ethical climate is related to higher levels of performance, job satisfaction, commitment to the organization, and intention to stay among salespeople—especially better-performing salespeople.[10] Organizations that have a positive ethical climate also have salespeople more committed to meeting the organization's goals and greater trust in management.[11]

Ethical conflicts often are not covered by company policies and procedures, and managers may not be available to provide advice. Thus, salespeople must make decisions on their own, relying on their ethical standards and understanding of the laws governing these situations.

Company Policies

To maintain good relationships with their companies and customers, salespeople need to have a clear sense of right and wrong so their companies and customers can depend on them when questionable situations arise. Many companies have codes of ethics for their salespeople to provide guidelines in making ethical decisions. Motorola's policy manual, for example, forbids the use of company funds for influential gifts, as well as acceptance of any gift. Further, it describes guidelines for examining whether any conflict of interest arises. Hewlett-Packard (HP) requires salespeople to take annual training courses regarding company policies, as well as laws and regulations, to ensure that they make informed decisions regarding ethics issues.

Values of Significant Others

People acquire their values and attitudes about what is right and wrong from the people they interact with and observe. Some important people influencing the ethical behavior of salespeople are their relatives and friends, other salespeople, and their sales managers.

Sales managers are particularly important because they establish the ethical climate in their organization through the salespeople they hire, the ethical training they provide for their salespeople, and the degree to which they enforce ethical standards.[12] Salespeople who trust their sales managers are more likely to engage in ethical behaviors.[13]

Students tend to be idealistic in terms of what they expect to encounter in business, though some hesitate to pursue a sales career because they think selling will force them to compromise their principles.[14] No matter the industry, research finds that ethical behavior leads to higher customer satisfaction, trust, loyalty, and repeat purchases. As one of our former students now selling commercial real estate told us, "Unethical reps are run out of our industry." Good ethics are good business, and experienced sales managers and salespeople know that.

Laws

In this chapter we examine ethical and legal issues in personal selling. *Laws* dictate which activities society has deemed to be clearly wrong–the activities for which salespeople and their companies will be punished. Some of these laws are reviewed later in the chapter. However, most sales situations are not covered by laws. Salespeople have to rely on their own codes of ethics and/or their firms' and industries' codes of ethics to determine the right thing to do.

A Personal Code of Ethics

Long before salespeople go to work they develop a sense of what is right and wrong–a standard of conduct–from family and friends. Although salespeople should abide by their own codes of ethics, they may be tempted to avoid difficult ethical choices by developing "logical" reasons for unethical conduct. For example, a salesperson may use the following rationalizations:

- All salespeople behave "this way" (unethically) in this situation.
- No one will be hurt by this behavior.
- This behavior is the lesser of two evils.
- This conduct is the price one has to pay for being in business.

Salespeople who use such reasoning want to avoid feeling responsible for their behavior and being bound by ethical considerations. Even though the pressure to

Values of significant others, such as spouses and family, can influence a salesperson's ethical choices.

make sales may tempt some salespeople to be unethical and act against their internal standards, maintaining an ethical self-image is important. Compromising ethical standards to achieve short-term gains can have adverse long-term effects. When salespeople violate their own principles, they lose self-respect and confidence in their abilities. They may begin to think that the only way they can make sales is to be dishonest or unethical, a downward spiral that can have significant negative effects.

Short-term compromises also make long-term customer relationships more difficult to form. As discussed earlier, customers who have been treated unethically will be reluctant to deal with those salespeople again. Also, they may relate these experiences to business associates in other companies.

Exhibit 2.4 lists some questions you can ask yourself to determine whether a sales behavior or activity is unethical. The questions emphasize that ethical behavior is determined by widely accepted views of what is right and wrong. Thus, you should engage only in activities about which you would be proud to tell your family, friends, employer, and customers.

Your firm can strongly affect the ethical choices you will have to make. What if your manager asks you to engage in activity you consider unethical? There are a number of choices you can make that are discussed in greater detail in Chapter 16, when we focus on relationships with your manager. From a personal perspective, however, here are several of those choices:

1. *Ignore your personal values and do what your company asks you to do.* Self-respect suffers when you have to compromise principles to please an employer. If you take this path, you will probably feel guilty and quickly become dissatisfied with yourself and your job.
2. *Take a stand and tell your employer what you think.* Try to influence the decisions and policies of your company and supervisors.
3. *Refuse to compromise your principles.* There are really two choices here—express your feelings to leadership or just simply ignore the pressure. If the leadership of the company won't change, refusing to join in may mean you will get fired or be forced to quit. Long-term benefits, though, can accrue as customers find that you are trustworthy.

Exhibit 2.4

Checklist for Making Ethical Decisions

1. Would I be embarrassed if a customer found out about this behavior?
2. Would my supervisor disapprove of this behavior?
3. Would most salespeople feel that this behavior is unusual?
4. Am I about to do this because I think I can get away with it?
5. Would I be upset if a salesperson did this to me?
6. Would my family or friends think less of me if I told them about engaging in this sales activity?
7. Am I concerned about the possible consequences of this behavior?
8. Would I be upset if this behavior or activity were publicized in social media?
9. Would society be worse off if everyone engaged in this behavior or activity?

If the answer to any of these questions is yes, the behavior or activity is probably unethical, and you should not do it.

4. *Agree to comply but then don't.* What happens in the field isn't always observed by management, so some salespeople may say they'll do what their management wants them to, but then choose to avoid the unethical behavior.

You should not take a job with a company whose products, policies, and conduct conflict with your standards. Before taking a sales job, investigate the company's procedures and selling approach to see whether they conflict with your personal ethical standards. The issues concerning the relationship between salespeople and their companies are discussed in more detail in Chapter 16, and methods for evaluating companies are presented in Chapter 17.

SELLING ETHICS AND RELATIONSHIPS

The core principle at work in considering ethics in professional selling is that of fairness. The buyer has the right to make the purchase decision with equal and fair access to the information needed to make the decision; further, all competitors should have fair access to the sales opportunity. Keeping information from the customer or misrepresenting information is not fair because it does not allow the customer to make an informed decision. Kickbacks, bribes, and other unethical activities are unfair to both the customer's organization and to competitors. Those types of activities do not allow fair access to the sales opportunity. These and other situations can confront salespeople in their relationships with their customers, competitors, and colleagues (other salespeople).

RELATIONSHIPS WITH CUSTOMERS

The most common areas of ethical concern involving customers include using deception; offering bribes, gifts, and entertainment; providing special treatment; divulging confidential information; and engaging in backdoor selling.

Using Deception

Deliberately presenting inaccurate information, or lying, to a customer is illegal. Further, misleading customers by telling half-truths or withholding important information can also lead to legal consequences but is more often a matter of ethics. Some salespeople believe it is the customer's responsibility to uncover potential product problems. These salespeople answer questions, perhaps incompletely, and don't offer information that might make a sale more difficult. For example, a salesperson selling life insurance may fail to mention that the policy won't pay off under certain circumstances.

Customers expect salespeople to be enthusiastic about their firm and its products and recognize that this enthusiasm can result in a certain amount of exaggeration as part of the persuasion process. Customers also expect salespeople to emphasize the positive aspects of their products and spend little time talking about the negative aspects. But practicing **deception** by withholding information or telling lies is clearly manipulative and therefore unethical. Such salespeople take advantage of the trust customers place in them. When buyers uncover these deceptions, they will be reluctant to trust such salespeople in the future. Not only that, but sophisticated buyers recognize such deceptions and assume the worst anyway.[15]

Salespeople who fail to provide customers with complete information about products lose an opportunity to develop trust. Trust is created through many actions, such as keeping all promises, especially the small promises like calling back when you say you will. In Building Partnerships 2.1 we develop this concept of trust more completely.

BUILDING Partnerships 2.1

SERVICE LEVEL AGREEMENTS

Bruce Culbert is the chief revenue officer of one of Atlanta's fastest-growing companies, the Pedowitz Group. This company provides marketing services to clients all over the United States, companies as varied as Purina and the Boston Bruins.

"A client pays us because we help them create sales-ready leads through better marketing technology. That means they give us responsibility for their sales revenue, which puts us in a very humbling position," notes Culbert.

In any services field, one reason the contract is so important is because the product isn't tangible. The contract specifies what the services are, when they will be delivered, when they are considered finished, and the like. Each level of service agreed to in the contract is called a service level agreement (SLA). If the SLA requires 24-hour turnaround, then 24 hours is the metric by which the service is measured.

"The reality, though, is that we can hit the SLAs in a contract and still not deliver on the goal, which is to increase a customer's sales," says Culbert. "SLAs only cover things like how quickly we do things or how many things we do, not how well we do them."

"Our clients can fire us at any time, contract or no contract. But we do what we say we will, and we won't cut corners. We respond to our customers quickly, but more importantly, we respond with the right answers." Culbert believes that customers trust the Pedowitz Group because he and his colleagues do what they say they will—from the smallest things to the delivery of results.

Source: Bruce Culbert, personal interview.

Offering Bribes, Gifts, and Entertainment

Bribes and kickbacks may be illegal. **Bribes** are payments made to buyers to influence their purchase decisions, whereas **kickbacks** are payments made to buyers based on the amount of orders placed. A purchasing agent personally benefits from bribes and kickbacks, but these payments typically have negative consequences for the purchasing agent's firm because the product's performance is not considered in buying decisions.

Entertaining clients is an accepted business practice in most industries, and this is an acceptable way to build relationships as long as the entertainment is not too lavish.

©Andersen Ross/Blend Images LLC RF

Taking customers to lunch is a commonly accepted business practice. Most salespeople take customers to lunch occasionally or frequently, and in many instances salespeople use this time to get to know the buyer better rather than pitch business. However, some companies take customers to sporting events, to play golf, or even on overnight trips to the company's plant or headquarters. In some cases these trips can become quite lavish; the pharmaceutical industry, for example, came under close governmental regulation for questionable practices regarding exotic and expensive trips for doctors who prescribe certain medications.

Determining which gifts and entertainment activities are acceptable and which are not brings up ethical issues. To avoid these issues, many U.S. companies have policies that forbid employees to accept gifts (more than pencils or coffee cups) or entertainment from suppliers. These firms require that all gifts sent to the employee's home or office be returned. IBM does not allow any gifts, even coffee cups; Walmart, the largest retailer in the world, makes no allowance for entertainment because all contact between buyers and vendors can occur only at business meetings at Walmart's or the vendor's headquarters. On the other hand, many companies have no policy on receiving gifts or entertainment. Some unethical employees will accept and even solicit gifts, even though their company has a policy against such practices.

To develop a productive, long-term relationship, salespeople need to avoid embarrassing customers by asking them to engage in activities they might see as unethical. If a salesperson wants to give a gift out of friendship or invite a customer to lunch to develop a better business relationship, she or he should phrase the offer so the customer can easily refuse it. For example, a salesperson with a large industrial firm might have this conversation with a customer:

SALESPERSON: John, we have worked well together over the last five years, and I would like to give you something to show my appreciation. Would that be OK?

BUYER: That's very nice of you, but what are you thinking of giving me?

SALESPERSON: Well, I want to give you a Mont Blanc pen. I really enjoy using my pen, and I thought you might like one also. Is that OK?

BUYER: I would appreciate that gift. Thank you.

Buyers typically are sensitive about receiving expensive gifts, according to Shirley Hunter, account manager for Oracle. "It's like getting five dozen roses after a first date. It's embarrassing if anyone finds out, and you have to wonder what's the catch?"[16] Some industries used promotional items frequently, but in pharmaceutical sales, government regulations have increasingly forbidden the use of gifts because no one wants the choice of a prescription to be influenced by a salesperson's gift to a doctor. Some guidelines for gift giving are as follows:

- Check your motives for giving the gift. The gift should be given to foster a mutually beneficial, long-term relationship, not to obligate or pay off the customer for placing an order.
- Make sure the customer views the gift as a symbol of your appreciation and respect with no strings attached. Never give customers the impression that you are attempting to buy their business with a gift.
- Make sure the gift does not violate the customer's or your firm's policies.
- The safest gifts are inexpensive business items imprinted with the salesperson's company's name or logo.

Even when customers encourage and accept gifts, lavish gifts and entertainment are both unethical and bad business. Treating a customer to a three-day fishing trip is no substitute for effective selling. Sales won this way are usually short lived. Salespeople who offer expensive gifts to get orders may be blackmailed into continually providing these gifts to obtain orders in the future. Customers who can be bribed are likely to switch their business when presented with better offers.

Providing Special Treatment

Some customers try to take advantage of their status to get special treatment from salespeople. For example, a buyer may ask for expedited shipment. Providing this extra service may upset other customers who do not get the special attention. In addition, spending time expediting that customer's shipment instead of making sales calls can reduce the salesperson's productivity. Salespeople should be diplomatic but careful about undertaking requests to provide unusual services.

Divulging Confidential Information

During sales calls salespeople often encounter confidential company information, such as new products under development, costs, and production schedules. Offering information about a customer's competitor in exchange for an order is unethical. Many times, though, the request is not that obvious. For example, a customer asks how well your product is selling, and you reply, "Great!" The customer then asks, "Well, how is it doing at HEB?" If the customer is told how many cases are sold at HEB, then HEB's right to confidentiality was violated. We discuss legal issues around privacy later in this chapter, but there are ethical issues regarding confidentiality that are not always covered by law.

Sometimes salespeople have to sign a **nondisclosure agreement (NDA)**, which is a contract that specifies what information is owned by the customer and how or if that information can be shared with anyone. That's because salespeople may have access to information that, if it became public, could damage the customer. For example, a customer may be working on a new product, and if competitors found out, they might preempt the new product launch with a similar product of their own. Long-term relationships can develop only when customers trust salespeople to maintain confidentiality. By disclosing confidential information, a salesperson will get a reputation for being untrustworthy. Even the customer who solicited the confidential information will not trust the salesperson, who will then be denied access to information needed to make an effective sales presentation.

Engaging in Backdoor Selling

Sometimes purchasing agents require that all contacts with the prospect's employees be made through them because they want to be fully informed about and control the buying process. In many instances, there are sole source contracts that may be in place requiring all purchases of a certain category to be made from a specified supplier. This policy can make it difficult for a new supplier to get business from a customer using a competitor's products.

Sharing customers' information with one of their competitors, such as how much they sell your product, isn't fair to them. Remember, that information belongs to them, not to you.

© JGI/Jamie Grill/Blend Images LLC RF

Salespeople engage in **backdoor selling** when they ignore the purchasing agent's policy, go around his or her back, and contact other people directly involved in the purchasing decision. Backdoor selling can be risky and unethical. If the purchasing agent finds out, and they usually do when the order is placed, the salesperson may never be able to get any sale. To avoid these potential problems, the salesperson needs to convince the purchasing agent of the benefits to be gained by direct contact with other people in the customer's firm.

Research on buyers in general suggests additional behaviors that they think are unethical or inappropriate. Exhibit 2.5 summarizes that research. Even cheating at golf can lead to a lost opportunity! John Palley, an attorney, tells the story of playing golf with a potential vendor's salesperson. The salesperson hit a ball into the rough, then after a short search, claimed to find it on the edge of the fairway. Palley

Exhibit 2.5
What Buyers Hate about Salespeople

- Exaggerates benefits of product.
- Passes the blame for something he or she did to someone else.
- Lies about product availability.
- Misrepresents guarantees.
- Lies about competition.
- Pushes products that people do not need.
- Makes oral promises that are not legally binding.
- Is not interested in customer needs.
- Answers questions even when he or she does not know the correct answer.
- Sells hazardous products.

Source: William Bearden, Thomas Ingram, and Raymond LaForge, *Marketing: Principles and Perspectives* (New York: McGraw-Hill/Irwin, 2004).

says, "I walked 20 feet and pointed to his original ball (with his company logo on it). He said, 'Ohhhh, that must be the one I lost the last time I played.'" Palley says he could have given that salesperson a lot of business but he never did. "If a person cheats at golf, I don't think I could trust him."[17]

RELATIONSHIPS WITH THE SALESPERSON'S COMPANY

Because salespeople's activities in the field cannot be closely monitored, their employers trust them to act in the company's best interests. Professional salespeople do not abuse this trust. They put the interests of their companies above self-interest. Taking this perspective may require them to make short-term sacrifices to achieve long-term benefits for their companies and themselves. Some problem areas in the salesperson–company relationship involve handling expense accounts ethically, reporting work time information and activities, and switching jobs.

Handling Expense Accounts Ethically

Many companies provide their salespeople with cars, smartphones, and data plans, as well as reimburse them for travel and entertainment expenses. Developing a reimbursement policy that prevents salespeople from cheating and still allows them the flexibility they need to cover their territories and entertain customers is almost impossible. Moreover, a lack of tight control can tempt salespeople to use their expense accounts to increase their income.

To do their jobs well, salespeople need to incur expenses. However, using their expense accounts to offset what they consider to be inadequate compensation is unethical. A salesperson who cannot live within the company compensation plan and expense policies has two ethical alternatives: (1) persuade the company to change its compensation plan or expense policy or (2) find another job. Salespeople are given expense accounts to cover legitimate expenses, such as for travel. Act as though you are spending your own money; an expense account does not mean you should stay in the most luxurious hotel in town.

Reporting Work Time Information and Activities

Employers expect their salespeople to work full-time. Salespeople on salary are stealing from their employers when they waste time on coffee breaks, long lunches, or unauthorized days off. Even salespeople paid by commission cheat their companies by not working full-time. Both their incomes and company profits decrease when salespeople take time off.

To monitor work activities, many companies use customer relationship management (CRM) software, such as Salesforce.com. This software not only helps salespeople keep track of customer contact information, it also links up to their calendar. As the software

SALES Technology 2.1

COMPLIANCE AND SALES SOFTWARE

Salespeople use customer relationship management (CRM) software to keep their own records of whom they have called on, what happened on each sales call, what needs to be done next and when, and so forth. Sales managers can access all of this information, too, and use it to determine if the salesperson is working hard enough.

Now, though, that same software has become a tool for making sure that salespeople and sales managers comply with laws and regulations. Salesforce.com, one of the leading vendors in CRM software, recently added Shield, a series of features that financial services firms can use to ensure that financial advisors meet their fiduciary responsibility to act in the best interest of their clients.

"CRM by its very nature allows advisers to record information with transactions with clients, so on the face of it, CRM is good for the mandates of the DOL law," said John Rourke, chief executive of Starburst Labs, the creator of Wealthbox CRM. "The heart of this is recording and compliance."

According to Shaun Calderwood, a CRM consultant, the CRM system helps maintain CAN-SPAM compliance. Not only can the system be used to create e-mail templates that comply with the law, CRM software can also monitor activity and generate reports alerting management to potential violations.

These are just two of the situations where technology is providing transparency into salesperson activities for the purpose of monitoring for compliance. Such uses will continue to grow as regulations become more complex.

As Sue Glover, owner of Sue Glover & Associates, says, "The CRM can't do it alone, but it does help ensure (salespeople) are doing their due diligence."

Sources: Shaun Calderwood, "7 Technical Tips to Handling Canada's Anti-Spam Legislation," *Perpetual West*, May 19, 2014; "Salesforce Adds Compliance Features to Financial Services CRM for DOL Fiduciary Rule," *ICT Monitor Worldwide*, July 26, 2016.

is updated by salespeople after each call (or at the end of the day), managers can pull reports to keep tabs on their salespeople's activities. Most salespeople dislike the clerical task of updating the information. Some provide false information, including calls they never made, just to hit activity goals. Giving inaccurate information or bending the truth is clearly unethical.

Switching Jobs

When salespeople decide to change jobs, they have an ethical responsibility to their employers. The company often makes a considerable investment in training salespeople and then gives them confidential information about new products and programs. Over time, salespeople use this training and information to build strong relationships with their customers.

For that reason, some companies require salespeople to sign a contract that contains a **noncompete clause**. While the legality of such a clause can vary from state to state, essentially the company wants to guard against your taking customers with you when you switch to a new company. If you switch jobs in the same industry, you may need to seek legal advice regarding any noncompete clauses. A salesperson may have good reasons to switch jobs. However, if a salesperson goes to work for a competitor, she or he should not say negative things about the past employer. Also, disclosing confidential information about the former employer's business is improper. The ethical approach to leaving a job includes the following:

- *Give ample notice.* If you leave a job during a busy time and with inadequate notice, your employer may suffer significant lost sales opportunities. Do not be surprised, though, if you are escorted out that day. Many companies are concerned about the loss of information by, as well as lack of productivity of, someone who has turned in notice, so the policy may be that you are turned out that day.

- *Offer assistance during the transition phase.* Help your replacement learn about your customers and territory, if given the opportunity, as Jim Keller did at Teradata (see From the Buyer's Seat 2.1 at the beginning of the chapter).
- *Don't burn your bridges.* Don't say things in anger that may come back to haunt you. Remember that you may want to return to the company or ask the company for a reference in the future. You may even find that the people you worked with move to a company you want to work for or sell to!
- *Don't take anything with you that belongs to the company.* That includes all your records and notes on companies you called on, even if you are going to a noncompeting company. In many states, customer records are considered **trade secrets,** or information owned by the company by which the company gains a competitive advantage. Trade secrets are protected by law, so if you take customer records with you, you could face a civil lawsuit.

RELATIONSHIPS WITH COLLEAGUES

To be effective, salespeople need to work together with other salespeople. Unethical behavior by salespeople toward their coworkers, such as engaging in sexual harassment and taking advantage of colleagues, can weaken company morale and harm the company's reputation.

Engaging in Sexual Harassment

Sexual harassment includes unwelcome sexual advances; requests for sexual favors, jokes or graffiti; posting sexually explicit material on bulletin boards or cubicle walls; and physical conduct. Harassment is not confined to requests for sexual favors in exchange for job considerations such as a raise or promotion; creating a hostile work environment can be considered sexual harassment. Some actions that are considered sexual harassment are engaging in suggestive behavior, treating people differently because they are male or female, making lewd sexual comments and gestures, sharing by e-mail jokes that have sexual content, showing obscene photographs, alleging that an employee got rewards by engaging in sexual acts, and spreading rumors about a person's sexual conduct.

Customers as well as coworkers can sexually harass salespeople. Salespeople are particularly vulnerable to harassment from important customers who may seek sexual favors in exchange for their business. Following are some suggestions for dealing with sexual harassment from customers:

- Don't become so dependent on one customer that you would consider compromising your principles to retain the customer's business. Develop a large base of customers and prospects to minimize the importance of one customer–a good idea for a lot of reasons, and not just because you might be concerned about sexual harassment.
- Tell the harasser in person or write a letter stating that the behavior is offensive, is unacceptable, and must be stopped. Clearly indicate that you are in control and will not be passive.
- Use the sexual harassment policies of your firm and your customer's firm to resolve problems. These policies typically state the procedure for filing a complaint, the person responsible for investigating the complaint, the time frame for completing the investigation, and the means by which the parties will be informed about the resolution.

Research indicates that sexual harassment is rare; one study found only an average of 1.3 cases per year per company in all areas of the company, not just sales.[20] That study also found that companies are much more worried about making sure their employees have a safe environment in which to work than any fear of lawsuits; in other words, executives want to make sure their people have a good environment in which to work because it is the right thing to do, not because they may get sued if they fail to do so.

Taking Advantage of Other Salespeople

Salespeople can behave unethically when they are too aggressive in pursuing their own goals at the expense of their colleagues. For example, it is unethical to steal potential customers from other salespeople. This practice is called **poaching**. In some companies, sales territories are defined by a customer list, and customers are open to being called on until they are on the list. Should the account go dormant, it can become open again. But some salespeople will try to take over accounts, while others will try to make dormant accounts look active in order to keep them. Colleagues usually discover such unethical behavior and return the lack of support. If the company has policies protecting customers or territories, such behavior can lead to immediate termination.

RELATIONSHIPS WITH COMPETITORS

Making false claims about competitors' products or sabotaging their efforts is clearly unethical and often illegal. For example, a salesperson who rearranges the display of a competitor's products in a customer's store to make it less appealing is being unethical. This type of behavior can backfire. When customers detect these practices, the reputations of the salespeople and their companies may be permanently damaged.

Another questionable tactic is criticizing a competitor's products or policies. Although you may be tempted to say negative things about a competitor, this approach usually does not work. Customers will assume you are biased toward your own company and its products and discount negative comments you make about the competition. Some customers may even be offended. If they have bought the competitor's products in the past, they may regard these comments as a criticism of their judgment.

LEGAL ISSUES

Society has determined that some activities are clearly unethical and has created a legal system to prevent people from engaging in these activities. Salespeople who violate these laws can cause serious problems for themselves and their companies—problems more serious than being considered unethical by a buyer. By engaging in illegal activities, salespeople expose themselves and their firms to costly legal fees and millions of dollars in fines.

The activities of salespeople in the United States are affected by three forms of law: statutory, administrative, and common. **Statutory law** is based on legislation passed either by state legislatures or by Congress. The main statutory laws governing salespeople are the Uniform Commercial Code (UCC) and antitrust laws. **Administrative laws** are established by local, state, or federal regulatory agencies. The Federal Trade Commission (FTC) is the most active agency in developing administrative laws affecting salespeople. However, the Securities and Exchange Commission regulates stockbrokers, and the Food and Drug Administration regulates pharmaceutical salespeople. Finally, **common law** grows out of court decisions. Precedents set by these decisions fill in the gaps where no laws exist.

The laws affecting salespeople are ever changing. Some affect specific industries, such as laws affecting pharmaceutical and medical supply companies and their salespeople. Others, like the UCC, are more general and affect all salespeople. But even if there is no single law passed regarding a specific industry, the U.S. government issues new rules and regulations every year, and the rate is growing. In 2013 alone, over 26,700 pages of regulations affecting salespeople were issued.[19]

This section discusses current laws affecting salespeople, but every year important new laws are developed and court decisions rendered. Thus you should contact your firm for advice when a potential legal issue arises.

UNIFORM COMMERCIAL CODE

The **Uniform Commercial Code (UCC)** is the legal guide to commercial practice in the United States. The UCC defines a number of terms related to salespeople.

Agency

A person who acts in place of his or her company is an **agent**. Authorized agents of a company have the authority to legally obligate their firm in a business transaction. This authorization to represent the company does not have to be in writing. Thus, as a salesperson your statements and actions can legally bind your company and have significant financial impact.

Sale

The UCC defines a **sale** as "the transfer of title to goods by the seller to the buyer for a consideration known as price." A sale differs from a **contract to sell**. Anytime a salesperson makes an offer and receives an unqualified acceptance, a contract exists. A sale is made when the contract is completed and title passes from the seller to the buyer.

The UCC also distinguishes between an offer and an invitation to negotiate. A sales presentation is usually considered to be an **invitation to negotiate**. An **offer** takes place when the salesperson quotes specific terms. The offer specifically states what the seller promises to deliver and what it expects from the buyer. If the buyer accepts these terms, the parties will have established a binding contract.

Salespeople are agents when they have the authority to make offers. However, most salespeople are not agents because they have the power only to solicit written offers from buyers. These written offers, called **orders**, become contracts when they are signed by an authorized representative in the salesperson's company. Sometimes these orders contain clauses stating that the firm is not obligated by its salesperson's statements. However, the buyer usually can have the contract nullified and may even sue for damages if salespeople make misleading statements, even though they are not official agents.

This buyer is inspecting a shipment of various products. Because the products were shipped FOB destination, the buyer is not responsible for the merchandise until it shows up at the buyer's location. The buyer can even turn down the sale now if the products are not up to standard.

Title and Risk of Loss

If the contract terms specify **free on board (FOB) destination**, the seller has title until the goods are received at the destination. In this case any loss or damage incurred during transportation is the responsibility of the seller. The buyer assumes this responsibility and risk if contract terms call for **FOB factory**. The UCC also defines when titles transfer for goods shipped cash on delivery (COD) and for goods sold on consignment. Understanding the terms of the sale and who has title can be useful in resolving complaints about damaged merchandise.

thinking it through

If a salesperson is not an agent, then what is the salesperson? Does not being an agent change the salesperson's obligations to the company in any way? Or to the customer?

Oral versus Written Agreements

In most cases oral agreements between a salesperson and a customer are just as binding as written agreements. Normally, written agreements are required for sales over $500. Salespeople may be the legal representatives of their firms and thus must be careful when signing written agreements.

Obligations and Performance

When the salesperson and the customer agree on the terms of a contract, both firms must perform according to those terms in "good faith," which means they have to try to fulfill the contract. In addition, both parties must perform according to commonly accepted industry practices. Even if salespeople overstate the performance of their products, their firms have to provide the stated performance and meet the terms of the contract.

Warranties

A **warranty** is an assurance by the seller that the products will perform as represented. Sometimes a warranty is called a *guarantee.* The UCC distinguishes between two types of warranties: expressed and implied. An **expressed warranty** is an oral or a written statement by the seller. An **implied warranty** is not actually stated but is still an obligation defined by law. For example, products sold using an oral or a written description (the buyer never sees the products) carry an implied warranty that the products are of average quality. However, if the buyer inspects the product before placing an order, the implied warranty applies only to any performance aspects that the inspection would not have uncovered. Typically an implied warranty also guarantees that the product can be used in the manner stated by the seller.

Problems with warranties often arise when the sale is to a reseller (a distributor or retailer). The ultimate user–the reseller's customer–may complain about a product to the reseller. The reseller, in turn, tries to shift the responsibility to the manufacturer. Salespeople often have to investigate and resolve these issues.

MISREPRESENTATION OR SALES PUFFERY

In their enthusiasm salespeople may exaggerate the performance of products and even make false statements to get an order. Over time, common and administrative laws have defined the difference between illegal misrepresentation and sales puffery. Not all statements salespeople make have legal consequences. However, misrepresentation, even if legal, can destroy a business relationship and may involve salespeople and their firms in lawsuits.

Glowing descriptions such as "Our service can't be beat" are considered to be opinions or **sales puffery**. Customers cannot reasonably rely on these statements. Following are some examples of puffery:

- This is a top-notch product.
- This product will last a lifetime.

- Our school bus chassis has been designed to provide the utmost safety and reliability for carrying the nation's most precious cargo–schoolchildren.
- The most complete line of reliable, economical gas heating appliances.

However, statements about the inherent capabilities of products or services, such as "Our system will reduce your inventory by 40 percent," may be treated as statements of fact and become warranties. Here are examples of such statements found to be legally binding:

- Mechanically, this oil rig is a 9 on a scale of 10.
- Feel free to prescribe this drug to your patients, doctor. It's nonaddicting.
- This equipment will keep up with any other machine you are using and will work well with your other machines.

Rich Kraus owned a company providing document shredding services using special trucks that contain high-speed shredders. When purchasing a new truck, he looked to another small company. The salesperson was the owner's son, and his pride came through as he gave a demo and rattled off the capabilities of the equipment. Compared to Kraus's current model, this shredder was 40 percent faster and had 30 percent more capacity for storing shredded material, so he placed an order for the $250,000 truck.

Unfortunately he quickly realized the truck was capable of holding only 60 percent of the paper that the salesperson said it could. When the problem was discussed with the engineer, he admitted that the salesperson had provided incorrect information. However, he didn't want to correct the owner's son in front of a prospective customer. He added that the salesperson was a good honest person and that his enthusiasm probably just got the best of him.

Only after threatening legal action did Kraus get his money back and order a truck from his original vendor. Since then, Kraus sold his company to a larger company that purchases an average of 50 trucks per year, all from Kraus's original vendor.

As Kraus says, "Since that time we have had dozens of associates in the industry ask us about our experience with this company. It's hard to fathom how many orders it lost as a result." Risking the reputation of the company for even a single unit just wasn't worth it.[18]

The **False Claims Act**, or Lincoln Law, was passed in 1863 during the Civil War to encourage citizens to press claims against vendors that fraudulently sold to the U.S. government (all states now have their own version, too). During the war, defense contractors were selling all manner of products (including mules) that could not live up to the claims made by the salespeople. As a result, the government was losing money and the war. This law enabled a person bringing a claim of fraud to share in the proceeds if the contractor was found guilty and damages are assessed. Although this law is well over 100 years old, as you read in the opening profile, today's businesspeople like Jessica Lehrer at ThyssenKrupp Elevator still have to ensure that their claims are accurate, especially when selling to the government.

U.S. salespeople need to be aware of both U.S. laws and laws in the host country when selling internationally. All countries have laws regulating marketing and selling activities. In Canada all claims and statements made in advertisements and sales presentations about comparisons with competitive products must pass the **credulous person standard**. This standard means the company and the salesperson have to pay damages if a reasonable person could misunderstand a statement. Thus, a statement like "This is the strongest axle in Canada" might be considered puffery in the United States but be viewed as misleading in Canada unless the firm had absolute evidence that the axle was stronger than any other axle sold in Canada.

To avoid legal and ethical problems with misrepresentation, you should try to educate customers thoroughly before concluding a sale. You should tell the customer as much about the specific performance of the product as possible. Unless your firm has test results concerning the product's performance, you should avoid offering an opinion about the product's specific benefits for the customer's application. If you don't have the answer to a customer's question, don't guess. Say that you don't know the answer and will get back to the customer with the information.

ILLEGAL BUSINESS PRACTICES

The Sherman Antitrust Act of 1890, the Clayton Act of 1914, the Federal Trade Commission Act of 1914, and the Robinson-Patman Act of 1934 prohibit unfair business practices that may reduce competition. The Federal Trade Commission is often tasked with enforcing these laws, though the Justice Department may also bring cases. The courts use these laws to create common law that defines the illegal business practices discussed in this section.

Business Defamation

Business defamation occurs when a salesperson makes unfair or untrue statements to customers about a competitor, its products, or its salespeople. These statements are illegal when they damage the competitor's reputation or the reputation of its salespeople.

Following are some examples of false statements made about competitors that have been found to be illegal:

- Company X broke the law when it offered you a free case of toilet paper with every 12 cases you buy.
- Company X is going bankrupt.
- You shouldn't do business with Company X. Mr. Jones, the CEO, is really incompetent and dishonest.

You should avoid making negative comments about a competitor, its salespeople, or its products unless you have proof to support the statements.

Reciprocity

Reciprocity is a special relationship in which two companies agree to buy products from each other. For example, a manufacturer of computers agrees to use microprocessors from a component manufacturer if the component manufacturer agrees to buy its computers. Such interrelationships can lead to greater trust and cooperation between the firms. However, reciprocity agreements are illegal under the Sherman Antitrust Act if one company forces another company to join the agreement. Reciprocity is legal only when both parties consent to the agreement willingly.

Tying Agreements

In a **tying agreement** a buyer is required to purchase one product in order to get another product. For example, a customer who wants to buy a copy machine is required to buy paper from the same company, or a distributor that wants to stock one product must stock the manufacturer's entire product line. Because they reduce competition, tying agreements typically are illegal under the Clayton Act. They are legal only when the seller can show that the products must be used together–that is, that one product will not function properly unless the other product is used with it.

Tying agreements are also legal when a company's reputation depends on the proper functioning of equipment. Thus, a firm can be required to buy a service contract for equipment it purchases, although the customer need not buy the contract from the manufacturer.

Conspiracy and Collusion

An agreement between competitors before customers are contacted is a **conspiracy**, whereas **collusion** refers to competitors working together while the customer is making a purchase decision. For example, competitors are conspiring when they get together and divide up a territory so that only one competitor will call on each prospect. Collusion occurs when competitors agree to charge the same price for equipment that a prospect is considering. These examples of collusion and conspiracy are illegal because they reduce competition.

Interference with Competitors

Salespeople may illegally interfere with competitors by doing the following:

- Trying to get a customer to break a contract with a competitor.
- Tampering with a competitor's product.
- Confusing a competitor's market research by buying merchandise from stores.

Restrictions on Resellers

Numerous laws govern the relationship between manufacturers and resellers–wholesalers and retailers. At one time it was illegal for companies to establish a minimum price below which their distributors or retailers could not resell their products. Today this practice, called **resale price maintenance**, is legal in some situations.

Manufacturers do not have to sell their products to any reseller that wants to buy them. Sellers can use their judgment to select resellers if they announce their selection criteria in advance. One sales practice considered unfair is providing special incentives to get a reseller's salespeople to push products. For example, salespeople for a cosmetics company may give a department store's cosmetics salespeople prizes based on sales of the company's product. These special incentives, called **spiffs (push money)**, are legal only if the reseller knows and approves of the incentive and it is offered to all the reseller's salespeople. *Spiff* stands for "special promotion incentive fund" and dates back to a time when there was more selling by retail salespeople. Even if they are legal, though, not everyone agrees that spiffs are ethical.[21]

Price Discrimination

The Robinson-Patman Act became law because independent wholesalers and retailers wanted additional protection from the aggressive marketing tactics of large chain stores. Principally, the act forbids price discrimination in interstate commerce. Robinson-Patman applies only to interstate commerce, but most states have passed similar laws to govern sales transactions between buyers and sellers within the same state.

Court decisions related to the Robinson-Patman Act define **price discrimination** as a seller giving *unjustified* special prices, discounts, or services to some customers and not to others. To justify a special price or discount, the seller must prove that it results from (1) differences in the cost of manufacture, sale, or delivery; (2) differences in the quality or nature of the product delivered; or (3) an attempt to meet prices offered by competitors

Using spiffs to promote one product over another, such as computer display, is legal, but research shows consumers believe the practice to be unethical.

©Digital Vision/SuperStock RF

in a market. Different prices can be charged, however, if the cost of doing business is different or if a customer negotiates more effectively. For example, a customer who buys in large volume can be charged a lower price if the manufacturing and shipping charges for higher-volume orders are lower than they are for smaller orders.

In general, firms also may not offer special allowances to one reseller unless those allowances are made available to competing resellers. Because most resellers compete in limited geographic areas, firms frequently offer allowances in specific regions of the country. However, recent Supreme Court decisions allow some leeway in offering discounts to resellers who are engaged in competitive bids. These discounts do not necessarily have to be offered uniformly to all resellers for all customers but can be selectively offered to meet specific competitive situations. In one case a Volvo truck dealer sued Volvo, citing discounts given to other Volvo dealers in situations where the dealers were all bidding on the same customer's contract. The Supreme Court ruled that these instances did not violate the law because they were negotiated individually to meet bids from non-Volvo providers.

Privacy Laws

Privacy laws limit the amount of information that a firm can obtain about a consumer and specify how that information can be used or shared. The Gramm-Leach-Bliley Act, passed in 1999, requires written notification of customers regarding privacy policies. Note that the law does not discriminate in how the information was obtained. In other words, the law is the same for a customer who fills out a credit application or a customer who responds to questions from a salesperson. Although this law applies primarily to financial institutions, a second phase of the act became law in 2003, broadening its application. Further, any company that publishes a privacy policy is expected, by regulation of the FTC, to follow that policy and is liable to prosecution if it uses customer information inappropriately.

European Union (EU) law is even more stringent than U.S. law. The application of privacy applies to many more settings, and transfer of information is forbidden in nearly all circumstances. Further, the law can apply to information that could be shared among non-EU subsidiaries, which means that in some instances an account manager in Europe cannot share information with an American colleague.

Do-Not-Call Law

The federal **Do-Not-Call Registry** originally took effect in 2003 and was strengthened in 2007 and limits the conditions under which anyone on the registry may be telephoned at home or on a cell phone. A salesperson, for example, cannot call the number of someone on the registry if the person has not been customer within the past 18 months. This registry was set up by the FTC under its ability to set rules for commerce, and is an administrative law. However, the FTC can levy fines against companies and individuals that violate the rules, as some companies have already learned. The rules do not apply to business phones, nor do they apply to solicitations by nonprofits and political organizations.

CAN-SPAM Act

The **CAN-SPAM Act** was intended to reduce deceptive e-mails and usually contains specifications, such as an opt-out process and complete contact information, that are allowable. The U.S. CAN-SPAM law specifies a fine up to $40,000 for each e-mail sent, so you can see that violations can quickly add up; individuals can and have gone to jail for violating the law. Like many laws involving privacy, European legislation is much stiffer and more likely to lead to prosecution; even in Canada, companies are more likely to be fined. E-mails that contain information about a transaction or relationship that the receiver already has with the sender are usually OK; the problem is when the e-mail is a commercial message with the intent to sell something. To comply with the law, commercial messages cannot be deceptive and must include opt-out information and full contact information (including a postal address) for the sender. Opt-outs also have to be processed and honored quickly. These rules do not mean that a salesperson can't send promotional messages to new prospects, only that the e-mails meet those requirements.

Few salespeople have been prosecuted for violating CAN-SPAM, but U.S. companies have been fined. One of the early fines was just under $1 million; recently a company was fined $200,000 because the opt-out process didn't work.[22] The lesson, though, for most salespeople is to let the marketing department handle promotional e-mails sent to people you don't know.

INTERNATIONAL ETHICAL AND LEGAL ISSUES

Ethical and legal issues are complex for selling in international markets. Value judgments and laws vary widely across cultures and countries. Behavior that is commonly accepted as proper in one country can be completely unacceptable in another country. For example, a small payment to expedite the loading of a truck is considered a cost of doing business in some Middle Eastern countries but may be viewed as a bribe in the United States.

Many countries make a clear distinction between payments for lubrication and payments for subordination. **Lubrication** involves small sums of money or gifts, typically made to low-ranking managers or government officials, in countries where these payments are not illegal. The lubrication payments are made to get the official or manager to do the job more rapidly–to process an order more quickly or to provide a copy of a request for a proposal. For example, Halliburton, the company hired to rebuild Iraq, says, "Sometimes the company [Halliburton] may be required to make facilitating or expediting payments to a low-level government employee or employees in some other countries than the United States to expedite or secure the routine governmental action. . . . Such facilitating payments may not be illegal. . . . Accordingly, facilitating payments must be strictly controlled, and every effort must be made to eliminate or minimize such payments."[23] The policy goes on to say that any such payments must have advance authorization from the company's legal department so there will be no question whether the payment is lubrication or subordination. **Subordination** involves paying larger sums of money to higher-ranking officials to get them to do something that is illegal or to ignore an illegal act. Even in countries where bribery is common, subordination is considered unethical.[24]

RESOLVING CULTURAL DIFFERENCES

What do you do when the ethical standards in a country differ from the standards in your country? This is an old question. Cultural relativism and ethical imperialism are two extreme answers to this question. **Cultural relativism** is the view that no culture's ethics are superior. If the people in Indonesia tolerate bribery, their attitude toward bribery is no better or worse than that of people in Singapore who refuse to give or accept bribes. When in Rome, do as the Romans do. But is it right for a European pharmaceutical company to pay a Nigerian company to dispose of the pharmaceutical company's highly toxic waste near Nigerian residential neighborhoods, even though Nigeria has no rules against toxic waste disposal?

On the other hand, **ethical imperialism** is the view that ethical standards in one's home country should be applied to one's behavior across the world. This view suggests, for example, that Saudi Arabian salespeople working for a U.S. firm should go through the same sexual harassment training U.S. salespeople do, even though the strict conventions governing relationships between men and women in Saudi Arabia make the training meaningless and potentially embarrassing.

Adopting one of these extreme positions is probably not the best approach. To guide your behavior in dealing with cultural differences, you need to distinguish between what is merely a cultural difference and what is clearly wrong. You must respect not only core human values that should apply in all business situations but also local traditions and use the cultural background to help you decide what is right and what is wrong. For example, exchanging expensive gifts is common in Chinese business relationships, although it may be considered unethical in Western cultures. Most Western firms operating in China accept this practice as an appropriate local tradition.

Salespeople, particularly those who operate in foreign cultures, need significant corporate support and guidance in handling cultural ethical differences. Even a high level of personal morality may not prevent an individual from violating a law in a sales context, so it is imperative that companies establish specific standards of conduct, provide ethical training, and monitor behavior to enforce standards as uniformly as possible around the globe.[25]

LEGAL ISSUES

Regardless of the country in which U.S. salespeople sell, they are subject to U.S. laws that prohibit participating in unauthorized boycotts, trading with enemies of the United States, or engaging in activities that adversely affect the U.S. economy. The **Foreign Corrupt Practices Act (FCPA)** makes it illegal for U.S. companies to pay bribes to foreign officials; however, an amendment to the act permits small lubrication payments when they are customary in a culture. Violations of the law can result in sizable fines for company managers, employees, and agents who knowingly participate in or authorize the payment of such bribes. Recently Samsung heir and executive Jay Y. Lee was arrested in the Unites States for bribery for actions that allegedly took place in Korea. Note that Jay Lee was personally charged with violating the law, while the company was not indicted.[26] Companies can get into trouble too; GlaxoSmithKline had to pay about $600 million in one case (and sales executives faced up to four years in prison), but the record seems to be held by two Brazilian companies that had to pay nearly $4 billion.[27] One method companies can use to protect themselves, in the event an employee does violate the law, is to include the FCPA in the company's code of ethics. If the company takes specific steps, such as mentioning the law in company policy, the government's assumption is that the employee acted on his or her own and is individually responsible.

The U.S. laws concerning bribery are much more restrictive than laws in other countries. For example, in Italy and Germany bribes made outside the countries are clearly defined as legal and tax deductible.

SELLING YOURSELF

Most college students do not give much thought to their reputation, at least in terms of a professional reputation. Yet your actions in class, around campus, and on social media add up to a professional reputation in the sense that faculty form an opinion that is shared with recruiters and others who make important decisions. For example, faculty recommendations may be necessary for scholarships, membership in prestigious organizations, and, of course, jobs. Professors and instructors base their recommendations not only on what they observe but also on what they hear.

Carrying your weight in group projects, contributing your share in study groups, and doing your own work are actions that exhibit more than a professional work ethic; they also show your integrity. Other small things, like coming to class and leaving your cell phone silent in your backpack during class, can also contribute to a professor's estimation of a student's overall professional demeanor.

Of course, obvious actions such as claiming illness without any documentation, cheating on an exam (or even giving the appearance of cheating), or collaborating too closely with another student on an independent exercise can damage your credibility. Students may believe they can get away with such actions in classes not in their major and still get good faculty recommendations, but in reality reputation is much bigger than that. Although not every faculty member will learn a student's complete reputation, most of us learn enough from our colleagues and our students to know whom to recommend and whom to avoid.

Similarly, many students think they can put anything they want on social media. What they don't realize is that potential employers can, and do, access that information.

When you meet guest speakers, when you work on projects that involve companies, and when you complete that internship, you are adding to your professional reputation. What does it say about a student, for example, who accepts a job but continues to interview? The professional reputation is significantly damaged if that first job ends up getting turned down. Start working on your professional reputation now. Whether or not you decide to create one intentionally, you are building that reputation anyway.

SUMMARY

This chapter discussed the legal and ethical responsibilities of salespeople. These responsibilities are particularly important in personal selling because salespeople may face conflicts between their personal standards and the standards of their firms and customers. However, the evolution of selling has raised ethical standards and expectations; building long-term relationships with customers doesn't allow for unethical behavior.

Salespeople's ethical standards determine how they conduct relationships with their customers, employers, and competitors. Ethical issues in relations with customers involve the use of entertainment and gifts and the disclosure of confidential information. Ethical issues in relations with employers involve expenses and job changes. Finally, salespeople must be careful in how they talk about competitors and treat competitive products.

Many companies have ethical standards that describe the behavior expected of their salespeople. In evaluating potential employers, salespeople should consider these standards.

Salespeople also encounter many situations not covered by company statements and therefore must develop personal standards of right and wrong. Without personal standards, salespeople will lose their self-respect and the respect of their company and customers. Good ethics are good business. Over the long run, salespeople with a strong sense of ethics will be more successful than salespeople who compromise their own and society's ethics for short-term gain.

Statutory laws (such as the Uniform Commercial Code) and administrative laws (such as Federal Trade Commission rulings) guide the activities of salespeople in the United States. Selling in international markets is complex because of cultural differences in ethical judgments and laws that relate to sales activities in various countries.

KEY TERMS

administrative law 44
agent 45
backdoor selling 40
bribes 38
business defamation 48
CAN-SPAM Act 51
canned sales pitch 31
collusion 49
common law 44
conspiracy 49
contract to sell 45
credulous person standard 47
cultural relativism 52
Do-Not-Call Registry 50
deception 37
ethical imperialism 52
ethics 30
expressed warranty 46
False Claims Act 47
FOB factory 46
Foreign Corrupt Practices Act (FCPA) 52
free on board (FOB) destination 45
implied warranty 46
invitation to negotiate 45
kickbacks 38
lubrication 51
manipulation 33
noncompete clause 42
nondisclosure agreement (NDA) 40
offer 45
order 45
persuasion 33
poaching 44
price discrimination 49
privacy law 50
reciprocity 48
resale price maintenance 49
sale 45
sales puffery 46
sexual harassment 43
spiffs (push money) 49
statutory law 44
subordination 51
trade secrets 43
tying agreement 48
Uniform Commercial Code (UCC) 45
warranty 46

QUESTIONS AND PROBLEMS

1. There are certainly many ethical and legal issues in selling, as this chapter demonstrates. Do you think there are more ethical and legal issues in selling than other jobs, such as accounting, finance, retail store management, or the like? Which issues raised in the chapter are likely to be present, no matter the job, and which are likely to be specific to sales jobs?
2. Do you think that social media and the Internet have made companies more or less ethical? Why?
3. How has the evolution of selling influenced ethics in professional selling?
4. What's the difference between manipulation and persuasion? Give two examples of what would be considered manipulation and alternatives of acceptable persuasion. Then describe how your examples of manipulation might fall into the realm of illegal activity and under which law or laws.
5. Some professors believe that ethics cannot be taught; only laws need to be taught. Do you agree? Why or why not? What do you think Jim Keller's (in The Buyer's Seat 2.1) answer would be to this question? Why? Would his answer differ from that of someone who sells to consumers?
6. Your customer asks what you think of a competitor's product. You know from experience with other customers that it is fine for low

volumes of usage, but given this particular customer's needs, you expect that the volume would lead to a lot of breakdowns. How do you respond? Be specific about what you would say.

7. Using the scenario from question 6, you have a product that competes directly against the competitor's product brought up by the customer and costs about the same–do you bring up the costs? Your product that serves the customer's needs best costs 20 percent more and you know that budget is an issue. What do you do? Again, write out exactly what you would say.
8. One of our students, whose father sells million-dollar equipment, shared the story of how his family was able to spend their vacation on a private Caribbean island–no exaggeration–as a guest of one of his father's clients. While that may be extreme, what might the ethical issues be with accepting a gift from a customer? How should you respond if offered a gift?
9. For each of the following situations, evaluate the salesperson's action and indicate what you think the appropriate action would be:
   - **a.** A salesperson prints out all of the customer contact information from the customer information software, then quits his job. He then joins a company that sells to the same market, using the printout to begin making calls.
   - **b.** A customer asks if you can remove a safety feature because it slows down the operators of the equipment.
   - **c.** A customer puts out a request for bids, saying that the lowest bid that meets the specifications will be awarded the job. The purchasing agent calls you when the bids are opened and says if you lower your price 8 percent, you can get the job. You ask who the lowest qualified bidder was and the buyer says it wasn't you.
   - **d.** A few months after joining a company, you learn about a credit card that gives you a 20 percent cash refund on meals at certain restaurants. You get the card and start taking clients only to restaurants offering the rebate, pocketing the rebate.
   - **e.** A customer gives a salesperson a suggestion for a new service. The salesperson does not turn in the idea to her company, even though the company's policy manual states that all customer ideas should be submitted with the monthly expense report. Instead, the salesperson quits her job and starts her own business using the customer's suggestion.

CASE PROBLEMS

case 2.1

Barton Hargrave

Holly Thompson joined Barton Hargrave, an architectural engineering firm, after graduating from college with a degree in sales. She spent six months learning the services of her firm and how to put together pricing proposals before she got her first territory, Denver and Colorado Springs. Barton Hargrave had once been a leader in that region and still enjoyed a strong reputation, but the previous salesperson hadn't worked very hard. As a result, Holly was able to show strong sales growth by simply working hard.

Within six months, however, she began to get the same e-mail from client after client. "Holly, please explain your firm's pricing to us, line item by line item." After the fifth such e-mail, she forwarded it to her manager, Barry McNichols, who was based in Chicago at Barton Hargrave's corporate headquarters.

As soon as he saw the e-mail, Barry picked up the phone and called Holly. "You need to be careful; it looks like you've got Ruhter and Associates trying to pick off your customers," he told her. "Its strategy is to tell customers our prices are higher and prove it by showing a line-item comparison. But actually, it's how the company defines each line that differs, and when you add it up, we're less expensive by some 15 to 20 percent."

"How do I prove that we're not more expensive?," asked Holly.

"It's hard because Ruhter won't show the client a full price list. To make matters worse, we also filed a lawsuit against Ruhter because its salespeople keep telling clients we're going out of the architectural engineering business."

"Oh, that explains why I've gotten that question a few times recently."

Questions

1. How do you respond to the pricing issue if you can't actually prove Ruhter is lying? How would you handle a customer who goes with Ruhter and then realizes it costs more?
2. How do you respond to the question about leaving the business? What if a client asked about the lawsuit directly, saying, "I hear your company filed suit against Ruhter. Wasn't that a cheap shot at a competitor?"

Note: This scenario is based on a situation faced by one of our former students. The names and industry have been changed, but the situation is real.

case 2.2

MoxyChem

MoxyChem manufactures and distributes chemicals in the western United States, Mexico, and Canada. Usually the company sells to a distributor, which sells to the customer that uses the chemicals. Hudgins ChemSupply is the biggest distributor in Idaho and represents nearly 15 percent of Josh Carter's annual sales. Recently Josh acquired a new account in the same area, Boise Chemicals, which has the potential to be just as large. His most recent meeting with Marsha Hudgins, owner of Hudgins ChemSupply, though, went like this:

"Look, Boise Chemicals underbid us on the Canuck contract by 10 percent. You must be offering Boise a better price than us, and I want to know why," said Marsha.

Josh knew that Boise bid that job with no profit in order to win the Canuck contract, with plans to grow margins once it was able to prove better service. Moreover, the price Josh quoted Boise was actually 5 percent more than Marsha's. "Marsha, I'm not giving Boise a better price–it doesn't buy as much as you do from us, so I can't."

"Huh. You'll have to do better than that. You know that the Farley solvents contract is coming up, and it is going to be big. I want to know what Boise intends to do about it."

"Marsha, if I told you Boise's strategy, as if I knew it, why would you ever trust me with your information?"

"C'mon. I'm your biggest customer. We have to stick together."

"Well, I don't know Boise's strategy."

"Try to find out. And while you're at it, I think I can get the Mohawk Paper account away from Durcon if you'll give me just a 5 percent discount on those products."

Durcon wasn't one of Josh's distributors and the Mohawk Paper account was big, at least $100,000 per month, but Josh also knew he was as low as he could go with Hudgins on price. Maybe he could get by with sending some product as "free samples"?

Questions

1. What should Josh do about the Boise situation? Should he try to find out if Boise plans to bid on the Farley contract and, if so, what its strategy is?
2. What should Josh do about the Mohawk account?
3. Describe Josh's relationship with Marsha. Where should he go with this account in the future?

ROLE PLAY CASE

(*Note:* If you've not completed the Role Play Case in Chapter 1, you should review it before starting this role play. If you need product information, visit Gartner.com/ncsc.)

You are working with the CIO at Legacy Management, a capital investment fund that buys troubled companies and installs its own executives who turn the companies around. Then it takes the companies public or sells to other investors. The company just merged with another one, and the cultures are not merging well.

It's time to ask for the order. You should summarize how Gartner's research provides the client with proven processes that lead to desirable outcomes. For Legacy, this means that it should see a more unified culture, with everyone pulling in the same direction. Once you've summarized, ask for a commitment of $200,000 to cover training. Each buyer will be given a sheet with information about how to respond.

ADDITIONAL REFERENCES

Agnihotri, Raj, and Michael T. Krush. "Salesperson Empathy, Ethical Behaviors, and Sales Performance: The Moderating Role of Trust in One's Manager." *Journal of Personal Selling and Sales Management* 35, no. 2 (2015), pp. 164–72.

Bartlett, Katharine T., and Mitu Gulati. "Discrimination by Customers." *Iowa Law Review* 102, no. 1 (November 2016), pp. 223–57.

Bateman, Connie, and Sean Valentine. "The Impact of Salesperson Customer Orientation on the Evaluation of a Salesperson's Ethical Treatment, Trust in the Salesperson, and Intentions to Purchase." *Journal of Personal Selling and Sales Management* 35, no. 2 (2015), pp. 125–42.

Bush, Victoria, Alan J. Bush, Jared Oakley, and John E. Cicala. "The Sales Profession as Subculture: Implications for Ethical Decision Making." *Journal of Business Ethics* 142, no. 3 (May 2017), pp. 549–65.

Chawla, Vaibhav. "Workplace Spirituality Governance: Impact on Customer Orientation and Salesperson Performance." *Journal of Business and Industrial Marketing* 31, no. 4 (2016), pp. 498–506.

Chressanthis, George A., Andrew Sfekas, Pratap Khedkar, Nitin Jain, and Prashant Poddar. "Determinants of Pharmaceutical Sales Representative Access Limits to Physicians." *Journal of Medical Marketing* 14, no. 4 (November 2014), pp. 220–43.

Cicala, John E., Alan J. Bush, Daniel L. Sherrell, and George D. Deitz. "Does Transparency Influence the Ethical Behavior of Salespeople?" *Journal of Business Research* 67, no. 9 (September 2014), pp. 1787–94.

DeConinck, James B., Mary Beth DeConinck, and Hollye K. Moss. "The Relationship among Ethical Leadership, Ethical Climate, Supervisory Trust, and Moral Judgment." *Academy of Marketing Studies Journal* 20, no. 3 (2016), pp. 89–99.

Hansen, John D., Donald J. Lund, and Thomas E. DeCarlo. "A Process Model of Buyer Responses to Salesperson Transgressions and Recovery Efforts: The Impact of Salesperson Orientation." *Journal of Personal Selling and Sales Management* 36, no. 1 (2016), pp. 59–69.

Hill, Ronald Paul, and Justine M. Rapp. "Codes of Ethical Conduct: A Bottom-Up Approach." *Journal of Business Ethics* 123. no. 4 (September 2014), pp. 621–30.

Hochstein, Bryan W., Leff Bonney, and Melissa Clark. "Positive and Negative Social Reactions to Salesperson Deviance." *Journal of Marketing Theory and Practice* 23, no. 3 (Summer 2015), pp. 303–20.

Hoeppner, Sven. "The Unintended Consequence of Doorstep Consumer Protection: Surprise, Reciprocation, and Consistency." *European Journal of Law and Economics* 38, no. 2 (October 2014), pp. 247–76.

Jaramillo, Fernando, Belén Bande, and Jose Varela. "Servant Leadership and Ethics: A Dyadic Examination of Supervisor Behaviors and Salesperson Perceptions." *Journal of Personal Selling and Sales Management* 35, no. 2 (2015), pp. 108–15.

Kasabov, Edward. "What We Know, Don't Know, and Should Know about Confusion Marketing." *European Journal of Marketing* 49, no. 11/12 (2015), pp. 1777–1808.

Lo, Desmond Ho-Fu, Wouter Dessein, Mrinal Ghosh, and Francine Lafontaine. "Price Delegation and Performance Pay: Evidence from Industrial Sales Forces." *Journal of Law Economics & Organization* 32, no. 3 (August 2016), pp. 508–12.

Milovic, Alex, and Rebecca Dingus. "Everyone Loves a Winner . . . or Do They? Introducing Envy into a Sales Contest to Increase Salesperson Motivation." *American Journal of Management* 14, no. 4 (November 2014), pp. 27–32.

Oh, Joon-hee, Jungkun Park, and Brian N Rutherford. "Management of Frontline Financial Sales Personnel." *Journal of Financial Services Marketing* 19, no. 3 (September 2014), pp. 208–20.

Paterson, Jeannie Mari, and Gerard Brody. " 'Safety Net' Consumer Protection: Using Prohibitions on Unfair and Unconscionable Conduct to Respond to Predatory Business Models." *Journal of Consumer Policy* 38, no. 3 (September 2015), pp. 331–55.

Riggs, John F., Scott Widmier, and Richard E Plank. "The Impact of Pharmaceutical Industry Salesperson Regulations, Guidance Statements, and Laws on Their Sales Behaviors: A Taxonomy with Managerial Insight." *International Journal of Pharmaceutical and Healthcare Marketing* 10, no. 2 (2016), pp. 161–91.

Schwepker, Charles H., and Roberta J. Schultz. "Influence of the Ethical Servant Leader and Ethical Climate on Customer Value Enhancing Sales Performance." *Journal of Personal Selling and Sales Management* 35, no. 2 (2015), pp. 93–107.

Tanner, Emily C., John F. Tanner Jr., and Kirk Wakefield. "Panacea or Paradox? The Moderating Role of Ethical Climate." *Journal of Personal Selling and Sales Management* 35, no. 2 (2015), pp. 175–88.

Tseng, Lu-Ming. "Blowing the Whistle on Workplace Sexual Harassment: Examining the Role of Harasser Status and Types of Sexual Harassment." *Equity, Diversity, and Inclusion: An International Journal* 33, no. 6 (2014), pp. 510–22.

©tdub303/Getty Images RF

chapter 3

BUYING BEHAVIOR AND THE BUYING PROCESS

SOME QUESTIONS ANSWERED IN THIS CHAPTER ARE

- What are the different types of customers?
- How do organizations make purchase decisions?
- Which factors do organizations consider when they evaluate products and services?
- Who is involved in the buying decision?
- What should salespeople do in the different types of buying situations?
- Which changes are occurring in organizational buying, and how will these changes affect salespeople?

PROFILE

> ***"Recognizing buyer behavior is something that can make or break a call in a matter of minutes."***
>
> *Taylor Dixon, 3M*

Courtesy of Taylor Dixon

PROFILE I had been warned about this buyer. He was a big fish in a little pond, and he knew it. Known for being a bit of a "playboy," my boss didn't even let me meet with him for the first time alone. His office walls are covered with awards, trophies, and pictures of his success. In the far corner of the room there's a fireplace with a bearskin rug. Over the top? Maybe, but a clear indication into what his buyer behavior was. In order to win him over I had to make him look good. I knew this instantly upon walking into the room.

After graduating from Baylor University, I joined 3M. I'm currently the Midwest sales representative covering eight states and representing 3M's consumer product line as a whole. The consumer product line is extensive with thousands of SKUs [stock-keeping units], but we're most well known in my channel for our Post-it® Notes and Scotch® Tape. My customers vary from large office supplies distributors where I'm working with their salespeople to push my products, to retail accounts where I meet with the customer to put programs in place or set planograms for their stores. Recognizing buyer behavior is something that can make or break a call in a matter of minutes. In my world I primarily wear three hats: the analyst, the marketer, and the salesperson. Depending on whom I'm meeting with, I wear one of the three.

Certain buyers want to know *why*. Why should they buy my product? "Give me numbers and proof that I'll make money with this product." They want to know every little detail about the product from specs to country of origin. For calls with the *why* buyer I always have to make sure my analyst hat is on and I'm prepared with information to support bringing in this product. Since I work with both retail accounts and distributors, inventory and shelf space is precious. Buyers are eager to bring in things that will fly off the shelves, not sit there for months at a time. It's my job to show them how my product will drive more business and growth in their category.

Some buyers want to know *when*. They've already accepted my product, perhaps because of the strong brand associated with it or because of our relationship. The question they have is, "When do I bring it in and when do I promote it?" They're interested in getting the most out of this new product as possible. For the *when* buyer, I have to put on my marketer hat. It's extremely important that I'm in close communication with our marketing team in these situations as they can provide the assets and schedules associated with the promotion of the product. Naturally, some products sell better during certain seasons and at certain times of the year. For example, people aren't likely buying winter coats in the middle of July. By providing buyers with the marketing calendar for each product, they can promote it appropriately and grow the business most efficiently.

The final buyer I run into wants to know *what*. The *what* buyer typically asks, "What will this product do for me and my business as a whole?" Meetings with *what* buyers require me to put on my salesperson hat. They want to know that not only will my product grow their business, but my company is there to support them throughout the entire process. *What* buyers need to be sold on the big picture. I'm there to show them not only what my product can do for their customers, but also what the product can do for their business.

It was important that I recognized my buyer I mentioned earlier as a *what* buyer. He believed in the product and my company as a whole, but wanted to know what was in it for him. In recognizing his buying behavior, I've been able to present and effectively communicate with him in a way that has grown his direct business with 3M over the past year. Being in sales is much more than just being salespersons. We have to recognize buyer behavior in order to succeed and mold ourselves to match their wants and needs.

Visit our Web site at: www.3M.com.

Taylor Dixon, Salesperson, 3M Company, Used with permission.

WHY PEOPLE BUY

In general, people buy to satisfy a want or desire, to solve a problem, or to satisfy an impulse. Even in situations where people are buying as part of their jobs, like all people, buyers have personal goals and aspirations. They want to get a raise, be promoted to a high-level position, have their managers recognize their accomplishments, and feel they have done something for their company or demonstrated their skills as a buyer or engineer. These needs can complicate buying decisions that are made on behalf of an employer, not forgetting that there are also the basic needs that the product or service solves.

To complicate matters further, there may be needs associated with how the person wants to buy. Think, for a moment, about what you have purchased for yourself via the Internet. You may have many reasons for using the Internet, none of which have anything to do with the product you purchased. But the *way* you bought met certain needs—maybe a need for convenience or a need for greater variety than the local store could provide. As salespeople, we have to be acutely aware of the needs we are solving: the needs that the product solves directly, the individual's needs that are served indirectly, and the needs that are solved by selling the way the buyer wants to buy.

TYPES OF CUSTOMERS

Business is full of a wide variety of customers, including producers, resellers, government agencies, institutions, and consumers. Each of these customer types has different needs and uses a different process to buy products and services. In many situations salespeople will have only one type of customer, but in other territories they may have many different types of customers. Thus salespeople may need to use different approaches when selling to different types of customers.

MANUFACTURERS

Manufacturers buy products and services to manufacture and sell their products and services to customers. Buyers working for manufacturers are involved in two types of buying situations: buying products that will be included in the products the company is manufacturing, or buying products and services to support the manufacturing operation.

OEM Purchasers

Buyers for **original equipment manufacturers (OEMs)** purchase goods (components, subassemblies, raw and processed materials) to use in making their products. An example of an OEM buyer is Dell. Dell may use Intel processors in its computers, making Dell the OEM. Sometimes, though, Dell sells computers to other OEM manufacturers. For example, when you use a kiosk at the airport to print your boarding pass, the computer inside it is a Dell, but the kiosk is put together and sold by someone else.

Salespeople selling OEM products need to demonstrate that their products help their customers produce products that will offer superior value. For example, Tim Pavlovich, OEM salesperson for Dell, says that one reason why Dell gets contracts like the kiosk contract is because Dell has a worldwide service team already in place and can fix the computers anywhere in the world.

Most OEM products are bought in large quantities on an annual contract. The purchasing department negotiates the contract with the supplier; however, engineering and production departments play a major role in the purchase decision. Engineers evaluate the products and may prepare specifications for a custom design. The production department works with the supplier to make sure the OEM products are delivered "just in time."

OEM customers are building long-term relationships with a limited number of OEM suppliers. Thus, relationship building with more than one department in a customer firm is particularly important when selling OEM products.

End Users

When manufacturers buy goods and services to support their own production and operations, they are acting as **end users**. End-user buying situations include the purchase of capital equipment; maintenance, repair, and overhaul (MRO) supplies; and services. **Capital equipment** items are major purchases, such as mainframe computers and machine tools that the producer uses for a number of years. **MRO supplies** include paper towels and replacement parts for machinery. **Services** include Internet and telephone connections, employment agencies, consultants, and transportation.

Because capital equipment purchases typically require major financial commitments, capital equipment salespeople need to work with a number of people involved in the purchase decision, including high-level corporate executives. These salespeople need to demonstrate the reliability of their products and their support services because an equipment failure can shut down the producer's operation. Capital equipment buying often focuses on lifetime operating cost rather than the initial purchase price because the equipment is used over a long period. Thus, capital equipment salespeople need to present the financial implications as well as the operating features and benefits of their products.

MRO supplies and services are typically a minor expense and therefore are usually less important to businesses than are many other items. Purchasing agents typically oversee MRO buying decisions. Because they often do not want to spend the time to evaluate all suppliers, they tend to purchase from vendors who have performed well in the past, creating functional relationships.

Although the cost of MRO supplies is typically low, availability can be critical. For example, if you've ever had a flight delayed because maintenance had to wait for a part to come from a far-off hangar, you have experienced the importance of MRO product availability. In fact, one of the authors had a flight delayed because the maintenance person had to drive to a hardware store to buy caulk because there was an air leak around the windshield in the cockpit. The hour delay to buy a $3 tube of caulk caused 50 passengers to miss their connection, which then led to 50 interactions with passengers to re-book, costing the airline much more than the $3!

RESELLERS

Resellers buy finished products or services with the intention to resell them to businesses and consumers. Hormel sells precooked meats, such as pepperoni for pizza toppings, to resellers–distributors who then sell to restaurants. Other examples of resellers include McKesson Corporation, a wholesaler that buys health care products from manufacturers and resells those products to drugstores; Brazos Valley Equipment, a dealer for John Deere, selling tractors, harvesters, combines, and other agricultural implements to farmers; and Dealer's Electric, selling lighting, conduit, and other electrical components to electricians and contractors. All these are resellers, and they buy for similar reasons.

Resellers consider three elements when making decisions about which products to sell: profit margin, turnover, and effort. Resellers want to maximize their return on investment (ROI), which is a function of **profit margin**, or how much they make on each sale; **turnover (TO)**, or how quickly a product will sell; and how much effort it takes to sell the product. Buyers for resellers often simplify their decisions by a focus on either profit margin or turnover, but all resellers are interested in putting together an assortment of products that will yield the greatest overall ROI.

Salespeople work with resellers to help them build their ROI. Not only do salespeople help resellers choose which products to sell, but they also train resellers on how to sell and service products and build point-of-purchase displays and promotions and may also help resellers with developing advertising and marketing campaigns to boost sales. For example, with increasing competition between grocery chains, retailers are asking suppliers to create excitement and generate traffic in stores.

Rikki Ingram, marketing brand manager for Smithfield Foods, says,

Smithfield partners with grocers to promote the full line of Smithfield products with in-store displays, building sales for both Smithfield and the retailer.

©Daniel Acker/Bloomberg/Getty Images

> Increased competition amongst grocery retailers is absolutely changing the dynamics for manufacturers and salespeople. We have large European brands such as Aldi and Lidl shaking things up in the U.S., as well as Publix making its way North and Wegmans making its way South. Price is no longer the primary differentiator. You'll see more and more brick-and-mortar retailers leaning into the digital trend by offering online ordering and custom targeting through various social channels. For those consumers which still wish to walk the aisles, retailers are beginning to offer more experiential shopping experiences, deepening the emotional connection with their consumers. They're doing this with store layout changes (addition of wine and coffee bars, etc.) as well as putting pressure on their suppliers for superior freshness and quality. The reality is, consumers want to know more about the brands they're buying and manufacturers need to evolve and provide the transparency their consumers are seeking. For example, on the Smithfield brand we recently launched www.Smithfield-Rewards.com which is a loyalty site that allows consumers to visit the virtual town of Smithfield, Virginia. Through the site, consumers will be rewarded with great prizes and also given the opportunity to learn more about the brand and more about the rich history of the town we call home.

Source: Smithfield Foods

Note that the same customer can act as an OEM manufacturer, an end user, and a reseller. For example, Dell Inc. makes OEM buying decisions when it purchases microprocessors for its computers, acts as an end user when it buys materials handling equipment for its warehouse, and functions as a reseller when it buys software to resell to its computer customers when they place orders.

GOVERNMENT AGENCIES

The largest customers for goods and services in the United States are federal, state, and local governments, which collectively purchase goods and services valued at more than $1.7 trillion annually. Including government-owned utilities, federal, state, and local governments purchase the equivalent of 12 percent of the country's entire gross domestic product, making it the largest customer in the world.[1] Government buyers typically develop detailed specifications for a product and then invite qualified suppliers to submit bids. A contract is awarded to the lowest bidder. The government has also developed procedures for small purchases without a bid, streamlining the process and reducing costs.

Effective selling to government agencies requires a thorough knowledge of their unique procurement procedures and rules. Salespeople also need to know about projected needs so they can influence the development of the buying specifications. For example, Harris Corporation worked for six years with the Federal Aviation Administration and finally won a $1.7 billion contract to modernize air traffic communication systems.

Some resources available to salespeople working with the federal and state governments are the following:

- The *Commerce Business Daily* provides notice of new federal sales opportunities each day at www.cbd-net.com. Companies can sign up to be notified of opportunities in specific product categories.
- The National Association of State Purchasing Officials in Washington, DC, publishes information for all 50 states, including the availability of vendor guides, registration fees, and how to get on bidder lists (see www.NASPO.org).
- The Small Business Administration offers a Web site (www.sba.gov) that educates small businesses on how to sell to governments and also lists sales opportunities specifically available only to small businesses.
- FedBizOpps.gov is a Web site that lists all business opportunities greater than $25,000. At any given time, there are over 40,000 open sales opportunities described on this site.

Many international salespeople are selling to government agencies, even though private companies may be the biggest buyers of these products and services in the United States. For example, Nokia, a Finnish company that manufactures telephone equipment, sells not only to private companies such as Verizon and AT&T in the United States but also to the post, telephone, and telegraph (PTT) government agencies in many countries in Europe, Asia, and Africa.

Selling to foreign governments is challenging. The percentage of domestic product (countries may require that a certain percentage of the product be manufactured or assembled locally) and exchange rates (the values of local currencies in U.S. dollars) are as important as the characteristics of the product. Different economic and political systems, cultures, and languages also can make international selling difficult.

INSTITUTIONS

Another important customer group consists of public and private institutions such as churches, hospitals, and colleges. Often these institutions have purchasing rules and procedures that are as complex and rigid as those used by government agencies.

Packaged goods manufacturers, such as Smithfield and Hormel, sell to both resellers (supermarkets) and institutional customers (restaurants and hospitals), often through distributors such as Sysco and Frosty Acres Brands. These customers have different needs and buying processes. In some instances, institutions purchase more like resellers, worrying about the same needs, such as how fast the product will sell or be consumed. In other ways, institutions can be like producers, concerned with how their clients will view their services.

CONSUMERS

Consumers purchase products and services for use by themselves or by their families. A lot of salespeople sell insurance, automobiles, clothing, and real estate to consumers. However, college graduates often take sales jobs that involve selling to business enterprises, government agencies, or institutions. Thus, the examples in this text focus on these selling situations, and this chapter discusses organizational rather than consumer buying behavior.

In the next section we contrast the buying processes of consumers and organizations. Then we describe the buying process that organizations use in more detail, including the steps in the process, who influences the decisions, and how salespeople can influence the decisions.

ORGANIZATIONAL BUYING AND SELLING

Salespeople who sell to consumers and salespeople who call on organizations have very different jobs. Because the organizational buying process typically is more complex than the consumer buying process, selling to organizations often requires more skills and is more challenging than selling to consumers. Relationships, too, can differ because of the size of the organizations involved.

COMPLEXITY OF THE ORGANIZATIONAL BUYING PROCESS

The typical organizational purchase is much larger and more complex than the typical consumer purchase. Organizations use highly trained, knowledgeable purchasing agents to make these decisions. Many other people in organizations are involved in purchase decisions, including engineers, production managers, business analysts, and senior executives.

Organizational buying decisions often involve extensive evaluations and negotiations over time. The average time required to complete a purchase is five months, not counting straight rebuys, and during that period salespeople need to make many calls to gather and provide information.

Bill Dunne, account executive for EIPP Solutions, recalled one particular sale that he said was a good example of the normal sales process:

> First, they put out an RFP (request for proposal) and had a meeting where they invited anyone who might want to bid for the business. There were eight other vendors who attended. Two weeks later, I turned in a proposal. Several days later, I got a call saying that we were finalists and that they wanted to meet. During this meeting with their CFO, COO and CIO, they went through my proposal and asked me all types of detailed questions for more than two hours. A week after that, I gave them a tour of one of our facilities. Then I had one more meeting, this time with the President and CFO only. The next day, they informed me that I got the sale, but then we had another round of negotiations over terms and conditions. Finally, three months after issuing the RFP, they signed a contract with us.
>
> Source: Bill Dunne, account executive for EIPP Solutions

As Dunne noted, though, this level of diligence in selecting a vendor was important to the buyer because it expected to remain a customer for years.

The complexity of organizational purchase decisions means salespeople must be able to deal effectively with a wide range of people working for their customer and their company. For example, when selling a new additive to a food processor such as Nabisco, an International Flavors and Fragrances (IFF) salesperson may interact with advertising, product development, legal, production, quality control, and customer service people at Nabisco. The salesperson needs to know the technical and economic benefits of the additive to Nabisco and the benefits to consumers.

In addition, the IFF salesperson coordinates all areas of his or her own firm to assist in making the sale. The salesperson works with research and development to provide data on consumer taste tests, with production to meet the customer's

To sell a part for use in John Deere products, you may have to call on a buyer at their headquarters, shown here in Iowa, but you'll have to service plans in Brazil, India, Germany, and France as well as the US.

delivery requirements, and with finance to set the purchasing terms. (Working effectively within the salesperson's organization is discussed in more detail in Chapter 16.)

The complexity of organizational selling is increasing as more customers become global businesses. For example, IBM began moving away from regional purchasing to global sourcing in order to unify contracts, buy in larger quantities from a smaller number of vendors, and obtain more favorable terms.[2] John Deere has a special corporate unit that works with manufacturing plants to unify sourcing for the same reason. There's no doubt that global competitiveness is a key factor increasing the complexity of organizational buying, but global sourcing is also a key factor for achieving a sustainable competitive advantage.[3]

DERIVED VERSUS DIRECT DEMAND

Salespeople selling to consumers typically can focus on individual consumer or family needs. Organizational selling often requires salespeople to know about the customer's customers. Sales to OEMs and resellers are based on derived demand rather than direct demand. **Derived demand** means that purchases made by these customers ultimately depend on the demand for their products–either other organizations or consumers. For example, Micron Technology makes the microprocessors used in Apple products. The company enjoyed 58 percent growth in sales when Apple launched a new iPhone.[4]

HOW DO ORGANIZATIONS MAKE BUYING DECISIONS?

To effectively sell to organizations, salespeople need to understand how organizations make buying decisions. This section discusses the steps in the organizational buying process, the different types of buying decisions, and the people involved in making the decisions.

STEPS IN THE BUYING PROCESS

Exhibit 3.1 shows the eight steps in an organizational buying process.

Recognizing a Need or a Problem (Step 1)

The buying process starts when someone realizes a problem exists. Employees in the customer's firm or outside salespeople can trigger this recognition. For example, a supermarket cashier might discover that the optical scanner is making mistakes in reading bar code labels. Salespeople often trigger the buying process by demonstrating how their products can improve the efficiency of the customer's operation.

Defining the Type of Product Needed (Step 2)

After identifying a problem, organization members develop a general approach to solving it. For example, a production manager who concludes that the factory is not running efficiently recognizes a problem, but this insight may not lead to a purchase decision. The manager may think the inefficiency is caused by poor supervision or unskilled workers.

However, a production equipment salesperson might work with the manager to analyze the situation and show how efficiency could be improved by purchasing

Exhibit 3.1
Steps in the Organizational Buying Process.

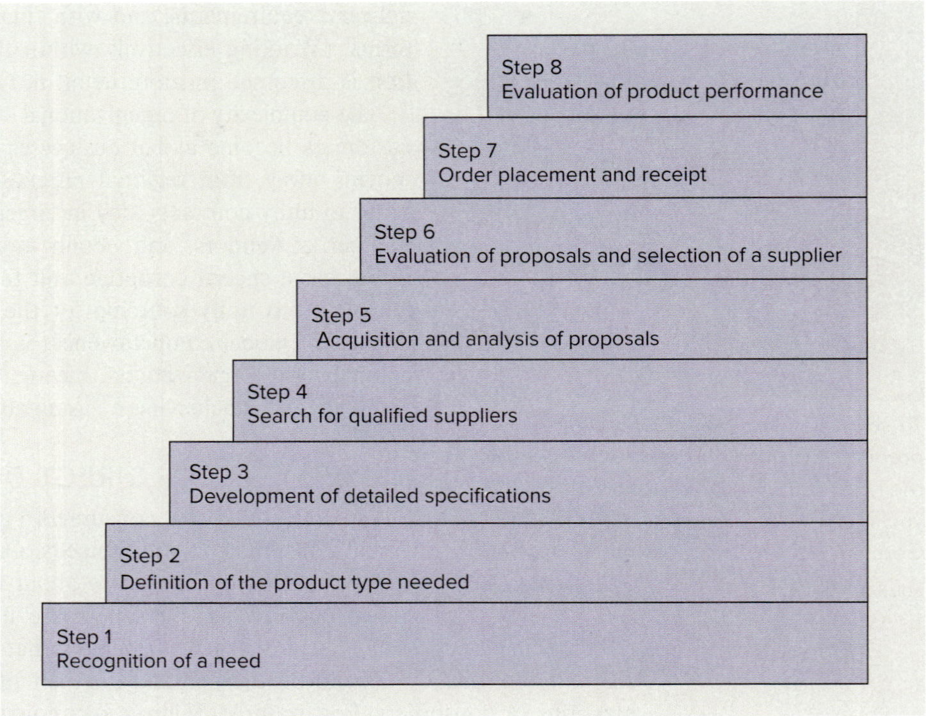

some automated assembly equipment. Thus, the problem solution is defined in terms of purchasing a product or service–the automated assembly equipment needed–and the buying process moves to step 3. If the decision to continue requires senior management participation, these executives may approve the manager's request to consider the purchase, then leave it up to the manager to cover the next few steps before stepping back in when a final decision is made.

Developing Product Specifications (Step 3)

In step 3 the specifications for the product needed to solve the problem are prepared. Potential suppliers will use these specifications to develop proposals. The buyers will use them to objectively evaluate the proposals.

Steps 2 and 3 offer great opportunities for salespeople to influence the outcome of the buying process. Using their knowledge of their firm's products and the customer's needs, salespeople can help develop specifications that favor their particular product. For example, Tim Simmons, a director of strategic business solutions at Teradata, was selling to a major retailer who was using another company's product. What the customer asked Tim to demonstrate was an add-on, but he asked a number of questions about specific problems they might be having. Knowing the competitor, Tim was pretty sure the customer had those problems. He then asked if it were more important to keep the competitor's equipment or solve the problems. By redefining the purchase on the basis of solving business problems rather than buying an add-on, he was able to get the product specifications changed to suit his product and to win a $4 million sale.

Searching for Qualified Suppliers (Step 4)

After the specifications have been written, the customer looks for potential suppliers. The customer may simply contact previous suppliers or go through an extensive search procedure: do a Web search, read customer reviews online, download case studies and position papers, and call customers found on a list on the potential suppliers' Web site. In fact, Forester (a research company that competes with Gartner) has found that 74 percent of business buyers gather at least half of the information needed to make a decision before ever speaking to a salesperson.[5]

Acquiring and Analyzing Proposals (Step 5)

In step 5 qualified suppliers are asked to submit proposals. Recall that Bill Dunne earlier described how he attended a pre-proposal meeting with the buyer so that he and competitors could get questions answered before preparing their proposal. Then Dunne went to work with people in his company to develop their proposal. In many instances, proposals are slide presentations delivered by the salesperson over the Web through Webex, Skype, or some other form of online conference call. In Dunne's case, it was e-mailed as a PDF and reviewed by the buyer privately, without Dunne's involvement, prior to a meeting with the buying company's executives.

Evaluating Proposals and Selecting a Supplier (Step 6)

Next, the customer evaluates the proposals. After a preferred supplier is selected, further negotiations may occur concerning price, delivery, or specific performance features.

Placing an Order and Receiving the Product (Step 7)

In step 7 an order is placed with the selected supplier. The order goes to the supplier, who acknowledges receipt and commits to a delivery date. After the product is shipped, the buying firm inspects the received goods and then pays the supplier for the product. During this step salespeople need to make sure the paperwork is correct and their firm knows what has to be done to satisfy the customer's requirements. In many instances, the customer may be responsible for placing the order through a secure Web site.

Evaluating Product Performance (Step 8)

In the final step of the purchasing process, the product's performance is evaluated. The evaluation may be a formal or informal assessment made by people involved in the buying process. The supplier is also evaluated on such characteristics as whether the billing was accurate, how quickly service calls were handled, and similar criteria.

Salespeople play an important role in this step. They need to work with the users to make sure the product performs well. In addition, salespeople need to work with purchasing agents to ensure that they are satisfied with the communications and delivery.

This after-sale support ensures that the salesperson's product will get a positive evaluation and that he or she will be considered a qualified supplier in future procurement. This step is critical to establishing successful long-term relationships. (Building relationships through after-sale support is discussed in more detail in Chapter 14.)

CREEPING COMMITMENT

Creeping commitment means a customer becomes increasingly committed to a particular course of action while going through the steps in the buying process. As decisions are made at each step, the range of alternatives narrows; the customer becomes more and more committed to a specific course of action and even to a specific vendor. As was noted earlier, salespeople who are not involved early in the process are at a disadvantage because the range of options gets narrower with each set of decisions.

In instances involving purchasing components or materials as part of new product development, buyers are more interested in early involvement by possible vendors than when buying other types of products. Called *early procurement involvement* or *early supplier involvement,* this strategy has potential suppliers participate in the actual design process for a new product.[6] EVCO, a plastics manufacturing company, promotes its engineering department's abilities in early supplier involvement as a competitive advantage. It argues that it is able to reduce operating costs by eliminating waste and design in other cost savings, as well as improve product design.[7] Whatever the reason, each design decision represents a creeping commitment to a final set of decisions that are difficult to undo.

thinking **it** through

What steps did you go through in making the choice to attend this university? How can you relate your decision-making process to the eight steps in the organizational buying process? Did any decisions you made early in the process affect decisions you made later in the process? What roles did your family and friends play in the decision process?

TYPES OF ORGANIZATIONAL BUYING DECISIONS

Many purchase decisions are made without going through all the steps just described. For example, a Frito-Lay salesperson may check the supply of his or her products in a supermarket, write a purchase order to restock the shelves, and present it to the store manager. After recognizing the problem of low stock, the manager simply signs the order (step 6) without going through any of the other steps. However, if the Frito-Lay salesperson wanted the manager to devote more shelf space to Frito-Lay snacks, the manager might go through all eight steps in making and evaluating this decision.

Exhibit 3.2 describes three types of buying decisions–new tasks, modified rebuys, and straight rebuys[8]–along with the strategies salespeople need to use in each situation. In this exhibit the "in" company is the seller that has provided the product or service to the company in the past, and the "out" company is the seller that is not or has not been a supplier to the customer.

NEW TASKS

When a customer purchases a product or service for the first time, a **new-task** situation occurs. Most purchase decisions involving capital equipment or the initial purchase of OEM products are new tasks.

Because the customer has not made the purchase decision recently, the company's knowledge is limited, and it goes through all eight steps of the buying process. In these situations customers face considerable risk. Thus, they typically seek information from salespeople and welcome their knowledge. Two studies found that organizational buyers rate salespeople as a more important information source than the Internet, particularly when the success of the purchase is likely to be difficult to achieve and to evaluate.[9]

From the salesperson's perspective, the initial buying process steps are critical in new-task situations. During these steps, the alert salesperson can help the customer define the characteristics of the needed product and develop the purchase specifications. By working with the customer in these initial steps, the salesperson can take advantage of creeping commitment and gain a significant advantage over the competition. The final step, postpurchase evaluation, is also vital. Buyers

Exhibit 3.2
Types of Organizational Buying Decisions

	New Task	Modified Rebuy	Straight Rebuy
Customer Needs			
Information and risk reduction	Information about causes and solutions for a new problem; reduce high risk in making a decision with limited knowledge.	Information and solutions to increase efficiency and/or reduce costs.	Needs are generally satisfied.
Nature of Buying Process			
Number of people involved in process	Many	Few	One
Time to make a decision	Months or years	Month	Day
Key steps in the buying process (Exhibit 3.1)	1, 2, 3, 8	3, 4, 5, 6, 8	5, 6, 7, 8
Key decision makers	Executives and engineers	Production and purchasing managers	Purchasing agent
Selling Strategy			
For in-supplier	Monitor changes in customer needs; respond quickly when problems and new needs arise; provide technical information.	Act immediately when problems arise with customers; make sure all of customer's needs are satisfied.	Reinforce relationship.
For out-supplier	Suggest new approach for solving problems; provide technical advice.	Respond more quickly than present supplier when problem arises; encourage customer to consider an alternative; present information about how new alternative will increase efficiency.	Convince customer of potential benefits from reexamining choice of supplier; secure recognition and approval as an alternative supplier.

making a new purchase decision are especially interested in evaluating results and will use this information in making similar purchase decisions in the future.

STRAIGHT REBUYS

In a **straight rebuy** situation, the customer buys the same product from the same source it used when the need arose previously. Because customers have purchased the product or service a number of times, they have considerable knowledge about their requirements and the potential vendors. MRO supplies and services and reorders of OEM components often are straight rebuy situations.

Typically, a straight rebuy is triggered by an internal event, such as a low inventory level. Because needs are easily recognized, specifications have been developed, and potential suppliers have been identified, the latter steps of the buying process assume greater importance.

Some straight rebuys are computerized. For example, many hospitals use an automatic reorder system developed by Baxter, a manufacturer and distributor of medical supplies. When the inventory control system recognizes that levels of supplies such as tape, surgical sponges, or IV kits have dropped to prespecified levels, a purchase order is automatically generated and transmitted electronically to the nearest Baxter distribution center.

When a company is satisfied and has developed a long-term supplier relationship, it continues to order from the same company it has used in the past. Salespeople at in-companies want to maintain the strong relationship; they do not want the customer to consider new suppliers. Thus, these salespeople must make sure that orders are delivered on time and that the products continue to get favorable evaluations.

Salespeople trying to break into a straight rebuy situation—those representing an out-supplier—face a tough sales problem. Often they need to persuade a customer to change suppliers, even though the present supplier is performing satisfactorily. In such situations the salesperson hopes the present supplier will make a significant mistake, causing the customer to reevaluate suppliers. To break into a straight rebuy situation, salespeople need to provide compelling information to motivate the customer to treat the purchase as a modified rebuy.

MODIFIED REBUYS

In a **modified rebuy** situation, the customer has purchased the product or a similar product in the past but is interested in obtaining new information. This situation typically occurs when the in-supplier performs unsatisfactorily, a new product becomes available, or the buying needs change. In such situations sales representatives of the in-suppliers need to convince customers to maintain the relationship and continue their present buying pattern. In-suppliers with strong customer relationships are the first to find out when requirements change. In this case customers give the supplier's salespeople information to help them respond to the new requirements.

Salespeople with out-suppliers want customers to reevaluate the situation and to actively consider switching vendors. The successful sales rep from an out-supplier will need to influence all the people taking part in the buying decision.

WHO MAKES THE BUYING DECISION?

As we discussed previously, a number of people are involved in new-task and modified rebuy decisions. This group of people is called the **buying center**, an informal, cross-department group of people involved in a purchase decision. People in the customer's organization become involved in a buying center because they have formal responsibilities for purchasing or they are important sources of information. In some cases the buying center includes experts who are not full-time employees. For example, consultants usually specify the air-conditioning equipment that will be used in a factory undergoing remodeling. Thus, the buying center defines the set of people who make or influence the purchase decision.[10]

Salespeople need to know the names and responsibilities of all people in the buying center for a purchase decision, and sometimes they need to make sure the right people are participating. For example, one of Bill Dunne's prospects for a customer relationship management software application was certain that the company would buy Bill's offering, a customized version of SugarCRM. Yet when it came time to buy, the CEO, who had not been involved in any prior meetings, stepped in and selected another vendor. Why? There was one key feature about the other vendor's product that he really liked, and while Bill had uncovered the CEO's interest in the feature, he didn't realize it would be a deal killer for him. "The lesson I learned," says Bill, "is to meet with every person who uses the system at least once."

USERS

Users, such as the manufacturing personnel for OEM products and capital equipment, typically do not make the ultimate purchase decision. However, they often have considerable influence in the early and late steps of the buying process—need recognition, product definition, and postpurchase evaluation. Thus users are particularly important in new-task and modified rebuy situations. Salespeople often attempt to convert a straight rebuy to a modified rebuy by demonstrating superior product performance or a new benefit to users.

INITIATORS

Another role in the buying process is that of **initiator**, or the person who starts the buying process. A user can play the role of the initiator, as in "This machine is broken; we need a new one." In fact, often it is users' dissatisfaction with a product used by the organization that initiates the purchase process.[11] In some instances, though, such as in OEM product decisions, the initiator could be an executive making a decision such as introducing a new product, which starts the buying process.

INFLUENCERS

People inside or outside the organization who directly or indirectly provide information during the buying process are **influencers**. These members of the buying center may seek to influence issues regarding product specifications, criteria for evaluating proposals, or information about potential suppliers. For example, the marketing department can influence a purchase decision by indicating that the company's products would sell better if they included a particular supplier's components. Architects can play a critical role in the purchase of construction material by specifying suppliers, even though the ultimate purchase orders will be placed by the contractor responsible for constructing the building. Influence can be technical, such as in product specifications, but can also involve finances and how a decision is made.

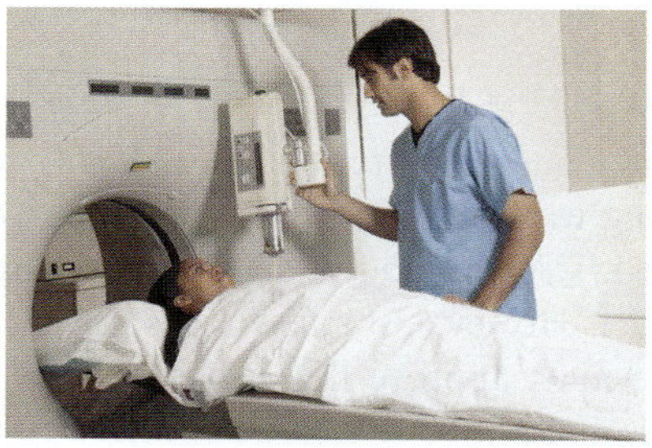

The buying center for radiology equipment includes (clockwise from upper left) the technicians operating the equipment (users), the radiologists (gatekeepers and influencers), and the hospital administrator (the decision maker).

(top): ©Plush Studios/Blend Images LLC RF; (top right): ©Image Source RF; (bottom center): ©Steve Debenport/Getty Images RF

Miller and Heiman, two noted sales consultants, assert that there are four types of influencers. One is the **economic influencer**, or person who is concerned about the financial aspects of the decision. Another is the user, which we will discuss later. A third is the **technical influencer**, a person who makes sure the technical requirements (including logistics, terms and conditions, quality measurements, or other specifications) are met. Miller and Heiman state that these people usually have the authority only to say no (meaning the salesperson did not meet the specifications, so the proposal is rejected), so they play a gatekeeping role (discussed more in a moment). The fourth role or type of influencer is the coach. The **coach** is someone in a buying organization who can advise and direct you, the salesperson, in maneuvering through the buying process in an effective fashion, leading to a sale. In addition, this person may advocate for you in private conversations among members of the buying center. As you can imagine, finding a coach is an important factor when decision processes are complex and involve a lot of people.[12]

GATEKEEPERS

Gatekeepers control the flow of information and may limit the alternatives considered. For example, the quality control and service departments may determine which potential suppliers are qualified sources.

ethics

Purchasing agents often play a gatekeeping role by determining which potential suppliers are to be notified about the purchase situation and are to have access to relevant information. In some companies, all new contacts must be made through purchasing agents. They arrange meetings with other gatekeepers, influencers, and users. Such gatekeeping activity is not a power play; rather, it ensures that purchases are consolidated under one contract, thus reducing costs and increasing quality. These single contracts are growing in popularity as a way to reduce costs globally.[13] When purchasing agents restrict access to important information, salespeople are tempted to bypass the purchasing agents and make direct contact. Direct contact is risky and can result in salespeople being excluded from sales opportunities. In Chapter 7 we discuss ethical strategies that salespeople can use to deal with this issue.

DECIDERS

In any buying center one or more members of the group, **deciders**, make the final choice. Determining who actually makes the purchase decision for an organization is often difficult. For straight rebuys the purchasing agent usually selects the vendor and places the order. However, for new tasks many people influence the decision, and several people must approve the decision and sign the purchase order.

In general, senior executives get more involved in important purchase decisions that have a greater effect on the performance of the organization. For example, the chief executive officer (CEO) and chief financial officer (CFO) play an important role in purchasing a telephone system because this network has a significant impact on the firm's day-to-day operations.

To sell effectively to organizations, salespeople need to know the people in the buying center and their involvement at different steps of the buying process. Consider the following situation. Salespeople selling expensive intensive care monitoring equipment know that a hospital buying center for the type of equipment they sell typically consists of physicians, nurses, hospital administrators, engineers, and purchasing agents. Through experience, these salespeople also know the relative importance of the buying center members in various stages of the purchasing process (see Exhibit 3.3). With this information the intensive care equipment salespeople know to concentrate on physicians throughout the process, nurses and engineers in the middle of the process, and hospital administrators and purchasing agents at the end of the process.

Exhibit 3.3
Importance of Hospital Buying Center Members in the Buying Process for Intensive Care Monitoring Equipment

Step in Buying Process	Physicians	Nurses	Hospital Administrators	Purchasing Engineers	Agents
Need recognition (step 1)	High	Moderate	Low	Low	Low
Definition of product type (step 2)	High	High	Moderate	Moderate	Low
Analysis of proposal (step 5)	High	Moderate	Moderate	High	Low
Proposal evaluation and supplier selection (step 6)	High	Low	High	Low	Moderate

SUPPLIER EVALUATION AND CHOICE

At various steps in the buying process, members of the buying center evaluate alternative methods for solving a problem (step 2), the qualifications of potential suppliers (step 4), proposals submitted by potential suppliers (step 5), and the performance of products purchased (step 8). Using these evaluations, buyers select potential suppliers and eventually choose a specific vendor.

The needs of both the organization and the individuals making the decisions affect the evaluation and selection of products and suppliers (see Exhibit 3.4). Often these organizational and personal needs are classified into two categories: rational needs and emotional needs.[14] **Rational needs** are directly related to the performance of the product. Thus, the organizational needs discussed in the next section are examples of rational needs. **Emotional needs** are associated with the personal rewards and gratification of the person buying the product. Thus, the personal

Exhibit 3.4
Factors Influencing Organizational Buying Decisions

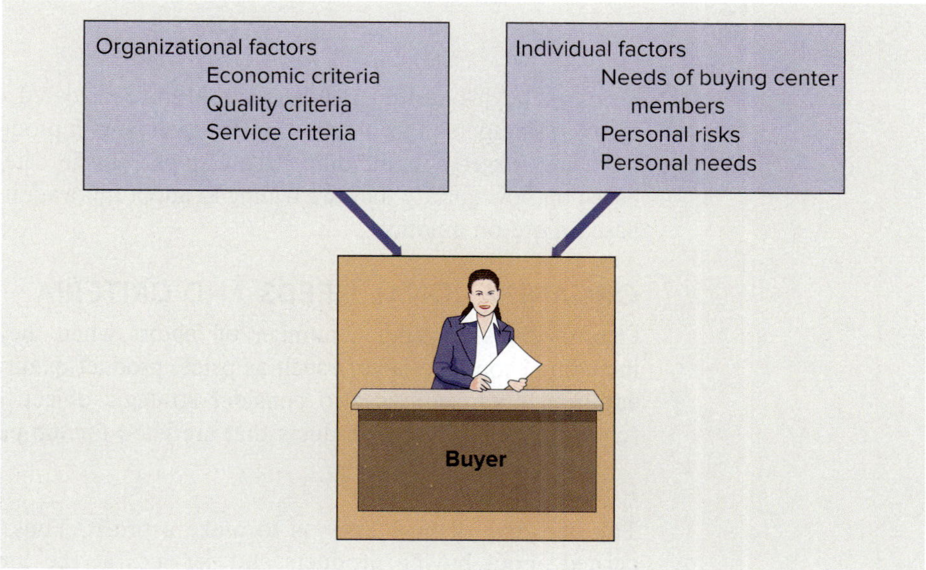

BUILDING Partnerships 3.1

FOUR TYPES OF BUYERS

Camille Sandler sells products that help surgical patients re-grow skin and other tissue. One application is for patients who need to have surgery on their face. As she says about one patient, "He would have looked like Frankenstein" were it not for her company's product.

Sound futuristic? To some doctors, as one of her prospects said, "That's crap. I don't believe it."

Camille has found that she's quickly able to identify four types of buyers, based on how willing they are to consider such a futuristic solution. This categorization helps her determine how to sell, and in some cases, whom to avoid.

"There are the early adopters—those who are eager to try new products and step out of the box to see what's new in the market. These buyers look for new ways to improve their business practices. Then there are the late adopters. These buyers buy products and services early on in the product life cycle but are not quite as eager to jump on the buying train as first adopters. After the late adopters come what you may call trend followers. When everyone else starts using a product and they see their colleagues buying it, then they too will become buyers. Lastly, there is the group that will never buy. They are not interested, nor will they ever be interested no matter how wonderful your product is. They are set in their ways and have no interest to change."

She believes she can identify buyer types within the first 20 seconds: "Reading your buyers' verbal and nonverbal body language can help you determine what category of buyer you are dealing with and how to approach them. In my industry of selling medical devices, figuring out your buyer type and then getting him or her on your team is critical for success in the buying process. Unfortunately, getting a 'yes, I want to buy' is not enough for a sale."

The buying process is more intricate than that. "I not only have to get the support of the surgeon, but the hospital must be on board as well. To make matters more complicated, many times the contracting department must get involved too. Our medical products must be approved at the hospitals we sell to in order for the surgeons to be able to use them. So getting the surgeon's support helps immensely when it comes time to sell to the hospital. If the surgeon will go up to bat for me, the process becomes a whole lot easier." For a futuristic product like the one Sandler sells, the contracting department needs to approve the product if the hospital's own surgeons are the ones backing the product.

But that takes first figuring out which surgeons are more likely to support it, and starting there. And yes, the one who told her that her product was "crap" became a customer not long after.

Source: Camille Sandler, Used with permission.

needs of buying center members often are considered emotional needs. Camille Sandler, salesperson for Acell, supplies doctors with products that help patients heal following surgery. In Building Partnerships 3.1 she categorizes doctors as buyers based on how quickly they are willing to adopt innovations, a categorization scheme based more on emotions.

ORGANIZATIONAL NEEDS AND CRITERIA

Organizations consider a number of factors when they make buying decisions, including economic factors such as price, product quality, and supplier service. In addition, organizations also consider strategic objectives, such as sustainability (choosing vendors and products that are good for the planet) and social diversity.

Economic Criteria

The objective of businesses is to make a profit. Thus, businesses are very concerned about buying products and services at the lowest cost. Organizational buyers are now taking a more sophisticated approach to evaluating the cost of equipment. Rather than simply focusing on the purchase price, they consider installation costs, the costs of needed accessories, freight charges, estimated maintenance costs, and operating costs, including forecasts of energy costs. Retail buyers also consider other financial factors, such as who pays for promotion plans–the retailer or the manufacturer.

Life-cycle costing, also referred to as the total cost of ownership, is a method for determining the cost of equipment or supplies over their useful lives.[15] Using this approach, salespeople can demonstrate that a product with a higher initial cost will have a lower overall cost. An example of life-cycle costing appears in Exhibit 3.5. (Approaches, that salespeople can use to demonstrate the value of their products to customers are discussed in more detail in Chapter 9.)

Quality Criteria

Many firms recognize that the quality and reliability of their products are as important to their customers as price. Firms expect their suppliers to support their efforts to provide quality products. A recent study in the UK indicates that suppliers are evaluated on both the quality of their service and the quality of their products because both impact the quality that the buyer can deliver to its customer.[16] Salespeople often need to describe how their firms will support the customer's quality objectives.

To satisfy customer quality needs, salespeople need to know what organizational buyers are looking for. Quality criteria can include such objective measures as the number of defects per thousand products, the amount of time a machine operates before needing service, or the number of items a system can process in a given period of time. Some buyers also utilize subjective measures, such as if a piece of office furniture looks sturdy or if the vendor has great ratings on the Web. Either way, the salesperson has to identify what criteria will be used to determine quality.

Service Criteria

Organizational buyers want more than products that are low cost, that perform reliably, and that are aesthetically pleasing. They also want suppliers that will work with them to solve their problems. One primary reason firms are interested in developing long-term relationships with suppliers is so they can learn about each other's needs and capabilities and use this information to enhance their products' performance.

Exhibit 3.5
Life-Cycle Costing

	Product A	Product B
Initial cost	$35,000	$30,000
Life of machine	10 years	10 years
Power consumption per year	150 MWh*	180 MWh
Power cost at $30/MWh	$45,000	$54,000
Estimated operating and maintenance cost over 10 years	$25,000	$30,000
Life-cycle cost	$105,000	$114,000

Note: A more thorough analysis would calculate the net present value of the cash flow associated with each product's purchase and use.

* MWh = megawatt-hour.

Service level agreements (SLAs) are standards for minimum service delivery for specific objective measures of how the vendor will perform services, and are written into a contract.[17] These are especially critical early in a relationship because SLAs guide both buyer and seller in making sure the appropriate level of service is delivered.

Value analysis is an example of a program in which suppliers and customers work together to reduce costs and still provide the required level of performance.[18] Representatives from the supplier and the purchasing department and technical experts from engineering, production, or quality control usually form a team to undertake the analysis. The team begins by examining the product's function. Then members brainstorm to see whether changes can be made in the design, materials, construction, or production process to reduce the product's costs but keep its performance high. Some questions addressed in this phase are the following:

- Can a part in the product be eliminated?
- If the part is not standard, can a standard (and presumably less expensive) part be used?
- Does the part have greater performance than this application needs?
- Are unnecessary machining or fine finishes specified?

Salespeople can use value analysis to get customers to consider a new product. This approach is particularly useful for the out-supplier in a straight rebuy situation. David Lenling, a sales representative for Hormel, used value analysis to sell pepperoni to a 35-unit group of pizzerias in the Cincinnati area. The owner had been using the same pepperoni and bacon topping for over 15 years and was reluctant to switch. Lenling showed how the Hormel pepperoni product cost $5 per case more but offered 1,200 more slices in a case with the same weight, which equated to an additional $12 of pepperoni, or a $7 per case net savings, enough to make about 35 more pizzas per case. The owner of the chain was unaware of these differences until Lenling actually weighed his current product. Through value analysis, Lenling was able to interrupt a straight rebuy. Further, Lenling's buyer agreed that the Hormel product tasted better and was less greasy, resulting in a better-looking and tastier pizza, which might result in customers coming back more often. Because Hormel products are of high quality and sell at a premium price, Lenling and other sales representatives have to prove that the products are worth the extra money. They use value analysis to help purchasing agents determine how much it costs to use the product rather than how much the product costs. That's why Lenling was able to win that large pizza chain's business.

INDIVIDUAL NEEDS OF BUYING CENTER MEMBERS

In the preceding section we discussed criteria used to determine whether a product satisfies the needs of the organization. However, buying center members are people. Their evaluations and choices are affected by their personal needs as well as the organization's needs.

Types of Needs

Buying center members, like all people, have personal goals and aspirations. They want to get a raise, be promoted to a high-level position, have their managers recognize their accomplishments, and feel they have done something for their company or demonstrated their skills as a buyer or engineer.

Salespeople can influence members of the buying center by developing strategies to satisfy individual needs. For example, demonstrating how a new product will reduce costs and increase the purchasing agents' bonus would satisfy the purchasing agents' financial security needs. Encouraging an engineer to recommend a product employing the latest technology might satisfy the engineer's need for self-esteem and recognition by his or her engineering peers.

Risk Reduction

In many situations, members of the buying center tend to be more concerned about losing benefits they have now than about increasing their benefits. They place a lot of emphasis on avoiding risks that may result in poor decisions, decisions that can adversely affect their personal reputations and rewards as well as their organization's performance. Buyers first assess the potential for risk and then develop a risk reduction strategy.[19] To reduce risk, buying center members may collect additional information, develop a loyalty to present suppliers, or spread the risk by placing orders with several vendors.

Because they know suppliers try to promote their own products, customers tend to question information received from vendors. Customers usually view information from independent sources such as trade publications, review sites on the Internet, colleagues, and outside consultants as more credible than information provided by salespeople and company advertising and sales literature. Therefore, they will search for such information to reduce risk when a purchase is important.

When making a buying decision, this woman's performance is being judged by others in the organization. Thus, she will seek to find ways to reduce her risk, while also reducing risk to the organization.

Advertising, the Internet, and sales literature tend to be used more in the early steps of the buying process. Word-of-mouth information from friends and colleagues is important in the proposal evaluation and supplier selection steps. Word-of-mouth information is especially important for risky decisions that will have a significant impact on the organization or the buying center member. Sales Technology 3.1 illustrates the importance of the Internet for word-of-mouth information, as well as company-created information.

Another way to reduce uncertainty and risk is to display **vendor loyalty** to suppliers—that is, to continue buying from suppliers that proved satisfactory in the past.[20] Converting buying decisions into straight rebuys makes the decisions routine, minimizing the chances of a poor decision. One name for this is **lost for good**; for all the out-suppliers, this account can be considered lost for good because the in-supplier has cemented this relationship for a long time. Organizations tend to develop vendor loyalty for unimportant purchase decisions, though they will often look to vendors who have proved trustworthy when beginning to search in a risky situation. In these situations the potential benefits from new suppliers do not compensate for the costs of evaluating these suppliers.

The consequences of choosing a poor supplier can be reduced by using more than one vendor. Rather than placing all orders for an OEM component with one

SALES Technology 3.1

THE POWER OF DIGITAL MARKETING

When business customers of Verizon need help, they often do an online search that brings up solutions and information from other customers. "The problem, though, is that while these postings are not always 100% accurate," says Ken Madrigal, senior digital strategist with Verizon, "our customers fully believe these sources." Getting the right information to come up first in a search and getting customers to trust it is a constant challenge.

Research shows that buyers rely heavily on sources of information from the Web. Just as with consumers, business buyers read customer reviews but they also use other sources of information. One recent study identified the following online sources, in addition to customer reviews:

White papers, research papers written for vendors that explain why their process or platform is best and under what conditions.

Case studies, papers that illustrate how a vendor's customer used the product.

Review reports, papers written by consultants that compare and contrast product performance for a group of competitive products against a rigorous set of standards.

Social media, which is really used more to find the white papers, case studies, and review reports than to read about specific complaints or compliments.

Yet in spite of the research that shows that buyers get a lot of information from these sources, the final decision is often based on the personal interaction and expertise of the sales team. As Bruce Culbert, chief revenue officer of the digital marketing agency The Pedowitz Group, says, "All we do is open the door for the salesperson to walk through and finish the job."

Sources: Ken Madrigal, March 18, 2017; Bruce Culbert, May 14, 2017; Julie Schwartz and Anna Whiding, "Persuading Buyers to Choose You," ITSMA, December 31, 2014.

supplier, for example, a firm might elect to purchase 75 percent of its needs from one supplier and 25 percent from another. Thus, if a problem occurs with one supplier, another will be available to fill the firm's needs. If the product is proprietary–available from only one supplier–the buyer might insist that the supplier develop a second source for the component. Such a strategy is called **"always a share,"** which means the buyer will always allocate only a share to each vendor.

These risk reduction approaches present a major problem for salespeople working for out-suppliers. To break this loyalty barrier, these salespeople need to develop trusting relationships with customers. They can build trust by offering performance guarantees or consistently meeting personal commitments. Another approach is to encourage buyers to place a small trial order so the salesperson's company can demonstrate the product's capabilities. On the other hand, the salesperson for the in-supplier wants to discourage buyers from considering new sources, even on a trial basis.

SUPPLY CHAIN MANAGEMENT AND PROFESSIONAL PURCHASING

The purchasing profession is undergoing dramatic changes. Companies have recognized the impact that effective purchasing can make on the bottom line. For example, if a company can save $5,000 on a purchase, $5,000 is added to net income. If sales go up $5,000, of which most is additional costs, only $500 may be added to net income. Savings, though, don't just come from reducing the purchase price–those savings come from better management of the supply chain. Most large firms have elevated their directors of purchasing to the level of senior vice president and added the supply chain management responsibility to reflect the increasing importance of this function.

SUPPLY CHAIN MANAGEMENT

Supply chain management (SCM) began as a set of programs undertaken to increase the efficiency of the distribution channel that moves products from the producer's facilities to the end user. More recently, however, SCM has become more than just logistics; it is now a strategy of managing inventory while containing costs. SCM includes logistics systems, such as just-in-time inventory control, as well as supplier evaluation processes, such as supplier relationship management systems.

The **just-in-time (JIT) inventory control** system is an example of a logistics SCM system used by a producer to minimize its inventory by having frequent deliveries, sometimes daily, just in time for assembly into the final product. In theory each product delivered by a supplier must conform to the manufacturer's specifications every time. It must be delivered when needed, not earlier or later, and it must arrive in the exact quantity needed, not more or less. The ultimate goal is to eventually eliminate all inventory except products in production and transit.

To develop the close coordination needed for JIT systems, manufacturers tend to rely on one supplier. The selection criterion is not the lowest cost, but the ability of the supplier to be flexible. As these relationships develop, employees of the supplier have offices at the customer's site and participate in value analysis meetings with the supplier. The salesperson becomes a facilitator, coordinator, and even marriage counselor in developing a selling team that works effectively with the customer's buying center. Resellers are also interested in managing their inventories more efficiently. Retailers and distributors work closely with their suppliers to minimize inventory investments and still satisfy the needs of customers. These JIT inventory systems are referred to as **quick-response (QR) systems** or **efficient consumer response (ECR) systems** in a consumer product distribution channel. (Partnering relationships involving these systems are discussed in more detail in Chapter 14.)

Automatic replenishment (AR) is a form of JIT where the supplier manages inventory levels for the customer. The materials are provided on consignment, meaning the buyer doesn't pay for them until they are actually used. These types of arrangements are used in industrial settings, where the product being consumed is a supply item used in a manufacturing process, as well as in retail settings. Efficient consumer response systems use automatic replenishment technology through **electronic data interchange (EDI)**, or computer systems that share data across companies. Exhibit 3.6 illustrates the communications associated with placing orders and receiving products that are transmitted electronically through EDI. Recent research

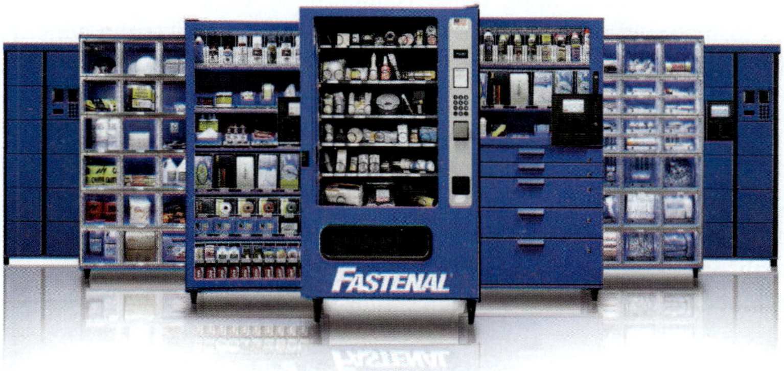

Fastenal places vending machines in clients' locations because this allows its customers to buy what they need when they need it–a form of just-in-time inventory management.

Courtesy of Fastenal

Exhibit 3.6
EDI Transactions

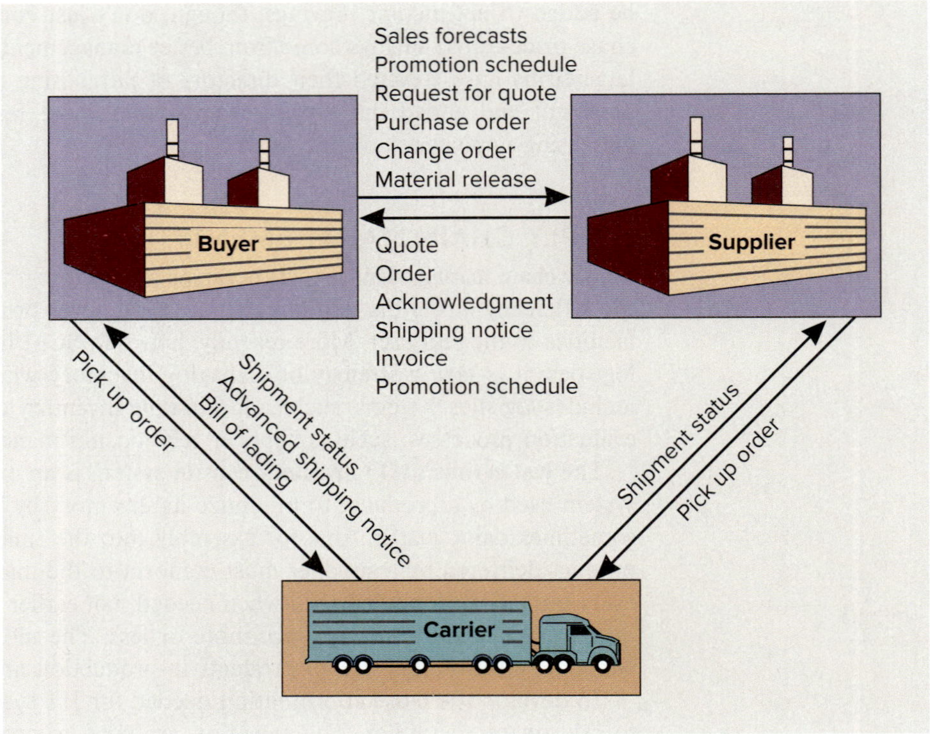

has indicated that adopting systems involving both EDI and quick-response or JIT delivers a number of benefits to the firm, in addition to lower costs. These benefits include greater flexibility in manufacturing, improved stability of supply, and other operating benefits.

Supplier relationship management (SRM) is a strategy by which organizational buyers evaluate the relative importance of suppliers and use that information to determine with whom they want to develop partnerships.[21] Being loyal to one vendor can create value, as illustrated in From the Buyer's Seat 3.1. The first step is to identify the **annual spend**, or amount that is spent with each vendor and for what products. One outcome is the ability to consolidate purchases and negotiate better terms. After the relative importance is identified, organizational buyers frequently use a formal method, called **vendor analysis**, to summarize the benefits and needs satisfied by a supplier. When using this procedure, the buyer rates the supplier and its products on a number of criteria, such as price, quality, performance, and on-time delivery. Note that the ratings of suppliers can be affected by the perceptions and personal needs of the buyers. Then the ratings are weighted by the importance of the characteristics, and an overall score or evaluation of the vendor is developed. The next section describes the multiattribute model, which is useful in analyzing how members of the buying center evaluate and select products. The model also suggests strategies salespeople can use to influence these evaluations.

SRM software is being used by companies like Procter & Gamble (P&G), makers of products such as Crest toothpaste. The software allows P&G to track suppliers' performance along metrics such as delivery reliability and invoice accuracy. At the same time, however, the software supports a larger strategy that

From the BUYER'S SEAT 3.1

THE VALUE OF LOYALTY

A recent study by Bain of 290 executives in 11 countries reported that two-thirds are less loyal than they used to be. At the same time, another study found that companies that have more loyal customers grow from 4 to 8 percent faster than their competitors. From the vendor side, customer loyalty is very important, but what about from the buyer side? And why is loyalty diminishing?

There are two types of loyalty. The first is behavioral, or repeat purchasing behavior over time. The second is attitudinal, or emotionally liking a brand, company, or salesperson. The fact that loyalty can be given to a brand, company, or salesperson independently, meaning a buyer may like the salesperson and be neutral about the brand, makes loyalty in business markets more complicated than consumer markets.

The goal for everyone, buyers and sellers alike, is attitudinal *and* behavioral loyalty. Buyers want companies and salespeople they can rely on and with whom they like doing business. As Deyan Sharkur, procurement supervisor for WuXi AppTec, says about his company's relationship with Staples, the office supply company, "The biggest advantage is the collaborative partnership. We have a team that really knows our business and is consistently reviewing our account to make sure we're getting the best value." According to Shakur, the relationship is about both value, defined as return on their spend, and relationship, or trusting the Staples team.

So if being loyal reduces risk and increases value, why is vendor loyalty declining?

One theory is the growth of online channels for buying. Without personal interaction, impersonal purchasing makes each transaction stand alone and reduces attitudinal loyalty.

Yet, salespeople and customer service people remain the key. "If I have a problem or need something that is not on the Staples website, I always reach out to my Staples Business Advantage account manager," says Sabrina Martinez, purchasing manager for Hotel Allegro, a chain of hotels in Chicago. "He researches it for me and tries to find a solution." In one instance, this meant bringing in an ergonomics specialist and building a custom desk.

Finding a product that works, from the buyer's seat, is a matter of sifting through the ones that don't. Finding a vendor worth the buyer's loyalty means finding a salesperson that works for the buyer.

Sources: Bain Company, *"Building Loyalty in B2B Companies"*; Staples, *"A Pain-Relieving Partnership"*; Staples, *"In Their Words: Procurement Professionals Share How Staples Business Advantage Gets the Job Done"*

includes early supplier involvement in product innovation because the company can combine purchases for better pricing and inventory management.[22]

SRM isn't always about improving profits. Sustainability, for example, is an important trend in purchasing and means making purchasing decisions that do not damage the environment. General Motors is trying to purchase only tires made from natural rubber but without deforestation or human rights violations. Using natural rubber will reduce the carbon impact associated with rubber made from petroleum but will take time due to the need for producers to invest in rubber plantations. But sustainability is an important goal for GM and worth the effort.[23]

thinking it through

Review the stages in the decision-making process described earlier in the chapter. Do you go through those stages when making an important purchase? How does the Internet affect the way you buy products and services? What effect does it have on each stage of the process?

MULTIATTRIBUTE MODEL OF PRODUCT EVALUATION AND CHOICE

The multiattribute model is a useful approach for understanding the factors individual members of a buying center consider in evaluating products and making choices. The multiattribute model is one approach that companies can take to making purchases and is most often used in complex decisions involving several vendors.[24] Many business decisions are straight rebuys, but the original vendor selection decision may have involved a multiattribute approach. The vendor analysis form used by Chrysler illustrates the use of this model in selecting vendors. The model also provides a framework for developing sales strategies.

The multiattribute model is based on the idea that people view a product as a collection of characteristics or attributes. Buyers evaluate a product by considering how each characteristic satisfies the firm's needs and perhaps their individual needs. The following example examines a firm's decision to buy laptop computers for its sales force. The computers will be used by salespeople to track information about customers and provide call reports to sales managers. At the end of each day, salespeople will call headquarters and upload their call reports.

PERFORMANCE EVALUATION OF CHARACTERISTICS

Assume the company narrows its choice to three hypothetical brands: Apex, Bell, and Deltos. Exhibit 3.7 shows information the company has collected about each brand. Note that the information goes beyond the physical characteristics of the product to include services provided by the potential suppliers.

Each buying center member (or the group as a whole in a meeting) might process this objective information and evaluate the laptop computers on each characteristic. These evaluations appear in Exhibit 3.8 as ratings on a 10-point scale, with 10 being the highest rating and 1 the lowest.

How do members of the buying center use these evaluations to select a laptop computer? The final decision depends on the relationship between the performance evaluations and the company's needs. The buying center members must consider the degree to which they are willing to sacrifice poor performance on one attribute for superior performance on another. The members of the buying center must make some trade-offs.

Exhibit 3.7
Information about Laptop Computers

Characteristic/Brand	Apex	Bell	Deltos
Reliability rating	Very good	Very good	Excellent
Weight (pounds)	3.0	4.5	7.5
Display size (inches)	15.0	13	10.1
Display visibility	Good	Very good	Excellent
Speed (clock rate in gigahertz)	2.4	3.0	2.4
RAM (memory in gigabytes)	2	2	4
Number of U.S. service centers	140	60	20

Exhibit 3.8
Performance Evaluation of Laptop Computers

Characteristic/Brand Rating	Apex	Bell	Deltos
Reliability	5	5	8
Weight	8	5	2
Display size	8	6	4
Display visibility	2	4	6
Speed	4	8	4
RAM	3	3	8
Service availability	7	5	3

No single product will perform best on all characteristics. For example, Apex excels on size, weight, and availability of convenient service; Bell has superior speed; and Deltos provides the best reliability and internal memory.

IMPORTANCE WEIGHTS

In making an overall evaluation, buying center members need to consider the importance of each characteristic. These importance weights may differ from member to member. Consider two members of the buying center: the national sales manager and the chief information officer (CIO). The national sales manager is particularly concerned about motivating salespeople to use the pad computers. He believes in pad computers because they are small and lightweight and have good screen visibility. On the other hand, the CIO foresees using the laptop computers to transmit orders and customer inventory information to corporation headquarters. She believes expanded memory and processing speed will be critical for these future applications and prefers laptops.

Exhibit 3.9 shows the importance these two buying center members place on each characteristic using a 10-point scale, with 10 representing very important and 1 representing very unimportant. In this illustration the national sales manager and the CIO differ in the importance they place on characteristics;

Exhibit 3.9
Information Used to Form an Overall Evaluation

	Importance Weights		Brand Ratings		
Characteristic	Sales Manager	CIO Director	Apex	Bell	Deltos
Reliability	4	4	5	5	8
Weight	6	2	8	5	2
Display size	7	3	8	6	4
Display visibility	8	5	2	4	6
Speed	1	7	4	8	4
RAM	1	6	3	3	8
Service availability	3	3	7	5	3
Overall evaluation					
Sales manager's			168	150	141
MIS director's			137	157	163

however, both have the same evaluations of the brands' performance on the characteristics. In some cases people may differ on both importance weights and performance ratings.

OVERALL EVALUATION

A person's overall evaluation of a product can be quantified by multiplying the sum of the performance ratings by the importance weights. Thus, the sales manager's overall evaluation of Apex would be as follows:

$$
\begin{aligned}
4 \times 5 &= 20 \\
6 \times 8 &= 48 \\
7 \times 8 &= 56 \\
8 \times 2 &= 16 \\
1 \times 4 &= 4 \\
1 \times 3 &= 3 \\
3 \times 7 &= \underline{21} \\
 & 168
\end{aligned}
$$

Using the national sales manager's and CIO's importance weights, the overall evaluations, or scores, for the three laptop computer brands appear at the bottom of Exhibit 3.9. The scores indicate the benefit levels the brands provide as seen by these two buying center members.

VALUE OFFERED

The cost of the computers also needs to be considered in making the purchase decision. One approach for incorporating cost calculates the value–the benefits divided by the cost–for each laptop. The prices for the computers and their values are shown in Exhibit 3.10. The sales manager believes Apex provides more value. He would probably buy this brand if he were the only person involved in the buying decision. On the other hand, the CIO believes that Bell and Deltos offer the best value.

SUPPLIER SELECTION

In this situation the sales manager might be the key decision maker, and the CIO might be a gatekeeper. Rather than using the CIO's overall evaluation, the buying center might simply ask her to serve as a gatekeeper and determine whether these computers meet her minimum acceptable performance standards on speed and

Exhibit 3.10
Value Offered by Each Brand

	Overall Evaluation (Benefits Points)	Assigned Value	
		Computer Cost	Benefit/Cost
Sales manager			
Apex	167	$1,600	$0.10
Bell	152	1,800	0.08
Deltos	143	1,800	0.08
CIO			
Apex	130	$1,600	0.08
Bell	169	1,800	0.09
Deltos	177	1,800	0.10

memory. All three computers pass the minimum levels she established of a 2-gigahertz clock rate and a 3-gigabyte internal memory. Thus, the company would rely on the sales manager's evaluation and purchase Apex laptops for the sales force.

Even if a buying center or individual members do not go through the calculations described here, the multiattribute model is a good representation of their product evaluations and can be used to predict product choices. Purchase decisions are often made as though a formal multiattribute model were used.

thinking it through

If you were selling the Bell computer to the national sales manager and CIO depicted in the text and in Exhibits 3.9 and 3.10, how would you try to get them to believe that your computer provides more value than Apex or Deltos does? What numbers would you try to change?

IMPLICATIONS FOR SALESPEOPLE

How can salespeople use the multiattribute model to influence their customers' purchase decisions? First, the model describes the information customers use in making their evaluations and purchase decisions. Thus, salespeople need to know the following information to develop a sales strategy:

1. The suppliers or brands the customer is considering.
2. The product characteristics being used in the evaluation.
3. The customer's rating of each product's performance on each dimension.
4. The weights the customer attaches to each dimension.

With this knowledge salespeople can use several strategies to influence purchase decisions. First, salespeople must be sure their product is among the brands being considered. Then they can try to change the customer's perception of their product's value. Some approaches for changing perceived value follow:

1. Increase the performance rating for your product.
2. Decrease the rating for a competitive product.
3. Increase or decrease an importance weight.
4. Add a new dimension.
5. Decrease the price of your product.

Assume you are selling the Bell computer and you want to influence the sales manager so he believes your computer provides more value than the Apex computer. Approach 1 involves altering the sales manager's belief about your product's performance. To raise his evaluation, you would try to have the sales manager perceive your computer as small and lightweight. You might show him how easy it is to carry—how well it satisfies his need for portability. The objective of this demonstration is to increase your rating on weight from 5 to 7 and your rating on size from 6 to 8.

You should focus on these two characteristics because they are the most important to the sales manager. A small change in a performance evaluation on these characteristics will have a large impact on the overall evaluation. You would not want to spend much time influencing his performance evaluations of speed or memory because these characteristics are not important to him. Of course your objectives when selling to the CIO would be different because she places more importance on speed and memory.

This example illustrates a key principle in selling. In general, salespeople should focus primarily on product characteristics that are important to the customer—characteristics that satisfy the customer's needs. Salespeople should not focus on the areas of superior performance (such as speed in this example) that are not important to the customer.

Approach 2 involves decreasing the performance rating of Apex. This strategy can be dangerous. Customers prefer dealing with salespeople who say good things about their products, not bad things about competitive products.

In approach 3 you try to change the sales manager's importance weights. You want to increase the importance he places on a characteristic on which your product excels, such as speed, or decrease the importance of a characteristic on which your product performs poorly, such as display visibility. For example, you might try to convince the sales manager that a fast computer will decrease the time salespeople need to spend developing and transmitting reports.

Approach 4 encourages the sales manager to consider a new characteristic, one on which your product has superior performance. For example, suppose the sales manager and CIO have not considered the availability of software. To add a new dimension, you might demonstrate a program especially developed for sales call reports and usable only with your computer.

Approach 5 is the simplest to implement: Simply drop your price. Typically firms use this strategy as a last resort because cutting prices decreases profits.

These strategies illustrate how salespeople can adapt their selling approach to the needs of their customers. Using the multiattribute model, salespeople decide how to alter the content of their presentation—the benefits to be discussed—based on customer beliefs and needs. (Chapter 4 describes adaptive selling in more detail and illustrates it in terms of the form of the presentation—the communication style the salesperson uses.)

SELLING YOURSELF

When you are selling your ideas or selling yourself in a job search, recognize that there is a buying center. Although a sales manager may make the final decision on whether you are hired, chances are that you'll interview with at least four people before the job offer will come. Who is the gatekeeper, who is the decider, and who are influencers? Similarly, once you have the job and you have an idea for a new program or product, you will have to sell that idea to management. That decision will likely include someone from finance, someone from operations, and so on, creating a buying center. Each member of the center will take on different roles and may be present for only part of the decision. Each member may also have different criteria.

Further, you need to understand the process by which the decision is made. In a job search, the decision to hire someone has been made before anyone talks to you. At that point your concern is making it from the large pool of college students they've interviewed at six different campuses to the group they bring into the office, to the final selection of new employees. Similarly, management approval of your idea is likely to follow a process not unlike that of any organizational purchase. Keep in mind that your idea is competing against other ideas from other people, just as your candidacy for a sales job is compared to other college students from your school and others. Therefore, take some time to understand who is involved in the decision, what criteria they will use, and what process they will use to reach a decision.

SUMMARY

Salespeople sell to many different types of customers, including consumers, business enterprises, government agencies, and institutions. This text focuses on selling to organizations rather than to consumers. Selling to organizations differs from selling to consumers because organizations are more concentrated, demand is derived, and the buying process is more complex.

The organizational buying process consists of eight steps, beginning with the recognition of a need and ending with the evaluation of the product's performance. Each step involves several decisions. As organizations progress through these steps, decisions made at previous steps affect subsequent steps, leading to a creeping commitment. Thus, salespeople need to be involved in the buying process as early as possible.

The length of the buying process and the role of various participants depend on the customer's past experiences. When customers have had considerable experience in buying a product, the decision becomes routine–a straight rebuy. Few people are involved, and the process is short. However, when customers have little experience in buying a product–a new task–many people are involved, and the process can be lengthy.

The people involved in the buying process are referred to as the buying center. The buying center is composed of people who are initiators, users, influencers, gatekeepers, and deciders. Salespeople need to understand the roles buying center members play to effectively influence their decisions.

Individuals in the buying center are concerned about satisfying the economic, quality, and service needs of their organization. In addition, these people have personal needs they want to satisfy.

Organizations face an increasingly dynamic and competitive environment. Purchasing is becoming a strategic weapon with the development of supply chain management and supplier relationship management strategies.

The Internet is playing a much more important role in business-to-business transactions than it plays in the widely publicized business-to-consumer e-businesses. Business-to-business applications of the Internet are designed to support salespeople's ability to build relationships with major customers.

KEY TERMS

always a share 78
annual spend 80
automatic replenishment (AR) 79
buying center 70
capital equipment 61
coach 72
creeping commitment 67
decider 72
derived demand 65
economic influencer 72
efficient consumer response (ECR) system 79
electronic data interchange (EDI) 79
emotional needs 73
end user 61
gatekeeper 72
influencer 71
initiator 71
just-in-time (JIT) inventory control 79
life-cycle costing 75
lost for good 77
manufacturer 60
modified rebuy 70
MRO supplies 61
new task 68
original equipment manufacturer (OEM) 60
profit margin 61
quick-response (QR) system 79
rational needs 73
reseller 61
service level agreement (SLA) 76
services 61
straight rebuy 69

supplier relationship management (SRM) 80
supply chain management (SCM) 79
technical influencer 72
turnover (TO) 62
user 71
value analysis 76
vendor analysis 80
vendor loyalty 77

ETHICS PROBLEMS

1. You sell services to city and county governments that help lower their costs in billing for services like water, trash collection, and the like. Your company is owned by two African American sisters. The mayor of a major city in your territory has publicly stated that the city has reached its goal of buying 15 percent of its services from women and minority-owned businesses, yet you've heard it said that the city is buying only about 5 percent from women and minority-owned business. To make matters worse, you can't get an appointment with the head of utilities but you know for a fact that your company could reduce operating costs by almost 20 percent. What do you do?
2. You are talking about this chapter to your parents, when they say, "What are they doing, teaching you how to manipulate people? Cheat them by using their buying style against them?" How do you respond?

QUESTIONS AND PROBLEMS

1. Assume that the federal government is going to make reducing obesity a major priority. The process it has adopted includes reducing sugar content in children's cereals, making vegetables more palatable, and reducing fat in the overall diet. Identify three product categories (not including vegetables) for which derived demand would influence manufacturers and producers of consumer packaged goods (foods sold to be cooked or heated and eaten at home). Include at least one product affected positively and one product affected negatively.
2. Read Building Partnerships 3.1. Camille Sandler described four types of buyers based on whether they were willing to consider a new innovation. What are some other ways she could classify buyers? How can she work with a contracting department run by someone who is not willing to innovate?
3. Assume you are a salesperson selling to OEMs. How would the purchasing decision process differ in the following situations? Which situation is a new task? A modified rebuy? A straight rebuy? How likely is the buyer to get other people in the organization involved? Which types of people are likely to get involved in each decision? Whom would you call on first? Which situation is likely to produce the slowest decision?
   a. The organization is purchasing a custom-designed machine to be used in the manufacturing of metal racks that house multiple monitoring systems.
   b. An organization reorders plastic shields that it uses in making medical monitoring equipment from a regular supplier, a supplier that it has bought from in the past.
   c. The organization is designing a new line of medical monitoring equipment and wants an improved and updated microprocessor. It is considering its past suppliers as well as some suppliers that it has not bought from before.
4. Review each purchase in question 3. What information would you need to conduct a value analysis for each? Note: You will need some different and some similar information in each situation.
5. A chain of restaurants wants to purchase a new order entry computer system tied into an accounting system that manages food inventory and automatically replenishes packaged food items and supplies. Which criteria for evaluating supplier proposals might be used by (a) the purchasing agent, (b) the information systems department, (c) a store manager, and (d) the head of the legal department? How would this purchase differ from a purchase of the same products by a company that resells store fixtures

and equipment to small restaurants? How would this purchase differ if the chain had 4 locations versus 400?

6. Fastenal sells maintenance, repair, and operations supplies. One of its strategies is to put vending machines on customers' sites, particularly for small tools, so that Fastenal carries the cost of inventory and the customer pays for it only when the product is actually needed. You have an account with the potential to be your largest, but it is under contract to a vendor that doesn't provide that service. The contract expires in six months. What do you do? (Feel free to visit the Fastenal website for more information www.fastenal.com/.)
7. When is vendor loyalty important to the buyer? Find at least one example in the chapter (there are several) where vendor loyalty would prove to be important and discuss why it was important in that particular instance. What can buyers do to improve vendor loyalty? When might vendor loyalty be inefficient or wasteful? Does it matter whether the loyalty that the buyer tries to curry is with the salesperson or the company?
8. Create a matrix of types of needs and types of customers (OEM, users, etc.). Which customer types share the same types of needs or express needs in the same way? Which ones differ? Why? Relate your chart to the multiattribute matrix. How would your chart help you prepare to sell?
9. Mitchell's Metal Shop is considering the purchase of a new press, a machine that bends sheet metal. The cost is $10,000, which is about 25 percent of the firm's profit for the quarter. Ford Motor Company is also considering buying new presses–30 of them. Discuss how risk is different for Frank Mitchell, owner of Mitchell's Metal Shop, and Ford.
10. How would your multiattribute matrix for a new car differ from that of your parents? How is it that you might have some of the same desires (such as high gas mileage) yet consider completely different cars?

CASE PROBLEMS

case 3.1

Going Out through the Back Door

Travis Bruns is a sales representative for Crown Lift Services in Houston, Texas. In his own words, he describes an ethics issue with a buyer.

I was in a real cutthroat bidding war for a $300,000-plus sales opportunity. Over the course of two months the competitive field had been narrowed down to two organizations, mine and the incumbent organization. The customer had set up a set of strict guidelines for the bidding process. One of those was that they had designated a "point of contact" (POC) that was to be the liaison through which all bids and proposals were to channel through to the VP. My organization and I had truly put our best foot forward on pricing and proposed service after the sale, and although the negotiations had been rough, we were able to sell the value of our solution, retain a fair amount of profit, and were told we had the deal: a true win-win. On the final day that the bid was open, I received a call from the point of contact asking me to lower my price. I was confused. I inquired about the previous discussions that had taken place in which we had mutually agreed that the price of our proposal was fair and good. I could hear some level of discomfort if not embarrassment in the POC's voice, so I came right out and asked him, "I get the sense that you are not comfortable with what is happening here either. What happened?"

He replied, "Well, Travis, [your competitor] called one of the other managers in the office and was able to find out the pricing in your proposal. He then went around me and called the VP directly and offered a much lower price. The VP then called me and asked me to get you to lower your price or the other company will get the business."

I was dumbfounded. I asked the customer, "If I cannot lower my price, are you telling me this deal is over for me?"

"I think so," he replied.

Travis Bruns. Used with permission.

Questions

1. What would you do? Do you lower your price or walk away? Why? Write out specifically what you would say next.
2. Do buyers have to follow the same ethics principles as sellers? For example, sellers have to fully disclose all information. Do buyers? Why or why not? What ethical principle violation occurred here?

case 3.2

DIMIS

Mark Swanson is a relatively new salesperson for DIMIS, a company that sells tools used in mining and oil fields. He was telling his boss, Sally Turcotte, about a call he just got from Betsy Price, the head of supply chain management for Austin Stone, a mining company.

"She said that Gary Herman, the company's production director, asked her if he could look into getting the new digital control system for their current production equipment," Mark reported to Sally. "But she also said that the CFO was against adding more costs."

The digital control system Betsy referenced is an add-on to certain forms of expensive tools that enables the tool to connect to the user's Wi-Fi. Through this connection, the tool can provide information into a software program that can monitor usage, which can then be used to optimize uptime by optimally scheduling maintenance or alerting users to potential problems such as overheating.

"Do you think she was serious about the costs?," asked Sally.

"I think so." Mark's face showed his lack of confidence in knowing the answer. "What I do know is that they have no budget set aside for it."

"How will they determine a budget? And what will their process be in making a decision?"

"I'm not sure," replied Mark. "But I do know they are going to put a committee together because she said new systems like this are difficult to justify."

"So who's going to be involved? Will they have their maintenance department and their welders involved or will it only be management? And is IT going to be involved?"

"Not sure, but I have a meeting with them next week, and I'd like you to go with me," Mark said.

Questions

1. What is the likely makeup of the buying center? Who plays or has played which roles? What would be the likely focus of each role in the buying center?
2. What type of purchase situation is this? What are the implications for Mark?
3. How can Mark use the multiattribute matrix to guide a sales plan?

ROLE PLAY CASE

During much of the rest of the semester, you will be calling on one of three accounts. The accounts are listed here with some information. Information that you gain on each call can be used in subsequent calls as you practice the skills and apply the concepts introduced in each chapter.

Asset Recovery Management: Asset Recovery Management (ARM) buys bad loan portfolios from banks and credit card companies, then tries to collect the debt. It built its business by building mathematical models that it uses to evaluate the loan portfolios, claiming that these models give the firm better insight on a portfolio's value. It also uses statistics to determine how best to recover the loans.

FSS: This company was originally called Fire Suppression Services because it was just a manufacturer of firefighting systems and began by selling fire suppression products to fire departments and to commercial property owners and builders. Now international, the company also manufactures other chemical products that serve the agriculture market (including forestry and golf course maintenance) and the fishing industry.

Mizzen Industries: Mizzen Industries works in the shipbuilding, chemical, and oil industry, painting ships, large tanks, and other unusual painting situations involving paint on to metal. The company, headquartered in Newport News, Virginia, grew rapidly by acquiring small paint companies in other shipbuilding ports, such as Jacksonville, Florida, Mobile, Alabama, and Houston, Texas.

Today, you have an appointment with the chief information officer, whom you met at a large conference. Start the sales call from the beginning as if you were entering the person's office. Reintroduce yourself and your company, thank the person for the appointment, and then tell the buyer you'd like to ask some questions. Your questions should be about the buying process and who is involved. Afterward, see if you can chart the buying center and the company's organizational structure.

ADDITIONAL REFERENCES

Anaza, Nwamaka A., Brian Rutherford, Minna Rollins, and David Nickell. "Ethical Climate and Job Satisfaction among Organizational Buyers: An Empirical Study." *Journal of Business and Industrial Marketing* 30, no. 8 (2015), pp. 962–72.

Chuah, Stephanie Hui-Wen, Philipp A. Rauschnabel, Malliga Marimuthu, Ramayah Thurasamy, and Bang Nguyen. "Why Do Satisfied Customers Defect? A Closer Look at the Simultaneous Effects of Switching Barriers and Inducements on Customer Loyalty." *Journal of Service Theory and Practice* 27, no. 3 (2017), pp. 616–41.

Sinčić Ćorić, D., Ivan-Damir Anić, Sunčana Piri Rajh, Edo Rajh, and Natasa Kurnoga. "Organizational Buying Decision Approaches in Manufacturing Industry: Developing Measures and Typology." *Journal of Business and Industrial Marketing* 32, no. 2 (2017), pp. 227–37.

Giovanis, Apostolos, Pinelopi Athanasopoulou, and Evangelos Tsoukatos. "The Role of Service Fairness in the Service Quality-Relationship Quality-Customer Loyalty Chain: An Empirical Study." *Journal of Service Theory and Practice* 25, no. 6 (2015), pp. 744–76.

Gould, A. Noel, Annie H. Liu, and Yang Yu. "Opportunities and Opportunism with High Status B2B Partners in Emerging Economies." *Journal of Business and Industrial Marketing* 31, no. 5 (2016), pp. 684–94.

Hollmann, Thomas, Cheryl Burke Jarvis, and Mary Jo Bitner. "Reaching the Breaking Point: A Dynamic Process Theory of Business-to-Business Customer Defection." *Journal of the Academy of Marketing Science* 43, no. 2 (March 2015), pp. 257–78.

Husser, Jocelyn, Laurence Gautier, Jean-marc André, and Véronique Lespinet-najib. "Linking Purchasing to Ethical Decision Making: An Empirical Investigation." *Journal of Business Ethics* 123, no. 2 (August 2014), pp. 327–38.

Keinänen, Hanna, and Olli Kuivalainen. "Antecedents of Social Media B2B Use in Industrial Marketing Context: Customers' View." *Journal of Business and Industrial Marketing* 30, no. 6 (2015), pp. 711–22.

Kozlenkova, Irina V., G. Tomas, M. Hult, Donald J. Lund, Jeannette A. Mena, and Pinar Kekec. "The Role of Marketing Channels in Supply Chain Management." *Journal of Retailing* 91, no. 4 (December 2015), pp. 586–609.

Makhitha, K. M. "Understanding the Organisational Buyer Behaviour of Craft Retailers in South Africa." *Journal of Applied Business Research* 31, no. 2 (2015), p. 501.

Mogre, Riccardo, Adam Lindgreen, and Martin Hingley. "Tracing the Evolution of Purchasing Research: Future Trends and Directions for Purchasing Practices." *Journal of Business and Industrial Marketing* 32, no. 2 (2017), pp. 251–57.

Poddar, Amit, Naveen Donthu, Daniel C Bello, and Jeff Foreman. "Decision Making under Parity: An Experimental Examination of Retailers' Choice among Parity Trade Promotions." *Journal of Marketing Theory and Practice* 25, no. 2 (Spring 2017), pp. 105–24.

Russo, Ivan, Ilenia Confente, David M Gligor, and Chad W Autry. "To Be or Not to Be (Loyal): Is There a Recipe for Customer Loyalty in the B2B Context?" *Journal of Business Research* 69, no. 2 (February 2016), pp. 888–92.

Scheer, Lisa K., C. Fred Miao, and Robert W. Palmatier. "Dependence and Interdependence in Marketing Relationships: Meta-Analytic Insights." *Journal of the Academy of Marketing Science* 43, no. 6 (November 2015), pp. 694–712.

Walsh, Gianfranco, Sharon E. Beatty, and Betsy Bugg Holloway. "Measuring Client-Based Corporate Reputation in B2B Professional Services: Scale Development and Validation." *Journal of Services Marketing* 29, no. 3 (2015), pp. 173–87.

©Jamie Grill/Blend Images-JGI/Getty Images RF

Knowledge and Skill Requirements

PART 1

chapter 4

USING COMMUNICATION PRINCIPLES TO BUILD RELATIONSHIPS

SOME QUESTIONS ANSWERED IN THIS CHAPTER ARE

- What are the basic elements in the communication process?
- Why are listening and questioning skills important?
- How can salespeople develop listening skills to collect information about customers?
- How do people communicate without using words?
- What are some things to remember when communicating via technology like phones, e-mail, texting, and social media?
- How does a salesperson adjust for cultural differences?

PROFILE

"No matter which way the client prefers to communicate, salespeople need to learn how to read them and adapt."

Rebecca Clark, White Lodging

Courtesy of Rebecca Clark

PROFILE My name is Rebecca Clark and I graduated from Northern Illinois University in 2014 with a bachelor of science degree in marketing and a certificate in professional sales. Before interviewing to be selected to get into the Advanced Professional Selling class with Dr. Peterson, he was already teaching the importance of communication skills without us even knowing. In order to get into the class, we needed to set up an interview, conduct an interview, and follow up with a "thank-you" note without having a lesson on it. He never failed to remind us of the importance of effective communication and understanding the customer's preference even before knowing us.

Throughout the course, we were required to send weekly recaps of what we accomplished and had a deadline each week, which taught us promptness and how to effectively communicate to a customer and/or manager electronically. At one point, I had to sell face-to-face to one of our corporate sponsors of our program. Learning all of this in the sales program made me feel much more advanced than the students that were my competition when it came to interviewing for postgraduate positions. That same corporate partner that I sold to in class, White Lodging, ended up giving me an offer and I have worked for the company for three years now. First impressions are very important. A first impression is not just how well salespeople can handle themselves in a conversation; body language such as eye contact, facial expressions, and placement of arms and legs are equally important when greeting a client, or in my case an interviewer. Three years have passed since I first learned all of this and it is something I still pay attention to when trying to read how my clients are reacting to my hotel.

With so many different generations in the workforce right now, there are so many different ways to communicate while selling and it is important that there is an understanding of all of them because sales professionals never know whom they will be selling to. Technology plays a huge role in everyday communication and it is important to learn how to get someone's attention in an e-mail; but face-to-face is still the most powerful because customers then have a face to relate to as opposed to an e-mail that can get lost in their inbox. No matter which way clients prefer to communicate, salespeople need to learn how to read them and adapt. The most important part of communication remains the same in any scenario, and that is listening.

All people love to talk about themselves. In order to get them to disclose their needs, it is important to prompt them with open-ended questions and then actively listen to them so the sales professional can summarize what the customers say and perform trial closes on them. They will then see the importance of the product being offered and be more open to listening to how the sales professional will fit their needs. The sales meeting is always going to be in the hands of the sales professionals, so they need to make sure they are continuing to move forward and controlling the conversation to get to their next step or close the business.

Visit our Web site at: www.whitelodging.com/.

BUILDING RELATIONSHIPS THROUGH TWO-WAY COMMUNICATION

As we will discuss further in Chapter 13, open and honest communication is a key to building trust and developing successful relationships. To develop a good understanding of each other's needs, buyers and sellers must effectively communicate with each other by actively talking and listening. This is an area in which most can improve, as recent studies suggest communicating is the biggest sales skill gap globally.[1]

THE COMMUNICATION PROCESS

Exhibit 4.1 illustrates the **two-way communication** process. The process begins when the sender, either the salesperson or the customer, wants to communicate some thoughts or ideas. Because the receiver cannot read the sender's mind, the sender must translate these ideas into words. The translation of thoughts into words is called **encoding**. Then the receiver must decode the message and try to understand what the sender intended to communicate. **Decoding** involves interpreting the meaning of the received message.

Consider a salesperson who is describing a complex product to a customer. At one point, a perplexed look flits across the customer's face. The salesperson receives this nonverbal message and asks the customer what part of the presentation needs further explanation. This **feedback** from the customer's expression tells the salesperson that the message is not being received. The customer then sends verbal messages to the salesperson in the form of questions concerning the operation and benefits of the product.

COMMUNICATION BREAKDOWNS

Communication breakdowns can be caused by encoding and decoding problems and the environment in which the communications occur. The following sales interaction between a copier salesperson and a prospect illustrates problems that can arise in encoding and decoding messages:

> *What the salesperson means to say:* We have an entire line of Toshiba copiers. But I think the Model 900 is ideally suited for your needs because it provides the basic copying functions at a low price.

Exhibit 4.1
Two-Way Flow of Information

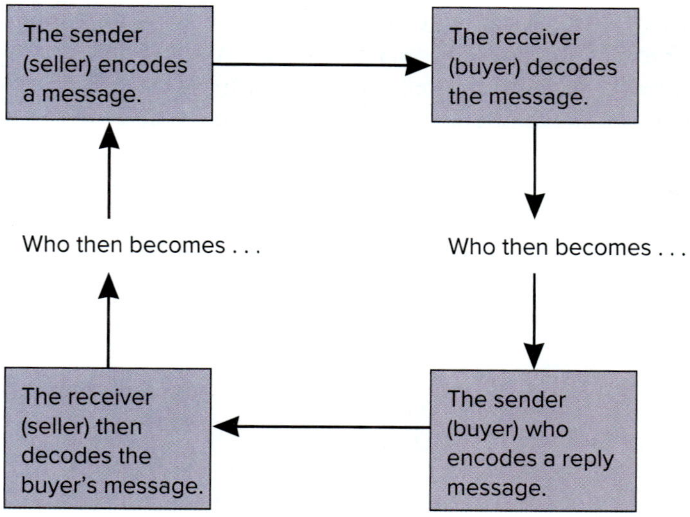

Background noise can hinder effective communication. The salesperson should attempt to move the discussion to a quieter location so the noise will not distract the customer.

©Image Source RF

What the salesperson actually says (encodes): The Model 900 is our best-selling copier, and it's designed to economically meet the copying needs of small businesses like yours.

What the customer hears: The Model 900 is a low-priced copier for small businesses.

What the customer thinks (decodes): This company makes cheap copiers with limited features, probably for businesses that don't have much money. But I need a copier with more features. I think I'd better look elsewhere for a better copier.

What the customer actually says: I don't think I'm interested in buying a copier now.

In this situation the salesperson assumed that price was very important to the prospect, and the prospect thought (incorrectly) that the salesperson's company made only low-priced, low-performance copiers.

Communication can also be inhibited by the environment in which the communication process occurs. For example, noises can distract the salesperson and the customer. **Noises** are sounds unrelated to messages being exchanged by the salesperson and the customer, such as ringing telephones or other conversations nearby. To improve communication, the salesperson should attempt to minimize noises in the environment by closing a door to the room or suggesting that the meeting move to a quieter place.

Other environmental issues must be dealt with before effective communication can occur. For example, people communicate most effectively when they are physically comfortable. If the room is too hot or too cold, the salesperson should suggest changing the temperature controls or moving to another room. These types of environmental issues and possible solutions are discussed in Chapters 7 and 8. For now, realize that effective communication can't occur without the proper environment.

Finally, it is important to note that buyers do not always follow this communication model perfectly. Some buyers—and sellers for that matter—have agendas that do not always result in honest, straightforward attempts to reveal truth. Rather, they may at times use communication as a tool to mask their true motives and intentions. You have probably done this yourself—when caught doing something wrong and wishing to avoid detection or punishment, you masked the truth or said things you hoped would be interpreted in ways that were favorable to you.

thinking it through

Think of a big disagreement you had with someone recently (perhaps with a friend, professor, or a relative). Did any miscommunication occur? Why was the communication poor? Was it due to noise, poor feedback, poor encoding, poor decoding, or what?

SENDING VERBAL MESSAGES EFFECTIVELY

A basic reason that salespeople communicate is to simply provide information to the buyer. Salespeople also often attempt to engage in **persuading**, the process by which the salesperson attempts to convince other people (e.g., buyers) to change their attitudes or behaviors regarding an issue while understanding that the other person is free to accept or reject the idea. This section will explore methods of communicating via verbal communication.

CHOICE OF WORDS

ethics

As Quintilion, the famous Roman orator, said, "Choice of words is the origin of eloquence." Salespeople don't have to be eloquent, but most could use some pointers to develop their skills in word choice. Use short words and phrases to demonstrate strength and force (like *accelerated* and *intervened*) or to provide charm and grace (like *crystal clear* and *crisp copies).* Avoid trite words such as *nice* and *good* and phrases that make you sound like an overeager salesperson such as *a great deal, I guarantee you will . . . ,* and *No problem!* Also avoid using off-color language, slang, and foul language, even with established customers.

Every salesperson should be able to draw on a set of words to best help present the features of a product or service. The words might form a simile, such as *This battery backup is like a spare tire;* a metaphor, such as *This machine is a real workhorse;* or a phrase drawing on sensory appeal, such as *smooth as silk* or *strong as steel.* To find the best way to use words, it often helps to listen to the way your customer talks.

Be careful about using words that have become so common in business conversations as to be almost meaningless. Words like *core competence, value added, enterprise-wide, fault-tolerant,* and *mission-critical* are often cited as examples. Avoid them because they can make you come across as phony.

Words have different meanings in different cultures and even in different subcultures of the United States. In England the hood of a car is called the *bonnet,* and the trunk is called the *boot.* In Boston a milkshake is simply syrup mixed with milk, whereas a frappe is ice cream, syrup, and milk mixed together.

VOICE CHARACTERISTICS

A salesperson's delivery of words affects how the customer will understand and evaluate his or her presentation. Poor voice and speech habits make it difficult for customers to understand a salesperson's message. **Voice characteristics** include rate of speech, loudness, inflection, and articulation.

Customers tend to question the expertise of salespeople who talk much slower or faster than the normal rate of 140 words per minute. Salespeople should vary their rate of speech depending on the nature of the message and the environment in which the communication occurs. Simple messages can be delivered at faster rates, and more difficult concepts should be presented at slower rates.

Loudness should be tailored to the communication situation. To avoid monotony, salespeople should learn to vary the loudness of their speech. Loudness can also be used to emphasize certain parts of the sales presentation, indicating to the customer that these parts are more important.

Inflection is the tone or pitch of speech. At the end of a sentence, the tone should drop, indicating the completion of a thought. When the tone goes up at the end of a sentence, listeners often sense uncertainty in the speaker. Use inflection to reduce monotony. If you speak with enthusiasm, it will help your customer

In order for the salesperson to communicate with these buyers, he must use words and stories that are meaningful and interesting to them.

©Guy Bubb/Gallo Images/Getty Images RF

connect emotionally. However, don't forget to be yourself. The buyer can be turned off if you're obviously just trying to copy the successful communication traits of someone else.

Articulation refers to the production of recognizable sounds. Articulation is best when the speaker opens his or her mouth properly; then the movements of the lips and tongue are unimpeded. When the lips are too close together, the enunciation of certain vowels and consonants suffers.

STORIES

While they are entertaining, stories can also make points most effectively. Great stories often include conflicts, trials, and crises and help the listener think through choices and outcomes of those decisions. Of course salespeople cannot assume all customers are familiar with trade jargon, and thus they need to check with their customers continually to determine whether they are interpreting sales messages and stories properly.

Salespeople can paint word pictures to help customers understand the benefits or features of a product. A **word picture** is a graphic or vivid story designed to help the buyer easily visualize a point. To use a word picture effectively, the salesperson needs to paint as accurate and reliable a picture as possible. Exhibit 4.2 provides an example of a word picture that a Toyota Highlander salesperson might use when calling on the owner of a real estate firm.

Effective stories often include an **analogy**, which is when the speaker attempts to draw a parallel between one thing and another. For example, to explain how a new machine controller is always monitoring and is ready to respond instantly, the seller could say this:

> It's kind of like a broadband Internet connection. It's always on. This controller never goes to sleep, never hangs up. This controller is sitting there, 24 hours a day, 7 days a week, 365 days a year, watching for the smallest malfunction and then taking immediate action to resolve the problem.

Exhibit 4.2
Example of a Word Picture

Situation

A Toyota salesperson is calling on Jill, the owner of a commercial real estate firm. The goal of the word picture is to demonstrate the value of the four-wheel-drive option.

Word Picture

Jill, picture for a moment the following situation. You have this really hot prospect—let's call him Steve—for a remote resort development. You're in your current car, a Cadillac XTS. You've been trying to get Steve up to the property for months, and today is his only free day for several weeks. The property, up in the northern Georgia mountains, is accessible only by an old logging road. The day is bright and sunny, and Steve is in a good mood. When you reach the foot of the mountains, the weather turns cloudy and windy. As you wind up the old, bumpy road, a light rain begins. You've just crossed a small bridge when a downpour starts; the rain is pelting your windshield. Steve looks a little worried. Suddenly your car's tires start spinning. You're stuck in the mud.

Now let's replay the story, assuming that you buy the Toyota Highlander we've been talking about. [Salesperson quickly repeats the first paragraph of this story, substituting "Toyota Highlander" for "Cadillac XTS."] Suddenly your car tires start spinning. You're stuck in the mud. Calmly you reach down and shift into four-wheel drive. The Toyota pulls out easily, and you reach the destination in about five minutes. Although it's raining, the prospect looks at the land and sees great potential. On the way back down the mountain, you discuss how Steve should go about making an offer on the property. Jill, I hope I've made a point. Can you see why the four-wheel-drive option is important for you, even though it does add to the base price of the car?

KEEP OPEN LINES OF COMMUNICATION

Although this might seem obvious, sometimes the obvious needs to be stated: As a salesperson you must always keep the lines of verbal communication with the buyer open. That means you must contact buyers often, keep them fully informed, and make sure you are accessible for their contact, as From the Buyer's Seat 4.1 indicates.

ACTIVE LISTENING

Many people believe effective communication is achieved by talking a lot. Inexperienced salespeople often go into a selling situation thinking they have to outtalk the prospect. They are enthusiastic about their product and company, and they want to tell the prospect all they know. However, salespeople who monopolize conversations cannot find out what customers need. One authority suggests an **80–20 listening rule**: Salespeople should try to listen 80 percent of the time and talk no more than 20 percent of the time.[2] Studies have shown that salespeople with outstanding communication skills actually support the value creation process.[3]

People generally speak at a rate of around 120 to 160 words per minute, but they can listen to more than 800 words per minute. This difference is referred to as the **speaking–listening differential**. Because of this differential, salespeople often become lazy listeners. They do not pay attention and often remember only 50 percent of what is said immediately after they hear it.

Effective listening is not a passive activity. There are three levels of listening, as Exhibit 4.3 illustrates. Salespeople who practice **active listening** project themselves into the mind of the speaker and attempt to feel the way the speaker feels. Firms are spending millions of dollars on speech analytics technology for their call centers so they can discover the customer's emotions during a phone conversation. Field salespeople should be able to do that more effectively because they are face-to-face with the customer. If a customer says she needs a small microphone, a Sony salesperson needs to listen carefully to find out what the term *small* means to this particular customer—how small the microphone has to be, why she needs a small

From the BUYER'S SEAT 4.1

CAN WE TALK?

Change is the new normal in retail; this is the main thing a sales representative needs to understand if he or she wants to grow my business and build a strong relationship with a buyer today.

I have been in purchasing for almost 10 years now. I have witnessed many sales representatives fail to navigate their business through the changing retail environment and shift in customer spending habits. The path for the few who do experience success is truly driven by strong communication skills and adaptation.

Strong communication skills in sales come down to timely, transparent, and direct two-way conversations. Conversations between parties (buyer and seller) can be through e-mail, text, in person, or phone call depending on the given circumstances. Here is an example of a strong business relationship and strong communication skills resulting in a positive sales outcome.

My business had been very turbulent, specifically in a particular shade of pink color tops. My customers were not consistently purchasing this color top and I was concerned that we had too much inventory and too much on the way in this color. Just about that same time, my vendor sent me a text to tell me he was concerned about production on a style of this color and he was going to work hard to maintain delivery for me. I asked him to call me and we discussed the current selling of the color along with his production concerns. Together we were able to work together to alleviate any risk by changing the color (a benefit for my customer) and working on an updating production timeline based on the change (a benefit for his team). It was a win-win for both.

I understand this example seems very simple. However, this is not always the route sales representatives take. Many reps will work really hard to make their customer happy and would not have reached out at the first sign of trouble ahead, instead opting to try to fix the problem. As a result of the timely and transparent communication of this sales representative we were able to collaborate to find a solution that benefited both of us and only strengthened our relationship.

Adaptation is critical in success as a sales representative in today's retail environment. In order to adapt, a sales representative must be open-minded and possess strong listening skills as well as communication skills. As retail is rapidly changing, the way a company does things and the way the customer purchases are evolving. Unfortunately, many sales representatives have a difficult time changing quickly enough to keep up with the retailer's needs or have a difficult time keeping up-to-date in communication. Here is an example of a sales representative who was one of my key representatives; now I no longer work with him as things changed:

Our customers had changed quickly. We simply were not evolving our trends fast enough to satisfy customer needs. We also found that our customers were frustrated that our product looked too similar to our competition's. The sales representative I worked with also sold to my competition and had a strong history with my company. This individual had grown familiar with looking at his own selling reports and what was selling at the competition to offer me suggestions on what to buy for my customers. I communicated to him that while that had worked for us for many years, our customers had changed, and I needed the supplier to evolve the product offering to be trendier. Our sales had slowed down and we needed to make a change. The sales rep did not want to change how he had worked with me. After each meeting I gave him the same feedback—I need to see newer product. Eventually the supplier communicated to me in a complaining manner about the decline in the sales of his product and I explained that he needed to change the way he was conducting business. He did not take this feedback seriously and continued to try to do things the way he had in the past without communicating to me and was not willing to work something out. Eventually, I had to tell the supplier that other sales representatives had been able to adapt to changing times and offer me newer product and had grown their business with us. I no longer needed to work with the original seller, as it was not offering me anything unique.

From my seat, the sales representatives that can focus on remaining open-minded and being transparent in their communication with their buyers will see their businesses grow. If a sales representative is unable to create this open dialogue relationship, it will be difficult for his or her to find success.

Sheena Guzzo personal correspondence, used with permission; other names kept confidential upon request.

Exhibit 4.3
Levels of Listening

Level	Name	Characteristics
1	Hearing	Tuning in and tuning out. Mainly paying attention to self. Not responding to the speaker. Often just pretending to listen.
2	Passive listening	Not making a great effort to understand what the speaker is trying to convey. Not listening to the deeper meaning of what the speaker is saying. Being more concerned with the content of the message than the speaker's feelings. Speaker thinking the listener is really listening.
3	Active listening	Actively trying to put self in the speaker's place. Seeing things from the speaker's point of view, including feelings. Reading speaker's body language carefully. Avoiding all distractions.

microphone, and what she will be willing to sacrifice to get a small microphone. Active listening enables the salesperson to recommend a type of microphone that will meet the customer's specific needs.

Listen to understand, not to respond. Read that sentence again! Listeners should attempt to understand what the seller is truly saying, and not spend that time trying to think about how they are going to respond. Listeners think while they listen, using the speaking–listening differential to their advantage. They think about the conclusions toward which the speaker is building, evaluate the evidence being presented, and sort out important facts from irrelevant ones. Active listening also means the listener attempts to draw out as much information as possible. Gestures can motivate a person to continue talking. Head nodding, eye contact, and an occasional *I see, Tell me more,* or *That's interesting* all demonstrate an interest in and understanding of what is being said. Take a moment to complete the questionnaire in Exhibit 4.4 to rate your active listening skills.

Suggestions for active listening include (1) repeating information, (2) restating or rephrasing information, (3) clarifying information, (4) summarizing the conversation, (5) tolerating silences, and (6) concentrating on the ideas being communicated.

REPEATING INFORMATION

During a sales interaction the salesperson should verify the information he or she is collecting from the customer. A useful way to verify information is to repeat, word for word, what has been said. This technique minimizes the chance of misunderstandings:

CUSTOMER: I'll take 20 cases of Nestlé milk chocolate hot cocoa and 12 cases of the rich chocolate.

SALESPERSON: Sure, Mr. Johnson, 20 cases of milk chocolate and 12 cases of rich chocolate.

CUSTOMER: Wait a minute. I got that backward. The rich chocolate is what sells the best here. I want 20 cases of the rich chocolate and 12 cases of the milk chocolate.

SALESPERSON: Fine. Twelve milk chocolate, 20 rich chocolate. Is that right?

CUSTOMER: Yes. That's what I want.

Salespeople need to be careful when using this technique, however. Customers can get irritated with salespeople who echo everything.

Exhibit 4.4
Test Your Active Listening Skills

	My performance could be improved substantially			My performance needs no improvement	
During a typical conversation:					
1. I project an impression that I sincerely care about what the person is saying.	1	2	3	4	5
2. I don't interrupt the person.	1	2	3	4	5
3. I don't jump to conclusions.	1	2	3	4	5
4. I ask probing questions.	1	2	3	4	5
5. I ask continuing questions like "Could you tell me more?"	1	2	3	4	5
6. I maintain eye contact with the person.	1	2	3	4	5
7. I nod to show the person that I agree or understand.	1	2	3	4	5
8. I read the person's nonverbal communications.	1	2	3	4	5
9. I wait for the person to finish speaking before evaluating what has been said.	1	2	3	4	5
10. I ask clarifying questions like "I'm not sure I know what you mean."	1	2	3	4	5
11. I restate what the person has stated or asked.	1	2	3	4	5
12. I summarize what the person has said.	1	2	3	4	5
13. I make an effort to understand the person's point of view.	1	2	3	4	5
14. I try to find things I have in common with the person.	1	2	3	4	5

Scoring: 60-70 = Outstanding; 50-59 = Good; 40-49 = Could use some improvement; 30-39 = Could definitely use some improvement; Under 30 = Are you listening?

Source: ILPS scale, Stephen B. Castleberry, C. David Shepherd, and Rick E. Ridnour, "Effective Interpersonal Listening in the Personal Selling Environment: Conceptualization, Measurement, and Nomological Validity," *Journal of Marketing Theory and Practice*, Winter 1999, pp. 30-38.

RESTATING OR REPHRASING INFORMATION

To verify a customer's intent, salespeople should restate the customer's comment in his or her own words. This step ensures that the salesperson and customer understand each other:

CUSTOMER: Your service isn't what I had expected it would be.

SALESPERSON: I see, you're a bit dissatisfied with the financial advisor services I've been giving you.

CUSTOMER: Oh, no. As a matter of fact, I've been getting better service than I thought I would.

CLARIFYING INFORMATION

Another way to verify a customer's meaning is to ask questions designed to obtain additional information. These can give a more complete understanding of the customer's concerns:

CUSTOMER: Listen, I've tried everything. I just can't get this drill press to work properly.

To be an effective listener, the salesperson demonstrates an interest in what the customer is saying and actively thinks about questions for drawing out more information.

©Paul/Getty Images RF

SALESPERSON: Just what is it that the drill press doesn't do?

CUSTOMER: Well, the rivets keep jamming inside the machine. Sometimes one rivet is inserted on top of the other.

SALESPERSON: Would you describe for me the way you load the rivets onto the tray?

CUSTOMER: Well, first I push down the release lever and take out the tray. Then I push that little button and put in the rivets. Next, I push the lever again, put the tray in the machine, and push the lever.

SALESPERSON: When you put the tray in, which side is up?

CUSTOMER: Does that make a difference?

This exchange shows how a sequence of questions can clarify a problem and help the salesperson determine its cause. A salesperson can also use **emotional labeling**, which is discovering and naming the emotions behind the buyer's statements. For example, the salesperson might state, "It sounds like you are really frustrated."

SUMMARIZING THE CONVERSATION

An important element of active listening is to mentally summarize points that have been made. At critical spots in the sales presentation, the salesperson should present his or her mentally prepared summary. Summarizing provides both salesperson and customer with a quick overview of what has taken place and lets them focus on the issues that have been discussed:

CUSTOMER: So I told him I wasn't interested.

SALESPERSON: Let me see whether I have this straight. A salesperson called on you today and asked whether you were interested in reducing your costs. He also said he could save you about $125 a month. But when you pursued the matter, you found out the dollar savings in costs were offset by reduced service.

CUSTOMER: That's right.

SALESPERSON: Well, I have your account records right here. Assuming you're interested in getting more for your company's dollar with regard to cell service costs, I think there's a way we can help you—without having to worry about any decrease in the quality of service.

CUSTOMER: Tell me more.

TOLERATING SILENCES

This technique could more appropriately be titled "Bite your tongue." At times during a sales presentation, a customer needs time to think.[4] This need can be triggered by a tough question or an issue the customer wants to avoid. While the customer is thinking, periods of silence occur. Salespeople may be uncomfortable during these silences and feel they need to say something. However, the customer cannot think when the salesperson is talking. The following conversation about setting a second appointment demonstrates the benefits of tolerating silence:

SALESPERSON: What day would you like me to return with the samples and give that demonstration to you and your team?

CUSTOMER: [*obviously thinking*]

SALESPERSON: [*silence*]

CUSTOMER: OK, let's make it on Monday, the 22nd.

CONCENTRATING ON THE IDEAS BEING COMMUNICATED

Frequently what customers say and how they say it can distract salespeople from the ideas the customers are actually trying to communicate. For example, salespeople may react strongly when customers use emotion-laden phrases such as *bad service* or *lousy product.* Rather than getting angry, the salesperson should try to find out what upset the customer so much. Salespeople should listen to the words from the customer's viewpoint instead of reacting from their own viewpoint.

READING NONVERBAL MESSAGES FROM CUSTOMERS

In addition to asking questions and listening, salespeople can learn a lot from their customers' nonverbal behaviors.[5] When two people communicate with each other, spoken words play a surprisingly small part in the communication process. Words are responsible for only 40 percent of the information people acquire in face-to-face communication. Voice characteristics account for 10 percent of the message received, and the remaining 50 percent comes from nonverbal communications.[6] In this section we discuss how salespeople can collect information by observing their customers' **body language**. Later in the chapter we examine how salespeople can use the three forms of **nonverbal communication**—body language, space, and appearance—to convey messages to their customers. Note that experts don't always agree on what nonverbal cues mean. The examples provided in this chapter are those commonly accepted by sales trainers.

Studies have shown that the brain can actually lose it's ability to understand nonverbals if face-to-face contact decreases. One fear of overuse of social media is that people will lose their nonverbal reading skills.

The customer in the upper panel is giving negative nonverbal signals of arms crossed and no smile. Both buyers and the seller in the lower panel are giving positive nonverbal signals.

©Gary Ombler/Dorling Kindersley/Getty Images; (bottom): ©Sigrid Olsson/PhotoAlto/Getty Images RF

BODY ANGLE

Back-and-forth motions indicate a positive outlook, whereas side-to-side movements suggest insecurity and doubt. Body movements directed toward a person indicate positive regard; in contrast, leaning back or away suggests boredom, apprehension, or possibly anger. Changes in position may indicate that a customer wants to end the interview, strongly agrees or disagrees with what has been said, or wants to place an order.

FACE

The face has many small muscles capable of communicating innumerable messages. Customers can use these muscles to indicate interest, expectation, concern, disapproval, or approval. The eyes are the most important area of the face. The pupils of interested or excited people tend to enlarge. Thus, by looking at a customer's eyes, salespeople can often determine when their presentations have made an impression. For this reason many Chinese jade buyers wear dark glasses so they can conceal their interest in specific items and bargain more effectively. Even the rate at which someone blinks can tell a lot about a person. The average blink rate for a relaxed person is 10 to 20 blinks per minute (bmp). During normal conversation, it increases to about 25 bmp. A bmp rate over 50, and particularly over 70, indicates high stress levels.

Eye position can indicate a customer's thought process. Eyes focused straight ahead mean a customer is passively receiving information but devoting little effort to analyzing the meaning and not really concentrating on the presentation. Intense eye contact for more than three seconds generally indicates customer displeasure. Staring indicates coldness, anger, or dislike.

Customers look away from the salesperson while they actively consider information in the sales presentation. When the customer's eyes are positioned to the left or right, the salesperson has succeeded in getting the customer involved in the presentation. A gaze to the right suggests the customer is considering the logic and facts in the presentation, and gazing to the left suggests more intense concentration based on an emotional consideration. When customers cast their eyes down, they may be thinking, *How can I get my boss to buy this product?* or *How can I get out of this conversation?* When customers look away for an extended period, they probably want to end the meeting.

Skin color and skin tautness are other facial cues. A customer whose face reddens is signaling that something is wrong. That blush can indicate either anger or embarrassment. Tension and anger show in a tightness around the cheeks, jawline, or neck.

ARMS

A key factor in interpreting arm movements is intensity. Customers will use more arm movement when they are conveying an opinion. Broader and more vigorous movement indicates the customer is more emphatic about the point being communicated verbally. Always remember cultural differences. For example, it's rude to cross your arms in Turkey.

The open hands on the left are a positive signal by a salesperson. The intertwined fingers in the middle indicate that the salesperson is expressing his power and authority. On the right the salesperson is playing with his hands, indicating underlying tension.

Courtesy of Stephen B. Castleberry

HANDS

Hand gestures are very expressive. For example, open and relaxed hands are a positive signal, especially with palms facing up. Self-touching gestures typically indicate tension. Involuntary gestures, such as tightening of a fist, are good indicators of true feelings. The meanings of hand gestures differ from one culture to another. For example, the thumbs-up gesture is considered offensive in the Middle East, rude in Australia, and a sign of OK in France. In Japan the OK sign made by holding the thumb and forefinger in a circle symbolizes money, but in France it indicates that something is worthless.

LEGS

When customers have uncrossed legs in an open position, they send a message of cooperation, confidence, and friendly interest. Legs crossed away from a salesperson suggest that the sales call is not going well. Note that crossing your feet and showing the bottoms of your shoes are insulting in Japan.

BODY LANGUAGE PATTERNS

Exhibit 4.5 illustrates the patterns of signals that generally indicate the customer is reacting positively or negatively to a salesperson's presentation. However, no single gesture or position defines a specific emotion or attitude. To interpret a customer's feelings, salespeople need to consider the pattern of the signals via a number of channels. For example, some men are most comfortable in informal conversations with their arms crossed. It doesn't necessarily mean they're against you or what you're saying.

In business and social situations, buyers often use nonverbal cues to try to be polite. As a result salespeople often have difficulty knowing what a customer is really thinking. For example, smiling is the most common way to conceal a strong emotion. Salespeople need to know whether a customer's smile is real or just a polite mask. The muscles around the eyes reveal whether a smile is real or polite. When a customer is truly impressed, the muscles around the eyes contract, the skin above the eyes comes down a little, and the eyelids are slightly closed.

Here are some verbal and nonverbal signals that customers may be hiding their true feelings:

- *Contradictions and verbal mistakes.* People often forget what they said previously. They may leak their true feelings through a slip of the tongue or a lapse in memory.

- *Differences in two parts of a conversation.* In the first part of a conversation, a customer may display some nervousness when asked about the performance of a competitor's product and then respond by outlining the competitor's product's faults. Later in the conversation, the evaluation of the competitor's product may be much more positive.
- *Contradictions between verbal and nonverbal messages.* For example, a facial expression may not match the enthusiasm indicated by verbal comments. Also, a decrease in nonverbal signals may indicate that the customer is making a cautious response.
- *Nonverbal signals.* Voice tone going up at the end of a sentence, hesitation in the voice, small shrugs, increased self-touching, and stiffer body posture suggest that the customer has concerns.

When customers disguise their true feelings, they are often trying to be polite, not deceptive. To uncover the customer's true feelings and build a relationship, the salesperson needs to encourage the customer to be frank by emphasizing that she or he will benefit from an open exchange of information. Here are some comments a salesperson can make to encourage forthright discussion:

- Perhaps there is some reason you cannot share the information with me.
- Are you worried about how I might react to what you are telling me?
- I have a sense that there is really more to the story than what you are telling me. Let's put the cards on the table so we can put this issue to rest.

SENDING MESSAGES WITH NONVERBAL COMMUNICATION

The preceding section described how salespeople can develop a better understanding of their customers by observing their body language. Salespeople can also use their own body language, spacing, and appearance to send messages to their customers. This section explores that aspect of body language.

USING BODY LANGUAGE

During a 30-minute sales call around 800 nonverbal signals are exchanged.[7] Astute salespeople use these signals to communicate more effectively with customers. For example, salespeople should strive to use the positive signals shown in Exhibit 4.5. Cooperative cues indicate to customers that the salesperson sincerely wants to help them satisfy their needs. Obviously salespeople should avoid using negative cues.

Exhibit 4.5
Patterns of Nonverbal Reactions to Presentation

Positive Signals	Negative Signals
Uncrossed arms and legs	Crossed arms or legs
Leaning forward	Leaning backward or turned away from you
Smiling or otherwise pleasant expression	Furrowed brow, pursed lips, frowning
Nodding	Shaking head
Contemplative posture	Fidgeting, distracted
Eye contact	No eye contact
Animated, excited reaction	Little change in expression, lifeless

In fact, salespeople should consider engaging in **mirroring**, which is where one person copies the nonverbals of another. In this case, salespeople should use their nonverbals carefully, hoping that the buyer will mirror their positive and open nonverbals.

Remember this word of warning: The most effective gestures are natural ones, not those you are forcing yourself to perform. A buyer can spot nongenuine nonverbals. Use as much of this information as you can, but don't become so engrossed in following all the rules that you can't be yourself.

And if you are in inside sales, you can use nonverbals to your advantage, even if the buyer can't see you. As R. J. Zimmerman, an inside salesperson, commented, "I've learned that if you're selling over the phone, it's a great idea to stand up while in a conversation. Standing naturally gives you a more upbeat attitude and the customer will be able to hear your positive attitude."[8]

Facial Muscles

Nonverbal communication is difficult to manage. Facial reactions are often involuntary, especially during stressful situations. Lips tense, foreheads wrinkle, and eyes glare without salespeople realizing they are disclosing their feelings to a customer. Salespeople will be able to control their facial reactions only with practice.

As with muscles anywhere else in the body, the coordination of facial muscles requires exercise. Actors realize this need and attend facial exercise classes to learn to control their reactions. Salespeople are also performers to some extent and need to learn how to use their faces to communicate emotions.

Nothing creates rapport like a smile.[9] The smile should appear natural and comfortable, not a smirk or an exaggerated, clownlike grin. To achieve the right smile, stand before a mirror or a video camera and put your lips in various smiling positions until you find a position that feels natural and comfortable. Then practice the smile until it becomes almost second nature.

Eye Contact

Appropriate eye contact varies from situation to situation. People should use direct eye contact when talking in front of a group to indicate sincerity, credibility, and trustworthiness. Glancing from face to face rapidly or staring at a wall has the opposite effect. However, staring can overpower customers and make them uncomfortable.

Gestures and Handshaking

Gestures can have a dramatic impact. For example, by exposing the palm of the hand, a salesperson indicates openness and receptivity. Slicing hand movements and pointing a finger are very strong signals and should be used to reinforce only the most important points. In most cases pointing a finger should be avoided. This gesture will remind customers of a parent scolding a child. When salespeople make presentations to a group, they often use too few hand gestures. Gestures should be used to drive home a point. But if a salesperson uses too many gestures, acting like an orchestra conductor, people will begin to watch the hands and miss the words.

The location of your hands during gestures can have a huge impact on the message received. For example, imagine a salesperson standing and giving a presentation to a small group of businesspeople. If she drops her hands down by her sides while presenting and keeps them there, she will come across as passive and lacking enthusiasm. Hand gestures presented at about the height of her navel help the salesperson come across as truthful. Gestures at chest level suggest she has real passion about a topic, while those above the head are interpreted as great passion. Try each of these locations of gestures in front of a mirror while saying "I love you" to see what impact the location of gestures has on the interpretation of the spoken words.

In terms of shaking hands, salespeople should not automatically extend their hands to prospects, particularly if a prospect is seated.[10] Shaking hands should be the prospect's choice. If the prospect offers a hand, the salesperson should respond with a firm but not overpowering handshake while maintaining good eye contact. Chances are that you have experienced both a limpid handshake–a hand with little or no grip–and a bone-crunching grip. Either impression is often lasting and negative. Also, if you tend to have sweaty hands, carry a handkerchief.

Women should shake hands in the same manner men do. They should avoid offering their hand for a social handshake (palm facing down and level with the ground, with fingers drooping and pointing to the ground). Likewise, a man should not force a social handshake from a woman in a business setting.

The salesperson selling in an international context needs to carefully consider cultural norms regarding the appropriateness of handshaking, bowing, and other forms of greeting. For example, the Chinese prefer no more than a slight bow in their greeting, whereas an Arab businessperson may not only shake hands vigorously but also keep holding your hand for several seconds. A hug in Mexico communicates a trusting relationship, but in Germany such a gesture would be offensive because it suggests an inappropriate level of intimacy. Germans tend to pump the hand only once during a handshake. Seventy-four percent of British adults admit they no longer reach out a hand to greet friends or colleagues.[11] Some African cultures snap their fingers after shaking hands, but other Africans would see this act as tasteless. And some Eastern cultures use the left hand for hygienic purposes, so offering a left hand would insult them.

Posture and Body Movements

Shuffling one's feet and slumping give an impression of a lack of both self-confidence and self-discipline. On the other hand, an overly erect posture, like that of a military cadet, suggests rigidity. Salespeople should let comfort be their guide when searching for the right posture.

To get an idea of what looks good and feels good, stand in front of a mirror and shift your weight until tension in your back and neck is at a minimum. Then gently pull your shoulders up and back and elevate your head. Practice walking by taking a few steps. Keep the pace deliberate, not halting; deliberate, controlled movements indicate confidence and empathy. Note cultural differences like the fact that Japanese people value the ability to sit quietly and can view a fidgety American as uncontrolled.

This buyer and seller are in the intimate zone.

THE ROLE OF SPACE AND PHYSICAL CONTACT

The physical space between a customer and a salesperson can affect the customer's reaction to a sales presentation. Exhibit 4.6 shows the four distance zones people use when interacting in business and social situations. The **intimate zone** is reserved primarily for a person's closest relationships, the **personal zone** for close friends and those who share special interests, the **social zone** for business transactions and other impersonal relationships, and the

Exhibit 4.6

Distance Zones for Interaction

public zone for speeches, teachers in classrooms, and passersby. The exact sizes of the intimate and personal zones depend on age, gender, culture, and race. For example, the social zone for Latinos is much closer than that for North Americans. Latinos tend to conduct business transactions so close together that North Americans feel uncomfortable.

Customers may react negatively when they believe salespeople are invading their intimate or personal space. To show the negative reaction, customers may assume a defensive posture by moving back or folding their arms. Although approaching too close can generate a negative reaction, standing too far away can create an image of aloofness, conceit, or unsociability.

In general, salespeople should begin customer interactions at the social zone and not move closer until an initial rapport has been established. If the buyer indicates that a friendlier relationship has developed, the salesperson should move closer.

In terms of touching, buyers fall into two touching groups: contact and noncontact. Contact people usually see noncontact people as cold and unfriendly. On the other hand, noncontact people view contact people as overly friendly and obtrusive. People who like to be touched tend to respond to touch with increased persuasion and liking for the salesperson. Although some customers may accept a hand on their backs or a touch on their shoulders, salespeople should generally limit touching to a handshake. Touching clearly enters a customer's intimate space and may be considered rude and threatening–an invasion.

APPEARANCE

Physical appearance, specifically dress style, is an aspect of nonverbal communication that affects the customer's evaluation of the salesperson. Two priorities in dressing for business are (1) getting customers to notice you in a positive way and (2) getting customers to trust you. If salespeople overdress, their clothing may distract from their sales presentation. Proper attire and grooming, however, can give salespeople additional poise and confidence. One salesperson for Smith & Nephew, a medical equipment company, says he always dresses like a chameleon. "Dress like your doctor" is his motto. If the doctor is in suit and tie, he wears a suit and tie; if the doctor prefers casual dress, the seller does likewise.

At one time dressing for work was simple: You just reached in the closet and picked from your wardrobe of blue, gray, and pinstripe suits. Today things are not that simple. With casual days and dress-down Fridays, styles and dress codes vary considerably from office to office. Salespeople should learn the norms for dress in their field and follow them closely.

During a given day a salesperson may have to visit his or her company's and customers' offices, each of which may have a different dress code. And sometimes the buyer will have dress codes that even visiting salespeople must follow. For example, Target has dress codes that apply to salespeople who want to make presentations at its company offices.

Vicki West has developed five timeless principles for a salesperson wanting to dress for success.[12] We describe these here.

Principle 1: Consider the Geography

The temperature: Clothing choices are obviously influenced by temperature trends and variations. San Francisco is different from Minneapolis, which differs from Austin, Texas, in humidity, temperature, and weather patterns. These factors dictate the fiber and type of clothing worn. Although linen and cotton are cool, warm-weather fabrics suitable almost the entire year in the southern part of the United States, they would be appropriate only in the late spring and summer in other locales.

The local cultural norms: Some cities are formal, and others are known for their casual culture. The economic and business sectors of a community often play a pivotal role in the local cultural norms for clothing choices. An example of a cultural norm difference within the short distance of 200 miles is that between Dallas and Austin, Texas. Dallas is more formal than Austin in most industry sectors. Dallas is known as a "headquarters" town with large regional and national businesses represented. Austin has a large segment of population employed in education, high technology, and the music industry, all of which typically have a younger, more casual workforce.

Principle 2: Consider Your Customers

Their appearance: Customers wear many different types of clothing, which are often dictated by the demands of their profession. Farmers, bankers, high-technology workers, and educators all dress differently depending on the functional demands of their daily work. A salesperson's appearance is certainly impacted by the customers' industry.

Their expectations for your appearance, however, generally reflect their impression of your industry. Salespeople representing the banking industry would be expected to dress differently from salespeople in the music recording industry.

Principle 3: Consider Your Corporate Culture

Norms for your industry should dictate the general parameters for appearance choices. It is obvious that corporate cultures change from time to time. The trend has been to dress more casually in the hot-weather months, even in conservative industries such as banking and finance. However, the consensus of many industry groups is that it is important to wear professional business attire regularly, with some exceptions based on geography and a salesperson's customer base.

Principle 4: Consider Your Aspirations

Top levels of your organization generally set the tone for an entire organization. If you aspire to reach a high level in the organization, it's important to note what expectations your organization might have for your general appearance.

An old rule is to dress *one level above your position.* Watch your immediate superior, who will decide whom to promote. If you want a promotion to the next level in the organization, dress as if you already have the position; then you will be perceived as a good fit for the job.

Principle 5: Consider Your Own Personal Style

Wait until you have the halo effect before making a personal style statement. The "halo effect" refers to the tendency to generalize one positive aspect of your behavior to all aspects of your behavior. This phenomenon can work to your benefit. No one wants to look like a corporate drone with no individual style, but the first week on the job may not be the best time to make your personal appearance statement. Wait until you have proved your professional skills, no matter what the industry, before wearing clothing that may be deemed inappropriate to your particular industry.

Be reasonable in your wardrobe choices. Being individualist and memorable can be a positive decision, depending on the range of choices that are acceptable to a specific industry group. However, choosing outrageous or completely unsuitable clothing is probably not in the best interests of your personal career development. Like it or not, large jewelry, piercings, tattoos, heavy perfumes and colognes, short skirts, shorts, revealing blouses or shirts, pink or turquoise hair, and so forth are simply considered inappropriate in most sales situations.

COMMUNICATING VIA TECHNOLOGY

In addition to face-to-face interactions, salespeople communicate with customers by using the telephone, voice mail, e-mail, texts, and social media. As shown in Exhibit 4.7, these methods vary in the interactivity of the communications, the ability to use verbal and nonverbal communication channels, and the quantity of information that can be conveyed. **Response time** is the time between sending a message and getting a response to it. Salespeople should use the communication method preferred by the buyer and should not overdo communicating with the buyer to the point of being a nuisance.

TELEPHONE AND VOICE MAIL

Salespeople need to use the phone correctly and effectively. Perfect your phone style by practicing alone before making any calls. Make sure you know what you want to say before placing the call. Many would argue that it is a polite gesture to

Exhibit 4.7
Comparison of Various Methods of Salesperson Communications

	Face-to-Face	Telephone	Voice Mail	Text	E-Mail
Response time	Fast	Fast	Slow	Slow	Slow
Salesperson can use verbal communications	Yes	Yes	Yes	No	No
Salesperson can hear buyer's verbal communications	Yes	Yes	No	No	No
Salesperson can read buyer's nonverbal communications	Yes	No	No	No	No
Quantity of information seller can send	Highest	Average	Lowest	Varies	Varies
Quantity of information buyer can send	Highest	Average	None	None	None

start by asking, "Is this a good time to talk?" Don't be too rushed to be nice; it is never acceptable to be rude. And don't forget to smile as you talk. Even though the prospect won't see it, he or she will hear it in your enthusiastic tone of voice.

Active listening is as important when conversing over the phone as when conversing in person. Take notes and restate the message or any action you have agreed to undertake. In addition, you will need to encourage two-way communication. If you have ever talked with two-year-olds over the phone, you know that if you ask them a yes-or-no question, they tend to shake their heads yes or no rather than verbalize a response. Similarly, you cannot nod your head to encourage someone to continue talking on the phone. Instead you must encourage conversations with verbal cues such as *Uh-huh, I see,* or *That's interesting.* Finally, just as in face-to-face conversation, you must be able to tolerate silences so customers have an opportunity to ask questions, agree or disagree, or relate a point to their circumstances.

It is important to set objectives for your phone call and strategize what you're going to say and why. Here is an example of using the phone to make an appointment:

1. [*State customer's name.*] Hello, Mr. Peterson? [*Pause.*]
2. [*Introduce yourself and show preparation.*] This is Amanda Lowden with Cisco Systems. I was talking to your director of operations, Marvin Schepp, and he suggested I talk with you.
3. [*Politely check time.*] I hope I didn't catch you in the middle of something urgent or pressing? [*Pause.*]
4. [*State purpose and build credibility.*] I'm calling to let you know about our new carrier routing system. I've shown it to several other systems engineers in town, and they found its self-healing and self-defending operating system to be something they wanted to explore further.
5. [*Commitment to action.*] I'd like to meet with you and share some feedback from your business associates. Could you put me on your calendar for 30 minutes next Monday or Tuesday?
6. [*Show appreciation and restate time, or keep door open.*] Thank you, Mr. Peterson. I'll be at your office at 9 a.m. on Tuesday. [*or*] I appreciate your frankness, Mr. Peterson. I'd like to get back to you in a couple of months. Would that be all right?

Use proper techniques and etiquette when leaving voice mail messages:[13]

- Leave a clear, concise message, while speaking slowly and distinctly.
- A little casual conversation up front is acceptable, but don't waste the prospect's time.
- Ask for a callback, and slowly repeat your name and phone number at the end of your message.

For your own voice mail system, use a fresh greeting on your system each day. Tell callers if a time limit exists for your voice mail, and if possible, offer the option to talk to someone immediately.

Technology enables salespeople to improve their communications with customers.

©Jason Homa/Blend Images LLC RF

TEXT MESSAGES AND E-MAIL

High tech doesn't replace face-to-face interactions; it merely supplements and enhances personal exchanges. For example, text messages can be used to communicate quickly with a buyer, assuming the buyer is OK receiving communications in that way.

But text messages are too abbreviated for more complex communications. Following are some suggestions for salespeople with regard to e-mail and text message communication:

- For e-mails, use proper capitalization and punctuation–use correct uppercase and lowercase. Maybe write your e-mail first in a word processing document; this will give you the ability to utilize its spelling and grammar-check function. And don't use chat room abbreviations, such as "LOL." Proofread, proofread, and proofread–the small things you may not notice when you are writing the e-mail may translate to carelessness in the eyes of the reader.
- When receiving an important e-mail, be sure to respond quickly. If more than 24 hours will be needed to provide a response, it is a great idea to send a quick reply explaining your delay.
- Don't be lulled into thinking that immediacy (fast) means the same thing as intimacy (close, friendly relationship) in communication. Buyers generally prefer face-to-face communications over other media types.
- Never respond to an e-mail or text if you are emotional (e.g., angry).
- Make sure the first few lines of the e-mail are important. Many people read only the first few lines before deleting a message.
- It is hard for buyers to read your nonverbal messages in e-mail or texts because they can't see them (and you can't read theirs). The receiver may not grasp the tone or your intent, and using complicated emoticons just makes it more confusing. If you can't convey tone correctly in an e-mail or text, then use face-to-face or the phone instead.
- Learn the customer's preferences for e-mail and texts. Adapt the content to the customer's preferred communication style.
- Don't send long e-mail messages or large attachments unless the buyer is expecting them.[14]
- Use effective e-mail openings, like "Did you know [interesting fact]. . . . Is [this] an issue for you right now?"[15]
- Use speed to impress customers–especially for damage control. Exceed a customer's expectations, such as responding immediately to urgent messages. E-mail and texts sent to you by customers should be answered by the end of the workday.
- Don't deliver bad news via e-mail or texts; rather, use these media to arrange a meeting to discuss the issue. And remember that e-mails and texts are easily shared and can be misused. They are also discoverable in litigation.
- If it is going to take more than two rounds of e-mails to resolve an issue, many buyers would rather you pick up the phone and call them instead.
- White space in an e-mail is a good idea, as it can make reading the e-mail easier. Consider using in-line subheads to make it even easier to read and digest.[16]

ethics

Discovering a person's e-mail address can be difficult at times. Here are some tools, but use them judiciously so as not to engage in unethical practices or be guilty of spamming. When companies issue a press release, the writer generally includes his or her e-mail address. With this information, the salesperson then knows the domain of the e-mail system of the prospect. Online tools, which you can use to try to guess at an e-mail address, using the domain include Mailtester.com, Email-format.com, Guesser.email, and anymailfinder.com.[17]

SALES Technology 4.1

SELLING THROUGH SOCIAL MEDIA

While it's not face-to-face communication, social media interaction can provide a salesperson with customer insight, feedback, and follow-up opportunities related to a service or product, a conversation that can generate interest and lead to a sale. Social media offer a unique ability to reach a plethora of individuals and create touch points all at once.

Buyers today have the capability to gather information more efficiently due to channels of social media and the Internet. Social media have given way to a technological version of word of mouth, a personal review and opinion for all to see, an influential aspect of product research. Research by McKinsey & Company found that recommendations from peers were 10 times more valuable than from salespeople.

Here are five steps to conduct sales through social media:

Step 1: *Choose the most viable platform to interact with prospects*

Know your client base prior to selecting a social media platform, otherwise valuable resources are wasted. Pick a platform that appeals best to your audience given the combination of available text, images, or video content. Bottom line: Identify where your target market is best represented and start there.

Step 2: *Join the community and develop an identity*

Commence by becoming familiar with the chosen platform. Create an account and profile, communicate, and identify norms and expectations without abusing the network. Stay true to you and your business uniqueness.

Step 3: *Form connections*

Favorite, like, follow, and connect with other profiles or friends that are similar to your market's clientele. Take time to research, to obtain knowledge about comparable products and firms in your industry. Form a connection that's valuable for both parties and build your network. Listen to their "story" by taking the time to read their background; this shows initiative and can help you distinguish their needs. Contact individuals privately, since that's more personal and helps avoids the stereotypical self-serving salesperson.

Step 4: *Develop meaningful relationships*

Focus on creating relationships that last. Current customers will in turn generate new leads. Word of mouth is a powerful tool. Observe what individuals are saying and be willing to engage. This shows you care. Once a foundation is built you can call attention to how your product and service could meet their needs.

Step 5: *Converse and follow up*

Avoid giving the elevator pitch by a message or post. You want to be genuine through your communication. State specifically how your product or service could be a solution to their unique needs. By listening to language on social media an opportunity can present itself without having to create an inquiry. Q&As also offer a chance to showcase your problem-solving capabilities and start dialogue.

Salespeople should respect the influence of social media on their product or service. By conducting yourself properly, online customers can increase awareness and grow your business free of charge.

Sources: Personal experience; Jacquelyn Smith, "How to Use Social Media to Make Sales," *Forbes*, January 10, 2014.

SOCIAL MEDIA

Salespeople are using social media such as blogs, LinkedIn, Twitter, Pinterest, and Facebook to communicate with customers and prospects. While many of the suggestions already covered in this chapter apply to these networks, salespeople should consider other issues as well. Sales Technology 4.1 provides an overview of how salespeople can approach using social media. Some suggestions for social media include the following:

- Fill out your profile completely to build trust and establish common bonds. Spend the time and money to get a great head shot photo and include it on your site. Make sure it is appropriate for business purposes. Update your profile regularly to keep it current and interesting. Remember that many members get updates every time someone changes his or her profile, so you're getting more exposure with every adjustment to your profile.

- Create contacts/friends lists such as "Family" and "Work Related" so you can better control the privacy of your profile and information.
- Follow all rules for the social media sites.
- Share articles and links to presentations and other information that might be helpful to prospects. Posting comments from experts will improve your credibility.
- Remember to post updates on your profile or wall about your business. Tell about upcoming events like webinars and conferences where you will be speaking.
- Combine your Facebook/LinkedIn account with other social media sites you participate in, like Twitter and Pinterest.
- Respond quickly to posts and queries.
- Add your Facebook/LinkedIn URL to your e-mail signature so prospects can learn more about you.
- And don't forget to put away your smartphone when you're in a meeting with a prospect. The last thing you want to do is to show disrespect. Interestingly, Union Pacific does not allow its salespeople to use any digital devices, whether in an internal or external meeting.

Businesses are starting to build relationships and stay connected to their customers and prospects with microblogging tools like Twitter. Due to the nature of Twitter, some additional considerations apply:

- Use a friendly and casual tone in messages. But make sure your tweets reflect the culture of your company.
- Make a link to things you think prospects would find interesting, like articles and Web sites. Tweets should have real value to the receiver.
- Don't create spam with Twitter.
- You can schedule when the tweets will be sent with add-ons like Social Oomph.
- Share interesting things about your community and nonbusiness items to help make yourself real. Remember that you are trying to create a friendly relationship.
- Remember to listen, not just send out tweets. Respond to at least some of the replying tweets. Don't feel guilty if you don't read or respond to all tweets.

Because of the growing use of social networking, Chapters 6 and 7 will discuss ways to use these tools to prospect and learn more about new customers. Building Partnerships 4.1 describes how one salesperson used technology to reach key decision makers.

ADJUSTING FOR CULTURAL DIFFERENCES

Communication in international selling often takes place in English because English is likely to be the only language salespeople and customers have in common. To communicate effectively with customers whose native language is not English, salespeople need to be careful about the words and expressions they use.[18,19] People who use English in international selling should observe the following rules:

- Slow down when speaking, but don't speak more loudly. You don't want to appear to be talking down to someone.

BUILDING Partnerships 4.1

BUILDING RELATIONSHIPS WITH CUSTOM MARKETING MESSAGES

Aptos is a partner of many of the top retailers in the world, consistently being rated as one of the top providers by our customers. We design software that helps our clients solve their business problems across areas such as point of sale, custom relationship management, merchandising, order management, and e-commerce, to name a few. As an account executive, my role is to find new business for Aptos from both existing accounts and in new accounts. Proper communication through technology plays a vital role in my typical process.

When I'm first assigned a new account, I will spend a few hours online researching their Web site, recent news, LinkedIn, and industry publications to obtain as much knowledge as I can about their company history, market niche, key individuals, and future aspirations as an organization. This process often allows me to learn their phone number, business locations, and even individuals' e-mail address, providing the opportunity to personally reach out and introduce myself. The next step is pooling everything I've learned to develop custom marketing messages, delivered through e-mail, phone, and U.S. mail to demonstrate the homework I've done to understand their business and connect it to how we've helped a competitor of theirs in a similar situation. It's much easier to leave a lasting impression in person, but still possible through a custom marketing message.

It takes a good bit of time to develop an effective message, with many rounds of revising. Here are some keys:

- Let your authenticity shine through.
- Each sentence and statement must have meaning; you're not persuading but offering a solution. This means either benefits must be communicated to the prospect or you must connect emotionally. The audience cannot be left asking what or why.
- Ditch clichés and jargon (a tough obstacle when not engaging in face-to-face communication). You don't want your audience failing to understand what your company can offer.
- The best communication is short, simple, and sweet. Avoid rambling on and on. Rather write clear and concise sentences to better articulate your message and achieve better sentence flow. This minimizes objection and friction.
- Any available feedback from a colleague always helps.

Let me share a story to prove how this works in real life. When I had just graduated from college I was a determined new salesperson seeking to build a customer base, make a name for myself, and make my employer proud. A national restaurant chain intrigued me. Using the technique described above, by researching online I came across the restaurant's e-mail address format (i.e., last_first@restaurant.com). Once learning of this e-mail format, I decided to be ambitious and reach out to its CEO (what is considered a top-down prospecting approach). After not hearing anything back for some time, I kept finding reasons to contact him, eliciting his interests while maintaining proper communication steps to create an effective message. Being patient and persistent and following up finally got me a return e-mail from the CEO. He wanted to know more about how Aptos could benefit the company, and after contacting back, an official sales meeting was set. My manager, along with my manager's boss, were also in attendance at this meeting. Prior to the meeting's start, the fellow company's CEO specifically said how persistent, patient, and determined I was and that he would not be here if it were not for my effort and hard work.

It felt great being a young salesperson earning my boss's admiration and approval and being appreciated by the other company's key individuals. The most important prospect I'd ever generated was standing right there eager to listen to what we could offer. In the end it didn't lead to a sale that day, but it created goodwill between both parties, was a career progression for me, and offered a learning experience. B2B sales is not easy, but persistence, faith, patience, and proper communication principles do pay off to help build relationships.

Source: Personal correspondence, used with permission, anonymous upon request.

This American salesperson needs to recognize the differences between communicating in an Arab culture and an American culture.

©Image Source/ Getty Images RF

- Use common English words that a customer would learn during the first two years of studying the language. For example, use *expense* rather than *expenditure* or *stop* instead of *cease.*
- Use words that do not have multiple meanings. For example, *right* has many meanings, whereas *accurate* is more specific. When you use words that have several meanings, recognize that nonnative speakers will usually use the most common meaning to interpret what you are saying.
- Avoid slang expressions peculiar to American culture, such as *slice of life, struck out, wade through the figures,* and *run that by me again.*
- Use rules of grammar more strictly than you would in everyday speech. Make sure you express your thoughts in complete sentences, with a noun and a verb.
- Use action-specific verbs, as in *start the motor,* rather than action-general verbs, as in *get the motor going.*
- Never use vulgar expressions, tell off-color jokes, or make religious references.
- Expect that it may take longer to build trust and relationships.

Even if you are careful about the words you use, misunderstandings can still arise because terms have different meanings, even among people from different English-speaking countries.[20] For example, in the United States *tabling a proposal* means "delaying a decision," but in England it means "taking immediate action." In England promising to do something by the end of the day means doing it when you have finished what you are working on now, not within 24 hours. In England *bombed* means the negotiations were successful, whereas in the United States this term has the opposite meaning.

International salespeople need to understand the varying perceptions of time in general and the time it takes for business activities to occur in different countries. For example, in Latin American and Arab countries people are not strict about keeping appointments at the designated times. If you show up for an appointment on time in these cultures, you may have to wait several hours for the meeting to start. Lunch is at 3:00 p.m. in Spain, 12:00 noon in Germany, 1:00 p.m. in England, and 11:00 a.m. in Norway. In Greece no one makes telephone calls between 2:00 p.m. and 5:00 p.m. The British arrive at their desks at 9:30 a.m. but like to do paperwork and have a cup of tea before getting any calls. The French, like the Germans, like to start early in the day, frequently having working breakfasts. Restaurants close at 9:00 p.m. in Norway–just when dinner is starting in Spain. The best time to reach high-level Western European executives is after 7:00 p.m., when daily activities have slowed down and they are continuing to work for a few more hours. However, Germans start going home at 4:00 p.m.

Significant cultural differences dictate the appropriate level of eye contact between individuals. In the United States salespeople look directly into their customers' eyes when speaking or listening to them. Direct eye contact is a sign of interest in what the customer is saying. In other cultures looking someone in the eye may be a sign of disrespect:

- In Japan, looking directly at a subordinate indicates that the subordinate has done something wrong. When a subordinate looks directly into the eyes of his or her supervisor, the subordinate is displaying hostility.

- In Muslim countries, eye contact is not supposed to occur between men and women.
- In Korea, eye contact is considered rude.
- Brazilians look at people directly even more than Americans do. Americans tend to find this direct eye contact, when held over a long period, to be disconcerting.

SELLING YOURSELF

You are about to go into an interview that you have been preparing for because it is your number one choice on your list of places you want to work and you are feeling very confident. You met someone at a job fair a couple weeks ago and you e-mailed him to set up this interview early so you would have plenty of time to prepare. He let you know you would be interviewing with the decision maker, who had a full day of interviewing other students, and gave you the time slot of 3:00 in the afternoon.

It is toward the end of the interviewer's day and she comes out to greet you and bring you back to the conference room. You notice that she is lacking any emotion on her face and she says she has already had eight other interviews today so she is tired. From there, it is completely up to you to turn her attitude around by your communication skills. In the past couple of weeks you have been following any press releases or news articles that have come out about the company, and you can use that information to get the interviewer to speak to you. Maybe it was a new rebranding you read about that will get her excited about the new changes happening, or the company had a record-breaking year in sales. The interviewer will be both impressed that you are keeping up with the company and it may get her talking about something she is passionate about. At this point, it is very important to make sure you are holding eye contact, taking notes if applicable, and sitting forward to let her know you are just as interested as she is in this interview.

Even though the interview is about you, everyone enjoys talking about himself or herself (or his or her company) and it will get the interviewer excited about talking to you and listening to you. It may take a couple minutes to build your rapport with her, but it is important to make sure you keep up her spirits throughout the interview by maintaining body language and speaking clearly and concisely for the remainder of the time you spend with her.

Not every interview is going to be like this, but it is very important to know how to react to this unforeseen situation. The most important part about any interview is to come prepared, maintain good body language, and be yourself and you will be able to handle any situation that you may come across.

Rebecca Clark, used with permission.

SUMMARY

This chapter discussed the principles of communication and how they can be used to build trust in relationships, improve selling effectiveness, and reduce misunderstandings. The communication process consists of a sender, who encodes information and transmits messages, and a receiver, who decodes the messages. A communication breakdown can occur when the sender does a poor encoding job, when the receiver has difficulty decoding, and when noise and the environment interfere with the transmission of the message.

Effective communication requires a two-way flow of information. At different times in the interaction, both parties will act as sender and receiver. This two-way process enables salespeople to adapt their sales approach to the customer's needs and communication style.

When communicating verbally with customers, salespeople must be careful to use words and expressions their customers will understand. Effective communication is facilitated through the use of word pictures and by appropriate voice characteristics like inflection, articulation, and the proper rate of speech and loudness.

Listening is a valuable communication skill that enables salespeople to adapt to various situations. To listen effectively, salespeople need to actively think about what the customer is saying and how to draw out more information. Some suggestions for actively collecting information from customers are to repeat, restate, clarify, summarize the customer's comments, and demonstrate an interest in what the customer is saying.

About 50 percent of communication is nonverbal. Nonverbal messages sent by customers are conveyed by body language. The five channels of body language communication are body angle, face, arms, hands, and legs. No single channel can be used to determine the feelings or attitudes of customers. Salespeople need to analyze the body language pattern composed of all five channels to determine how a customer feels.

Salespeople can use nonverbal communication to convey information to customers. In addition to knowing how to use the five channels of body language, salespeople need to know the appropriate distances between themselves and their customers for different types of communications and relationships. Salespeople should learn to use their physical appearance and dress to create a favorable impression on customers.

Learning how to communicate effectively with technology is critical in today's marketplace. Not only should salespeople learn how to use the phone and e-mail effectively; they should also master the use of texting and social networking like Facebook and LinkedIn, as well as Twitter and blogs, to connect with their customers and prospects.

Finally, two-way communication increases when salespeople adjust their communication styles to the styles of their customers. In making such adjustments, salespeople need to be sensitive to cultural differences when selling internationally and in diverse subcultures.

KEY TERMS

active listening 98
analogy 97
articulation 97
body language 103
decoding 94
80-20 listening rule 98
emotional labeling 102
encoding 94
feedback 94
inflection 96
intimate zone 108
loudness 96
mirroring 107
noises 95
nonverbal communication 103
personal zone 108
persuading 96
public zone 109
response time 111
social zone 108
speaking-listening differential 98
two-way communication 94
voice characteristics 96
word picture 97

ETHICS PROBLEMS

1. Assume you just told a story to help make a point in your sales presentation. The prospect laughs, and says, "Say, I've got one that can top that! . . ." the prospect then proceeds to tell you a rather raunchy story that is not only sexist but also racist. How should you react?
2. Assume you are making your first call on a prospect and reach out to shake his hand. The

prospect shakes your hand, but then continues to hold it. After a second you get the uneasy feeling that the prospect is physically attracted to you, although you have done nothing to encourage this. You are in an office alone with the buyer. What should you do?

QUESTIONS AND PROBLEMS

1. As a student, you likely encounter many distractions that affect your listening ability.
   a. List three things that distract your listening as a student.
   b. What can you do to reduce each of these distractions?
2. Have two friends score you using the listening test (see Exhibit 4.4) found in this chapter.
   a. Compare your friend's scores with the one you gave yourself.
   b. Did your two friends score you the same way? Discuss any differences.
3. Make a chart with three columns: *Items, What I Want This Item to Communicate to Others,* and *What Others Will Think My Item Is Communicating.* In the first column list the following: *my hairstyle, the clothing I'm wearing today,* and *any jewelry or body accents* (like earrings or tattoos). In the second column describe the message you want to communicate with each item. Have someone else complete the third column, describing what the items communicate to him or her. Discuss the differences between what you hope the items communicate versus what someone else thinks the items are communicating.
4. Develop a word picture that helps explain the merits of buying an LED television, assuming the person has never owned an LED appliance.
5. What do the following body language cues indicate?
   a. Staring at a wall while someone else is talking.
   b. Fidgeting and moving around in the seat a lot.
   c. Leaning forward, smiling broadly.
   d. Face that is reddening, with tightness in the mouth, jaw, and neck.
6. Word choice is important. Some words, by themselves, may be perceived negatively or unprofessional. Come up with a better word choice that could be more positive and professional for each of the following words/phrases: *cheaper, you guys, that's cool, we're the best.*
7. In Building Partnerships 4.1 the author stated that it is important to avoid jargon. Jargon can be defined as special words that are used often by a particular group of people but that are usually hard, if not impossible, for others to understand. Why should a salesperson not use jargon? Wouldn't that make you look smart and informed as a salesperson?
8. Randomly select five e-mail messages you received today. Evaluate them on the basis of the suggestions offered in this chapter for the proper use of e-mail.
9. Assume you sell tickets for a nearby symphony orchestra and you wish to use Twitter to build relationships with potential season ticket holders. Create two tweets that you would post to accomplish this objective.

CASE PROBLEMS

case 4.1

Lynch Landscaping

Johan Wolf, a salesperson for Yellow Book USA, has just entered the elaborate office of Britni Yvonne Lynch, owner of Lynch Landscaping, an upscale landscaping provider in Boston. Britni is seated behind a vast mahogany desk in a high-backed stylish executive chair working on some paperwork. She doesn't look up as Johan enters the room.

JOHAN [*walking around Britni's desk and extending his hand*]: Good morning, Britni! It's nice to finally meet you. [laughing] Forgive me for saying so, but I'll have to admit this is the most elegant office, and you're the most attractive person I've called on this month!

BRITNI: [*not looking up from her paperwork or extending her hand as she finally responds*]: Please have a seat, Mr. . . . what was your name?

JOHAN: [*dragging up a seat from the side of the room and placing it on the same side of the desk as Britni, then plopping down in the seat*]: Johan. Johan Wolf.

It's a scorcher out there! I believe it's one of the warmest days in Boston this summer! Say, here's a "good one" I heard yesterday. Because of this heat, a man fainted in the middle of Newbury Street, and traffic quickly piled up in all directions, so a woman rushed to help him. When she knelt down to loosen his collar, another man emerged from the crowd, pushed the woman aside, and said, "It's all right honey, I've had a course in CPR!" The woman stood up and watched as he took the ill man's pulse and prepared to administer artificial respiration. At this point she tapped him on the shoulder and said, "When you get to the part about calling a doctor, I'm already here." Ha ha ha!

BRITNI: [*not laughing but pushing her paperwork away from her and crossing her arms*]: What can I do for you, Mr. Wolf?

JOHAN: Well, Britni, want to get right down to business? Great. I like someone who knows what she wants. I'd like to see your company take out a bigger ad in the Yellow Pages. Can't beat the Yellow Pages for business, now can you?

BRITNI: [*turning in her chair to look out the window while looking at her watch*]: We provide professional lanscaping to high-end clients, depending mostly on word-of-mouth recommendations for new clients, Mr. Wolf.

JOHAN: [*taking out a pad of paper from his shirt pocket and searching his pockets for a pen*]: Now that's news to me, Britni. I thought you were like all the rest, desperately seeking ugly lawns to make them prettier. Ha ha ha!

BRITNI: [*making a steeple with her hands while still looking out the office window*]: I would guess you would, Mr. Wolf. [*swiveling in her chair to face Johan*] Yes, I would guess you would. [*pressing a button on her desk*] Ms. Deramus, Mr. Wolf has completed his interview with me. Will you kindly escort him out? [*eyeing Johan with a triumphant look on her face*] Have a good day, Mr. [*strongly emphasizing the word* Mr.] Wolf.

Questions

1. Evaluate the exchange.
2. What would you do differently if you were Johan?

case 4.2

Channel 6

Chase Stemper just graduated from college, and just accepted a job as a salesperson with Channel 6, the local CBS TV broadcasting company. In his new role, he is responsible for selling advertising to businesses and organizations in a five-county area.

Chase really loves technology and social media and uses it every chance he gets. Given his love for the tools, he decided to use them to try and build his sales. Here are some activities that Chase did in his first week on the job:

1. He sent e-mails to every prospect (approximately 720) in the list supplied by his company, and included several large .pdf files that showcased his products. To do this, he copied and pasted the e-mail addresses using the "cc" option. His opening line was "You've never met me before, so I wanted to introduce myself to you."
2. He used his personal Facebook page, which he always keep updated while in college to tell of his loves and pursuits of girls, and tried to connect with as many of his prospects as he could discover using the "search for friends" option of Facebook. To help make his page more appropriate for his prospects,

he took pictures of himself outside the TV's office building, pointing at the large CBS sign. His grin was a mile wide.

3. He got LinkedIn to as many prospects as he could. He also started posting articles on his LinkedIn that he thought might be useful to his prospects in running their own businesses. His LinkedIn profile remained pretty sparse because he never did see much use in filling out things like his work experience, current job, and interests.
4. He had to inform one customer that the advertisement that was supposed to run on *NFL Sunday Night Football* was being pulled, due to CBS taking that spot to run a promotion for a new series. Chase used e-mail to let the customer know.
5. He sent out the following tweet using his personal Twitter account: "Looking to do some TV advertising in the region? I've got some great rates! Call me at xxx or e-mail me at xxx right away! Chase"
6. He used his Facebook page to link friends to his Instagram photos and videos, and made sure that on his Instagram page he put photos and videos of some of the ads that were broadcast by his station. The purpose was to hopefully generate interest in advertising by prospects.
7. Since he had the personal cell phone number of one of the customers that he was given in his new role, he decided to just send a text that read: "How's it going today, George? I'm your new salesperson at the station. Let's have lunch."
8. One of the customers he was given to service at the station had asked for a quote for two 30-second ads on Friday night around 8:00. Chase, using e-mail, wrote this: "Friday night is busy and crowded. Will put together a quote ASAP, but FYI, it's going to take a bit to get the motor going."

Questions

1. Given what you know about best practices, evaluate the appropriateness of the activities listed.
2. How can a salesperson keep updated with what the norms are for the various social media and technology tools?

ROLE PLAY CASE

In this chapter's role play interaction, you are still meeting with the same person you did for Chapter 3. (If you did not do the role play at the end of Chapter 3, you will need to review that information now.) That person is telling you about the business. Feel free to ask questions, but your main objective is to listen and understand all you can about the business environment in which he or she operates. Practice active listening skills; after the role play, identify which listening techniques you used. Further, identify the three most important elements about the person's business that you need to understand. Interpret the buyer's body language. Finally, anytime you hear jargon, write down the word or phrase.

Note: For background information about these role plays, see Chapter 1.

To the instructor: Additional information needed to complete the role play is available in the Instructor's Manual.

ADDITIONAL REFERENCES

Anders, Abram, Joshua T. Coleman, and Stephen B. Castleberry. "Communication Preferences of Business-to-Business Buyers for Receiving Initial Sales Messages: A Comparison of Media Channel Selection Theories." *International Journal of Business Communication*, in press.

Barrett, Deborah J. *Leadership Communication.* New York: McGraw-Hill, 2014.

Burgoon, Judee K., Laura K. Guerrero, and Kory Floyd. *Nonverbal Communication.* London: Routledge, Taylor & Francis Group, 2016.

Gardner, Lenann McGookey. "Are You Sure You Understand the Basics of Successful Selling?" *American Salesman* 58, no. 3 (2013), pp. 3–6.

Hazeldine, Simon. *Neuro-sell: How Neuroscience Can Power Your Sales Success.* London: Kogan Page, 2014.

Koehl, Maryse, Juliet F. Poujol, and John F. Tanner. "The Impact of Sales Contests on Customer Listening: An Empirical Study in a Telesales Context." *Journal of Personal Selling and Sales Management* 36, no. 3 (2016), pp. 281–93.

Knapp, Mark L., Judith A. Hall, and Terrence G. Horgan. *Non-verbal Communication in Human Interaction.* New York: Wadsworth Publishing, 2013.

Kuhnke, Elizabeth. *Body Language: Learn How to Read Others and Communicate with Confidence.* Hoboken, NJ: Capstone, 2016.

Maryse, K., Juliet F. Poujol, and John F. Tanner Jr. (2016), "The Effects of Sales Contests on Salesperson Listening," *Journal of Personal Selling & Sales Management* 36.3, pp. 281-293.

Pullins, Ellen Bolman, Hanna Timonen, Timo Kaski, and Mari Holopainen. "An Investigation of the Theory Practice Gap in Professional Sales." *Journal of Marketing Theory and Practice* 25, no. 1 (2017), pp. 17–38.

Sobczak, Art. *Smart Calling: Eliminate the Fear, Failure, and Rejection from Cold Calling.* Hoboken, NJ: Wiley, 2013.

Solomon, Denise H., and Jennifer Theiss. *Interpersonal Communication: Putting Theory into Practice.* New York: Routledge, 2013.

Knowledge and Skill Requirements

PART 1

©Robert Daly/Getty Images RF

chapter 5

ADAPTIVE SELLING FOR RELATIONSHIP BUILDING

SOME QUESTIONS ANSWERED IN THIS CHAPTER ARE

- What is adaptive selling?
- Why is it important for salespeople to practice adaptive selling?
- What kind of knowledge do salespeople need to practice adaptive selling?
- How can salespeople acquire this knowledge?
- How can salespeople adapt their sales strategies, presentations, and social styles to various situations?

PROFILE

> *"When I present to buyers I find the best way to be adaptive is tailoring my message to each buyer's social style."*
>
> Chareen Bogner, McKesson

Courtesy of Chareen Bogner

PROFILE As a graduate of Northern Illinois University (NIU) I completed a BAA in marketing, a minor in psychology, and a certificate in professional selling. My sales curriculum at NIU started with Dr. Rick Ridnour who taught me the principles of selling. Then I continued my studies under Dr. Dan Weilbaker in Advanced Professional Selling. Last, Dr. Robert Peterson coached me in the sales competition, World Collegiate Sales Open. All three professors contributed immensely to my selling skills which helped me land an outside sales position with McKesson.

As an account manager at McKesson, building relationships with internal and external players in my market is critical to my long-term success. I find knowledge to be a key element of building and maintaining relationships. When I pair knowledge of my industry, my customers' needs, and my solution, it is a winning combination.

At the heart of business-to-business selling is problem solving. My lasting relationships hinge on my ability to help my current or prospective customers meet their goals for the upcoming fiscal year. I work diligently to gather knowledge about trends in the marketplace and the potential impact on my customers. I communicate often with my customers to understand the goals of various stakeholders in their organization. I use the knowledge gathered from the market to adapt my offerings.

When I present to buyers, I find the best way to be adaptive is tailoring my message to each buyer's social style. Often the social style gives me insight into which details of my offering would be most important to each buyer. For example, in the health care field I work with both clinical and executive buyers. Often, but not always, the clinical buyers are analytical so they focus on patient care outcomes and compliance. At the executive level the buyers typically focus on operational efficiency and cost savings. Social styles can also help you anticipate objections for each of your buyers. How I anticipate and handle objections creates trust between the customer and me.

For me, trust is the most important element in building business relationships. I find using my expertise, employing transparency, setting expectations, and delivering results to be critical. I work diligently to be an industry expert so I can consult my customers on major business decisions. I am open and honest about aspects of the market that could negatively impact their operations. In addition, I set expectations throughout the entire sales process. Last, I make sure I am delivering conclusive results. Always remember, your best business relationships with current customers will turn into your best references for prospective customers. Happy selling!

Visit our Web site at: www.mckesson.com.

Personal selling is the most effective marketing communication medium because it allows salespeople to tailor their presentations to each customer. They use their knowledge of the customer's buying process (Chapter 3) and finely tuned communication skills (Chapter 4) to learn about their customers and select effective sales strategies. Effective salespeople adapt their selling strategies and approaches to the selling situation. This chapter examines how salespeople can communicate effectively with their customers by practicing adaptive selling.

TYPES OF PRESENTATIONS

Salespeople can choose from a number of presentation types, which vary in the extent to which salespeople adapt to the circumstance. This text examines the three most common: (1) the standard memorized presentation, (2) the outlined presentation, and (3) the customized presentation.

STANDARD MEMORIZED PRESENTATION

The **standard memorized presentation**, also called a *canned presentation,* is a completely memorized sales talk. The salesperson presents the same selling points in the same order to all customers. Some companies insist that their inside salespeople, for example, memorize the entire presentation and deliver it word for word. Others believe that salespeople should be free to make some minor adjustments.

The standard memorized presentation ensures that the salesperson will provide complete and accurate information about the firm's products and policies. Because it includes the best techniques and methods, the standard memorized presentation can help bring new salespeople up to speed quickly and give them confidence. However, the effectiveness of the standard memorized presentation is limited because it offers no opportunity for the salesperson to tailor the presentation to the needs of the specific customer.

OUTLINED PRESENTATION

The **outlined presentation** is a prearranged presentation that usually includes a standard introduction, standard answers to common objections raised by customers, and a standard method for getting the customer to place an order. An example of an outlined presentation appears in Exhibit 5.1. Notice that the wording was just provided as an example for salespeople, but not what they were to follow word for word.

An outlined presentation can be very effective because it is well organized. It is more informal and natural than the standard memorized presentation and provides more opportunity for the customer to participate in the sales interaction. It also permits some flexibility in the approach used to present the key points.

CUSTOMIZED PRESENTATION

The **customized presentation** is a written and/or oral presentation based on a detailed analysis of the customer's needs. This type of presentation offers an opportunity to use the communication principles discussed in Chapter 4 to discover the customer's needs and problems and propose the most effective solution for satisfying those needs. The customer recognizes the sales representative as a professional who is helping provide real value, not just selling products, as From the Buyer's Seat 5.1 describes. The customized presentation lets the salesperson demonstrate empathy. Cultivating this view is an important step in developing a partnering relationship.

Each of the presentation types just discussed involves a different level of skill, cost, and flexibility. Standard memorized presentations can be delivered at a low

Exhibit 5.1
Example of an Outlined Presentation

Scenario: A Procter & Gamble Salesperson Calling on a Grocery Store Manager	
Step in Outlined Sales Presentation	**Say Something Like This**
1. Reinforce past success.	Good morning, Mr. Babcock. I was talking with one of your stockers, and he said that our Crest end-of-aisle display was very popular with customers last weekend. He said that he had to restock it three times. Looks like you made a wise decision to go with that program.
2. Reiterate customer's needs.	I know that profits and fast turns are what you are always looking for.
3. Introduce new Secret antiperspirant campaign.	We have a new campaign coming up for our Secret line.
4. Explain ad campaign and coupon drops.	We will be running a new set of commercials on CBS, NBC, and ABC programs. . . . Also, we'll be adding an insert in the Sunday coupon section with a 75-cents-off coupon.
5. Explain case allowances.	We are going to give you a $2.20 case allowance for every case of Secret you buy today.
6. Ask for end-of-aisle display and order of cases.	I propose that you erect an end-of-aisle display on aisle 7 . . . and that you order 20 cases.
7. Thank manager for order.	Thank you, and I know the results will be just as good as they were for our Crest promotion.

cost by unskilled salespeople with little training. On the other hand, the customized presentation can be costly, requiring highly skilled people to analyze the customer's needs. Salespeople have the greatest opportunity to adapt their presentations to customer needs when using the customized presentation and the least opportunity when using the standard memorized presentation. The next section discusses the importance of adapting sales presentations.

ADAPTIVE SELLING AND SALES SUCCESS

Salespeople practice **adaptive selling** when they react to different sales situations by changing their sales behaviors. An extreme example of nonadaptive selling is using the standard memorized presentation, in which the same presentation is used for all customers. The customized presentation illustrates adaptive selling because the presentation is tailored to the specific needs of the customer.

Adaptive selling is featured in this textbook because this approach forces the salesperson to practice the marketing concept. It emphasizes the importance of satisfying customer needs. And being adaptable increases buyer trust and commitment and results in higher sales performance. The communication principles described in Chapter 4 are required to practice adaptive selling successfully. For example, a Kohler sales representative may believe that a portable generator manufacturer is interested in buying an economical, low-horsepower gasoline motor. While presenting the benefits of a low-cost motor, the sales rep discovers, by observing nonverbal behaviors, that the customer is interested in discussing overall operating costs. At this point the rep asks some questions to find out whether the customer would pay a higher price for a more efficient motor with lower operating costs. Based on the customer's response, the rep may adopt a new sales strategy: presenting a more efficient motor and demonstrating its low operating costs.

From the BUYER'S SEAT 5.1

ADAPTING IN A REGULATED PUBLIC TRANSIT MARKET

First Transit, a subsidiary of First Group Inc., provides contract public transit services, transit management services, and consulting throughout North America. When the Minnesota Legislature created the Duluth Transit Authority (DTA) in 1969, one of its first actions was to enter into an agreement with what is now known as First Transit, for operation and management of the DTA. Of course, one thing the DTA must do is to purchase buses.

A new bus typically costs $480,000. Purchasing new equipment and parts, such as a bus fleet, requires large capital and a lengthy procurement process. After getting approval and funding to purchase a bus, a prebid meeting is held, after which a public open bid process begins. This is followed by a series of interviews all regulated by the Federal Transportation Administration (FTA), since federal funds are involved. For purchases within the DTA, we must perform an independent cost estimate (ICE), comparing competitor prices to provide assurances that taxpayer money is being spent well and that the DTA is held accountable such as not showing favoritism to a specific supplier. This means suppliers must meet specifications and adapt their product to DTA, state, and federal specifications.

After sending out a request for proposal, we buyers at the DTA do not just accept the lowest bid price; decisions are based on total value, including quality and how well the supplier satisfies specifications. Potential vendors therefore have to engage in adaptive selling to compete with the other suppliers to best meet the needs of the DTA, and add total value to outbid one another for business.

Procurement in the public transit industry allows for zero special treatment or relationship bias on any given bid due to fair public open bids required by federal regulations. Deciding to buy product A versus product B depends highly on the price, but also how well seller A compared to seller B best adapts his or her presentation (bid) to meet our needs and specifications in the bid. An excellent seller goes above and beyond to exceed our specifications and adapts the presentation bid to our needs by enhancing a particular product. Take, for example, a seller exceeding our specifications and offering a stainless steel chassis on its bus to equate for the corrosion from Duluth's winter salty roads, or a better heating system to keep riders warm.

A seller that researches our company details, equates for the environment we operate in, and adapts his or her product or bid offer to better our transit service is how a strong business relationship is built. It's also important to know that the seller can be relied on for parts and warranty service, and in so doing, may reap repeat business. Suppliers providing quality products that meet specifications and are offered at a fair price ensures the passengers are in good hands, as they are the number one priority. Providing the best public transit experience that we can offer is the DTA's goal.

Source: Dennis Jensen, Duluth Transit Authority, used with permission.

It is sometimes hard for people to realize that the world is not made up of people just like them.[1] Many people are much older than you, while some are younger than you. They practice different religions, enjoy different foods, and shop at stores where you would never think of shopping. They have different moral beliefs and different ideas about "the perfect product" and were raised in a totally different way. Their hopes and aspirations don't match yours. Many of them would be shocked to hear what your life's dreams and goals are.

We are not just talking about differences in people in other countries. We are talking about people who live next door to you, who are sitting next to you in your classroom. Millennials are different from baby boomers, who differ from the generations before them. One salesperson reported that grocery stores that cater to migrant farmers in the San Francisco area want a different product mix (such as more demand for Hormel SPAM) than a grocery store in midtown San Francisco (more demand for upscale, specialty Hormel meat products like Cure 81 ham). The sooner you realize that your world is made up of diverse people, the sooner you will realize the importance of becoming adaptive. Selecting the appropriate

BUILDING Partnerships 5.1

HOW I USED THE C LEVEL TO LEVERAGE A SALE

The highest-level executives at companies usually have titles that begin with the word *chief* (like chief executive officer, chief operating officer) resulting in a group of executives that is often simply referred to as the C-suite or C-level. Most salespeople are not comfortable selling at the C-level. There are many individual and organizational reasons for this, but my example will relate to my experience in a follow-up from an organizational meeting.

Initial stumbling blocks that I have experienced start with availability. How do I get the introduction; they won't return my call? Plus, there is the fear of creating friction with my current, lower-level contact by going around that individual. The greatest challenge I have, though, is fear or intimidation in getting the meeting and then having to present. Don't get me wrong! I'm not uncomfortable talking in front of other people, but what do I talk about, and how do I know what is important to them?

Selling a product or service to non-C-level types is fairly routine. My firm's marketing, product management, and other departments have provided all the right literature, samples, and talking points that the buyer or engineer is looking for when trying to better understand my product. I also have a myriad of additional competitive references, benchmarks, and examples of how other customers like them have gained efficiency, cost labor savings, and supply chain efficiencies. I'm confortable telling my story to lower-level buyers, and people like engineers, since I've a story to tell that I'm familiar with. I've created it and I'm comfortable telling it.

Now, what training or mentorship have I received on how to navigate the top-level executives? None, and the same is true of many other salespeople! I didn't fully realize the impact of this issue until I started joining organizations where the owners of my customers were attending. I wasn't in their office, but I was getting face time and was able to ask some informative questions. This was a dialog that was outside my typical points of discussion to a buyer or engineer. I wasn't selling these C-level people on product features, unless they specifically asked about some details. I had a colleague trying to hand out samples; it was poorly received, and I believe he was looked at only as a product information or order taker, not a partner to their business.

My approach was more fact finding on what was important to them, searching for their exact needs. I followed up by finding out who in their organization was responsible or would have the greatest impact that I should talk with.

Take this instance for reference: I attended a meeting for industrial packaging companies. Topics at the luncheon were around trends and industry conditions. I had listened and tried to make as many introductions to C-level people as I could. Weeks later I was in the lobby of my customer, Duravent, starting to walk back with my distributor and an engineer of Duravent. At that exact moment, the Duravent owner walked by, stopped to talk to me, and asked what I thought about our recent meeting. The impact was not product related, but I did have the full attention of the Duravent engineer for that next meeting! He did not ask about the relationship with the owner, but I could tell that he was influenced just by the fact that I apparently knew his bosses' boss. We were able to work through the design issues that morning and the Duravent engineer specified our product, and a sale was made!

Source: Anonymous, used with permission, names changed.

sales strategy for a sales situation and making adjustments during the interaction are crucial to successful selling.

Salespeople should also adapt to the customer's desire for a specific type of relationship. For example, if a customer is not interested in developing a strong, long-term relationship and is more interested in maintaining a less involved relationship, the salesperson should adapt to this desire.

Practicing adaptive selling does not mean salespeople should be dishonest about their products or their personal feelings.[2] It does mean salespeople should alter the content and form of their sales presentation so customers will be able to absorb the information easily and find it relevant to their situation. As Building Partnerships 5.1 illustrates, there are many ways to be adaptive as a salesperson.

thinking it through Do you act and talk differently to your professor than when you talk to your friends? Why do you adapt in that way?

The advantages and disadvantages of the three types of sales presentations illustrate the benefits and drawbacks of adaptive selling.[3] Adaptive selling gives salespeople the opportunity to use the most effective sales presentation for each customer.[4] However, uncovering needs, designing and delivering different presentations, and making adjustments require a high level of skill. The objective of this textbook is to help you develop the skills and knowledge required to practice adaptive selling.

ADAPTIVE SELLING: THE IMPORTANCE OF KNOWLEDGE

A key ingredient to be adaptive is knowledge.[5] Salespeople need to know about the products they are selling, the company they work for, and the customers they will be selling to. Knowledge enables the salesperson to build self-confidence, gain the buyer's trust, satisfy customer needs, practice adaptive selling, and have greater performance.

PRODUCT AND COMPANY KNOWLEDGE

Salespeople need to have a lot of information about their products, services, and company. Purchasing agents rate product knowledge as one of the most important attributes of good salespeople. Effective salespeople need to know how products are made, what services are provided with the products, how the products relate to other products, and how the products can satisfy customers' needs. Salespeople also need to know about their competitors' products as well as their own because they are frequently asked to compare their products to competitors' offerings.

KNOWLEDGE ABOUT SALES SITUATIONS AND CUSTOMERS

Equally important with product and company knowledge is detailed information about the different types of sales situations and customers salespeople may encounter, as Building Partnerships 5.1 discusses. For example, T-Mobile salespeople need to be knowledgeable about networking and information technology and have overall expertise in how businesses operate in order to sell cell phone service to their unique customer types.

This salesperson has acquired extensive knowledge of the customer's systems.

By developing categories of customer types or types of sales situations, salespeople reduce the complexity of selling and free up their mental capacity to think more creatively. The categories salespeople use can focus on the benefits the customer seeks, the person's role in the buying center, the stage in the buying process, or the type of buying situation. For example, a Colgate-Palmolive salesperson might divide buyers into several categories based on their decision-making style. When selling to emotional buyers, this salesperson might need to be more enthusiastic and engage in visual storytelling. When selling to rational buyers, this salesperson might want to stress the financial benefits of purchasing the new toothpaste.

The Challenger Sales model is built on the importance of knowledge about sales situations and customers.[6] The model, based on the results of thousands of interviews with sales managers, suggests that the most successful salespeople create winning proposals because they actually understand the prospect's world better than the prospect understands it. This approach requires that the salesperson's company invest time and resources to learn about the industry and the unique problems/opportunities that exist in that industry. It is this knowledge that the salesperson uses to secure the prospect's business.

HOW TO CREATE KNOWLEDGE

One source of knowledge would be top salespeople in the company you work for.[7] Some firms will collect and share this information with you. For example, AT&T conducted in-depth interviews with its top performers.[8] Through these interviews, it learned about the types of situations these salespeople encountered and what strategies they used in each situation. The company developed role plays for each sales situation and used them when training new salespeople. Such role playing enabled the new salespeople to experience the variety of situations they would actually encounter on the job. The strategies recommended by the top salespeople served as a starting point for the trainees to develop their own sales methods for handling these situations.

Salespeople also create knowledge by getting feedback from sales managers. This can be in the form of **performance feedback** ("Did you achieve the goals you set for this call?") or **diagnostic feedback** ("Let's talk about why you didn't achieve your goals"). Diagnostic feedback provides information about what you're doing right and wrong instead of just whether you made a sale.

The following example illustrates diagnostic feedback:

SALESPERSON: Why do you think I didn't make the sale?

SALES MANAGER: You stressed the low maintenance cost, but he wasn't interested in maintenance cost. Did you see how he kept looking around while you were talking about how cheap it is to maintain the product?

SALESPERSON: What do you think I should do next time?

SALES MANAGER: You might try spending more time finding his hot button. Maintenance cost isn't it.

Successful sales managers give their salespeople diagnostic feedback.

©Image Source RF

Other sources of knowledge include the Web, company sales manuals and newsletters, experts in the salesperson's firm, sales meetings, plant visits, and business and trade publications. Salespeople also collect information about competitors from customers, by visiting competitor displays at trade shows, and from viewing competitors' Web pages.

RETRIEVING KNOWLEDGE FROM THE KNOWLEDGE MANAGEMENT SYSTEM

Salespeople store much of their acquired knowledge in their own memory, and, as such, retrieval is merely accessing information in that memory.[9] Many companies also have customer relationship management (CRM) systems and knowledge management software to support their salespeople. Salespeople use programs like Salesforce.com CRM to store and retrieve critical knowledge about accounts, products, and competitors. For example, salespeople for the Iowa Wild hockey franchise use a CRM system to store and access information about their customers. They use this knowledge (whether season tickets were purchased in past, whether group tickets were purchased, time of season when tickets were purchased in the past, and so forth) when interacting with customers to develop sales strategies and purchase recommendations. Studies have shown that using a CRM system has a positive impact on being adaptive while selling.

It is important for salespeople to be able to retrieve brochures and other business collateral from the knowledge management system. But perhaps more important is the ability to tap the knowledge of in-house experts. One writer calls this "genius management," which implies going beyond document management to the realm of tapping knowledge from genius within your firm. Progressive firms are encouraging in-house experts, like engineers, product development specialists, and financial staff, to develop in-house blogs, wikis, and Web pages that are easily accessible and searchable by the sales force. Social networking sites like LinkedIn and Facebook can also be used to connect in-house experts with salespeople. Finally, firms are experimenting with tagging, which is including keywords with a person's name in company documents and on internal Web pages. The keywords indicate the areas of expertise for which that person can be contacted. The goal in all of this is to make it easier for salespeople to connect to experts in their own firms for ideas and assistance.

A number of popular sales training models are available that help salespeople develop and then retrieve knowledge in selling. For example, Accenture and the Miller Heiman Group have long trained salespeople to discover needs and effectively sell value.[10] They are considered process models, in that they both teach a complete system of selling that includes all elements of the sales process. There are also a number of proven effective techniques that can be incorporated into most any process model. We now turn our attention to one of the most highly regarded techniques, the social style matrix.

THE SOCIAL STYLE MATRIX: A TRAINING PROGRAM FOR BUILDING ADAPTIVE SELLING SKILLS

To be effective, salespeople need to use their knowledge about products and customers to adapt both the content of their sales presentations—the benefits they emphasize to customers and the needs they attempt to satisfy—and the style they use to communicate with customers.[11] The **social style matrix** is a popular training program that companies use to help salespeople adapt their communication styles.[12]

David Merrill and Roger Reid discovered patterns of communication behaviors, or social styles, that people use when interacting with one another.[13] Merrill and Reid found that people who recognize and adjust to these behavior patterns have better relationships with other people. The company conducts training using these concepts.[14]

Here is a quick preview of what you will learn about the social style training program. As you know, the world is made up of diverse people. For example, some are fast decision makers, whereas others are slow to make just about any kind of decision; some like to talk, whereas others are quiet. To make it easier, this system divides all people into four different types or categories that are based on two dimensions. Your goal as a salesperson is to first identify which of the four types you are. Next you figure out which of the four types your customer is. Finally you adjust your behavior to mirror or match that of your customer. This adaptation is often called **style flexing**. Now that you have a general idea of how the system works, let's look at it in more detail.

DIMENSIONS OF SOCIAL STYLES

This training program uses two critical dimensions to understand social behavior: assertiveness and responsiveness.

Assertiveness

The degree to which people have opinions about issues and publicly make their positions clear to others is called **assertiveness**. Simply having strong convictions does not make a person assertive; assertive people express their convictions publicly and attempt to influence others to accept these beliefs.

Assertive people speak out, make strong statements, and have a take-charge attitude. When under tension, they tend to confront the situation. Unassertive people rarely dominate a social situation, and they often keep their opinions to themselves. Exhibit 5.2 shows some verbal and nonverbal behavioral indicators of assertiveness.

Responsiveness

The second dimension, **responsiveness**, is based on how emotional people tend to get in social situations. Responsive people readily express joy, anger, and sorrow. They appear to be more concerned with others and are informal and casual in social situations. Less responsive people devote more effort toward controlling their emotions. They are described as cautious, intellectual, serious, formal, and businesslike. Exhibit 5.3 lists some indicators of responsiveness.

CATEGORIES OF SOCIAL STYLES

The two dimensions of social style, assertiveness and responsiveness, form the social style matrix shown in Exhibit 5.4. Each quadrant of the matrix defines a social style type.

Exhibit 5.2
Indicators of Assertiveness

Less Assertive	More Assertive
"Ask" oriented	"Tell" oriented
Go-along attitude	Take-charge attitude
Cooperative	Competitive
Supportive	Directive
Risk avoider	Risk taker
Makes decisions slowly	Makes decisions quickly
Lets others take initiative	Takes initiative
Leans backward	Leans forward
Indirect eye contact	Direct eye contact
Speaks slowly, softly	Speaks quickly, intensely
Moves deliberately	Moves rapidly
Makes few statements	Makes many statements
Expresses moderate opinions	Expresses strong opinions

Exhibit 5.3
Indicators of Responsiveness

Less Responsive	More Responsive
Controls emotions	Shows emotions
Cool, aloof	Warm, approachable
Talk oriented	People oriented
Uses facts	Uses opinions
Serious	Playful
Impersonal, businesslike	Personable, friendly
Moves stiffly	Moves freely
Seldom gestures	Gestures frequently
Formal dress	Informal dress
Disciplined about time	Undisciplined about time
Controlled facial expressions	Animated facial expressions
Monotone voice	Many vocal inflections

Exhibit 5.4
Social Style Matrix

Some examples of social styles (Hillary Clinton, Donald Trump, Barack Obama, Paul McCartney). Do you agree with where they are placed? Note that all these people may switch to a different style under certain conditions.

(top left): ©K2 images/Shutterstock.com RF; (top right): Source: Library of Congress [LC-DIG-ppbd-00607]; (bottom left): ©Peter Macdiamid/Getty Images; (bottom right): ©Eric Thayer/Getty Images

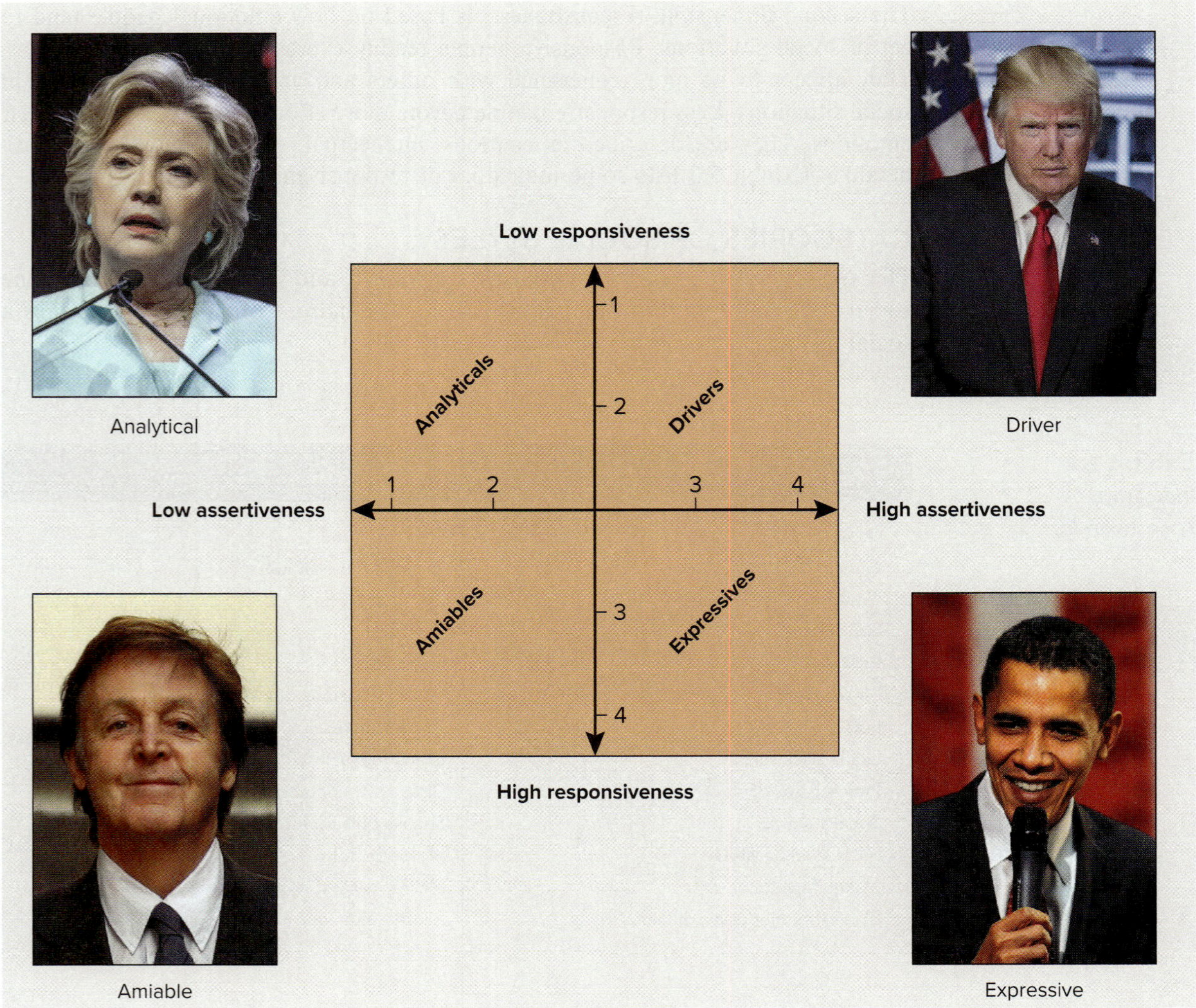

Drivers

Drivers are high on assertiveness and low on responsiveness. The slogan of drivers, who are task-oriented people, might be "Let's get it done now, and get it done my way." Drivers have learned to work with others only because they must do so to get the job done, not because they enjoy people. They have a great desire to get ahead in their companies and careers.

Drivers are swift, efficient decision makers. They focus on the present and appear to have little concern with the past or future. They generally base their decisions on facts, take risks, and want to look at several alternatives before making a decision. As compared to analyticals, who also like facts and data, drivers want to know how the facts affect results—the bottom line. They are not interested in simply technical information.

To influence a driver, salespeople need to use a direct, businesslike, organized presentation with quick action and follow-up. Proposals should emphasize the effects of a purchase decision on profits.

Expressives

Expressives are high on assertiveness and high on responsiveness. Warm, approachable, intuitive, and competitive, expressives view power and politics as important factors in their quest for personal rewards and recognition. Although expressives are interested in personal relationships, their relationships are primarily with supporters and followers recruited to assist expressives in achieving their personal goals.

People with an expressive style focus on the future, directing their time and effort toward achieving their vision. They have little concern for practical details in present situations. Expressives base their decisions on their personal opinions and the opinions of others. They act quickly, take risks, but tend to be impatient and change their minds easily.

When selling to expressives, salespeople need to demonstrate how their products will help the customer achieve personal status and recognition. Expressives prefer sales presentations with product demonstrations and creative graphics rather than factual statements and technical details. Also, testimonials from well-known firms and people appeal to expressives' need for status and recognition. Expressives respond to sales presentations that put them in the role of innovator, the first person to use a new product.

Amiables

Amiables are low on assertiveness and high on responsiveness. Close relationships and cooperation are important to amiables. They achieve their objectives by working with people, developing an atmosphere of mutual respect rather than using power and authority. Amiables tend to make decisions slowly, building a consensus among people involved in the decision. They avoid risks and change their opinions reluctantly.

Salespeople may have difficulty detecting an amiable's true feelings. Because amiables avoid conflict, they often say things to please others despite their personal opinions. Therefore, salespeople need to build personal relationships with amiables. Amiables are particularly interested in receiving guarantees about a product's performance. They do not like salespeople who agree to undertake activities and then do not follow through on commitments. Salespeople selling to amiables should stress the product's benefits in terms of its effects on the satisfaction of employees.

Analyticals

Analyticals are low on assertiveness and low on responsiveness. They like facts, principles, and logic. Suspicious of power and personal relationships, they strive to find a way to carry out a task without resorting to these influence methods.

Because they are strongly motivated to make the right decision, analyticals make decisions slowly, in a deliberate and disciplined manner. They systematically analyze the facts, using the past as an indication of future events.

Salespeople need to use solid, tangible evidence when making presentations to analyticals. Analyticals are also influenced by sales presentations that recognize their technical expertise and emphasize long-term benefits. They tend to disregard personal opinions. Both analyticals and amiables tend to develop loyalty toward suppliers. For amiables, the loyalty is based on personal relationships; analyticals' loyalty is based on their feeling that well-reasoned decisions do not need to be reexamined.

IDENTIFYING CUSTOMERS' SOCIAL STYLES

Exhibit 5.5 lists some cues for identifying the social styles of customers or prospects. Salespeople can use their communication skills to observe the customer's behavior, listen to the customer, and ask questions to classify the customer. Merrill and Reid caution that identifying social style is difficult and requires close, careful observation. Salespeople should not jump to quick conclusions based on limited information. Here are some suggestions for making accurate assessments:

- Concentrate on the customer's behavior and disregard how you feel about the behavior. Don't let your feelings about the customer or thoughts about the customer's motives cloud your judgment.
- Avoid assuming that specific jobs or functions are associated with a social style ("He must be an analytical because he is an engineer").
- Test your assessments. Look for clues and information that may suggest you have incorrectly assessed a customer's social style. If you look for only confirming cues, you will filter out important information.

Exhibit 5.5
Cues for Recognizing Social Styles

Analytical	Driver
Technical background. Achievement awards on wall. Office is work oriented, showing much activity. Conservative dress. Likes solitary activities (e.g., reading, individual sports).	Technical background. Achievement awards on wall. No posters or slogans on office walls. Calendar prominently displayed. Furniture is placed so that contact with people is across desk. Conservative dress. Likes group activities (e.g., politics, team sports).
Amiable	**Expressive**
Liberal arts background. Office has friendly, open atmosphere. Pictures of family displayed. Personal momentos on wall. Desk placed for open contact with people. Casual or flamboyant dress. Likes solitary activities (e.g., reading, individual sports).	Liberal arts background. Motivational slogans on wall. Office has friendly, open atmosphere. Cluttered, unorganized desk. Desk placed for open contact with people. Casual or flamboyant dress. Likes group activities (e.g., politics, team sports).

- Create, join, and participate in social media groups (e.g., LinkedIn, Twitter) to learn more about the social style of the buyer.

SOCIAL STYLES AND SALES PRESENTATIONS

In addition to teaching trainees how to assess social style, the Merrill and Reid program also assesses the trainees' social styles. Each person is asked to have a group of his or her customers complete a survey. These responses are used to determine the trainee's style. Trainees frequently are surprised by the difference between their self-perceptions and the perceptions of their customers. To get a rough idea of your own social style, you can complete the assessment in Exhibit 5.6.

Exhibit 5.6
Self-Assessment of Social Styles

Assertiveness Ratings I perceive myself as:				Responsiveness Ratings I perceive myself as:			
Quiet .... Talkative				Open .... Closed			
1	2	3	4	4	3	2	1
Slow to decide .... Fast to decide				Impulsive .... Deliberate			
1	2	3	4	4	3	2	1
Going along .... Taking charge				Using opinions .... Using facts			
1	2	3	4	4	3	2	1
Supportive .... Challenging				Informal .... Formal			
1	2	3	4	4	3	2	1
Compliant .... Dominant				Emotional .... Unemotional			
1	2	3	4	4	3	2	1
Deliberate .... Fast to decide				Easy to know .... Hard to know			
1	2	3	4	4	3	2	1
Asking questions .... Making statements				Warm .... Cool			
1	2	3	4	4	3	2	1
Cooperative .... Competitive				Excitable .... Calm			
1	2	3	4	4	3	2	1
Avoiding risks .... Taking risks				Animated .... Poker-faced			
1	2	3	4	4	3	2	1
Slow, studied .... Fast-paced				People-oriented .... Task-oriented			
1	2	3	4	4	3	2	1
Cautious .... Carefree				Spontaneous .... Cautious			
1	2	3	4	4	3	2	1
Indulgent .... Firm				Responsive .... Nonresponsive			
1	2	3	4	4	3	2	1
Nonassertive .... Assertive				Humorous .... Serious			
1	2	3	4	4	3	2	1
Mellow .... Matter-of-fact				Impulsive .... Methodical			
1	2	3	4	4	3	2	1
Reserved .... Outgoing				Lighthearted .... Intense			
1	2	3	4	4	3	2	1

Mark your answers above. Total the score for each side and divide each by 15. Then plot your scores on Exhibit 5.4 to see what social style you are. For fun, you may want to have several friends also score you.

Sources: David Merrill and Roger Reid, *Personal Styles and Effective Performance* (Radnor, PA: Chilton, 1981). See also Tom Kramlinger and Larry Wilson, *The Social Styles Handbook: Adapt Your Style to Win Trust*, 2nd ed. (Herentals, Belgium: Nova Vista Publishing, 2011).

Interpreting self-ratings requires great caution. Self-assessments can be misleading because we usually do not see ourselves the same way others see us. When you rate yourself, you know your own feelings, but others can observe only your behaviors. They don't know your thoughts or your intentions. We also vary our behavior from situation to situation. The indicators listed in Exhibits 5.2 and 5.3 merely show a tendency to be assertive or responsive.

Is there one best social style for a salesperson? No. None is "best" for all situations; each style has its strong points and weak points. Driver salespeople are efficient, determined, and decisive, but customers may find them pushy and dominating. Expressives have enthusiasm, dramatic flair, and creativity but can also seem opinionated, undisciplined, and unstable. Analyticals are orderly, serious, and thorough, but customers may view them as cold, calculating, and stuffy. Finally, amiables are dependable, supportive, and personable but may also be perceived as undisciplined and inflexible.

ethics

The sales training program based on the social style matrix emphasizes that effective selling involves more than communicating a product's benefits. Salespeople must also recognize the customer's needs and expectations. In the sales interaction, salespeople should conduct themselves in a manner consistent with customer expectations. Exhibit 5.7 indicates the expectations of customers with various social styles.

Although each customer type requires a different sales presentation, the salesperson's personal social style tends to determine the sales technique he or she typically uses. For example, drivers tend to use a driver technique with all customer types. When interacting with an amiable customer, driver salespeople will be efficient and businesslike, even though the amiable customer would prefer to deal with a more relationship-oriented and friendlier salesperson.

This sales training program emphasizes that to be effective with a variety of customer types, salespeople must adapt their selling presentations to customers' social styles. Versatility is the key to effective adaptive selling.

Exhibit 5.7

Customer Expectations Based on Social Styles

	Customer's Social Style			
Area of Expectation	Driver	Expressive	Amiable	Analytical
Atmosphere in sales interview	Businesslike	Open, friendly	Open, honest	Businesslike
Salesperson's use of time	Effective, efficient	To develop relationship	Leisurely, to develop relationship	Thorough, accurate
Pace of interview	Quick	Quick	Deliberate	Deliberate
Information provided by salesperson	Salesperson's qualifications; value of products	What salesperson thinks; whom he/she knows	Evidence that salesperson is trustworthy, friendly	Evidence of salesperson's expertise in solving problem
Salesperson's actions to win customer acceptance	Documented evidence, stress results	Recognition and approval	Personal attention and interest	Evidence that salesperson has analyzed the situation
Presentation of benefits	What product can do	Who has used the product	Why product is best to solve problem	How product can solve the problem
Assistance to aid decision making	Explanation of options and probabilities	Testimonials	Guarantees and assurances	Evidence and offers of service

VERSATILITY

The effort people make to increase the productivity of a relationship by adjusting to the needs of the other party is known as **versatility.** Versatile salespeople—those able to adapt their social styles—are much more effective than salespeople who do not adjust their sales presentations.[15] Here is a comparison of behaviors of more versatile and less versatile people:

Less Versatile	More Versatile
Limited ability to adapt to others' needs	Able to adapt to others' needs
Specialist	Generalist
Well-defined interests	Broad interests
Sticks to principles	Negotiates issues
Predictable	Unpredictable
Looks at one side of an issue	Looks at many sides of an issue

How can a salesperson improve his or her versatility? Many companies have sales training programs, using tools like the social style matrix that help teach salespeople the differences in buyers. Role playing is also used extensively for managers to spot problems in salesperson versatility and to teach new ways to help improve it. For example, sales training might suggest that effective salespeople adjust their social styles to match their customers' styles. In role plays, salespeople with a driver orientation need to become more emotional and less assertive when selling to amiable customers. Analytical salespeople must increase their assertiveness and responsiveness when selling to expressive customers. Exhibit 5.8 shows some techniques for adjusting sales behaviors in terms of assertiveness and responsiveness.

Exhibit 5.8
Adjusting Social Styles

	Adjustment	
Dimension	Reduce	Increase
Assertiveness	Ask for customer's opinion.	Get to the point.
	Acknowledge merits of customer's viewpoint.	Don't be vague or ambiguous.
	Listen without interruption.	Volunteer information.
	Be more deliberate; don't rush.	Be willing to disagree.
	Let customer direct flow of conversation.	Take a stand.
		Initiate conversation.
Responsiveness	Become businesslike.	Verbalize feelings.
	Talk less.	Express enthusiasm.
	Restrain enthusiasm.	Pay personal compliments.
	Make decision based on facts.	Spend time on relationships rather than business.
	Stop and think.	Socialize; engage in small talk.
		Use nonverbal communication.

SALES Technology 5.1

USING TECHNOLOGY TO INCREASE ADAPTABILITY BY INSIDE SALESPEOPLE

Technological revolution and innovation have developed the means by which businesses can influence customers from around the world through inside salespeople. Although this offers intriguing possibilities, there is still the need for inside sales reps to engage in adaptive selling techniques. These particular skills can help power a sales rep to a superior level by properly assessing unique needs and modifying his or her selling behaviors.

Customer relationship management (CRM) systems are a beneficial asset for inside salespeople to be adaptive. Through CRM systems (like Salesforce.com and NetSuite) and add-ons (like Talkdesk), salespeople can study all known information about a client or a prospect before contact. For example, Talkdesk offers salespeople a way to maintain an extensive and detailed database that provides an efficient mechanism to use knowledge about prospects and customers. Salespeople are able to classify customers as to their specific social style (analytical, driver, amiable, expressive). With this information, and with templates provided by Talkdesk, inside salespeople can help tailor a specific sales presentation. Talkdesk can help a salesperson work through different situations and objections raised by the prospect or customer.

Source: Talk Desk

RECAP: THE ROLE OF KNOWLEDGE IN ADAPTING

The social style matrix illustrates the importance of knowledge, organized into categories, in determining selling effectiveness through adaptive selling. Sales training based on the social style matrix teaches salespeople the four customer categories or types (driver, expressive, amiable, and analytical). Salespeople learn the cues for identifying them. Salespeople also learn which adjustments they need to make in their communication styles to be effective with each customer type. As Sales Technology 5.1 describes, there are ways to help inside salespeople adapt as well.

SYSTEMS FOR DEVELOPING ADAPTIVE SELLING SKILLS

The social style matrix developed by Merrill and Reid is one of several sales training methods based on customer classification schemes. Rather than using assertiveness and responsiveness, classification schemes by other sales trainers use dimensions like the following:

- Warm-hostile and dominant-submissive
- Dominance and sociability
- Relater, socializer, thinker, and director
- Logical (yellow), emotional (blue), conceptual (orange), and analytical (green)
- Skeptics, charismatics, thinkers, followers, and controllers
- Hawk, owl, dove, and peacock

Regardless of the training system used, it is imperative that salespeople adjust to their audience. Salespeople adjust for types of customers. They also adjust their style when selling to diverse cultures even within their own country. For example, Hispanic salespeople may need to alter their communication style when selling to Anglo-American customers.

Training methods such as the social style matrix are simply a first step in developing knowledge for practicing adaptive selling. They emphasize the need to practice adaptive selling–to use different presentations with different customers–and stimulate salespeople to base their sales presentations on an analysis of the customer. But these methods are limited; they present only a few types of customers, and classification is based on the form of communication (the social style), not on the content of the communication (the specific features and benefits stressed in the presentation).

In addition, accurately fitting customers into the suggested categories is often difficult. Customers act differently and have different needs in different sales encounters: A buyer may be amiable in a new task buying situation and be analytical when dealing with an out-supplier's salesperson in a straight rebuy. Amiable buyers in a bad mood may act like drivers. By rigidly applying the classification rules, salespeople may actually limit their flexibility, reducing the adaptive selling behavior these training methods emphasize.

SELLING YOURSELF

The chapter illustrates ways to adapt your selling to build relationships. The techniques shared can apply to many aspects of your life, both business and personal. Take some time to think of your friends and family. Can you identify their social style? Does it impact how you communicate with them?

The most important part of finishing your education is interviewing for your job upon graduation. You should treat every aspect of the interview process like a sales cycle, and adapt accordingly. First, do your research. When you gather knowledge about the company and the position, you will be able to match your skills and experiences to the job description. Ask your sales professors for alumni contacts who already work at the company you are researching. In addition, gather knowledge about your interviewers as they are asking you questions. You should watch their body language carefully to assess their reaction to your answers. Second, ask good questions. Often the best salespeople are the ones who ask the right questions. Ask meaningful questions that demonstrate your seriousness about the position. The answers you get will help you adapt to the specific situation. Third, always close the interview. You should start with trial closes to handle any potential objections about giving you the position. Then ask about the next steps you need to take to gain the position.

While you prepare for your interview remember how important it is to get your desired position. Your first job is an opportunity to build a foundation for your personal life goals. Take your skills, experiences, and relationships and apply them to the interview process. Research your competition for the position and find ways to stand out among the other candidates. Ask about the benefits and longevity of a career at your desired company. Show your drive, organization, work ethic, integrity, communication, and any other skills that demonstrate your ability to adapt and perform the job well.

Once you start your new job you should continue to sell yourself via branding. You should consider how you are building your brand with peers, leadership, customers, and industry stakeholders. Internal and external players in your market can often influence your ability to sell and get promoted. You should never miss an opportunity to create a relationship at any level inside or outside your company.

Best of luck interviewing and closing your dream job, and continued success in your future career!

Chareen Bogner, sales representative, McKesson. Used with permission.

SUMMARY

Adaptive selling uses one of the unique properties of personal selling as a marketing communication tool: the ability to tailor messages to individual customers and make on-the-spot adjustments. Extensive knowledge of customer and sales situation types is a key ingredient in effective adaptive selling.

To be effective at adapting, salespeople need considerable knowledge about the products they sell, the companies for which they work, and the customers to whom they sell. Experienced salespeople organize customer knowledge into categories. Each category has cues for classifying customers or sales situations and an effective sales presentation for customers in the category.

The social style matrix, developed by Merrill and Reid, illustrates the concept of developing categorical knowledge to facilitate adaptive selling. The matrix defines four customer categories based on a customer's responsiveness and assertiveness in sales interactions. To effectively interact with a customer, a salesperson needs to identify the customer's social style and adapt a style to match. The sales training program based on the social style matrix provides cues for identifying social style as well as presentations salespeople can use to make adjustments.

KEY TERMS

adaptive selling 127
amiable 135
analytical 135
assertiveness 133
customized presentation 126
diagnostic feedback 131
driver 135
expressive 135
outlined presentation 126
performance feedback 131
responsiveness 133
social style matrix 132
standard memorized presentation 126
style flexing 133
versatility 139

ETHICS PROBLEMS

1. Your boss tells you about one of your buyers, Erica: "Just talk about Cubs baseball, because she's a fanatic about the Cubs! If you do, she'll like you and buy just about anything. Even more than she needs because she hates to say no to someone who likes the Cubs!" What will you do in that situation?
2. You have a buyer, a driver, who is a real challenge. It seems as though she is always playing games with salespeople. For example, today she said she wouldn't answer questions about her needs or what she was currently buying from your leading competitor. She said, "You need to find some other way to discover what business your competitors are getting here." Then with a sly turn of her head, she added, "I think you're going to have to engage in some espionage, here as well as at your competitor's warehouse. Are you a good spy?" What will you do in this situation?

QUESTIONS AND PROBLEMS

1. A salesperson stated, "I just can't stand to deal with buyers who smile, ask about my family, and refuse to tell me why they can't buy from me that day." Based on this limited amount of information, what social style would you guess the salesperson to be? What would be your response to this salesperson?
2. While many salespeople have adopted technology tools to aid them in selling, some have refused. What would be your response to a salesperson

who says the following: "Look, I put a lot of information on my computer a few years ago, including all of my contacts, and notes about calls. Then my computer crashed and I lost everything! I'm not going to waste my time like that again!"

3. A salesperson made the following comment: "It's such a waste of time to read all of my company's internal blog posts and the white papers my company sends me about the industry I am selling to. Who has time to read all of that stuff?" Based on what you learned in this chapter about knowledge systems, what would be your response to this salesperson?
4. "A good salesperson can easily adapt to any customer type. That's why we hire them, right?" Do you agree? Why or why not?
5. In general, would a salesperson with an expressive social style be better at selling than a person with a driver or an analytical style? Why?
6. Some people object to the social style matrix training system because they don't want to "act." They just want to be themselves, and not "put on a show." What would you say to them?
7. What social styles would you assign to the following people? Why?
   a. Conan O'Brien.
   b. Your favorite instructor in high school.
   c. One of your parents.
   d. Kim Kardashian
8. The salesperson in Building Partnerships 5.1 used encounters with C-level executives at an industry meeting to help secure the attention of lower-level buyers and influencers in the firm. Can you think of at least one other way that a salesperson might use a C-level executive to influence decisions made by buyers and influencers lower in the firm?
9. Suppose that during a sales call on an electronics reseller, the buyer says, "I don't think iPhones are going to continue to be a best-selling item in the future!" How should you respond if this customer is an amiable? An expressive?
10. Market research by a company specializing in designing and installing custom counter tops in commercial kitchens identified two types of buyers. Type I is concerned only that the item is the absolute cutting edge in terms of style and materials. Type II is concerned about practical elements such as functionality and long wear. How would you adapt the selling of your custom countertops to each type?

CASE PROBLEMS

case 5.1

Won't Take No for an Answer

I'm in a buyer role at a Fortune 100 firm. Let me tell you a **true** story that happened to me last month. I was in my doorway about to leave my office to meet with a vice president. I had ended a meeting in my office about three minutes early to give myself the time to get up the three flights of stairs to her (the VP's) office in time.

A salesperson whom I had never met before stopped me in my doorway, and I explained that I was on my way to an important meeting. The salesperson proceeded to take my hand and shake it and introduce himself. He said he was asked to meet with me by a coworker to introduce his services. I reiterated that I needed to go to my meeting, but I would take his card and call him later. So you're thinking that ended the conversation, right? If so, you'd be wrong.

He refused to clear the doorway! This is only going to take a minute, he promised, and launched into his sales pitch. I interrupted him, explaining that I really didn't have a minute and that I would call him later.

It was as though he never heard me. He continued to explain his services which really frustrated me! His disregard for my time resulted in my standing there longer than I needed to and my being two minutes late for my meeting.

Questions

1. Based on the limited amount of information provided, what would you guess is the social style of the buyer? How about the social style of the seller? Explain your reasoning.
2. Make a list of five "rules" you could set for yourself as a salesperson to avoid making a buyer like this angry at you.

Source: Tracey Brill, used with permission.

case **5.2**

Zimmer

I'm Alexa and I sell orthopedic products, like hip, shoulder, elbow, and knee replacements, for Zimmer. One aspect of my selling job requires me to service what I sell, and in the case of replacement joints, that means going into the operating room with the surgeon and taking on the role of a technical expert when it comes to the capabilities, function, and surgical technique used with my company's hardware.

I took a survey and found out that I am definitely an expressive. People see me as warm and approachable, yet also not afraid to express my points of view with strong conviction. I tend to act rather quickly when making decisions, after I've had a chance to survey the opinions of others who are important to me.

There are three surgeons I'm going to be calling on tomorrow, to introduce a newly developed solution in cartilage repair. Let me tell you a bit about each one.

Dr. Avilia is a meticulous, detail-oriented knee and hip replacement surgeon. His office is so neat that it looks like he rarely even uses it. He keeps the top of his desk completely free of anything except for a small business card holder at one corner. He is a world-class surgeon with many awards displayed on the walls. I've heard that he wants to get right down to business and demands to know the bottom line immediately. He has little tolerance for someone who is not the best at what they do. If he thinks you are wasting his time, he will politely tell you so, before wishing you a nice day and sending you out the door. His favorite hobby is collecting fine wines.

Dr. Mokri, an accomplished knee surgeon, has been known to be a few minutes late to surgeries due to getting caught up in some conversation with a colleague or patient. His friends tend to think of him as a great big "teddy bear" whom everyone wants to be around. His personality is in some way magnetic, and he has many friends. He is an ultra-competitive tennis player and rarely loses, but when he does, he immediately demands a rematch for the next day if possible. He serves on five different medical boards and councils and is known as an influential leader in each. People have said that he is a visionary, both in the orthopedic surgery realm as well as his own personal life. He has toyed with running for political office and most friends think he would make a great debater if he did decide to run! His favorite hobby, other than playing tennis, is traveling to the Far East.

Dr. Rodriguez specializes in elbow replacements. While certainly friendly, she could hardly be called effusive with her affection or conversation. She seems to be totally task oriented, and wants to be the best elbow replacement surgeon in the northwest. She doesn't seem to understand the power struggles among the various surgeons and administrators at the hospital, and would rather spend her time reading the latest medical journals and conversing with surgeons around the globe on the latest surgical techniques. She sometimes is slow to adopt new techniques, however, wanting to be absolutely certain that any procedure is better than all other possible procedures before changing. Her favorite hobby is fly fishing.

Questions

1. What is the social style of each surgeon? Discuss facts that helped you determine that assessment.
2. How should Alexa adapt to each surgeon?

ROLE PLAY CASE

This role play requires some before-class preparation. Write a brief outline of how you would describe Gartner to someone who has never heard of it. Identify three features of Gartner's services that you think would benefit your buyer, based on the information you've learned so far this semester. Then write down what you would want to say about each feature. You will take turns presenting your sales presentations to your buyer. After you give your presentation, determine what the other person's social style was. Identify the hints the buyer gave you.

If you have been using Gartner role plays all along, you can use the same customer you have called on. If not, you will need to review the role play material at the end of Chapter 3. You can also review material about Gartner in the role play case at the back of this book to understand Gartner and what it does, as well as visit www.gartner.com/ncsc.

When you play the buyer, pick a social style different from your own. Interact with the seller in ways that give clues about your social style. Before the role play starts, think of at least five things you will do to hint at your new social style. Keep in mind that a social style includes both responsiveness and assertiveness, so make sure your hints combine both dimensions. After each role play, the salesperson should say what the other person's social style was and what clues were used to make that determination.

To the instructor: There is no additional information required for this role play if you have been using these all semester. Otherwise, see the note in the Instructor's Manual.

ADDITIONAL REFERENCES

Bolander, Willy, Cinthia B. Satornino, Douglas E. Hughes, and Gerald R. Ferris. "Social Networks within Sales Organizations: Their Development and Importance for Salesperson Performance." *Journal of Marketing* 79, no. 6 (2015), pp. 1-16.

Cardon, Peter W. *Business Communication: Developing Leaders for a Networked World.* New York: McGraw-Hill Irwin, 2014.

Chakrabarty, Subhra, Gene Brown, and Robert E. Widing. "Distinguishing between the Roles of Customer-Oriented Selling and Adaptive Selling in Managing Dysfunctional Conflict in Buyer–Seller Relationships." *Journal of Personal Selling and Sales Management* 33, no. 3 (2013), pp. 245-60.

Feller, Bryan. "The After Action Review and Your Sales Team: A Great Match." *American Salesman* 59, no. 6 (2014), pp. 3-7.

Friend, Scott B., Carolyn F. Curasi, James S. Boles, and Danny N. Bellenger. "Why Are You Really Losing Sales Opportunities? A Buyers' Perspective on the Determinants of Key Account Sales Failures." *Industrial Marketing Management* 43, no. 7 (2014), pp. 1124-35.

Grant, Terri, and M. M. Borcherds. *Communicating @ Work: Boosting Your Spoken, Written and Visual Impact.* Pretoria: Van Schaik Publishers, 2015.

Guenzi, Paolo, Artur Baldauf, and Nikolaos G. Panagopoulos. "The Influence of Formal and Informal Sales Controls on Customer-Directed Selling Behaviors and Sales Unit Effectiveness." *Industrial Marketing Management* 43, no. 5 (2014), pp. 786-800.

Jay, Joelle. "How to Get the Feedback You Didn't Really Want to Hear (But Really Need to Know)." *American Salesman* 61, no. 3 (2016), pp. 12-16.

Kara, Ali, Syed Saad Andaleeb, Mehmet Turan, and Serap Cabuk. "An Examination of the Effects of Adaptive Selling Behavior and Customer Orientation on Performance of Pharmaceutical Salespeople in an Emerging Market." *Journal of Medical Marketing* 13, no. 2 (2013), pp. 102-14.

Konrath, Jill. *Agile Selling: Getting up to Speed Quickly in Today's Ever-Changing Sales World.* New York: Portfolio/Penguin, 2014.

Murfield, Monique L. Ueltschy, and Terry L. Esper. "Supplier Adaptation: A Qualitative Investigation of Customer and Supplier Perspectives." *Industrial Marketing Management* 59 (2016), pp. 96-106.

Rippé, Cindy B., Suri Weisfeld-Spolter, Alan J. Dubinsky, Aaron D. Arndt, and Maneesh Thakkar. "Selling in an Asymmetric Retail World: Perspectives from India, Russia, and the US on Buyer–Seller Information Differential, Perceived Adaptive Selling, and Purchase Intention." *Journal of Personal Selling and Sales Management* 36, no. 4 (2016), pp. 344-62.

Román, Sergio, and Pedro Juan Martín. "Does the Hierarchical Position of the Buyer Make a Difference? The Influence of Perceived Adaptive Selling on Customer Satisfaction and Loyalty in a Business-to-Business Context." *Journal of Business and Industrial Marketing* 29, no. 5 (2014), pp. 364-73.

Shannahan, Rachelle J., Alan J. Bush, Kirby L. J. Shannahan, and William C. Moncrief. "How Salesperson Perceptions of Customers' Pro-Social Behaviors Help Drive Salesperson Performance." *Industrial Marketing Management* 51 (2015), pp. 100-14.

Singh, Ramendra, and Gopal Das. "The Impact of Job Satisfaction, Adaptive Selling Behaviors and Customer Orientation on Salesperson's Performance: Exploring the Moderating Role of Selling Experience." *Journal of Business and Industrial Marketing* 28, no. 7 (2013), pp. 554-64.

Tracy, Brian. *Sales Success.* New York: American Management Association, 2015.

Wang, Yichuan, Shih-Hui Hsiao, Zhiguo Yang, and Nick Hajli. "The Impact of Sellers' Social Influence on the Co-Creation of Innovation with Customers and Brand Awareness in Online Communities." *Industrial Marketing Management* 54 (2016), pp. 56-70.

Yeboah Banin, Abena, Nathaniel Boso, Magnus Hultman, Anne L. Souchon, Paul Hughes, and Ekaterina Nemkova. "Salesperson Improvisation: Antecedents, Performance Outcomes, and Boundary Conditions." *Industrial Marketing Management* 59 (2016), pp. 120-30.

The Partnership Process

2

PART

©monkeybusinessimages/Getty Images RF

chapter 6

PROSPECTING

SOME QUESTIONS ANSWERED IN THIS CHAPTER ARE

- Why is prospecting important for effective selling?
- Are all sales leads good prospects? What are the characteristics of a qualified prospect?
- How can prospects be identified? How can social media be used?
- How can the organization's promotional program be used in prospecting?
- How can an effective lead qualification and management system aid a salesperson?
- How can a salesperson overcome a reluctance to prospect?

PROFILE

> *"To become successful in any sales career, it is important to become an effective prospector. Prospecting is the heartbeat of your business."*
>
> *Karl Macalincag, GDP Technologies*

PROFILE My name is Karl Macalincag and I graduated from Kennesaw State University with a degree in business administration specializing in professional selling. I want to give a special thank you to Dr. Loe, Dr. Borders, and Professor Serkadakis from Kennesaw State for giving me the foundation to become a successful sales professional. Throughout my career at Kennesaw State, I was able to compete and become a top performer in several sales competitions as well as contribute to winning the National Collegiate Sales Competition in 2016.

Courtesy of Karl Macalincag

Upon graduation, I immediately accepted a position with GDP Technologies in which I am able to use the concepts I have learned from KSU to become successful.

To become successful in any sales career, it is important to become an effective prospector. Prospecting is the heartbeat of your business. If you are not a fanatical prospector, it becomes very difficult to hit your quota every month. After shadowing and learning about the top performers at GDP Technologies, I have found one commonality among them: They all have the capability of keeping their pipeline full by continuous quality prospecting. The number one mistake of a new salesperson is relying on one big deal that can make or break his or her month. You have a better chance of having a successful month by continuing to fill the funnel with qualified prospects. Qualified prospects include businesses that have a need for your service, are able to buy, and have the authority to buy. Ignoring these characteristics can lead to wasted time with prospects that will not help your business grow. No matter how busy a sales professional is throughout the day with appointments, administrative work, or demos, the sales professional should have a consistent routine of effectively prospecting every day.

In addition to prospecting, it is important to grow your network by participating in professional social events that your company offers. At GDP Technologies, the president of our company allows us to attend every Gwinnett, Georgia, Chamber of Commerce event. This gives us the opportunity to build strong personal relationships with C-level executives. Building familiarity with potential prospects at professional events can significantly impact your success as a sales representative. The more you build familiarity to prospects with your company and service, the more they are able to trust doing business with you. I have been able to develop a strong referral business by attending these events that are offered by the company.

Last, it is important to learn how to overcome the reluctance of prospecting to become successful in sales. I always focus on having a positive mindset and forming a habit of consistent activity. Your activity in sales is directly correlated to your mindset. If you believe in your product, service, leaders, and company you are able to produce more activity for your business. Activity leads to results, and results lead to more income for you and your family. Managing your mindset and activity can help you achieve your goals as a sales professional. As Zig Ziglar said, "You can have everything in life you want if you will just help enough other people get what they want."

Visit our Web site at: www.gdptechnologies.com.

An important activity for nearly all salespeople is locating qualified prospects. This chapter provides resources to help you prospect effectively and efficiently.

THE IMPORTANCE OF PROSPECTING

Prospecting, the process of locating potential customers for a product or service, is the most important activity that many salespeople do.[1]

Why is it so important? Salespeople must find new customers to replace those that switch to competitors, go bankrupt, move out of the territory, merge with noncustomers, or decide to do without a product or service. A salesperson often needs to prospect even in existing accounts because of downsizing, job changes, or retirements of buyers. Sales trainer Joe Girard uses a Ferris wheel metaphor to describe the important process of adding new customers (loading new accounts onto the Ferris wheel) to replace customers you lose (people getting off the Ferris wheel). Without replacing lost accounts, your Ferris wheel will soon be running with no one on board.

Of course, prospecting is more important in some selling fields than in others. For example, the financial advisor or real estate sales representative with no effective prospecting plan usually doesn't last long in the business. Sales positions such as these may require 100 contacts to get 10 prospects who will listen to presentations, out of which 1 person will buy. Each sale, then, represents a great deal of prospecting. It is also important in these fields to prospect continually. Some sales trainers relate this process to your car's gas tank: You don't wait until the gas gauge is on empty before you fill up!

Some sales positions require less emphasis on locating new contacts. For example, a Lockheed Martin salesperson assigned exclusively to sell the F-16 tactical fighter jet to South Korea and Singapore would not spend any time trying to locate new governments to call on. For these types of sales positions, prospecting as we normally think of it (that is, looking for new leads) is not an important part of the sales process. Nevertheless, salespeople cannot ignore these obvious leads, as the next section discusses. Salespeople still have to assess whether leads are good prospects.[2]

CHARACTERISTICS OF A GOOD PROSPECT

Prospecting actually begins with locating a **lead** (sometimes called a "suspect")—a potential prospect that may or may not have what it takes to be a true prospect. Some salespeople mistakenly consider every lead a prospect without first taking the time to see whether these people really provide an opportunity to make a sale.

Exhibit 6.1
The Sales Funnel

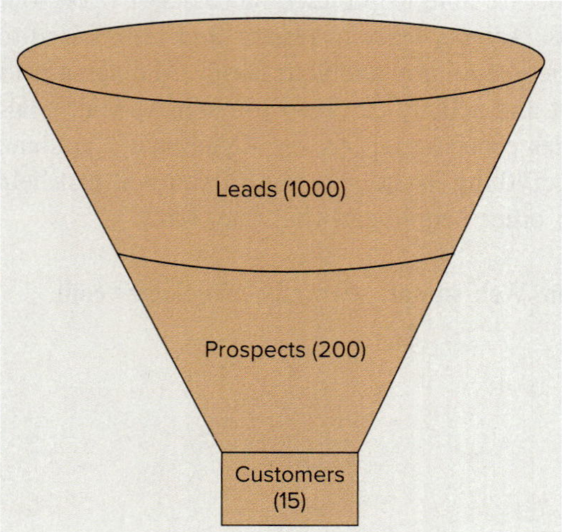

To avoid that mistake, the salesperson must **qualify the lead**. Qualifying is the process of determining whether a lead is in fact a **prospect**. If the salesperson determines that the lead is a good candidate for making a sale, that person or organization is no longer considered a lead and instead is called a prospect. Note that many leads do not become prospects. Exhibit 6.1 illustrates this process. One thousand leads might be needed, for example, to generate 200 prospects, of which only 15 might become customers. Some companies break down this **sales funnel** into more levels, depending on how complex the purchase process and sales cycle are.

The following five questions are used by many organizations to help qualify leads and pinpoint the good prospects.

ethics

DOES A WANT OR NEED EXIST?

Research has supplied no infallible answers to why customers buy, but it has found many reasons. As we pointed out in Chapter 3, customers buy to satisfy practical needs as well as intangible needs, such as prestige or aesthetics.

By using high-pressure tactics, sales attempts may be made to those who do not need or really want a product. Such sales benefit no one. The buyer will resent making the purchase, and a potential long-term customer will be lost.

DOES THE LEAD HAVE THE ABILITY TO PAY?

For example, the commercial real estate agent usually checks the financial status of each client to determine the price range of office buildings to show. A client with annual profits of $100,000 and cash resources of $75,000 may be a genuine prospect for office space in the $30,000 to $50,000 annual rental bracket. An agent would be wasting time, however, by showing this client space listed at $100,000 annual rent. The client may have a desire for the more expensive setting, but the client is still not a real prospect for the higher-priced office space if he or she doesn't have the resources to pay for it.

Ability to pay includes both cash and credit. Many companies subscribe to a credit-rating service offered by firms such as Dun & Bradstreet. Salespeople use information from these sources to determine the financial status and credit rating of a lead. They can also qualify leads with information obtained from local credit agencies, consumer credit agencies such as Experian, noncompetitive salespeople, and the Better Business Bureau. Salespeople are sometimes surprised at their leads' credit ratings. Some big-name firms have poor ratings.

DOES THE LEAD HAVE THE AUTHORITY TO BUY?

Knowing who has the authority to make a purchase saves the salesperson time and effort and results in a higher percentage of closed sales. As discussed in Chapter 3, many people can be involved in a purchase decision, and it can be unclear who has the authority to buy.

Because of downsizing, some firms are delegating their purchasing tasks to outside vendors. These service vendors, called **systems integrators**, have the authority to buy products and services on behalf of the delegating firm. Systems integrators usually assume complete responsibility for a project from its beginning to follow-up servicing. An example would be Lockheed Martin acting as a systems integrator for the complete mail-processing system of a new postal sorting facility in Germany. In that scenario every potential vendor would actually be selling to Lockheed Martin, not to the German government. When systems integrators are involved, salespeople need to delineate clearly who has the authority to purchase. Sometimes the overall buyer (the German government in this example) will retain veto power over potential vendors.

CAN THE LEAD BE APPROACHED FAVORABLY?

Some leads simply are not accessible to the salesperson. For example, the president of an international bank, a major executive of a large manufacturing company, or the senior partner in a well-established law firm would not normally be accessible to a young college graduate starting out as a financial advisor for Edward Jones. Getting an interview with these people may be so difficult and the chances of making a sale may be so small that the sales representative should eliminate them as possible prospects.

IS THE LEAD ELIGIBLE TO BUY?

Eligibility is an equally important factor in finding a genuine prospect. For example, a salesperson who works for a firm that requires a large minimum order should not call on leads that could never order in such volume. Likewise, a representative who sells exclusively to wholesalers should be certain the individuals he or she calls on are actually wholesalers, not retailers.

Another factor that may determine eligibility for a particular salesperson is the geographic location of the prospect. Most companies operate on the basis of **exclusive sales territories**, meaning that a particular salesperson can sell only to certain prospects (such as doctors in only a three-county area) and not to other prospects. A salesperson working for such a company must consider whether the prospect is eligible, based on location or customer type, to buy from him or her.

Salespeople should also avoid targeting leads already covered by their corporate headquarters. Large customers or potential customers that are handled exclusively by corporate executives are often called **house accounts**.[3] For example, if Marriott Hotels considers Ingersoll Rand a house account, a Marriott Hotel salesperson (who sets up events and conventions at the hotel) located in New York City should not try to solicit business from one of Ingersoll Rand's divisions located in New York City. Instead all Ingersoll Rand business would be handled by a Marriott executive at Marriott corporate headquarters.

OTHER CRITERIA

Leads that meet the five criteria are generally considered excellent prospects by most companies. Some sellers, however, add other criteria. For example, DEI Management Group instructs its salespeople to classify leads by their likelihood of buying.

Some firms look at the timing of purchase to determine whether a lead is really a good prospect. Relevant questions to consider include these: When does the prospect's contract with our competitor expire? Is a purchase decision really pending? How do we know? Still other firms look at the long-term potential of developing a partnering relationship with a lead. Here are some questions to ponder: What is the climate at the organization–is it looking to develop partnering relationships with suppliers? Do any of our competitors already have a partnering relationship there?

The Corporate Executive Board takes an entirely different approach to prospecting and qualifying leads, which it terms **insight selling**.[4] Under this approach, salespeople evaluate prospects who do not necessarily have a clear understanding of what they need but are in a state of flux and have been shown to be quite agile in making changes (that is, they are able and willing to act quickly when a compelling case is made to them). This approach also encourages salespeople to interact with people in the buying firm who are skeptical rather than friendly information providers and then coach these skeptical decision makers how to buy the seller's solution. Why this approach? Proponents claim that buyers today already know a great deal about the marketplace and understand many of their options and that salespeople who follow the proposed approach are more successful in gaining commitment.

HOW AND WHERE TO OBTAIN PROSPECTS

Prospecting sources and methods vary for different types of selling. A sales representative selling corrugated containers for Citation Box & Paper Company, for example, may use a system different from what banking or office products salespeople

Exhibit 6.2
Overview of Common Sources of Leads

Source	How Used
Satisfied customers	Current and previous customers are contacted for additional business and leads.
Endless chain	Salesperson attempts to secure at least one additional lead from each person he or she interviews.
Networking	Salesperson uses personal relationships with those who are connected and cooperative to secure leads.
Center of influence	Salesperson cultivates well-known, influential people in the territory who are willing to supply lead information.
Social media	Salesperson uses online tools like LinkedIn, Facebook, and Twitter to prospect for new customers and maintain contact with existing customers.
Other Internet uses	Salesperson uses Web sites, e-mail, listservs, bulletin boards, forums, roundtables, and newsgroups to secure leads.
Marketing department	Salespeople use the marketing department of their firm to generate leads.
Shows, fairs, and merchandise markets	Salespeople use trade shows, conventions, fairs, and merchandise markets for lead generation.
Webinars and seminars	Salespeople use seminars and online webinars to generate leads.
Lists and directories	Salesperson uses secondary data sources, which can be free or fee based.
Databases and data mining	Salespeople use sophisticated data analysis software and the company's databases to generate leads.
Cold calling	Salesperson tries to generate leads by calling on totally unfamiliar organizations.
Spotters	Salesperson pays someone for lead information.
Inside salespeople	Inside salespeople are used to generate leads.
Expertise	Salespeople use their personal talks and speeches as well as written communication like blogs to showcase their expertise.
Sales letters	Salesperson writes personal letters to potential leads.
Other sources	Salesperson uses noncompeting salespeople, people in his or her own firm, friends, and so on to secure information.

would use. Exhibit 6.2 presents an overview of some of the most common lead-generating methods. Note that there is some overlap among the methods.

SATISFIED CUSTOMERS

Satisfied customers, particularly those who are truly partners with the seller, are the most effective sources for leads.[5] In fact some trainers argue that successful salespeople should be getting the vast majority of their new business through referrals from customers, and firms are now encouraged to calculate **customer referral value (CRV)**, which is the monetary value of the referral as well as the costs to get and maintain the referral. Referrals of leads in the same industry are particularly useful because the salesperson already understands the unique needs of this type of organization (if you have sold to a bank already, you have a better understanding of banks' needs). Referrals in some cultures, like Japan, are even more important than they are in North America.

To maximize the usefulness of satisfied customers, salespeople should follow several logical steps. First they should make a list of potential references (customers who might provide leads) from among their most satisfied customers.

Salespeople use referral events to generate leads.

©Purestock/SuperStock RF

This task will be much easier if the salespeople have maintained an accurate and detailed database of customers. Some current customers could be called **promoters** or evangelists. These are your most loyal customers who not only keep buying from you but also urge their friends and associates to do the same. Next salespeople should decide what they would like each customer to do (such as have the customer write a personal letter or e-mail message of introduction to a specific prospect, see whether the customer would be willing to take phone inquiries, have the customer directly contact prospects, or have the customer provide a generic letter of reference or write a recommendation for you on LinkedIn). Finally salespeople should ask the customer for the names of leads and for the specific type of help she or he can provide.

Salespeople sometimes gather leads at **referral events**, which are gatherings designed to allow current customers to introduce prospects to the salesperson. For example, a northwestern financial advisor might invite a group of current clients to a ski resort for a weekend. The skiing weekend is free for clients who bring one or more prospects. Other events that salespeople use include sporting events, theater visits, dinner at a nice restaurant, a short cruise, or golf lessons by a pro. The key is that the gathering should be fun and sociable and a way for a salesperson to gather leads. The name of a lead provided by either a customer or a prospect, known as a **referred lead**, is generally considered the most successful type of lead.

Satisfied customers not only provide leads but also are usually prospects for additional sales. This situation is sometimes referred to as **selling deeper** to a current customer. Salespeople should never overlook this profitable opportunity. Sales to existing customers often result in more profits than do sales to new customers. For example, if a midsize company increased its customer retention by just 5 percent, its profits would double in only 10 years. Chapter 15 explores account development more fully. Of course it is also possible that a customer could be the other kind of referrer–one who tells others about how poorly you or your product performed. This **negative referral** is not the kind of referral a salesperson likes to get, and every effort should be made to ensure that the customer is satisfied and stays satisfied with the solution offered by the salesperson. This also will be discussed in more detail in Chapter 14.

Finally, salespeople who leave one company can bring their sales clients with them to the new company for which they work. Phil Birt did that when he was laid off from Seagate Technology during a downturn in the economy and went to work for Bell Micro. At Bell Micro, Birt grew the revenue of one customer by $400,000 in four months and that of another customer by $100,000 in a single month.[6] Of course salespeople who change jobs must always follow the agreements signed with their first employers before transferring such business.

ENDLESS-CHAIN METHOD

In the **endless-chain method** sales representatives attempt to get at least one additional lead from each person they interview. This method works best when the source is a satisfied customer and partner; however, it may also be used even when a prospect does not buy. Exhibit 6.3 illustrates how a sales representative successfully used the endless-chain method.

Exhibit 6.3
Example of the Endless-Chain Method of Prospecting

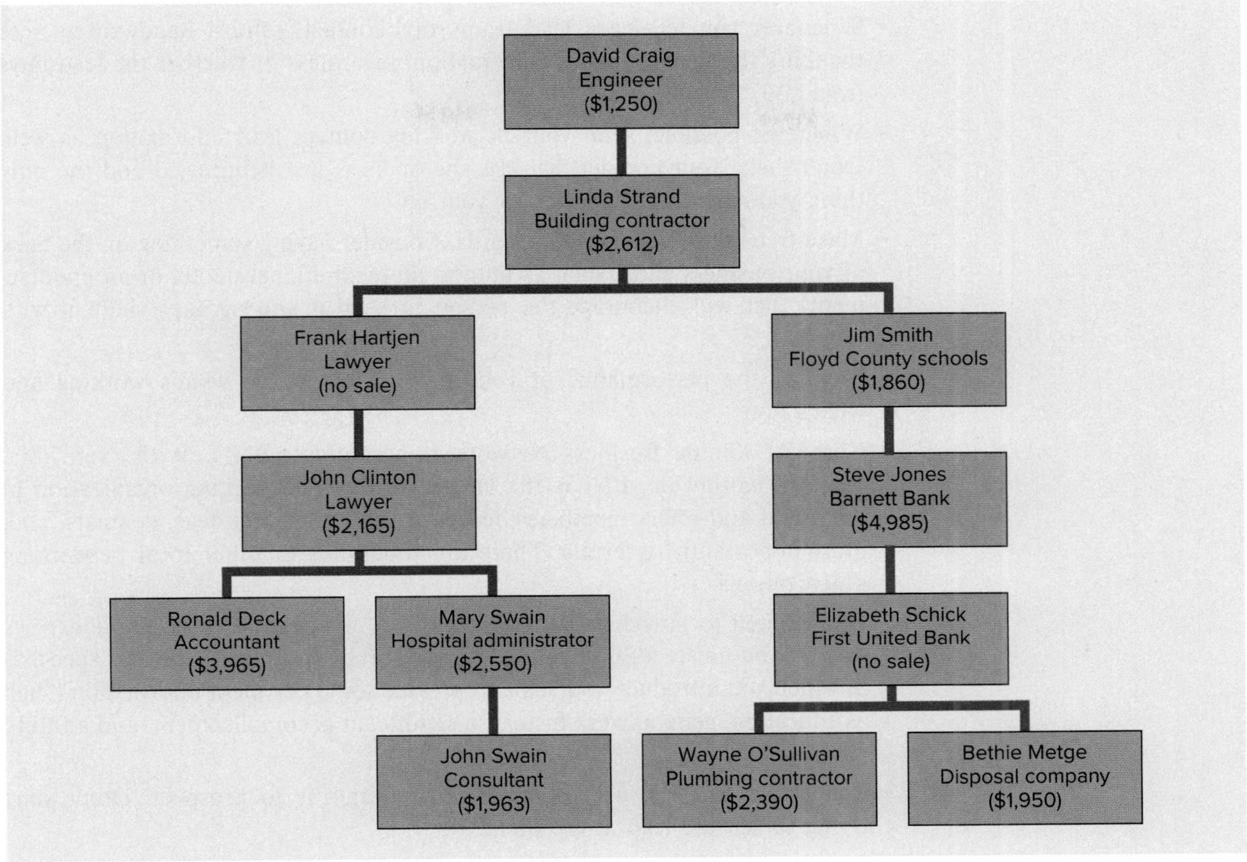

The sales representative used the endless-chain method to produce $25,690 in business (selling fax machines) within a 30-day period. All the sales resulted directly or indirectly from the first referral from an engineer to whom the sales rep had sold a mere $1,250 worth of equipment.

NETWORKING AND CENTER OF INFLUENCE

Networking is the utilization of personal relationships by connected and cooperating individuals for the purpose of achieving goals. In selling, networking simply means establishing connections to other people and then using those networks to generate leads, gather information, generate sales, and so on. Networking can, and often does, include satisfied customers.

Networking is crucial in many selling situations. For example, trying to sell in China without successful networking, called *guanxi* in China, would be disastrous.

Successful networkers offer a number of practical suggestions:

- Call at least two people per day, and go to at least one networking event every week to increase your exposure and time with your contacts.
- Make a special effort to move outside your own comfort zone in a social setting. Learn to mingle with people you don't already know. One expert calls this behavior acting like a host instead of like a guest.
- Spend most of your initial conversation with a new contact talking about his or her business, not yours, and don't forget to learn about the person's non-business interests.

- Follow up with your new contact on a regular basis with cards, notes of congratulations about awards or promotions, and articles and information that might help her or him.
- Whenever you receive a lead from your contact, send a handwritten note thanking the person for the information, regardless of whether the lead buys from you.
- Whenever possible, send your networking contact lead information as well. Don't make your contact feel like she or he is just being used and the only thing you care about is leads for yourself.
- Make free use of your business cards. Consider having something on the back of your business card (such as humor, an inspirational quote, or an endorsement) that will encourage the person to keep it and perhaps share it with others.
- Monitor the performance of your networking to see what's working and what's not.
- Consider joining Business Network International (BNI). With over 7,800 chapters worldwide, BNI is the largest business networking organization in the world and offers members the opportunity to share ideas, contacts, and, most importantly, referrals. There are thousands of other local networking organizations.
- Be prepared to introduce yourself succinctly in social settings. Some experts suggest you create a 30-second commercial (also called an "elevator speech") in which you introduce yourself and provide some pertinent information (such as education, general work history, a significant accomplishment, and a future goal).
- Remember that the goal of networking events is to prospect. Don't start trying to sell the lead at the event.

In one form of networking, the **center-of-influence method**, the salesperson cultivates a relationship with well-known, influential people in the territory who are willing to supply the names of leads.[7] Here is how an industrial cleaning service salesperson used the center-of-influence method when meeting with a well-known and respected maintenance engineer:

> Now that you've had the opportunity to learn more about me and my service, I wonder if you will do me a favor? You mentioned that it was probably the best-designed package you've seen. I know that as an engineer you wouldn't personally need my services, but can you think of any of your business associates who could benefit from such a plan? Does one come to mind?

thinking it through

Who is a center of influence for you right now? How could a salesperson who wanted to sell you something learn who your center of influence is?

In industrial sales situations the centers of influence are frequently people in important departments not directly involved in the purchase decision, such as quality control, equipment maintenance, and receiving. The salesperson keeps in close touch with these people, solicits their help in a straightforward manner, and keeps them informed about sales that result from their aid.

Centers of influence tend to be those who enjoy being very socially involved in their communities. And people in the community not only trust these individuals but also seek their advice. One true story illustrates the method's use. A Xerox representative found that decision makers from several companies would get together from time to time. These accounts formed a **buying community**: a small, informal group of people in similar positions, often from several companies, who communicate regularly, both socially and professionally. The salesperson also found that one particular decision maker in that group, or community, would share the results of any sales call with the other members of the community. Thus a call on that account had the power of seven calls. By working carefully with this center of influence, the salesperson closed nine orders from the seven accounts, with sales that totaled more than $450,000.

SOCIAL MEDIA

As described in Chapter 4, salespeople are using social media, like LinkedIn, Facebook, blogs, and Twitter, to communicate with buyers.[8] Given the growing importance of these channels, these types of tools can also be used to prospect for new customers. However, salespeople should not rely only on social media for prospecting.[9]

Salespeople should first determine their overall approach for using social media, involving either a push or a pull strategy. As salespeople, are we trying to push ourselves, our companies, and our products to prospects? If so, then the seller can use social media tactics, such as live question-and-answer sessions on the seller's Facebook page, using LinkedIn to gather prospect names, and so forth. As salespeople, are we trying to pull customers toward us and our products? If so, tactics might include the use of seller blogs, wikis, video blogs (called vlogs), microblogs like Twitter, and so forth.[10]

Here are some tips on the use of social media for prospecting by salespeople:[11]

- Go to the prospect's Web site. Read blogs posted there and register yourself to receive any type of material the prospect might occasionally send out.
- Go to LinkedIn and search for the company and the person you want to call on. Try to get connected to the individual through a connection you already have.[12]
- Even if you find a LinkedIn account for a top-level executive, do not expect that that person is the one using the account. Very often an executive assistant is the one using the account.[13]
- Once you are connected, review the prospect's LinkedIn page carefully. Look for things you have in common. See what organizations and groups your prospect belongs to or follows. Follow the same procedure for other social networking sites like Facebook, and make sure you tailor messages to fit the mission and tone of each specific networking site.
- Follow the prospect (both the company and the individual you will be calling on) on Twitter. Sometimes a prospect won't have a Twitter account showing on the company Web site, so you will need to do a company search on Twitter to find the prospect (search.twitter.com). Also, see whom your prospect is following on Twitter.
- If the prospect decides to follow you on Twitter, send her or him a direct message. If the prospect doesn't follow you on Twitter, you can still send a message by commenting on one of his or her tweets using Twitter's @ feature.

- Search for the prospect and the company on networking sites like YouTube and SlideShare.
- If your company has just launched a new product or service, ask users what they think about it via Twitter.[14] Or ask any question. Twitter is great for getting opinions from people.
- Upload your contacts from your e-mail program to LinkedIn and Facebook to search for more connections.
- Use Find Friends in Facebook to find other people whom you might be able to add to your network.
- Look at your friends' lists of friends. Invite them to link to you or ask your friend to initiate this linking.
- Start a group page for your product in Facebook.
- Use the Search feature in Facebook to find groups and fan pages that might be related to your business.
- Use the search updates feature in LinkedIn and data intelligence tools like InsideView to see if prospects have secured any new business, are developing new products, and so forth.
- Create a blog that includes your opinions, educates prospects, provides news, and encourages reactions and postings from prospects. Carefully establish a personal brand identity for yourself in all social media venues.[15]
- Follow competitors' social media postings to gather competitor intelligence.
- Monitor your social media sites for comments/postings by competitors and unsatisfied customers.
- Use the TweetDeck feature to be alerted whenever a keyword (like your company name or your product) has appeared in any tweet. Use other social media monitoring tools, like HootSuite, to pick up when someone needs help or is dissatisfied.

As an example of the effectiveness of using social networking, an employee of SoftBrands was trying to find a way to connect with the software giant SAP. The employee decided to start following the tweets of a local SAP worker, and this resulted in some small talk via tweets about sports. Eventually this moved to a face-to-face meeting with the prospect and a profitable sale.[16] As another example, IBM has set up Web sites that allow its sales reps to create blogs with feeds tied directly to LinkedIn and Twitter.[17] IBM reps also use Twitter to provide customers information about events and news.

OTHER INTERNET USES

Successful salespeople are using their companies' Web sites, e-mail, listservs, bulletin boards, forums, roundtables, and newsgroups to connect and learn more about individuals and companies that may be interested in their products or services. Building Partnerships 6.1 describes how a medical device salesperson does this.

For example, John Deere, which sells construction and agriculture equipment, uses its Web site to give leads information about products, show them where the nearest dealers are located, and gather their names and addresses if they desire more information. One advantage of Web-based promotions is the number of international leads that can be secured, and John Deere realizes this benefit by making its Web site available in many different languages.

Personal Medicine, a start-up company that is bringing the house call back to medicine, had trouble enlisting both doctors and patients. Its solution was to use

BUILDING Partnerships 6.1

MEDICAL SALES PROSPECTING

I work in medical device sales, specifically orthopedics, so my end users are orthopedic surgeons. I have worked for Smith&Nephew, Inc. for 12+ years across several divisions, with the last 7 being in the Advanced Surgical Division focusing on sports medicine. My customers can also include hospitals and surgery centers, but the decision makers tend to be the surgeons when it comes to the products being used in the operating room.

When prospecting orthopedic surgeons I like to be as thorough as possible. I strongly believe that in order to provide value to the surgeons' practice a salesperson needs to have the ability to empathize as much as possible with them. To do this I believe a person must gather as much information as possible prior to contacting the doctors. I always start by doing a Google search. From that I can find out where they went to medical school and did their residency and fellowship (if they did one). I have a good sense of the philosophy of many of the training programs for orthopedics in the country, so this helps me start to get an idea of how the doctors were trained and, more importantly, who trained them. If I need more information about where they trained I can find more information online, but I also call our local people in the area who usually work at the training hospital. They typically know the system and the attending surgeons well. In my experience, surgeons who have recently finished training (0-3 years out) are less likely to change what they did in training. This information will help me adjust my approach and expectations.

Another area I look for while online is if the surgeons have had any articles published in a medical journal. If so, this will give indications as to what topics they have particular interest or expertise in. Further online research will bring me to social media sites. If these are public I can learn if they are married, have children, and what they like to do socially or what hobbies they have. This sort of research may seem invasive, but as an example I like to know if surgeons have a family to go home to at the end of the day. This will adjust the times when I will try to see them. I can often find out if I have similar interests outside of work with them such as sports, music, art, etc., and if we have any mutual friends.

I also do plenty of research offline. Talking to people who work with the surgeons both in the clinic and the operating room give me a great sense of how they conduct their days, what motivates them, what type of practice they have, how their schedules tend to run and, importantly, what products they are using now and with what techniques. Different surgeons have different priorities, but the top priority is almost always patient outcomes. I take that as a given and then try to get a sense of what else matters most to them. It could be speed, economics, evidence-based medicine, solid scientific data, etc. The people who work with them give me a good sense of this. I have found that by knowing as much as possible prior to contact sends a subtle message that I appreciate the value of the time I have with the doctors and that I appreciate the serious nature of the job. In the end I want to partner with the doctors to help improve the quality of life of their patient population. I take my role in that very seriously.

Once I have gathered as much of this information as I can I will be much better prepared to figure out when and how to approach the surgeons. When and how are of equal value to me. These are very busy professionals who have a very stressful job. Oftentimes I see people in my business focus mostly on the "how" and disregard the "when." If I approach these surgeons to pitch them a product at the wrong time I am doomed before I open my mouth. As I stated previously, empathy is the key.

As a medical device representative my job also involves going into the operating room with the surgeons once they have agreed to try my product, and at that point I become a technical support person. Knowing as much about the surgeons as possible is critical to success, which will make or break the deal in most instances.

Source: Brendan Brooks, orthopedic medical device sales representative. Used with permission.

LeadShare, a Web tool offered by SlideShare. With LeadShare marketers post interesting and important information online (in the form of PowerPoint slides, PDF documents, and so forth). To review that information, the viewer must supply contact information. That information is then sent to the organization posting the information and forms the basis for sales leads.

Firms are also developing **extranets**–Internet sites that are customized for specific target markets. Extranets are usually used to build relationships with current customers, but some companies are also using these sites to generate leads. For example, Turner Broadcasting owns CNN, Cartoon Network, Adult Swim, and truTV. Turner set up an extranet that is accessible only to media buyers. Buyers can access programming information, cable research data, and Turner's salespeople from the site.

MARKETING DEPARTMENT

Firms' marketing departments have developed sophisticated systems to generate inquiries from leads, often including a toll-free number to call for more information, by using advertising and direct mail.[18] For example, Fiskars, a Finnish scissors manufacturer, used a direct marketing campaign targeted at purchasing managers and directors at high-volume German hardware stores. The company sent a special package to each individual that included a unique form of a letter, with each word carefully cut out letter by letter in a single piece of paper, along with a pair of Fiskars to clip out a redeemable coupon for more information. The result was a 19 percent increase in orders during that month.[19]

Marketing departments are more than just tools for filling the sales funnel, however. Account-based marketing efforts use an enterprise account sales/marketing team devoted to the customer. In these teams, marketing, working with the sales team, actually helps develop the account plan, rather than just supply the sales force with contact information, and so forth.

SHOWS, FAIRS, AND MERCHANDISE MARKETS

Many companies display or demonstrate their products at trade shows, conventions, fairs, and merchandise markets.[20] Sales representatives, usually stationed at booths, are present to demonstrate products to visitors, many of whom salespeople have not called on before. In some cases a manufacturer lives or dies by how well it does in these special selling situations. WestRock, a company that manufactures office products such as calendars, depends heavily on the annual national office products association show. Its salespeople report that selling year-round is easier due to the impression the company makes on prospects at the show. And don't forget that one way to prospect is to simply "walk" the show and meet and learn about people who are working at other booths.

Trade shows and fairs help salespeople discover and qualify leads.

Trade shows are short (usually less than a week), temporary exhibitions of products by manufacturers and resellers. In Europe trade shows are called **trade fairs**. Once the show is over, all vendors pack up and leave. The Consumer Electronics Show (with 2.5 million square feet of space) showcases electronics products each year. The more than 2,500 vendors at this show are all manufacturers looking for dealers for their products; the end users of the products are not admitted. Dealers often make an entire year's worth of purchases at the show, so the show is a make-or-break situation for many manufacturers. The New York National Boat Show differs in that it has a dual audience: Vendors exhibit to end users (the boating public) as well as to resellers.

Even firms that do not use resellers may have salespeople involved in trade shows. At many trade shows all attendees are customers. For example, when the Texas High School Athletic Directors hold its annual convention, it also invites manufacturers of products and services to exhibit their products. The trade show is an adjunct of the convention, with the audience composed entirely of end users. Suppliers, like Riddell Helmets, create elaborate booths, develop contests and interesting takeaways, and do on-site demonstrations at these events.

Merchandise markets are places where suppliers have sales offices and buyers from resellers visit to purchase merchandise. The Dallas Market Center, for example, hosts more than 50 separate markets for children's wear, western apparel, linens, and other soft goods. The sellers are the manufacturers or distributors, and they sell only to resellers, not to the public. Sellers may lease showroom space permanently or only during market weeks. Sellers who lease space permanently usually bring in buyers during off-market periods or when no markets are being held.

Buyers visit many vendors during markets, selecting the products they will carry for the next season. In some industries, almost all sales to resellers occur during markets.

Instead of mechanically asking, Are you enjoying the show? or Can I help you with something today? sharp salespeople try to discover whether the lead has a need or a want they can meet. The seller then gives the lead helpful information and gathers information that will be used later in further qualifying the lead and preparing for a sales call. Timely follow-up of leads is critical if sales are to follow a show.

WEBINARS AND SEMINARS

Many firms use seminars and **webinars** (online seminars) to generate leads and to provide information to prospective customers. For example, a local pharmaceutical representative for Bristol-Myers Squibb will set up a seminar for 8 to 10 oncologists and invite a nationally known research oncologist to make a presentation. The research specialist usually discusses some new technique or treatment being developed. During or after the presentation, the pharmaceutical representative for Bristol-Myers Squibb might describe how Squibb's drug Taxol helps in the treatment of ovarian and breast cancer.

What are some key things to keep in mind when planning a webinar or seminar? Make sure your seminar appeals to a specialized market and invite good prospects, especially those prospects who might not be willing to see you one-on-one. The subject should be something your attendees have a strong interest in, while your speaker must be considered an authority on the topic. Try to go as high quality as possible (remember, you're building an image) and consider serving food. Finally, you should take an active role before, during, and after the seminar.

LISTS AND DIRECTORIES

Individual sales representatives can develop prospect lists from sources such as public records, telephone directories, chamber of commerce directories, newspapers, trade publications, club membership lists, and professional or trade membership lists. Secondary sources of information from public libraries also can be useful. For example, industrial trade directories are available for all states. It is often useful to know the **Standard Industrial Classification (SIC)** code or the **North American Industry Classification System (NAICS)** code, which is a uniform classification for all countries in North America, when researching using secondary sources.

Salespeople can purchase a number of prospecting directories and lead-generating publications. You can purchase mailing lists for all gerontologists (specialists in geriatrics), Lions clubs, T-shirt retailers, yacht owners, antique dealers, Catholic high schools, motel supply houses, multimillionaires, pump wholesalers, and thousands of other classifications. These lists can be delivered as printed mailing labels or secured directly from the Web from such sources as www.salesgenie.com.

Salespeople should keep in mind that lists may not be current and may contain inaccurate information regardless of any guarantee of accuracy. In international selling situations, procuring lists can be much more difficult.

DATABASES AND DATA MINING

Sophisticated firms are developing interactive **databases** that contain information about leads, prospects, and customers. For example, Pioneer, one of the country's largest producers of seed corn, has a dynamic database of 600,000 farm operators in the United States and Canada that everyone in the firm can access. The system has resulted in better sales prospecting and more tailored sales presentations.

Companies are using **data mining**, which consists of artificial intelligence and statistical tools, to discover insights hidden in the volumes of data in their databases. For example, Eagle Equipment of Norton, Massachusetts, uses iMarket software to target its sales calls to the best prospects. Using the company's database, the software identifies prospects most likely to buy something and then matches that profile against a database of 12 million businesses. Sales Technology 6.1 describes the importance of using data mining, while Chapter 15 more fully examines the use of data mining and databases.

COLD CALLING

Before learning about other prospecting methods, college students often assume that salespeople spend most of their time making cold calls. In using the **cold canvass method**, or **cold calls** (by call we usually mean a personal visit, not a telemarketing call), a sales representative tries to generate leads for new business by calling on totally unfamiliar organizations. Cold calling can waste a salesperson's time because many companies have neither a need for the product nor the ability to pay for it. This fact stresses the importance of qualifying the lead quickly in a cold call so as not to waste time. Also, today cold calling is considered rude by many purchasing agents and other professionals.

Salespeople often rate making cold calls as the part of the job they like least. Thus, as mentioned earlier, most firms now encourage their salespeople to qualify leads instead of relying on cold calls. In fact, Ameriprise banned cold calling for its salespeople nationwide years ago. This policy forced the reps to use other methods, such as networking and referrals. But sometimes firms require their salespeople to start making cold calls, especially in downtimes. From the Buyer's Seat 6.1 shares some thoughts from one buyer about salespeople who cold call.

Still, some companies use cold calling.[21] And some companies use a selective type of cold calling they refer to as a **blitz:** A large group of salespeople attempts to call on all the prospective businesses in a given geographic territory on a specified day. For example, an office machine firm may target a specific four-block area in Guadalajara, Mexico; bring in all the salespeople from the surrounding areas; and then

SALES Technology 6.1

STREAMLINING PROSPECTING THROUGH THE USE OF BIG DATA

Given the competitive market today, sales organizations' success hinges on solutions to meet customers' needs. New technologies are helping streamline this process; analyzing large amounts of customer and prospect data, referred to as Big Data, provides specific insight into purchasing habits and needs of customers. Today, it is estimated that, on average, only 15 percent of data, that happens to be at a company's disposal, is actually analyzed.

While Big Data are not the only solution to effective prospecting, analytic tools can put salespeople on a more successful track to profitable prospecting. To effectively grow sales, research on which analytical data sources are the best to implement must still be conducted. The best strategy is to find a partner that can best offer a reliable data source to push prospecting efforts.

Traditional prospecting required cold calling, an outdated time-consuming and resource-intensive practice, and that was just to find leads who still needed qualifying. Then came the acquisition of contact lists by lead providers that sometimes resulted in wasted effort. Now, by the way of advanced technology and data analytics of customers and prospects, firms can identify potential customers who have a better chance of building a relationship and turning into a client. For example, companies in the biopharmacy industry are generating customer value analytics (CVA) using Big Data to help find the best way to approach leads and consistently meet the needs of omnichannel prospects and customers, all while lowing customer acquisition costs (CAC). Cold calling is now warm calling with the ability to build rapport to tailor a unique sales message and build long-lasting relationships.

Prospecting through Big Data develops leads in both B2C and B2B sales environments. Furthermore, Big Data help firms better know how to construct targeted messages and successfully predict how a buyer will probably respond to a sales presentation. In summary, Big Data provide a tool to help an organization become most efficient in gaining clients and achieving sales profitability.

Sources: Louis Columbus, "Ten Ways Big Data Is Revolutionizing Marketing and Sales," May 9, 2016, *Forbes.com*; Ilya Semin, Young Entrepreneur Council, "The Sales Shakeup: How Data Is Redefining Sales Prospecting," *The Huffington Post*, December 17, 2015

have them, in one day, call on every business located in that four-block area. The purpose is to generate leads for the local sales representative as well as to build camaraderie and a sense of unity among the salespeople.

SPOTTERS

Some salespeople use **spotters**, also called **bird dogs**. These individuals will, for a fee, provide leads for the salesperson. The sales rep sometimes pays the fee simply for the name of the lead but more often pays only if the lead ends up buying the product or service. Spotters are usually in a position to find out when someone is ready to make a purchase decision. For example, a janitor who works for a janitorial service company and notices that the heating system for a client is antiquated and hears people complaining about it can turn over this information to a heating contractor.

A more recent development is the use of outside paid consultants to locate and qualify leads. Small firms attempting to secure business with large organizations are most likely to use this approach. For example, Synesis Corporation, a small firm specializing in computerized training, used the services of a consultant to identify and develop leads. The result of one lead was a major contract with AT&T.

ethics

Use caution, however, when offering a cash payment to a customer for spotting. Your action may be misconstrued by the customer as exploiting the relationship.

From the **BUYER'S SEAT** 6.1

YES, I'M A PROSPECT...SO DO YOUR HOMEWORK BEFORE SEEING ME!

As a senior buyer in the public sector (the city of Rochester) it's often more difficult for sellers to develop an in-depth relationship with me due to the process surrounding bids and projects. Any purchase below $5,000 can be conducted through the purchasing department, but anything over that requires a public bid opening with sealed bids, such as contracting for construction or the design behind a project. The type of buying and contracting I am involved with changes based on the time of year and weather seasons; in the spring a lot of effort goes toward construction projects. For instance, in the spring there can be trail projects, which require contracting with an organization that has a design service background to first get an estimate of costs and set of specifications; then we'll request and eventually purchase a bid.

Although my procurement process differs, I've experienced many types of prospecting from sellers. Many salespeople make cold calls on me, and the sellers are just trying to push a product or service on me. Yes it sounds cliché, but salespeople can be pushy (a selling technique you will want to avoid if you're calling on me!). From my end this comes across as lack of care. I'll just wait for the conversation to end, hang up, and that'll be the end of it.

For example, recently I had a pushy new salesperson, I'll call her Julie, inquire about a project the city was planning. The problem was, after talking with Julie and informing her to touch base at a later time, she had no interest in following the timeline to respond or follow up at the date that I provided. Zero patience. When buying for the government, there are many t's that must be crossed and i's dotted; each "piece of the puzzle" must fit, meaning it must be in the best interest of the public and best interest politically/economically. In other words, each Rochester city department has to be totally on board. Here, a government purchase must meet certain thresholds and be signed off by multiple city council members, who happen to meet only three times a month. Julie continually called back inquiring about this particular project, which was waiting to be okayed by the city. This sales behavior is very aggressive and Julie came across as interested only in generating a revenue stream, like a car salesman seeking commission and nothing more.

Salespersons prospecting must be willing to listen for needs and be forthcoming in developing a business. They should have my best interests in mind. The most appropriate way to reach out to me is to conduct prior research, whether it's Google or our city Web site. Only then should a seller begin to state how she believes her product or service could help my organization. I encourage you to ask for further information to be provided about a project or request of bid, and show that you care and are truly interested in mutual benefits. Prospecting successfully doesn't just require understanding and accommodating to me as a buyer; it is all about timing as well.

In my point of view, personalities and emotional intelligence dictate how prospecting should be conducted based off the individuals involved. It's easy to identify when that has not been done beforehand! For example, we'll take bids for something such as a body camera for police. A requester from the city will have expertise on a certain product such as a body camera and will determine specs a good product must have and pass it along to us to bid out.

Prospecting for a project goes a long way not only to ensure a smooth and fair bidding process, but we can also do repeat business, especially with consistently low bid prices as a factor. If I find you to be assertive, with poor emotional intelligence and not understanding me and my needs, you will not do well. As a buyer I'll always ask, why? Why your company? Why your product? What makes you unique and valuable?

Source: Anonymous. Used with permission. Names have been changed.

Also, some customers' firms may prohibit such behavior. Sometimes it is better to send a personal thank-you note or small gift to the customer instead.

INSIDE SALESPEOPLE

Firms combine efforts of inside and field salespeople to prospect effectively (inside sales reps were discussed in Chapter 1). For example, Motorola's government division,

Firms combine the efforts of inside and field salespeople to prospect effectively, often using the phone as a first tool for contact with a lead.

©Ingram Publishing RF

which sells mobile communication systems to such entities as police stations and fire departments, can use inside salespeople to generate and then qualify leads. Qualified leads are turned over to field sales representatives if the order is large enough to warrant a personal visit to the buying organization. If the prospect needs a smaller system, the inside salesperson will actually handle the account.

EXPERTISE

Salespeople can prospect by developing their expertise in their field, resulting in prospects seeking information from them. Admittedly, that won't happen for most salespeople when they first graduate from college, but over time they can develop their expertise and seek avenues to showcase their talent.

Salespeople have many ways to demonstrate their expertise in a particular subject. Some will engage in public speaking on topics related to their expertise. Speeches at industry conventions, at luncheons and dinners hosted by prospects and industry representatives, and on college campuses provide outlets for expertise to be disseminated. Salespeople can also demonstrate their expertise in written form, including writing journal articles, publishing articles in trade publications, hosting a blog, and posting on other's blogs. Blogs can be particularly effective since they are an accepted way to reach professionals, are easy to create and share, and can be written in a conversational style that leads enjoy reading.

SALES LETTERS

Prospecting sales letters can be integrated into an overall prospecting plan. One way to make sales letters stand out is to include a promotional item with the mailer. Here are some good examples:[22]

- First National Bank of Shreveport, Louisiana, targeted certified public accountants (CPAs) for one mailer. The bank timed the mailers to arrive on April 16, the day after the federal income tax filing deadline. Included in each mailer was a small bottle of wine, a glass, and cheese and crackers–a party kit designed to celebrate the end of tax season. The bank followed up with telephone calls two days later and ultimately gained 21 percent of the CPAs as new customers.
- Office Depot sent top executives at a large bank a metal suitcase filled with piles of fake money. The box also contained an MP3 player that included videos of how Office Depot could meet that bank's specific needs.
- Sprint sent top decision makers a personal meeting invitation housed in a specially designed attractive box with a Louisville Slugger bat enclosed. Those who agreed to meetings would receive professional baseball jerseys for their favorite baseball teams.

thinking it through What would be your reaction if you received the Louisville Slugger bat just described as part of a direct mail piece? Would there be a better way to gain your attention in such a mailing? If so, how could a salesperson learn what that would be?

The salesperson must first consider the objective of any written communication (like a sales letter or e-mail message) and the audience. What action does the salesperson desire from the reader? Why would the reader want to undertake that action? Why would the reader not want to undertake the action? These questions help guide the salesperson in writing the letter.

The opening paragraph must grab the reader's attention, just as a salesperson's approach must get a prospect's attention in a face-to-face call. The opening gives the readers a reason to continue reading, drawing them into the rest of the letter. Another way to gain attention is to have a loyal client whom the prospect respects write the introduction (or even the entire letter) for the salesperson. Here's an example of an opening paragraph:

> Thanks for stopping by the Datasource booth at the ACUTA Conference in Chicago last week. I hope you enjoyed the show and had some fun shooting hoops with us! Were you there when one highly energetic attendee shot the basketball clear over into the Mac booth? I'll fill you in on the details of what happened next, but first I'd like to invite you to something I know you're not going to want to miss.

The next paragraph or two, the body of the letter, considers why the reader would and would not want to take the desired action. Benefits of taking the action should be presented clearly, without jargon, and briefly. The best-presented benefits are tailored to the specific individual, especially when the salesperson can refer to a recent conversation with the reader. A reference such as the following example can truly personalize the letter:

> As you said during our visit at the show, you're looking for a software firm that can work with a small business like yours without making you feel like a second-class citizen. At Datasource, we've committed ourselves to working exclusively with small to midsize firms like yours.

If the salesperson and the buyer do not know each other, part of the body of the letter should be used to increase credibility. References to satisfied customers, market research data, and other independent sources can be used to improve credibility:

> You may have heard that last year we won the prestigious Youcon Achievement Award, presented by the Tennessee Small Business Development Center in recognition for outstanding service specifically to small businesses. In fact, the small businesses themselves are the voters for the award. We're proud of that award because it tangibly reflects the commitment we've shown. And we have dedicated ourselves to continue in that tradition.

The final paragraph should seek commitment to the desired course of action. Whatever the action desired, the letter must specifically ask that it take place. The writer should leave no doubt in the prospect's mind about what he or she is supposed to do. The writer should make the action for the prospect easy to accomplish, fully explain why it should be done now, and end with a positive picture. Here's an example:

> So I want to personally invite you to a free lunch seminar at Datasource. You'll hear from our partners about the very latest solutions to your technology challenges. The food promises to be great, and the information will be presented in a casual,

small group setting. Please take a moment to reserve your spot at the lunch by visiting our Web site at www.datasourceinc.com or calling 800-999-xxxx. You'll be glad you did.

A postscript (or PS) can also be effective. Postscripts stand out because of their location and should be used to make an important selling point. Alternatively, they can be used to emphasize the requested action, such as pointing out a deadline.

While you are writing, remember to check your work carefully for misspelled words and grammar problems. Make sure you know the correct word to use of the following pairs, and many others like them: it's and its, they're and their, affect and effect, compliment and complement, discreet and discrete.[23]

Proof your work carefully because you often don't see problems in a quick glance, as the following paragraph illustrates:[24]

> i cdnuolt blveiee taht I cluod aulaclty uesdnatnrd waht I was rdanieg. The phaonmneal pweor of the hmuan mnid, aoccdrnig to a rscheearch at Cmabrigde Uinervtisy, it dseno't mtaetr in waht oerdr the ltteres in a wrod are, the olny iproamtnt tihng is taht the frsit and lsat ltteer be in the rghit pclae. The rset can be a taotl mses and you can sitll raed it whotuit a pboerlm. Tihs is bcuseae the huamn mnid deos not raed ervey lteter by istlef, but the wrod as a wlohe.

And of course spell check won't catch everything; the following passed with flying colors:[25]

> I have a spelling checker, it came with my PC. It plainly marks four my revenue mistakes I cannot sea. I've run this poem threw it, I'm sure your pleased too no, its letter perfect in it's weigh, my checker tolled me sew.

Finally, read over your letter to make sure it is crystal clear. You don't want to be guilty of sending out something as confusing as the following (which were official British instructions for storing warheads):[26]

> It is necessary for technical reasons that these warheads should be stored with the top at the bottom, and the bottom at the top. In order that there may be no doubt as to which is the top and which is the bottom, for storage purposes, it will be seen that the bottom of each head has been labeled with the word TOP.

OTHER SOURCES OF LEADS

Many salespeople find leads through personal observation. For example, by reading trade journals carefully, salespeople can learn the names of the most important leaders (and hence decision makers) in the industry. Sellers also read general business publications (such as the *Wall Street Journal*) and local newspapers.

Leads can be found in many other places as well. Some prospect while doing something they enjoy, such as belonging to a cycling club. Salespeople for noncompeting but related products can often provide leads, as can members of trade associations. You can find leads while volunteering in your community, doing things like helping build a house for Habitat for Humanity. Good friends can also provide leads. Of course one of the best ways to learn about new business opportunities is to keep up with regional, national, and world trends from industry surveys, like the U.S. Industrial Outlook.

Nonsales employees within the salesperson's firm can also provide leads. Some companies strongly encourage this practice. For example, Computer Specialists Inc., a computer service firm, pays its nonsales employees a bonus of up to $1,000 for any names of prospective customers they pass along. In one year the program resulted in 75 leads and 9 new accounts.

Government agencies can also supply lead information. The FedBizOpps site, for example, provides information about federal government bid opportunities and can be viewed at www.fbo.gov.

LEAD QUALIFICATION AND MANAGEMENT SYSTEMS

Salespeople need to develop a process for qualifying leads, often called a **lead qualification system.** As mentioned early in this chapter, salespeople must ensure that their leads meet the five basic criteria of a prospect. Let's look more closely at this process.

Many firms view prospecting as a funneling process in which a large number of leads are funneled (or narrowed down) into prospects and some, finally, into customers. Marketing often generates these leads, but it is interesting that most leads thus generated by marketing departments are not followed up by salespeople.[27]

To help salespeople use their time wisely and to increase the number of leads that sellers actually follow up with, firms engage in lead filter and assessment, sometimes called **prequalification,** before turning them over to the field sales force. This can include data verification (making sure the phone number, address, e-mail address is correct), fraud screening (to weed out bots and other devices), and grading/scoring and prioritization of the leads. Many lead qualification systems assign points to a prospect, rather than simply designating them as hot or cold, offering the salesperson more insight into the lead's value. Sometimes the prequalification process is as simple as purchasing a prequalified list.

Salespeople must not only qualify leads but also carefully analyze the relative value of each lead. This part of the process is called a **lead management system**, which is discussed more fully in Chapter 15. Part of the decision process often includes a valuation of the prospects' expected customer lifetime value or return on investment, as well as an appraisal of what types of value the selling firm can add to the prospect. Grading prospects and establishing a priority list result in increased sales and the most efficient use of time and energy. There is even an association dedicated to helping companies manage their leads more effectively: the Sales Lead Management Association.[28]

The use of technology makes lead qualification and management more efficient and effective. For example, IBM has tied its lead generation and management system into its CRM system (CRM systems are more fully discussed in Chapter 15). The results have been better tracking and prioritization of leads and prospects. The scoring system recommended by the Corporate Executive Board rates leads on five traits (organizational basics, operating environment, view of the status quo, receptivity to new or disruptive ideas, and potential for emerging needs) and then, based on the score, offers suggestions on whether to pursue the opportunity.

Salespeople can get leads during volunteering activities.

©Hero Images/Getty Images RF

Any good lead management system, like IBM's, should evaluate the profitability of sales resulting from various lead-generating activities instead of just counting the number of names a particular method yields. Sales analytics analysis may show that the present

BUILDING Partnerships 6.2

KEEP ACCURATE DATA ON CUSTOMERS AND PROSPECTS

The saying "garbage in equals garbage out" rings true with a few of the salespeople who have worked for me over the years. For example, one salesperson who works for me made a prospecting call on a business in her new sales territory. The prospect was very busy and the business owner's wife was not friendly and did not want to be interrupted by a salesperson. She told the salesperson to leave the premises. The salesperson asked her name and if she could give her one of her business cards with her contact information. She replied, "No, I really do not want you coming here anymore, LEAVE NOW."

The salesperson was upset but wanted to document the call. She hoped that the prospect was just having a bad day. In order to document the call in the CRM system the salesperson simply recorded the contact person's name as "Crabby Lady," since she never got the woman's name. She then described in the CRM system how the call went and to wait a long time before calling on the business again.

About a year and a half later the company sent a mailing to the potential prospects in that type of business located in the database. The letter was mailed to the business and was addressed to "Crabby Lady." This obviously did not go over very well with the prospect and blew any opportunity of future sales.

Source: Jim Sodomka, sales and marketing manager, company name withheld upon request, used with permission.

system does not produce enough prospects or the right kinds of prospects. Salespeople may, for example, depend entirely on referred names from company advertising or from the service department. If these two sources do not supply enough names to produce the sales volume and profits desired, other prospecting methods should be considered.

As one uses a lead management and CRM system, care should be taken to ensure mistakes that could backfire in the future don't occur, as Building Partnerships 6.2 illustrates.

OVERCOMING A RELUCTANCE TO PROSPECT

People often stereotype salespeople as bold, adventurous, and somewhat abrasive. But salespeople often struggle with a reluctance to prospect that persists no matter how well they have been trained and how much they believe in the products they sell.

Research shows a number of reasons for reluctance to call, including worrying about worst-case scenarios; spending too much time preparing; being overly concerned with looking successful; being fearful of making group presentations, of appearing too pushy, of losing friends or losing family approval, and of using the phone for prospecting; and feeling intimidated by people with prestige or power or feeling guilt at having a career in selling.

Reluctance to call can and must be overcome to sell successfully. Several activities can help:

- Start by listening to the excuses other salespeople give to justify their call reluctance behavior. Evaluate their validity. You'll usually be surprised to find that most excuses really aren't valid.

Salespeople must learn how to overcome a reluctance to prospect. Managers indicate that some salespeople seem to just want to stay in the office and talk with coworkers, rather than go out and prospect for new customers.

- Engage in sales training and role-playing activity to improve your prospecting skills and your ability to handle questions and rejections that arise.
- Make prospecting contacts with a supporting partner or sales manager. Just his or her presence will often provide additional needed confidence (you won't feel so alone).
- Set specific goals for all your prospecting activity. Put them on your "to do" list. Chapter 15 will provide more direction in this activity.
- Realize the economic value of most prospecting activities. For example, if you keep good records, you may discover that every phone call you make (regardless of whether that particular prospect buys) results in an average of $22 commission in the long run.
- Stop negative self-evaluations from ruling your behavior. Learn to think positively about the future instead of focusing on your past blunders.
- Remember that you are calling on prospects to solve their needs, not just so you can line your pocket with money. You are performing a vital, helpful, important service to your prospects by calling on them. (If this isn't true, maybe you should find another sales job.)
- Control your perceptions of what prospects might say about you, your company, or your products. You don't know what their reactions will be until you meet with the prospects. Leads do buy from salespeople.
- Learn and apply relaxation and stress-reducing techniques.
- Recount your own prospecting successes or those of others.

SELLING YOURSELF

Using these concepts discussed in this chapter can help you find an opportunity that will be perfect for you after graduation. There will be plenty of companies that you will have to qualify to see if they are the best fit for you. Based on your skill set, you can make a decision on whether or not you are a good match for the company. Some questions you may want to ask yourself about the company include: Do I fit the culture of the company? Does the company give you the opportunity to grow professionally? Can you add value to the organization to help fulfill its goals? Does the income opportunity help achieve your goals? Asking these types of questions can help you narrow down your job search after graduation.

Being involved with the resources and opportunities offered by your school can make the decision easier for you. Many schools offer sales clubs, internships, and networking events that will give you a better view of what company is the best fit for you. These opportunities allow you to build long-term business relationships for the future and help you qualify companies that are better suited for you. During these networking events, it is very important to know how to sell yourself. Companies should know why you will be an asset to their team and what you can bring to the table. There will be many candidates applying for the same position, and your ability to sell yourself will be the difference maker in whether or not you will be offered the position.

On the other hand, it is important to know that reluctance to prospecting can hold you back from finding the company that best fits your skill set. More than ever, universities and colleges around the country give students the opportunity to network and connect with many different companies. It is important to take advantage of these opportunities by prospecting many companies based on the criteria you are looking for within a company. Lack of interviewing and connecting with companies will give you less chance of finding the ideal company for you.

Continuing to prospect companies that are best qualified for your skill set will help you reach success earlier in your career. Just like this chapter discussed, reluctance to prospect qualified companies can hold you back from your potential to become a successful sales professional. Prospecting is important in your career as well as when finding a new job.

Karl Macalincag, technology consultant, GDP Technologies. Used with permission.

SUMMARY

Locating prospective customers is the first step in the sales process. New prospects are needed to replace old customers lost for a variety of reasons and to replace contacts lost in existing customers because of plant relocations, turnover, mergers, downsizing, and other factors.

Not all sales leads qualify as good prospects. A qualified prospect has a need that can be satisfied by the salesperson's product, has the ability and authority to buy the product, can be approached by the salesperson, and is eligible to buy.

Many methods can be used to locate prospects. The best source is a satisfied customer. Salespeople can also use the endless-chain method, networking, social media, lists and directories, cold canvassing (including blitzes), spotters, and becoming known as experts via blogs, speeches, and so forth. Companies provide leads to salespeople through promotional activities such as the Internet, inquiries from advertising and direct mail, telemarketing, trade shows, merchandise markets, and webinars/seminars.

Effective prospecting requires a strong plan that hinges on developing a lead qualification and management system and overcoming reluctance to prospect.

KEY TERMS

bird dog 161
blitz 160
buying community 155
center-of-influence method 154
cold call 160
cold canvass method 160
customer referral value (CRV) 151
database 160
data mining 160
endless-chain method 152
exclusive sales territories 150
extranet 158
house accounts 150
insight selling 150
lead 148
lead management system 166
lead qualification system 166
merchandise market 159
negative referral 152
networking 153
North American Industry Classification System (NAICS) 160
prequalification 166
promoter 152
prospect 148
prospecting 148
qualifying the lead 148
referral event 152
referred lead 152
sales funnel 148
selling deeper 152
spotter 161
Standard Industrial Classification (SIC) 160
systems integrator 149
trade fair 158
trade show 158
webinar 159

ETHICS PROBLEMS

1. Suppose you're attending a Chamber of Commerce event. You strike up a conversation with a person you have never met, who turns out to be a sales rep for a competitor. She starts talking about her territory and how she wishes you didn't compete so hard against her. "Tell you what," she says after a moment of thought, "What if you take the northern two counties and I'll just stop making calls there? And I'll take the southern two counties, and you can stop trying to prospect there. Sound good?" What would you say?
2. Suppose a friend of yours hears that you are trying to have a positive presence via a blog you've started. The blog is targeted to your present as well as prospective customers. Your friend says, "That's pretty cool. And I know how I can help. I'll start making comments on your blog that are really positive and I'll link your blog postings to my LinkedIn account, Twitter, and Facebook. And I'll have all of my friends do that same. We'll all pretend to be in the same industry you're selling to, so that will give you a lot of positive word of mouth. Pretty helpful, huh?" How would you reply to your friend?

QUESTIONS AND PROBLEMS

1. Describe a referral event that could be created, assuming you are a salesperson for a local hotel that has a group of conference rooms that can easily host up to 50 people. Your target market consists of local firms and organizations like clubs that have not used the conference rooms before.
2. Describe a time when you had a bad experience with a product or service and told others about it. In essence, you acted as a negative referral. What could the company or salesperson have done to cause you to not be a negative referral?
3. Describe a product or service that is pretty substantial in terms of cost that you hope or intend to buy in the next year. Now, assume that there is a salesperson who would like to know of your interest and hopefully sell you that product or service. Who would be an effective center of influence in this situation? In other words, whom do you know that a salesperson for that product could talk to in order to learn more about your interests and desires?
4. Assume you are a salesperson for large farm implements like tractors and combines. Whom might you use as paid spotters to generate leads?
5. The fear of rejection is one reason that some salespeople have a reluctance to prospect. What can you do now, while you're in school, to help avoid having a fear of rejection when you become a salesperson?
6. Assume you sell office furniture to commercial accounts. Locate at least one merchandise mart and one trade show or fair where you might be able to display your products.
7. How would you develop a prospect list under the following situations?
   a. You belong to a Kiwanis that needs to recruit new members.
   b. You sell paper shredding and disposal services (for sensitive documents) to businesses.
8. Building Partnerships 6.1 described how one medical salesperson engages in prospecting. Using what you know from this chapter, briefly describe three other ways that a medical device salesperson could probably prospect.
9. From the Buyer's Seat 6.1 described the traits of successful and unsuccessful salespeople who sell in the public sector (like to a city). Using the Internet as a source, discover the names and titles of some of the city employees (buyers, engineers, accountants, city councilors, and so forth) where or near where you live. Provide this information for three people.
10. If you were a salesperson for the following, how would you develop a prospect list?
    a. A new line of light fixtures that are energy efficient.
    b. A travel agency specializing in medical tourism (for people traveling to a country other than their own to obtain medical treatment).
    c. A manufacturer of commercial baking and pastry supplies.

CASE PROBLEMS

case 6.1

Haiku Lighting

You are a salesperson for Haiku, a premier manufacturer of lighting fixtures and fans. Today, you're looking to locate prospects for the new Haiku Light fixture. The black fixture easily installs into any can or standard flush setting. The new Haiku light fixtures conserve energy automatically by using smart technology built into the light itself. Thanks to an onboard motion sensor, the light is turned on or off when you enter and leave a room, thereby greatly reducing energy consumption.

Of significant note, the Haiku Lights have 16 brightness settings that adjust automatically. The fixtures can shift color temperature from warm amber (perfect for when you just want to relax) to cool white (which is ideal for the daylight hours), allowing the user to easily set the mood of the room. All of the features can be accessed using a remote controller (included), or via a wireless app, available in all of the common smart phone operating systems. The fixture produces 50% more light than the average 60-watt incandescent bulb, and can last up to 30 times longer. It retails for just $199.

As a salesperson for this new product you would like to identify leads and prospect for new customers. Your territory consists of commercial users and residential home builders.

Questions

1. Create a LinkedIn posting targeted to commercial lighting consultants that would serve as a form of prospecting.
2. Create a series of three tweets that you might send with the hope of informing prospective residential home builders of the new product.

Source: Haiku Home

case 6.2

Chicago Marriott Downtown Magnificent Mile

The Chicago Marriott Downtown Magnificent Mile is a Windy City landmark on Michigan Avenue's Magnificent Mile. Located in the heart of world-class shopping and dining, this hotel is within walking distance of top attractions, including the Navy Pier, Shedd Aquarium, Millennium Park, as well as the landmark Chicago Theater District. The hotel rooms and suites have state-of-the-art flat-screen TVs, deluxe bedding, and ergonomic furnishings. With 66,400 square feet of event space, including 54 meeting rooms, this luxury hotel creates a distinguished venue for business engagements, social gatherings, and elegant wedding receptions. The largest meeting room is the Grand Ballroom with maximum meeting space of 19,193 square feet and a maximum seating capacity of 2,200. The hotel is known for its outstanding service coupled with magnificent style.

Assume that you are a salesperson for the Chicago Marriott Downtown Magnificent Mile. Your goal is to book meetings and conventions from businesses and not-for-profit organizations.

Questions

1. First, study the website for the hotel, so you can become more familiar with its ambience and offerings (search for "Chicago Marriott Downtown Magnificent Mile").
2. Tell how you would use satisfied customers to prospect for meetings and conventions for the upcoming year on your schedule.

Source: Marriot

ROLE PLAY CASE

You recently got your latest copy of *City Business*, which featured the top 10 fastest-growing companies in your city. So you took that list, of which 2 are already customers, and identified several that you think might make good prospects. You then began researching them, finding out who the executive officers are and what the companies are about.

One company, Premiere, is a mattress and pillow manufacturer. It recently developed a line of foam products that it is selling direct to consumers over the Web, a line of business growing very rapidly for the company.

You learned that the company was founded by Jesse Hughes, and he is still the president. His daughter, Shelby Hughes Brock, is the CFO. The CIO is Alex Boyle. But that's all you have time for, as you have a Chamber of Commerce luncheon to attend.

As you are registering for the luncheon at the Longwood Convention Center, you see one of those three registering next to you. You have approximately 45 seconds, as the two of you walk into the ballroom where the luncheon will be held, to introduce yourself and Gartner, and ask for an appointment.

Note: For background information about Gartner, if you haven't been using Gartner all semester, please see the Role Play case information at the back of the book.

To the instructor: Additional information needed to complete the role play is available in the Instructor's Manual.

ADDITIONAL REFERENCES

Belew, Shannon. *The Art of Social Selling: Finding and Engaging Customers on Twitter, Facebook, Linkedin, and Other Social Networks.* New York: AMACOM, 2014.

Blount, Jeb. *Fanatical Prospecting: The Ultimate Guide for Starting Sales Conversations and Filling the Pipeline by Leveraging Social Selling, Telephone, Email, and Cold Calling.* Hoboken, NJ: Wiley, 2015.

Dapko, Jennifer L., and Andrew B. Artis. "Writing Effective Prospecting Emails: An Instructional Guide." *Journal of Selling* 16, no. 1 (2017), pp. 33–47.

Fellingham, Charles. *How to Sell: Succeeding in a Noble Profession: The Complete Guide to Prospecting, Selling, and Negotiating to Win.* New York: Morgan James Publishing, 2016.

Hughes, Tim, and Matt Reynolds. *Social Selling: Techniques to Influence Buyers and Changemakers.* Philadelphia: Kogan Page, 2016.

Hunter, Mark. *High-Profit Prospecting: Powerful Strategies to Find the Best Leads and Drive Breakthrough Sales Results.* New York: American Management Association, 2017.

Kumar, V., J. Andrew Petersen, and Robert P. Leone. "Defining, Measuring, and Managing Business Reference Value." *Journal of Marketing* 77, no. 1 (2013), pp. 68–86.

Nguyen, Bang, Xiaoyu Yu, T. C. Melewar, and Junsong Chen. "Brand Innovation and Social Media: Knowledge Acquisition from Social Media, Market Orientation, and the Moderating Role of Social Media Strategic Capability." *Industrial Marketing Management* 51 (2015), pp. 11–25.

Read, Nicholas A. C. *Target Opportunity Selling: Top Sales Performers Reveal What Really Works.* New York: McGraw-Hill Education, 2014.

Smilansky, Oren. "Six Steps to Social Selling Success." *CRM Magazine* 20, no. 6 (2016), pp. 32–35.

Stratten, Scott. *UnMarketing: Everything Has Changed and Nothing Is Different.* Hoboken, NJ: Wiley, 2016.

Tanner, J. F., Jr. *Dynamic Customer Strategy: Today's CRM.* New York: Business Expert Press, 2013.

Tanner, J. F., Jr. *Turning Models into Customers, in Analytics and Dynamic Customer Strategy: Big Profits from Big Data.* Hoboken, NJ: Wiley, 2014.

©Pressmaster/Shutterstock.com RF

chapter 7

PLANNING THE SALES CALL

SOME QUESTIONS ANSWERED IN THIS CHAPTER ARE

- Why should salespeople plan their sales calls?
- What precall information is needed about the individual prospect and the prospect's organization?
- How can this information be obtained?
- What is involved in setting call objectives?
- Should more than one objective be set for each call?
- How can appointments be made effectively and efficiently?

PROFILE

> *"Precall planning has been the key to my success at Enterprise Fleet Management."*
>
> *Christine Cortina, Enterprise Fleet Management*

PROFILE My name is Christine Cortina and I graduated from Northern Illinois University (NIU) in 2014 with a bachelor's degree in marketing, as well as certificates in Professional Selling and Social Entrepreneurship. During my time at NIU, I took Advanced Professional Selling (MKTG 450) with Dr. Rob Peterson, which has directly impacted my professional and personal life more than any other course I have ever taken. As you may have already realized, the best way to learn is through experience. Advanced Professional Selling gave me the opportunity to learn from experience as an undergraduate. This jump-started my growth as a sales professional and gave me the skill set I needed to land my first job directly out of college.

Courtesy of Christine Cortina

I work for Enterprise Fleet Management, an affiliate of Enterprise Holdings, which owns the Enterprise Rent-A-Car brand. I provide fleet management consulting services and solutions for companies, nonprofits, and government agencies that utilize vehicles as a part of their daily operations. I develop long-term strategic partnerships that help companies and organizations better align their fleet with their overall business objectives and growth plans. I consult with business leaders at the C-suite level, and my role is focused entirely on new business.

Precall planning has been the key to my success at Enterprise Fleet Management. For any organization with a fleet, its vehicles directly correlate to its ability to generate revenue and/or provide services. Depending on the size of the business, a fleet can also be one of its largest expenses. Therefore, there tends to be a lot of people at each company involved in the fleet management decision-making process. Precall planning helps me determine who the true decision maker is and what the best method of and time to contact him or her is. Since I sell to business owners and C-level executives, it can take a long time to get an initial meeting set up. Being more strategic with precall planning can help shorten this process.

Furthermore, I need to be well versed in details regarding my prospect or his or her industry. My potential clients are from a diverse range of industries, ownership types, revenue brackets, and geographic footprints. If I understand the prospect's business environment and what may be affecting the company, I can tailor the reasons to do business with me accordingly. Precall planning helps me prepare impactful questions to ask, so that I gain a better understanding of what is important to my potential client.

As a rule, my minimal objective is to secure the next meeting; my primary goal is to get the next meeting and gather more data; and my ultimate goal is to earn the business. I use my objectives to keep myself on task and control the sales process.

Visit our Web site at: www.efleets.com.

From the BUYER'S SEAT 7.1

HOW I WISH SALESPEOPLE WOULD PLAN FOR A MEETING WITH ME

I'm a buyer at General Electric in the IT department. The types of purchases I deal with on a daily basis are buying contracts, specifically software licensing agreements. This requires a lot of reading on my behalf, with the purpose of mitigating risk of what I'm purchasing. Typically, I work with our attorney on a daily basis to address various things surrounding a contract. Furthermore, I purchase HR contracts (typically buying services; time and materials).

I can tell you this: No buyer ever enjoys receiving cold calls, especially at a high rate! Although this is often a part of the salesperson's job and the buyer's job is to work with salespeople, it's nowhere near the most desirable or efficient form of communication. To obtain a sale I much prefer to see salespeople put forth the effort and dedicate some time to set up an actual meeting and get to know me. It means a lot when a salesperson asks how my family is doing. And even though each buyer has a different communication style, being personable can go a long way.

In my experience the larger the companies, the more their salespeople struggle at successful communication. I recall a time when Xerox constantly kept cold calling me—different salespeople each time as a matter of fact, many not even knowing my name. In this instance it appeared as though they did not document dialogue from past calls since it was the same software pitch each and every time. It's constructive and reassuring when salespeople actually put forth the effort to meet face-to-face and at least portray genuine interest in creating a meaningful relationship.

There are many examples where a company didn't try to build a relationship. A software company, instead of providing a sales call, actually sent a USB drive and file for me to download and learn about its products. This is a very poor sales strategy in my opinion. In another case, I received an e-mail with a link to educate me, the buyer, about the products. Are you kidding? This practice requires buyers to do all the grunt work, and assumes they have the time and knowledge to do it well. In many cases, as a buyer of software I am not the expert on the products. Instead, the expert is the engineer or management, who also at times receive the same annoying e-mails, telling them to learn about the product before some eventual sales call might take place. Another poor practice that can be frustrating to me as a buyer is if company B salespeople constantly contact me when we are already in a contract with company A for the same service. Most contracts last three to five years at set pricing, so if you are company B, it's okay to maintain a relationship with me so when our contract is over you can send in a bid. With that being said, don't become a nuisance where we end up screening your calls. Plan to reach out and touch base periodically, make a relationship, then send in a bid after we post a request for proposal.

I can say as technology has advanced, cold calls have been reduced. Software selling companies are planning more for the meetings and doing more homework, actually identifying our needs prior to an actual meet. That type of planning is appreciated as a buyer.

Finally, I will offer a few more tips. Never be guilty of engaging in the practice of "junk mail" (common in software sales). If you're thinking of working in sales be aware of the sales culture before joining. And always study the culture of the buyer's company prior to planning a sales call. In my experiences, sales culture varies geographically. I understand a salesperson's time is valuable, but so is mine. With proper planning we can achieve a win-win relationship.

Source: Lindsey Buran, used with permission, company name changed, as requested.

WHY PLAN THE SALES CALL?

Successful salespeople know that advance planning of the sales call is essential to achieve in selling. The salesperson should remember that the buyer's time is valuable. Without planning the sales call, a salesperson may cover material in which the buyer has no interest, try to obtain an order even though that is an unrealistic expectation for this sales call, or strike off into areas that veer from what the buyer needs to hear. The results are wasted time and an annoyed prospect, as From the Buyer's Seat 7.1 describes. However, by having a clear plan for the call, the salesperson more likely will not only obtain commitment but also win the buyer's respect and confidence.

Exhibit 7.1

A Flow Diagram of the Planning Process

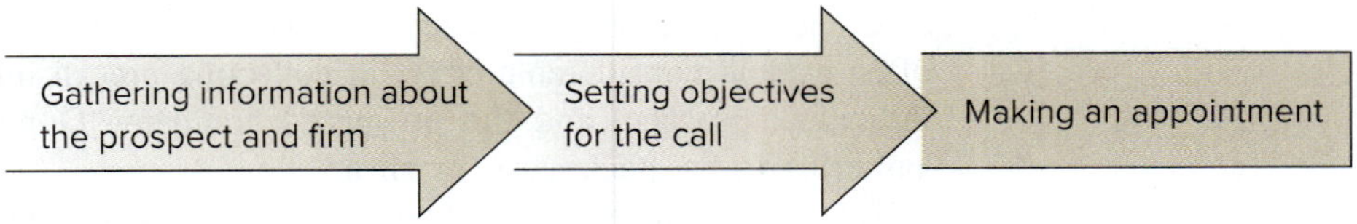

Salespeople should also remember the value of their own time. Proper planning helps them meet their call objectives efficiently and effectively. They then have more time to make additional calls, conduct research on customers, fill out company reports, and complete other necessary tasks. The result is better territory management. (See Chapter 15 for more discussion of time and territory management.)

Of course planning must fit into the salesperson's goals for the account. Some accounts have greater strategic importance and thus require more planning. (See Chapter 13 for a discussion of the types of relationships that a seller can have with a buyer and Chapter 15 about classifying accounts and prospects.) Accounts with which a firm is partnering obviously need the most planning, whereas smaller accounts may warrant less planning. Also, salespeople must not make planning an end in itself and a way to avoid actually making calls. Exhibit 7.1 shows how the concepts in this chapter are related.

OBTAINING PRECALL INFORMATION

Often the difference between making and not making a sale depends on the amount of homework the salesperson does before making a call. The more information the salesperson has about the prospect, the higher the probability of meeting the prospect's needs and developing a long-term relationship. However, the salesperson must be aware of the costs involved in collecting information. At some point, the time and effort put into collecting information become greater than the benefits obtained. And of course, for some cold calls, there will be little if any precall information collected.

Gathering information from individuals in the prospect's firm before making a call on the prospect is often a wise investment of time.

Clearly a salesperson who has been calling regularly on a prospect or customer may not need to collect a lot of additional information; records and notes from prior calls may be adequate to prepare for the sales call. The same holds true for a new salesperson if the previous one kept good records. But beware! In this fast-paced world, things are changing every day. Consider the following dialogue:

SALESPERSON [*walking up to the receptionist of one of his best customers*]: Hello, Jim. I'm here to see Toby. I have some information I promised to share with her about our new manufacturing process. She was pretty excited about seeing it!

RECEPTIONIST [*looking tired*]: Sorry, Jeff. Toby was transferred last week to our Toronto plant. Haven't you heard about our latest reorganization? Just went into effect two weeks ago. I'm still trying to figure it out. It seems that all our engineering people are moving to the Toronto site.

The key: Don't assume that your knowledge about the account is automatically up-to-date.

Of course, before you make an initial call on an important prospect, you will often expend considerable effort in collecting precall information about both the individual prospect and the prospect's company. Don't expect this information gathering to be quick, easy, or cheap.

It is important to learn and maintain current knowledge about both the prospect as an individual and his or her firm. The sections that follow examine these areas more closely. Of course the salesperson should keep in mind privacy concerns, as related in Chapter 2.

THE PROSPECT/CUSTOMER AS AN INDIVIDUAL

Depending on the situation, the following includes information that salespeople might learn about a prospect or a customer (some during the planning phase, and some during relationship development):

ethics

Personal (Some of This Information Can Be Confidential)

- Name (including pronunciation).
- Education.
- Career aspirations.
- Interests (such as hobbies) and disinterests.
- Social style (driver or another category–see Chapter 5).

Attitudes

- Toward salespeople.
- Toward your company.
- Toward your product.

Relationships

- Formal reporting relationships.
- Important reference groups and group norms.
- Bonds that the prospect may have with other salespeople.

Evaluation of Products/Services

- Product attributes that are important.
- Product evaluation process (see Chapter 3 for details).

THE PROSPECT'S/CUSTOMER'S ORGANIZATION

Information about the prospect's or customer's company obviously helps the salesperson understand the customer's environment. This type of information lets the salesperson identify problem areas more quickly and respond accordingly.

For example, in a modified rebuy situation it would not be necessary to educate the prospect about general features common to the product class as a whole. Using the prospect's valuable time by covering material he or she already knows is minimized. Information like the following about the prospect's organization would be helpful (again, some of this will be learned precall, while other will come during relationship development):

Demographics

- Type of organization (manufacturing, wholesaling, retailing).
- Size; number of locations.

- Products and services offered.
- Financial position and its future.
- Overall culture of the organization (risk averse, highest ethical standards, forward thinking).

Prospect's Customers

- Types (consumers, retailers, wholesalers).
- Benefits they seek from the prospect's products and services.

Prospect's Competitors

- Who they are.
- How they differ in their business approaches.
- Prospect's strategic position in the industry (dominant, strong, weak).

Historical Buying Patterns

- Amount purchased in the product category.
- Sole supplier or multiple suppliers. Why?
- Reason for buying from present suppliers.
- Level of satisfaction with suppliers.
- Reasons for any dissatisfaction with suppliers or products currently purchased.

Current Buying Situation

- Type of buying process (new task, straight rebuy, or modified rebuy—see Chapter 3).
- Strengths and weaknesses of potential competitors.

People Involved in the Purchase Decision

- How they fit into the formal and informal organizational structure.
- Their roles in this decision (gatekeeper, influencer, or the like).
- Who is most influential.
- Any **influential adversaries** (carry great influence but are opposed to us)?
- Current problems the organization faces.
- Stage in the buying cycle.

Policies and Procedures

ethics

- About salespeople.
- About sales visits.
- About purchasing and contracts.

thinking it through

It's your first week on the job as a new salesperson. Your sales manager tells you to collect a lot of information about the prospects you call on, including their preferred political party and their children's names. What would be your reaction to her request? If you didn't want to ask these personal questions, how would you approach the situation with your manager?

SOURCES OF INFORMATION

Gathering all the information listed in the preceding sections for every prospect and organization is initially impossible. The goal is to gather what is both possible and profitable. Remember, your time is valuable! Also, you don't want to fall into the trap sometimes referred to as **analysis paralysis**, which can occur if you prefer to spend practically all your time analyzing situations and finding information instead of making sales calls. Salespeople must strike a proper balance between time spent in acquiring information and time spent making calls. The Marine Corps teaches what it calls the 70 percent solution: If you've got 70 percent of the information, have done 70 percent of the analysis, and feel 70 percent confident, then act!

It is important to gather useful information—not just piles of trivial facts about a prospect. In addition, salespeople need to check the quality of any data gathered rather than assuming they are good. Salespeople must also be concerned about information overload, which can be detrimental to their jobs. As Sales Technology 7.1 describes, there are new technology tools available to help in that process.

RESOURCES WITHIN YOUR COMPANY

One of the best sources of information can be the records in your own company, especially if your firm has developed a CRM system, as introduced in Chapter 6.[1] The most useful CRM systems include, in addition to standard demographic information, information about any direct contacts with the prospect (from direct mail inquiries, inside sales calls, online requests, social media contact, or the like), a sales history for the firm, whether anyone from your company has called on the prospect, and the results of any sales meetings.

Firms are devising many ways to keep the field sales force well informed. Some are using **sales portals**: online databases that include many sources of information in one place. This information can include items like account data, competitor intelligence, and news about the company, the industry, and the economy. All the salesperson has to do is use a single log-on to access all this information. For example, Delta Air Lines salespeople can log in to their company's portal and quickly and easily access key insights about their business customers.

Even if your firm doesn't have such a database, you should try to gather information about your prospect. For example, wouldn't it be nice to find out before, as opposed to during, a sales call that the prospect used to be a big customer of your firm but quit for some reason?

For important sales, you may well be working with a sales team that interacts with a prospect (a topic more fully addressed in Chapter 16). This team, sometimes called a **selling center**, consists of all the people in the selling organization who participate in a selling opportunity. Members of the team may be able to provide or help you secure needed information.

THE INTERNET AND SOCIAL MEDIA

A first place to look for information would be the prospect company's own Web page. It is amazing what you can find on company Web pages.

Don't forget to use social media like LinkedIn and Facebook to learn more about prospects, as described in Chapter 6. And there are many business information providers online, like InsideView, DiscoverOrg, Pipl.com, and ZoomInfo, that salespeople can use to extract information about companies and people from millions of published sources. Some of this information is free, and some requires payment for more exact information.

SALES Technology 7.1

SALES ACCELERATION TECHNOLOGY

A new category of sales software being utilized is referred to as "sales acceleration technology." This acceleration technology seeks to capitalize on sales revenue by influencing the most efficient and effective sales practices, from precall processes to follow-up processes. With automation serving as an aid in all sales processes, this not only increases the pace of sales but also provides opportunity for sales reps to grow their business by generating leads, more effectively plan for the call, and having more enlightening conversations in needs identification. Sales technology is being implemented in many business organizations, and it is predicted that in just a few years, all big companies such as the Fortune 500 will be utilizing some combination of sales acceleration technology, which is also referred to as a sales stack.

Below is a list and brief description of some sales acceleration technology to help sales planning:

Configure price quote (CPQ) software—Helps companies produce accurate sales price quotes and proposals.

E-mail tracking software—Provides templates for e-mail and lead tracking capability.

Call tracking software—Allocates leads effectively for inside salespeople.

Lead prioritization software—Prioritizes revenue by classifying sales-ready leads.

Predictive analytics software—Uses data to accurately predict sales opportunities by modeling.

Sales content management software—Provides relevant content to sales reps at the appropriate stage in the sales process.

In the past the sales industry lagged behind the utilization of technological tools compared to other business industries, such as marketing. Prior to this arrival of automated technologies, organizations entered business data manually whether it was in spreadsheets, charts, or note taking, and decisions about planning were just skills that salespeople had developed over time. Sales systems such as CRM then provided a boost in productivity and efficiency of individual salespersons due to the customer data storage capabilities. With that being said, even though the process has changed through the use of a CRM system, in some cases the outcome hasn't. Sales acceleration takes it to the next level. These tools link sales calls with client data to properly position available resources in the right framework. In that way, sales acceleration tools are more advanced systems to benefit salespeople and fully capitalize on already existing CRM systems.

Using sales acceleration, buyer patterns are more transparent and sales procedures are updated. The era of going door-to-door or just explaining a product's specifications in a presentation are long gone. With so much information available buyer's usually conduct thorough research on their own. Sophisticated automated tools, like sales acceleration technology, are helping managers and salespeople plan a sales call and better meet customer needs with the outcome of increasing revenues and achieving long-term success.

Sources: Jesse Davis, "What Is Sales Acceleration Technology?"; *Young Entrepreneur Council*, "The Sales Shakeup: How Data Is Redefining Sales Prospecting", *The Huffington Post*, December 17, 2015; "Sales Stack 2017: The Tools", April 27, 2017.

SECRETARIES AND RECEPTIONISTS

ethics

Secretaries and receptionists in the prospect's firm usually are a rich source of information. Be courteous, however, because secretaries and receptionists are accustomed to having salespeople pry for all sorts of free information. Prioritize your questions and provide justification for asking them. Above all, treat secretaries and receptionists with genuine respect. Dawn Hedges, a Zimmer salesperson who sells surgical joint replacements, has built tremendous relationships with the receptionists she calls on. For example, she knows one receptionist who doesn't let Dawn's competitors in to see the doctors. And the receptionist collects any brochures left with her by competitors and then calls Dawn and gives her the information.[2]

NONCOMPETING SALESPEOPLE

Another source for precall information is noncompeting salespeople. In fact, one of the best sources of information is the prospect's own salespeople because they empathize with your situation.

TRADITIONAL SECONDARY SOURCES

Traditional secondary data sources can also be helpful. Firms such as Standard & Poor's, Hoover's, and Moody's publish a number of informative documents in print and online that are available in many public libraries. These sources can help answer questions about brand names, key contacts, historical information, the current situation and outlook for the firm and the industry, location of plants and distribution centers, market shares, and so on.

THE PROSPECT

Much information can be gleaned directly from the prospect. However, don't expect prospects to sit down and answer any and all questions you might have, especially for topics where the information is fairly easy to get (like what products the prospect makes or sells). Prospects don't have time to fill you in on all the details of their business. If you don't know the basics, many prospects will justifiably refuse to deal with you.

It is also worth mentioning that just as you are gathering information about the prospect prior to a meeting, the prospect often does collect information about you. Even before the sale your prospect can request price quotes via e-mail. He or she can also view your Web page as well as your competitors' Web pages. And the prospect can easily chat with colleagues and read about you on newsgroups, review sites, blogs, and social media sites to learn about you and your firm. Any salesperson who doesn't understand these realities won't be prepared for the kinds of questions a prospect might ask or for comments a prospect might make.

OTHER SOURCES

Many other sources can provide information. Some information may have been gleaned at a trade show the prospect attended. Much information will be in the lists and directories from which the prospect's name came. For example, a center of influence will often be able to provide information to a Merrill Lynch financial advisor about her friends. Your current customers can often provide information about new clients. Occasionally a prospect will be important enough to warrant hiring an outside consultant to collect information, especially if you are gathering precall information for international selling. Although some information about foreign companies is available, much will not be obtainable. Salespeople in the United States are often amazed at the lack of information about foreign companies. Two good sources are the U.S. government's export portal and the U.S. Commercial Service Market Research Library (with over 100,000 industry and country-specific market reports).

SETTING CALL OBJECTIVES

The most important step in planning is to set objectives for the call.[3] Merely stating the objective "I want to make a sale" or "to tell her about my product" will not suffice. The customer's decision-making process (see Chapter 3) involves many steps, and salespeople need to undertake many activities as they guide customers through the process.

Yet, as Neil Rackham, an internationally respected sales researcher, notes, "It's astonishing how rarely salespeople set themselves call objectives of any kind—let alone effective ones. Although most books on selling emphasize the importance of clear call objectives, it's rare to see these exhortations turned into practice."[4] Why? Probably because many salespeople want to start doing something instead of "wasting time" planning. But without a plan, they actually increase their chances of wasting time.

As a first step in setting objectives, the salesperson should review what has been learned from precall information gathering. Any call objectives should be based on the results of this review. Also, the seller must keep in mind the relationship the firm wishes to have with the prospect. Not all prospects will or should become strategic partners with the seller's firm. Call objectives should not be created in a vacuum. They should be developed while taking into account the firm's goals, the sales team's goals, and the salesperson's goals. As has been said, "If you don't know where you're going, you may wind up somewhere else," and "If you don't know where you're going any road will take you there."

In their well-received sales training seminars and books about strategic selling, Miller and Heiman stress the importance of sales call planning being related to the firm's strategic goals for the account.[5] This important topic is covered in Chapter 15. For now, realize that call objectives are based on strategic decisions about the account.

CRITERIA FOR EFFECTIVE OBJECTIVES

All objectives should be specific, realistic, and measurable. A call objective that meets only one or two of these criteria will be an ineffective guide for the salesperson. We now examine each criterion in more detail.

An objective must be specific to be effective. It should state precisely what the salesperson hopes to accomplish, what the objective targets are, and any other details (suggested order quantity, suggested dates for future meetings, length of time needed for a follow-up survey, or the like). Specific objectives help the salesperson avoid "shooting from the hip" during the presentation and perhaps moving the prospect along too rapidly or too slowly.

Objectives must also be realistic. Inexperienced salespeople often have unrealistic expectations about the prospect's or customer's response in the sales call. For example, if Kia Motors currently uses Sony radios in all of its models, a Philips salesperson who expects Kia to change over to Philips radios in the first few sales calls has an unrealistic objective. It is important for sellers to plan objectives for a call that can be accomplished within the time allocated for that sales call. That doesn't mean the objectives should be easy. In reality, challenging but reachable goals tend to lead to better performance.

For objectives to be realistic, the salesperson needs to consider factors such as cultural influences. For example, some firms have an extremely conservative corporate culture. Creating change in such a culture is time consuming and often frustrating for the seller. The national culture is important in selling to international prospects. When selling to Arab or Japanese businesses, salespeople should plan to spend at least several meetings getting to know the other party. Developing relationships with Chinese businesspeople requires a great deal of entertaining. Selling in Russia is often slowed because of bureaucracy and incredible amounts of red tape. As these examples illustrate, culture is an important consideration in attempts to set realistic call objectives.

Finally, call objectives must be measurable so salespeople can objectively evaluate each sales call at its conclusion and determine whether the objectives were met. This suggests they should be written down. If a salesperson's stated objective is to get acquainted with the prospect or to establish rapport, how can the salesperson assess whether this goal was achieved? How can someone measure "getting acquainted"? To what extent would the salesperson have to be acquainted with the prospect to know that he or she achieved the sales call objective? A more measurable sales call objective (as well as a more specific and realistic one) is something like the following: to get acquainted with the prospect by learning which clubs or organizations she or he belongs to, which sports the prospect follows, what his or her professional background is, and how long the prospect has held the current position. With this revised call objective, a salesperson can easily determine whether the objective was reached.

A simple way to help ensure that objectives are measurable is to set objectives that require a buyer's response. For example, achievement of the following objective is easy to measure: to make a follow-up appointment with the buyer.

Successful salespeople in almost every industry have learned the importance of setting proper call objectives. Pharmaceutical salespeople for Novartis set clear objectives for each sales call they make to a physician. Then they lay out a series of objectives for subsequent calls so they know exactly what they hope to accomplish over the next several visits. One industrial products sales manager recommends that her salespeople keep their call objectives in view while they are on the sales call, helping them focus on the true goals of the sales call. Both these examples share a common theme: The salesperson needs to set specific, realistic, measurable call objectives. Exhibit 7.2 lists examples of call objectives that meet these criteria.

Some trainers use the acronym SMART to help salespeople remember how to set proper call objections. SMART suggests that call objectives should be specific, measurable, and achievable but realistic and time based.

Exhibit 7.2
Examples of Call Objectives

Objectives Related to the Process Leading Up to the Sale

- To have the prospect agree to come to the Atlanta branch office sometime during the next two weeks for a hands-on demonstration of the copier.
- To set up another appointment for one week from now, when the buyer will allow me to do a complete survey of her printing needs.
- To inform the doctor of the revolutionary anticlotting mechanism that has been incorporated into our new drug and have her agree to read the pamphlet I will leave.
- To have the buyer agree to pass my information along to the buying committee with his endorsement of my proposal.
- To have the prospect agree to call several references that I will provide to develop further confidence and trust in my office-cleaning business.
- To have the prospect agree on the first point (of our four-point program) and schedule another meeting in two days to discuss the second point.
- To have the prospect initiate the necessary paperwork to allow us to be considered as a future vendor.

Objectives Related to Consummating the Sale

- To have the prospect sign an order for 100 pairs of Calvin Klein jeans.
- To schedule a co-op newspaper advertising program to be implemented in the next month.
- To have the prospect agree to use our brand of computer paper for a trial period of one month.
- To have the retailer agree to allow us space for an end-of-aisle display for the summer promotion of Raid insect repellent.

Even a salesperson who fails to achieve the primary call objective will be encouraged to at least achieve the minimum call objective.

SETTING MORE THAN ONE CALL OBJECTIVE

Salespeople have learned the importance of setting multiple objectives for a sales call. Not only do they set a **primary call objective** (the actual goal they hope to achieve) before each sales call; they also set a **minimum call objective** (the minimum they hope to achieve) because they realize the call may not go exactly as planned (the prospect may be called away or the salesperson may not have all the necessary facts). On the other hand, the call may go better than the salesperson originally thought it would. Thus, although rarely achieved, an **optimistic call objective** (the most optimistic outcome the salesperson thinks could occur) is also set. The optimistic call objective will probably relate to what the salesperson hopes to accomplish for the account over the long term (that is, the account objectives–see Chapter 15).

The primary call objective, for example, of a Nestlé rep might be to secure an order from a grocer for 10 cases of Nestlé Semi-Sweet 12-ounce Morsels for an upcoming coupon promotion. That is what the seller realistically hopes to accomplish in the call. A minimum call objective could be to sell at least 5 cases of the Morsels, whereas an optimistic call objective would be to sell 20 cases, set up an end-of-aisle display, and secure a retail promotional price of $5.68.

Multiple objectives for a single call have many benefits. First, they help take away the salesperson's fear of failure because most salespeople can achieve at least their stated minimum objective. Second, multiple objectives tend to be self-correcting. Salespeople who always reach their optimistic objective realize they are probably setting their sights too low. On the other hand, if they rarely meet even their minimum objective, they probably are setting their goals too high.

It is possible to have more than one primary call objective for a single call. For example, several primary objectives a salesperson might hope to accomplish in a single meeting are to sell one unit, be introduced to one other member of the buying center, and have the prospect agree to send along a packet of information to an executive. In this example, if the salesperson genuinely hopes and expects to achieve all three objectives in the next meeting, they will all be considered primary call objectives. To aid in planning the call, some trainers suggest that the salesperson further prioritize these primary objectives into two groups: The most important primary objective is called the primary call objective, whereas the remaining ones become **secondary call objectives.** So, in this example, if selling the product is the most important thing to accomplish in the next meeting, the objectives will be as follows:

Primary call objective	Sell one unit.
Secondary call objectives	Be introduced to one other member of the buying center.
	Have the prospect agree to send along a packet of information to an executive.

SETTING OBJECTIVES FOR SEVERAL CALLS

By developing a series of specific objectives for future calls, the salesperson can develop a comprehensive strategy for the prospect or customer. This approach is especially important in a partnering relationship. To illustrate the use of multiple call objectives, Exhibit 7.3 gives a set of call objectives for visits over a period of

Exhibit 7.3
Multiple Call Objectives of a Samsung Salesperson Selling to Johnson Electronics

Overall Plan Developed on Oct. 1		Actual Call Results	
Expected Date of the Call	Call Objective	Date of Call	Call Results
Oct. 10	Secure normal repeat orders on F88 and F92. Increase normal repeat order of F100 LED Smart TV from three to five units. Provide product information for new LED Smart TV F104.	Oct. 10	Obtained normal order of F88. Steve decided to drop F92 (refused to give a good reason). Purchased only four F100 Smart TVs. Seemed responsive to F104 but needs a point-of-purchase (POP) display.
Oct. 17	Erect a front-counter POP display for F104 and secure a trial order of two units.	Oct. 18	Steve was out. His assistant didn't like the POP (thought it was too large). Refused to use POP. Did order one F104. Told me about several complaints with F100.
Nov. 10	Secure normal repeat orders for F88, F92, and F100. Schedule one co-op newspaper ad for the next 30 days featuring F104. Secure an order for 6 F104s.	Nov. 8	Obtained normal orders. Steve agreed to co-op ad but bought only five F104s. Thinks the margins are too low.
Nov. 17	Secure normal repeat orders of F88, F92, and F100. Secure an order for 10 F104s.	Nov. 18	Obtained normal order on F88, but Steve refused to reorder F100. Claimed the competitor product (Sony) is selling much better. Obtained an order of 15 units of F104.

time. The left side of the exhibit contains the long-term plan and each call objective that the Samsung salesperson developed for Johnson Electronics. Note the logical strategy for introducing the new product, the F104 LED Smart TV. The right side of Exhibit 7.3 shows the actual call results.

The salesperson was not always 100 percent successful in achieving the call objectives. Thus, several subsequent objectives needed to be modified. For example, because the meeting on October 10 resulted in the buyer dropping F92 LED Smart TVs, the call objectives on November 10 and November 17 need to reflect that Johnson Electronics no longer carries the F92 LED Smart TVs. The seller may also want to add a call objective for October 17: to discuss more about the situation with the F92 (because of the outcome of the October 10 meeting) and perhaps try to reintroduce it. This example illustrates the importance of keeping good records, making any necessary adjustments in the long-term call objectives, and then preparing for the next sales call. One sales vice president for a large sales force has some specific advice about setting multiple call objectives:

> The primary objective of the first session is to have another chance to visit. What this allows you to do is have your standards relatively low because you are trying to build a long-term relationship. You should be very sensitive to an opportunity to establish a second visit. What you want to do is identify aspects of the business conversation that require follow-up and make note of them. . . . The key is not the first visit . . . it is the second, the third, the twenty-second visit.[6]

Some industries typically have a long interval between when a prospect is first visited and when an actual sale is consummated. If so, this factor needs to be considered when setting up multiple call objectives and may imply that others get involved in the selling cycle. For example, the typical sale of a Silicon Optronics Image Sensor scanner (an image sensor for automated inspection applications in industrial plants) could take several years to close. After having its field sales force demonstrate the image-sensing scanner, the company can use inside sales reps (see Chapter 1 for a description of inside salespeople) to keep the prospects updated in a fashion that is consistent with the prospects' buying time frames. Silicon Optronics may also send out newsletters and updates several times a year to prospects. It is important for salespeople to consider the company's other promotional efforts when developing multiple call objectives for a prospect.

When setting multiple call objectives, the salesperson should obviously consider whom to call on in upcoming meetings. Although it seems obvious that the decision maker (who is often a middle manager for many products and services) should be included in those calls, visiting briefly with senior-level managers may also make sense. But what information would you share with the CEO, for example? As discussed in Chapter 1, the answer is the **customer value proposition (CVP)**: a written statement (usually one or two sentences) that clearly states how purchasing your product or service can help solve the customer's perceived business issue ("BI"). Further, the CVP focuses on what an individual manager needs to address and resolve to be able to better contribute to overall company objectives. The customer value proposition will be more fully discussed in Chapter 9 and will include numerous examples. Frequently the problem needing assistance involves a significant impediment to the firm's revenues and profits. Four common "BI's" include the following:[7]

- Increase revenue, market share, and shareholder value.
- Increase efficiency and productivity.
- Manage costs.
- Control quality and reliability.

Often a very important consideration is the success of the individual who is your contact within the customer's firm. And there needs to be a struggle (distinct emotion) associated with it.

Appointments increase the chances of seeing the right person and having uninterrupted time with the prospect.

©iStockphoto/Getty Images RF

BUYERS ARE SETTING GOALS ALSO

Salespeople must understand that buyers are often also setting objectives for the salesperson's sales call. These objectives are based on perceptions of how the salesperson's product or service can add value, as described in Chapters 1 and 3. The salespeople's job is to discover what customers value and then find ways to improve customer value relative to their own products or services.

What are some things that buyers look for to increase value? Purchasing managers continually point to the following areas, for which they set goals: on-time delivery, products that are exactly to specifications, competitive pricing, proper packaging/paperwork, technical support/service, level of technological innovation, and good emergency response.

MAKING AN APPOINTMENT

After gathering precall information and setting objectives, the salesperson's next step is generally to make an appointment. Appointments dignify the salesperson and help get the sales process off to a good start by putting the salesperson and the prospect on the same level—equal participants in a legitimate needs solution process. Appointments also increase the chances of seeing the right person and having uninterrupted time with the prospect.

Sales representatives use different contact methods for different customers. It's also important to point out that attitude (and the salesperson's mood) can have a tremendous impact on success in making appointments. This section describes how to see the right person at the right time and the right place, how to interact with gatekeepers, and how to gain an appointment.

THE RIGHT PERSON

Some experts emphasize the importance of going right to the top and making the first call on the highest-level decision maker. After carefully studying more than 35,000 sales calls, Neil Rackham offers a radically different view.[8] His research suggests that a salesperson should initially try to call on the **focus of receptivity**—the person who will listen receptively and give the seller needed valuable information. Note that this person may not be the decision maker or the one who understands all of the firm's problems. In fact, this person might not even be in the buying center. (See Chapter 3 for details about various people who serve as buying center members.) But this person will talk to the salesperson and provide information.

The focus of receptivity, according to the research, will then lead the salesperson to the **focus of dissatisfaction:** the person who is most likely to perceive problems and dissatisfactions. Finally, the focus of dissatisfaction leads to the **focus of power:** the person who can approve, prevent, and/or influence action. Getting to the focus of power too quickly can lead to disaster because the seller has not yet built a relationship and does not really know the buyer's needs. In summary, Rackham notes, "There's a superstition in selling that the sooner you can get to the decision maker the better. Effective selling, so it's said, is going straight to the focus of power. That's a questionable belief."[9]

Recent research has indicated that a salesperson should work with specific types of individuals because they are better at generating consensus in the buying firm.[10] These include "go-getters," those who are always on the lookout for good ideas; "teachers," those who love to share insights and ideas with others in the firm; and "skeptics," those who tend to be cautious and generally slow down the adoption of new processes. These three groups, collectively called "mobilizers," will question, be skeptical, yet help the firm move in the right direction when convinced.

Often someone needs to introduce you to the decision maker, especially in some cultures. For example, to do business with companies in Mideast countries, it is often necessary to have introductions by trusted individuals. Former senators, ambassadors, and even celebrities provide this role.

Frequently in industrial selling situations, as Chapter 3 described, no single person has the sole authority to buy a product because it is a team buying decision. For example, a forklift sales representative for Clark may have to see the safety engineer, the methods engineer, the materials-handling engineer, and the general superintendent before selling the product to a manufacturing company. In this case the salesperson should usually try to arrange a meeting with the entire group as well as with each individual.

Videoconferencing makes it easy for a U.S. salesperson to make a presentation in Germany.

THE RIGHT TIME

There is little agreement on the subject of the best time for a sales interview; obviously the most opportune time to call will vary by customer and type of selling. The salesperson who calls on wholesale grocers, for example, may find from experience that the best times to call are from 9 a.m. to 11 a.m. and from 1:30 p.m. to 3:30 p.m. A hospital rep, on the other hand, may discover that the most productive calls on surgeons are made between 8:30 a.m. and 10 a.m. and after 4 p.m. For most types of selling, the best hours of the day are from approximately 9 a.m. to 11:30 a.m. and from 1:30 p.m. to 4 p.m.

Is there a best day to call on a prospect? According to InsideSales.com, Thursday is best, followed by Wednesday, with Tuesday being the worst day.[11]

THE RIGHT PLACE

ethics

Meetings can occur just about anywhere, including by video on the Internet. The sales call should take place in an environment conducive to doing business. Such is not always the case, however. For example, some salespeople still take customers to topless bars. In addition to distractions, topless bars present a number of problems for the salesperson who uses them to achieve sales. For example, is it ethical to gain business by using such tactics? Also, once a buyer has purchased on the basis of this entertainment, chances are the seller will have to keep it up or lose the customer. Salespeople should also understand that their companies do care about where they meet a client and are tracking that information for a number of purposes.

Videoconferencing–meetings in which people are not physically present in one location but are connected via voice and video–is growing in usage. In a variant on videoconferencing, called **Webcasting** or **virtual sales calls**, the meeting is broadcast over the Internet.[12] For example, due to downsizing, emWare, Inc. has only eight salespeople. According to Michael Nelson, CEO of emWare, the use of virtual sales calls is now necessary and is actually quite successful. Salespeople should learn how to plan for such meetings. One key is to carefully plan all technical elements of the presentation and to rehearse them as much as possible. (Chapter 9 provides more insight into practicing and avoiding problems.)

CULTIVATING RELATIONSHIPS WITH SUBORDINATES

Busy executives usually have one or more subordinates who plan and schedule interviews for them. These **screens** (or **barriers**, as salespeople sometimes call them) often make seeing the boss difficult. These screens can also take on the role of gatekeepers for the buying center (Chapter 3 discusses gatekeepers).

Sales strategists have identified several ways to interact with a screen:

ethics

- The salesperson can work "through the screen." The seller has to convince the gatekeeper that a meeting with the boss is in the boss's best interests.
- The salesperson can go "over the screen." While talking to the screen, the seller drops names of people higher up in the organization. The screen may allow the seller in to see the boss right away for fear of getting into trouble.

Salespeople should work to achieve friendly relationships with the prospect's subordinates.

- The salesperson can go "under the screen" by trying to make contact with the prospect before or after the screen gets to work (or while the screen is taking a coffee break). This is a strategy that can easily backfire. For example, having pushy, aggressive salespeople who constantly bypass screens and formal committees can result in customer dissatisfaction, and even refusal to do business with the seller.

TELEPHONING FOR APPOINTMENTS

Field salespeople can save many hours by phoning, or having others phone for them, to make appointments. Chapter 4 provided many insights on how to use the phone effectively and suggested a way to gain an appointment with a prospect.

The goal of this type of telephone call is to make an appointment, not to sell the product or service. Exhibit 7.4 shows appropriate responses to common objections that Xerox copier salespeople encounter when making appointments. Salespeople need to anticipate objections and decide exactly how to respond, as Chapter 10 will more fully discuss.

Exhibit 7.4
Responses to Objections concerning Appointments

Objection from a Secretary	Response
I'm sorry, but Mr. Wilkes is busy now.	What I have to say will take only a few minutes. Should I call back in a half hour, or would you suggest I set up an appointment?
We already have a copier.	That's fine. I want to talk to Mr. Wilkes about our new paper flow system design for companies like yours.
I take care of all the copying.	That's fine, but I'm here to present what Xerox has to offer for a complete paper flow system that integrates data transmission, report generation, and copiers. I'd like to speak to Mr. Wilkes about this total service.
Objection from the Prospect	**Response**
Can't you mail the information to me?	Yes, I could. But everyone's situation is different, Mr. Wilkes, and our systems are individually tailored to meet the needs of each customer. Now . . . [benefit statement and repeat request for appointment].
Well, what is it you want to talk about?	It's difficult to explain the system over the telephone. In 15 minutes, I can demonstrate the savings you get from the system.
You'd just be wasting your time. I'm not interested.	The general objection is hiding a specific objection. The salesperson needs to probe for the specific objection: Do you say that because you don't copy many documents?
We had a Xerox copier once and didn't like it.	Probe for the specific reason of dissatisfaction and have a reply, but don't go too far. The objective is to get an appointment, not sell a copier.

BUILDING Partnerships 7.1

PLANNING FLEXIBILITY IN DENTISTRY SALES CALLS

Plan for being flexible in your sales calls. I am in dental sales (I am referred to as a dental representative), and so my clients are key staff members including doctors of dentistry (dentists) and dental hygienists. Right now my sales meetings usually occur like clockwork, a revolving three-week set routine of planned sales calls with my current customers. So much so that one time when I "missed" a sales call, the dental office contacted me asking if I was all right. Needless to say the wrong week but right day was marked on its calendar.

Plans in life often change; this can be true in sales as well. For example, I can be scheduled to have a sales call in Wabash on Monday afternoon, but suddenly have to change plans if that given office becomes too busy. In this industry an office can get jam-packed because emergencies can make for a chaotic day, causing its schedules to be filled up. In that case a planned sales call will have to be delayed. As I navigate through the day, I must be prepared to possibly add or cancel planned sales calls.

My visits on a given day can include 500 miles of traveling, resulting in a limited number of calls I can make. If an office is swamped, plans of that day must be changed and a new scheduled time booked. This is made easier when I'm in Seattle, my hometown. Although I make more calls on those days, time slots can be altered more easily with closer offices and much less travel time.

My job has a few interesting twists. For example, while I sell my own products, occasionally manufacturers' reps will actually reach out to me to introduce their products for them. I've also served as something like a delivery service, running our tool kits over to an office. For example, I'll actually make runs out to our nearby warehouse where we have extra supplies, such as sterilized instruments and ultrasonic "plug and play" equipment. One other thing I do is to provide best practice suggestions to dental offices. Being in the industry for a long time, I'm able to offer suggestions based on what I've seen at other offices. I know how a certain dental office may function and understand the challenges as well as insight to improve daily practice or clinical dentistry.

Sales are maintained and built through relationships, and sometimes those relationships are with other noncompeting suppliers. For example, sometimes I work with another manufacturers' rep for a company such as 3M or Oral B to better my chances of getting an appointment or getting into a specific office. This process helps me get past the front-door conversation and actually meet face-to-face with a dentist. The key in all of this is to plan and be flexible!

Source: Anonymous, as requested. Used with permission. All names have been changed.

ADDITIONAL PLANNING

A successful salesperson thinks ahead to the meeting that will occur and plans accordingly. For example, salespeople should plan how they intend to make a good first impression and build credibility during the call. It is also important to plan how to further uncover the customer's needs and strengthen the presentation. Salespeople should anticipate the questions and concerns the prospect may raise and plan to answer them helpfully. These issues are discussed in detail in the next several chapters. For now, be aware that these activities should be planned before the meeting begins. Of course, it is always important for a salesperson to build flexibility into all of this planning, as Building Partnerships 7.1 describes.

Before making the sales call, it is important to practice. How long should a rep spend practicing? Longer than many would think. As Mark Twain wrote, "It usually takes more than three weeks to prepare a good impromptu speech." Some have even suggested that for very important presentations, the seller spend 30 minutes preparing and practicing for each minute of presentation time. While often broken, the rule does indicate the importance of planning and practicing the presentation. Of course the time spent in practicing would depend on how much time the seller has and on the goals of the presentation.

One other thing that salespeople do is **seeding**—that is, sending the customer information that could be useful to the customer, but this does not include sales related information like pricing, brochures, and so on. For example, a rep can constantly search the news, blogs, and social media postings for material that may be useful for a prospect. This material is sent to the prospect with a note saying something like, "Jim, I thought you would find this article useful!" Remember that the material being sent is not sales material, and it does not include the selling firm's catalogs, brochures, pricing, and so on. Rather, it is good, useful information that will help the prospect's business. The result? The buyer views the seller as someone trying to be truly helpful and as someone who really understands the buyer's business.

SELLING YOURSELF

The ultimate goal of pre-call planning is to make yourself more effective (due to preparation) in the upcoming situation. The need for thoughtful preparation is not just a concept that applies to the business world. Pre-call planning techniques can be used in your personal life as well. You will find opportunities to use it in many situations, such as a job interview or finding a place to live.

As a college student, you know how important it is to find a job before you graduate. When I was in college, I always viewed my goal as finding a career. It is very common for new graduates to jump around to different companies for the first few years after college. I did not want that to happen to me. My call objective for each interview and shadow day was to make sure that my first post-college employer was the right fit for me. Therefore, I wanted to collect information about daily routine, training programs, corporate culture, compensation, opportunity for promotion, company values, etc. The ultimate goal would be to move on in the interview process. Employers judge you just as much by your questions as they do by your answers to theirs. Pre-call planning is an important step in setting yourself apart from the competition.

Depending on your situation, you may have had to take a serious look at renting your own place prior to college graduation. Whether it's your first time searching for your own place or not, if you apply pre-call planning skills to this process, it can organize your approach. Let's say you are looking to rent an apartment. You need to figure out what your primary and minimal objectives are. What's important to you? Price, space, location, commute, amenities, etc.? The primary objective is to find a place that has everything you are looking for. The minimal objective is to find a place that has what's most important to you. Pre-call planning can help you make an efficient, confident decision about where you live—which directly correlates to your quality of life.

My advice is to look at each situation in terms of the objectives you are trying to accomplish, and look for methods to plan ahead for the next step. It does not matter if you end up with a career in sales, you will need to apply this crucial sales skill throughout your personal and professional life.

Source: Christine Cortina, salesperson, Enterprise Fleet Management, used with permission.

SUMMARY

This chapter stressed the importance of planning the sales call. Developing a clear plan saves time for both salespeople and customers. In addition, it helps salespeople increase their confidence and reduce their stress.

As part of the planning process, salespeople need to gather as much information about the prospect as possible before the first call. They need information about both the individual prospect and the prospect's organization. Sources of this information include lists and directories, secretaries and receptionists, noncompeting salespeople, and direct inquiries made by the prospect.

To be effective, a call objective should be specific, realistic, and measurable. In situations requiring several calls, the salesperson should develop a plan with call objectives for each future call. Also, many salespeople benefit from setting multiple levels of objectives–primary, minimum, and optimistic–for each call.

As a general rule, salespeople should make appointments before calling on customers. This approach enables the salesperson to talk to the right person at the customer's site.

A number of methods can be used to make appointments. Perhaps the most effective is the straightforward telephone approach.

KEY TERMS

analysis paralysis 180
barriers 189
customer value proposition (CVP) 187
focus of dissatisfaction 188
focus of power 188
focus of receptivity 188
influential adversaries 179
minimum call objective 185
optimistic call objective 185
primary call objective 185
sales portals 180
screens 189
secondary call objectives 185
seeding 192
selling center 180
videoconferencing 189
virtual sales call 189
Webcasting 189

ETHICS PROBLEMS

1. Suppose that during your information-gathering phase you identify a hostile influential adversary named Dirk. You know that Dirk will do everything possible to see your competitor get the business. In talking about this with your sales manager, she suggests that you find some way to covertly strip Dirk of his credibility and thus cause him to be a nonissue. Would you follow your manager's advice? What kinds of things would you be willing to do? What would you be uncomfortable doing?

2. During precall planning, you learn that an important prospect enjoys being treated by salespeople to visit casinos, of which there are several in your area. Your firm doesn't have any policy about whether you can visit one of these with a client and you've never visited one with a client before. How will these facts affect your planning for your upcoming sales visit to this prospect? What will you do?

QUESTIONS AND PROBLEMS

1. Think about either a best friend you have now, or one you had before. Assume that a salesperson wanted to sell that person an important product or service. The salesperson would like to find a good focus of receptivity for your friend. Whom would that be? Do you think the focus of receptivity you just identified would cooperate with the salesperson?
2. In Sales Technology 7.1 you were introduced to the concept of sales acceleration technology. Using the Web, look up information about one such tool, name the tool, and briefly report on it is how it is used.
3. This chapter listed a number of information items that a salesperson could find out about a prospect/customer as an individual. Assume you are going to sell your instructor a new iPhone. See how much information you can supply from the list in the text.
4. Evaluate the following objectives for a sales call:
   - **a.** Demonstrate the entire line of 15 watches.
   - **b.** Find out more about what the buyer has used in the past.
   - **c.** Have the buyer trust me.
   - **d.** Determine which service the prospect is currently using for office cleaning and how much it costs.
   - **e.** Have the buyer agree to hold our next meeting at a nice restaurant.
   - **f.** Get an order for a 20-month subscription to our R30 Service Contract.
   - **g.** Reduce the buyer's concern that we've been in business for only six months.
5. Think for a moment about trying to secure a job. Assume you are going to have your second job interview next week with Fastenal for a sales position. The interview will take place over the phone with the senior recruiter. You've already had one 30-minute informational interview on campus, where most of the time was spent explaining what Fastenal offers new job seekers. Most candidates go through a set of four interviews. List your primary objective, minimum objective, and optimistic objective for your second interview.
6. In From the Buyer's Seat 7.1 the buyer encouraged salespeople to learn about the culture of the buying organization. List three ways in which a salesperson can learn about the buyer's organizational culture.
7. Evaluate the following approach for getting an appointment: Mr. Peters, I'm actually going to be in your area next Thursday morning. Would it be OK if I stopped by for a few minutes, say, sometime between 8:30 and 11:00 in the morning?
8. Although there is no firm rule, list what you think to be the best time of day to call on the following individuals:
   - **a.** A college computer/bookstore manager (to sell computer accessories).
   - **b.** A manager at a glass installation and repair company (to sell a new tool to remove broken glass shards).
   - **c.** A condominium complex manager (to sell a new camera security system).
   - **d.** An air conditioner contractor (to sell a new brand of air conditioning system).
9. For each of the individuals identified in question 8 identify the worst time of year to call on each individual.
10. Suppose you have graduated and you belong to the alumni association of your school. Your association plans to raffle off a number of donated items to raise funds for a new multimedia center at your school. To be a success, the event will need many donated raffle prizes.
    - **a.** Which sources will you use to identify potential sponsors?
    - **b.** What information do you need to qualify them properly?

CASE PROBLEMS

case 7.1

Presidential Aviation (Part A)

Presidential Aviation has provided charter flights to a wide array of customers, including business travelers worldwide. Thanks to the Presidential online booking system, business travelers can secure reliable quotes and book both domestic and international flights. Presidential has a sizable fleet of aircraft, including jets (light, midsize, and large jets) and turboprops.

The company is known for its ability to cater to passengers' every desire, including gourmet meals, special beverages, entertainment while in the air, and other luxury accommodations. Presidential also staffs a full-service VIP jet concierge program, similar to what major airlines offer.

Miguel Lopez is a salesperson for Presidential Aviation. He is currently planning an important first visit to Jorge Morales, a procurement officer at Regent Seven Seas Cruises. Company officials travel across the country a great deal in their work. Miguel would like to tell Jorge how Presidential can provide outstanding benefits to the Regent Seven Seas Cruises. Some of the special features for business travelers include the following:

- Privacy–you have the entire aircraft to yourself and can travel with passengers you know and enjoy.
- Comfort–including extra-roomy leather seats, in-flight movies, fully stocked bar, and gourmet meals that you choose.
- Ease–no time-consuming check-in process. You drive right up to the plane, and your luggage goes from your car into the plane.
- Point-to-point travel–there are no set schedules, so you fly when you want. Presidential uses 10 times more airports than commercial airlines, so you can fly from less congested airports closer to where you live.

Questions

1. What kind of information should Miguel gather about Jorge before their meeting?
2. What kind of information should Miguel gather about Regent Seven Seas Cruises before his meeting?
3. Which sources can Miguel use to gather that needed information?

Sources: RSSC; Presidential Aviation

case 7.2

SportsEvents Magazine

The primary goal of *SportsEvents* magazine is to assist event planners of amateur sporting events and competitions to achieve more success with their events. The magazine includes plenty of "how-to" articles that are authored by leading event planners as well as news and information that sports planners could use. The magazine also provides stories on important topics such as information about sports complexes, interviews with leading event planners, and other things that would help planners be successful in their jobs.

Akimi Hamaski is an advertising salesperson for *SportsEvents*, and his territory includes all of the states west of the Mississippi River in the United States. In a few weeks, Akimi will be calling on Patrick Goldman, general manager of the Minnesota Sports Facilities Authority (MSFA), the owner and operator of the U.S. Bank Stadium in Minneapolis, Minnesota. MSFA has never advertised in *SportsEvents* magazine. Akimi is not sure if anyone from his magazine has ever even called on Patrick or the MSFA.

Questions

1. Assume that you are Akimi Hamaski. List your call objectives for your first call with the general manager for the Minnesota Sports Facilities Authority.
2. Develop a three-call follow-up schedule and list the objectives for each call.

Sources: US Bank Stadium, *SportsEvents* Magazine.

ROLE PLAY CASE

This role play continues with the same customer firm you have been selling to: ARM, FSS, or Mizzen. (If you have not done role plays before, you will need to review the information about the various role play customers that can be found at the end of Chapter 3.)

Your buyer has agreed to allow you to meet with the rest of the buying center. Now it is time to plan the sales call. Write out your sales call objectives. In case you need assistance, here is some additional information from your previous calls, and feel free to ask your buyer for additional information. In addition to your call objectives, outline an agenda, or what you plan to do step-by-step.

BANCVUE: You are planning for a sales call with the VP of sales and marketing. You know that the company is growing about 15 percent per year. There are 45 salespeople, managed by four regional sales managers.

GELTECH: Your sales call will be with the same person plus some of the agents who have contact management software that they bought. The ultimate decision will be made by Mr. McLane, but he is likely to buy whatever this group recommends.

HIGHPOINT SOLUTIONS: You are going to meet with the two VPs of sales. Recall that one manages a sales force of 59 salespeople and sells to distributors, while the other has institutions and government agencies as accounts, with 18 salespeople.

Once you've written your objectives, review them with your group. Make sure they meet the criteria for objectives as specified in the chapter.

Note: For background information about these role plays, please see Chapter 1.

To the instructor: Additional information needed to complete the role play is available in the Instructor's Manual.

ADDITIONAL REFERENCES

Atkinson, William. "The Key to Value Selling." *Material Handling & Logistics,* April 2013, pp. 6–7.

Kato, Junichi, and Richard Schoenberg. "The Impact of Post-Merger Integration on the Customer-Supplier Relationship." *Industrial Marketing Management* 43, no. 2 (2014), pp. 335–45.

Mandják, Tibor, Zsuzsanna Szalkai, Edit Neumann-Bódi, Mária Magyar, and Judit Simon. "Emerging Relationships: How Are They Born?" *Industrial Marketing Management* 49 (2015), pp. 32–41.

Offenberger, Brian. "10 Things Prospects Hate." *SDM: Security Distributing & Marketing* 46, no. 3 (2016), p. 72.

Palmatier, Robert W., Mark B. Houston, Rajiv P. Dant, and Dhruv Grewal. "Relationship Velocity: Toward a Theory of Relationship Dynamics." *Journal of Marketing* 77, no. 1 (2013), pp. 13–30.

Sanders, T. *Dealstorming: The Secret Weapon That Can Solve Your Toughest Sales Challenges.* New York: Portfolio/Penguin, 2016.

Spina, Gianluca, Federico Caniato, Davide Luzzini, and Stefano Ronchi. "Past, Present and Future Trends of Purchasing and Supply Management: An Extensive Literature Review." *Industrial Marketing Management* 42, no. 8 (2013), pp. 1202–12.

Töytäri, Pekka, and Risto Rajala. "Value-Based Selling: An Organizational Capability Perspective." *Industrial Marketing Management* 45 (2015), pp. 101–12.

The Partnership Process

2

PART

©Brand X/Getty Images RF

chapter 8

MAKING THE SALES CALL

SOME QUESTIONS ANSWERED IN THIS CHAPTER ARE

- How should the salesperson make the initial approach to create a good impression and gain the prospect's attention?
- How can the salesperson develop rapport and increase source credibility?
- Why is discovering the prospect's needs important, and how can a salesperson get this information?
- How can the salesperson most effectively relate the product or service features to the prospect's needs?
- Why is it important for the salesperson to make adjustments during the call?
- How does the salesperson recognize that adjustments are needed?
- How can a salesperson effectively sell to groups?

PROFILE

"The transportation industry has many different aspects when it pertains to safety, so during the call it is important to actively listen to identify opportunities."

Seth Bleiler, 3M

Courtesy of Seth Bleiler, 3M

PROFILE I graduated with both my BS in management in 2013 and my MBA in 2015 from Texas State University. During my undergraduate degree, I studied professional selling under Professor Vicki West, director of the Center for Professional Sales. Upon entry into the MBA program, I took on the role as graduate assistant for the Center for Professional Sales, in which I assisted undergraduate students in their professional selling course work. After graduation, I entered the Frontline Internship Program for 3M in the Personal Safety Division. Upon completion of the internship I accepted a full-time position with 3M Traffic Safety and Security Division as a government transportation safety specialist.

I am the government transportation safety specialist for Tennessee and Arkansas. I work with everyone from the contractors all the way up to state government officials. My main focus is to sell high-quality pavement markings and reflective sign sheeting for the roadways to enhance the safety of the motoring public. In addition, I work with the local and state governments to create specifications to make it a priority to increase roadway safety through my products. Ultimately, by selling these specifications I can increase profits for my territory and our division. Regardless of whether I am going to a sales call with a contractor or a state senator, a crucial part in the sales process is making the sales call.

Making the sales call opens the door to building professional and profitable relationships. I always research the company, gather data-based research, and ask open-ended questions, as it is crucial to be effective during the sales call. The transportation industry has many different aspects when it pertains to safety, so during the call it is important to actively listen to identify opportunities. Once opportunities have been identified, I present data-driven research that explains the benefits of my company's products and how they would be beneficial in meeting the customer's needs and goals.

In the transportation industry, local and state governments have many different vendors fighting to get their products on the roadways. This can make building rapport and credibility a difficult task. So I keep up with industry standards and legislation that can be beneficial to my customers and this helps not only in building rapport, but also in building credibility. I have become a resource for many customers on how the transportation industry is growing and changing to make safer roadways.

Ultimately, those customers whom I'm meeting with have dreams of making transportation and roadways safer for motorists, and by effectively making the sales call, I can open the door to help make their dreams a reality.

Visit our Web site at: www.3m.com.

Seth Bleiler, government transportation safety specialist, 3M. Used with permission.

Exhibit 8.1
Essential Elements of the Sales Call

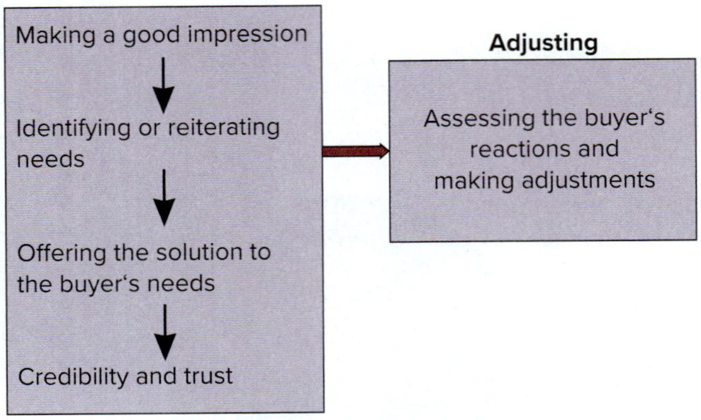

At this point in the sales process, we assume that an appointment has been made, sufficient information about the prospect and his or her organization has been gathered, and the salesperson has developed strong objectives for the call. In this chapter we discuss how to make the actual sales call. The content of a sales call depends on the specific situation the salesperson encounters as well as the extent of the relationship the salesperson has already established with the other party.[1] Exhibit 8.1 provides an organizing framework for our discussion. We start by considering how to make a good impression and begin to develop a long-term relationship. We then examine the initial needs assessment phase of a relationship and how to relate solutions to those needs. Finally, we discuss the relationship between adaptability and successful sales calls. Knowledge, adaptability, and trust are critical for successful sales to occur.

There are, of course, many conceptualizations of the selling process. For example, one trainer finds value in describing the selling process as the **Four A's** (*a*cknowledge, *a*cquire, *a*dvise, and *a*ssure).[2] First the seller acknowledges the buyer by greeting/welcoming/honoring and building trust. Next the seller acquires information via needs analysis and a summary of that analysis outlining the agreement between buyer and seller about the current situation and the desired solution. Advising comes next, during which the seller narrows the possible choices to specific options, sells benefits of those options (not just features), watches for buying signals, and asks for the order. Finally, the seller assures the buyer after the sale by enhancing satisfaction with the buying decision and giving proper follow-up and referrals.

MAKING A GOOD IMPRESSION

When salespeople arrive late, make a poor entrance, fail to gain the buyer's interest, or lack rapport-building skills, it is difficult for them to secure commitment and build partnerships.[3] This section discusses how salespeople can manage the buyer's impression of them, a process termed **impression management**.[4] Most of the information presented here assumes that the salesperson is making a first call on a prospect. However, impression management continues throughout calls.

One of the most important ways to ensure a good first impression is to be well prepared (as we discussed in Chapter 7). Smart salespeople prepare a checklist of things to take to the presentation so they won't forget anything.

WAITING FOR THE PROSPECT

Being on time for a scheduled sales call is critical to avoid giving the buyer a negative impression. With cell phones, there is no good reason for not calling if you're going to be a few minutes late to the appointment.

Salespeople should use waiting time effectively.

©Lane Oatey/BJI/blue jean images/Getty Images RF

Every salesperson must expect to spend a certain portion of each working day waiting for sales interviews. Successful salespeople make the best possible use of this time by working on reports, studying new product information, checking e-mail and text messages, planning and preparing for their next calls, and obtaining additional information about the prospect. (Chapter 15 covers time management more fully.)

Some trainers suggest that salespeople not wait for any prospect, under normal circumstances, more than 15 minutes after the appointment time. Why? To demonstrate that the seller's time is also important. Exceptions are necessary, of course, depending on the importance of the customer, the reason the customer is running late, and the distance the salesperson has traveled. In all cases salespeople should keep things in perspective, realizing that their time is also valuable. Chapter 15 discusses just how valuable that time really is.

When the salesperson arrives, the receptionist may merely say, "I'll tell Ms. Schimpf that you are here." After the receptionist has spoken with Ms. Schimpf, the salesperson should ask approximately how long the wait will be. If the wait will be excessive or the salesperson has another appointment, it may be advisable to explain this tactfully and to ask for another appointment. Usually the secretary either will try to get the salesperson in to see the prospect more quickly or will arrange for a later appointment.

FIRST IMPRESSIONS

In the first meeting between a salesperson and a prospect or customer, the first two or three minutes can be very important. Making a favorable first impression usually results in a prospect who is willing to listen. A negative first impression, on the other hand, sets up a barrier that may never be hurdled.

Salespeople may make a poor impression without realizing it. They may know their customer's needs and their own product but overlook seemingly insignificant things that can create negative impressions. As Chapter 4 related, how you dress can affect the message you send to the buyer. Also, studies have shown that the physical attractiveness and gender of salespeople can influence purchase intentions of buyers. And don't forget that according to generation gap experts, it can be challenging for a millennial (born 1980–1999) salesperson to relate to a baby-boom (born 1946–1964) buyer.

So what should a seller do to create a good first impression? You should be well groomed and enter confidently (but not arrogantly) by using erect posture, lengthy stride, and a lively pace, and among the first words out of your mouth should be something like, "Thanks for seeing me." And don't forget to smile. Watch what happens when you look at someone and smile. In 99 out of 100 cases, you will receive a smile in return.

But here's a caveat to the counsel just offered: Observe the prospect's state and modify your behavior as needed. When some customers are in a bad mood, the last thing they want is a happy, bouncy salesperson. In fact, in such a situation, the prospect might be inattentive or even refuse to meet with such a salesperson. Adapt and even ask if this is not a good time to meet if you perceive that the buyer is very stressed. Also, be aware that many buyers are repulsed by a salesperson who enters the room with exaggerated and false enthusiasm that her product is for sure going to solve all of the buyer's problems. It's better to be humble than to be cocky.[5]

It is also important to remember prospects' names and how to pronounce them (www.hearnames.com provides verbal pronunciation of many hard-to-say names). There are many ways to try to remember someone's name–such as giving your full attention when you hear it and then repeating the name immediately, associating it with someone else you know with the same name, associating it with the person's most prominent feature or trait, using it during the conversation, and writing it down phonetically.

ethics

Some experts argue that the customer's name should be used in the opening statement. Dale Carnegie, a master at developing relationships, said a person's name is "the sweetest and most important sound" to that person. Using a person's name often indicates respect and a recognition of the person's unique qualities. Others disagree with this logic, claiming that using the person's name, especially more than once in any short time, sounds phony and insincere. A compromise is to use the prospect's name in the opening and then to use it occasionally during the rest of the call.

thinking it through

You walk into a prospect's office confidently. Even though you've never met her before, you aren't nervous. You've done your homework and have strong objectives for this meeting. After you introduce yourself to the prospect and sit down, you suddenly remember that you left your iPad in your car. And in that iPad is your entire presentation! Your car is several blocks away. What should you do? What would you say to the prospect?

SELECTING A SEAT

When selecting a seat, it is a good idea to look around and start to identify the prospect's social style and status (see Chapter 5). For example, in the United States important decision makers usually have large, well-appointed, private offices. But this isn't always true. In Kuwait, a high-ranking businessperson may have a small office and lots of interruptions. Don't take that environment to mean he or she is a low-ranking employee or is not interested. Walmart buyers interview salespeople in rough conditions to help instill the idea that they want the lowest prices they can get.

Asking permission to sit down is usually unnecessary. The salesperson should read the prospect's nonverbal cues to determine the right time to be seated. And note that many calls will not involve sitting down at all, such as talking to a store manager in a grocery store aisle, conversing with a supervisor in a warehouse, or asking questions of a surgeon in a post-op ward.

GETTING THE CUSTOMER'S ATTENTION

Recall from Chapter 5 that there are several types of sales presentations, including standard memorized, outlined, and customized. In this chapter we assume that the salesperson has chosen a customized presentation.

Getting the customer's attention is not a new concept. Getting the attention of another person is also the goal of many other activities you are familiar with, such as advertising, making new friends, writing an English composition, giving a speech, or writing a Facebook post. Also, gaining the prospect's attention can be started before the sales call via social media tools (like sending surveys and polls via LinkedIn to generate interest in your idea).

Time is valuable to prospects, and prospects concentrate their attention on the first few minutes with a salesperson to determine whether they will benefit from the interaction. The prospect is making a decision: Do I want to give this salesperson 15 minutes of my time? Thirty minutes of my time? None of my time? This decision is made even while the salesperson is walking in the door and selecting a seat. Some claim that salespeople have less than six minutes to establish credibility with a client. The first few words the salesperson says often set the tone of the entire sales call. The **halo effect** (how and what you do in one thing changes a person's perceptions of other things you do) seems to operate in many sales calls. If the salesperson is perceived by the prospect as effective at the beginning of the call, he will be perceived as effective during the rest of the call and vice versa. There are many ways to open a presentation. An **opening** is a method designed to get the prospect's attention and interest quickly and to make a smooth transition into the next part of the presentation (which is usually to more fully discover the prospect's needs). Because each prospect and sales situation is unique, salespeople should be adaptable and be able to use any or a combination of openings. Again, keep in mind that openings are generally less important with partnering customers whom the salesperson has already met. Exhibit 8.2 provides details about a number of possible openings. But remember, many prospects won't like what they deem to be "canned" approaches and will react negatively.

Exhibit 8.2

Openings That Salespeople Can Use to Gain Attention

Opening Method	Example	Things to Consider
Introduction opening (simply introduce yourself).	Ms. Hallgren, thank you for seeing me today. My name is Daniel Mundt, and I'm with ServiceMaster.	Simple, but may not generate interest.
Referral opening (tell about someone who referred you to the buyer).	Mr. Schaumberg, I appreciate you seeing me today. I'm here at the suggestion of Ms. Fleming of Acumen Ornamental Iron Works. She thought you would be interested in our line of wrought iron products and railings.	Always get permission. Don't stretch the truth.
Benefit opening (start by telling some benefit of the product).	Mr. Penney, I would like to tell you about a color copier that can reduce your copying costs by 15 percent.	Gets down to business right away.
Product opening (actually demonstrate a product feature and benefit as soon as you walk up to the prospect).	[Carrying an iPad into an office] Ms. Hemming, you spend a lot of time on the road as an investigative lawyer. Let me show you how this little handheld item can transform your car (or any place you go) into an efficient, effective office.	Uses visual and not just verbal opening; can create excitement.
Compliment opening (start by complimenting the buyer or the buyer's firm).	I was calling on one of your customers, Jackson Street Books, last week, and the owner couldn't say enough good things about your service. It sure says a lot about your operation to have a customer start praising you out of the blue.	Must be sincere, not just flattery. ethics
Question opening (start the conversation with a question).	Ms. Borgelt, what is your reaction to the brochure I sent you about our new telemarketing service?	Starts two-way communication.

DEVELOPING RAPPORT

Rapport in selling is a close, harmonious relationship founded on mutual trust.[6] You build rapport when the prospect perceives you to be like him or her in some way. Ultimately the goal of every salesperson should be to establish rapport with each customer. Often salespeople can accomplish this with some friendly conversation early in the call. Part of this process involves identifying the prospect's social style and making necessary adjustments (see Chapter 5).

The talk about current news, hobbies, mutual friends, and the like that usually breaks the ice for the actual presentation is often referred to as **small talk**. One of the top traits of successful salespeople is the ability to be sociable. Examples include the following:

> I understand you went to Nebraska? I graduated from there with a BBA in 2016.
>
> Did you see the Houston Rockets game on ESPN last night?
>
> I read in the paper that you won the bass fishing tournament last weekend. That's pretty cool!
>
> So did you have trouble getting home from work last week with that snowstorm?
>
> Your receptionist was very helpful when I set this appointment. I never would have found this building if she hadn't told me where to park.
>
> You don't happen to remember Marla Jones, do you? She said she went to college with you and said to say hi.

Customers are more receptive to salespeople with whom they can identify–that is, with whom they have something in common. Thus, salespeople will be more effective with customers with whom they establish such links as mutual friends, common hobbies, or attendance at the same schools. Successful salespeople engage in small talk more effectively by first performing **office scanning**: looking around the prospect's environment for relevant topics to talk about.

Sharing letters from satisfied customers helps a salesperson establish credibility.

Be careful, however, when engaging in small talk because it can be to your detriment. One salesperson told of a client who asked her opinion about the economic outlook. The seller said she thought it was going down. The buyer had a different opinion, and it took months to repair the relationship. It is generally best to avoid controversial topics like politics and religion. Don't talk about your personal problems in an effort to get sympathy. Don't complain about others (boss, wife) or gossip about your competitors. Also, especially for first calls on prospects, you want to avoid using trite phrases like "How are you doing today?" because they don't sound sincere.

Of course salespeople should consider cultural and personality differences and adapt the extent of their nonbusiness conversation accordingly. For example, an AT&T rep would probably spend considerably less time in friendly conversation with a New York City office manager than with, say, a manager in a rural Texas town. Businesspeople in Africa place such high value on establishing friendships that the norm calls for a great deal of friendly conversation before getting down to business. Chinese customers want a lot of rapport building before they get down to business. Amiables and expressives tend to enjoy such conversations, whereas drivers and analyticals may be less receptive to spending much time in nonbusiness conversation. Studies show that salespeople who adapt and mirror their prospects are more successful in gaining desired results. Also, there could be less need for small talk if the salesperson uses a question or product opening when getting the customer's attention.

At this point in the sales call, after gaining the prospect's attention and establishing some rapport, a salesperson will often share his or her goals or agenda for the meeting with the prospect. This step can help build further rapport and trust. For example:

> Just so you know, my goal today is simply to verify what your needs might be and then, as I promised in the phone call, to share with you the results of the lab test we conducted last fall.

WHEN THINGS GO WRONG

Making and maintaining a good impression is important. How nice it would be if the beginning of every call went as smoothly as we have described here. Actually, things do go wrong sometimes. The best line of defense when something goes wrong is to maintain the proper perspective and a sense of humor. It's not the first thing you have done wrong and won't be your last.

For example, assume that a seller accidentally scratched a prospect's desk with her portfolio. The worst response by this salesperson would be to faint, scream, or totally lose control. A better response would include a sincere apology for the scratch and an offer to pay for any repairs.

What if you say something that is truly embarrassing? According to Mark Twain, "Man is the only animal that blushes, or needs to." For example, one salesperson calling on an older buyer motioned to a picture of a very young lady on the buyer's desk. "Is that your daughter," the seller stated, smiling. "That's my wife," the buyer replied, frowning. In another sales call, the salesperson saw a picture on the prospect's desk and said, "Oh wow! What a great picture! How'd you ever get a picture of yourself with John Madden, the football guy!" The buyer replied angrily, "That's not John Madden, that's my wife!"[7] Obviously both sellers made major blunders. The first thing you should do in such a situation is to apologize sincerely. Then change the subject or move on in your presentation. Try to relax and put the incident behind you. And learn this lesson: Think before you speak!

Of course you can get into trouble without even saying a word. As Chapter 4 indicated, you must be careful when using gestures in other cultures because they often take on different meanings. And there is technology to help evaluate sales calls and offer suggested changes, as Sales Technology 8.1 describes.

SALES Technology 8.1

TECH-POWERED SELLING

Technology is finding new ways to have a profound effect on sales calls. Gryphon Networks, for example, is a business headquartered in Boston that helps companies analyze actual sales calls. Systems can track and evaluate everything from where the conversation left off and what appointments were made, to notifying salespeople of scheduled follow-up calls. The current status of sales leads is also documented. This advanced tech support more efficiently uses resources and bypasses manual documentation. By using such a system salespeople have more time to conduct profit-contributing activities.

Technology such as the one offered by Gryphon also evaluates the salesperson's efforts during a sales call and offers valuable advice in future sales training activities. An example could be a salesperson using slang or informal language during communication that may hinder the effectiveness of the sales call, or empty communication that just clutters dialogue or insinuates false promissory service. Furthermore, when making sales in such an industry like financial services that is heavily regulated, if a mistake is made on the salesperson's end (like inappropriately using a word such as *promise* or *guarantee*) a manager or oversight person can correct the individual on the misquote. All of the collected data can also be pooled together to provide an extensive report in chart or table form to better training and improve sales growth. Each system can be tailored to the business it serves or the individual it analyzes to track performance.

The systems can amass both quantitative and qualitative data to improve customer response and help build mutually beneficial business relationships. For example, Gryphon Network helped a Belmont savings bank see a 20 percent increase in its sales conversions once it got accustomed to the system provided by the partnership.

Sources: Gryphon Networks; Bryan Yurcan, "Tech Can't Replace a Sales Call (Yet), but It Can Make One Better," *American Banker*, November 23, 2016.

IDENTIFYING THE PROSPECT'S NEEDS: THE POWER OF ASKING QUESTIONS

A story is told of a woman who walks into a new doctor's office. The doctor, knowing nothing about her at all, asks the woman's name. "Janet Louden," she replies. The doctor scribbles for a minute on a prescription pad, hands the prescription to her, and then walks out. What's missing in that story? The doctor had no idea what the woman's needs were, but proceeded to try to solve her "problem." The chances of success in such a situation are infinitesimally small. The same is likely to be the true when a salesperson tries to make a presentation without knowing the customer's needs.[8]

Once the salesperson has entered and captured the buyer's attention, it is time to identify the buyer's needs. Remember that this might have occurred in the pre-approach and might involve more than one buyer and more than one sales call. To begin this process, a salesperson might use transition sentences like the following (assuming a product approach was used to gain attention):

> Well, I'm glad you find this little model interesting. And I want to tell you all about it. But first I need to ask you a few questions to make sure I understand what your specific needs are. Is that OK?

If the buyer gives permission, the salesperson begins to ask questions about the buyer's needs. Don't be surprised if the buyer is reluctant to provide confidential

Exhibit 8.3

Discovering the Root Cause of the Need

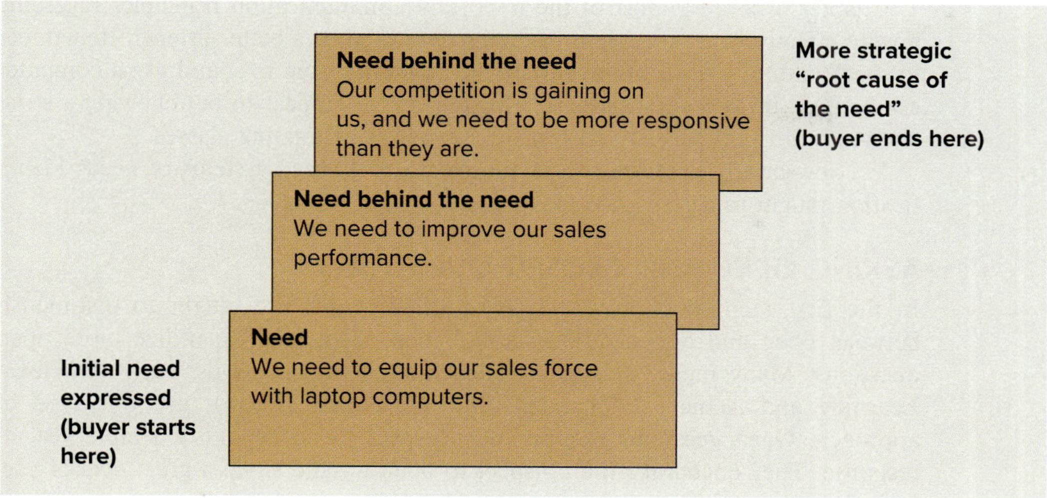

information. There are many people out there trying to steal valuable company information. The seller has to establish credibility and trust.

Occasionally a salesperson makes the mistake of starting with product information rather than with a discussion of the prospect's needs. The experienced salesperson, however, attempts to uncover the prospect's needs and problems at the start of the relationship. In reality, discovering needs is still a part of qualifying the prospect.

There is an underlying reason for every customer need, and the salesperson must continue probing until he or she uncovers the root problem or need. This process could be called "discovering the root cause of the need" and is graphically illustrated in Exhibit 8.3.

Needs vary greatly. However, here are some examples:

- Need to decrease total dollars spent on maintenance each year.
- Need to increase sales of our current line of toasters.
- Need to increase awareness of our new bank location.

This salesperson is discovering the prospect's needs before describing the services he offers.

As you discover needs, keep in mind that this process can be uncomfortable for the prospect. The prospect may resent your suggesting that there could be a problem or a better way to do things. When faced with direct evidence that things could be better, the prospect may express fear (fear of losing her job if things are not corrected or of things changing and the situation getting worse than it is now). Also, remember that the time needed to discuss needs varies greatly depending on the type of industry, the nature of the product, how well the salesperson and buyer know each other, and so forth. We will come back to this issue after we examine methods of identifying needs.

Chapter 4 covered most of the important communication principles regarding how to effectively ask questions of the prospect and be a better listener. Remember to speak naturally while asking questions. You don't want to sound like a computer asking a set of rote questions. Nor do you want to appear to be following a strict word-for-word outline that you learned in your sales training classes.

We now briefly describe two of the most widely used systems of needs identification taught to salespeople today.

ASKING OPEN AND CLOSED QUESTIONS

In the first method of needs discovery, salespeople are taught to distinguish between open and closed questions and then encouraged to utilize more open questions. Many highly respected sales training organizations, such as Wilson Learning and Achieve Global (the Miller Heiman Group), use this type of approach. **Open questions** require the prospect to go beyond a simple yes–no response. They encourage the prospect to open up and share a great deal of useful information. For example:

What kinds of problems have the new federal guidelines caused for your division?

What projects are crucial for your company right now?

What are your decision-making criteria for choosing the successful vendor?

Closed questions require the prospect to simply answer yes or no or to offer a short, fill-in-the-blank type of response. Examples include the following questions:

Have you ever experienced computer downtime as a result of an electrical storm?

Do you have a favored vendor?

Did you make the decision that resulted in your current vendor?

Who else will be involved in the decision-making process?

In most cases salespeople need to ask both open and closed questions. Open questions help paint the broad strokes of the situation, whereas closed questions help zero in on specific problems and attitudes. Some trainers believe simple, closed questions are best at first. Prospects become accustomed to talking and start to open up. After a few closed questions, the salesperson moves to a series of open questions. At some point he or she may revert back to closed questions.

Angie Main, a radio advertising salesperson, likes to ask her prospects the following two open questions to discover their needs:

What misconceptions do people have about your business?

If you could tell people one thing about your business, what would you want to tell them?[9]

Notice how these questions focus on the needs of the prospect rather than the solution (how her radio station can meet those needs).

Exhibit 8.4 contains an illustrative dialogue of a bank selling a commercial checking account to a business. In this sales presentation the salesperson's questions follow a logical flow. Note that follow-up probes are often necessary to clarify the prospect's responses. At the conclusion of asking open and closed questions, the salesperson should have a good feel for the needs and wants of the prospect.

Exhibit 8.4
Using Open and Closed Questions to Discover Needs

Salesperson's Probe	Prospect's Response
Have you ever done business with our bank before? [closed]	No, our firm has always used First of America Bank.
I assume, then, that your checking account is currently with First of America? [closed]	Yes.
If you could design an ideal checking account for your business, what would it look like? [open]	Well, it would pay interest on all idle money, have no service charges, and supply a good statement.
When you say "good statement," what exactly do you mean? [open]	It should come to us once a month, be easy to follow, and help us reconcile our books quickly.
Uh-huh. Anything else in an ideal checking account? [open]	No, I guess that's about it.
What things, if any, about your checking account have dissatisfied you in the past? [open]	Having to pay so much for our checks! Also, sometimes when we have a question, the bank can't answer it quickly because the computers are down. That's frustrating!
Sure! Anything else dissatisfy you? [open]	Well, I really don't like the layout of the monthly statement we get now. It doesn't list checks in order; it has them listed by the date they cleared the bank.
Is there anything else that I need to know before I begin telling you about our account? [open]	No, I think that just about covers it all.

One final suggestion is to summarize the prospect's needs:

> So let me see if I have this right. You write about 35 checks a month, you keep about a $5,000 balance, and you are looking for a checking account that pays interest on your unused balance and has overdraft protection. . . . Is that correct?

Summarizing helps solidify the needs in the prospect's mind and ensures that the prospect has no other hidden needs or wants.

SPIN® TECHNIQUE

The SPIN method of discovering needs was developed by Huthwaite, an international research and training organization, after analyzing thousands of actual sales calls.[10] The results indicated that successful salespeople go through a logical needs identification sequence, which Huthwaite labeled **SPIN**: *s*ituation questions, *p*roblem questions, *i*mplication questions, and *n*eed payoff questions. SPIN works for salespeople involved in a **major sale**: one that involves a long selling cycle, a large customer commitment, an ongoing relationship, and large risks for the prospect if a bad decision is made. Major sales can occur anywhere but often involve large or national accounts. For example, both SC Johnson and Bridgestone have used SPIN for their major accounts but may use other techniques for smaller accounts.

SPIN actually helps the prospect identify unrecognized problem areas. Often, when a salesperson simply asks an open question such as "What problems are you having?," the prospect replies "None!" The prospect isn't lying; he or she may not realize that a problem exists. SPIN excels at helping prospects test their current opinions or perceptions of the situation. Also, SPIN questions may be asked over the course of several sales calls, especially for large or important buyers. As an overview, an abbreviated needs identification dialogue appears in Exhibit 8.5; it demonstrates all components of SPIN for a salesperson selling cell phone services.

Exhibit 8.5
Using the SPIN Technique to Sell Cell Phone Internet Access

Salesperson: Do your engineers use cell phones in their work? [situation question]

Prospect: Yes, we supply each field engineer with a cell phone.

Salesperson: Do you have many problems with cell calls being lost while an engineer is talking? [problem question]

Prospect: Not really. Most of our engineers work in the city, and there are plenty of towers here to take care of calls.

Salesperson: Sure. Have you ever had engineers who need to access the Internet for details about a client's situation while onsite? Or a need to access files from your central server? [problem question]

Prospect: Well, now that you mention it, that is starting to be a problem. Most engineers like to carry paper copies of the documents they will need, but there are times when a document is back at the office.

Salesperson: What happens if an engineer doesn't have the document she needs while at a client's location? [implication question]

Prospect: That happened just last week to Carlee. She was at a client and thought she had all the paperwork. Turns out there was a spreadsheet she needed but didn't have. She had to drive back to the office to get it. Our client got pretty upset because their staff had to just stand around and wait for Carlee to get back.

Salesperson: If I can show you a way to make sure your engineers have access to all of their important files as well as complete Internet access while at the clients' locations and do so for no more than 10 percent above what you're paying for cell service now, would you be interested? [need payoff question]

Prospect: Sure. The more I think about it, the more I realize that we need to give our engineers the tools that our competitors are using. I'd hate to lose business because we're too cheap to invest in the right tools.

Situation Questions

Early in the sales call, salespeople may ask **situation questions**, which are general data-gathering questions about background and current facts. The goal of these questions is to better understand the prospect's current situation.

Salespeople should not assume they can ask lots of situation questions in a sales call, and successful salespeople learn to limit them; prospects quickly become bored or impatient if they hear too many of them. Inexperienced and unsuccessful salespeople tend to ask too many situation questions. In fact, most situation-type questions should be answered through precall information gathering and planning. If a salesperson asks too many situation questions, the prospect will think the salesperson is unprepared. Here are some examples of situation questions:

What's your position? How long have you been here?

How many people do you employ? Is the number growing or shrinking?

What kind of handling equipment are you using at present? How long have you had it?

Problem Questions

When salespeople ask about specific difficulties, problems, or dissatisfactions the prospect has, they are asking **problem questions**. The goal is to discover a problem. Here are some examples of problem questions:

Is your current machine difficult to repair?

Do your operators ever complain that the noise level is too high?

Do you get fast turnaround when you outsource your work?

Is the cost of maintaining your own server becoming an issue?

If a seller can't discover a problem using problem questions, then she might need to ask additional situation questions first to uncover more issues that might lead to better problem questions.

Implication Questions

Questions that logically follow one or more problem questions and are designed to help the prospect recognize the true ramifications of the problem are **implication questions**. Implication questions cannot be asked until some problem area has been identified (through problem questions). The goal of implication questions is for the prospect to see that the identified problem has some serious ramifications and implications that make the problem worthy of being resolved. These questions attempt to motivate the prospect to search for a solution to the problem.

Implication questions relate back to some similar issues that were described in the multiattribute model in Chapter 3. In the multiattribute model, customers weigh various attributes differently in terms of importance. In the same way, some problems that are identified by problem questions have more weight (are more serious in the eyes of the buyer) than others. The goal of the salesperson is to identify problems that have high importance to the buyer.

Examples of implication questions include these:

What happens if you ship your customer a product that doesn't meet specs?

What does having to pay overtime do to your price, as compared to your competitors'?

Does the slowness of your present system create any bottlenecks in other parts of the process?

What happens if you miss a deadline?

Could that situation have repercussions for your job security?

Do you think competitors will notice what is going on and attempt to gain market share at your expense due to the problem?

If the buyer answers these questions in a way that indicates she doesn't see serious implications of the problem identified, the seller would have to go back and ask additional implication questions, problem questions, and maybe even situation questions. The seller doesn't move ahead to need payoff questions until the prospect sees that there are serious ramifications if he does not solve the problem.

Need Payoff Questions

When salespeople ask questions about the usefulness of solving a problem, they are asking **need payoff questions**. In contrast to implication questions, which are problem centered, need payoff questions are solution centered:

If I can show you a way to eliminate paying overtime for your operators and therefore reduce your cost, would you be interested?

Would you like to see a reduction in the number of products that don't meet quality specifications?

Would an increase in the speed of your present system by 5 percent resolve the bottlenecks you currently experience?

If the prospect responds negatively to a need payoff question, the salesperson has not identified a problem serious enough for the prospect to take action. In that case, the salesperson should probe further by asking additional problem questions, implication questions, and then a new need payoff question.

Conclusions about SPIN

One critical advantage of SPIN is that it encourages the prospect to define the need. During the questioning phase the salesperson is focusing on problems and isn't focusing on her product. As a result, the prospect views the salesperson more as a consultant trying to help instead of someone trying to push a product. Building Partnerships 8.1 describes the importance of being a consultant and discovering needs before talking about solutions.

SPIN selling has been taught to thousands of salespeople. For example, Fastenal uses a technique modeled after SPIN when selling thousands of commercial products.[11] Many salespeople quickly master the technique, whereas others have more difficulty. The best advice is to practice each component and to plan implication and need payoff questions before each sales call. SPIN works well for buyers that have a real problem (like inventory piling up). It is perhaps more difficult to use when the seller is only discussing an opportunity (no real problems, but "my solution could help you make more money").

REITERATING NEEDS YOU IDENTIFIED BEFORE THE MEETING

The salesperson may fully identify the needs of the prospect before making the sales call. In that case reiterating the needs early in the sales call is advisable so that both parties agree about the problem they are trying to solve. For example:

> Mr. Reed, based on our several phone conversations, it appears that you are looking for an advertising campaign that will position your product for the rapidly growing senior citizen market, at a cost under $100,000, using humor and a well-known older personality, and delivered in less than one month. Is that an accurate summary of your needs? Has anything changed since we talked last? Is there anything else I need to know at this point?

Likewise, in multiple-call situations, going through a complete needs identification at every call is unnecessary. But it is still best to briefly reiterate the needs identified to that point:

> In my last call we pretty much agreed that your number one concern is customer satisfaction with your inventory system. Is that correct? Has anything changed since we met last time, or is there anything else I need to know?

ADDITIONAL CONSIDERATIONS

How many questions can a salesperson ask to discover needs? It depends on the situation. Generally, as the buyer's risk of making the wrong decision goes up, so does the amount of time the salesperson can spend asking the prospect questions.

Salespeople should remember that buyers are empowered today with much information, as Chapter 1 described. In fact, it is not uncommon for the buyer to initiate the first contact with the seller, after the buyer identifies their own needs, researches potential vendors, and develops criteria for solving their needs.

Occasionally the prospect will refuse to answer important questions because the information is confidential or proprietary. The salesperson can do little except emphasize the reason for asking the questions. Ultimately the prospect needs to trust the salesperson enough to divulge sensitive data. Chapters 13 and 14 discuss trust-building strategies.

BUILDING Partnerships 8.1

MAKING THE SALES CALL

When I started in sales I was planning for my first sales call to a longstanding customer of our company. Having checked with one key contact that supported the account, I thought I had all the information I needed and had confidence for the meeting. My key contact had indicated that all was great and that I should expect zero issues. During my meeting, however, I learned that I should have looked at the other areas of support for feedback also. For example, one of the smallest parts of our support, which I had not checked with prior to my important meeting, had the most issues that were ongoing. From that day forward, I always check with all support areas and take their issues into account to avoid walking into a land mine.

After finding out who is who, I conduct each visit and phone call with the key people, keeping in mind the unique issues that are important to each one of them. For instance, customers that I engage with are in the financial, procurement, safety, security, operations, maintenance, and administration management departments. Each area requires a unique approach as to what is important to that person's job. If a person's job is safety related, I need to focus case study information and technical specification items that set my product apart from a safety standpoint from competitors. The same applies for other areas as well.

Making successful sales calls also includes getting to know the gatekeepers. Those are the people at the front desk and those who have access to their manager's calendars. This comes in handy when you need to get time coordinated on the calendar of many people.

When I make a sales call, I like to make sure I speak with all levels and areas of the customer's organization. That is important because people retire and quit their jobs, and one never knows who might be promoted to the vacated positions.

Before arriving, I review my meeting report notes from my last visit and any communication I have had leading up to this meeting. I do this to ensure I successfully followed up with my customer to resolve any issues he or she might have had in the last visit, as well as to think about current issues/questions we might deal with in this call.

In a sales call we discuss current and future needs, and I probe with questions to determine if other areas need attention. Sometimes people do not know they have an issue until you point it out. That is rarer, but when you help them identify an area of need, and then have the solution to that need, it makes you look more professional in their eyes. An example can be a subcomponent with an issue that hasn't failed in the field for the customer yet, but would show signs of early failure. Pointing out what to look for helps resolve an issue before it begins. At the conclusion of each meeting, I always summarize things I need from them (data, photos, inventory), and give them a summary of things I will do after I leave. It is always good to clarify who is responsible for what, and what action you will take on a subject matter.

I find that coming in with a smile is the most important part of starting a sales call. People are more willing to give you time when they feel comfortable with you. I once met with a guy who said he normally gives vendors only a short window in his schedule, but always seems to give me more time. I think the key is that I don't always thunder on my sales agenda. I prefer to ask and speak on personal topics (hobbies, family, stories) that gets someone in the mood to talk. I subtly slip in my sales agenda needs in the conversation or at the tail end as I get ready to go.

The most important part of my sales call is the relationship and partnership I am building with each customer. I have customers I call on who do not buy my products and might not due to political motivations at their agency. However, they may not stay at their current location or the political atmosphere may change and I don't want them to think I ignored them and will call on them only when they have money to spend with me. You never know what tomorrow brings, so the least you can do is prepare yourself for what might occur.

Source: Chad Engle, GILLIG, LLC, Used with permission.

At times buyers do not answer questions because they honestly don't know the answers. The salesperson should then ask whether the prospect can get the information. If the prospect cannot do so, the salesperson can often ask the buyer's permission to probe further within the prospect's firm.

ethics

On the other hand, some buyers will not only answer questions but also appear to want to talk indefinitely. In general, the advice is to let them talk, particularly in many cultures. For example, people in French-speaking countries tend to love rhetoric, the act and art of speaking; attempts to cut them off will only frustrate and anger them.

thinking it through

Prospects often provide sensitive and confidential information when they reveal facts about their situations and needs. Assume that a prospect at Allied reveals to you her firm's long-term strategy for taking business away from her number one competitor, Baker's. You are close friends with the buyer at Baker's, which is one of your biggest customers. Will you share the confidential information with the Baker's buyer?

DEVELOPING A STRATEGY FOR THE PRESENTATION

In order for both the buyer and seller to be working with the same assumptions and toward common goals, some trainers suggest that the salesperson present an agenda for the sales call. The buyer is then encouraged to make suggested changes to the agenda. In the same spirit of mutual understanding, at the conclusion of the sales call the salesperson summarizes the call and creates a follow-up plan, again with input and suggestions from the buyer.

Based on the needs identified, a strategy should be developed for how best to meet those needs. This process includes sorting through the various options to see what is best for this prospect, prioritizing the needs identified. Decisions have to be made about the exact product or service to recommend, the optimal payment terms to present for consideration, service levels to suggest, product or service features to stress during the presentation, and so on. Chapter 7 also talks about developing a strategy.

Products have many, many features, and one product may possess a large number of features that are unique and exciting when compared to competitive offerings. Rather than overload the customer with all the great features, successful salespeople discuss only those that specifically address the needs of the prospect. Talking about lots of features of little interest to the customer is a waste of time and is sometimes called **feature dumping**.

OFFERING VALUE: THE SOLUTION TO THE BUYER'S NEEDS

After developing a strategy for the presentation based on a customer's needs, it is time to relate product or service features that are meaningful to the buyer, assess the buyer's reaction to what is being said, resolve objections (covered in Chapter 10), and obtain commitment (the topic of Chapter 11).

The salesperson usually begins offering the solution with a transition sentence, something like the following: "Now that I know what your needs are, I would like to talk to you about how our product can meet those needs." The seller's job is then to translate product features into benefits for solving the buyer's needs. To

Exhibit 8.6

An Example of Features and Benefits

Courtesy of Renowned Builders Inc.

do this effectively, the salesperson must know the metrics of the prospect's decision; that is, on what criteria and in what way is the prospect evaluating possible solutions? This will be discussed more in Chapter 9 and in other chapters.

RELATING FEATURES TO BENEFITS

A **feature** is a quality or characteristic of the product or service. Every product has many features designed to help potential customers. A **benefit** is the way in which a specific feature will help a particular buyer and is tied directly to the buying motives of the prospect. A benefit helps the prospect more fully answer the question "What's in it for me?" Exhibit 8.6 shows a list of features and sample benefits for a product. The way in which a salesperson shows how a product addresses the buyer's specific needs is sometimes called the **customer benefit proposition**. This concept will be described more fully in Chapter 9.

The salesperson usually includes a word or a phrase to make a smooth transition from features to benefits:

> This china is fired at 2,600°F, and what that means to you is that it will last longer. Because it is so sturdy, you will be able to hand this china down to your children as an heirloom, which was one of your biggest concerns.

Our service hotline is open 24 hours a day, which means that even your third-shift operators can call if they have any questions. That should be a real help to you because you said your third-shift supervisor was inexperienced in dealing with problems.

Some trainers suggest going beyond mentioning features and benefits. One variation, **FAB**, has salespeople discussing *f*eatures, ***a*dvantages** (why that feature would be important to anyone), and *b*enefits. For example:

This car has antilock brakes [*feature*], which help the car stop quickly [*advantage*], which provides the safety you said you were looking for [*benefit*].

In another variation, **FEBA** (*f*eatures, *e*vidence, *b*enefits, *a*greement), salespeople mention the feature, provide evidence that the feature actually exists, explain the benefit (why that feature is important to the buyer), and then ask whether the buyer agrees with the value of the feature and benefit. For example:

This car has the highest-quality antilock brakes on the market today [*feature*] as proved by this test by the federal government [*evidence*]. They will provide the safety you said you were looking for [*benefit*]; don't you agree [*agreement*]?

Buyers are not interested in facts about the product or the seller's company unless those facts help solve their wants or needs. The salesperson's job is to supply the facts and then point out what those features mean to the buyer in terms of benefits and value creation. Neil Rackham, noted sales training leader, emphasizes this theme:

The world has changed and so has selling. Today, the primary sales job is to create value–to add problem solving and creativity, so that the customer buys the advice and expertise of the salesperson as much as they buy the product . . . [in a survey] product pitches were the number one complaint from customers, with comments such as "It's quicker, more convenient, and more objective to go to the Internet than to listen to a product pitch."[12]

Exhibit 8.7 illustrates how one trainer incorporates these concepts into a problem/solution model. The customer's needs are called "business model." The salesperson knows some, but not all, of the buyer's needs before the sales call, represented by the first three lines under "Business model (needs)." However, by actively listening (see Chapter 4), the seller learns more needs during the presentation, represented by lines 4 and 5 under "Business model (needs)." Using all identified needs, the seller talks about the relevant features and benefits. While doing this, the salesperson offers proof of these assertions, based on the customer's social style (see Chapter 5). The salesperson also engages in activities to help the buyer realize the importance of meeting his or her needs sooner, providing reasons to buy now. The end result is increased sales and profits for the seller.

Buyers typically consider two or more competitive products when making a purchase decision. Thus, salespeople need to know more than just the benefits their products provide. They need to know how the benefits of their products are superior or inferior to the benefits of competitive products. Of course, as you explain the benefits of your service, you must make sure the prospect is interested in those benefits.

Sometimes, when selling certain commodities, it is important to sell the features and benefits of the seller's firm instead of the product. For example, Ray Hanson of Fastenal sells fasteners such as bolts and nuts. He states, "In the fastener industry I have found that a generic product, such as a nut or bolt, doesn't have too many features and benefits. We talk to our potential customers about the features our company has and how these features could benefit them as our customers."[13]

Exhibit 8.7
The Problem/Solution Model

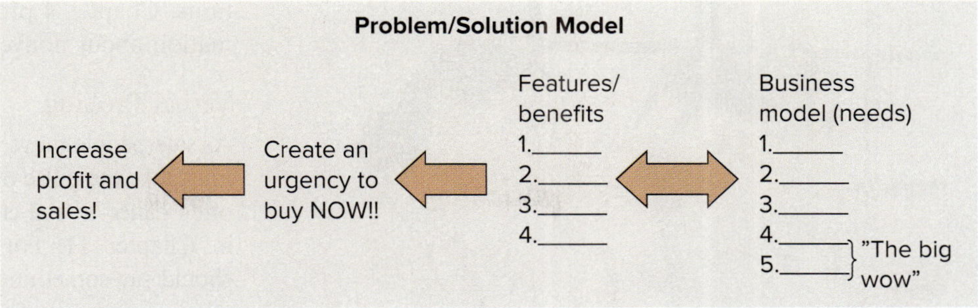

Source: Carl Sooder, used with permission.

When selling to resellers, salespeople have two sets of benefits to discuss with the prospect: what the features of the product will do for the reseller and what the product features will do for the ultimate consumer of the product. Covering both sets of features and benefits is important. Exhibit 8.8 illustrates the two sets of features.

ASSESSING REACTIONS

While making a presentation, salespeople need to continually assess the reactions of their prospects. The prospect needs to agree that the benefits described would actually help his or her company. By listening to what buyers say and observing their body language (see Chapter 4 to review how to be a better listener), salespeople can determine whether prospects are interested in the product. If buyers react favorably to the presentation and seem to grasp the benefits of the proposed solution, the salesperson will have less need to make alterations or adjustments. But if a prospect does not develop enthusiasm for the product, the salesperson will need to make some changes in the presentation.

Using Nonverbal Cues

An important aspect of making adjustments is interpreting a prospect's reactions to the sales presentation. By observing the prospect's five channels of nonverbal communication, salespeople can determine how to proceed with their presenta-

Exhibit 8.8
Features and Benefits of Yummy Earth Organic Gummy Bears, as Presented to a Grocery Store

Features	Benefits
Important to the Final Consumer	
Organic.	You want organic products, and this product is certified organic.
Only 90 calories per serving.	You can enjoy a treat without worrying about its effect on your weight.
100 percent of daily need for vitamin C in every serving.	You are getting needed nutrition from a snack.
Important to the Grocery Store	
Test marketed for two years.	Because of this research, you are assured of a successful product and effective promotion; thus, your risk is greatly reduced.
$500,000 will be spent for consumer advertising in the next 18 months.	Your customers will come to your store looking for the product.
40-cent coupon with front positioning in the national Sunday insert section.	Your customers will want to take advantage of the coupon and will be looking for the product in your store.

Nonverbal cues help salespeople know when to make adjustments.

tions. Chapter 4 provides more detailed information about nonverbal cues.

Verbal Probing

As salespeople move through a presentation, they must take the pulse of the situation. This process, often called a **trial close**, is more fully described in Chapter 11. For example, the salesperson should say something like the following:

> How does this sound to you?
>
> Can you see how these features help solve the problem you have?
>
> Have I clearly explained our program to you?
>
> Do you have any questions?

The use of such probing questions helps achieve several things. First, it allows the salesperson to stop talking and encourages two-way conversation. Without such probing, a salesperson can turn into a rambling talker while the buyer becomes a passive listener. Second, probing lets the salesperson see whether the buyer is listening and understanding what is being said. Third, the probe may show that the prospect is uninterested in what the salesperson is talking about. This response allows the salesperson to redirect the conversation to areas of interest to the buyer. This kind of adjustment is necessary in almost every presentation and underscores the fact that the salesperson should not simply memorize a canned presentation that unfolds in a particular sequence.

Salespeople must listen. Often we hear only what we want to hear. This behavior is called **selective perception**, and everyone is guilty of it at times. For example, read the following sentence:[14]

> Finished files are the result of years of scientific study combined with the experience of years.

Now go back and quickly count the number of *f*'s in that sentence. Most non-native English speakers see all six *f*'s, whereas native English speakers see only three (they don't count the *f*'s in *of* because it is not considered an important word). The point is that once salespeople stop actively listening, they miss many things the buyer is trying to communicate.

Making Adjustments

Salespeople can alter their presentations in many ways to obtain a favorable reaction. For example, a salesperson may discover during a sales presentation that the prospect simply does not believe the seller has the appropriate product knowledge. Rather than continue with the presentation, the salesperson should redirect her or his efforts toward establishing credibility in the eyes of the prospect.

Other adjustments might require collecting additional information about the prospect, developing a new sales strategy, or altering the style of presentation. For example, a salesperson may believe a prospect is interested in buying an economical, low-cost motor. While presenting the benefits of the lowest-cost motor, the salesperson discovers the prospect is interested in the motor's operating costs. At this point the salesperson should ask some questions to find out whether the prospect would be interested in paying a higher price for a more efficient motor with lower operating costs. On the basis of the prospect's response, the salesperson can adopt a new sales strategy, one that emphasizes operating efficiency rather than the motor's initial price. In this way the sales presentation is shifted from features and benefits based on a low initial cost to features and benefits related to low operating costs.

BUILDING CREDIBILITY DURING THE CALL

To develop a close and harmonious relationship, the salesperson must be perceived as having **credibility**—that is, he or she must be believable and reliable.[15] A salesperson can take many actions during a sales call to develop such a perception.[16] From the Buyer's Seat 8.1 provides an example of when a seller did not achieve that goal.

To establish credibility early in the sales call, the salesperson should clearly delineate the time she or he thinks the call will take and then stop when the time is up. How many times has a salesperson said, "This will take only 5 minutes!" and 30 minutes later you still can't get rid of him or her? No doubt you would have perceived the salesperson as more credible if, after 5 minutes, he or she stated, "Well, I promised to take no more than 5 minutes, and I see our time is up. How would you like to proceed from here?" One successful salesperson likes to ask for half an hour and take only 25 minutes.[17]

Another way to establish credibility is to offer concrete evidence to back up verbal statements. If a salesperson states, "It is estimated that more than 80 percent of the households in America will own LED HD televisions by 2025," he or she should be prepared to offer proof of this assertion—for instance, hand the prospect an article from a credible source. Ways to establish credibility are discussed in greater detail in Chapter 9.

Some trainers suggest adding a **credibility statement** early in the sales call that includes features of yourself and your company. The purpose of the statement is to help the buyer realize you are capable of meeting her needs. The statement can be strengthened by proving its assertions with such items as testimonials and test results (more about these in the next chapter). Here's an example of a credibility statement:

> Hank, I don't know how much you may know about Apple Valley Savings and Loan. We were founded by a Swedish immigrant back in 1932 whose stated goal was to offer the best service in the Midwest. We've now grown into the third-largest savings bank in the upper Midwest with assets exceeding $23 billion and are the only savings bank in the Midwest earning the coveted Pinnacle Award for Excellence eight years in a row. We have over 32 branches in the five-state region. I've been with the bank for the last 14 years and have spent the last 6 years working closely with higher education institutions like yours. In terms of investments, we have focused a great deal of effort on higher education. For example, we recently provided a $2.3 million loan to West Valania State University to expand its ice hockey rink.

ethics

Of course, one way to establish credibility is to avoid making statements that do not have the ring of truth to them. For example, some suggest you should avoid using a phrase like "We're the best" or "We're number one." As one skeptical buyer noted, "Just how many number ones are there in the world, anyway?" Salespeople should also remember that, in addition to damaging credibility, truth-stretching comments can come back to haunt them in the form of legal liability (see Chapter 2 for a review of legal issues).

From the BUYER'S SEAT 8.1

I'M NOT SURE I CAN EVER TRUST YOU AGAIN

As a buyer I place a great deal of importance on whether or not I can trust a salesperson. My trust for a salesperson is developed through interactions where I assess how able, honest, and reliable the seller is. I expect promises and guarantees a salesperson makes during a sales call/presentation to be followed through on. The same thing goes once a supplier is actually contracted for its services or products. Adhering to the things set forth in the contract and purchasing agreement is important. If a salesperson needs to make a change, then keep in contact with me and continue making sales calls to update me. If needed, we can make adjustments in the contract or scheduling, and this will help maintain a win-win relationship for both. Lacking initiative as a salesperson rubs me and other buyers the wrong way, so please salesperson, when you promise something, intend to keep that promise.

Let me give you an example. I am a buyer at the Hunter Davis Los Angeles Drydocks and Shipyard, which provides a broad range of services and capabilities to keep Los Angeles barges, freighters, vessels, and tugs functioning in peak condition. At the moment, the majority of my time is being occupied on a large project with a deadline timetabled for November of this year. I received several sales calls by various salespeople expressing interest in supplying parts for this project, and the equipment parts were bid out to multiple vendors before commencement of the work.

One of our salespeople for a current supplier we work with, Michael, was very quick to respond to our inquiry and help us achieve what was needed for pricing. In the end, Michael ended up winning the bid for a very important set of parts. After receiving a further sales call and a bit of negotiating, our order was promised with a delivery date in March.

We are now in May, almost two months past the promised delivery date, and have still not received the parts. After two weeks of unreturned communications (both phone calls and e-mails), Michael finally responded stating that the parts were backordered and were planned to actually ship the same day. That was well over a month ago and none of the parts have arrived. How can I ever trust Michael and this supplier again?

With these parts being crucial to our timeline it is vital that vendors hold up their guaranteed delivery date and inform us of any delays so we can adjust accordingly. If Michael would have made a call and relayed new shipping information to us right away, we could have made some adjustments to our build schedule. Instead, some of our business could be lost, all because the requirements promised during the sales call or stated in the contract were not met in a timely manner. Going forward, I will be forever skeptical of what Michael says and whether or not he can get parts delivered when we need them.

Source: Anonymous upon request, used with permission, all names changed.

Many salespeople have found that the most effective way to establish credibility is to make a **balanced presentation** that shows all sides of the situation—that is, to be totally honest. Thus, a salesperson might mention some things about the product that make it less than perfect or may speak positively about some exclusive feature of a competitor's product. Will this approach defeat the seller's chances of a sale? No. In fact, it may increase the chances of building long-term commitment and rapport. Salespeople can keep customers happy and dedicated by helping them form correct, realistic expectations about a product or service.

ethics

Salespeople can build credibility by recognizing cultural differences, not only in foreign markets but also in North America. How? By demonstrating sensitivity to the needs and wants of specific subcultures and avoiding biased or racist language. See Chapter 4 for more information about cultural differences.

In selling complex products, sales representatives often must demonstrate product expertise at the beginning of the sales process—for example, by telling the customer, without bragging, about their special training or education. They can also strengthen credibility with well-conceived, insightful questions or comments.

When selling complicated technical products and services, Todd Graf notes, "You have to keep it simple. Teach as you go. Make transitions slow and smooth and always ask if they understand (half the time they don't). This is key because they may have to go back and explain some of your features to the decision maker who isn't present in this meeting."[18]

Being willing to say "I'm sorry, I was wrong on that" or "I don't know the answer to that, but I'll get it to you" will also go a long way toward establishing credibility. A seller should never use a word if he or she doesn't know the exact definition. Some buyers may even test the salesperson. Here's an example from a real salesperson who was calling on a doctor:[19]

SALESPERSON: Because product X acts as an agonist at the kappa receptor, miosis will occur.

DOCTOR: What does *miosis* mean?

SALESPERSON: It means the stage of disease during which intensity of signs and symptoms diminishes.

DOCTOR: No! *Miosis* means contraction of the pupils.

At this point the doctor walked out of the room, and the seller thought she had lost all credibility. Actually, he had just gone out and grabbed a dictionary. The first definition was the contraction of the pupils, and the second was the seller's definition. The salesperson's definition, not the doctor's, fit the use of the term for this medication. The doctor then shook the seller's hand and thanked her for teaching him a new definition of the word. The salesperson's credibility certainly increased.

SELLING TO GROUPS

Selling to groups can be both rewarding and frustrating. On the plus side, if you make an effective presentation, every member of the prospect group becomes your ally. On the down side, groups behave like groups, with group standards and norms and issues of status and group leadership.

When selling to groups, the salesperson must gather information about the needs and concerns of each individual who will attend. Salespeople should discover (for each prospect group member) member status within the group, authority, perceptions about the urgency of the problem, receptivity to ideas, knowledge of the subject matter, attitude toward the salesperson, major areas of interest and concern, key benefits sought, likely resistance, and ways to handle this resistance. Chapter 3 discusses many things that salespeople should consider about buying centers.

It is important to develop objectives not only for the meeting but also for what the seller hopes to accomplish with each prospect present at the meeting. Planning may include the development of special visual aids for specific individuals present. The seller must expect many more objections and interruptions in a group setting compared to selling to an individual.

An informal atmosphere in which group members are encouraged to speak freely and the salesperson feels free to join the group's discussion usually works best in these situations. Thus an informal location (such as a corner of a large room as opposed to a formal conference room) is preferred. Formal presentation methods, such as speeches, that separate buyers and sellers into them-versus-us

Selling to groups requires special skills in monitoring several individuals at once, as well as being able to respond to customers with occasionally conflicting needs.

sides should be avoided. If the group members decide that the meeting is over, the salesperson should not try to hold them.

Of course, most things you have learned about selling to individuals apply equally to groups. You should learn the names of group members and use them when appropriate. You should listen carefully and observe all nonverbal cues. When one member of the buying team is talking, it is especially important to observe the cues being transmitted by the other members of the buying team to see whether they are, in effect, agreeing or disagreeing with the speaker.

There are several types of group selling situations. If the group meeting is actually a negotiation session, many more things must be considered. As a result, we devote an entire chapter (Chapter 12) to the topic of formal negotiations. Also, sometimes a salesperson makes a call on a prospect as part of a selling team from his firm (for example, the team might consist of his sales manager, someone from technical support, someone from customer support, and a sales executive from the firm). These situations require coordination and teamwork. Because of the importance of the various selling team scenarios, the issue of selling teams is more fully discussed in Chapter 16.

SELLING YOURSELF

Selling yourself is a skill that can be used in all aspects of life, from scoring your first job to getting a first date. Each step in this chapter will help you accomplish your sales and interview goals. With these steps you will be able to figure out your potential employer's needs as well as differentiate yourself from the rest of the pool of applicants.

First impressions can set the tone for your interview. One key proponent to making a great first impression is to dress to impress. Dressing professionally not only makes you feel confident but also shows the interviewer that you are serious about interviewing for the position. Though you may not think looking pristine before you interview is a key aspect, it can set you apart from the other applicants. Additionally, always be sure to smile and give a firm handshake before sitting down to start the interview. Whether you are trying to score your dream job or meeting with your customer the first time, first impressions lay the foundation for how your interview or sales call will go.

If you haven't researched the interviewer's needs already, be direct and ask what the company is looking for in the role you for which you are interviewing. For example:

"Mr./Ms. Interviewer, tell me more about your expectations for this role."

"Explain to me some of the daily tasks that are required for this role in order to be successful."

"Describe to me what type of customers I would be dealing with on a daily basis."

By asking these types of questions, you will be able to uncover the company's needs and then relate them directly to your features and how they can benefit the company. Your features and benefits should tie directly to your portfolio/résumé and the accomplishments within it. This creates and reinforces a consistent message during your interview and will help build credibility.

Finally, in order to effectively sell yourself you need to *be* yourself. Good interviewers and customers can tell whether you are genuine and sincerely care about the job or product/service you are trying to sell. Being comfortable in your own shoes will reinforce each step in the selling process and make an interview or your sales call go as planned.

Seth Bleiler, government transportation safety specialist, 3M. Used with permission.

SUMMARY

Salespeople need to make every possible effort to create a good impression during a sales call. The first few minutes with the prospect are important, and care should be taken to make an effective entrance by giving a good first impression, expressing confidence while standing and shaking hands, and selecting an appropriate seat.

The salesperson can use any of several methods to gain the prospect's attention. Salespeople should adopt the opening that is most effective for the prospect's personality style. Also critical is the development of rapport with the prospect, which can often be enhanced by engaging in friendly conversation.

Before beginning any discussion of product information, the salesperson can establish the prospect's needs by using open and closed questions. The SPIN technique is very effective for discovering needs in a major sale. In subsequent calls the salesperson should reiterate the prospect's needs.

When moving into a discussion of the proposed solution or alternatives, the salesperson translates features into benefits for the buyer. The salesperson also makes any necessary adjustments in the presentation based on feedback provided by the buyer's nonverbal cues and by verbal probing.

A close, harmonious relationship will enhance the whole selling process. The salesperson can build credibility by adhering to stated appointment lengths, backing up statements with proof, offering a balanced presentation, and establishing his or her credentials.

When selling to groups, the salesperson must gather information about the needs and concerns of each individual who will attend. The seller should also uncover the ego involvement and issue involvement of each group member. It is important to develop objectives not only for the meeting but also for what the seller hopes to accomplish with each prospect present at the meeting.

Now that you know how to start the sale, discover needs, relate features to specific benefits for the buyer, and build credibility, it is time to look more closely at how to communicate your ideas more effectively. That's the topic of the next chapter.

KEY TERMS

advantages 216
balanced presentation 220
benefit 215
benefit opening 203
closed questions 208
compliment opening 203
credibility 219
credibility statement 219
customer benefit proposition 215
FAB 216
feature 215
feature dumping 214
FEBA 216
Four A's 200

halo effect 203
implication questions 211
impression management 200
introduction opening 203
major sale 209
need payoff questions 211
office scanning 204
open questions 208
opening 203
problem questions 210
product opening 203
question opening 203
rapport 204
referral opening 203
selective perception 218
situation questions 210
small talk 204
SPIN 209
trial close 218

ETHICS PROBLEMS

1. You're an account executive for Wells Fargo Financial in Seattle. You had an initial appointment with a customer, Katlin, to find out what her goals were financially. The meeting went just as a typical first meeting should go, and there was a beneficial product you could create for her. However, her husband could not meet with you. After weeks of work and preparation, you have a loan that makes sense. The loan meets the goals Katlin wanted, so you have a second appointment with her to go over exact terms, again without her husband. You asked when her husband could come in and sign the loan documents, and she discloses to you that her husband is not aware of the $35,000 of credit card debts the loan is going to pay off. Both the husband and the wife must be present at the time of the loan. Legally you can call the husband and tell him about the loan application. What should you do?

   Source: Erik Abrahamson, Wells Fargo Financial; used with permission.
2. You're giving a presentation and it's going very well. Your prospect has already commented on how professional your information has been presented. You've been using a feature-benefit chart that you created late the night before to show how your new product is going to be introduced to the market. While the prospect is asking a question, you happen to glance down at your feature benefit chart again. You almost gasp out loud when you notice that the chart claims that $5,000,000 is going to be spent in advertising the new product launch, when in fact it should say $500,000. Will you admit the mistake to your prospect?

QUESTIONS AND PROBLEMS

1. Assume you're going to be meeting with one of your professors next week. You've never met with him or her before. What can you do, before and during that meeting, to develop rapport and build credibility with your professor?
2. "I don't need to discover my prospect's needs. I sell Hershey's candy to grocery and convenience stores. I know what their needs are: a high profit margin and fast turnover of products!" Comment.
3. Develop the FEBA for one of the features shown in Exhibit 8.8: 40-cent coupon with front positioning in the national Sunday insert section.
4. Assume that you are selling plumbing maintenance and repair services to a large hotel. Develop a series of open and closed questions to discover the prospect's needs.
5. Assume that you represent your school's placement service. You are calling on a large business

nearby that never hires graduates from your college. Generate a list of SPIN questions, making any additional assumptions necessary.

6. Prepare a list of features and benefits that could be used in a presentation to other students at your college. The objective of the presentation is to encourage them to participate in an attempt to break the world record in creating and eating the longest banana split. Students would be asked to secure pledges from family and friends for their participation, with all money raised going to the American Cancer Society.
7. Sales Technology 8.1 told about technology tools that help evaluate sales calls, including the use of slang and informal language. How might that be especially helpful when selling internationally?
8. In Building Partnerships 8.1 you read how one salesperson feels it is important to smile during a sales call. This chapter also talked about the importance of smiling. For an exercise to test this, observe what happens in 10 regular conversations you have with others. In 5 of the conversations, make sure you smile, while in the other 5 five intentionally avoid smiling. Report your observations of the differences between the two groups of conversations.
9. As a salesperson, should you use the prospect's first name (like, "Hello, George") or last name (like, "Hello, Ms. Carlin") in the following circumstances? Why? Assume in each case that this is your first call on the prospect.
   a. Calling on the 72-year-old president of a regional air cargo service.
   b. Calling on a 32-year-old supervisor of a manufacturing plant.
   c. Calling on a 44-year-old owner of a trendy nightclub.
10. You're selling a new line of chewing gum to a convenience store (choose some brand of gum). Write a list of features and benefits for the convenience store, as well as a list of features and benefits for the store's customers (the shoppers who come in and buy gum).
11. In From the Buyer's Seat 8.1 you heard the reflections of one buyer about a seller who did not keep his promises. Make a spreadsheet that includes headings of "Reasons I Might Not Keep a Promise as a Salesperson" and "Alternative Behavior I Might Do, Rather Than Breaking the Promise." Populate both columns with five entries, assuming the scenario as laid out in From the Buyer's Seat 8.1. In the end, hopefully you will have generated a list of excuses to break your word, followed by a better approach (than actually breaking your word).

CASE PROBLEMS

case 8.1

Presidential Aviation (Part B)

Presidential Aviation has provided charter flights to a wide array of customers, including business travelers worldwide. The company is known for its ability to cater to passengers' every desire, including gourmet meals, special beverages, entertainment while in the air, and other luxury accommodations. Miguel Lopez is a salesperson for Presidential Aviation. Today he will be making his first visit to Jorge Morales, a procurement officer at Regent Seven Seas Cruises.

For more details about Presidential Aviation and Regent Seven Seas Cruises, see Case 7.1 in Chapter 7.

Questions

1. Develop a set of open and closed questions to fully discover Jorge Morales's needs.
2. Develop a set of SPIN questions to discover Jorge Morales's needs.

Sources: RSSC; Presidential Aviation

case 8.2

The Walt Disney Studios

Assume you are making a call on the senior procurement agent of the Walt Disney Studios in Burbank, California. The Disney Studios, with annual revenues of about $3 billion, makes blockbuster movies each year with titles such as *The Jungle Book, Finding Dory, Captain America: Civil War,* and *Rogue One.*

On set, during setup and filming, the various personnel need to communicate with one another. In the past, each person has used his or her own private cell phone, or director's shouting, or walkie talkies to achieve this communication. The use of private cell phones can sometimes be challenging, however, due to various plans, phone types, differences in charging cords, and other technical issues. If all personnel had a single type of phone, then the studio could contact them more easily. Plus, each phone could be set up with private access to a wealth of information and private apps to link to such things as scripts, scene takes, communication and updates about schedules, and so forth.

You are making a call with the intention of eventually securing an order for 500 smartphones that will be used by the various people on set. The phones will be fully functional, allowing the use of all features, with the exception of overseas long-distance calls.

Questions

1. Choose any single cell phone model you wish. Then go to the Web and learn about its features.
2. Create a feature-benefit chart specifically for the Walt Disney Studios, taking into the account the information provided in this case. Make sure you communicate about benefits that are important to Disney in this specific situation.

Source: Disney

ROLE PLAY CASE

We are going to start over again, "from the top" as they say in the theater. Start from the beginning of the sales call, from when you knock on the door through the needs identification stage, ending just before your presentation. All that you have learned in previous role plays about the account continues to hold true. If you've been selling to ARM, you'll continue to do so, but you are now meeting with a different member of the buying center. The same is true for FSS and Mizzen. New buyer sheets will be passed out. You can have the same person play the new role or someone else in class. (*Note:* If you have not done role plays before, you will need to review the information about the various role play customers that can be found at the end of Chapter 3.)

If your class is divided into groups of three, the person who is watching should create a check sheet. Write *S, P, I,* and *N* down the left side of the paper. As the salesperson asks a question, check whether it is a situation, problem, implication, or needs payoff question. Also note if and how he or she identified or verified the decision process. *Don't forget:* At the start of the sales call, identify the type of opening used (introduction, benefit, product, curiosity, or some other form).

ARM: You will meet with the VP of sales and marketing. This is an appointment that was set up by the CIO you called on earlier. You've never talked to this person before.

FSS: Mr. McLane, the owner, has asked to see you. You weren't expecting this from your earlier sales calls, but you welcome the opportunity to meet the decision maker. His secretary called and made the appointment.

Mizzen Industries: You are meeting with one of the VPs of sales. The other VP was fired, but you don't know why. The meeting was set up by the CIO you called on earlier, who also told you about the firing, but she didn't know what had happened.

Note: For background information about these role plays, please see Chapter 1.

To the instructor: Additional information needed to complete the role play is available in the Instructor's Manual.

ADDITIONAL REFERENCES

Booher, Dianna Daniels. *What More Can I Say?: Why Communication Fails and What to Do about It.* New York: Prentice Hall Press, 2015.

Cardon, Peter W. *Business Communication: Developing Leaders for a Networked World.* New York: McGraw-Hill Irwin, 2014.

Conlow, Rick, and Doug Watsabaugh. *Superstar Sales: A 31-Day Plan to Motivate People, Build Rapport, and Close More Sales.* Pompton Plains, NJ: Career Press, 2013.

Freese, Thomas A. *Secrets of Question Based Selling: How the Most Powerful Tool in Business Can Double Your Sales Results.* Naperville, IL: Sourcebooks, 2013.

Kane, Nick, and Justin Zappulla. *Critical Selling: How Top Performers Accelerate the Sales Process and Close More Deals.* Hoboken, NJ: Wiley, 2016.

Kumar, V., and Werner Reinartz. "Creating Enduring Customer Value." *Journal of Marketing* 80, no. 6 (2016), pp. 36–68.

Paolo Guenzi , Luigi M. De Luca, and Rosann Spiro. "The Combined Effect of Customer Perceptions about a Salesperson's Adaptive Selling and Selling Orientation on Customer Trust in the Salesperson: A Contingency Perspective." *Journal of Business and Industrial Marketing* 31, no. 4 (2016), pp. 553–64.

Prendergast, Gerard Paul, Sze Sze Li, and Connie Li. "Consumer Perceptions of Salesperson Gender and Credibility: An Evolutionary Explanation." *Journal of Consumer Marketing* 31, no. 3 (2014), pp. 200–11.

Tyler, M., and J. Donovan. *Predictable Prospecting: How to Radically Increase Your B2B Sales Pipeline.* New York: McGraw-Hill Education, 2016.

Ulke, Anne-Kathrin, and Laura Schons. "CSR as a Selling of Indulgences: An Experimental Investigation of Customers' Perceptions of CSR Activities Depending on Corporate Reputation." *Corporate Reputation Review* 19, no. 3 (2016), pp. 263–80.

Zhang, Annie Liqin, Roger Baxter, and Mark S. Glynn. "How Salespeople Facilitate Buyers' Resource Availability to Enhance Seller Outcomes." *Industrial Marketing Management* 42, no. 7 (2013), pp. 1121–30.

The Partnership Process

PART 2

©Ingram Publishing/Getty Images RF

chapter 9

STRENGTHENING THE PRESENTATION

SOME QUESTIONS ANSWERED IN THIS CHAPTER ARE

- How can salespeople use verbal tools to strengthen a presentation?
- Why do salespeople need to augment their oral communication through tools such as visual aids, samples, testimonials, and demonstrations?
- What methods are available to strengthen a presentation?
- How can salespeople use visual aids and technology most effectively?
- What are the ingredients of a good demonstration?
- Is there a way to quantify the salesperson's solution to a buyer's problem?
- How can salespeople reduce presentation jitters?

PROFILE

> *"I've learned if I design my presentation with engagement at its core, magic happens."*
>
> *Justin Carter, Hewlett Packard Enterprise*

Courtesy of Justin Carter

PROFILE Prior to ever presenting to Fortune 500 companies, I gained life-changing information from the late Greg Graham and Ellen Daniels at Kent State University. I am a sales specialist at Hewlett Packard Enterprise. My role is to become a trusted advisor with major corporations while helping them along their IT transformation journey. Through my professional life, I've learned my success relies on how well I can present information. Studies show that your ability to captivate an audience within the first few moments are critically important. In a content-driven world, it is likely your customer will have viewed multiple presentations around your product or industry. The overall success of your presentation depends on your ability to articulate a topic well in its simplist form. The challenge is that there are also many other competitors trying to compete for the same mindshare. With that understanding, through my experience I have learned some valuable presentation skills.

1. *Speak with conviction and have a vested interest in the risks/challenges of your client's business*

Customers ultimately buy from who they like. With that being said, clients like advisors with as much concern for their business as they have. In any journey your client takes, they want to know that you are just as concerned/interested as they are. This comes through in the way you present information. When speaking, it is important to use the term "we" instead of "you". "We" says that I have a vested interest in this exchange and am looking to sell a solution. Share how you will be a part of the journey with them to mitigate perceived risk with your solution. It is important that they know how you will be a value added extension of their business.

2. *Present information that encourages a dialogue instead of a monologue*

It is painful for anyone to sit through a presentation that suppresses his or her ability to engage. I've learned if I design my presentation with engagement at its core, magic happens. The customers may share things they have never shared before. You may go into a presentation thinking their solution is A, but engagement may uncover their solution is really B. Set the tone early in your presentation and you may have clients who get out of their seats because you've peaked their interest.

3. *Tell stories*

Often a concept may not become clear to your clients unless you paint a mental picture. Your trustworthiness can also be built when you use cases. Often in my presentation I will discuss what we've done for other customers with similar challenges. Walking a client through an example of how you solved another customer's challenges can be the game changer. If you don't have a personal example, use one from a colleague.

In conclusion, balance is key. Well-built slides won't make up for poor communication and vice versa. Keeping slides easy to understand with concise talking points can be extremely helpful to your audience. Adding value is the best thing you can do, and it often starts at the presentation level. Practicing often, rehearsing objections and perceived concerns can be a game changer.

Visit our Web site at: www.hpe.com/us/en/home.html.

CHARACTERISTICS OF A STRONG PRESENTATION

Communication tools such as visual aids, samples, testimonials, demonstrations, and the use of stories and humor are important ingredients in most sales calls. Use of such tools focuses the buyer's attention, improves the buyer's understanding, helps the buyer remember what the salesperson said, offers concrete proof of the salesperson's statements, and creates a sense of value.

KEEPS THE BUYER'S ATTENTION

How many times has your mind wandered during classroom lectures while the instructor earnestly discussed some topic? What happened? The instructor lost your attention. In contrast, your attention probably remains more focused in a class when the instructor uses stories and humor effectively, brings in guest speakers, and finds ways to get you actively involved in the discussion.

The same is true of buyer-seller interactions. Unless you can get the buyer actively involved in the communication process doing more than just passively hearing you talk, the buyer's attention will probably turn to other topics. Building Partnerships 9.1 provides some helpful hints on communicating effectively with clients and presents some other important perspectives on how to succeed in sales.

The buyer's personality can also affect his or her attention span. For example, one would expect an amiable to listen more attentively to a long presentation than, say, a driver would. Thus an effective salesperson should consider the social style of the prospect and adapt the use of communication aids accordingly (see Chapter 5 for more about personality styles).

IMPROVES THE BUYER'S UNDERSTANDING

Many buyers have difficulty forming clear images from the written or spoken word. An old Chinese proverb says, "Tell me–I'll forget. Show me–I may remember. But involve me, and I'll understand." Appeals should be made to as many of the senses (hearing, sight, touch, taste, and smell) as possible. Studies show that appealing to more than one sense with **multiple-sense appeals** increases understanding dramatically, as Exhibit 9.1 illustrates. For example, in selling Ben & Jerry's ice cream novelties to a grocery store manager, the salesperson may describe the product's merits (an appeal to the sense of hearing) or show the product and invite the merchant to taste it (appeals to sight, touch, and taste). Appeals to the grocer's fifth sense, smell, are also possible. On the other hand, salespeople who sell machinery are limited to appeals that will affect the buyers' senses of hearing, sight, and touch.

HELPS THE BUYER REMEMBER WHAT WAS SAID

On average, people immediately forget 50 percent of what they hear; after 48 hours they have forgotten 75 percent of the message. This is unfortunate because securing an order often requires multiple visits, and in many situations the prospect must relay to other people information learned in a sales call. In these circumstances it becomes more critical for the seller to help the buyer remember what was said.

Even selling situations involving one call or one decision maker will be more profitable if the buyer remembers what was said. Vividly communicated features create such a strong impression that the buyer remembers the seller's claims and is more likely to tell others about them.

BUILDING Partnerships 9.1

MY "SECRET SAUCE" FOR SALES SUCCESS

My name is Beth Jeanetta. I work as a sales account executive at an amazing company, where our goal and motive is to help companies stop wasting their money in regard to their IT expenditures. The way we achieve such results is by conducting business through our 14 enterprise-class data centers located in six states, featuring multitenant and private cloud solutions, IT consulting, and related managed technical services.

I'll explain what I consider my "secret sauce" for sales. My success in the approach and sales pitches and presentations lies within the "Be's":

- Be Authentic/Be Yourself—Do *not* try to be "just like somebody else," even if they are rock star salespeople. You can capitalize on tips, tricks, knowledge, and experience but you have to execute in your own style, otherwise it will look and feel fake.
- Be Available—Give your clients/prospects your contact information and always respond promptly.
- Be Knowledgeable—Know about your products and services. *Never* be afraid to loop in resources for help or resolution if you are unsure of an answer during a presentation.
- Be Transparent—Clients/prospects value honesty, so always maintain a transparent relationship.
- Be Friendly—People will buy from people they *like*. Build genuine relationships with your prospects/clients, which is essential for repeat business.
- Be Organized/Communicate—Keeping organized and communicating well internally and externally will benefit your sales team as well as buyers.
- Be Reliable—Do what you say you are going to do, when you say you are going to do it. If you make a guarantee during a presentation to a buyer, be sure to follow through.
- Be Prepared—Before you even schedule an appointment with a potential client, do the research! Look up information online; use LinkedIn connections; ask colleagues, clients, and friends for warm introductions; find out if the potential client is in any local networking groups, and so forth. Have your catchy "elevator pitch" with your follow-up responses thought out and rehearsed. Mine is the first paragraph of this article. From there, I tailor the presentation to the individual client's needs.
- Be Connected—Attend networking groups that will drive your business forward. Create your own networking and lead share groups where you host, present, and foster those relationships as being the "industry expert." You will create a name for yourself that can be beneficial in conversation and increase sales influence.
- Be Educated—We all can learn more about sales techniques, our industry, and other related subjects to foster our personal growth.
- Be Passionate—If you aren't passionate about your job, quit. Find something you can be passionate about because it will show through personally and professionally in your sales results and your body language.
- Be Able to Find Balance—Balance your personal, professional, and spiritual life. This will hopefully lead to a balanced sales presentation.
- Be Aware of Your Time—Time is money for someone in sales.
- Be Trustworthy—Always present solutions with your client's best interest in mind; this will lead to a lasting relationship with your client.
- Be Succinct—Be brief while being factual.
- Be Confident—Confidence can be the difference between being a good salesperson and a great salesperson. Express confidence throughout your interactions, presentations, and your life in general.
- Be Able to Have Fun!—Enjoy the process, be creative, have fun with it! It will show through in the results.

Sales can be a very rewarding career but it also has its challenges. Don't be afraid to fail! It is through our failures that oftentimes we learn our most valuable lessons. I can assure you that over your career, you will lose sales; we all do. Learn and move on. Accept responsibility, personally and professionally, for your results. If you do that, it will help in your future sales approach and presentation.

(Continued)

MY "SECRET SAUCE" FOR SALES SUCCESS (*Continued*)

I manage my sales career as if it were my own business, because it is. I make sure to spend my budget dollars wisely, attending events that will help grow my business. I do an honest self-reflection of where I am at and how my funnel is forecasting. how I can improve, and then develop a plan to get there. As my next step, I execute against my sales plan. If something doesn't work in my pitch, I stop, regroup, and try something different since there is not one set way to generate sales. There isn't any mystery in what makes a great sales presentation other than hard work, attitude, and perseverance. You will know you are doing it right when you start getting referrals, renewals, client compliments, testimonials, and white papers, all of which lead to more opportunities for pitches, presentations, and an increase in sales.

Source: Beth Jeanetta, sales account executive, prefers company name anonymous, used with permission.

Exhibit 9.1
How We Learn

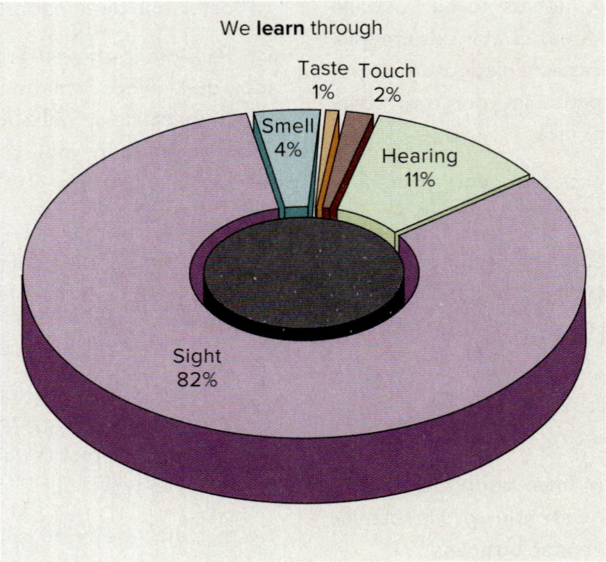

Lasting impressions can be created in many ways. One salesperson swallows some industrial cleanser to show that it is nontoxic; another kicks the protective glass in the control panel of a piece of machinery to show that it is virtually unbreakable in even the roughest conditions. Whatever the method used, the prospect is more likely to remember a sales feature if it is presented skillfully in a well-timed demonstration.

OFFERS PROOF OF THE SALESPERSON'S ASSERTIONS

Let's face it: Most people won't believe everything a salesperson tells them. Many of the communication tools we discuss in this chapter provide solid proof to back up a salesperson's claims. For example, a salesperson can easily claim that a cellphone screen can't be scratched, but the claim is much more convincing if the salesperson uses her keys and tries hard to scratch her cellphone screen right in front of the prospect.

CREATES A SENSE OF VALUE

The manner in which a product is handled suggests value. Careful handling communicates value, whereas careless handling implies that the product has little value. For example, a delicate piece of china will be perceived as more valuable if the salesperson uses appropriate props, words, and care in handling it.

HOW TO STRENGTHEN THE PRESENTATION

Salespeople should ask themselves the following questions: How can I use my imagination and creativity to make a vivid impression on my prospect or customer? How can I make my presentation a little different and a little stronger? With this frame of mind, salespeople will always try to do a better and more effective job of meeting their customers' needs. In this section we explore the many tools available to strengthen a presentation.

Before we describe the various methods, it is important to reiterate a point made in the preceding chapter. A seller should not grab a method because it sounds trendy or because it worked in a previous sales call or because it is highly entertaining. Rather, a seller should strategically select methods and media that will helpfully address the needs of the buyer. This process includes responding to the buyer's unique style (see Chapter 5 to review social styles):

- Expressives like to see strong, intense colors and lots of photos, cartoons, fancy fonts, and positive images (smiles).
- Analyticals prefer visuals that are clean and simple, a list of references, and lots of details.
- Amiables prefer visuals with people in them and a relatively slow-moving presentation.
- Drivers want crisp, professional visuals with bold lettering to highlight important points.

Strategizing also includes considering such elements as how many people will attend the presentation, which stage of the buying process they are in, what information they need, what type of situation this is (new task, modified rebuy, straight rebuy), and so on (see Chapter 3 for more buying factors to consider). In all cases, it is important to get your prospects involved and keep the focus of attention centered on them.

VERBAL TOOLS

Storytelling and Word Pictures

The power of the spoken word can be phenomenal. To communicate effectively, the salesperson needs to remember all the hints and tools found in Chapter 4. The latest neuroscience tells us that there are basically three paths to the subconscious mind (habits, beliefs, and emotions), and stories are ways to tap into all of those paths.[1] Word pictures (see Chapter 4 for a full discussion of word pictures) and stories of all types can be effective.[2] Here are some points to keep in mind when using stories:

- It is best to use stories from your own life. If you borrow one, don't act as if it is your personal story.
- Make sure you have a reason for telling the story.
- Consider using a prop, like a glove or a suitcase or something that helps tell the story and will help the prospect remember the story.
- Use the "hook" of the story to tie back directly into your presentation.

- Be accurate and vivid with the words you choose. Learn to paint a clear picture.
- Pace the story, watching your audience for cues. Use silence, loudness, softness, and pauses.
- Choose stories that fit your own style. Don't try to be someone you're not.
- Remember, stories can be short—even a few sentences.
- Want to learn how to tell stories better? Listen to some experts at www.themoth.org and www.thisamericanlife.org.

Humor

Another way a salesperson can help keep the buyer's attention is through the use of humor. The wonderful effects of laughter will put everyone more at ease, including the salesperson. Use humorous stories from your own experience, borrowed humor, or humor adapted from another source. Here are some things to keep in mind:

- Don't oversell the joke (Here's one that'll really break you up!).
- Don't apologize before telling a joke (I wasn't ever good at telling a joke, but here goes).
- Identify any facts that are absolutely necessary for the punch line of the story to make sense (Jerry Joyner, my next-door neighbor who was always sticking his nose in other people's business, . . .).
- Use humor from your own life. Most have already heard jokes circulating in e-mail or on the Web.
- Enjoy yourself by smiling and animating your voice and using nonverbals.
- Practice telling the joke different ways to see which exact wording works best.
- Make sure your punch line is clear.

ethics

Beware of overdoing humor or using off-the-wall or offensive humor. Both can backfire, as one presenter found out when he used the following opening line about an overweight attendee: "Pull up two chairs and have a seat." The presenter knew right away that it was a big mistake. Always be cautious about using insider jokes, especially if you're still considered an outsider.

thinking it through

What humor have you seen backfire? How can you be sure the humor you are using isn't going to offend someone?

Also, understand that what is funny to one person or group may not be funny to others. For example, a foreigner from Egypt may not appreciate someone from America making fun of Egyptian culture—but someone from Egypt can tell that same joke and get plenty of laughs.

VISUAL TOOLS

A salesperson can use various visually oriented tools to strengthen a presentation. This section explores the content and use of those tools, followed by a discussion of the various media available to display the results.

Graphics and Charts

Graphics and charts help illustrate relationships and clearly communicate large amounts of information. Charts may show, for example, advertising schedules, a breakdown of typical customer profiles, details of product manufacture, profit margins at various pricing points, or the investment nature of purchasing a product.

Here are hints for developing charts and related visuals:[3]

- Know the single point a visual should make, and then ensure that it accomplishes that point.
- Customize charts by including the name of the prospect's company in one corner or by some other form of personalization.
- Use current, accurate information.
- Don't place too much information on a visual; on text visuals, don't use more than five or six words per line or more than five lines or bullets per visual. Don't use complete sentences; the speaker should verbally provide the missing details.
- Use bullets (dots or symbols before each line) to differentiate issues and to emphasize key points.
- Don't overload the buyer with numbers. Use no more than five or six columns, and drop all unnecessary zeros.
- Clearly label each visual with a title. Label all columns and rows.
- Recognize the emotional impact of colors, and choose appropriate ones. An abundance of green connected to a humorous graph might be offensive in Islamic countries because green is a religious color. In Brazil and Mexico, purple indicates death. In America, blue indicates confidence and safety, black connotes a strong sense of power, and white indicates sophistication and formality.[4]
- If possible, use graphics (like diagrams, pie charts, and bar charts) instead of tables. Tables are often needed if actual raw numbers are important; graphics are better for displaying trends and relationships.
- Use high-quality drawings and photographs instead of clip art if possible.
- Use consistent art styles, layouts, and scales for your collection of charts and figures. Consistency makes it easier for the buyer to follow along.
- For PowerPoint slides, use 28-point type for the titles and 24-point type for the text, using Arial or Helvetica. And use transition effects and sound clips sparingly.
- Check your visuals closely for typographical errors, misspelled words, and other errors.
- Know and obey copyright laws. You can't just grab images off the Web and use them.

Salespeople should use humor to get and keep the customer's attention.

©John Burke/Getty Images RF

Models, Samples, and Gifts

Visual selling aids such as models, samples, and gifts may be a good answer to the problem of getting and keeping buyer interest. For example, Mul-T-Lock salespeople carry along a miniature working model of the company's electronic door locks when calling on prison security system buyers. The model allows the salesperson to show how the various components work together to form a fail-safe security network.

Other salespeople use cross-sectional models to communicate with the buyer. For example, salespeople for Motion Industries use a cutaway model of a power transmission friction reduction product. This model helps the buyer, usually an industrial engineer, clearly see how the product is constructed, resulting in greater confidence that the product will perform as described.

ethics

Depending on the service or product, models, samples, and gifts can make excellent sales aids and help maintain the prospect's interest after the call. Loctite displayed the superior holding power of its glue by suspending a man by his shoes at a trade show, held in place by the Loctite adhesive. In a Johnson's Wax sales campaign, salespeople called on buyers of major chains to describe the promotion. Salespeople walked into each buyer's office with a solid oak briefcase containing cans of aerosol Pledge, the product to be highlighted during the promotion. During the call the sales representative demonstrated the Pledge furniture polish on the oak briefcase. At the conclusion of the visit, the rep gave the buyer not only the cans of Pledge but also the briefcase. Of course gift giving must be done with care and not violate the rules of the buyer's company.

Catalogs and Brochures

Catalogs and brochures can help salespeople communicate information to buyers effectively. The salesperson can use them during a presentation and then leave them with the buyer as a reminder of the issues covered. Brochures often summarize key points and contain answers to the usual questions buyers pose, as the example in Exhibit 9.2 illustrates.

Exhibit 9.2

A Brochure with Great Visual Appeal

©Peter Brooker/REX/Shutterstock.com RF

Photos, Illustrations, Ads, and Maps

Photos are easy to prepare, are inexpensive, and permit a realistic portrayal of a product and its benefits. Photographs of people may be particularly effective. For example, leisure made possible through savings can be communicated via photographs of retired people at a ranch, a mountain resort, or the seashore. Illustrations drawn, painted, or prepared in other ways also help dramatize needs or benefits. Copies of recent or upcoming ads may contribute visual appeal. Detailed maps can be easily developed, for example, to show how a magazine's circulation matches the needs of potential advertisers.

Testimonials and Test Results

Testimonials are statements written by satisfied users of a product or service. For example, company representatives who sell air travel for major airlines have found case histories helpful in communicating sales points. Air Canada recounts actual experiences of business firms, showing the variety of problems that air travel can solve.

The effectiveness of a testimonial hinges on the skill with which it is used and a careful matching of satisfied user and prospect. In some situations the testimony of a rival or a competitor of the prospective buyer would end all chance of closing the sale; in other cases this type of testimony may be a strong factor in obtaining commitment. As much as possible, the person who writes the testimonial should be above reproach, well respected by his or her peers, and perhaps a center of influence (see Chapter 6). For example, when selling to certified public accountants (CPAs), a good source for a testimonial would be the president of the state's CPA association.

Before using a testimonial, the salesperson needs to check with the person who wrote it and frequently reaffirm that he or she is still a happy, satisfied customer. One salesperson for Unisys routinely handed all prospects a testimonial from a satisfied customer of a new software package. But unknown to the salesperson, the "satisfied customer" became an unsatisfied one and actually returned the software. The salesperson kept handing out the letter until one of his prospects alerted him to the situation. He will never know how many other prospects lost interest after contacting that customer.

Salespeople should not hand out a testimonial to every prospect. Such letters should be used only if they help address the buyer's needs or concerns. Also, be aware that prospects probably discount testimonials, thinking that the seller is presenting letters only from very satisfied customers.

Salespeople can also use test results to strengthen the presentation. Tests on the product or service may have been conducted by the seller's firm or some third-party organization (such as Consumer Reports or Underwriters Laboratories). Generally, tests conducted by independent, recognized authorities have more credibility for the prospect than tests done by the seller.

Using Media to Display Visuals

Many media are available to display the types of items just mentioned. New media and improvements to existing media are being introduced almost every week (like 3D interactive viewing, virtual reality, and so forth). Salespeople are encouraged to choose media that are appropriate for the exact situation and not merely choose a tool because it is new or exciting. Sales Technology 9.1 describes how salespeople can use technology to spice up presentations.

Most salespeople have developed a **portfolio**, which is a collection of visual aids, often placed in a binder or on a computer. Salespeople do not intend to use

SALES Technology 9.1

POWERPOINT? OUT WITH THE OLD, IN WITH THE NEW

Sales presentations are a key to a representative's job success and are the first steps toward reaching a beneficial business relationship. Microsoft approximated that 30 million PowerPoint presentations are shown each day, while your competition and every other salesperson in your industry are contending for your prospect's business. You do not want to leave your audience feeling unimpressed and unenthusiastic. The following tools can help capture that audience and grow your sales.

SlideShark

Today almost all business professionals, like buyers, come equipped to a meeting with some form of laptop or tablet, yet not many salespeople are willing to take advantage. Conference rooms can be large and attendees sitting at a distance are likely to disengage or daydream at times. The solution? Personally stream your presentation to their device and leave an impression that can't be otherwise achieved. It might seem counterproductive as a salesperson to encourage your audience to ignore maintaining eye contact with you, but many do so anyways.

With an application such as SlideShark you have the ability to merely provide a link and transmit your slides in real time so prospects and clients can see the same on their own personal device (laptop, tablet, smartphone). While presenting from any streaming device, like a smartphone, you can configure SlideShark to emphasize significant points of the presentation and highlight various elements on your prospect's device. Time is of the essence, so rather than wasting time setting up your presentation, capture your audience's attention by uploading your presentation to your prospect's devices. Plus, using your phone you can easily navigate slides or broadcast your slides to a remote audience so they can follow along.

Haiku Deck

Yes, PowerPoint is still widely used, but let's face it, it can be perceived as boring and commonplace. "Death by PowerPoint" is a phrase often used for a reason; you do not want your prospect to feel the same. Haiku Deck provides salespersons with properties at their disposal to change PowerPoint into an influential aspect of the presentation. Offered as a free app, it includes default inventive templates, endless amounts of photos, and a user-friendly interface to design beautiful visuals and text.

Prezi

Prezi creates a fun and interactive presentation platform that draws in the attention of the viewer with entertaining story-enhancing visuals. Prezi, unlike most other platforms, is exciting due to its expansive graphical features and zoom ability through various waypoints, maximizing the flow of a presentation. This platform infuses videos, images, and transition effects at the sales rep's desire. With the ability for unique presentations individual personality comes to light. Furthermore, this portrays you as a sales rep current with the times, and can help infer that you can be depended on to keep the client up-to-date on technological industry trends.

Source: Robyn Schelenz, "Using Technology to Improve Your Sales Presentations," *National Association of Sales Professionals* Web site

everything in the portfolio in a single call; rather, the portfolio should contain a broad spectrum of visual aids the salesperson can find quickly should the need arise. When showing visuals in your portfolio, make sure the portfolio is turned so the buyer can see it easily. The portfolio should not be placed, like a wall, between you and the buyer. Remember to look at the buyer, not at your visual; maintaining eye contact is always important.

Video is another tool salespeople can use. Salespeople use video to help buyers see how quality is manufactured into a product (showing the production process at the manufacturing plant), how others use a product or service (showing a group of seniors enjoying the golf course at a retirement resort), promotional support offered with the product (showing an upcoming TV commercial for a product), and even testimonials from satisfied users. When using video, make sure the video is fast paced and relatively short. Don't show more than four minutes of a video at one time.

Salespeople have adopted laptops, iPads, and other portable devices for use in sales calls. For example, Merck pharmaceutical salespeople carry laptops with a database of technical information, as well as complete copies of articles from medical journals. Progressive firms, like Aetna, are investing in **digital collateral management systems** (also called **sales asset management systems**) to archive, catalog, and retrieve digital media and text. **Collateral** is a collection of documents that are designed to generate sales, such as brochures, sales flyers and fact sheets, and short success stories. Digital collateral management systems simplify the collection and make it possible for salespeople to easily secure and adapt these selling tools for specific situations. For example, salespeople using the SAVO digital collateral management system (www.savogroup.com) can easily call up photos, videos, audio files, PowerPoint templates, Web pages, legal documents, streaming media, and just about anything else that has been digitally entered into the system.

Some salespeople use PowerPoint to give presentations. However, it is critical that salespeople not merely progress from one slide to the next. Presentations should use visuals that encourage two-way conversation rather than an endless group of slides.

thinking it through

You turn down the lights for a PowerPoint computer slide presentation. A few minutes later, you start to panic when your eye catches an unusual jerking movement made by the buyer—she's falling asleep! What do you do now?

Computers not only offer excellent visuals and graphics but also allow the salesperson to perform what-if analyses. For example, when a grocery buyer asked a Procter & Gamble rep what would happen if a new product were sold for $3.69

Examples of sales collateral for an industrial product.

©McGraw-Hill Education/Jill Braaten, photographer

instead of the $3.75 suggested retail price, the salesperson was able to easily change this number in the spreadsheet program. Instantly all charts and graphs were corrected to illustrate the new pricing point, and comparisons with the competitor's product were generated.

When using computers, be prepared. Have backup batteries, adapters, and so forth. Really get to know your hardware and software so you can recover if the system crashes. And make sure both you and your customer can comfortably view the output.

Images can also be displayed using other media. **Document cameras**, also called **visual presenters**, are capable of displaying any three-dimensional object without the use of a transparency. **Electronic whiteboards**, commonly referred to as SMART boards, interactive whiteboards, or digital easels, are used by salespeople, especially when working with customers who prefer to brainstorm an issue or problem. These are great at encouraging a group to interact with a presentation rather than merely watch it.

PRODUCT DEMONSTRATIONS

One of the most effective methods of appealing to a buyer's senses is through product demonstrations or performance tests.[5] Customers and prospects have a natural desire to prove a product's claims for themselves. For example, orthopedic surgeons are like carpenters for human bodies: They repair damage and build new skeletons. They don't want a salesperson merely to tell them about new products; these surgeons want to touch them, feel them, and use them to see if they are good. When selling hip replacements to such doctors, sales reps demonstrate their products right in the surgery room. Because there is a definite sterile field, sales reps have to stand outside that field and use a green laser pointer to show where the surgeon should place the appliance.

One enterprising sales representative was having trouble convincing the buyer for a national retailer that the salesperson's company could provide service at all the retailer's scattered outlets. On the next trip to the buyer, the sales representative brought along a bag of darts and a map marked with the chain's hundreds of stores and service locations. The buyer was invited to throw darts at the map and then find the nearest stores. The test pointed out that the nearest location for service was always within 50 miles. This "service demonstration" helped win the representative's company a multimillion-dollar order.

Salespeople use electronic tools to display important information.

©Potstock/Shutterstock.com RF

Another salesperson was selling feeding tubes to a hospital. A nurse took the salesperson to a patient's bed and stated, "Here, you do it. You said it was easier to insert. Let me see you insert it."[6]

Some products can be sold most successfully by getting the prospect into the showroom for a hands-on product demonstration. Showrooms can be quite elaborate and effective. For example, Kohler operates a marketing showroom in Kohler, Wisconsin. Prospects (architects and designers) from across the world can view and try all of Kohler's kitchen and bath fixtures. **Executive briefing centers**, which are rooms set

An executive briefing center.

©Onoky/SuperStock RF

aside to highlight a company's products and capabilities, are the ultimate presentation room.

Here are a number of helpful hints for developing and engaging in effective demonstrations:

- Be prepared. Practice your demonstration until you become an expert. Plan for everything that could possibly go wrong.
- Secure a proper place for the demonstration, one free of distractions for both you and the buyer. If the demonstration is at the buyer's office, make sure you have everything you need (power supply, lighting, and so on). Remember, it can even be an online presentation as Chapter 7 described.
- Check the equipment again to make sure it is in good working order prior to beginning the presentation. Have necessary backup parts and supplies (like paper or bulbs).
- Get the prospect involved in a meaningful way. In a group situation, plan which group members need to participate.
- Always relate product features to the buyer's unique needs.
- Make the demonstration an integral part of the overall presentation, not a separate, unrelated activity.
- Keep the demonstration simple, concise, and clear. Long, complicated demonstrations add to the possibility that the buyer will miss the point. Limit technical jargon to technically advanced buyers who you know will understand technical terms.
- Plan what you will do during any dead time–that is, time in which the machine is processing on its own. You can use these intervals to ask the buyer questions and have the buyer ask you questions.
- Find out whether the prospect has already seen a competitor's product demonstration. If so, strategically include a demonstration of features the buyer liked about the competitor's product. Also, plan to show how your product can meet the prospect's desires and do what the competitor's product will not do.
- Find out whether any buyers present at your demonstration have used your product before. Having them assist in the demonstration may be advantageous if they view your product favorably.
- Probe during and after the demonstration. Make sure buyers understand the features and see how the product can help them. Also, probe to see whether buyers are interested in securing the product.

Remember Murphy's law: What can go wrong will go wrong! If a demonstration "blows up" for any reason, your best strategy usually is to appeal to fate with a humorous tone of voice: "Wow, have you ever seen anything get so messed up? Maybe I should run for Congress!" Don't let technical glitches embarrass or frustrate you. Life is not perfect, and sometimes things just don't work out the way you plan them. If it will help, remember that prospects also are not perfect, and sometimes they mess things up as well. Maintaining a cool and level head will probably impress the prospect with your ability to deal with

Getting the buyer actively involved during the call is important.

a difficult situation. It may even increase your chances of a sale because you are demonstrating your ability to handle stress (something that often occurs during the after-sale servicing of an account).

HANDOUTS

Handouts are written documents provided to help buyers remember what was said. A well-prepared set of handouts can be one of the best ways to increase buyer retention of information, especially over longer periods. A common practice is to make a printed copy of the presentation visuals and give that to the buyers at the conclusion of the presentation.

Others would argue that your use of handouts should be more strategically focused. Thus, handouts are not a last-minute thought but rather are a tool that needs to be carefully planned while you are preparing your presentation. For example, you could draw a line on a piece of planning paper and on the left side list the things you will do and say during the presentation while on the right side listing the items that should go into the handout. In that way the two will work together and be complementary.

What things can go into a handout? Complex charts and diagrams can be included. Because you want to keep your presentation visuals relatively simple (see the preceding hints), your handouts can supply more complete, detailed information. You may also want to include some company reports or literature. However, to avoid making the buyer wade through a lot of nonrelevant information, include only important sections. Other items to include are Web addresses with a description of each site, case studies, magazine articles, and a copy of your presentation visuals themselves (with room to take notes if you're going to give the buyer your handout during the presentation). Whatever you choose, here are some tips:

- Consider highlighting important sections of the handout.
- Don't forget the goal of your meeting. That should drive all your decisions about what to include in your handouts.
- Make sure the handouts look professional. Use graphics instead of text whenever possible.
- Don't cram too much information on a page. White space is fine. Try not to fill more than two-thirds of any page with information.
- Don't drown your prospect in information. Include only helpful information in your handouts.
- Handouts are even more important for foreign buyers, especially those who are nonnative English speakers. You might even consider giving them a copy of your handouts before your meeting so they can become more comfortable and familiar with concepts and phrases. Including a glossary, with definitions, will also be appreciated by foreign buyers.
- Make sure your handouts have "legs," and are easy to follow and understand so that when they are passed from the buyer to others in the buyer's organization, they can make sense of what they're seeing.

WRITTEN PROPOSALS

In some industries written proposals are an important part of the selling process.[7] Some proposals are simple adaptations of brochures developed by a corporate marketing department. But in industries that sell customized products or require competitive bidding (as many state and local governments do), a written proposal may be necessary for the buyer to organize and compare various offerings.

The RFP Process

A document issued by a prospective buyer asking for a proposal may be called a **request for proposal (RFP),** request for quote (RFQ), or request for bid (RFB). For brevity's sake, we will refer to all of these as RFPs.

The RFP should contain the customer's specifications for the desired product, including delivery schedules. RFPs are used when the customer has a firm idea of the product needed. From the salesperson's perspective, being a part of the specifying process makes sense. Using the needs identification process, the salesperson can help the customer identify needs and specify product characteristics.

Writing Proposals

Proposals include an **executive summary**—a one- or two-page summary that provides the total cost minus the total savings, a brief description of the problem to be solved, and a brief description of the proposed solution. The summary should satisfy the concerns of an executive who is too busy or unwilling to read the entire proposal. The executive summary also piques the interest of all readers by allowing a quick glance at the benefits of the purchase.

The proposal also includes a description of the current situation in relation to the proposed solution and a budget (which details costs). Some firms have even developed computer programs to automatically generate sales proposals in response to a set of questions the salesperson answers about a particular customer.[8] This is especially helpful because sometimes buyers use RFPs to keep their current suppliers in check. In such a case, a seller might want to minimize the amount of time spent responding to an RFP. (A familiar saying in sales is "You can't cash an RFP.")

When writing proposals, remember to use your most polished writing skills. Skip buzzwords, focusing on actual results that the prospect can gain from going with your proposal.

Presenting the Proposal

Prospects use proposals in many different ways. Proposals can be used to convince the home office that the local office needs the product, or proposals may be used to compare the product and terms of sale with those of competitors. As we mentioned earlier, the intended use will influence the design of the proposal; it will also influence how the salesperson presents the proposal.

When the proposal is going to be sent to the home office, it is wise to secure the support of the local decision maker. Although that person is not the ultimate decision maker, the decision may rest on how much effort that person puts into getting the proposal accepted. Buying centers often use proposals to compare competitive offerings, and the salesperson is asked to present the proposal to the buying committee.

There are several options if you are going to give an oral presentation of your proposal. First, you can give the buyers a copy of the complete proposal before your presentation. During the meeting you would spend about 5 to 10 minutes summarizing the proposal and then ask for questions. Second, if you choose to give the written proposal to the buyers during the oral presentation, you may want to distribute the proposal a section at a time to avoid having them read ahead instead of listening to your oral presentation.

VALUE ANALYSIS: QUANTIFYING THE SOLUTION

To recap what we've described throughout this book, salespeople are selling value. As mentioned in Chapter 3, one of the trends in buying is more sophisticated analyses by buyers. Buyers today are looking at the total cost of ownership over the lifetime of the product or service. This section explores methods available to help the buyer conduct these types of analyses.

Quantifying a solution is more important in some situations than in others. Some products or services (like replacement parts or repairs) pose little risk for the prospect. These products are so necessary for the continuation of the prospect's business that little quantifying of the solution is usually needed. Other products pose moderate risk (such as expanding the production capacity of a plant for an existing successful product) or high risk (like programs designed to reduce costs or increase sales; these present higher risk because it is hard to calculate the exact magnitude of the potential savings or sales). For moderate-risk and high-risk situations, quantifying the solution becomes increasingly important. Finally, certain products pose super-high risk (brand-new products or services, which are riskier because no one can calculate costs or revenues with certainty). Attempts at quantifying the solution are imperative in super-high-risk situations. In summary, the higher the risk to the prospect, the more attention the salesperson should pay to quantifying the solution.

Salespeople can strengthen a presentation by showing the prospect that the cost of the proposal is offset by added value; this process is often called **quantifying the solution** or **value analysis**. Some of the most common ways to quantify a solution are value propositions, cost–benefit analysis, return on investment, payback period, net present value, and opportunity cost. For retail buyers, the seller usually must prove turnover and profit margins. The key is to offer information that will help buyers evaluate your offering based on their metrics. Thus, if a buyer is evaluating proposals on the basis of ROI, that's the metric you should focus on in your presentation.

Customer Value Proposition

A **customer value proposition (CVP)**, also called a *value proposition,* is the way in which your product will meet the prospect's needs and how that is different from the offerings of competitors, especially the next-best alternative.[9] Honeywell sales reps create basic value propositions for each market segment and then further refine them for each individual customer. The value bundle contained in a solid customer value proposition includes the features and benefits (financial and emotional) tailored to the prospect, the proof that those benefits actually exist, and the value of the seller and the seller's firm as the solutions provider. Simply having a superior product or delivering on your promises is no longer sufficient. Rather, what distinguishes you is how you make your customers feel while using your product. The experience is what bonds your customers to you.

As you write your customer value proposition, remember that what it contains is tailored to the individual prospect, so it needs to address three key issues: What is important to this specific prospect (which requires we understand the customer's business model)? How does our solution create value for this specific prospect? And how can we demonstrate our capability (which means we have to communicate the value to the customer)?

Here are some weak examples of customer value proposition statements, none of which tell how the prospect is really going to benefit or how the seller can demonstrate that she is able to accomplish the goals for the account:

- It's the most technologically advanced system on the market today.
- We reduce training time more than any of our competitors.
- Our service was rated number one by an independent service lab.

Now here are examples of good customer value proposition statements, which include the elements discussed:[10]

- According to your CFO, dispatching multiple service vans to a customer site has been costing an estimated $20,000 a year in extra fuel costs. When you add that to the cost of unproductive personnel time and missed revenue, the loss is $850,000 per year. When you implement our Call Tracker system you will be able to reduce repeat customer service calls by 20 percent, resulting in a monthly savings of $250,000. This will require an investment of $2 million, which will be returned in only eight months. We implemented a similar solution at Acme Transfer, which began achieving a monthly savings of $500,000 within 90 days of installation. And I have personally overseen 15 such installations and will be there to ensure that all parties are fully trained in use of the new system.
- In this era of heightened airport security concerns, Advanced Engineering, a leading manufacturer of state-of-the-art explosives detective devices, offers a unique solution. The complete "Senso-37 Detection System" for major airports like yours requires a $200,000 investment, fully installed. Our superior system has been shown to save lives, lower human security guard costs, and decrease passenger processing time. My analysis reveals that Orlando International Airport will decrease its general security guard expenses at the major passenger screening area by $80,000 per year for the next four years, giving you a payback in just 2.5 years and also giving you and your passengers peace of mind that *all* passengers are being screened with state-of-the-art technology. When you install the system you also get an added advantage: my commitment and supervision, as one of the top salespeople in my company, that your system will be installed at Orlando International Airport on time and as promised and that your security staff will be trained efficiently and effectively.

Customer value propositions should contain four main parts:

- One or more key features of the product/service complete with external proof
- The tangible and intangible benefits, both economical and emotional
- Positioning your company as the prospect's long-term partner
- Offering yourself as the personal problem solver

How do you create a customer value proposition? Having solid, clear information is critical, as From the Buyer's Seat 9.1 illustrates. Try brainstorming with your sales team and look for statements that truly tell your customers how your solution is going to solve their problems. Every time you write one down, keep asking, "So what difference does that make?" For example, if you write "saves time," ask, "So what does it matter if it saves time?" By doing so, you will eventually be able to reach the core value that your customer will achieve by adopting your product. Another helpful way to create a customer value proposition is by talking to your

From the BUYER'S SEAT 9.1

SELL ME VALUE, AND THEN DELIVER ON THAT VALUE

As an owner of my own construction business, I serve both as a salesperson and as a buyer. As a salesperson I need to maintain balance, meaning I don't want to get greedy and bite off more than I can chew. On the other hand, big projects and contracts give my business and others longevity and financial security and can build trust among my suppliers, subcontractors, and the clients I'm building for. I also have to buy quality products from suppliers and services from subcontractors.

In meeting with suppliers (lumber, window companies) and subcontractors (electricians, plumbers, concrete contractors) I purchase large amounts of building supplies or services. Salespeople can bolster their presentation by doing their research, attending conventions to learn about the latest offerings and trends, reading about new products in their industry, visiting other properties to get a sense of what buyers use or what they provide for their clients, and any anything else to help strengthen their business sense and prepare them for the objections that I am bound to offer.

A common thing salespeople struggle with is their inability to accept feedback, criticism, or the answer "no." I've done business with individuals on a project where there was a mistake made by them or some promise was not met, and the salespersons/suppliers couldn't take accountability for their actions or admit a mistake was made. For instance, salespeople who say "I told him so" or "Honestly it was not my fault" or "It wasn't on my end" are viewed negatively, as deflecting is a warning sign to me. This severely damages the future opportunities for these companies or individuals, as I likely won't consider their business again. If salespeople take accountability, they're much more likely to garner my respect and get another chance. Remember, I have to deliver what was promised to my client in order to be successful.

Furthermore, no buyer wants cheap. I refuse to present a cheap end product to my customers; that's not what they deserve or pay for. Nor do I expect a cheap end product from my suppliers or subcontractors. Buyers do not pursue the most expensive either. To improve your sales presentation, focus on the value you can offer, what about your product or service provides me with the best value proposition. Take into account what will "wow" your buyer, how your product can give that extra edge. Choosing between good, better, or best, I generally prefer the middle. For example, a subcontractor who provides better service with a 5 to 10 percent premium makes my life easier as I get a better product and the best value. The most expensive purchase is unreasonable financially and in turn viewed as overpriced.

Last, I value when my suppliers and subcontractors can show examples from other builds and provide customer testimonials. To me this shows both initiative and their ability to not only market, but also stand behind their business with confidence. Believing in what you're selling is one of the most successful skills a salesperson can portray, because it can reassure the buyer. An example of this is when I had a salesperson who supplied our house wrap (goes underneath siding) change the product he was offering. At first I was unwilling to switch products, but after the trusted salesperson offered credible testimonials along with the belief that this was indeed the best house wrap, I purchased the new product, all because he took initiative, he had my best interests in mind, and he believed in his product.

These sales practices better my company and build strong business relationships.

Source: Andrew Knutson, president, Knutson Custom Construction, used with permission.

customers. They know what value you can bring to a prospect because they have experienced it firsthand and are usually willing to offer suggestions.

Cost-Benefit Analysis

Perhaps the simplest method of quantifying a solution is to list the costs to the buyer and the savings the buyer can expect from the investment, often called a **simple cost-benefit analysis**. For this analysis to be realistic and meaningful,

Exhibit 9.3
Cost-Benefit Analysis for a Mobile Radio

Monthly Cost		
Monthly equipment payment (five-year lease/purchase)*		$1,555.18
Monthly service agreement		339.00
Monthly broadcast fee		+ 533.60
Total monthly cost for entire fleet		$2,427.78
Monthly Savings		
Cost savings (per truck) by eliminating backtracking, unnecessary trips (based on $0.36/mile × 20 miles × 22 days/month)		$158.40
Labor cost savings (per driver) by eliminating wasted time in backtracking, etc. ($8/hour × 25 minutes/day × 22 days/month)		+ 73.33
Total cost savings per vehicle		231.73
Times number of vehicles		× 32
Total monthly cost savings for entire fleet		$7,415.36
	Years 1-5	**Year 6+**
Monthly savings	$7,415.36	$7,415.36
Less: monthly cost	− 2,427.78	− 872.85
Monthly benefit	4,987.58	6,542.51
Times months per year	× 12	× 12
Annual benefit	$59,850.96	$78,510.12

*Payment reflects ongoing cost of service agreement and broadcast fees.

information needed to calculate savings must be supplied by the buyer. Exhibit 9.3 shows how one salesperson used a chart to compare the costs and benefits of purchasing a two-way radio system.

In many situations the salesperson does a **comparative cost-benefit analysis** by comparing the present situation's costs with the value of the proposed solution or the seller's product with a competitor's product. For example, a company with a premium-priced product may justify the higher price on the basis of offsetting costs in other areas. If productivity is enhanced, the increased productivity has economic value.

Return on Investment

The **return on investment (ROI)** is simply the net profits (or savings) expected from a given investment, expressed as a percentage of the investment:

$$\text{ROI} = \text{Net profits (or savings)} \div \text{Investment}$$

Thus, if a new product costs $4,000 but saves the firm $5,000, the ROI is 125 percent ($5,000 ÷ $4,000 = 1.25). Many firms set a minimum ROI for any new products, services, or cost-saving programs. Salespeople need to discover the firm's minimum ROI or ROI expectations and then show that the proposal's ROI meets or exceeds those requirements. For an ROI analysis to be accurate, it is important for the seller to collect meaningful data about costs and savings that the buyer can expect.

Payback Period

The **payback period** is the length of time it takes for the investment cash outflow to be returned in the form of cash inflows or savings. To calculate the payback period, you simply add up estimated future cash inflows and divide them into the

For large capital outlays, the prospect usually needs to see the return on investment, payback period, and/or net present value.

investment cost. If expressed in years, the formula is as follows:

Payback period = Investment ÷ Savings (or profits) per year

Of course the payback period could be expressed in days, weeks, months, or any other period.

As an example, suppose a new machine costs \$865,000 but will save the firm \$120,000 per year in labor costs. The payback period is 7.2 years (\$865,000 ÷ \$120,000 per year = 7.2 years).

Thus, for the buyer, the payback period indicates how quickly the investment money will come back to him or her and can be a good measure of personal risk. When a buyer makes a decision, his or her neck is "on the line," so to speak, until the investment money is at least recovered. Hence, it's not surprising that buyers like to see short payback periods.

We have kept the discussion simple to help you understand the concept. In reality the calculation of the payback period would take into account many other factors, such as investment tax credits and depreciation.

Net Present Value

As you may have learned in finance courses, money left idle loses value over time (a dollar today is worth more than a dollar next week) because of inflation and the firm's cost of capital. Thus, firms calculate the value of future cash inflows in today's dollars (this process is called *discounting the cash flows*). One tool to assess the validity of an opportunity is to calculate the **net present value (NPV)**, which is simply the net value today of future cash inflows (discounted back to their present value today at the firm's cost of capital) minus the investment. The actual method of calculating NPV is beyond the scope of this book, but many computer programs and calculators can calculate NPV quickly and easily:

Net present value = Future cash inflows discounted into today's dollars − Investment

As an example of the preceding formula, let's assume that a \$50 million investment will provide annual cash inflows over the next five years of \$15 million per year. The cash inflows are discounted (at the firm's cost of capital), and the result is that they are actually worth \$59 million in today's dollars. The NPV is thus \$9 million (\$59 million − \$50 million).

As with ROI and payback period, many firms set a minimum NPV. In no case should the NPV be less than \$0. Again, we have kept this discussion simple to help you understand the basic concept.

Opportunity Cost

The **opportunity cost** is the return a buyer would have earned from a different use of the same investment capital. Thus, a buyer could spend \$100 million to buy any of the following: a new computer system, a new production machine, or a controlling interest in another firm.

Successful salespeople identify other realistic investment opportunities and then help the prospect compare the returns of the various options. These comparisons can be made by using any of the techniques we have already discussed (cost-benefit analysis, ROI, payback period, NPV). For example, a salesperson might help the buyer determine the following information about the options identified:

	NPV	Payback Period
Buying a new telecommunications system	$1.6 million	3.6 years
Upgrading the current telecommunications system	0.4 million	4.0 years

Salespeople should never forget that prospects have a multitude of ways to invest their money.

Selling Value to Resellers

When resellers purchase a product for resale, they are primarily concerned with whether their customers will buy the product and how much they will make on each sale. For example, when an Xbox salesperson meets with Walmart to sell video games, he is armed with data showing how much profit is made every time Walmart sells a game and how fast the games sell. The Walmart buyer uses this information to compare the performance of Xbox video games with objectives and with other products sold in the same category, such as Sony's PlayStation.

PROFIT MARGIN **Profit margin** is the net profit the reseller makes, expressed as a percentage of sales.

$$\text{Profit margin \%} = (\text{Selling price} - \text{Cost}) \div \text{Selling price}$$

So, if a product costs me $1, and I sell it for $2 (that is a markup of $1), then the profit margin is 50 percent [($2 – $1) ÷ $2 = 0.50, which is the same as 50 percent].

It is calculated, and thus influenced, by many factors. For example, if Linz Jewelers bought 100 rings for $1,000 each ($100,000), spent $45,000 in expenses (for advertising, salesperson commission, store rent, and other items), and sold them all at an average price of $3,000 ($300,000 in revenue), the profit would be $155,000, with a profit margin of 52 percent ($155,000 ÷ $300,000 = 0.52).

There are other formulas that are derived from the one we're using here, which salespeople often need to know:

$$\text{Selling price} = \text{Cost} \div (1 - \text{Margin \%})$$
$$\text{Cost} = \text{Selling Price} \times (1 - \text{Margin \%})$$

INVENTORY TURNOVER **Inventory turnover** is typically calculated by dividing the annual sales by the average retail price of the inventory on hand, and can be calculated several ways:

Inventory turnover (in dollars) = Annual sales $ ÷ Average inventory $

Inventory turnover (in units) = Annuals sales units ÷ Average inventory in units

Inventory turnover (at cost) = Annualized cost of goods sold ÷ Average inventory at cost

Thus it measures how fast a product sells relative to how much inventory has to be carried—how efficiently a reseller manages its inventory. The reseller would like to have in the store only the amount needed for that day's sales because inventory represents an investment. Thus, large retailers such as Cub Foods receive daily delivery of some products. If the reseller is able to reduce its inventory level, it can invest this savings in stores or warehouses or in the stock market.

For example, if Linz Jewelers usually kept eight rings in stock, inventory turnover would be calculated by dividing total sales in units (100 rings) by average inventory (8 rings). Thus inventory turnover would be 100 ÷ 8, or 12.5 times. The answer represents the number of times that Linz sold the average inventory level. Another way to calculate this is to divide total sales ($300,000 in the Linz example) by the average price of inventory (8 units at $3,000, or $24,000). The answer is the same: 12.5 times.

A reseller does not necessarily want to increase inventory turnover by reducing the amount of inventory carried. Several negative consequences can result. For example, sales may fall because stockouts occur more frequently and products are not available when customers want to buy them. Expenses can increase because the reseller has to order more frequently. Finally, the cost of goods sold may increase because the reseller pays higher shipping charges and does not get as big a quantity discount.

Sellers provide resellers with information to prove that inventory turnover can be improved by buying from them. They describe their **efficient consumer response (ECR) system**, **quick-response (QR) system**, **automatic replenishment (AR)**, and just-in-time (JIT) inventory management systems designed to reduce the reseller's average inventory and transportation expenses but still make sure products are available when end users want them. Chapter 3 described the use of these information systems in depth.

As an example, the September 11, 2001, tragedy created an outpouring of patriotic feelings among Americans. Within 24 hours there was a shortage of American flags, and there is only one major American flag manufacturer. The company had 80,000 flags in inventory on September 11. By the close of business September 12, both Target and Walmart had completely sold out of flags—over 150,000 each. When the stores opened September 13, Walmart had 80,000 more flags, whereas Target had none. How? Walmart's QR system was updated every five minutes, whereas Target didn't update its inventory system until the stores were closed in the evening. Walmart had an order placed with expedited shipping before the stores closed and before Target knew it was out of flags! Similar situations occurred in other product categories, such as flashlights, batteries, battery-powered radios, bottled water, guns, ammunition, and other products that frightened Americans wanted. As you can see, EDI and ECR systems can give resellers significant competitive advantage.

Electronic data interchange (EDI) is a computer-to-computer transmission of data from a reseller, such as Walmart, to vendors (such as American Flag Company) and back. Resellers and vendors that have ECR or QR relationships use EDI to transmit purchase orders and shipping information.

RETURN ON SPACE A key investment that resellers make is in space—retail store space and warehouse space. A measure that retailers use to assess the return on their space investment is sales per square foot or sales per shelf foot. In a grocery store or a department store, shelf or display space is a finite asset that is used to capacity. Products therefore must be evaluated on how well they use the space allocated to them. For example, if a retailer generates $200 per square foot in sales with Tommy Hilfiger merchandise and only $150 selling Ralph Lauren merchandise, it may increase the space allocated to Tommy Hilfiger and reduce the space allocated to Ralph Lauren.

DEALING WITH THE JITTERS

Let's face it. For many people, giving a presentation is a frightening experience. Even seasoned salespeople can get the jitters when the presentation is for a very important client or when the prospect has been rude in an earlier meeting. It all comes down to fear: the fear of being embarrassed or failing, the fear of exposing our lack of knowledge in some area, or the fear of losing our train of thought. The reasons don't even have to be valid. If you have the jitters, you need to help resolve them.

Here are some tips from the experts on how to reduce presentation jitters:

- Know your audience well.
- Know what you're talking about. Keep up-to-date.
- Prepare professional, helpful visuals. These not only help your audience understand the presentation, but also can help you remember important points.
- Be yourself. Don't try to present like someone else.
- Get a good night's sleep.
- For presentations to groups, feed off the energy and enthusiasm of several friendly, happy-looking people in your audience. (That's what professors often do!)
- Recognize the effect of fear on your body and reduce the accompanying stress manifestations by stretching, taking deep breaths to relax breathing, and so on.
- Visualize your audience as your friends–people who are interested and eager to hear what you have to say.
- Psych yourself up for the presentation. Think of the successes you have had in your life (previous presentations that went well or other things you have done well).
- Realize that everyone gets nervous before a presentation at times. It is natural. In fact, it can help you keep from being cocky.
- *Practice, practice, practice!* And finally, practice.

SELLING YOURSELF

You are unique, and having a fresh perspective is valuable and often rare. There are a minimum of three things that are unique to you that nobody can exactly replicate: your fingerprint, your voice, and your eyes. These three are specific to you and when selling yourself should be your modus operandi. Your touch is different, noticeable by how you perform tasks. Your voice is different, noticeable by what you say and how you say it. Your eyes are different, noticeable by your perspective and how you view things.

The key to selling yourself is being yourself! Understanding strengths and working in those areas will easily separate you from the rest. Many people in sales are trying to understand how to fit in instead of stand out. Know you are always being interviewed whether you know it or not. You could find yourself receiving promotions that you did not interview for.

Whether you are in the board room or at the local grocery store, you never know who could have your next opportunity in their hands. Sales is not about fitting the stigma of being the used car salesperson, but rather about being relational. Through building rapport and being curious, you can stumble on great information to build your case.

As a college student, you may need to sell yourself to a potential employer. Being honest can go a long way when selling. I know what it feels like to appear knowledgeable about something I am not. This often does not end well. People are much more appreciative if you say you do not know the answer but will find it.

Justin Carter, sales specialist, Technology Services, Hewlett Packard Enterprise, Used with permission.

SUMMARY

Strengthening communication with the buyer is important. It helps focus the buyer's attention, improves the buyer's understanding, helps the buyer remember what was said, and can create a sense of value.

Many methods of strengthening communication are available. These include such items as word pictures, stories, humor, charts, models, samples, gifts, catalogs, brochures, photos, ads, maps, illustrations, testimonials, and test results. Media available include portfolios, video, computers, and visual projectors.

A backbone of many sales presentations is the product demonstration. It allows the buyer to get hands-on experience with the product, something most other communication methods do not offer. Handouts and written proposals can also strengthen presentations.

It is often important to quantify a solution so the buyer can evaluate its costs in relation to the benefits he or she can derive from the proposal. Some of the more common methods of quantifying a solution include simple cost-benefit analysis, comparative cost-benefit analysis, return on investment, payback period, net present value, and calculation of opportunity cost, turnover, and profit margins. Salespeople should be prepared to present a clear customer value proposition that offers real value to the customer.

All communication tools require skill and practice to be used effectively. Outstanding salespeople follow a number of guidelines to improve their use of visuals, demonstrate their products more effectively, and reduce their nervousness.

KEY TERMS

automatic replenishment (AR) 250
collateral 239
comparative cost-benefit analysis 247
customer value proposition (CVP) 244
digital collateral management system 239
document camera 240
efficient consumer response (ECR) system 250
electronic data interchange (EDI) 250
electronic whiteboard 240
executive briefing center 240
executive summary 243
handouts 242
inventory turnover 249
multiple-sense appeals 230
net present value (NPV) 248
opportunity cost 248
payback period 247
portfolio 237
profit margin 249
quantifying the solution 244
quick-response (QR) system 250
request for proposal (RFP) 243
return on investment (ROI) 247
sales asset management system 239
simple cost-benefit analysis 246
testimonial 237
value analysis 244
visual presenter 240

ETHICS PROBLEMS

1. Assume you are calling on a male buyer. As you engage in small talk, he offers up a joke involving strong sexual innuendo, including a derogatory statement about women. Will you laugh? How will you respond?

2. You realize that a piece of software you are going to demonstrate to a prospect has a complicated data entry requirement for a certain report to run correctly. You also know from past experience that buyers of this software

complain about how complicated and nonintuitive it is. You share your concern with your manager. She replies, "Well, that's easy to correct! Just have everything already inputted before the demo even begins. That way you can run the report and it will look smooth and easy!" You know that doing it in this way will deceive the prospect into thinking it is all easy, which it isn't. What will you say to your boss? What will you do during the demonstration?

QUESTIONS AND PROBLEMS

1. Assume you plan a demonstration to prove some of the claims you have made for a new treadmill (exercise equipment). How would the demonstration differ for each of these three individuals: an overweight 35-year-old man who is very concerned about losing weight, a 28-year-old Marathon runner, and a 60-year-old woman in good health?
2. How could you demonstrate the following products?
   - **a.** A new brand of moist dog food to a kennel owner.
   - **b.** A new line of polyester fleece fabric to a fabric buyer for Walmart.
   - **c.** A set of industrial cookware to a high school cafeteria.
3. Which communication tools would you use to provide solid proof to address the following concerns expressed by prospects?
   - **a.** I don't think that set of cookbooks would sell well in a store like ours. People don't come to Sam's Club to buy cookbooks!
   - **b.** I'm not convinced there is a need for another line of synthetic oil at our quick lube stations. We already carry one of the major brands.
   - **c.** That trampoline won't hold up under rough play by teenage boys.
   - **d.** Why should we add greeting cards to our store. Most people send electronic greeting cards these days!
4. This chapter generally accepts the use of humor as a positive, useful tool for salespeople. Are there times when the use of humor could actually be detrimental to communication effectiveness? Explain.
5. Which communication tools would you use to communicate the following facts?
   - **a.** We have been in business since 1997.
   - **b.** This new controller is going to make your PlayStation users have a much more realistic experience as they play.
   - **c.** These dress shirts will not need ironing even after 50 washings.
   - **d.** This cordless drill will operate at maximum output nonstop for two hours before it needs recharging.
   - **e.** These cabinet drawer knobs will never lose their shiny silver coat.
6. Assume that you are selling a complete line of weather-resistant patio, pool, and deck furniture to a large hotel to replace all of its current furniture. The total cost will be $275,000. You expect that repairs/replacements will drop by $19,000 a year over the next 10 years. At the outfitter's cost of capital, the discounted cash inflows have a value today of $335,000. Use this information to calculate the following:
   - **a.** Return on investment.
   - **b.** Payback period.
   - **c.** Net present value.
7. Assume that ACME Tools buys 125 drill presses for $969 each and then spends $2,000 in expenses for advertising, salesperson commission, and store rent. The generators sell for $1,695 each. ACME keeps 90 generators in stock at all times. Average annual sales are 500 generators. Calculate the following:
   - **a.** Profit margin percentage.
   - **b.** Inventory turnover in units.
8. Assume you will be selling a new line of skis to a reseller (a ski shop). You will be selling the skis to the shop for $150 each, and suggesting they retail the skis for $220. You anticipate their annual sales revenue for this new line of skis to be $5,500 (25 pair of skis), and an average inventory on hand of $1,760 (8 pair of skis). Calculate the following, showing all of your work:
   - **a.** Profit margin percentage.
   - **b.** Inventory turnover in dollars.
   - **c.** Inventory turnover in units.
9. In Building Partnerships 9.1 the writer encouraged salespeople to be able to find balance in life. Do a Web search on the topic of work-life balance, and report five things you found that might be helpful advice in your own life to maintain proper work-life balance.

CASE PROBLEMS

case 9.1

Zadro Inc. (Part A)

There are many harmful germs found in the home, in public places, and in hotels while traveling. The Programmable UV Sanitizing Wand, made by Zadro, can effectively kill up to 99.99 percent of germs and viruses in just 10 seconds. It can also kill dust mites in mattresses, pillows, and carpets. Since the wand is portable, it can travel with you wherever you travel, removing harmful substances regardless of where you are. The user simply waves the scanner within a quarter inch of the surface for 10 seconds to kill the substances.

The scanner is 1½ inches high × 20 inches wide × 1¾ inches deep and runs on three C batteries. An optional AC adapter is sold separately. The scanner includes an electronic child lock to prevent misuse. A stand is provided and is used to go over keyboards, butcher blocks, and so on for hands-free operation. The programmable unit can be set for 10-, 20-, 40-, and 60-second times as well as two to five minutes, depending on the surface area that needs to be scanned. The unit is not designed to be used on humans or animals. The scanner, which is laboratory certified and tested, retails for $99, and all units come with a 90-day limited warranty. Resellers are offered the units for $60, with a quantity discount price of $50 for all units over 100 in a single order.

Questions

1. Describe how you would use the communication tools described in this chapter to sell the Programmable UV Sanitizing Wand to Target. Target would then resell to its consumers. Make any assumptions necessary.
2. Develop a short (five-minute) slide show that you can use to introduce the product to potential buyers at a retailer trade show.

Source: Zadro Inc.

case 9.2

Passport Health

Each year up to 20 percent of people suffer from the results of the flu. Thankfully there are vaccinations that can help reduce the incidence of the flu. The Centers for Disease Control and Prevention (CDC) claims, "The first and most important step in preventing flu is to get a flu vaccination each year." Yet many people claim they are just too busy to get to a clinic, or that the local drugstore that provides the vaccinations is too crowded. That's where Passport Health can help.

Passport Health will provide onsite flu clinics at your workplace. Trained nurses administer the shots, and Passport Health provides all of the coordination, administration, and any registration needed. The results should be fewer sick days and lower health care costs, which should result in a more efficient and productive workforce.

Assume you are a salesperson for Passport Health. Today you are calling on a large manufacturing plant (or service provider) in your area. You have never called on this organization before.

Questions

1. Create an effective story that can help strengthen your presentation. This story should help the buyer understand how important it is to get a flu vaccination. The story should be from your own experiences, or from experiences of others whom you personally know. In other words, don't just go to the Web and find a story. Your story might tell how someone suffered from the flu who didn't get a flu shot, or how someone avoided a common flu that was rampant because that person got the flu shot, or some other story that makes the point effectively.
2. Create a second effective story that can help strengthen your presentation. This story should help the buyer understand that clinics and storefront providers of flu shots are often crowded, or inconvenient in some way for the average "9 to 5" employee.

Sources: CDC; Passport Health USA

ROLE PLAY CASE

You will now present to the same person whose needs you identified in Chapter 8. (If you have not done role plays before, you will need to review the information about the various role play customers that can be found at the end of Chapter 3. If you did not do the role play at the end of Chapter 8, choose one of the three companies to sell to.) If you sold to ARM, you'll do so again; the same goes for FSS and Mizzen. Begin by summarizing the buyer's needs and gaining agreement that these are all the needs. Then make your presentation.

As a buyer, do not offer any objections today. Just listen, add your thoughts on how the product might help if asked, and agree. Ask questions if something seems vague or confusing. Further, ask for proof. For example, if the salesperson says everyone loves it, ask to see a testimonial letter or something of that sort.

When you are the odd person out and observing, look for the following:

- Did the seller tie the features to the buyer's needs? Or did the seller present features that were not needed?
- Did the seller try to gain agreement that the buyer recognized and valued the benefit?
- Did the seller use visual aids as proof sources effectively?
- Did the seller use specific language versus general or ambiguous language (for example, "It's the best")?

Note: For background information about these role plays, please see Chapter 1.

To the instructor: Additional information needed to complete the role play is available in the Instructor's Manual.

ADDITIONAL REFERENCES

Frey, Robert S. *Successful Proposal Strategies for Small Businesses: Using Knowledge Management to Win Government, Private-Sector, and International Contracts*. 6th ed. Norwood, MA: Artech House, 2013.

Friend, Scott B., Carolyn F. Curasi, James S. Boles, and Danny N. Bellenger. "Why Are You Really Losing Sales Opportunities? A Buyers' Perspective on the Determinants of Key Account Sales Failures." *Industrial Marketing Management* 43, no. 7 (2014), pp. 1124–35.

Jaques, Emma. *The Winning Bid: A Practical Guide to Successful Bid Management.* Philadelphia, PA: Kogan Page, 2013.

Kumar, V., and Werner Reinartz. "Creating Enduring Customer Value." *Journal of Marketing* 80, no. 6 (November 2016), pp. 36–68.

Liinamaa, Johanna, Mika Viljanen, Anna Hurmerinta, Maria Ivanova-Gongne, Hanna Luotola, and Magnus Gustafsson. "Performance-Based and Functional Contracting in Value-Based Solution Selling." *Industrial Marketing Management* 59 (2016), pp. 37–49.

Lombardoa, Sebastiano, and Francesca Cabiddub. "What's in It for Me? Capital, Value and Co-creation Practices." *Industrial Marketing Management* 61 (February 2017), pp. 155–69.

Macdonald, Emma K., Michael Kleinaltenkamp, and Hugh N. Wilson. "How Business Customers Judge Solutions: Solution Quality and Value in Use." *Journal of Marketing* 80, no. 3 (2016), pp. 96–120.

Prior, Daniel D. "Supplier Representative Activities and Customer Perceived Value in Complex Industrial Solutions." *Industrial Marketing Management* 42, no. 8 (2013), pp. 1192–1201.

Sheridan, Matt. *A+ Demonstrations: Excellence in Sales Engineering.* Waltham, MA: Boston Writers Publishing, 2014.

Wagner, Janet, and Sabine Benoit (née Moeller). "Creating Value in Retail Buyer-Vendor Relationships: A Service-Centered Model." *Industrial Marketing Management* 44 (2015), pp. 166–79.

Zhang, Jonathan Z., George F. Watson IV, Robert W. Palmatier, and Rajiv P. Dant. "Dynamic Relationship Marketing." *Journal of Marketing* 80, no. 5 (2016), pp. 53–75.

©Moodboard/SuperStock RF

The Partnership Process

PART 2

chapter 10

RESPONDING TO OBJECTIONS

SOME QUESTIONS ANSWERED IN THIS CHAPTER ARE

- How should salespeople sell value and build relationships when responding to objections?
- When do buyers object?
- What objections can be expected?
- Which methods are effective when responding to objections?
- How do you deal with tough customers?

PROFILE

"When an objection is presented, actively listening is imperative. Are they expressing a legitimate concern that would halt moving forward or just simply an excuse not to buy?"

Molly Gilleland, Comcast Spotlight

Courtesy of Molly Gilleland

PROFILE My name is Molly Gilleland, and I graduated from the Kennesaw State University (KSU) sales program in 2014. It was, in fact, an earlier edition of this textbook that changed the course of my career! I've always had an interest in sales, but it wasn't until I had the privilege of being taught and coached by Dr. Terry Loe, Dr. Gary Selden, Dr. Leila Borders, and Mr. Michael Serkedakis that I found a passion for not only sales, but for people. After all, a career in sales is based on building relationships with clients and effectively finding ways to add value to their businesses. Since my graduation from KSU, I have been fortunate to find my calling in the advertising industry where I have been a local account executive in Atlanta for the past two years.

Cold calling, needs identification meetings, and presentations are all daily tasks for me. Although these activities are all different in nature, I always find one common thread among them—objections! No matter where you are in the sales process, objections are bound to come up. In the sales world, how you respond to objections is especially important because this is where the best salespeople are able to educate, add value, and deepen relationships with clients and prospects.

Educating the client on how advertising can help their business is a huge part of our sales process, and when learning new information, it is human nature to question things. Because of this, I am able to anticipate objections that will likely arise and use the technique of forestalling to proactively address them.

When an objection is presented, actively listening is imperative. Are they expressing a legitimate concern that would halt moving forward or just simply an excuse not to buy? I'm able to find out only by paying attention, being empathetic to the client's concern, and asking open-ended questions to get to the root of their issues.

As an example: A new gym is about to open up in town.

GYM OWNER: Sorry, Molly, we aren't interested at this time. We have too much going on with the renovations and grand opening.

ME: Mr. Gym Owner, I can understand that. Being a new business in town, how are you planning on drawing in new members once everything is set up?

GYM OWNER: Our other franchises rely solely on social media and that's really worked for them.

ME: That's great! Are you finding that's the case for you too? Based on our conversation, it sounds like having to consistently update your social media takes your focus off getting the gym renovated for the grand opening. Using commercials to target the potential gym members in your area could help with branding before your opening and take some of the work off your plate. Would you be interested in that?

Once I completely understand their true need, I am able to confidently yet genuinely address it while reminding them of the benefits of what we have to offer. During this, watching for nonverbal cues from clients can be especially telling. Are they nodding their head in agreement or looking confused? Always circle back to get the clients' thoughts and to make sure that they understand and accept your solution. After successfully responding to an objection, you should feel as if you have advanced closer to not only closing the sale, but also deepening the relationship with your client or prospect—a win-win situation!

Visit our Web site at: www.comcastspotlight.com.

Molly Gilleland, account executive, Comcast Spotlight. Used with permission.

THE GOAL IS TO BUILD RELATIONSHIPS AND SELL VALUE

An **objection** is a concern or a question raised by the buyer.[1] Salespeople should do everything they can to encourage buyers to voice concerns or questions. The worst type of objection is the one the buyer refuses to disclose because a hidden objection cannot be dealt with. Many sales have been lost because salespeople didn't find out the objections or didn't helpfully respond to them.

Salespeople should keep in mind that the goal with regard to objections is the same as with every other part of the sales call: to sell real value to the buyer. Having a positive attitude about objections is paramount in this regard. Proper attitude is shown by answering sincerely, refraining from arguing or contradicting, and welcoming—even inviting—objections. Objections should be expected and never taken personally.

Simply pretending to be empathetic is useless; buyers can easily see through such pretense. Also, once the buyer gets the idea that the salesperson is talking for effect, regaining that buyer's confidence and respect will be almost impossible. Empathy shows as much in the tone of voice and facial expressions as in the actual words spoken.

The greatest evidence of sincerity comes from the salesperson's actions. One successful advertising agency owner states, "I have always tried to sit on the same side of the table as my clients, to see problems through their eyes." Buyers want valid objections to be treated seriously; they want their ideas to be respected, not belittled. They look for empathetic understanding of their problems. Real objections are logical to the prospect regardless of how irrational they may appear to the salesperson. Salespeople must assume the attitude of helper, counselor, and advisor and act accordingly. To do so, they must treat the prospect as a friend, not a foe. In fact, buyers will feel more comfortable about raising objections and will be much more honest the more they trust the salesperson, the better the rapport, and the stronger the partnering relationship.

The reality is that salespeople run into more rejection in a day than most people have to absorb in weeks or months. Because of the emotional strain, many see selling as a tough way to make a living. However, salespeople must remember that objections present sales opportunities. People who object have at least some level of interest in what the salesperson is saying. Further, objections provide feedback about what is really on the prospect's mind. Only when this openness exists can a true partnering relationship form. This attitude shows in remarks such as the following:

I can see just what you mean. I'd probably feel the same way.

That's a great question!

If I were purchasing this product, I'd want an answer to that same question.

WHEN DO BUYERS RAISE OBJECTIONS?

Salespeople can expect to hear objections at any time during the buyer–seller relationship (see Chapter 3 for a review of the buying process). Objections are raised when the salesperson attempts to secure an appointment, during the approach, during the presentation, when the salesperson attempts to obtain commitment, and during the after-sale follow-up. Objections can also be made during formal negotiation sessions (see Chapter 12).

SETTING UP AN INITIAL APPOINTMENT

Prospects may object to setting the appointment times or dates that salespeople request to introduce the product. This type of objection happens especially when products, services, or concepts are unfamiliar to the buyer. For example, a commercial benefits salesperson for CLS Partners might hear the buyer make the following statement when asked to meet and learn more about a cafeteria-style benefits package: "No, I don't need to see you. I've not heard many good things about the use of cafeteria-style packages for dental coverage. Most employees just get confused!"

THE PRESENTATION

Buyers can offer objections during the beginning of the presentation (see Chapter 8). They may not like or believe the salesperson's attention-getting opening statement. They may not wish to engage in small talk or may not agree with statements made by the seller attempting to build rapport. Buyers may object to the salesperson's stated goals for the meeting.

Objections often come up to points made in the presentation. For example, a computer disaster recovery salesperson for Rackspace Hosting might hear this objection: "We've never lost a lot of computer data files before! Why should I pay so much money for a service I may never use?"

Such objections usually show the prospect's interest in the topic; thus, they can actually be desirable. Compared to a prospect who just says, "No thanks," and never raises his or her concerns, selling is easier when buyers voice their concerns because the salesperson knows where the buyers stand and that they are paying attention.

ATTEMPTING TO OBTAIN COMMITMENT

Objections may be voiced when the salesperson attempts to obtain commitment. For example, an AK Steel salesperson who has just asked the buyer's permission to talk to the buyer's chief engineer may hear this objection: "No, I don't want you talking to our engineers. My job is to keep vendors from bugging our employees."

Skill in uncovering and responding to objections is very important at this stage of the sales call. Also, knowing the objections that are likely to occur helps the salesperson prepare supporting documentation (letters of reference, copies of studies, and so on).

Salespeople who hear many objections at this point in the sales call probably need to further develop their skills. An excessive number of objections while obtaining commitment may indicate a poor job of needs identification and the omission of significant selling points in the presentation, as Building Partnerships 10.1 describes. It may also reveal ineffective probing during the presentation to see whether the buyer understands or has any questions about what is being discussed.

AFTER THE SALE

Even buyers who have agreed to purchase the product or service can still raise objections. During the installation, for example, the buyer may raise concerns about the time it is taking to install the equipment, the quality of the product or service, the customer service department's lack of friendliness, or the credit department's refusal to grant the terms the salesperson promised. To develop long-term relationships and partnerships with buyers, salespeople must carefully respond to these objections. After-sale service is more fully discussed in Chapter 14.

BUILDING Partnerships 10.1

SOME THOUGHTS FROM A BOLIVIAN SALESPERSON

As a dental equipment salesperson in Bolivia, here are some sales behaviors that I try to enact each and every day:

Actively listen—As a salesperson, it is always important to take notes because once you start dealing with multiple clients and multiple projects, you may forget important details about your conversations.

Listen more than you speak—The best way to understand your customers' needs is by listening carefully. It is the best way to find out what your customers' problems are and help them find solutions.

Be prepared—One of the biggest problems with salespeople is that they don't know what they are selling, don't know their clients, or don't have a sales plan. Before contacting a client, the salesperson should know what information the client has, what he or she doesn't know, what the client needs to know, and how the salesperson plans to provide it. The salesperson should make a plan and do the "homework" before contacting or visiting the lead or client. Steve Jobs once said, "The client doesn't care how much effort you put into something, he is only worried on how you delivered." Therefore, be prepared for everything. If you don't know something about your client, your product, service, or solution, learn more about it because if you don't know what you're talking about, your lead or client will lose interest or trust.

Be honest—Another big problem is that salespeople prefer talking their way out of problems (even if they don't know what they are talking about) rather than being honest and saying the magic words "I don't know." By being honest, clients will know that you are more concerned about their interests than yours. Also, lying to get away with not knowing what you are talking about will not work with a client who knows more about your products or services than you. If clients know that you are being dishonest, they could ruin your reputation with negative word to mouth. Although being honest and saying "I don't know" can work at times, if that is your answer for every hard question that clients ask, you will also lose their trust and interest. Therefore, always be prepared.

Be organized—Organization can go a long way. If you stay organized, you will know exactly what you need to succeed and how to be resourceful for your clients. Also, if you present organized work to your clients, they will feel assured that they are working with a competent provider.

Stop selling and begin helping—I have learned that the best way to sell is by actually caring about my clients. I always keep in mind that my customers' success is my success. By helping customers instead of just trying to sell to them, I will be able to build a better relationship with them, understand their needs (they will feel comfortable enough to open up about problems or needs that they have), sell more by offering a variety of products and services, and build loyalty with me and my company.

So, here's a story that reflects some of what I've just mentioned. I work for a company that provides dental products and services for dentists and the dental technicians who make crowns. John, a technician who had difficulties working with Blue Company, the market leader, came to our office looking for Zirconia blocks to make crowns for his clients, the dentists. He was having problems with Blue Company because it was not understanding his needs. When he came to my office, I sat down with John, listened to his needs, and discussed the benefits of working with our products and our company. When the meeting concluded, we reached an agreement to provide him with over $50,000 in Zirconia blocks. In addition to those materials, he now buys other products from us on a monthly basis and is constantly sending us pictures that he posts on Facebook of the crowns that he has made with our Zirconia blocks. We have built a great relationship and he has referred many technicians and dentists to our company. It has lead to a 15 percent increase in sales compared to the previous year.

Source: Juan Guillermo Peredo, commercial manager, Technodent S.R.L., used with permission.

COMMON OBJECTIONS

Prospects raise many types of objections. Although listing every objection is impossible, this section attempts to outline the most common buyer objections.

It should be noted that some buyers like to raise objections just to watch salespeople squirm uncomfortably. (Fortunately, most buyers aren't like that!) Seasoned buyers, especially, sometimes like to make life difficult for sellers–particularly for young, nervous sellers. For example, Peggy, a manufacturer's salesperson for Walker Muffler, used to call on a large auto parts store in an attempt to have the store carry her line of mufflers. Jackie, the store's buyer, gave Peggy a tough time on her first two calls. At the end of her second call, Peggy was so frustrated with the way she was being treated that she decided never to call there again. However, as she was walking out of the store, she ran into a Goodyear rep who also called on Jackie to sell belts and hoses. Because the two salespeople were on somewhat friendly terms, Peggy admitted her frustrations to the Goodyear rep. He replied, "Oh, that's just the way Jackie operates. On the third call he is always a nice guy. Just wait and see." Sure enough, Peggy's next call on Jackie was not only pleasant but also productive! Buyers like Jackie usually just want to see the sales rep work hard for the order.

The following sections examine the five major types of objections (objections related to needs, product, source, price, and time), which are summarized in Exhibit 10.1, as well as several other objections that salespeople sometimes hear.

OBJECTIONS RELATED TO NEEDS

I Do Not Need the Product or Service

A prospect may validly state that the company has no need for what the salesperson is selling. A manufacturer that operates on a small scale, for example, may have no use for expensive machinery designed to handle large volumes of work. Similarly, a salesperson who is selling an accounts receivable collection service will find that a retailer that sells for cash does not require a collection service.

Exhibit 10.1

Five Major Types of Objections

Objections Related to Needs
I do not need the product or service.
I've never done it that way before.

Objections Related to the Product
I don't like the product or service features.
I don't understand.
I need more information.

Objections Related to the Source
I don't like your company.
I don't like you.

Objections Related to the Price
I have no money.
The value does not exceed the cost.

Objections Related to Time
I'm just not interested today.
I need time to think about it.

Salespeople may encounter such objections as "My business is different" or "I have no use for your service." These objections, when made by an accurately qualified buyer, show that the buyer is not convinced that a need exists. This problem could have been prevented with better implication and need payoff questions (see Chapter 8).

If the salesperson cannot establish a need in the buyer's mind, that buyer can logically be expected to object. In **pioneer selling**–selling a new and different product, service, or idea–the salesperson has more difficulty establishing a need in the buyer's mind. For example, salespeople for Alken-Murray often hear "I don't think we need it" when the buyer is asked to carry a line of biodegradable citrus degreasers.

I've Never Done It That Way Before

Most human beings are creatures of habit. Once they develop a routine or establish a custom, they tend to resist change. Fear of a new product's failure may be the basis for not wanting to try anything new or different. For example, Target Corporation's buyers are evaluated annually on the products they choose to buy, including such metrics as sales results, gross margins, and guest experience surveys.

Habits and customs also help insulate the prospect from social risks to some degree. For example, suppose you are selling a new line of marine engines to Newton, a newly promoted assistant buyer. If Jane, the previous assistant buyer and now the senior buyer, bought your competitor's product, Newton would appear to take less risk by continuing to buy from your competitor. If Newton buys from you, Jane may think, "I've been doing business with the other firm for 15 years. Now, Newton, you come in here and tell me I've been doing it wrong all these years? I'm not sure you're going to be a good assistant buyer."

OBJECTIONS RELATED TO THE PRODUCT

I Don't Like the Product or Service Features

Often the product or service has features that do not satisfy the buyer. At other times the prospect will request features currently not available. Customers may say things like these: It doesn't taste good to me! I was looking for a lighter shade of red. It took a month for us to receive our last order.

This buyer doesn't understand the point the salesperson is trying to make.

©John Lund/Marc Romanelli/Blend Images/Getty Images RF

I Don't Understand

Sometimes objections arise because customers do not understand the salesperson's presentation. Because these objections may never be verbalized, the seller must carefully observe the buyer's nonverbal cues. (See Chapter 4 for a discussion of nonverbal communication.) Misunderstandings frequently occur with customers who are unfamiliar with technical terms, unaware of the unique capabilities of a product, or uncertain about benefits arising from services provided with the product, such as warranties. Unfortunately buyers often will not admit that they do not understand something.

I Need More Information

Some buyers offer objections in an attempt to get more information. They may have already decided that they want the product or service but wish to fortify themselves with logical reasons they can use to justify the purchase to others. Also, the salesperson may not have provided enough credible proof about a particular benefit.

Conflict may also exist in the buyer's mind. One conflict could be a struggle taking place between the dictates of emotion and reason. Or the buyer may be concerned about the risk, and the seller hasn't sufficiently sold value. The buyer may be trying to decide between two competitive products or between buying and not buying. Whatever the struggle, buyers who object to get more information are usually interested, and the possibility of obtaining commitment is good.

OBJECTIONS RELATED TO THE SOURCE

I Don't Like Your Company

Most buyers, especially industrial buyers, are interested in the sales representative's company because the buyer is put at risk if the seller's firm is not financially sound, cannot continually produce the product, and so forth. These buyers need to be satisfied with the selling company's financial standing, personnel, and business policies. Buyers may ask questions such as these: How do I know you'll be in business next year? Your company isn't very well known, is it? Why does your company have a bad image in the industry?

Of course buyers who don't want to be rude may not actually voice these concerns. But unvoiced questions about the sales rep's company may affect their decisions and the long-term partnerships the sales rep is trying to establish.

I Don't Like You

Sometimes a salesperson's personality clashes with a prospect's. Effective salespeople know they must do everything possible to adjust their manner to please the prospect. At times, however, doing business with some people appears impossible.

Prospects may object to a presentation or an appointment because they have taken a dislike to the salesperson or because they feel they cannot trust the salesperson. Candid prospects may say, "You seem too young to be selling these. You've never worked in my industry, so how can you be trained to know what I need?" More commonly, the prospect shields the real reason and says, "We don't need any."

ethics

In some situations, the buyer may honestly have difficulty dealing with a particular salesperson. If the concern is real (not just an excuse), the seller's firm sometimes institutes a **turnover (TO)**, which simply means the account is given to a different salesperson. Unfortunately, TOs occasionally occur because the buyer has gender, racial, or other prejudices or because the salesperson is failing to practice adaptive selling behaviors.

thinking it through

Assume that you have worked as a salesperson for an industrial chemical firm for six months. You have attended a two-week basic selling skills course but have not yet attended any product knowledge training classes. You are making a sales call with your sales manager. The buyer says, "Gee, you look too young to be selling chemicals. Do you have a chemistry degree?" Before you get a chance to respond, your manager says, "Oh, he [*meaning you*] has already completed our one-month intensive product knowledge course. I guarantee he knows it all!" What would you say or do? What would you do if the buyer later asked you a technical question?

OBJECTIONS RELATED TO THE PRICE

I Have No Money

Companies that lack the resources to buy the product may have been misclassified as prospects. As indicated in Chapter 6, the ability to pay is an important factor in lead qualification. An incomplete or poor job of qualifying may cause this objection to arise.

When leads say they cannot afford a product, they may have a valid objection. If so, the salesperson should not waste time; new prospects should be contacted.

The Value Does Not Exceed the Cost

Buyers usually object until they are sure that the value of the product or service being acquired more than offsets the sacrifice. Exhibit 10.2 illustrates this concept. The question of value received often underlies customers' objections.

Whatever the price of a product or service, somebody will object that it is too high or out of line with the competition. Here are some other common price objections: I can beat your price on these items. We can't make a reasonable profit if we have to pay that much for the merchandise. I'm going to wait for prices to come down.

Exhibit 10.2

Value: The Relationship between Costs and Benefits

Note: If costs outweigh benefits, the decision will be not to buy. If benefits outweigh costs, the decision will be to buy.

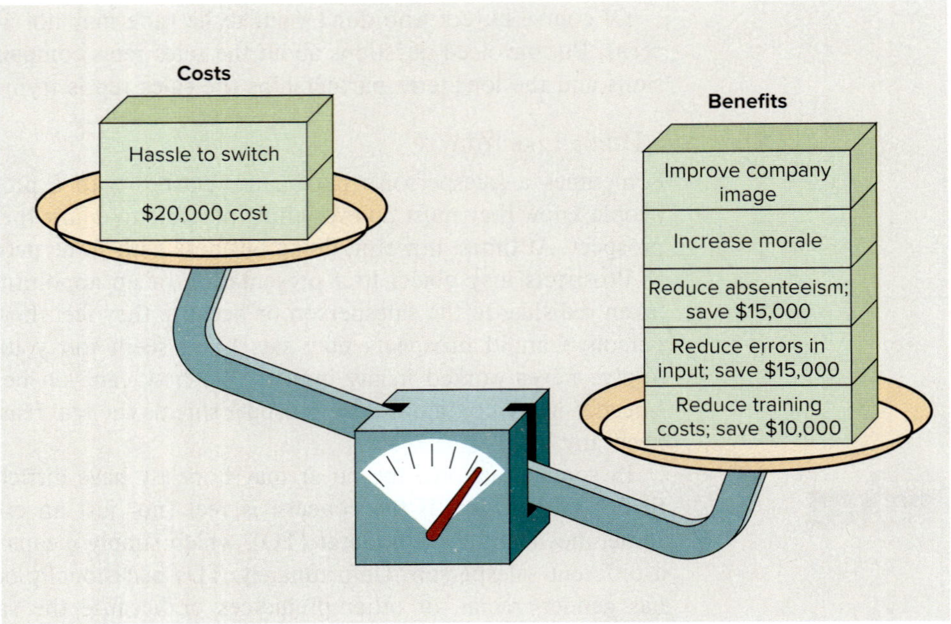

A more complete discussion of dealing with price objections appears later in this chapter. Implicit in many price objections is the notion of product or service quality. Thus, the buyer who states that your price is too high may actually be thinking, "The quality is too low for such a high price."

OBJECTIONS RELATED TO TIME

I'm Just Not Interested Today

Some prospects voice objections simply to dismiss the salesperson. The prospect may not have enough time to devote to the interview, may not be interested in the particular product or service, may not be in the mood to listen, or may have decided because of some unhappy experiences not to face further unpleasant interviews.

These objections often occur when salespeople are cold calling (see Chapter 6) or trying to make an appointment. Particularly aggressive, rude, impolite, or pesky salespeople can expect prospects to use numerous excuses to keep from listening to a presentation.

I Need Time to Think about It

Buyers often object to making a decision "now." Many, in fact, believe that postponing an action is an effective way to say no. Salespeople can expect to hear objections such as the following, especially from analyticals and amiables (see Chapter 5): I haven't made up my mind. I'd like to talk it over with my partner. Just leave me your literature; I'll study it and then let you know what we decide.

OTHER OBJECTIONS

Listing every possible objection that could occur under any situation would be impossible. However, following are a number of additional objections that salespeople often hear:

We have no room for your line.

There is no demand for your product.

ethics

Sorry, but I just don't do business with people of [your gender or your race or your ethnicity or your sexual preference or your religion and so forth].

I've heard from my friends that your insurance company isn't the best one to use.

Sure, we can do business. But I need a little kickback to make it worth my time and trouble.

I believe we might be able to do business if you are willing to start seeing me socially.

It's a lot of hassle in paperwork and time to switch suppliers.

Exhibit 10.3

Responding to Objections: Behaviors of Successful Salespeople

They anticipate objections and prepare helpful responses.

They address known problems before the prospect does; that is, they forestall known concerns.

They relax and listen and never interrupt the buyer.

They make sure that the objection is not just an excuse.

They always tell the truth.

BEHAVIORS OF SUCCESSFUL SALESPEOPLE

With regard to objections, successful salespeople anticipate objections and forestall known concerns, listen without interrupting, evaluate objections before answering, and always tell the truth (see Exhibit 10.3). Responding to objections in a helpful manner requires careful thought and preparation. Some trainers suggest that salespeople use the **LAARC Method** to respond to objections: Listen, Acknowledge, Assess (the validity of the objection), Respond, and Confirm (that the objection has been answered).[2]

ANTICIPATE OBJECTIONS

Salespeople must know that at some time, objections will be made to almost everything concerning their products, their companies, or themselves. Common sense dictates that they prepare helpful, honest answers to objections that are certain to be raised.

Many companies draw up lists of common objections and helpful answers and encourage salespeople to become familiar with these lists. Most firms also videotape practice role plays to help salespeople become more proficient in anticipating objections and responding effectively in each situation. Successful sales representatives may keep a notebook and record new objections they encounter. Please remember that buyers are also creating lists of objections, as From the Buyer's Seat 10.1 describes.

FORESTALL KNOWN CONCERNS

Good salespeople, after a period of experience and training, know that certain features of their products or services are vulnerable, are likely to be misunderstood, or are materially different from competitors' products. The salesperson may have products with limited features, may have to quote a price that seems high, may be unable to offer cash discounts, may have no service representatives in the immediate area, or may represent a new company in the field.

In these situations, salespeople often forestall the objection. To **forestall** is to prevent by doing something ahead of time. In selling, this means salespeople raise objections before buyers have a chance to raise them. For example, one salesperson forestalled a concern about the different "feel" of a split computer keyboard (the ones that are split down the middle to relieve stress and strain on the hands and wrists):

> I know you'll find the feel to be different from your old keyboard. You're going to like that, though, because your hands won't get as tired. In almost every split keyboard I've sold, typists have taken only one day to get accustomed to the new feel, and then they swear that they would never go back to their old-fashioned keyboards again!

From the **BUYER'S SEAT** 10.1

THE ART OF BUYING: KNOWING WHAT OBJECTIONS TO RAISE

I am tasked with purchasing new motorcycles (bikes) and also our "used trade-in agreements." We pick and choose what to purchase from BMW based off availability and our needs; the only thing BMW regulates is a minimum advertised price. As a business we make our bread and butter in the spring and summer, so the procurement of motorcycles plays a huge part in whether or not we are going to succeed financially during a quarter or year. In regard to purchasing motorcycles, regional climate up north has a great effect on our business. Customers may not know exactly what they want but they want it now—there is a short riding season and customers demand preference and priority.

The start of the procurement process of us buying a used motorcycle would be a client walking in and coming in contact with an associate. The first step would be to schedule a meeting to bring the bike in so the service department can evaluate it. We want to conduct this as soon as possible because the seller (our supplier) could go to a different dealership and we would lose out on the business. It's a very cutthroat business due to the shortness of available riding time. We conduct the service department evaluation in order to state our objections when buying, involving both cosmetic and mechanical issues. Our objections may focus on whether or not we feel any more money needs to be put into the bike to make it as "sellable" as possible, because after purchasing bikes we want to turn around and sell them for as much as we can. We may not even buy the bike if it doesn't fit our customer base or if it's a poor investment value.

Based on the scaled results of our analysis, our purchasing equation provides a ballpark value and we negotiate a deal with the seller. To minimize objections we explain to our sellers why we valued the bike at that price point. Objections always arise around price concerning how much a competitor will purchase a bike for or how much it will offer on trade-in value, or how much the customers could sell the bike for themselves. Knowledge and understanding of your market is essential as a buyer, and this is helpful when negotiating with your suppliers.

Source: Anonymous, names changed as requested. Used with permission.

A salesperson might bring up a potential price concern by saying, "You know, other buyers have been concerned that this product is expensive. Well, let me show you how little it will really cost you to get the best."

Some salespeople do such a good job of forestalling that buyers change their minds without ever going on record as objecting to the feature and then having to reverse themselves.[3] Buyers are more willing to change their thinking when they do not feel constrained to defend a position they have already stated. Although not all objections can be preempted, the major ones can be spotted and forestalled during the presentation. Forestalling can be even more important in written proposals (see Chapter 9) because immediate feedback between buyer and seller is not possible. Such forestalled objections can be addressed throughout the proposal. For example, on the page describing delivery terms, the seller could insert a paragraph that begins this way: "You may be wondering how we can promise an eight-day delivery even though we have such a small production capacity. Actually, we are able to . . . because. . . ." Another option for forestalling objections in written proposals is to have a separate page or section titled something like "Concerns You May Have with This Proposal." The section could then list the potential concerns and provide responses to them.

This person is listening carefully.

©ONOKY-Eric Herchaft/Getty Images RF

RELAX AND LISTEN—DO NOT INTERRUPT

When responding to an objection, listen first and then answer the objection.[4] Allow the prospect to state a position completely. A wise man said, "He that answereth a matter before he heareth it, it is folly and shame unto him."[5]

Do not interrupt with an answer, even if the objection to be stated is already apparent to you. Listen as though you have never heard that objection before.

Unfortunately too many salespeople conduct conversations somewhat like the following:

SALESPERSON: Mr. Clark, from a survey of your operations, I'm convinced you're now spending more money repairing your own motors than you would by having us do the job for you–and really do it right!

CUSTOMER: We're probably doing it fine right now. Now, I'm sure your repair service is good, but you don't have to be exactly an electrical genius to be able to . . .

SALESPERSON: Hang on! It isn't a matter of anyone being a genius. It's a matter of having a heavy investment in special motor repair equipment and supplies like vacuum impregnating tanks and lathes for banding armatures, boring bearings, and turning new shafts.

CUSTOMER: Yeah I know all that, but you missed my point. See, what I'm driving at . . .

SALESPERSON: I know what you're driving at, but you're wrong! You forget that even if your own workers are smart cookies, they just can't do high-quality work without a lot of special equipment.

CUSTOMER: But you still don't get my point! The maintenance workers that we now have doing motor repair work . . .

SALESPERSON: Could more profitably spend their time on plant trouble-shooting! Right?

CUSTOMER: That isn't what I was going to say! I was trying to say that between their troubleshooting jobs, instead of just sitting around and shooting the bull . . .

SALESPERSON: Now wait a minute, Mr. Clark. If you think that a good motor rewinding job can be done in someone's spare time, you're wrong!

Obviously attitudes and interruptions like these are likely to bring the interview to a quick end.

Salespeople should plan to relax as buyers offer objections. It's even OK to plan on using humor in your answers to objections. For example, if the buyer objects to the standard payments and asks how low your company could go, you could respond as follows: "Well, if I could get the bank to send you money each month, would you buy it?"

After laughing, the seller could talk about the various payment options. Using humor, as in this example, may help defuse the nervousness that both buyer and seller are feeling during this part of the process. For more insight into the use of humor, see Chapter 4.

What if the buyer asks a question for which you've already covered the material? Don't say, "I've already covered that!" Instead let the buyer finish asking the question and then answer the question with enthusiasm.

EVALUATE OBJECTIONS

To truly sell value and establish a relationship, the seller must evaluate objections before answering.[6] Objections may be classified as unsatisfied needs (that is, real objections) or excuses. **Excuses** are concerns expressed by the buyer that mask the buyer's true objections. Thus, the comment "I can't afford it now" would simply be an excuse if the buyer honestly could afford it now but did not want to buy for some other reason.

A buyer seldom says, "I don't have any reason. I just don't want to buy." More commonly the buyer gives a reason that appears at first to be a real objection but is really an excuse: "I don't have the money" or "I can't use your product." The tone of voice or the nature of the reason may provide evidence that the prospect is not offering a sincere objection.

Salespeople need to develop skill in evaluating objections. No exact formula has been devised to separate excuses from real objections. Sometimes it is best to follow up with a question:

BUYER: I just wish your company sold the full range of insurance products, you know, things like variable annuities.

SELLER: If we did offer variable annuities, would you be interested in having all of your insurance needs met by me?

If the buyer says yes, you know the concern is real. If the buyer says no, you know the buyer is just offering the objection about annuities as an excuse.

Circumstances can also provide a clue to whether an objection is a valid concern. In cold calling, when the prospect says, "I'm sorry, I don't have any money," the salesperson may conclude that the prospect does not want to hear the presentation. However, the same reason offered after a complete presentation has been made and data on the prospect have been gathered through observation and questioning may be valid. Salespeople must rely on observation, questioning, knowledge about why people buy (see Chapter 3), and experience to determine the validity of reasons offered for objections.

ALWAYS TELL THE TRUTH

In dealing with prospects and customers, truthfulness is an absolute necessity for dignity, confidence, and relationship development. Recall that our purpose is not to manipulate but to persuade so that the buyer can make the most effective decision. Lying and deception are not part of a successful long-term relationship. Over time it will be hard to remember which lie you told to which customer. Salespeople should avoid even white lies and half-truths when they answer objections.

ethics

Salespeople who tell lies, even small ones, need to recognize they have a problem and then find ways to change. One way to avoid lies is to spend more time gaining knowledge about their products and the products of their competitors. Sellers who do so aren't as tempted to lie to cover up the fact that they don't know some information requested by the prospect. Sellers also should commit to tell the truth, even if competitors don't follow suit. It is simply the right thing to do.

EFFECTIVE RESPONSE METHODS

Any discussion of specific methods for responding to objections needs to emphasize that no perfect method exists for answering all objections completely. Some prospects, no matter what you do, will never believe their objections have been adequately addressed.

In some instances, spending a lot of time trying to convince the prospect may not be wise. For example, when an industrial recycling salesperson contacts a prospect who says, "I don't believe in recycling," the salesperson may better spend available time calling on some of the vast number of people who do.

This section describes seven common methods for responding to objections. As Exhibit 10.4 indicates, the first two, direct denial and indirect denial, are used only when the prospect makes an untrue statement. The next five methods–compensation, referral, revisiting, acknowledgment, and postponement–are useful when the buyer raises a valid point or offers an opinion.

Before using the methods described in this section, salespeople almost always need to probe to help the prospect clarify concerns and to make sure they understand the objection. This method is often called the **probing method**. If the prospect says, "Your service is not too good," the salesperson can probe by saying, "I'm not sure I understand," or by asking a question. For example, the seller could ask one or more of the following: Not too good? What do you mean by not too good? Exactly what service are you referring to? Is service very important to you? Can you explain what you mean?

While this probing is usually verbal, it can also include nonverbal probing. For example, Professor Donoho at Northern Arizona University teaches a method called the **friendly silent questioning stare (FSQS)** to encourage buyers to elaborate or explain more fully what their concerns are.

Many serious blunders have occurred because a salesperson did not understand a question, answered the wrong question, or failed to answer an objection fully. For example, a sales training manager was listening to a representative for a consulting firm talk about her services. At one point in the conversation, the manager asked, "Has anyone in the electrical products industry ever used this training

Exhibit 10.4
Common Methods for Responding to Objections

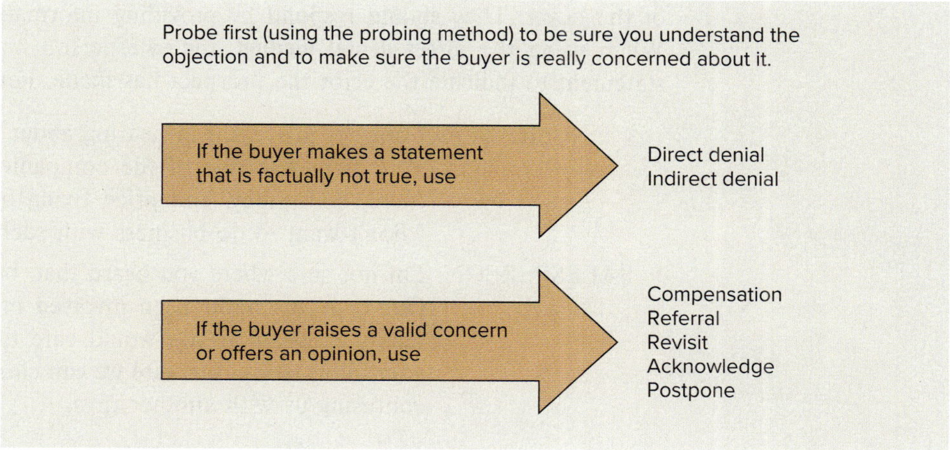

package before?" The consultant answered, "Sure, we have sold this package to several firms. Why, just last week I received a nice letter from Colgate-Palmolive, one of the largest consumer products company, that had nothing but good things to say. . . ." The manager did not buy the training package; he figured that if the consultant did not even know how to listen, the sales training package she was selling could not be very good either. (Chapter 4 provides many helpful suggestions regarding the art of questioning and probing.)

A salesperson who doesn't know the answer to the buyer's objection might say, "I don't know the answer to that question. But I'll find out and get the answer to you." The seller should paraphrase the buyer's question, write it down (this step helps jog the seller's memory as well as demonstrate to the buyer that the seller really intends to follow up), gather the information, and follow up quickly and exactly as promised. If you call the customer with the information and he or she is not available, leave the information on voice mail and then call later to verify that the prospect got the information. And don't forget that it is your responsibility to know most facts, so be prepared the next time for similar and additional questions and concerns. You can be sure your competitor is going to try to have complete answers ready.

thinking it through

How can the use of technology (such as databases, computers, and communication technology) help prevent a seller from having to answer, "I don't know the answer to that question. But I'll find out and call you with the information as soon as I can get it"?

Finally, most buyers would give you this rule to follow: Don't malign or disparage the competition. Sell your product or service on its own merits, not by trying to do so by making the competitive product sound inferior. For some buyers, cutting competition by salespeople is an automatic reason for discontinuing the conversation.

As you think about how you might respond, don't forget to use all tools you have. And one of your options is using social media, as Sales Technology 10.1 describes.

DIRECT DENIAL

At times salespeople face objections based on incomplete or inaccurate information of the buyer. They should respond by providing information or correcting facts. When using the **direct denial method**, the salesperson makes a relatively strong statement to indicate the error the prospect has made. For example:

BUYER: I am not interested in hearing about your guidance systems. Your firm was one of the companies recently indicted for fraud, conspiracy, and price fixing by a federal grand jury. I don't want to do business with such a firm.

SALESPERSON: I'm not sure where you heard that, but it simply is not true. Our firm has never been involved in such activity, and our record is clean. If you would care to tell me the source of your information, I'm sure we can clear this up. Maybe you're confusing us with another firm.

SALES Technology 10.1

HOW TO HELP RESOLVE OBJECTIONS USING SOCIAL MEDIA

Salespeople hear many objections in a given day, and there are a number of ways to resolve them. Social media offer new methods to help in this resolution. For example, here are a few common objections, and how social media might help.

Objection: I'm not sure you've done this enough to really understand my needs.

This objection is usually a question by the prospect as to whether you can be trusted to meet her needs. How can social media help? How about infusing your LinkedIn page with proof of your skills? You can list certifications, show education completed, have copies of white papers you've written, include a link to your blog, and of course, host recommendations from current and previous satisfied customers.

Objection: I'm going to need to find a time that my engineer, who is located in another city, can also meet with us.

Why not suggest that you connect via Google Hangout or Skype, and have the three-way meeting now? There are many social media options for connecting multiple people in a single meeting, and the quality of such interactions just gets better each year, technologically.

Objection: I'm not sure that would work in an organization of our size.

From the customer's social media pages, you can easily find links to her firm, and assess the approximate size of the organization. Plus, your LinkedIn page can include many recommendations from current customers, including some that are of the same size. You can also show tweets from satisfied customers, and pictures of successful implementations from your Instagram links.

These are but a few examples of how social media can be a real asset in helping resolve objections in a sales call.

Sources: Personal utilization by the authors; Kevin Thomas Tully, *"4 Popular Objections and How to Overcome Them Using Social Selling,"* October 21, 2014; *"Using Social Media in Your Objection Handling"*

No one likes to be told that he or she is wrong, so direct denial must be used with caution. It is appropriate only when the objection is blatantly inaccurate and potentially devastating to the presentation. The salesperson must also possess facts to back up such a denial. Direct denial should never be used if the prospect is merely stating an opinion or if the objection is true. For example, direct denial would be inappropriate to this objection: "I don't like the feel of simulated leather products." Direct denial should be avoided even for a false statement if the objection is of little importance to the buyer. An indirect denial would be more appropriate in that case.

INDIRECT DENIAL

In the **indirect denial method**, the salesperson denies the objection but attempts to soften the response. The salesperson takes the edge off the response by agreeing with the prospect that the objection is an important one. Prospects expect salespeople to disagree; instead, a salesperson who recognizes the sincerity of the objection will carefully respect the prospect's view. This approach avoids a direct contradiction and confrontation. To begin an answer, a salesperson would do well to agree with the prospect, but only to the extent that the agreement does not weaken the validity of the salesperson's later denial. For example:

BUYER: Your machines break down more often than those of most of your major competitors.

SALESPERSON: I can see why you might feel that way. Just 10 years ago that statement would have been right on target. However, things have changed with our new quality assurance program.

In fact, just last year Syncos Ratings, a well-respected independent evaluator of quality in our industry, rated us as number one for fewest breakdowns.

The important features of indirect denial are that salespeople recognize the position of the customer who makes the objection and then continues by introducing substantial evidence. The beginning statement should always be true and assure the prospect that the question is a good one. Examples of such statements follow:

With the market the way it is today, I can certainly see why you're concerned about that.

I'll bet 90 percent of the people I call on voice the same concern.

That's really an excellent question, and it allows me to clear up a misconception that perhaps I've given you.

Indirect denial should never be used if the prospect has raised a valid point or is merely expressing an opinion. It can be used for all personality types and is especially effective for amiables and analyticals because they like less assertive salespeople.

COMPENSATION METHOD

Every product has some advantages and some disadvantages compared to competing products. Also, an absolutely perfect product or service has never been developed; the firm always has to make cost–benefit decisions about what features to include.

Buyers note these trade-offs and often object because the salesperson's product is less than perfect. The wise salesperson will admit that such objections are valid and then proceed to show any compensating advantages. This approach is called the **compensation method** of responding to objections. Here is an example:

PROSPECT: This machine has only four filling nozzles. Your competitor's has six nozzles.

SALESPERSON: You're absolutely right. It has only four nozzles, but it costs $4,000 less than the competitor's models, and you said you needed a model that is priced in the lower range. Also, our nozzles are designed for easy maintenance. You have to remove only four screws to get to the filter screens. Most other models have at least 10 screws.

The compensation method is an explicit use of the multiattribute model discussed in Chapter 3. A low score on one attribute can be compensated for by a high score on another attribute. In fact, the compensation method is often referred to as the **superior benefit method** because the benefit of one attribute overcomes a concern about a less important attribute. The method can be effective for many objections and concerns. It seems most appropriate for analyticals, who are accustomed to conducting trade-off analyses. However, it is useful for all other personality types as well.

Of course the buyer may not value the compensating advantages. The buyer may really need the features at issue (perhaps the machine must have six nozzles to work with another piece of the prospect's equipment). In such cases salespeople can recommend a different product (from their own line, if available, or from a competitor) or search for other prospects.

Another time that the compensation method may be used is when the prospect says, "I'm just going to think about it. I'll be in touch with you later." The seller can show

A buyer may question the credibility and knowledge of a salesperson. In this situation the salesperson can use the referral method to help resolve those concerns.

©Image Source RF

how acting today more than compensates for the "pain" of making a decision today. These reasons usually include explaining the hidden costs of delaying the decision (it will go off sale, you will be saving money over your current system each month that you have our proposed system, our product may be out of stock when you need it, summer is a particularly good time to install a new system, or the like).

REFERRAL METHOD

When buyers' objections reflect their own attitudes or opinions, the salesperson can show how others held similar views before trying the product or service. In this method, called the **referral method** or the **feel-felt-found method**, the salesperson goes on to relate that others actually found their initial opinions to be unfounded after they tried the product:

PROSPECT: I don't think my customers will want to buy a Smart TV with all these fancy features.

SALESPERSON: I can certainly see how you feel. Bob Scott, down the road in Houston, felt the same way when I first proposed that he sell these. However, after he agreed to display them next to his current TV line, he found that his customers were very interested. In fact, he called me four days later to order more.

Those who teach this as the feel-felt-found method highlight the importance of the proper sequence, as well as the person or people identified in each stage. The sequence should be as follows: I can see how *you* feel . . . *others* felt the same way . . . yet *they* found. . . . Inexperienced salespeople often mix up the order or the parties identified (for example, by saying ". . . yet you will find").

Proof of the salesperson's assertion in the form of a testimonial letter strengthens the method; in fact, some trainers refer to this approach as the **third-party-testimony method**. If a letter is not available, the salesperson might be able to supply the name and phone number of the third party. The salesperson should always secure the third party's permission first, however. (See Chapter 9 for suggestions about testimonials and references.)

Although the referral method can be used for all personality types, it seems most appropriate for expressives and amiables. Both types tend to care about what other people think and are doing.

REVISIT METHOD

When using the **revisit method** (also called the **boomerang method**) of responding to objections, the salesperson turns the objection into a reason for buying the product or service. This method can be used in many situations (when making an appointment, during the presentation, when attempting to secure commitment, and in postsale situations):

BUYER: I don't think these would sell in my gun shop. They're really drab looking.

SALESPERSON: It's interesting that you mention that. In fact, their drab color is probably their best selling point and the reason you should carry them. You see, when a hunter is in the field, the last thing she wants to do is attract attention to herself. Thanks to the finish we use on this gear . . .

The revisit method requires care. It can appear very pushy and "salesy." This method does have useful applications, however. Often the product or service is actually designed to save the buyer substantial amounts of time or money. If the buyer objects to spending either the time to listen or the money, the revisit method may be a powerful tool to help the buyer see the benefit of investing these resources.

This method works with most personality types. Drivers may require the revisit method more often than other buyers because drivers tend to erect time constraints and other barriers and are less willing to listen to just any salesperson's presentation.

ACKNOWLEDGE METHOD

At times the buyer voices opinions or concerns more to vent frustration than anything else. When this occurs, the best strategy may be to use the **acknowledge method**, also called the **pass-up method**. Simply let the buyer talk, acknowledge that you heard the concern, pause, and then move on to another topic.

BUYER: Hey, you use Beyoncé in your commercials, don't you? Sure you do. Now I want to tell you that I don't like what she stands for! Kids today need a role model they can look up to. What happened to the kind of role models we used to have?

SALESPERSON: I certainly understand your concern. I remember my dad talking about some of his role models and the respect he had for them. [*Pause*] What were we talking about? Oh, yes, I was telling you about the coupon drop we are planning.

In this example the salesperson used the acknowledge method because the buyer apparently was just blowing off steam. A buyer who really wanted some response from the salesperson would have used the salesperson's pause to ask a direct question (Can't you change your commercials?) or make a statement (I refuse to do business with companies that use stars like Beyoncé in their commercials!).

In reality a salesperson often can do little about some prospects' opinions. What are the chances that this salesperson's firm will pull a $5 million ad campaign because one buyer objects? It is doubtful that a firm would take such action unless the buyer had tremendous power in the relationship.

Sometimes the salesperson can use the acknowledge method by simply agreeing with the prospect and then moving on, which suggests to the buyer that the concern really should not be much of an issue. For example:

BUYER: You want $25 for this little plastic bottle?

SELLER: Uh-huh. That's what they cost . . . [*Pause*] Now do you see the switch on this side? It's used if you ever need to . . .

The acknowledge method should not be used if the objection raised is factually false. Also, it should not be used if the salesperson, through probing, could help clarify the buyer's thinking on the topic. Experience is the key to making such a determination. In general, though, the acknowledge method should be used sparingly.

POSTPONE METHOD

In the early part of a sales interview, the prospect may raise objections that the salesperson would prefer to answer later in the presentation, after discovering the prospect's needs. Using the **postpone method**, the salesperson would ask permission to answer the question at a later time:

BUYER [*very early in the call*]: How much does the brass engraving equipment cost?

SALESPERSON: If you don't mind, I would prefer to answer that question in a few minutes. I really can't tell you how much it will cost until I learn more about your engraving needs and know what kinds of features you are looking for.

The prospect will seldom refuse the request if the sales representative appears to be acting in good faith. The sales representative then proceeds with the presentation until the point at which the objection can best be answered.

Some objections are best answered when they occur; others can be responded to most effectively by delaying the answer. Experience should guide the sales representative. The salesperson should take care not to treat an objection lightly or let it appear that he or she does not want to answer the question. Another danger in postponing is that the buyer will be unable to focus on what the salesperson is saying until the concern is addressed. On the other hand, the salesperson is responsible for helping the buyer to critically evaluate the solution offered, and often the buyer can process information effectively only after learning preliminary facts.

Salespeople make the most use of the postponement method when a price objection occurs early in the presentation. However, this method can be used for almost any type of objection or question. For example, postponing discussions about guarantees, delivery schedules, implementation time frames, and certain unique product features until later in the presentation is often preferable.

What if the buyer is convinced that he or she needs the answer right now? Then the salesperson should answer the objection now. Salespeople usually have more to lose by demanding that the buyer wait for information than by simply providing the answer when the buyer strongly requests it. For example:

PROSPECT: What are the delivery schedules for this new product?

SALESPERSON: I would really prefer to discuss that after we talk about our unique production process and extensive quality control measures.

PROSPECT: No, I want to know now!

SALESPERSON: Well, keep in mind that my later discussion about the production process will shed new light on the topic. We anticipate a four- to five-month delivery time after the contract reaches our corporate headquarters.

USING THE METHODS

The seven methods just discussed appear in sales training courses across all industries and geographic boundaries. To help you more easily distinguish the differences among the various methods, Exhibit 10.5 provides an example of the use of each method for the objection, "Your product's quality is too low."

Salespeople often combine methods when answering an objection. For example, a price objection may initially be postponed and then be discussed later using the compensation method. At other times several methods can be used in one answer. Here is an example:

BUYER: I don't think this product will last as long as some of the other, more expensive competitive products.

Exhibit 10.5
Responding to Objections: Using Each Method

Objection: Your product's quality is too low.

Responses*

Direct denial: That simply is not true. Our product has been rated as the highest in the industry for the last three years.

Indirect denial: I can certainly see why you would be concerned about quality. Actually, though, our product quality has been rated as the highest in the industry for the last three years.

Compensation: I agree that our quality is not as high as that of some of our competitors. However, it was designed that way for consumers who are looking for a lower-priced alternative, perhaps just to use in a weekend cottage. So you see, our somewhat lower quality is actually offset by our much lower price.

Referral: I can certainly understand how you feel. Mortimer Jiggs felt the same way before he bought the product. But after using it, he found that the quality was actually equal to that of other products.

Revisit: The fact that the quality is lower than other products is probably the very reason you should buy it. You said that some of your customers are looking for a low-priced product to buy for their grandchildren. This product fills that need.

Acknowledge: I understand your concern. You know, one of the things I always look for is how a product's quality stacks up against its cost. [*Pause*] Now, we were talking about . . .

Postpone: That's an interesting point. Before discussing it fully, I would like to cover just two things that I think will help you better understand the product from a different perspective. OK?

* These are not necessarily good answers to the stated objection. Also, the choice of method would depend on whether the objection is factual. Thus, the replies given here are designed simply to differentiate the various methods.

SALESPERSON: That's probably the very reason you should buy it [*revisit method*]. It may not last quite as long, but it is less than half the cost of competitive products [*compensation method*]. I can certainly understand your concern, though. You know, Mark Hancock felt the way you do. He was concerned about the product's life. But after he used our product for one year, he found that its life expectancy didn't create any problems for his production staff [*referral method*].

Sometimes the buyer will ask multiple questions at once–for example, "How much did you spend on R&D last year, what percentage of your revenue does that represent, and what is your R&D model going forward?" What is a seller to do? Remembering the questions so they don't get lost, the salesperson answers them one by one.

Make sure the buyer agrees before moving on.

CONFIRMING THAT THE OBJECTION HAS BEEN ANSWERED

Before moving on with the presentation, the salesperson needs to make sure that the buyer agrees that all objections have been completely answered. Without this commitment, the salesperson does not know whether the buyer understands the answer or whether the buyer's concerns have been fully addressed. To achieve this commitment, the salesperson can use one or more of the following types of phrases: Did I answer your question? Does that make sense? Do you see why that issue is not as important as you originally thought? Did that resolve your concern?

OBJECTIONS WHEN SELLING TO A GROUP OF BUYERS

Selling to a group of buyers (see Chapter 8) requires some extra care. If one person offers an objection, the seller should try to get a sense of whether other buyers share the concern. At times it may make sense to throw the issue back to the group. For example, if a buyer says that the people in his or her department won't attend the type of training sessions being proposed, the seller might respond as follows: Does anyone else have that same problem in their department? You all know your organizational climate better than I do. Have any of you found a way to deal with that issue that you would like to share with us? Any response from the seller should usually be directed to all buyers, not just the one who asked the question. After responding, the seller needs to make sure that all buyers are satisfied with the answer before moving on.

THE PRICE OBJECTION

Price is the perhaps the most frequently mentioned obstacle to obtaining commitment. In fact, about 20 percent of buyers are thought to buy purely on the basis of price (which means that a full 80 percent buy for reasons other than price). And as international competition continues to strengthen, salespeople can expect more price objections. As a result, all salespeople need to prepare for price objections.[7] For examples of common price objections, see the earlier section in this chapter. Since price objections are so pervasive, we now relate the concepts covered in this chapter to price objections.

Price is still an issue even between partnering firms. One leading firm in its industry has estimated that only 3 percent of its orders are sold at list price; the rest are price discounted.[8]

Unfortunately the first response of many salespeople to a price objection is to lower the price. Inexperienced salespeople, desiring to gain business, often quote the lowest possible price as quickly as possible. They forget that for a mutually beneficial long-term relationship to exist, their firm must make a fair profit. Also, by cutting prices the firm has to sell more to maintain profit margins, as Exhibit 10.6 clearly illustrates.

When faced with a price objection, salespeople should ensure that they have up-to-date information, establish the value of the product, and use communication tools effectively.

USE UP-TO-DATE INFORMATION

Successful salespeople make sure they have the most current pricing information available to them, including not only their prices but competitors' prices as well. Firms are helping salespeople in this regard. For example, many firms have developed intranet sites for their salespeople. If a salesperson finds that the company's price points are a little higher than the competition, the salesperson can use the intranet site to look for some sales or trade-in program that she or he can leverage to get the deal.

ESTABLISH THE VALUE

The product's value must be established before the salesperson spends time discussing price. The value expected determines the price a prospect is willing to pay. Unless the salesperson can build value to exceed the price asked, a sale will not occur. As a rule, value cannot be established during the early stages of the presentation.

Price objections are best handled with a two-step approach. First, the salesperson should try to look at the objection from the customer's viewpoint, asking questions

Exhibit 10.6

Look before You Cut Prices! You Must Sell More to Break Even

	Present Gross Profit					
Cut Price	5.0%	10.0%	15.0%	20.0%	25.0%	30.0%
1%	25.0	11.1	7.1	5.3	4.2	3.4
2	66.6	25.0	15.4	11.1	8.7	7.1
3	150.0	42.8	25.0	17.6	13.6	11.1
4	400.0	66.6	36.4	25.0	19.0	15.4
5	–	100.0	50.0	33.3	25.0	20.0
6	–	150.0	66.7	42.9	31.6	25.0
7	–	233.3	87.5	53.8	38.9	30.4
8	–	400.0	114.3	66.7	47.1	36.4
9	–	1,000.0	150.0	81.8	56.3	42.9
10	–	–	200.0	100.0	66.7	50.0
11	–	–	275.0	122.2	78.6	57.9
12	–	–	400.0	150.0	92.3	66.7
13	–	–	650.0	185.7	108.3	76.5
14	–	–	1,400.0	233.3	127.3	87.5
15	–	–	–	300.0	150.0	100.0
16	–	–	–	400.0	177.8	114.3
17	–	–	–	566.7	212.5	130.8
18	–	–	–	900.0	257.1	150.0
19	–	–	–	1,900.0	316.7	172.7
20	–	–	–	–	400.0	200.0
21	–	–	–	–	525.0	233.3
22	–	–	–	–	733.3	275.0
23	–	–	–	–	1,115.0	328.6
24	–	–	–	–	2,400.0	400.0
25	–	–	–	–	–	500.0

A business truism says that you can cut, cut, cut until you cut yourself out of business. This can certainly apply to cutting p-ices in an effort to increase profits. The two don't necessarily go together. For example, select the gross profit being earned at present from those shown at the top of the chart. Follow the left column down until you line up with the proposed price cut. The intersected figure represents the percentage of increase in unit sales required to earn the same gross profit realized before the price cut. Obviously it helps to know this figure so you don't end up with a lot of work for nothing.

See for yourself: Assume that your present gross margin is 25 percent and that you cut your selling price 10 percent. -ocate the 25 percent column under Present Gross Profit. Now follow the column down until you line up with the 10 percent cut in selling price in column 1. You will need to sell 66.7 percent more units to earn the same margin dollars as at the previous price.

to clarify the customer's perspective: "Too high in what respect, Mr. Jones? Could you tell me hcw much we are out of line? We are usually quite competitive on this model, so I am surprised you find our price high. . . . Are the other quotes you have for the same size engine?"[9]

After learning more about the customer's perspective, the next step is to sell value and quality rather than price (see Chapter 9 for a full discussion of the customer value proposition). Most customers prefer to buy less expensive products if they believe they will receive the same benefits. However, many customers will pay more for higher quality when the quality benefits and features are pointed out to them. Many high-quality products appear similar to lower-quality products; thus, salespeople need to emphasize the features that justify a difference.

For example, a salesperson who sells industrial fasteners and supplies may hear this objection: "That bolt costs $750! I could buy it elsewhere for $75." The salesperson should reply, "Yes, but that bolt is inside your most important piece of production equipment. Let's say you buy that $75 bolt. How much employee time and production downtime would it take to disassemble the machine again and replace that one bolt?" The salesperson can then engage in a complete cost-benefit analysis (see Chapter 9) to solidify the point.

A supplier of integrated circuits (ICs) was competing with another company whose price was 10 cents less. The buyer asked for a price concession, noting that the competitor's product was obviously less expensive. Unbeknownst to the supplier, however, the buyer had already examined the value propositions of the two companies and determined that the higher-priced one was actually worth 12 cents more than the less expensive one, due to services offered. Thus, in reality, the buyer had already realized that the higher-priced one was actually less expensive in terms of value (12 cents more in value minus the 10 cents higher in price = 2 cents higher in value per IC). The higher-priced supplier caved in and gave the buyer a 10-cent reduction in price, costing his firm $500,000 (5 million units at 10 cents each) in potential profits! And the sad fact is that the buyer was already planning on going with the higher-priced supplier.[10]

Intangible features can also provide value that offsets price. Some of these features are services, company reputation, and the salesperson:

- Good service in the form of faster deliveries, technical advice, and field assistance is but one of the many intangibles that can spell value, savings, and profits to a customer. For example, one company cut its prices in response to buyers' demands. However, the company later found that what the customers really wanted was technical support. As the company cut its prices, it had only reinforced its image as low priced with little technical support.
- For a customer tempted to buy on price alone, salespeople can emphasize the importance of having a thoroughly reliable source of supply: the salesperson's company. It has been demonstrated time and again that quality is measured by the reputation of the company behind it.
- Customers value sales representatives who go out of their way to help with problems and promotions–salespeople who keep their word and follow through when they start something. These services are very valuable to customers.

USE COMMUNICATION TOOLS EFFECTIVELY

One pharmaceutical salesperson often hears that her company's drug for migraines is too expensive. Her response is to paint a word picture:[11]

DOCTOR: How much does this product cost?

SALESPERSON: It costs about $45. . . . There are 15 doses per bottle, so it ends up about $3 per dose.

DOCTOR: That's too much money!

SALESPERSON: Consider your patients who have to lie in the dark because their headaches are so bad they can't see straight, can't think straight, and are nauseated by migraine pain. A price of $3 is really inexpensive to relieve these patients' pain, wouldn't you agree?

Probing questions can often help the buyer think through the ramification of price, like the following:

- Too expensive compared to what?
- How much will doing nothing cost you?
- Is it a cash flow issue or a budget issue?
- What is the ROI or profit margin you were looking to get?
- Let's say money was no object. Would our product/service help solve your problem?
- In your own business, is your offering always the lowest price one?

Just telling customers about quality and value is not enough; they must be shown. Top salespeople use the communication tools discussed in Chapter 9 to describe more clearly the quality and value of their products. This process includes activities such as demonstrating the product, showing test results and quality control procedures, using case histories, and offering testimonials.

DEALING WITH TOUGH CUSTOMERS

Sellers need to maintain the positive attitude discussed earlier, even with rude, hard-to-get-along-with prospects. It's not easy, and it's not fun.[12]

Sellers need to realize that we all have bad days. Maybe the buyer is having one. If the rudeness is quite blatant and the seller believes that this behavior is just due to the timing of the visit, the seller might say, "I'm sensing that this might not be the best time to talk. Should we reschedule for another time?"

If the buyer continues to communicate aggressively, being downright rude, you probably need to call attention to the fact. After all, to develop a long-term win-win relationship and partnership, you both need to be on the same footing. Perhaps saying something like this will clear the air: "I'm sorry, Joe. I don't know quite how to say this. But it seems to me that you wish to argue more than learn about my products. I'll gladly continue if you think we can both approach this problem with professionalism and courtesy." By doing so, you are asserting yourself and confronting the issue head-on. At the same time, you are avoiding an emotional reaction of anger. Of course it is important to keep in mind the various personalities that buyers can have (see Chapter 5) and the adjustments suggested for each.

Also remember that the buyer's culture often dictates how he or she will respond to a seller. For example, Germans are known as being thorough, systematic, and well prepared, but they are also rather dogmatic and thus lack flexibility and the desire to compromise. As a result, sellers not accustomed to such a culture could have difficulty dealing with a German prospect who raises a price objection in a strong tone of voice.

Believe it or not, some of the toughest customers aren't those who are noisy and boisterous. Rather, they are often the passive ones, the quiet ones–the ones who don't object, don't question, and don't buy. What should a seller do? Be open, direct, and honest. Stop talking. Ask questions. Try your best to get the buyer involved. Establish trust so the buyer can feel confident enough to ask

Salespeople must learn to deal with tough prospects and customers.

©Sunabe syou/Alamy Stock Photo RF

Believe it or not, the hardest prospects can be the quiet ones.

©Westend61/SuperStock RF

questions. If the buyer is still quiet, use a trial close. If this doesn't result in gaining commitment, ask the prospect what he or she would like to do at this point.

SELLING YOURSELF

Understanding how to effectively answer objections is not just a skill that will help you while at work, but one that is relevant in all areas of your life. Think about some situations where you have already noticed the need for answering tough questions. You are likely to think of college applications, job interviews, while in any sort of leadership role, or even in your personal relationships. By practicing the methods found in Chapter 10, successfully responding to objections in your life will become second nature.

Imagine that you are on a student advisory board at your university. While going over the curriculum to be taught to new students entering your program that year, you see an opportunity to enhance it by making tablets more readily available for student use. Knowing that the program's department head is not technology-savvy, what steps do you take to get these new tablets into the classroom?

After putting your presentation together that is filled with the benefits of tablets in the classrooms, it is important to anticipate and prepare for any potential objections from the department head. A list of potential objections could be budget restrictions, ROI concerns, fear of change, and tablet quality. After making a list of possible concerns, prepare exactly how you would address them. Doing this will help you remain cool, calm, and collected while in your big meeting with the department head.

While forestalling is critical, it is likely that there will still be unforeseen objections in your meeting. What if the department head tells you, "I'm not so sure about this. We may not have time to train the professors on the new tablets before the first classes begin." Although this didn't come in the form of a question, it is still an objection. Before responding, it is crucial to make sure that you understand the root of the objection, or the actual need. Is he actually worried about the implementation time or does he have a fear of change? Try asking the department head what steps would need to be taken to make him feel comfortable with the new tablets. Once you have an understanding of the department head's need, you can begin to overcome the objection.

Start by being patient and empathetic of the department head's concern. If he is not technology-savvy, then adding new tablets to the classrooms could be intimidating! Assure him that his concern is absolutely valid, but something that you can get through together. Be honest, clear, concise, and reinforce your response to the objection with the benefits that the tablets would bring to the classrooms.

Once you feel as if you've overcome the objection, check with the department head to make sure that he feels the same way and that the objection is no longer a concern for him. By following these basic steps, you will be able to navigate past all the department head's objections and achieve your goal of getting more tablets into the classroom!

Molly Gilleland, account executive, Comcast Spotlight. Used with permission.

SUMMARY

Responding to objections is a vital part of a salesperson's responsibility. Objections may be offered at any time during the relationship between buyer and salesperson. They are to be expected, even welcomed, and they must be handled with skill and empathy.

Successful salespeople carefully prepare effective responses to buyers' concerns. Salespeople need to develop a positive attitude, commit to always telling the truth, refrain from interrupting, anticipate and forestall known objections, and learn how to evaluate objections.

Buyers object for many reasons. They may have no money, or they may not need the product. They may need more information or misunderstand some information already offered. They may be accustomed to another product, may not think the value exceeds the cost, or may not like the product's features. They may want to get rid of the salesperson or may not trust the salesperson or his or her company. They may want time to think or may object for many other reasons.

Effective methods of responding to objections are available, and their success has been proved. Methods exist both for concerns that are not true and for objections that either are true or are only the buyer's opinion. Sensitivity in choosing the right method is vital. Salespeople need to develop skill in responding to price objections and in dealing with tough customers. Nothing will substitute for developing skill in these areas.

KEY TERMS

acknowledge method 274
boomerang method 273
compensation method 272
direct denial method 270
excuses 268
feel-felt-found method 273
forestall 265
friendly silent questioning stare (FSQS) 269
indirect denial method 271
LAARC method 265
objection 258
pass-up method 274
pioneer selling 261
postpone method 275
probing method 269
referral method 273
revisit method 273
superior benefit method 272
third-party-testimony method 273
turnover (TO) 263

ETHICS PROBLEMS

1. In this chapter you learned about the acknowledge method (pass-up method) where you let the buyer talk, acknowledge that you heard the concern, pause, and then move on to another topic. Given that you are not actually answering the buyer's concern, how can that be ethical? Wouldn't the ethical thing to do be to answer the concern directly?
2. Why not just use the direct denial method for objections or concerns that are raised by the buyer that are factually inaccurate? Isn't using the indirect denial just a trick to keep the buyer liking you?

QUESTIONS AND PROBLEMS

1. Categorize each of the following into the five basic types of objections. Then illustrate one way to handle each:
   a. After a sales presentation, the dairy farmer says, "You've made some good points, but your competitor's feed supplements can do just about everything yours can do."
   b. After the Nike salesperson answers an objection, the prospect remarks, "I guess your product is all right, but as I told you

when you walked in, things are going pretty well for us right now without your product."

c. After a thorough presentation about new educational resources for early childhood students, the prospect answers, "Are you kidding me? You want how much money for that online access to those articles?"

d. The industrial maintenance customer says, "I can buy those cleaning supplies online for a lot less than what you're selling them for."

2. Derrick Hamlin spent considerable time working with a prospective buyer. He thought a good order would be forthcoming on his next call. A portion of his conversation with the buyer went as follows:

BUYER: You know, I like what I hear about your emergency food delivery system. But how can I be sure it will be available on the days that we actually experience an emergency need for food?

DERRICK: I've never had any complaints before. I'm pretty sure they will be easily available.

BUYER: You are sure of that?

DERRICK: Well, I've never heard of any problems that I can remember.

BUYER: [*appearing unconvinced and looking at some papers on his desk without glancing up*]: I'll let you know later what I plan to do. Thanks for dropping by.

How can you improve on Derrick's answer to the buyer's concern?

3. Describe the differences between the compensation method and the referral method for responding to objections. Then, making any assumptions necessary, provide a clear example of each for this objection: "This new virtual reality training headset is way too expensive. I can buy some virtual reality headsets much cheaper than buying your units!"

4. Occasionally a buyer will offer several objections at one time. How would you respond if a buyer made the following comments without pausing? "Say, what is the estimated delivery time for these units, and how can I be sure they will arrive on time? Oh, and what happens if my needs change before our contract were to end?"

5. In Building Partnerships 10.1, the seller offered this advice: "Stop selling and begin helping" Give an example of how you might be able to do that if you were selling group tickets to a business for a sporting event on your campus.

6. Choose a hotel in your town. Assume that you work at that hotel and are planning to make calls to local civic organizations like the Kiwanis Club, the Lions Club, and so forth. Assume that the hotel has a private meeting room available that will seat 25 people. Your objective is to have officers of the clubs schedule their monthly meetings at the hotel.

a. Make a list of three objections you may expect to encounter.

b. List the answers to those three objections, and label the methods used.

7. In Sales Technology 10.1, you learned that salespeople can help in answering objections by infusing their LinkedIn page with proof of their skills. Go to LinkedIn, and view the profile of two people who are currently salespeople. Evaluate how effectively they have infused their LinkedIn page with these types of helpful items.

8. You have been describing to an IT security officer (that deals with computers at the company) and her boss a new security protection system that your firm just introduced. The new system has tracking features that make it easier for IT security personnel to assess in real time the current security situation of the network at organizations. The security officer says, "I would really like that!" The boss says, "Well, if it's what you think we need, OK. How much does it cost?" At your reply, "This one is $2,498 per month," the boss exclaims, "That seems outrageous!" What should you say or do?

9. For each of the following objections, provide answers that clearly demonstrate the direct denial and indirect denial methods. Assume each objection is *not* true:

a. My architectural customers wouldn't be impressed with the ability to see their proposed design plan in a 3-D virtual walkthrough. It's enough for me to just explain it to them and show them two-dimensional drawings.

b. The cost of replacing the power supply system will be more than just buying a new unit.

c. I heard that the flame retardant used in manufacturing your systems might cause cancer.

d. I know I can buy this cheaper online.

10. For each of the following objections, provide answers that clearly demonstrate the compensation method and referral method. Assume all the objections are either true or are the prospect's opinion, and make any assumptions necessary:

   a. Your after-incident cleanup service, for buildings damaged by storms and fires, costs a lot of money!

   b. I don't think our customers will like the new bluetooth speakers you're selling.

   c. Your repair technicians aren't certified by the international certification agency.

   d. My customers have never asked for this brand of air freshener.

CASE PROBLEMS

case 10.1

Zadro Inc. (Part B)

There are many harmful germs found in the home, in public places, and in hotels while traveling. The Programmable UV Sanitizing Wand, made by Zadro, can effectively kill up to 99.99 percent of germs and viruses in just 10 seconds. It can also kill dust mites in mattresses, pillows, and carpets. Since the wand is portable, it can travel with you wherever you travel, removing harmful substances regardless of where you are. The user simply waves the scanner within a quarter inch of the surface for 10 seconds to kill the substances.

The scanner is 1½ inches high × 20 inches wide × 1¾ inches deep and runs on three C batteries. An optional AC adapter is sold separately. The scanner includes an electronic child lock to prevent misuse. A stand is provided and is used to go over keyboards, butcher blocks, and so on for hands-free operation. The programmable unit can be set for 10-, 20-, 40-, and 60-second times as well as two to five minutes, depending on the surface area that needs to be scanned. The unit is not designed to be used on humans or animals. The scanner, which is laboratory certified and tested, retails for $99, and all units come with a 90-day limited warranty. Resellers are offered the units for $60, with a quantity discount of $50 for all units over 100 in a single order.

Assume that you are selling the Programmable UV Sanitizing Wand to Target Corporation for it to resell.

Questions

1. What objections could the buyer raise? Make any assumptions necessary to develop this list.
2. Provide a response to each objection you listed in question 1 (make any assumptions necessary to create your responses). Include the name of the method you recommend for each objection.

Source: Zadro Inc.

case 10.2

The London *Telegraph*

The Telegraph (which publishes *The Daily Telegraph, The Sunday Telegraph*, and the online version of *The Telegraph*), founded in 1855, is widely viewed as the national "newspaper of record" in England. Due to its many awards and news-breaking journalism, it holds a strong, international reputation as one of the highest-quality newspapers in the world. The newspapers's circulation is around 500,000, down a great deal from its high of around 1.5 million. You can view more details about the paper at its Web site: www.telegraph.co.uk/.

Assume that today you are calling on Skylyn Richards, senior advertising manager of Barnebys Auctions. Barnebys has opened a series of Web sites that feature online auctions of art, antiques, and design. You can view more details about Barnebys at its Web site: www.barnebys.com/.

You are planning to discuss having Barnebys place ads in both the online and print version of *The Telegraph*.

Questions

1. Here is a list of possible objections you think might occur during this first meeting with Skylyn. Assume that each objection for this question is actually an untrue statement. For each objection, provide a possible response, and label the method you used. Make any assumption necessary to create your responses.
   a. Your paper has been involved in a scandal for taking bribes from politicians so you will give them favorable editorial treatment.
   b. Advertising with you costs more than with other papers in London.
   c. You have never dealt with an auction house before, so you couldn't know what our needs are or how to address them.
   d. I read that your circulation is down to about 200,000 daily.
2. Here is a list of possible objections you think might occur during this first meeting with Skylyn. Assume that each objection for this question is actually a true statement or an opinion. For each objection, provide a possible response, and label the method you used. Make any assumption necessary to create your responses.
   a. I never did like your paper because it is too conservative-leaning.
   b. The circulation of your paper is way down from its high of years ago. I'm afraid it could fold.
   c. You published a nasty letter-to-the-editor from someone who had very unkind things to say about Barnebys.
   d. The *London Evening Standard* is a better paper.

Sources: The London Telegraph; Barnebys

ROLE PLAY CASE

You will repeat your role play presentation from Chapter 9. (If you have not done role plays before, you will need to review the information about the various role play customers that can be found at the end of Chapter 3. If you didn't do the role play for Chapter 9, you will need to review that material also, which can be found at the end of Chapter 9.) When you act as the observer today, you should identify what objection-handling method the seller used and if it was done effectively. The professor will give you a sheet to use as a buyer, listing objections for you to use during the role play. When you sell, try to use a variety of objection-handling methods.

Note: For background information about these role plays, please see Chapter 1.

To the instructor: Additional information needed to complete the role play is available in the Instructor's Manual.

ADDITIONAL REFERENCES

Arndt, Aaron, Kenneth Evans, Timothy D. Landry, Sarah Mady, and Chatdanai Pongpatipat. "The Impact of Salesperson Credibility-Building Statements on Later Stages of the Sales Encounter." *Journal of Personal Selling and Sales Management* 34, no. 1 (2014), pp. 19–32.

DeGroot, Robert P. *Objection Free Selling: How to Prevent, Preempt, and Respond to Every Sales Objection You Get.* Cape Coral, FL: Sales Training International, 2016.

Hoffeld, David. *The Science of Selling: Proven Strategies to Make Your Pitch, Influence Decisions, and Close the Deal.* New York: TarcherPerigee, 2016.

Rowe, William J., and Steven J. Skinner. "Delegating Slotting Allowance Authority to the Sales Force." *Industrial Marketing Management* 57 (2016), pp. 159–65.

©Abel Mitja Varela/Getty Images RF

The Partnership Process

PART 2

chapter 11

OBTAINING COMMITMENT

SOME QUESTIONS ANSWERED IN THIS CHAPTER ARE

- How much emphasis should be placed on closing the sale?
- Why is obtaining commitment important?
- When is the best time to obtain commitment?
- Which methods of securing commitment are appropriate for developing partnerships?
- How should pricing be presented?
- What should a salesperson do when the prospect says yes? When the prospect says no?
- What causes difficulties in obtaining commitment, and how can these issues be overcome?

PROFILE

"Ask if you have earned the right to have their business."

Kimberly Drumm, Electronic Systems, Inc.

Courtesy of Kimberly Drumm

PROFILE "Always be closing." Most everyone in the sales profession has heard this statement. Alec Baldwin coined this phrase as he profanely chastised a lackadaisical sales team in the movie *Glengarry Glen Ross*. If you can filter through the abusive "motivation" bestowed in this film, these three key words made famous by this movie are essential to the success of any salesperson: Always. Be. Closing.

When *do* you start "closing," or asking for commitment? Interview 100 salespeople and a majority of them will tell you, the *closing* appointment is the most important step in the sales cycle—that's when you get the order.

I strongly disagree. Closing begins in your very first interaction with customers, on the initial appointment. As you start to build rapport with the decision maker, as you ask him or her questions and learn about the company and its business needs, you are starting to close. You are closing for the right to learn more about the company's initiatives. You are closing for the next step in the sales cycle. You are closing for the opportunity to share with the customer how you and your company may help accomplish goals. You are closing for the chance to provide the customer with a quote or proposal.

So how do you accomplish these "micro closes"? There are several ways, but I find that most of the time the direct route is the shortest and, often, the most appreciated. You simply say, "Mr/s. Customer, based on our conversation today, there are several areas in which (my company name) has been able to assist other companies like (another client's business name) improve (insert problem uncovered during questions). May I share with you how we were able to do that?" Then close for the next step: "Would Wednesday at 9 a.m. or Thursday at 2 p.m. work better for you?"

Or perhaps you have sailed (or stumbled!) through the first few meetings and would like to be able to quote the customer for a current or future opportunity—ask for that opportunity!

Or you just finished presenting your proposal to the decision maker. You were up late the night before ensuring the details were perfect, double-checking your spelling, and triple-checking your pricing! Your heart raced as you stepped through the first few pages of your presentation, but you settled down and hit your stride as you explained how your proposed solution would address the pain points and headaches the customer had described to you several meetings ago. You presented your recommendations and pricing to the customer and now you sit in an echoing silence waiting for him or her to say, well—something. Now what? If you insist on violating one of the cardinal rules of sales by breaking that quiet air, at least do it with a question. Close the customer! Ask for the order. Ask the customer to do business with you. Ask the client to move forward with your company. If you don't, someone else will. So, take a deep breath and ask the customer if he or she can see the benefits of partnering with your company. Ask if you have earned the right to be the provider of (insert your incredible product or service there). Always. Be. Closing.

And then go get yourself a cup of coffee. After all, coffee *is* for closers!

Visit our Web site at: www.esi.net.

From the BUYER'S SEAT 11.1

WHAT BUYERS HATE ABOUT SALESPEOPLE

The stereotypical bad salesperson is one who is overly aggressive, overly friendly, and doesn't seem to care about the customer. While these behaviors are annoying, a recent survey of business buyers found that 70 percent of salespeople were just unprepared and unable to answer questions. This lack of knowledge means they really can't help buyers.

Buyers want to buy solutions for problems their company is facing. According to Amy Bible, director of acquisition sales for Dun & Bradstreet, buyers want short, easy sales processes—or, in their mind, buying processes. "When a buyer tells you that they're still making a decision, respond by asking for more insight into the decision-making process. This gives you an opportunity to learn what's not working and to help create a more streamlined process."

Sources: Amy Bible, *"Three Reasons Why Buyers Hate Your Sales Process,"*; Mary Shea, *"Why Buyers Don't Want to Meet with Your Salespeople and What to Do about It."*

SECURING COMMITMENT TODAY

Asking for the buyer's business, often called **closing**, has always received a great deal of emphasis in sales training. Hundreds of books, videos, and seminar speakers have touted the importance of closing–just search "close sales" at Amazon, and over 4,000 book titles will appear. Almost all are devoted to a method or methods that will make the decision maker say yes.

Look a little closer at those titles, however, and you'll notice that most of them are old. Some of the books may even be older than your parents! Today's sales professionals recognize that securing a sale is the reason for their existence, but getting that sale should be due to the value created, not the technique used.

Research shows that an emphasis on getting the sale no matter what damages trust and raises the possibility of losing commitment altogether.[1] Cheesy sales tricks also insult a buyer's intelligence. Buyers want to buy, not to be sold.

Solid research provides strong evidence that questions the value of closing techniques. The research, based on more than 35,000 sales calls over 12 years, has found that in a major sale, reliance on closing techniques instead of engaging in identifying needs and providing solutions actually reduces the chances of making a sale.[2]

So why even cover closing at all? The simplest answer is provided by Kimberly Drumm in the profile at the beginning chapter: "If you don't (ask for the sale), someone else will." But asking for the sale is not always easy; get it wrong and the sale might be lost. From the Buyer's Seat 11.1 shows how some salespeople get it wrong.

Without a buyer's commitment, no sale takes place. Buyers rarely volunteer to make a purchase even when that decision is obviously the right thing to do. This chapter covers the topic of obtaining commitment in a manner that is consistent with the theme of the book: developing and building long-term partnerships.

PART OF THE PROCESS

The process of obtaining commitment occurs throughout the natural, logical progression of any sales call. Recall from Chapter 3 that creeping commitment occurs when a customer becomes committed to a particular course of action throughout the buying process. Salespeople actually gain commitment repeatedly: when asking

Exhibit 11.1

Examples of Commitments Salespeople May Attempt to Obtain

Examples of Presale Commitments

- To have the prospect agree to come to the office sometime during the next two weeks for a hands-on demonstration of the equipment.
- To set up another appointment for one week from now, at which time the buyer will allow me to do a complete survey of her printing needs.
- To have the buyer agree to pass along my information to the buying committee with his endorsement of my proposal.
- To have the prospect agree to call several references that I will provide to develop further confidence and trust in my office-cleaning business.
- To have the prospect agree on the first point (of our four-point program) and schedule another meeting in two days to discuss the second point.
- To have the prospect initiate the necessary paperwork to allow us to be considered as a future vendor.

Examples of Commitments That Consummate the Sale

- To have the prospect sign an order for 100 pairs of jeans.
- To schedule a co-op newspaper advertising program to be implemented in the next month.
- To have the prospect agree to send three employees to our training program as a trial.
- To have the retailer agree to allow us space for an end-of-aisle display for the summer presentation of Raid insect repellent.

for an appointment, when checking to see whether the customer's entire needs have been identified, and when asking whether the prospect would like to see a demonstration or receive a proposal. Commitment, of course, is more than just securing an order. As Exhibit 11.1 illustrates, salespeople will attempt to obtain a commitment that is consistent with the objectives of the particular sales call.

Obtaining commitment is also important in moving the account through the relationship process. Once a sale is made, salespeople begin to plan for the next sale or for the next level of commitment that indicates a deepening relationship. At the same time, commitment is a two-way street. Salespeople also make commitments to buyers when the sale is made.

THE IMPORTANCE OF SECURING COMMITMENT

Overall, gaining commitment tells the salesperson what to do next and defines the status of the client. For example, gaining a needs identification appointment may mean that you have a "suspect"; at the end of that call, gaining commitment for a demonstration means you have a prospect. Gain an order and you gain a customer. Without gaining commitment, the salesperson may waste time doing the wrong things.

Salespeople need to become proficient in obtaining commitment for several other good reasons. First, if they fail to obtain commitment, it will take longer (more sales calls) to obtain a sale, if a sale occurs at all. Taking more time with one sale means fewer sales overall because you lose time for prospecting and other important activities. Second, assuming the product truly satisfies the prospect's needs, the sooner the prospect buys, the sooner she or he can realize the benefits of the product or service. Third, the company's future success depends on goodwill and earning a profit. Finally, securing commitment results in financial rewards for the salesperson; in addition, meeting needs is also intrinsically rewarding for the seller.

One thing to remember is that if you have done your job well and you have a product that the buyer truly needs, then you deserve the sale. The buyer is not doing you a favor by buying, and he or she expects you to ask for the sale if you've done your work professionally. Not only is gaining commitment important for you and your company, it is the professional thing to do. What is not professional is a high-pressure close; typically, high-pressure closing is necessary (and inappropriate) when the salesperson has not done a good job throughout the entire process.[3]

thinking it through

Think for a moment about a major purchase that you or a family member made, such as a new TV or a car. During the shopping process, what were some of the worst closes you experienced? What salesperson behavior really angers you when you try to shop for major purchases? What made the difference between those experiences and the ones you found satisfying?

Before we get into how to obtain commitment, some time should be spent on the importance of terms and conditions of the sale and how these influence the total cost. Sometimes terms are an important need and may be presented early in the call. But we present the credit terms here because often a buyer decides what to buy and then explores the financial terms that are available.

FINANCIAL TERMS AND CONDITIONS

Most salespeople try to hold off on presenting price until the end. Yet price is often the first question asked. The final price is really a function of the terms and conditions of the sale and depends on several factors.

Cash flow is an issue for many buyers and can stop a sale. Generally, companies pay 30 days after receiving products they've purchased. Yet the producer of those products had to pay all of the employees who made them, as well as the suppliers who parts or raw materials. Somehow, cash coming in has to be more than cash going out. No matter how badly they may want or need the product, not having the cash can delay or even prohibit a sale. Santosh Natarajan, of SSI-India, experienced such a challenge when developing a software application for Korcett. The company was growing so fast that all cash was being used up in production, leaving no cash for an important software upgrade. Santosh worked out a payment plan that matched his invoices to receipt of payments from customers. There was added risk for SSI-India, but it was worth it.

Factors that affect price are the use of quantity and other discounts, as well as credit and shipping terms. Figuring out the final actual price can be difficult, especially in situations with many options and packages rather than standardized products. Sales Technology 11.1 describes how some companies use special pricing software to put it all together.

DISCOUNTS

Discounts are given for many reasons and may be based on the type of customer (such as wholesaler or retailer, senior citizen, or younger adult), quantity purchased, or some other factor. The most common type of discount is the quantity discount.

Quantity discounts encourage large purchases by passing along savings resulting from reduced processing costs. Businesses offer two types of quantity discounts: (1) the single-order discount and (2) a cumulative discount. An office equipment company offering a 10 percent discount on a single order for five or more facsimile

SALES Technology 11.1

COMPLEX PRICING SOLUTIONS

More salespeople are involved in creating and offering custom solutions, which means pricing out the sale can be challenging—especially since so many of us didn't enter sales because we like math! Fortunately, there are technology solutions that help, and not just with the pricing but also with the actual product design.

A company can input its product catalog into a software system called a product configurator, making it easy for salespeople to work with customers to design the products they want. For example, *Powertrak*, made by Axonom, can not only be used to generate proposals and price quotes, it also can be used to design the final product. The system can even apply virtual reality to give the buyer a better look at what is being purchased.

Shimadzu Scientific Instruments chose the Powertrak configure/price/quote (or CPQ, as the type of solution is called in the industry) in part so that new salespeople could become productive more quickly. But the benefits weren't just for new salespeople. The system doesn't allow the user to make mistakes, like putting two incompatible parts together, which means that fewer approvals are needed. Fewer approvals means faster response to customer inquiries, resulting in more sales.

Shimadzu Scientific Instruments manufactures highly complex medical testing instruments. Karen Sasaki, manager of information technology at the company, said, "Powertrak (the CPQ it uses) not only gives us control to create kits and execute sales quotes more efficiently and accurately, but its robustness allows us to apply multiple quotes, that may include multiple product kits, to any given opportunity in Microsoft Dynamics CRM and forecast one or more quotes for pipeline management."

Arkos Field Services found that a CPQ system cut its proposal preparation and approval time from days to minutes. The company, which serves the oil and gas industry, sells replacement compressors and other equipment used in the field. "Successfully completing a job quote was an excruciating time-consuming task. Our sales managers were required to understand the job, scope it, contact the OEM about parts and pricing, and calculate service expenditures, all before finalizing the quote," said Eric May, director of project management office (PMO) at Arkos. But with a CPQ, the process became much easier. The result is that Arkos's sales engineers can spend more time going after new business, rather than working on proposals.

Sources: Anonymous, *"Arkos Field Services Speeds Service Quoting Time from Days to Minutes"*; Anonymous, *"Analytical Instruments Manufacturer Finds Powertrak Improves Sales Quoting Accuracy."*

machines is an example of a single-order discount. When offering a **cumulative discount**, that same company might offer the 10 percent discount on all purchases over a one-year period, provided the customer purchases more than five fax machines. The customer may sign an agreement at the beginning of the year promising to buy five or more machines, in which case the customer will be billed for each order at the discounted price (10 percent off). If the customer fails to purchase five fax machines, a single bill will be sent at the end of the year for the amount of the discount (10 percent of the single-unit price times the number of fax machines actually purchased). Another method is to bill the customer at the full price and then rebate the discount at the end of the year, based on the actual number of fax machines purchased.

CREDIT TERMS

Most U.S. sales are made on a credit basis, with **cash discounts** allowed for early payment. These cash discounts are the last discount taken, meaning that if a quantity discount is also offered, the cash discount is calculated after the quantity discount is taken off. A common discount is 2/10, n/30, which means that the buyer can deduct 2 percent from the bill if it is paid within 10 days from the date of invoice. Otherwise the full amount must be paid in 30 days. Another common discount is 2/10, EOM, which means that the 10-day period begins at the end of the month. For example, if the customer receives $1,000 worth of supplies on February 15 with terms of 2/10, EOM and pays the bill on March 5, the customer would pay $980 (that is, $1,000 at 2% = $20 discount for paying cash; $1,000 - $20 = $980). But if the customer pays on March 11, the bill would be the full $1,000.

Credit terms can be very important in managing cash flow, particularly for operational purchases. For example, if a retailer buys 1,000 pounds of Smithfield ham at $2 per pound, Smithfield may want payment upon receipt. But the retailer hasn't sold it yet so where does that cash come from? The longer the retailer can take to pay Smithfield, the more ham that can be sold to pay the bill. Smithfield, though, needs to pay the workers who processed the pork into ham—where does that cash come from? Managing cash flow is why companies closely monitor statistics such as how many days it takes to get paid, because buyers are using payment terms to manage their own cash.[4]

Other forms of credit, such as leasing and financing, are important for capital equipment purchases. Students may be familiar with auto leasing options, and commercial leasing is a similar option to purchasing. For example, Delta Leasing purchases commercial trucks that its clients want to lease. Delta Leasing owns everything from pickup trucks to specialized oilfield equipment and leases those assets to the companies that use them.[5] Tim Simmons with Teradata often works with GE Capital to prepare proposals for his clients, like Hallmark, so that they can acquire the Teradata solution.

SHIPPING COSTS

The terms and conditions of sale include shipping costs. Recall from Chapter 2 that the term *free on board (FOB)* is used to determine the point at which the buyer assumes responsibility for both the goods and the costs of shipping them. Thus, FOB destination means the buyer will take responsibility for the goods once they reach the buyer's location, and the seller will pay the freight.

Suppose Hormel quotes an FOB origin price. It will load the truck at its Chicago plant, but the buyer will pay for shipping. If Hormel sold a truckload of pepperoni to Coppoli's Deli under terms of FOB destination, Hormel would pay for shipping and would have the pepperoni delivered to Coppoli's Deli's warehouse, where warehouse personnel would unload the truck.

If Hormel quotes a price for pepperoni that's FOB origin, then Coppoli's Deli pays for shipping. If the price is FOB destination, then Hormel pays for shipping.

©Ariel Skelley/Blend Images LLC RF

Another form of FOB is *FOB installed,* meaning that title and responsibility do not transfer until the equipment is installed and operating properly. In some instances FOB installed can also mean that operator training must be provided before title transfers. These are important terms because there are significant costs associated with the technical installation and operator training for many pieces of sophisticated equipment. Buyers want to know the total price and what it includes.

The terms and conditions of a sale, including but not limited to price, can often play as important a role as the product itself in determining what is purchased. Creative salespeople understand the terms and conditions they have to work with so they can meet the needs of their buyers while also meeting the profit objectives of their own companies.

PRESENTING PRICE

Price is often discussed at the end of the presentation simply because the salesperson may not know what that price will be until the final solution is agreed on. Because price is so important to the buyer, it is worth considering how price should be presented.

Most firms set prices after careful study of competitors' offerings, the value delivered by the product or service, and the cost of providing the product or service. For these reasons the price should represent a reasonable and fair picture of the product's or service's value. Therefore, never apologize for a price or present the price apologetically; rather, present it with confidence.

Bruce Culbert, now chief service officer with the Pedowitz Group, says that salespeople sometimes negotiate against themselves. When he was at IBM,

> I had an account manager who was under pressure to make quota for the quarter. In presenting a proposal to a prospective customer, the salesperson did as was agreed and sent the proposal via e-mail a full two weeks prior to quarter end because the client said they would be able to make a decision by the end of the month. If this deal closed, the salesperson would hit quota. Several days call went by, and there was no response from the prospect. A follow-up e-mail and phone call went unanswered. In a panic the salesperson began to submit revised proposals each time, lowering the price in an attempt to get the prospect to respond positively. A week went by with no response. During the week two revised proposals had been submitted, each time lowering the price almost 10 percent. On the Tuesday before the quarter closed the client responded favorably to the original proposal with their apologies that they had not responded sooner but they were on vacation the past week and were just now catching up on e-mail. Needless to say the salesperson was ecstatic to learn of the good fortune just prior to quarter close. About 10 minutes later the salesperson received an additional e-mail from the client informing them to ignore the previous note and that they would like to accept proposal revision 2, which was almost 20 percent less than the original proposal.[6]

As Bruce says, here is a salesperson who panicked and lost the company 20 percent. Sometimes, companies can add to the pressure on salespeople, as you can see in Building Partnerships 11.1.

In addition to presenting the price with confidence, remember that price is not the focus of your presentation. The real issue is satisfying the needs of the buyer, of which budget is only one. True, a budget limitation can halt progress toward a sale. The real issue, though, is the total cost of ownership, which means the buyer should also factor in the value of the benefits delivered.

WHEN TO ATTEMPT TO OBTAIN COMMITMENT

Novice salespeople frequently ask themselves these questions: Is there a right time to obtain commitment? How will customers let me know they are ready to buy? Should I make more than one attempt? What should I do if my first attempt fails?

The right time to attempt to gain commitment is when the buyer appears ready, as evidenced by buying signals. Some salespeople say that one psychological moment in each sales presentation affords the best opportunity to obtain

BUILDING Partnerships 11.1

TIMING AND PRICING

What's it like to be closed—especially for a big deal? Steve Schlesinger is a sales guy who tells this story: "Just last week, we had a significant purchase to make, not just because it was an expensive or large purchase but because it represented a major change in strategy. Our strategy for information technology has been to build our own. In many ways, we were ahead of the market, and off-the-shelf programs did not fit our needs." His company reconsidered this approach when it came time to upgrade its customer management software. "Our first thought was that it was too expensive. Two years ago, we had looked at software for customer management, and it just didn't make sense."

He called a friend at Salesforce.com, and they went to work on a solution. "The development meeting was excellent, the integration piece was developed, and then they came back with a good cost/benefit analysis." But then the decision got tougher. "With offices across the United States and United Kingdom, we realized everyone who works with clients would need access to the software. This decision increased our license from 10 users to 70 or 80. That raises the costs substantially, and suddenly, that cost/benefit analysis wasn't looking so good." But it was two days before the end of the fiscal year for Salesforce.com, so it slashed the price and got the deal done.

Steve says it wasn't a hard, aggressive sale. The Salesforce.com team was transparent, "they needed to get it done and told us, and they gave me the leeway in the terms that I needed. They were very professional." But Steve clearly believes he got a better deal because of the timing.

LeeAnne Pearson conducted a study for a company that asked for anonymity. During the study, salespeople complained that top management would slash prices at the end of each quarter in order to get sales up and look good on Wall Street. "These salespeople were frustrated that they were giving up margin and commission in order for top management to look good and stock prices to go up. Worse yet, they also said buyers recognized the practice and purposively timed purchases and negotiated fiercely, knowing they could get bargains by waiting until the end of the quarter." These are sales of half a million dollars or more—yet salespeople are under the same pressure to close deals that car salespeople face every month!

Sources: LeeAnne Pearson, *"Sales Practices: A Comparison of Top and Bottom Salespeople,"* Research Paper 11-1, Baylor University's Center for Professional Selling (September 1, 2011); Steve Schlesinger's quotes are from personal interview, February 5, 2010.

commitment, and if this opportunity is bypassed, securing commitment will be difficult or impossible. This belief is not true, however. Seldom does one psychological moment govern the complete success or failure of a sales presentation.

Most buyers will commit themselves only when they clearly understand the benefits and costs of such a decision. At times this point occurs early in the call. A commitment to purchase a large system, however, usually will not occur until a complete presentation and several calls have been made and all questions have been answered.

Buying signals, or indications that the buyer is ready to buy, can be evidenced both in the buyer's comments and nonverbally. Buying signals are also called **closing cues**.

BUYER COMMENTS

A customer's comments often are the best indication that he or she is considering commitment. A prospect will seldom say, "All right, I'm ready to endorse this product to our buying committee." Questions about the product or terms of sale and comments in the form of requirements or benefit statements signal readiness to buy, as do responses to trial closes.

Buyer Questions

Here are some examples of questions that signal readiness to buy:

> If I agree to go with this cooperative advertising program, do you have any ads already developed that I could use?
>
> Do you have any facilities for training our employees in the use of the product?
>
> How soon would you be able to deliver the equipment?

Not all questions signal a readiness to buy. But if the question concerns implementing the purchase and points toward when, not if, the purchase is implemented, the prospect may be getting ready to buy.

Requirements

Requirements are conditions that have to be satisfied before a purchase can take place. For example:

> We need a cash discount for a supply order like this.
>
> We need to get this in weekly shipments.

Requirements that are stated near the end of the presentation are need statements that reflect a readiness to buy when they relate to how the purchase will be consummated. As the examples illustrate, requirements relating to financial terms or shipping indicate that the decision to buy the product has been made and now it is time to work out the details.

Benefit Statements

Sometimes prospects offer their own benefit statements, such as these:

> Oh, I like the way this equipment is serviced–it will make it much easier on my staff.
>
> Good, that color will match our office decor.

Such positive statements reflect strong feelings in support of the purchase–a sign that the buyer is ready.

Responses to Trial Closes

Salespeople can solicit such comments by continually taking the pulse of the situation with **trial closes**, which are questions regarding the prospect's readiness to buy (first discussed in Chapter 8). Throughout the presentation, the salesperson should be asking questions:

> How does this sound to you so far?
>
> Is there anything else you would like to know at this point?
>
> How does this compare with what you have seen of competing products?

Such questions are an important element of any sales process because trial closes serve several purposes, including identifying the customer's proximity to making the decision, gaining agreement on minor points, and creating a true dialogue in which the ultimate close is a natural conclusion. Note that these are more general questions than simply gaining agreement on benefits (discussed in Chapter 8), say as part of a FEBA.

One approach is to try a soft third-party trial close, such as by asking, "At this point, do you feel comfortable in recommending our product/service to others in your organization?" If you know that the buying process is likely to involve others, you can ask the question more specifically, such as, "Are you comfortable in bringing this to the [insert the appropriate title or name] attention?"

When a seller asks a trial close question, the buyer responds, thus creating a dialogue. Issues can be raised as objections or questions by the buyer, which tell the seller what to cover. Then, because the salesperson has been asking closing questions all along, the final close is just a natural part of the ongoing dialogue, as it should be.

NONVERBAL CUES

As in every phase of the presentation, nonverbal cues serve as important indicators of the customer's state of mind, as discussed in Chapter 4. While attempting to gain commitment, the salesperson should use the buyer's nonverbal signals to better identify areas of concern and see whether the buyer is ready to commit. Facial expressions most often indicate how ready the buyer is to make a commitment. Positive signals include eyes that are open and relaxed, face and mouth not covered with hands, a natural smile, and a relaxed forehead. The reverses of these signals indicate that the buyer is not yet ready to commit to the proposal.

Customers' actions also often indicate readiness to buy or make a commitment. For example, the prospective buyer of a fax machine may get a document and operate the machine or place the machine on the table where it will be used. The industrial buyer may refer to a catalog to compare specifications with competing products. A doctor, when told of a new drug, may pick up the pamphlet and begin carefully reading the indications and contraindications. A retailer considering whether to allow an end-of-aisle display may move to the end of an aisle and scan the layout. Any such actions may be signals for obtaining commitment; they should be viewed in the context of all available verbal and nonverbal cues.

As you can see in Building Partnerships 11.2, sometimes there are reasons to not accept a buyer's offer to buy. Such was the case for Les Dossey, and it was nonverbals that tipped him off.

HOW TO SUCCESSFULLY OBTAIN COMMITMENT

Do the two buyers on the right look like they are ready to commit to a purchase?

To obtain commitment in a nonmanipulative manner, salespeople need to follow several principles, including maintaining a positive attitude, letting the customer set the pace, being assertive instead of aggressive, and selling the right product in the right amounts.

MAINTAIN A POSITIVE ATTITUDE

Confidence is contagious. Customers like to deal with salespeople who have confidence in themselves, their products, and their companies. On the other hand, unnecessary fear can be a self-fulfilling prophecy. The student who fears essay exams usually does poorly; golfers who believe they will miss short putts usually do. So it is with salespeople: If they fear customers will not accept their proposals, the chances are good they will be right.[7]

BUILDING Partnerships 11.2

SELL ANYONE WHO WILL BUY?

Les Dossey had the interesting job of selling sales training. He met with the owner of a large commercial window cleaning and tinting company, a company that sold to the property managers of large office buildings. Since the company had hired experienced salespeople from all over, there was no single sales methodology that everyone used, making it difficult to manage for optimal performance. The president wanted to change that.

"I qualified: he had money and was the decision maker—he could buy." After presenting the sales training program, Les asked, "How would you like to proceed?"

The buyer replied, "I'd like to sign up. What do we do now?" The answer was to write a check for a 50 percent deposit. The buyer wrote the check and slid it across the table, "but I could tell by his body language that he wasn't ready. I knew if I took his check, we'd have problems and I knew that, for whatever reason, he wasn't going to be happy so I leaned back and said, 'I don't think you're ready for this. I don't want you to be alarmed, but I'm not going to accept this check.' I tore it in half and slid it back. Of course he was shocked, but you could see the relief just flow off his shoulders." They parted friends.

Les is happy to point out that the buyer actually came back several weeks later and bought at a lower level—then developed into a good referral for other business. "If all I cared about was myself, that could have easily gone the wrong way."

Sometimes, though, a buyer may be very happy about making a purchase that the salesperson knows is the wrong thing to do. Do you take the sale or refuse?

Tim Simmons, with Teradata, had that experience when selling to the outdoors outfitter Cabela's, now part of Bass Pro. The company had issued an RFP that explicitly stated that the new system had to sit on top of, not replace, its old system. But no add-on would deliver the results it really wanted. So finally Tim asked, "Is it more to accomplish your marketing goals or keep the old system? Because if it's necessary to keep the old system, then I'm not sure we should do business—you'll never be happy with the performance. But if you would consider buying a complete new system from us, I'll show you how we can meet your performance objectives, and justify the additional expense."

Tim says he could have easily just sold the add-on, but he believed the risk in losing the customer completely was justified by the better solution. Tim was true to his word, demonstrating how a complete replacement with a Teradata solution would meet the company's needs more completely. Cabela's bought the system and went on to be a showcase customer for Tim and for Teradata.

Sometimes the best option is to be willing to walk away from what you know to be a bad deal, even when the buyer is willing to buy.

Mark Hunter is a salesperson himself, but recently had this encounter as a buyer that left him in search of a different vendor. "It didn't take long for me to realize that the person with whom I was dealing was either a new salesperson or new to the department we were in. . . . He clearly knew what he was talking about, he was able to respond to my questions and, on a couple of occasions, he elaborated far more than he needed to. However, the reason he was unable to close the sale was that he didn't have any confidence in what he was saying and he was very uncomfortable talking to someone who could have been twice his age."[8]

LET THE CUSTOMER SET THE PACE

Attempts to gain commitment must be geared to fit the varying reactions, needs, and personalities of each buyer. Thus, the sales representative needs to practice adaptive selling. (See Chapter 5 for a complete discussion of adaptive selling.)

Some buyers who react slowly may need plenty of time to assimilate the material presented. They may ask the same question several times or show they do not understand the importance of certain product features. In these circumstances the salesperson must deliver the presentation more slowly and may have to repeat certain parts. Trying to rush buyers is unwise when they show they are not yet ready to commit.

As we discussed earlier in the book, buyers' decision-making styles vary greatly. Japanese and Chinese buyers tend to move more slowly and cautiously when evaluating a proposition. In contrast, buyers working for Fortune 500 firms located in the largest U.S. cities often tend to move much more quickly. The successful salesperson recognizes such potential differences and acts accordingly.

BE ASSERTIVE, NOT AGGRESSIVE

Over 30 years ago, research by Marvin Jolson identified three types of salespeople: aggressive, submissive, and assertive, a typology that is still effective.[9] Exhibit 11.2 summarizes the differences among assertive, aggressive, and submissive salespeople's handling of the sales interview. **Aggressive** salespeople control the sales interaction but often fail to gain commitment because they prejudge the customer's needs and fail to probe for information. Too busy talking to do much listening, they tend to push the buyer too soon, too often, and too vigorously. They might say, "I can't understand why you are hesitant," but they do not probe for reasons for the hesitancy. One buyer posted this on the web about one salesperson: "Told him our budget was set for the year, and it wasn't happening. He actually got even more aggressive and started making snarky comments about our budget and insulting the company. I just said I think we're done here, and hung up. Fortunately, I think he had the brainpower to realize how stupid that was, and never tried calling me back. The thing is that I was actually mildly interested in their products, but their sales techniques completely turned me off to them, to the point where I warn colleagues away from them."[10]

Submissive salespeople often excel as socializers. With customers they spend a lot of time talking about families, restaurants, and movies. They establish rapport quite effectively. They accept the customers' statements of needs and problems but do not probe to uncover any latent needs or opportunities. One recent study suggested that submissive salespeople rarely try to obtain commitment because they may fear rejection too much.[11]

Exhibit 11.2

How Aggressive, Submissive, and Assertive Salespeople Handle Sales Activities

	Selling Style		
Selling Activity	Aggressive	Submissive	Assertive
Defining customer needs	Believe they are the best judge of customer's needs.	Accept customer's definition of needs.	Probe for need-related information that customer may not have volunteered.
Controlling the presentation	Minimize participation by customer.	Permit customer to control presentation.	Encourage two-way communication and customer participation.
Closing the sale	Overwhelm customer; respond to objections without understanding.	Assume customer will buy when ready.	Respond to objections, leading to somewhat automatic close.

Assertive salespeople, the third type, are self-confident and positive. They maintain the proper perspective by being responsive to customer needs. Rather than aggressively creating new "needs" in customers through persuasion, they look for buyers who truly need their products and then use questions to acquire information, even listening assertively.[12] Their presentations emphasize an exchange of information rather than a one-way presentation.

SELL THE RIGHT ITEM IN THE RIGHT AMOUNTS

The chance of obtaining commitment improves when the right product is sold in the right amount. Although this principle sounds obvious, it often is not followed. Sometimes salespeople try to get the biggest order they can. Customers have long memories, they will refuse to do business again with someone who oversells, and they may also lack confidence in someone who undersells.

ethics

For example, SC Johnson, maker of Off! and Johnson Wax, created a sales program called Sell to Potential because it knows the importance of selling the right number of products. Sell too few units and the store will run out of stock during a promotion; sell too many units and the store will be stuck with excess inventory after the promotion. The chances to obtain commitment diminish rapidly when the salesperson tries to sell too many or too few units or the wrong grade or style of product.

Also, salespeople should not rely solely on trial orders. A **trial order** is a small order placed by a buyer to see if the product will work and should not be confused with a trial close. A trial order is no commitment, and all too often a buyer will agree to a trial just to get rid of the salesperson. Further, if the product requires training to learn how to use it properly, a customer who agrees to a trial might be unwilling to invest the time necessary to fully learn the product and will not fully realize the benefits. The product will be rejected often because customers don't have time to give fair trials. Trial orders can work well when the product is easy to implement (such as selling a new product to a retailer for resale) or when the benefits can be realized only by seeing the product in use.

EFFECTIVE METHODS

ethics

"If closing is seen by so many sales experts as manipulative and insulting, are effective methods those that are manipulative but not insulting?," asked one of our students. It is a fair question, and the answer has two elements. First, the salesperson's purpose is to sell the right product in the right amounts. If the prospect does not need what is being sold, the salesperson should walk to the next door and start again. Thus, there should never be a need for manipulation (review Chapter 2 for a discussion of manipulation). Second, in addition to selling only what the customer needs, the salesperson should also sell in a fashion consistent with the way the buyer prefers to buy. Therefore, the salesperson should gain commitment in a manner that will help the buyer make the choice, consistent with the principle of persuasion. We use the word *choice* here to mean that the buyer can say no. Salespeople do try to persuade buyers, but with persuasion, the choice remains with the buyer. Manipulative techniques are designed to reduce or eliminate choice; partnering methods are not.

Studying successful methods and techniques enables salespeople to help prospects buy a product or service they want or need. Buyers sometimes have a need or a want but still hesitate to buy the product or service that will satisfy it. For example, an industrial buyer for a candy manufacturer refused to commit to a change in sweeteners, even though she needed better raw material. Why? Because the sweetener rep had met with her on four separate occasions, and the buyer had difficulty remembering all that was said and agreed on. Each call was like starting over. Had the salesperson used the appropriate method (the benefit summary method, discussed later in this section), commitment might have been obtained.

There are literally hundreds of different methods of asking for commitment, whether that level of commitment is to buy or to recommend to someone else, or to simply agree to an appointment. What we describe here are some of the more commonly used methods that are consistent with a *Building Partnerships* philosophy.

DIRECT REQUEST

The most straightforward, effective method of obtaining commitment is simply to ask for it, called the **direct request method**. However, salespeople need to be wary of appearing overly aggressive when using this direct request method. Decisive customers, such as drivers, appreciate getting down to business and not wasting time. Here are some examples:

Can I put you down for 100 pairs of model 63?

Can we meet with your engineer next Thursday to discuss this further?

Will you come to the home office for a hands-on demonstration?

Can you call the meeting next week?

BENEFIT SUMMARY

Early in the interview salespeople discover or reiterate the needs and problems of the prospect. Then, throughout the presentation, they show how their product can meet those needs. They do this by turning product or service features into benefits specifically for that buyer. As they present each benefit, they ask if that benefit meets the need. When using this approach, called the **benefit summary method**, the salesperson simply reminds the prospect of the agreed-on benefits of the proposal. This nonmanipulative method helps the buyer synthesize points covered in the presentation to make a wise decision. For example, a salesperson attempting to obtain a buyer's commitment to recommend a proposal to a buying committee might say this:

> You stated early in my visit that you were looking for a product of the highest quality, a vendor that could provide quick delivery, and adequate engineering support. As I've mentioned, our fasteners have been rated by an independent laboratory as providing 20 percent higher tensile strength than the closest competitor, resulting in a life expectancy of more than four years. We also discussed the fact that my company can deliver fasteners to your location within 3 hours of your request and that this promise holds true 24 hours a day. Finally, I discussed the fact that we have four engineers on staff whose sole responsibility is to provide support and develop specifications for new fasteners for existing customers. Would you be willing to give the information we discussed to the buying committee along with your endorsement of the proposal?

One advantage of the benefit summary method over the direct request method is that the seller can help the buyer remember all the points discussed in the presentation. The summary becomes particularly important in long presentations and in selling situations involving several meetings prior to obtaining commitment. The salesperson cannot assume that the buyer will remember all the major points discussed in the presentation.

BALANCE SHEET METHOD

Sometimes referred to as the *Ben Franklin method* because Franklin described using it to make decisions, the **balance sheet method** aids prospects who cannot make a decision, even though no reason for their behavior is apparent. Such a prospect may be asked to join the salesperson in listing the pros and cons of buying now or buying later, of buying the salesperson's product or that of a competitor, or of buying the product or not buying it at all.

However, like many nonmanipulative sales techniques, this method can insult a buyer's intelligence if used inappropriately. The salesperson may start to obtain commitment with the following type of statement:

> You know, Mr. Thacker, Ben Franklin was like you, always determined to reach the right decisions and avoid the wrong ones. I suppose that's how you feel. Well, he suggested taking a piece of paper and writing all the reasons for deciding yes in one column and then listing the reasons for deciding no in a second column. He said that when you make this kind of graphic comparison, the correct decision becomes much more apparent.

That close may seem manipulative; it certainly sounds silly. A more effective start may be to simply draw a *T* on a plain piece of paper, place captions on each side of the crossbar, and leave space below for the insertion of specific benefits or sales points. Then ask the buyer to list pros and cons of making the purchase. For example, assume the product is National Adhesives's hot-melt adhesive used to attach paper labels to plastic Coke bottles. Coca-Cola is currently using a liquid adhesive made by Ajax Corporation. The top of the *T* might look like this:

Benefits of Adopting the National Adhesives Hot-Melt Method	Benefits of Staying with the Ajax Liquid Adhesives

The salesperson may say something like, "Making a decision like this is difficult. Let's see how many reasons we can think of for your going with the National Adhesives system." The salesperson would write the benefits (not features) in which the customer has shown interest on the left side of the *T*. Next the salesperson would ask the customer to list reasons to stay with the Ajax adhesive on the right side. When completed, the *T* lists should accurately reflect all the pros and cons of each possible decision. At that point the buyer is asked, "Which method do you think is the wisest?"

When used properly, the balance sheet method can help hesitant buyers express their feelings about the decision in a manner similar to the multiattribute matrix (see Chapter 3), which gives the salesperson an opportunity to deal with those feelings. It is especially appropriate for a buyer who is an analytical but would make less sense for an expressive. However, the balance sheet approach takes time and may appear "salesy," particularly if relatively unimportant benefits are considered to be equal to more important reasons not to buy. Also, the list of benefits of the product being sold will not always outnumber the list on the other side of the *T*.

PROBING METHOD

In the **probing method** sales representatives initially attempt to obtain commitment by another method, perhaps simply asking for it (the direct request method). If unsuccessful, the salesperson uses a series of probing questions designed to discover the reason for the hesitation. Once any reason becomes apparent, the salesperson asks a what-if question. (What if I could successfully resolve this concern? Would you be willing to commit?) An illustrative dialogue follows:

SALESPERSON: Could we make an appointment for next week, at which time I would come in and do a complete survey of your needs? It shouldn't take more than three hours.

PROSPECT: No, I don't think I am quite ready to take that step yet.

SALESPERSON: There must be some reason why you are hesitating to go ahead now. Do you mind if I ask what it is?

PROSPECT: I'm just not convinced that your firm is large enough to handle a customer of our size.

SALESPERSON: In addition to that, is there any other reason why you would not be willing to go ahead?

PROSPECT: No.

SALESPERSON: If I can resolve the issue of our size, then you would allow me to conduct a survey?

PROSPECT: Well, I wouldn't exactly say that.

SALESPERSON: Then there must be some other reason. May I ask what it is?

PROSPECT: Well, a friend of mine who uses your services told me that often your billing department sends him invoices for material he didn't want and didn't receive.

SALESPERSON: In addition to that, is there any other reason for not going ahead now?

PROSPECT: No, those are my two concerns.

SALESPERSON: If I could resolve those issues right now, would you be willing to set up an appointment for a survey?

PROSPECT: Sure.

This dialogue illustrates the importance of probing in obtaining commitment. The method attempts to bring to the table all issues of concern to the prospect. The salesperson does not claim to be able to resolve the issues but simply attempts to find out what the issues are. When probing has identified all the issues, the salesperson should attempt to resolve them as soon as possible. After successfully dealing with the concerns of the buyer, the salesperson should then ask for a commitment.

There are many modifications of the probing method. Another way to achieve the same results is the following:

SALESPERSON: Are you willing to buy this product today?

PROSPECT: No, I don't think so.

SALESPERSON: I really would like to get a better feel of where you are. On a scale of 1 to 10, with 1 being absolutely no purchase and 10 being purchase, where would you say you are?

PROSPECT: I would say I'm about a 6.

SALESPERSON: If you don't mind my asking, what would it take to move you from a 6 to a 10?

Also, keep cultural differences in mind. For example, if a Japanese businesswoman wants to tell an American salesperson that she is not interested, she might state, "Your proposal would be very difficult," just to be polite. If the seller attempts to use the probing method, the Japanese businesswoman may consider the seller to be pushy or a poor listener. In the same way, an Arab businessperson will never say no directly, a custom that helps both sides avoid losing face.[13]

This salesperson is presenting two campaign choices to her client, using the alternative choice close.

Courtesy of Jazmin Elliot

ALTERNATIVE CHOICE

In many situations a salesperson may have multiple options to present to a buyer. For example, Teo Schaars sells diamonds directly from cutters in the Netherlands to consumers in the United States. When he started in sales, he would display several dozen diamonds on a purple damask-covered table. Sales were few until his father, a Dutch diamond broker, suggested that he limit his customers' choices; there were simply too many diamonds to choose from, overwhelming the buyer. Schaars found his father's comments to be wise advice. Now Schaars spends more time probing about budget and desires and then shows only two diamonds at a time, explaining the key characteristics of each. Then he allows the customer to express a preference. Schaars may have to show half a dozen or more diamonds before a customer makes the final decision, but he rarely shows more than two at a time (www.anschardiamonds.com).

TRIAL OFFERS

One strategy that can be effective but is also very tricky is the trial offer. This approach is also called "the puppy dog close," based on the idea that once you take a puppy home, you won't want to give it up. If your product is simple to use and the benefits are obvious only in use, a trial offer can be effective. If the product is complicated, however, prospects may not want to make the investment in learning how to use it and conclude it is too difficult to learn. A fear that some sales managers have is that salespeople will rely too much on the approach as a way to avoid actually asking for the order.

If you plan to use the approach, it's best to do the following:

- Set a specific time for training, if needed, and make sure the user is comfortable with the product.
- Document that the decision criteria are concrete—and that the trial is needed to achieve those criteria.
- Agree on when a decision will be made. Otherwise, they may just want to use your product for free until they can get the next trial.

Some salespeople, such as in the car or office equipment business, find that prospects may use trials as a way to simply borrow the product and solve a short-term need. Setting proper expectations at the outset can aid in avoiding those situations.

OTHER METHODS

Literally hundreds of techniques and methods to obtain commitment have been tried. Exhibit 11.3 lists a number of traditional methods. Most of them, however, tend to be ineffective with sophisticated customers; nevertheless, many can be used in a nonmanipulative manner if appropriate. For example, the minor-point close can be appropriate if there really is a need to make a choice between two options; the factor that makes the method manipulative is the assumption that the minor choice is the equivalent to making the sale.

Exhibit 11.3
Some Traditional Closing Methods

Method	How It Works	Remark
Minor-point close	The seller assumes it is easier to get the prospect to decide on a very trivial point than on the whole proposition: What color do you like, blue or red?	This method can upset a prospect who feels he or she is being manipulated or tricked into making a commitment. Even unsophisticated buyers easily spot this technique.
Continuous yes close	Throughout the presentation, the seller constantly asks questions for which the prospect most logically would answer yes. By the end of the discussion, the buyer is so accustomed to saying yes that when the order is requested, the natural response is yes.	This method is based on self-perception theory. As the presentation progresses, the buyer begins to perceive himself or herself as being agreeable. At the close, the buyer wants to maintain this self-image and almost unthinkingly says yes. Use of this method can destroy long-term relationships if the buyer later feels manipulated.
Assumptive close	The seller, without asking for the order, simply begins to write it up. A variation is to fill out the order form as the prospect answers questions.	This method does not even give the buyer the courtesy of agreeing. It can be perceived as being very pushy and manipulative.
Standing-room-only close	The seller attempts to obtain commitment by describing the negative consequences of waiting. For example, the seller may state, "If you can't decide now, I'll have to offer it to another customer."	This method can be effective if the statement is true. However, if the prospect really does need to act quickly, this deadline should probably be discussed earlier in the presentation to reduce possible mistrust and the feeling of being pushed.
Benefit-in-reserve close	First the seller attempts to obtain commitment by another method. If unsuccessful, the seller says, "Oh, if you order today I can offer you an additional 5 percent for your trade-in."	This method can backfire easily. The buyer tends to think, "If I had agreed to your first attempt to obtain commitment, I would not have learned about this new enticement. If I wait longer, how much better will your offer be?" The buyer may then seek additional concessions in every future sale attempt.
Emotional close	The seller appeals to the buyer's emotions to close the sale. For example, the seller may say, "This really is a good deal. To be honest with you, I desperately need to secure an order today. As you know, I work on a straight commission basis. My wife is going to have surgery next week, and our insurance just won't cover. . . ."	Many obvious problems arise with this method. It is an attempt to move away from focusing entirely on the buyer's personal needs. It does not develop trust or respect. Do not use this close!

ethics

No method of obtaining commitment will work if the buyer does not trust the salesperson, the company, and the product. Gaining commitment should not require the use of tricky techniques or methods to force buyers to do something they do not want to do or to manipulate them to buy something they do not need.

IF COMMITMENT IS OBTAINED

The salesperson's job is not over when commitment is obtained. In fact, in many ways the job is just beginning. This section describes the salesperson's responsibilities that accrue after the buyer says yes.

NO SURPRISES

Customers do not like surprises, so now is the time to go over any important information they will need to fully enjoy the benefits of the product or service. For example, if you are selling life insurance and a physical is required, give the customer as much detail as possible to prepare him or her for that experience. Or if a company is going to lease a piece of heavy equipment, let the customer know that delivery will occur after a credit check and how long that credit check will take. John Branton, president of Safe Harbor Financial, requires his salespeople to make sure the client understands how the product works and, if any negative consequences can occur, make sure the client is prepared for it. No customer wants to be surprised with a tax bill later, for example, even if the purchase was still the best choice available.[14]

CONFIRM THE CUSTOMER'S CHOICE

Customers like to believe they have chosen intelligently when they make a decision. After important decisions, they may feel a little insecure about whether the sacrifice is worth it. Such feelings are called **buyer's remorse** or **postpurchase dissonance.** Successful salespeople reassure customers that their choice was the right one. For example:

> I know you will enjoy using your new office machines. You can plan on many months of trouble-free service. I'll call on you in about two weeks to make sure everything is operating smoothly. Be sure to call me if you need any help before then.
>
> Or
>
> Congratulations, Mr. Jacobs. You are going to be glad you decided to use our service. There is no finer service available. Now let's make certain you get off to the right start. Your first bulletin will arrive on Tuesday, March 2.
>
> Or
>
> You've made an excellent choice. Other stores won't have a product like this for at least 30 days and with our promotion plan, you'll enjoy sales results before anyone else.

GET THE SIGNATURE

The buyer's signature often formalizes a commitment. Signing the order is a natural part of a well-planned procedure. The order blank should be accessible, and the signing should be treated as a routine matter. Ordinarily the customer has decided to buy before being asked to sign the order. In other words, the signature on the order blank merely confirms that an agreement has already been reached. The decision to buy or not to buy should not focus on a signature.

The salesperson needs to remember several important points: (1) Make the actual signing an easy, routine procedure; (2) fill out the order blank accurately and promptly; and (3) be careful not to exhibit any excess eagerness or excitement when the prospect is about to sign.

SHOW APPRECIATION

All buyers like to think that their business is appreciated even if they purchase only small quantities. Customers like to do business with salespeople who show that they want the business.

Salespeople may show appreciation by writing the purchaser a letter. Is an e-mail message adequate? Eleanor Brownell doesn't think so. She says, "It [a handwritten note] makes you memorable."[15] Jackson Keyes came up with an unusual idea–he and his business partner write "Thank you!" and the buyer's name on a whiteboard, then take a selfie posting it on Snapchat. Given that their brand is beach-style fashions, this laid-back approach seems to work well. Showing appreciation develops goodwill with customers especially after large purchases and with new customers. In some situations a small gift, such as a pen with the selling company's name on it, may also be an effective thank you. Yusef Trowell closed a big job with a construction company, so he gave the decision maker a miniature construction helmet with her company's logo on it. Salespeople should always thank customers personally, and the thanks should be genuine.[16]

CULTIVATE FOR FUTURE CALLS

In most fields of selling, obtaining commitment is not the end of a business transaction; rather, it is only one part of a mutually profitable business relationship. Obtaining commitment is successful only if it results in goodwill and future commitment. Keep in mind that research shows that it is how the salesperson treats the customer that is the biggest determinant of future sales. How the customer gets treated determines loyalty, which then influences repurchase.[17]

Customers like to do business with salespeople who do not lose interest immediately after securing commitment. What a salesperson does after achieving commitment is called **follow-up**. As Jeffrey Bailey, sales director for Oracle, recognizes, "Making the sale is only the beginning." After making the sale, the salesperson must follow up to make sure the product is delivered when promised, set up appropriately, and so forth. We talk more about follow-up in later chapters. The point here is that the sale does not end with the customer's signature on the order form. Research shows that the quality of follow-up service is an important contributing factor in perceptions of salesperson quality and long-term relationships.[18]

REVIEW THE ACTIONS TO BE TAKEN

An important step, particularly when commitment is next in the buying process, is to review what each party has agreed to do. In the case of a multiple-visit sales cycle, the salesperson must review not only what the client will do but also what the salesperson will do to prepare for the next meeting. To be welcomed on repeat calls, salespeople must be considerate of all the parties involved in buying or using the product. They must pronounce and spell all names correctly, explain and review the terms of the purchase so no misunderstandings will occur, and be sociable and cordial to subordinates as well as those in key positions. In addition, the buyer or user must get the service promised. The importance of this point cannot be overemphasized. Chapter 13 provides detailed information about how to service the account and build a partnership.

IF COMMITMENT IS NOT OBTAINED

When asking for commitment, salespeople can often encounter objections. One important consideration is to recognize that these objections are no different than any others; they just happen at a time when you might think they're more important because the process is near the end. One approach is to respond with a question that checks the importance of the objection. For example, if the buyer objects to price, ask, "If price weren't an issue, is there anything else preventing us from moving forward?" If the answer is yes, then you probe to determine what those issues are, as price was likely just a screen for the real concerns. If the answer is no, then you can explore financial terms and other financial options. Other objections can serve as excuses to screen the real one, but price is the most often used screen.

Naturally the salesperson does not always obtain the desired commitment. The salesperson should never take this situation personally (which is easier said than done). Doing everything right does not guarantee a sale. Situations change, and customers who may have really needed the product when everything started may find that other priorities make a purchase impossible.

Many times, when a buyer says no, the seller is wise to treat it as "No, not now" rather than "No, never." Kenneth Young, CEO of Tymco, once told a salesperson that he just didn't have the budget to make the decision now but that he'd consider it again the following year. "The salesperson stayed in touch, and when it came time to plan the budget, I made sure she was given a chance to give us all of the cost details so we could plan for the purchase."

thinking it through

Many students report that asking for the order is the hardest part of selling. Why is it difficult? Does the customer need you to ask for the sale? Have you ever needed a salesperson to ask you to buy? Why or why not?

This section describes some of the common reasons for failing to obtain commitment and offers practical suggestions for salespeople who encounter rejection.

SOME REASONS FOR LOST OPPORTUNITIES

In this discussion, we are assuming that the salesperson did an appropriate qualifying job and understood the buyer's needs. Some buyers are being asked to attend a meeting or take the next step in the purchase process when no need is present. Clearly asking for commitment when there's no need is foolish. The real question is why would you lose a sale if the customer clearly had a need? Here's a few reasons.

Wrong Attitudes

As discussed earlier in the chapter, salespeople need to have a positive attitude. A fear that obtaining commitment will be difficult may be impossible to hide. Inexperienced salespeople naturally will be concerned about their ability to obtain commitment; most of us have an innate fear of asking someone else to do anything. Some salespeople even fail to ask for the sale because if they never ask, they will never hear no. As a result, they always have more prospects but fewer customers than everyone else. But all salespeople know they need to focus on obtaining commitment to keep their jobs.

Some salespeople display unwarranted excitement when they see that prospects are ready to commit. Research suggests that nonverbals are very important cues and can signal trustworthiness or a lack thereof to buyers. A salesperson who appears excited or overly eager may display nonverbal cues that suggest dishonesty or a lack of empathy, though cues vary from culture to culture.[19]

One of the main reasons for salespeople's improper attitudes toward obtaining commitment is the historical importance placed on closing the sale. Closing has often been viewed as a win-lose situation (if I get the order, I win; if I don't get the order, I lose). Until salespeople see obtaining commitment as a positive occurrence for the buyer, these attitudes will persist.

A boring presentation can be one reason for failure to obtain commitment.

Poor Presentation

Prospects or customers who do not understand the presentation or see the benefits of the purchase cannot be expected to buy. The salesperson must use trial closes (see Chapter 8) and continually take the pulse of the interview.

A poor presentation can also be caused by haste. The salesperson who tries to deliver a 60-minute presentation in 20 minutes may skim over or omit important sales points. Forgoing the presentation may be better than delivering it hastily. Further, a sales presentation given at the wrong time or under unfavorable conditions is likely to be ineffective.

Another reason for not obtaining commitment is lack of product knowledge. In fact, lack of product knowledge is often cited as an important barrier to obtaining commitment.[21] If the salesperson does not know what the product does, you can be certain the buyer will not be able to figure it out either.

Poor Habits and Skills

Obtaining commitment requires proper habits and some measure of skill. The habit of talking too much rather than listening often causes otherwise good presentations to fail. Knowing when to quit talking is just as important as knowing what to say. Some salespeople become so fascinated by the sound of their own voices that they talk themselves out of sales they have already made. A presentation that turns into a monologue is not likely to retain the buyer's interest.

DISCOVERING THE CAUSE

The real reasons for not obtaining commitment must be uncovered. Only then can salespeople proceed intelligently to eliminate the barriers. Some firms have developed sophisticated systems to follow up on lost sales. Sales software, such as Microsoft Dynamics or salesforce.com, can also identify points in the selling process where a salesperson may be having difficulty. If the sales cycle involves a demonstration, for example, and the salesperson turns fewer leads into demonstrations, the fault may lie in the needs identification skills of that salesperson.

Dave Alexander, account executive for SGA, Inc., says his company does a postsale analysis whether it wins or loses the sale. This discipline causes the sales team to focus on the factors that really lead to success.[20] Dave Stein, author of *How Winners Sell,* says that all too often salespeople will lay the blame for failure on price or the product but will take personal credit for any successes.[22] Both Stein and Alexander agree, however, that an effective win-loss system forces the salesperson to examine the real causes and, if the sale was not won, consider personal strategies for improvement.

SUGGESTIONS FOR DEALING WITH REJECTION

Maintain the Proper Perspective

Probably the inexperienced salesperson's most important lesson is that when a buyer says no, the sales process has not necessarily ended. A no may mean "Not now," "I need more information," "Don't hurry me," or "I don't understand." An answer of no should be a challenge to seek the reason behind the buyer's negative response.

In many fields of selling, most prospects do not buy. The ratio of orders achieved to sales presentations may be 1 to 3, 1 to 5, 1 to 10, or even 1 to 20. Salespeople may tend to eliminate nonbuyers from the prospect list after one unsuccessful call. This practice may be sound in some cases; however, many sales result on the second, third, fourth, or fifth call. Tim Pavlovich, sales executive for Dell, had one client require over 50 sales calls before closing. Of course, the sale was worth over $100 million annually, so it was pretty complicated. When an earlier visit has not resulted in commitment, careful preparation for succeeding calls becomes more crucial.

Another perspective is that when a buyer says no it is because the buyer is not yet fully informed; otherwise the buyer would have said yes. Consequently, if the buyer has given the salesperson the opportunity to make a presentation, the buyer recognizes that a need exists or is going to exist. What has not happened yet is that match between the offering and the need. At the same time, however, no does not mean "Sell me again right now." As we discussed earlier, no may mean "Sell me again later."

The salesperson should have a clear objective for each sales call. When commitment cannot be obtained to meet that objective, the salesperson will often attempt to obtain commitment for a reduced request (a secondary or minimum objective). For example, the salesperson may attempt to gain a trial order instead of an actual order, although, as we discussed earlier, this opportunity should be offered as a last resort.

Recommend Other Sources

A sales representative who uses the consultative selling philosophy (as described in Chapter 5) may recommend a competitor's product to solve the prospect's needs. When recommending other sources, the sales rep should explain why his or her product does not meet the prospect's needs and then provide the name of the competitive product. The goodwill generated by such a gesture should lead to future opportunities when the timing and needs are right.

After recommending other sources, the salesperson usually should ask the prospect for names of people who might be able to buy the seller's product. Also, the salesperson should emphasize the desire to maintain contact with the prospect in the event the seller's firm develops a competitive offering.

Use Good Manners

If obtaining commitment fails for any reason, the salesperson should react good-naturedly. Salespeople have to learn to accept no if they expect to call on prospects again. Even if salespeople do not obtain commitment, they should thank prospects for their time. Arguing or showing disappointment gains nothing. The salesperson may plan to keep in contact with these prospects through e-mail, an occasional phone call, a follow-up letter, or product literature mailings. One salesperson likes to make the following statement at the conclusion of any meeting that does not result in commitment: "I'll never annoy you, but if you don't mind, I'm going to keep in touch."

Many salespeople consider leaving something behind that will let the prospect contact the salesperson in the future. Some firms use promotional products, such as a pen with the company's name and phone number, as a gift after each call to remind the prospect of the salesperson's company. Others may simply use brochures and business cards.

BRINGING THE SALES CALL TO A CLOSE

Few buyers are interested in a prolonged visit after they commit. Obviously the departure cannot be abrupt; the salesperson should complete the sales call smoothly. But goodwill is never built by wasting the buyer's time after the business is concluded.

Remember that most sales take several calls to complete. If an order wasn't signed (and often getting an order isn't even the objective of the call; see Chapter 7) and the prospect wishes to continue considering the proposal, the salesperson should leave with a clear action plan for all parties. An example of the kind of dialogue the salesperson might pursue follows:

SALESPERSON: When will you have had a chance to look over this proposal?

BUYER: By the end of next week, probably.

SALESPERSON: Great, I'll call on you in about 10 days, OK?

BUYER: Sure, send me a meeting invite by e-mail.

SALESPERSON: Is there anything else I need to do for you before that next meeting?

The salesperson should always make sure the next step is clear for both parties. Therefore, review what you will do next, what the customer will do next, and when you will meet again.

Follow up promptly with a thank-you and reminder note after the sales call. If you are following up after a sales call in which you gained commitment for the next sales call, an e-mail message is not only sufficient but the best idea. For example, Bruce Culbert of the Pedowitz Group follows up each sales call with an e-mail that summarizes what happened, what each person promised to do (including what the buyer promised), and when the next meeting is. The sales cycle may take months, and such documentation is necessary to avoid losing momentum. Even when he is told no, his follow up e-mail includes a simple thank-you for the opportunity, along with a time frame for a follow-up. When he finally gets the sale, he'll follow up with a handwritten note and, in some cases, a "launch" dinner with the client to celebrate the new relationship.

Shirley Hunter, an account executive with Oracle, will follow up a sale with a handwritten thank-you note. She may also personally present a thank-you gift (her product costs half a million dollars, so a sale is worth celebrating). Her choice of a gift, though, will reflect the situation–a box of Lifesavers for the executive who got behind the purchase, a box of crayons for an architect, or something equally creative.

SELLING YOURSELF

When James Cobell wanted to start a sales club at Old Dominion University, he had to gain the support of others who had taken sales classes. "Getting someone to say they will do something is a lot easier than actually getting them to do it," says Cobell.

Like many companies, Southwest Airlines regularly works to improve the customer experience. John Tanner is part of the team working on the information technology infrastructure that will support those improvements. "There are many choices we can make," says Tanner, "and some may not pay off immediately." To get these changes approved, he relies on his sales experience from a previous position. "I have to be able to prove financial benefits first and foremost. But in all cases, these major decisions require me to convince others that these ideas are right for Southwest."

When selling internally, in your college now or in your company later, gaining real commitment can mean the difference between a program's success or failure. Just because the choice seems obvious to you–"It's the best decision for our customer and our company!"–doesn't mean that others in the company see it the same way. Nor can someone always order an employee to do something and expect the task to be done well. Commitment skills when selling yourself are critical to a successful career, whether you go into sales or something else altogether.

What's also important to remember is that when selling internally, you have to live with the consequences of the selling process much more intimately than when selling to a customer. Using pushy or cheesy techniques contributes to a reputation that makes future decisions or actions more difficult to secure.

Finally, it's important to remember to ask for commitment. Be specific–who will do what and when? When you are selling ideas, just getting someone to agree is easy. As Cobell says, getting someone to do something is much more difficult. But getting them to do it is what you need.

SUMMARY

Commitment cannot be obtained by some magical or miraculous technique if the salesperson has failed to prepare the prospect to make this decision throughout the presentation. Salespeople should always attempt to gain commitment in a way that is consistent with the objectives of the meeting. Obtaining commitment begins with the salesperson's contact with the prospect. It can succeed only when all facets of the selling process fall into their proper place. All sellers need to keep in mind this old saying: "People don't buy products or services; they buy solutions to their problems!"

The process of obtaining commitment is the logical progression of any sales call. Commitment is important for the customer, the seller's firm, and the seller. Commitment should result in a win-win situation for all parties concerned.

Pricing is an important element of any sale and is usually presented at the time of closing. Quantity discounts, payment terms, and shipping terms can affect the final price charged to the buyer as well as influence the decision.

There is no one "right" time to obtain commitment. Salespeople should watch their prospects closely and recognize when to obtain commitment. Successful salespeople carefully monitor customer comments, their buyers' nonverbal cues and actions, and their responses to probes. Comments can be in the form of questions, requirements, benefits, and responses to trial closes.

To successfully obtain commitment, the salesperson needs to maintain a positive attitude, allow the customer to set the pace, be assertive rather than aggressive, and sell the right item in the right amounts. Engaging in these practices will result in a strong long-term relationship between buyer and seller.

No one method of obtaining commitment works best for all buyers. The direct request method is the simplest to use; however, the prospect often needs help in evaluating the proposal. In those instances other methods may be more appropriate, such as the alternative choice, the benefit summary, the balance sheet method, or the probing method. No method of obtaining commitment will work if a buyer does not trust the salesperson.

If commitment is obtained, the salesperson should immediately assure the buyer that the choice was judicious. The salesperson should show genuine appreciation as well as cultivate the relationship for future calls.

If commitment is not obtained, the salesperson should analyze the reasons. Difficulties in obtaining commitment can be directly traced to wrong attitudes, a poor presentation, and/or poor habits and skills. Even if no commitment is obtained, the salesperson should thank the prospect for his or her time.

KEY TERMS

aggressive 298
assertive 299
balance sheet method 301
benefit summary method 300
buyer's remorse 305
buying signals 294
cash discount 291
closing 288
closing cues 294
cumulative discount 291
direct request method 300
follow-up 306
postpurchase dissonance 305
probing method 302
requirements 295
submissive 298
trial close 295
trial order 299

ETHICS PROBLEMS

1. In the opening profile, Kimberly Drumm says to "Always be closing." Some have interpreted this statement to mean to ask for the sale as early and as often as it takes to get the deal. Is that what she meant? One buyer stated, "All closing methods are devious and self-serving! How can a salesperson use a technique but still keep my needs totally in mind?" How would that buyer react to the methods offered by Kimberly? What might lead a buyer to take that perspective? Integrate into your discussion the concepts of persuasion versus manipulation.

2. A customer asked the salesperson, "How do you intend to solve my problem?" The salesperson told the customer his approach and provided a timeline on when each step would be completed. When asked for the sale, the customer said, "Oh, I'll just do it myself." Now that she had the process spelled out for her, she felt that she no longer needed the salesperson. Was her behavior appropriate? Why or why not? And, whether appropriate or not, how can salespeople avoid such situations? (*Note:* This happened to one of the authors recently when selling consulting services.)

QUESTIONS AND PROBLEMS

1. Review Exhibit 11.3 and discuss which social style would be best suited to which method of closing. Note that some of the methods are appropriate for multiple styles if worded differently. Give an example of how you would word one differently to address two different styles.
2. The sales process has gone well. You identified two important needs and shown how your product meets those needs. Your product costs $2,000 per month on a 24-month lease, or $100,000 to purchase plus a $200 per month maintenance agreement. Delivery and installation is $5,000, whether they lease or purchase. Supplies to operate the equipment are likely to run about $1,000 per month, based on the volume shared by the prospect. When the prospect asks, "How much will this cost?," how do you answer? What additional information would you like to know to help this buyer make the best decision?
3. What is the relationship between value analysis in Chapter 3, the value proposition in Chapter 9, and pricing? How does your response influence your perception of gaining commitment?
4. You've made six sales calls over a month with one prospect, during which you identified needs with three separate influencers, and you finally get to see the decision maker. You make your presentation and it seems to go well. All of the influencers are there; they are all nodding yes, so as you wrap up, you ask when they'd like to get started. The decision maker replies, "I'd like to think this over." Two of the influencers look surprised while the third looks confused. "OK," you reply, "is next Tuesday OK to check back?" How could you improve on your answer? Be specific; what exactly would you say?
5. One sales manager who worked for a refrigeration equipment company taught his salespeople the following close: Ask questions that allow you to fill out the contract. Assume the sale is made and hand the contract to the buyer, along with a pen. If the buyer doesn't immediately take the pen, drop it and make the buyer pick it up. Once the buyer has the pen in hand, he or she is more likely to use it to sign the contract, so just wait silently until the buyer does.
   a. Would you label this seller as assertive or aggressive?
   b. Is this a trick (manipulative) or merely dramatization (persuasive)?
   c. How would you respond to this behavior if you were the buyer?
6. You've identified a process by which your company could recycle packaging material, saving the company about 10 percent of the packaging costs. But when you talk this over with the person in charge of shipping, he says, "You're just a sales rep! Go sell something and let me do my job!" What do you think is driving his reaction? How would you respond? What would you do next?
7. As you think about the concept of creeping commitment, identify four different times in a sales call that a salesperson might ask for commitment other than asking for the sale.
8. Todd Pollock, vice president of the Vegas Golden Knights (the NHL's new hockey team), says he heard no at least 10 times and sometimes as many as 20 for every yes. How do you deal with rejection? What strategies would you try if you were in Todd's situation?
9. What would you say to a friend to gain his or her commitment to go on a ski trip for winter break? Describe exactly what you would say to your friend using each of the following methods (make any assumptions necessary):
   a. Alternative choice.
   b. Direct request.
   c. Benefit summary.
   d. Balance sheet.
   e. Probing.
10. A customer is willing to order 100 cases listed at $20 per case to get a 15 percent quantity discount. Terms are 2/10, n/30, FOB destination. The customer pays five days after receiving the invoice. How much did the customer pay?

CASE PROBLEMS

case 11.1

Global Sourcing for Allied?

Using radio frequency identification (RFID) technology, ClearScan manufactures inventory management and tracking systems. Used in any environment where tracking inventory location is important, these devices track movement of products within a warehouse, within a manufacturing facility, and even while on a truck or train. Sean Gardner was calling on Sarah Ford, senior purchasing director for Allied Signal, a company that makes low-energy products for commercial applications. Sarah has global responsibility for purchasing standardization, and developing a common inventory management system across all of Allied's 24 locations in eight countries is a task she has to complete this year. Sean's primary call objective was to have Sarah agree to set up an appointment in the next several weeks for Sean to present to the supply chain committee that will review proposals and narrow the choices to three systems.

SEAN: Our scanning systems can support the digital standards of both the United States and Europe, which means that, with some engineering changes in your computer network, your locations can use the same scanners.

SARAH: Sean, I've really been thinking that the RFID scanners made by Alcatel are industry standard, and I'm concerned about our China plant. What has ClearScan done differently with these scanners?

SEAN: Quality is something we take very seriously at ClearScan, but having the best-built old product isn't enough, is it? So we've also built probably the finest engineering staff over the past five years that you'll find anywhere. The result is a product line that was just awarded the Dubai Engineering Innovation World Cup award only last month.

SARAH: That's impressive, and you're right. A well-built product using yesterday's technology is of no benefit to us. But how important is bicontinental use at the scanning level? It's not like we ship from our European plants to the States; seems to me we could use local-made products and just merge data later when we need to.

SEAN: Yes, you can, but that's really inconsistent with the overall strategy of minimizing the number of vendors and having global suppliers. How do you serve Latin America or Africa?

SARAH: Well, we don't have a lot of business in Africa yet, but it's growing. And in Latin America, we supply both from China and the United States, so I see your point.

SEAN: Then you may have seen a report issued by Gartner that indicates some users have had data problems that were difficult to identify until something goes horribly wrong. Just merging data from disparate systems isn't always the best option.

SARAH: I've seen those data from Gartner as well as an article in the last issue of *Supply Chain Management.* But we've had no plans for a global RFID process.

SEAN: Why is that?

SARAH: We don't know that it is necessary—we don't think we've got that many locations where scanning is a necessity.

SEAN: How many sites do you consider scanning to be a necessity? And what separates those sites from others?

SARAH: Volume—we have maybe two or three locations where the volume is high enough to justify the expense. What are others experiencing?

SEAN: We've got several, maybe four, that have standardized with us globally and another group of about two dozen that use us in the United States or Europe. How does that sound?

SARAH: Intriguing, though we're not the same as others.

SEAN: I know. That's why I'd like to set up a meeting with your supply chain team in the near future. But we'll probably also need someone there from logistics, right?

SARAH: Yes, I suppose we would.

SEAN: Will I have your endorsement at the meeting?

SARAH: We'll have to wait and see. I'll need some documentation on the figures you've given me, and I'd like to get that before we set up the meeting.

Questions

1. What form of closing did Sean use to gain Sarah's commitment to the idea? Was that appropriate? Why or why not?
2. List how you would attempt to obtain commitment using three other methods of your choice. Write out exactly what you would say for each method (and be sure to identify the method).
3. Although you have been shown only a portion of the conversation, evaluate Sean's performance in terms of the following:
   a. Selling benefits, not features.
   b. Using trial closes.
   c. Using communication aids to strengthen the presentation.
   d. Responding to objections.
   e. Attempting to gain commitment at the proper time.

case 11.2

Prodio

When Bob Starr began his job as a salesperson for Prodio, he thought it would be easy. After all, the service he sold saved clients thousands of dollars. "What we do," said Nancy Gordon, chief sales officer, "is verify all of the credentials a doctor or other health care professional has when hired by a hospital or clinic. As it turns out, it can take up to six months to verify all of the licenses a doctor has to carry. We can do it with our proprietary software solution in under 30 days." She gave him several case studies showing savings of more than $100,000 because of revenue that was being lost waiting for the physician's credentials to be verified and another $50,000 on average for eliminating staff used in the verification process. So he began calling hospitals and asking for the head of human resources. Several times, he was put through and the conversation would go something like this.

"I'd like to meet with you to discuss an exciting new service, Prodio, which handles credentialing. The best thing is it's only $250 per doctor, saving most hospitals well over $150,000!"

"$250 per doctor? That's crazy! I've got no budget for anything like this! No thanks!"

So Bob called Nancy and said, "I'm not really getting anywhere. Can I work with someone to see how they are successful?"

The following Monday, he found himself in San Diego, meeting Carmen Lopez for coffee before going out on a few sales calls.

Carmen recommended waiting to give the price until the prospect had offered information regarding the number of doctors it was credentialing and what that cost was, as well as how long it took. "You can't sell price until they know what their current costs are," she advised. "This first call is a great example. The hospital CEO asked me to meet with the director of HR to get that information, which I did last week. Today, I'll present the costs and benefits and ask for the sale."

In the hospital's conference room, Carmen and Bob sat on one side of the table facing the CEO, John Blankenship, and Shirley Price the HR director. "John," said Carmen, "based on the information Shirley gave me, you'll reduce the credentialing period from an average of 90 days to under 30. For your more advanced specialties, it will go from six months to under 45 days. Shirley couldn't total the lost revenue you'll save by shortening the period, but we were able to determine that you'll also be able to eliminate two positions, saving another $138,000 versus spending just under $60,000 per year." She then handed the contract to the CEO.

There was a momentary silence and Bob could hear the antique clock ticking away on the credenza.

Shirley squirmed, visibly upset. When John looked at her, she said, "John, I don't want to fire two people. And I don't have other things for them to do."

John replied, "But this is one of those things we're going to have to do—financially, it's the right thing for the hospital."

As John turned his attention to signing the contract, Shirley stood and said, "Well, congratulations Carmen. Bob, nice to meet you," and she left the room.

An awkward pause ensued, broken when John handed the contract back to Carmen. "Does this contract mean we have to do all of our credentialing through you?"

"No," replied Carmen. "It just specifies the cost and our performance guarantees."

"OK. You work with Shirley to transition over. I'm not going to fire anyone, so until we can place them in other positions, you'll have to wait."

Questions

1. Assess Carmen's approach to presenting price. Is her approach something Bob should emulate?
2. Presenting price as the attention getter doesn't seem to work. If Bob does emulate Carmen's approach, what should he do when he calls to gain commitment to have that first meeting?
3. Carmen will need to work very closely with Shirley and her people, and it doesn't appear that Shirley is happy about the sale. What could Carmen have done to avoid this situation? How might this have gone differently if Shirley had been the initiator instead of John?

ROLE PLAY CASE

Once again you will give your presentation to the same buyer (ARM, FSS, and Mizzen) that you did after Chapters 9 and 10 (if you did not do role plays after those chapters, review that material now). This time you will complete your presentation, first summarizing the needs and going all the way to asking for the sale.

You will have an opportunity to work on presentation, objection handling, and closing skills.

If two people are involved in the sale (a seller and a buyer) while a third observes, the observer should do the following:

1. Identify any objection-handling methods used.
2. Determine whether the seller is focused on benefits or only features.
3. Note when trial closes are used.
4. Identify the closing method used.

The professor will pass out new buyer sheets.

ADDITIONAL REFERENCES

Alavi, Sascha, Jan Wieseke, and Jan H. Guba. "Saving on Discounts through Accurate Sensing: Salespeople's Estimations of Price Importance and Their Effects on Negotiation Success." *Journal of Retailing* 92, no. 1 (March 2016), pp. 40–55.

Arndt, Aaron, Kenneth Evans, Timothy Landry, Sarah Mady, and Chatdanai Pongpatipat. "The Impact of Salesperson Credibility-Building Statements on Later Stages of the Sales Encounter." *Journal of Personal Selling and Sales Management* 34, no. 1 (2014), pp. 19–32.

Guenzi, Paolo, Luigi M. De Luca, and Rosann Spiro. "The Combined Effect of Customer Perceptions about a Salesperson's Adaptive Selling and Selling Orientation on Customer Trust in the Salesperson: A Contingency Perspective." *Journal of Business and Industrial Marketing* 31, no. 4 (2016), pp. 553–64.

Inamizu, Nobuyuki, Hidenori Sato, and Fumihiko Ikuine. "Five Steps in Sales and Its Skills: The Importance of Preparing before an Interview with Customers." *Annals of Business Administrative Science* 16, no. 1 (2017), pp. 1–13.

Jelinek, Ronald. "Beyond Commitment: Entrenchment in the Buyer-Seller Exchange." *Journal of Personal Selling and Sales Management* 34, no. 4 (2014), pp. 272–84.

Johnson, Jeff S., Scott B. Friend, and Avinash Malshe. "Mixed Interpretations of Sales Proposal Signals." *Journal of Personal Selling and Sales Management* 36, no. 3 (2016), pp. 264–80.

Kadic-Maglajlic, Selma, Irena Vida, Claude Obadia, and Richard Plank. "Clarifying the Influence of Emotional Intelligence on Salesperson Performance." *Journal of Business and Industrial Marketing* 31, no. 7 (2016), pp. 877–88.

Ku, Hsuan-Hsuan, and Chih-Yun Huang. "Prompting Additional Services While Providing Service: Does It Offend the Customer?" *Journal of Service Theory and Practice* 26, no. 5 (2016), 657–80.

Limbu, Yam B., C. Jaychandran, Barry J. Babin, and Robin T. Peterson. "Empathy, Nonverbal Immediacy, and Salesperson Performance: The Mediating Role of Adaptive Selling Behavior." *Journal of Business and Industrial Marketing* 31, no. 5 (2016), pp. 654–67.

Mcfarland, Richard G., Joseph Rode, and Tasadduq A. Shervani. "A Contingency Model of Emotional Intelligence in Professional Selling."*Journal of the Academy of Marketing Science* 44, no. 1 (January 2016), pp. 108–18.

Missaoui, Yosra. "Non-verbal Communication Barriers When Dealing with Saudi Sellers." *International Journal of Organizational Leadership* 4, no. 4 (2015), pp. 392–402.

Plouffe, Christopher R., Willy Bolander, and Joseph A. Cote. "'Which Influence Tactics Lead to Sales Performance?' It Is a Matter of Style." *Journal of Personal Selling and Sales Management* 34, no. 2 (2014), 141–54.

Singh, Rakesh, and Pingali Venugopali. "The Impact of Salesperson Customer Orientation on Sales Performance via Mediating Mechanism." *Journal of Business and Industrial Marketing* 30, no. 5 (2015), pp. 594–607.

Wisker, Zazli Lily, and Athanasios Poulis. "Emotional Intelligence and Sales Performance: A Myth or Reality?" *International Journal of Business and Society* 16, no. 2 (May 2015), pp. 185–200.

Zboia, James, Ronald A. Clark, and Diana L. Haytko. "An Offer You Can't Refuse: Consumer Perceptions of Sales Pressure." *Journal of the Academy of Marketing Science* 44, no. 6 (November 2016), pp. 806–21.

©Nick White/Getty Images RF

The Partnership Process

PART 2

chapter 12

FORMAL NEGOTIATING

SOME QUESTIONS ANSWERED IN THIS CHAPTER ARE

- What is negotiation selling? How does it differ from nonnegotiation selling?
- What items can be negotiated in selling?
- What type of planning needs to occur prior to a negotiation meeting? How should a seller set objectives?
- How can the negotiation session be effectively opened? What role does friendly conversation play?
- Which negotiation strategies and tactics do buyers use? How should negotiators respond?
- What are the salesperson's guidelines for offering and requesting concessions?

PROFILE

"Arriving at agreed-upon terms is not always easy, and sometimes I need to walk away from the sale, but formal negotiations will always fail without mutual trust."

Eric LaBelle, Vista Outdoor

Courtesy of Eric LaBelle

PROFILE My name is Eric LaBelle. I learned the fundamentals of selling from Dr. Stephen Castleberry both in selling class at the University of Minnesota-Duluth and in a Selling Ideas at Work course during my graduate studies at the University of Wisconsin-Eau Claire. Currently I am a senior national account manager for Vista Outdoor, a manufacturer and marketer of consumer products for the outdoor sports and recreation markets. I sell Vista Outdoor's vast product offerings (like Bushnell, CamelBak, Savage, Stevens, Bell) to multiple national sporting goods chains. The sales process occurs with a team of buyers at each account, and formal negotiations are plentiful.

A sales role is made exponentially easier the more your relationship with the customer grows. While it often takes time to develop the trust needed to form a prosperous partnership, determining the type of sales professional you want to become up front is instrumental to your success. The mentality I take to the office every day is this: If I can put my best effort forward to ensure the mutual success of both Vista Outdoor and my customer, then I have succeeded. Arriving at agreed-upon terms is not always easy, and sometimes I need to walk away from the sale, but formal negotiations will always fail without mutual trust.

Negotiations are part of business for all companies, whether big or small. The success of a negotiation is determined long before meeting with the customer. Preparing to meet with my buyers starts with a clear understanding of what is to be accomplished. Setting concise goals, oftentimes with the head buyer in a prenegotiation phone call or e-mail exchange, establishes the groundwork needed to prepare for the meeting. If the agreed-upon goal of a meeting is to determine the final assortment of binoculars the retailer is going to carry next year, I now know my homework assignment. Prior to the meeting, I will research every detail of the retailer's current assortment, including peg space and margin requirements, as well as competitors' prices, features, and pitfalls. I will then match the competitors' products to my own and create a compelling argument why adjusting its current assortment will be beneficial to the retailer. I will talk with our product experts to verify my argument, and finally I will practice for the negotiation session until I am confident with my delivery and any objections the buyer may have.

Not once has a negotiation session proceeded exactly as I had planned! However, since I have prepared extensively for such contingencies, I am confident I can steer the meeting in the direction of mutually agreed-upon terms which both sides view as a win-win. Navigating through a successful negotiation may be cause for celebration, but the deal is not complete until a formal purchase order is received. Following up after a customer meeting is oftentimes just as important as the meeting itself.

Remember, formal negotiations are inevitable in the business world. Spending the time to prepare for a negotiation session will guide you down the path to a successful business relationship.

Visit our Web site at: www.vistaoutdoor.com/.

Eric LaBelle, senior national account manager, Vista Outdoor. Used with permission.

We have all engaged in negotiations of some type. Most of these were informal (such as with your parents about attending a concert) and dealt with relatively minor issues, although they may have been intensely important to you at the time. This chapter discusses formal negotiations that occur between buyers and salespeople. The skills you will learn can also be used in your day-to-day negotiations with friends, parents, and people in authority positions.

THE NATURE OF NEGOTIATION

The bargaining process through which buyers and sellers resolve areas of conflict and arrive at agreements is called **negotiation**. Areas of conflict may include minor issues (like who should attend future meetings) as well as major ones (such as cost per unit or exclusive purchase agreements). The ultimate goal of both parties should be to reduce or resolve the conflict.

Two radically different philosophies can guide negotiations. In **win-lose negotiating** the negotiator attempts to win all the important concessions and thus triumph over the opponent. This process resembles almost every competitive sport you have ever watched. In boxing, for example, one person is the winner, and the other is, by definition, the loser.

In the second negotiating philosophy, **win-win negotiating**, the negotiator attempts to secure an agreement that satisfies both parties. You have probably experienced social situations similar to this. For example, if you want to attend a football game and your friend wants to attend a party, you may negotiate a mutual agreement that you both attend the first half of the game and still make it to the party. If this arrangement satisfies both you and your friend, you have engaged in win-win negotiating.

The discussion in this chapter assumes that your goal as a salesperson is to engage in win-win negotiating. In fact, this entire book has emphasized developing relationships, which is a win-win perspective. Partners attempt to find solutions that benefit both parties because each party is concerned about the other party's welfare.

However, the buyer may be using a win-lose strategy, whereby the buyer hopes to win all major concessions and have the seller be the loser. To help you spot and prepare for such situations, we discuss many of these tactics as well.

NEGOTIATION VERSUS NONNEGOTIATION SELLING

How does negotiation differ from the sales presentations we have discussed up to this point? This textbook has already covered many aspects of negotiating an agreement between buyer and seller. For example, in Chapter 10 we discussed the negotiations that occur as the seller is helping the buyer deal with objections. And in Chapter 11 we talked about obtaining commitment, which often requires negotiating on some key points. Importantly, however, we assumed that many, if not most, factors during a regular sales call are constrained, and not open to change or negotiation. For example, the price of one Allsteel Quip brand ergonomic chair has been set at $499. The Allsteel salesperson will not lower that price unless, of course, the buyer agrees to purchase large quantities. Even then the buyer will receive just a standard quantity discount as outlined in the seller's price manual. In essence, the salesperson's price book and procedure manual form an inflexible set of rules. If the buyer objects, an attempt to resolve the conflict will occur by using techniques discussed in Chapter 10 (such as the compensation method or the revisit method).

Formal negotiations usually involve multiple buyers and multiple sellers.
©Moodboard/SuperStock RF

In contrast, if the Allsteel seller enters formal negotiations with the same buyer, the price and delivery schedules will be subject to modification. The buyer neither expects nor wants the seller to come to the negotiation meeting with any standard price book. Instead the buyer expects most policies, procedures, and prices to be truly negotiable.

Negotiations also differ from regular sales calls in that they generally involve more intensive planning and a larger number of people from the selling firm. Prenegotiation planning may go on for six months or more before the actual meeting takes place. Planning participants usually represent a wide spectrum of functional areas of the firm, such as production, marketing, sales, human resources, accounting, purchasing, and executive officers.

Finally, formal negotiations generally take place only for very large or important prospective buyers. For example, Hormel might negotiate with some of the largest food chains, such as Walmart and Cub Foods, but would not engage in a large, formal negotiation session with small local or mom-and-pop grocery stores. Negotiating is an expensive endeavor because it uses so much of so many important people's time. The firm wants to invest the time and costs involved in negotiating only if the long-term nature of the relationship and the importance of the customer justify the expense.

WHAT CAN BE NEGOTIATED?

If the customer is large or important enough, almost anything can be negotiated. Salespeople who have not been involved in negotiations before often find it hard to grasp the fact that so many areas are subject to discussion and change. Exhibit 12.1 lists some items that are often negotiated between buyers and sellers. But in reality, no single negotiation session covers all the areas listed. Each side comes to the bargaining table with a list of prioritized issues; only important points for which disagreement exists are discussed.

Exhibit 12.1

Items That Are Often Negotiated between Buyers and Sellers

- Inventory levels the buyer must maintain.
- Inventory levels the seller must keep on hand to be able to restock the buyer quickly.
- Details about the design of the product or service.
- Web page development.
- How the product will be manufactured.
- Display allowances for resellers.
- Advertising allowances and the amount of advertising the seller does.
- Sales promotion within the channel of distribution.
- Delivery terms and conditions.
- Retail and wholesale pricing points for resellers.
- Prices and pricing allowances for volume purchases.
- Amount and location of shelf positioning.
- Special packaging and design features.
- Service levels after the sale.
- Disposing of unsold or obsolete merchandise.
- Credit terms.
- How complaints will be resolved.
- Order entry and ease of monitoring orders.
- Type and frequency of communication between the parties.
- Performance guarantees and bonds.

ARE YOU A GOOD NEGOTIATOR?

All of us are negotiators; some of us are better than others. We have negotiated with parents, friends, professors, and, yes, sometimes even with opponents. However, the fact that you have engaged in many negotiations in your lifetime does not mean you are good at negotiating.

The traits necessary to successfully negotiate vary somewhat, depending on the situation and the parties involved. Some characteristics, however, are almost universal. For example, a good negotiator must have patience and endurance; after two hours of discussing the same issue, the negotiator needs the stamina and willingness to continue until an agreement is reached. Also, a willingness to take risks and the ability to tolerate ambiguity become especially critical in business negotiations because it is necessary to both accept and offer concessions during the meeting without complete information.

Successful salespeople do not always make great negotiators. In fact, negotiating may be the most difficult skill for any salesperson to develop. Many managers have to coach reps on their negotiating skills because many reps don't want to risk ruining a relationship they worked hard to build. The unconscious reaction of most salespeople in negotiations often ends up being the opposite of the correct thing to do. For example, what if, in preparation for the upcoming negotiation session, the customer asks for detailed specifications about your product? Most salespeople would gladly supply reams of technical data, full glossy pictures, an offer of plant tours, and the like. The problem with that approach lies in the possibility that the customer will pick several features that he or she does not need and then pressure for price concessions. (Look, I don't need that much memory capacity and don't want to pay for something I'm not going to use. So why don't you reduce your price? I shouldn't have to pay for something I'm not planning on ever using!) A salesperson who is a good negotiator would avoid this situation by supplying information to the customer only in exchange for the right to ask the customer more questions and thus gain more information.

People who fear conflict usually are poor negotiators. In fact, some negotiating strategies are actually designed to increase the level of conflict to bring all the issues to the table and reach an equitable settlement. Along the same lines, people who have a strong need to be liked by all people at all times tend to make very poor negotiators. Other undesirable traits include being closed-minded, unorganized, dishonest, and downright belligerent.

Of course cultural differences do exist. For example, Brazilian managers may believe competitiveness is more important in a negotiator than integrity. Chinese managers in Taiwan may emphasize the negotiator's rational skills less than his or her interpersonal skills.

As this discussion indicates, being a truly excellent negotiator requires a careful balance of traits and skills. Take a moment and complete the questionnaire in Exhibit 12.2 to rate your negotiating skills. Don't be discouraged by a low score.

Exhibit 12.2
Negotiation Skills Self-Inventory

Place a check by each item that accurately reflects your personality and traits on an average, normal day.

______ 1. Helpful	______ 20. Receptive
______ 2. Risk taker	______ 21. Easily influenced
______ 3. Inconsistent	______ 22. Enthusiastic
______ 4. Persistent	______ 23. Planner
______ 5. Factual	______ 24. Stingy
______ 6. Use high pressure	______ 25. Listener
______ 7. Self-confident	______ 26. Controlled
______ 8. Practical	______ 27. Think under pressure
______ 9. Manipulative	______ 28. Passive
______ 10. Analytical	______ 29. Economical
______ 11. Arrogant	______ 30. Gullible
______ 12. Impatient	______ 31. Afraid of conflict
______ 13. Seek new approaches	______ 32. Endurance
______ 14. Tactful	______ 33. Tolerate ambiguity
______ 15. Perfectionist	______ 34. Have strong need to be liked
______ 16. Stubborn	______ 35. Organized
______ 17. Flexible	______ 36. Honest
______ 18. Competitive	______ 37. Belligerent
______ 19. Gambler	

How to score the checklist:

All of the traits listed are positive except for the following negative traits: 3, 6, 9, 11, 12, 15, 16, 19, 21, 24, 28, 30, 31, 34, and 37. To arrive at a total score, give yourself one point for all positive traits and subtract one point for all negative traits. To interpret your total score: 19–22 = excellent; 15–18 = good; 11–14 = fair.

You cannot easily change personality traits, but the rest of this chapter suggests ways to improve your skills.

PLANNING FOR THE NEGOTIATION SESSION

Preparation and planning are the most important parts of negotiation, according to many expert sources. And that planning includes preparing ourselves emotionally for the stress that will occur within a negotiation session. In Chapter 7 we discussed how to gather precall information and plan the sales call. All of that material is equally relevant when planning for an upcoming negotiation session—for example, learning everything possible about the buying team and the buyer's organization.

The meetings the salesperson will have with the buyer before the actual negotiation session facilitate this learning. The buyer may also be, or have been, a customer of the salesperson, with the upcoming negotiation session designed to review contracts or specify a new working relationship. Even in such scenarios, negotiators will want to carefully review the players and learn as many facts about the situation as possible.

LOCATION

Plan to hold the negotiation at a location free from distraction for both teams. A neutral site, one owned by neither party, is usually best; it removes both teams from interruptions by business associates, and no one has a psychological ("home court") advantage. Experienced negotiators find the middle of the workweek best for negotiations and prefer morning to afternoon or evening (because people are more focused on their jobs rather than after-hours and weekend activities).

Some negotiations are now occurring online. Research shows that using these new forms can affect the behavior of negotiators. For example, reciprocity doesn't occur as frequently or in the same way. Those who are the first to offer a concession often don't find the other party giving a similar one in return, regardless of the power in the relationship. Furthermore, contrary to face-to-face negotiations, having more power in a relationship doesn't result in the other party giving larger concessions. Sales Technology 12.1 describes cloud software to help manage online negotiations.

Sales reps need to set aside time to plan for a negotiation session.

TIME ALLOTMENT

As you are probably aware, negotiations can take a tremendous amount of time. Some business negotiations take years. But how much time should be set aside for one negotiation session? The answer depends on the negotiation objectives and the extent to which both sides desire a win-win session. Studies have shown that high time pressure will produce nonagreements and poor outcomes when one or more sides take a win-lose perspective, but if both sides have a win-win perspective, high outcomes are achieved regardless of time pressure.

NEGOTIATION OBJECTIVES

Power is a critical element when developing objectives. The selling team must ask, Do we need them more than they need us? What part of our service is most valuable

SALES Technology 12.1

CLOUD-BASED NEGOTIATING SOFTWARE

The ever-expanding Internet and innovative technologies are constantly reshaping the sales industry. Parley Pro, a cloud-based negotiation software, allows buyer and sellers to negotiate online. With this Internet platform, potentially more individuals could participate in the negotiation process because parties need not be present in a central location.

Parley Pro automates the workflow from contract introduction to close. This discussion-centered all-in-one software substitutes e-mails, attachments, and use of manual documents with a chat-like negotiation procedure. This inventive software eliminates the wasted time of sending numerous documents between parties. Managers and higher up company individuals can quickly review facts and transcripts of the conversation history or view the current state of the negotiation. Interactive dashboards and analytics manage negotiations and track milestones. A dashboard displays current status and performance indicators for portfolio of contracts. This process streamlines negotiating and makes it more effective and more transparent. The ultimate value of Parley Pro lies in the transparency of the negotiating process.

Sources: Docusign, "How to Use Technology to Simplify Sales," *Influencive*, December 13, 2017.

to them? Can they get similar products elsewhere? Optimally both parties share balanced power, although this situation is rare in practice. The best scenario is one in which the selling team feels like it can exit the negotiation if the other side does not meet the seller's minimum objectives.

In developing objectives for the session, keep in mind that the seller will almost certainly have to make concessions in the negotiation meeting. Thus, setting several objectives, or positions, is extremely important.

The **target position** is what your company hopes to achieve at the negotiation session. Your team should also establish a **minimum position**, which is the absolute minimum level you will accept. Finally, an **opening position**–the initial proposal–should be developed.

For example, for a Fenwal salesperson negotiating the price for a blood collection and transfusion system at a blood bank, the target position could be $2.5 million, with a minimum position of $2 million and an opening position of $3 million. In negotiations over service levels by Gallovidian Fresh Foods in the United Kingdom with Morrisons grocery stores with regard to fresh vegetables, the seller's opening position might be weekly delivery, the target position delivery twice a week, and the minimum position (the most the seller is willing to do) delivery three times a week.

To allow for concessions, the opening position should reflect higher expectations than the target position. However, the buyer team may consider a very high opening position to be unrealistic and may simply walk away. You have probably seen this happen in negotiations between countries that are at war. To avoid this problem, negotiators must be ready to support that opening position with solid information. Suppose the opening position for a Colgate-Palmolive negotiating team is to offer the grocer a display allowance of $1,000 (with a target position offering of $1,500). The team must be ready to prove that $1,000 is reasonable. When developing objectives, negotiators need to sort out all issues that could arise in the meeting, prioritizing them by importance to the firm. Then the negotiators

Exhibit 12.3
Comparing Buyer and Seller Price Positions.

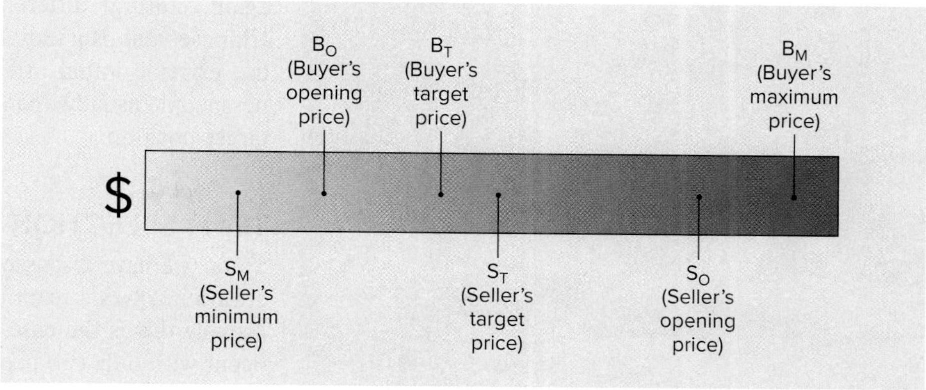

should develop contingency plans to get a good idea, even before the meeting begins, of their planned reactions and responses to the buyer's suggestions.

Talking over these issues beforehand helps the negotiation team avoid "giving away the store" during the heat of the negotiation session. It also allows the team to draw on the expertise of company experts who will not be present during the session.

The buyer team also develops positions for the meeting. Exhibit 12.3 presents a continuum that shows how the two sets of positions relate. With the positions illustrated, the parties can reach an agreement somewhere between the seller's minimum (S_M) and the buyer's maximum (B_M). However, if B_M falls to the left of S_M (has a lower maximum acceptable price), no agreement can be reached; attempts at negotiation will be futile. For example, if the buyer is not willing to pay more than \$200 (B_M) and the seller will not accept less than \$250 (S_M), agreement is impossible. In general, the seller desires to move as far to the right of S_M (as high a price) as possible, and the buyer desires to move as far to the left of B_M (as low a price) as possible.

Negotiators need to try to anticipate these positions and evaluate them carefully. The more information collected about what the buyer hopes to accomplish, the better the negotiators will be able to manage the meeting and arrive at a win-win decision.

Negotiators create a plan to achieve their objectives. However, the chance of failure always exists. Thus, planners need to consider strategy revisions if the original plan should fail. The development of alternative paths to the same goal is known as **adaptive planning**. For example, a firm may attempt to secure a premium shelf position by using any of the following strategies:

- In return for a 5 percent price discount.
- In return for credit terms of 3/10, n/30.
- In return for a 50–50 co-op ad campaign.

The firm would attempt to secure the premium shelf position by using, for example, the first strategy; if that failed, it would move to the second strategy; and so forth. Fortunately, with laptops and spreadsheets such as Excel, negotiators can quickly calculate the profitability of various package deals for their firms.

Many firms will engage in a brainstorming session to try to develop strategies that will meet the firm's objectives. A **brainstorming session** is a meeting in which people are allowed to creatively explore various methods of achieving goals. Once

The salesperson's team must prepare for an upcoming negotiation session. Remember that the buyer's team is also planning.

again, cultural differences exist.[1] For example, Chinese and Russian businesspeople habitually use extreme initial offers, whereas Swedish businesspeople usually open with a price close to their target position.

TEAM SELECTION AND MANAGEMENT

So far we have discussed negotiation as though it always involves a team of both buyers and sellers. Usually this is the case. However, negotiations do occur with only two people present: the buyer and the salesperson.

Teams offer both pros and cons. Because of team members' different backgrounds, the group as a whole tends to be more creative than one individual could be. Team members can help one another and reduce the chances of making a mistake. However, the more participants, the more time generally required to reach agreement. Also, team members may voice differing opinions among themselves, or one member may address a topic outside his or her area of expertise. Such things can make the seller's team appear unprepared or disorganized.

In general the seller's team should be the same size as the buyer's team. Otherwise the sellers may appear to be trying to exert more power or influence in the meeting. Whenever possible, strive for the fewest team members possible. Unnecessarily large teams can get bogged down in details; and the larger the team, the more difficult reaching a decision generally becomes.

Each team member should have a defined role in the session. For example, experts are often included to answer technical questions; executives are present as more authoritative speakers on behalf of the selling firm. Exhibit 12.4 lists the types of team members often chosen for negotiations. Many of these people take part in prenegotiation planning but do not actually attend the negotiation session.

Team members should possess the traits of good negotiators, although it often does not work out that way. For example, many technical experts have no tolerance for ambiguity and may fear conflict. As a result, the team leader needs to help them see clearly what their role is, as well as what they should not get involved in, during the session.

The team leader will manage the actual negotiation session. Because of their intimate knowledge of the buyers and their needs, salespeople, rather than the executives on the team, often fill this post. When selecting a team leader, the seller's management also needs to consider the anticipated leader of the buyer team. It is unwise to choose a leader for the selling team who may be intimidated by the buyer's leader.

The team usually develops rules about who will answer what kinds of questions, who should be the first to respond to a concession offered by the buyers, who will offer concessions from the seller's standpoint, and so on. A set of nonverbal and verbal signals is also developed so team members can communicate with one another. For example, they may agree that when the salesperson takes out a breath mint, all team members are to stop talking and let the salesperson handle all issues; or when the executive places her red book inside her briefcase, the team should move toward its target position, and the salesperson should say, "OK, let's look at some alternatives."

Exhibit 12.4
People Who May Serve on the Selling Negotiation Team

Title	Possible Role
Salesperson	Coordinates all functions.
Field sales manager (district manager, regional manager, etc.)	Provides additional local and regional information. Secures necessary local funding and support for planning and presentations. Offers information about competitors.
National sales manager/ vice president of sales	Serves as a liaison with corporate headquarters. Secures necessary corporate funding and staff support for planning and presentation. Offers competitor information.
National account salesperson/national account sales manager	Provides expertise and support in dealing with issues for important customers. Offers information about competitors.
Marketing department senior executives, product managers, and staff	Provide suggestions for product/service applications. Supply market research information as well as information about packaging, new product development, upcoming promotional campaigns, etc. Offer information about competitors.
Chief executive officer/ president	Serves as an authority figure. Facilitates quicker decisions regarding changes in current policy and procedures. As a peer, can relate well with buyer's senior officers.
Manufacturing executives and staff	Provide information about current scheduled production as well as the possibility/cost of any modifications in the schedule.
Purchasing executives and staff	Provide information about raw materials inflows. Offer suggestions about possible quantity discounts from suppliers.
Accounting and finance executives and staff	Source of cost accounting information. Supply corporate target returns on investment, cost estimates for any needed changes in the firm under various buying scenarios, and information about order entry, billing, and credit systems.
Information technology executives and staff	Provide information about current information systems and anticipated changes needed under various buying scenarios. Help ensure that needed periodic reports for the buyers can be generated in a timely fashion.
Training executives and staff	Provide training for negotiation effectiveness and conduct practice role plays. Also provide information about and suggestions for anticipated necessary buyer training.
Outside consultants	Provide any kind of assistance necessary. Especially helpful if the firm has limited experience in negotiations or has not negotiated with this type of buyer before.

To ensure that team members really understand their respective roles and that all rules and signals are clearly grasped, the team should practice. This process usually involves a series of videotaped role play situations. Many firms, such as Taylor Communications, involve their sales training department in this practice. Trainers, using detailed information supplied by the team, realistically play the roles of the buying team members.

The selling team will likely have many meetings before the negotiation session. These will be internal meetings, with members of the selling team, and also meetings with the buyers. Because not every selling team member can be at all meetings, sometimes it is hard for team members to keep abreast of developments.

INDIVIDUAL BEHAVIOR PATTERNS

The team leader needs to consider the personality style of each member of both teams to spot any problems and plan accordingly. Of course one method would be to sort the members into analyticals, amiables, expressives, and drivers based on the dimensions of assertiveness and responsiveness (see Chapter 5 for a full

Exhibit 12.5
Conflict-Handling Behavior Modes

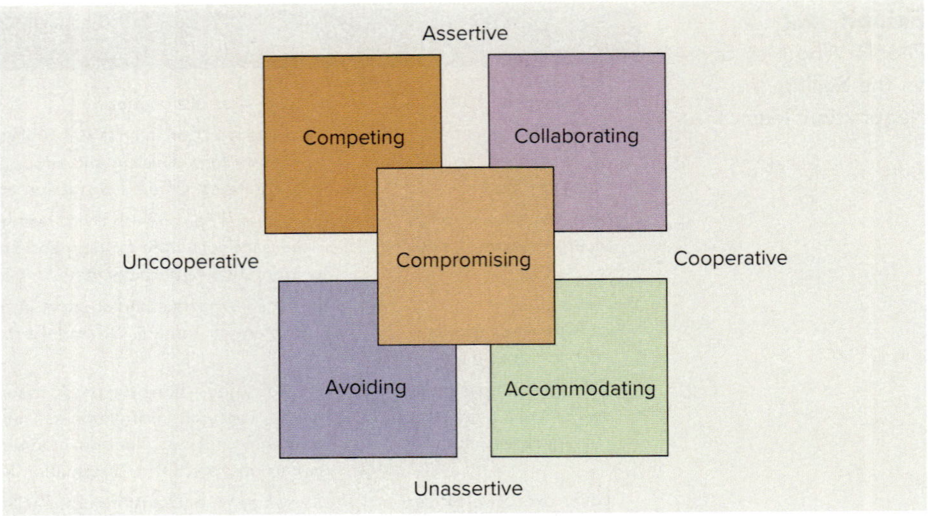

Source: Kenneth Thomas, "Conflict and Conflict Management," in *The Handbook of Industrial and Organizational Psychology*, ed. Marvin Dunnette (Skokie, IL: Rand McNally, 1976).

discussion). Some researchers have developed personality profiles specifically for negotiations. This section presents one of the most widely used sets of negotiation profiles.

After studying actual conflict situations, a number of researchers arrived at a set of basic conflict-handling modes based on the dimensions of assertiveness and cooperativeness.[2] Exhibit 12.5 presents these five modes: competing, accommodating, avoiding, compromising, and collaborating. Note that these five styles are different from the social styles (drivers, amiables, expressives, and analyticals) that we have been using throughout the book. Because all negotiations involve some degree of conflict, this typology is appropriate for use by salespeople preparing for a negotiation session.

People who resolve conflict in a **competing mode** are assertive and uncooperative. They tend to pursue their own goals and objectives completely at the expense of the other party. Often power oriented, they usually surround themselves with subordinates (often called "yes-men") who go along with their ideas. Team members who use the competing mode look for a win–lose agreement: They win, the other party loses.

Individuals in the **accommodating mode** are the exact opposite of competing people. Unassertive and highly cooperative, accommodators focus on the needs and desires of the other party and seek primarily to satisfy the concerns of the other party. Although they do not necessarily wish to lose, they do want to make sure the other side gets all they want. Accommodators can be spotted by their excessive generosity; their constant, rapid yielding to another's point of view; and their obedience to someone else's order, even if it is obviously not something they desire to do.

Some people operate in the unassertive and uncooperative **avoiding mode**. These people do not attempt to fulfill their own needs or the needs of others. In essence, they simply refuse to address the conflict at all. They do not strive for a win–win agreement; in fact, they do not strive for any agreement.

The **compromising mode** applies to people "in the middle" in terms of cooperativeness and assertiveness. A compromiser attempts to find a quick, mutually acceptable solution that partially satisfies both parties. A compromiser gives up more than a competing person but less than an accommodating person. In many ways the compromiser attempts to arrive at a win–win solution. However, the

People exhibit different conflict-handling modes. Can you spot someone in this photo who may be in the avoiding mode? The collaborating mode?

agreement reached usually does not maximize the satisfaction of the parties. For example, a compromising person might quickly suggest, "Let's just split the difference." Although this sounds fair, a better solution—one that would please both parties more—may be reached with further discussion.

Finally, people in the **collaborating mode** are both assertive and cooperative. They seek to maximize the satisfaction of both parties and hence to reach a truly win–win solution. Collaborators have the motivation, skill, and determination to really dig into an issue or a problem and explore all possible solutions. The best situation, from a negotiation standpoint, would be to have on both teams a number of people who generally use a collaborating mode.

As with the social style matrix described earlier, one person can exhibit different modes in different situations. For example, a buying team negotiator who perceives that his or her position on an issue extremely vital to the long-term welfare of the company is correct may revert from a collaborating mode to a competing mode. Likewise, when potentially heavy damage could occur from confronting an issue, that same buyer might move to an avoiding mode.

INFORMATION CONTROL

What do buyers do while selling teams engage in preparation? They prepare too! Keep in mind that buyers have read as many books and attended as many seminars about negotiation as sellers have because this training is one of their best negotiating tools. Buyers try to learn as much as they can about the seller's team and plans, including the seller's opening, target, and minimum positions. Buyers also are interested in the seller's team membership and decision rules. As a result, the selling team leader needs to emphasize the need for security: Don't give everyone access to all information. In fact, many team members (such as technical support) do not need to have complete and exhaustive knowledge of all the facts surrounding the negotiation.

As an example, one Fortune 500 firm was negotiating a $15 million deal with one of its customers. The selling team's leader had to leave the room for a few minutes, and while he was gone, the plant manager for the selling firm came in. The plant manager, though intending to do no harm, bragged about how his company had already invested $2 million in a prototype and retooling just to prepare for the customer's expected commitment. Needless to say, when the seller's team leader returned to the room, the buyer said he had all the information he needed. Two days later the buyer was a very tough negotiator, armed with the knowledge that the seller had already committed to the project. It pays to control the flow of information!

THE NEGOTIATION MEETING

Before discussing what occurs in the negotiation meeting, we should note that some buyers will attempt to engage in a win–lose tactic of beginning to negotiate when the other party does not expect it. This tactic has been called **ambush negotiating** or a **sneak attack**. It can occur during meetings prior to the negotiation meeting or even during installation of the new product. For example, during the first week of installation of a new telecommunications system, the buyer may state, "We're going to have to renegotiate the price of this system. Since we signed that contract, we have learned of a new system being introduced by one of your competitors." The seller should never negotiate in such a situation until prepared to deal with the issue completely.

At the negotiation meeting the buyer team and seller team physically come together and deliberate about topics important to both parties, with the goal of arriving at decisions. As mentioned earlier, this meeting usually has been preceded by one or more smaller buyer-seller meetings designed to uncover needs and explore options. Informal phone conversations probably were used to set some aspects of the agenda, learn about team members who will be present, and so on. Also, the negotiation itself may require a series of sessions to resolve all issues.

PRELIMINARIES

Engaging in friendly conversation to break the ice before getting down to business is usually a good idea. Use this time to learn and use the names of all members on the buyer team. This preliminary activity is especially important in many international negotiation meetings. For example, Japanese businesspeople usually want to spend time developing a personal relationship before beginning negotiations, and alcohol is usually a part of this. Not so in Saudi Arabia, where customs dictate strict abstinence.

Every effort should be made to ensure a comfortable environment for all parties. Arranging ahead of time for refreshments, proper climate control, appropriate size of room, adequate lighting, and correct layout of furniture will go far to establish an environment conducive to negotiating.

Most negotiations occur at a rectangular table. Teams usually sit on opposite sides, with the team leaders at the heads of the table. If possible, try to arrange for a round table or at least a seating arrangement that mixes members from each team together. This seating plan helps the parties feel that they are facing a common task and fosters a win-win atmosphere.

If the buyer team has a win-lose philosophy, expect all kinds of ploys to be used. For example, the furniture may be too large or too small or may be uncomfortable to sit in. The buyers may sit in front of large windows to force you to stare directly into sunlight. You may discover that the sellers' seats are all placed beneath heat ducts and the heat is set too high. You should not continue with the meeting until all unfavorable physical arrangements have been set right.

As far as possible the selling team should establish a win-win environment. This environment can be facilitated by avoiding any verbal or nonverbal threatening gestures, remaining calm and courteous, and adopting an attitude of investigation and experimentation. The leader might even comment,

> I can speak for my team in saying that our goal is to reach agreements today that we can all be proud of. We come to this meeting with open minds and look forward to exploring many avenues toward agreement. I am confident that we will both prosper and be more profitable as a result of this session.

thinking it through

What if you do everything in your power to establish a win-win relationship with the buyer team, but the buyers insist on viewing the negotiation session as a series of win-lose maneuvers? That is, your team consists mostly of collaborators who are trying to see that both sides are winners, whereas the buyers are mostly in the competing mode where they hope to win and hope you lose. Since they won't play by win-win "rules," should you?

Exhibit 12.6

Preliminary Negotiating Session Agenda

> **Preliminary Agenda**
>
> Meeting between FiberCraft and Rome Industrial Inc.
>
> Proposed New Spin Machine for 15 FiberCraft Plants
>
> November 21
>
> 1. Introductions by participants.
> 2. Agree on the meeting agenda.
> 3. Issues:
>   a. Who will design the new machine?
>   b. Who will pay the costs of testing the machine?
>   c. Who will have ownership rights to the new machine (if it is ever built for someone else)?
>   d. Who will be responsible for maintaining and servicing the new machine during trial runs?
>   e. Who will pay for any redesign work needed?
> 4. Coffee break.
> 5. Issues:
>   a. How and when will the machines be set up in the 15 locations? Who will be responsible for installation?
>   b. What percentage will be required for a down payment?
>   c. What will the price be? Will there be any price escalation provisions? If not, how long is this price protected?
> 6. Summary of agreement.

An **agenda**, a listing of what will be discussed and in what sequence, is important for every negotiation session. It helps set boundaries and keeps everyone on track. Exhibit 12.6 offers an example of a negotiation agenda. The selling team should come to the meeting with a preliminary typed agenda. Don't be surprised when the buyer team also comes with an agenda; in that case the first thing to be negotiated is the agenda itself. In general, putting key issues not at the very first in the agenda is advantageous. This approach allows time for each party to learn the other's bargaining style and concession routines. Moreover, agreement has already been reached on some minor issues, which, in a win–win situation, supports an atmosphere for reaching agreement on the major issues.

GENERAL GUIDELINES

To negotiate effectively, the seller team must put into practice the skills discussed throughout this book. For example, listening carefully is extremely important. Careful listening involves not only being silent when the buyer talks but also asking good probing questions to resolve confusion and misunderstanding.

The team leader must keep track of issues discussed or resolved. During complicated negotiations many items may be discussed simultaneously. Also, some issues may be raised but not fully addressed before someone raises a separate issue. The leader can provide great assistance by giving periodic status reports, including what has been resolved and the issues being discussed. More important, he or she can map out what still needs to be discussed. In essence this mapping establishes a new agenda for the remainder of the negotiation session.

Once again, cultural differences are important in negotiations. For example, most Canadians and Americans are uncomfortable with silence; most Japanese, on the other hand, are much more comfortable with extended periods of silence. North Americans negotiating with Japanese businesspeople usually find this silence stressful. Negotiators must prepare themselves for such probabilities and learn ways to reduce stress and cope in this situation.

If negotiations require an interpreter, carefully select someone well qualified for the job. And don't expect everything you say to be translated correctly. Here are some items that have been translated into English from another language (so you can get a sense of the problem of translation errors):[3]

- In a family-style restaurant in Hong Kong: Come broil yourself at your own table.
- From an Italian hotel in the mountains: Standing among the savage scenery, the hotel offers stupendous revelations. There is a French window in every room. We offer commodious chambers, with balcony imminent to a romantic gorge. We hope you want to drop in. In the close village you can buy jolly memorials for when you pass away.
- In a Moscow newspaper under the heading "INTERPRETING": Let us you letter of business translation do. Every people in our staffing know English like the hand of their back. Up to the minute wise-street phrases, don't you know, old boy!

- In a Sarajevo hotel: Guests should announce abandonment of their rooms before 12 o'clock, emptying the rooms at the latest until 14 o'clock for the use of the room before 5 at the arrival or after the 16 o'clock at the departure will be billed as one more night.

Finally, keep in mind that during negotiations, people need to save **face**, which is the desire for a positive identity or self-concept. Of course not all people strive for the same face (some want to appear "cool," some "macho," some "crass," and so on). Negotiators will at least try to maintain face and may even use the negotiation session to improve or strengthen this identity.

DEALING WITH WIN-LOSE NEGOTIATORS

Many books have been written and many consultants have grown rich teaching both buyers and sellers strategies for effective negotiating. Unfortunately many of these techniques are designed to achieve a win-lose situation. We describe several to illustrate the types of tactics buyers might engage in during negotiations. This knowledge will help the negotiating team defend its position under such attacks.

ethics

Both buyers and sellers occasionally engage in the win-lose strategies described here. However, because we are assuming that sellers will adopt a win-win perspective, this section focuses on how to handle buyers who engage in these techniques. Exhibit 12.7 presents an effective overall strategy for dealing with win-lose negotiators.

Good Guy-Bad Guy Routine

You have probably seen the **good guy-bad guy routine** if you watch police movies or TV shows.[4] A tough police detective interrogating the suspect gets a little rough. The detective uses bright lights and intimidation. After a few minutes a second officer (who has been watching) asks his companion to "go out and get some fresh

Exhibit 12.7
What to Do When the Buyer Turns to Win-Lose Strategies

Detach yourself.	Don't respond right away. Instead give yourself time to think about the issue. Say something like "Hold on, I'm not sure I follow you. Let's go back over what you just said again." Use the time you have gained to rethink your positions and what would be in the best interests of both parties.
Acknowledge their position and then respond.	In using this tool, you are trying to create a favorable climate for your response. You would start off by mentioning that you agree with them by saying something like "Yes, you have a good point there when you said . . ." After agreeing, you then make your point. For example, you might conclude by saying, "and I would like to make sure you continue to have minimal downtime. And for that to happen, you know, we really need to have someone from your firm attend the training." This tool is somewhat similar to the indirect denial and revisit techniques discussed in Chapter 10.
Build them a bridge.	Come up with a solution that incorporates the buyer's suggestion. For example, "building on your idea, what if we . . ." or "I got this idea from something really neat you said at our meeting last Friday." This approach helps the buyer save face.
Warn, but don't threaten.	Sometimes you may have to help a buyer understand the consequences of his or her position. For example, if the buyer indicates that she or he must have a cheaper fabric for the furniture in an office building, you can say, "I know how important the choice of fabric is to your firm's image, but if you choose that fabric, you won't achieve the image you're really looking for. How much will that cost you in lost clients who might not get a sense that you are very successful?" A warning is not the same thing as a threat. A threat is what will happen if you don't get *your way;* a warning is what will happen if they do get *their* way.

air." While the tough detective (the "bad guy") is outside, the other detective (the "good guy") apologizes for his partner's actions. The good guy goes on to advise the crook to confess now and receive better treatment rather than wait and have the bad guy harass him or her some more. The routine works on the "hurt and rescue" principle: The bad guy offers discomfort and tension, and then the good guy offers escape and a way to bring closure to the situation.

Negotiators often try the same routine. One member of the buyer team (the bad guy) makes all sorts of outlandish statements and requests:

> Look, we've got to buy these for no more than $15 each, and we must have credit terms of 2/10, net 60. After all the business we've given you in the past, I can't believe you won't agree to those terms!

Then another member of the buyer team (the good guy) takes over and appears to offer a win-win solution by presenting a lower demand:

> Hang on, Jack. These are our friends. Sure, we've given them a lot of business, but remember they've been good to us as well! I believe we should let them make a decent profit, so $15.50 would be more reasonable.

According to theory, the sellers are so relieved to find a friend that they jump on the good guy's suggestion.

As an effective defense against such tactics, the selling team must know its position clearly and not let the buyer's strategy weaken it. Obviously the selling team needs the ability to spot a good guy–bad guy tactic. A good response might be the following:

> We understand your concern. But based on all the facts of the situation, we still feel our proposal is a fair one for all parties involved.

Lowballing

You may also have experienced **lowballing**, which occurs when one party intentionally underestimates or understates a cost.[5] Car dealers have used it for years. The salesperson says, "This car sells for $29,613." After you agree to purchase it, what happens? "Oh, I forgot to tell you that we have to charge you for dealer prep and destination charges, as well as an undercoating already applied to the car. So let's see, the total comes to $31,947. Gee, I'm sorry I didn't mention those expenses before!" Most people go ahead and buy. Why? They have already verbally committed themselves and do not want to go against their agreement. Also, they do not want to start the search process again.

The technique is also used in buyer–seller negotiations in industrial situations. For example, after the sellers have signed a final agreement with the buyer team, one of the buyer team members says, "Oh, I forgot to mention that all of our new contracts must specify FOB destination, and the seller must assume all shipping insurance expenses."

The best response to lowballing is just to say no. Remind the buyer team that the agreement has been finalized. The threat of lowballing underscores the importance of getting signatures on contracts and agreements as soon as possible. If the buyers insist on the new items, the selling team will simply be forced to reopen the negotiations. (Try this tactic on car dealers too!)

A variation of lowballing, **nibbling**, is a small extra, or add-on, the buyer requests after the deal has been closed. Compared to lowballing, a nibble is a much smaller request. For example, one of the buyers may state, "Say, could you give us a one-time 5 percent discount on our first order? That would sure make our boss happy and make us look like we negotiated hard for her." Nibbling often works because the request is so small compared to the entire agreement.

If a member of the buying team engages in an emotional outburst tactic, the seller should never respond in like fashion.

©George Doyle/Stockbyte/Getty Images RF

The selling team's response to the nibble depends on the situation. It may be advantageous to go ahead and grant a truly small request that could be easily met. On the other hand, if the buyer team uses nibbling often, granting these requests may need to be restricted. Again, the best strategy is to agree on the seller's position before the meeting begins and set guidelines for potential nibbles. Often the seller grants a nibble only if the buyer agrees to some small concession in return.

Emotional Outbursts

How do you react when a close friend suddenly starts crying, gets angry, or looks very sad? Most of us think, What have I done to cause this? We tend to feel guilty, become uneasy, and try to find a way to make the person stop crying. That is simply human nature.

Occasionally buyer teams will appeal to your human nature by engaging in an **emotional outburst tactic**. For example, one of the buyers may look directly at you, shake his or her head sadly, slowly look down, and say softly,

> I can't believe it's come to this. You know we can't afford that price. And we've been good partners all these years. I don't know what to say.

This statement is followed by complete silence among the entire buyer team. Members hope you will feel uncomfortable and give in to their demands. In an extreme case one or more buyers would actually walk out of the room or begin to shout or cry.

The selling team, once again, needs to recognize this behavior as the technique it is. Assuming no logical reason exists for the outburst, the negotiators should respond with a gentle but firm reminder of the merits of the offer and attempt to move the buyer group back into a win-win negotiating frame of mind.

Budget Limitation Tactic

In the **budget limitation tactic**, also called a **budget bogey**, the buyer team states something like the following:

> The proposal looks great. We need every facet of the program you are proposing in order for it to work in our business. But our budget allows us only $250,000 total, including all costs. You'll have to come down from $300,000 to that number, or I'm afraid we can't afford it.

This statement may be absolutely true. If so, at least you know what you have to work with. Of course claims of budget ceilings are sometimes just a ploy to try to get a lower price.

The best defense against budget limitations is to do your homework before going into the negotiation session. Learn as much as you can about budgets and maximums allowed. Have alternative programs or proposals ready that incorporate cost reduction measures. After being told of a budget limitation during the negotiation session, probe to make sure that the claim is valid. Check the possibility of splitting the cost of the proposal over several fiscal years. Probe to find out whether the buyer would be willing to accept more risk for a lower price or to have some of the installation work done by the buyer's staff. See if there are nonprice changes that might have more value to the buyer, as Building Partnerships 12.1 describes. You can also help forestall this tactic by working closely with the buyer before the negotiation meeting, providing reasonable ballpark estimates of the cost of the proposal.

BUILDING Partnerships 12.1

HOW TO NEGOTIATE WITHOUT PRICE CHANGES

I sell ticket packages for a major sports entity in the United States. In my professional sports team we have, as much as possible, chosen to not negotiate surrounding price when attempting to sell ticket contracts. In essence we stick with our price and firms can either agree to that or they can choose a different opportunity. However, this does not mean other factors are not negotiable. Aspects that are negotiable include how we can construct the sale to happen and what particular benefits or extra incentives we can offer. What makes certain negotiations possible is asking probing questions on the front end to determine what is important to that particular customer and understanding why the customer is electing to purchase our ticket packages in the first place.

In our industry, relationships with customers take you only so far. Take, for example, a business customer who is a fan of our team and is interested in purchasing a full season ticket plan, but is uncertain about the number of games or price. In this case, I would most likely ask, "Who is your favorite player?" or "Have you ever had the chance to be on a Major League Baseball field prior to a game?" I would then say, "What if I told you I could get you on the field before the game to stand next to a player on the team, i.e., Clayton Kershaw, during the National Anthem?" Something as simple and sincere as that costs my organization and me nothing, but makes a major sale possible to achieve. Aspects such as this are something I can easily negotiate.

The same practice can be done for a company looking for a "wow" factor to influence clients to make upsell or cross-sell opportunities possible. Negotiating incentives like batting practice passes or an autographed jersey to give to a top client can make all the difference in turning $2 to 3K of tickets sales into $15 to 20K of tickets. Negotiation is not and should never be limited to price only, since other factors are pertinent to a sale and negotiation provides the opportunity to discuss various offerings.

Another way my department negotiates is by simply inquiring, "How can we make this sale happen today?," when talking about purchasing some product of ours. Throwing out ideas like jerseys, batter's practice field passes, and so on sometimes isn't the best way to negotiate, as it is not something they may view as important. To successfully negotiate a win-win deal it could be something as little as seeking a ticket upgrade for a game, which is less expensive for us than getting an autographed jersey. On the other side, individuals may say, "I want to meet a player," which often just is not possible, but it still gives people in my position a benchmark of where negotiations should start. From there, I can suggest, "Well I can't do that, but I could get you batting practice passes for a game or upgrade to this unique package," and we can negotiate back and forth until we reach something agreeable and satisfactory for both parties.

The most ineffective salesperson behavior I see is not asking enough questions. I think most salespeople have been there when they are meeting with a big company or a super wealthy consumer, where I basically think, "You have a lot of money. You should spend a lot of money with me because you have it." It goes back to assessing what they need, and what their goals and challenges are. Remember that your goal in negotiating is to achieve a win-win for both parties.

Source: Anonymous, names changed as requested.

Browbeating

Sometimes buyers will attempt to alter the selling team's enthusiasm and self-respect by **browbeating** them. One buyer might make a comment like the following:

> Say, I've been reading some pretty unflattering things about your company in *The Wall Street Journal* lately. Seems like you can't keep your unions happy or your nonunion employees from organizing. It must be tough to get out of bed and go to work every day, huh?

If the selling team feels less secure and slightly inferior after such a comment, the tactic was successful.

You should not let browbeating comments influence you or your proposal. That's easier said than done, of course. Presumably you were able to identify in prenegotiation meetings that this buyer had this type of personality. If so, you could prepare by simply telling yourself that browbeating will occur but you will not let it affect your decisions. If you can make it through one such comment, buyers usually will not offer any more because they can see that browbeating will not help them achieve their goals.

One response to such a statement would be to practice **negotiation jujitsu**.[6] In negotiation jujitsu the salesperson steps away from the opponent's attack, rather than attacking his or her position, and then directs the opponent back to the issues being discussed. Instead of striking back, the seller breaks the win-lose attempt by not reacting negatively. The seller may even ask for clarification, advice, or criticism, but will not try to defend her ideas. The goal in all of this is to calm the buyer, giving the person a chance to release anger or frustration and make his or her position more clear while helping the seller maintain control of her own emotions. For example, the salesperson may say,

> I hear what you're saying. We're concerned about our employees and are working to resolve all problems as quickly as we can. If you have any ideas that would help us in this regard, we'd sure like to hear them. . . . Now, we were discussing price . . .

Other Win-Lose Tactics

Of course many other tactics are used, and it is beyond the purpose of this book to list them all. However, here are a few more:

- Limited authority: "Sorry, but we don't have the authority to make that decision here today." Solution: Verify the truth of that statement. If true, get the person with authority to the table.
- **Red herring** (bringing up a minor point first to distract the other side from considering the main issue): "We're going to have to have Saturday delivery in our agreement." Solution: Ask to set it aside temporarily until more substantive issues are dealt with.
- **Trial balloon** (floating an idea without really offering it as a concession or agreement; the goal is just to get information): "So have you considered going to a deferred shipping plan?" Solution: Don't just supply the information; ask "Well, if we did, what would your offer be?"
- Total silence by the buyer after you make an offer (most salespeople are uncomfortable with silence and will start offering some solution to break the buyer's silence): [Buyers just sit there and stare at the sellers.] Solution: Restate your offer, but don't offer new suggestions until they have acted on what you suggested. Just repeat your terms.

MAKING CONCESSIONS

One of the most important activities in any negotiation is the granting and receiving of concessions from the other party. One party makes a **concession** when it agrees to change a position in some fashion. For example, if your opening price position was $500, you would be granting a concession if you agreed to lower the price to $450.

Based on many successful negotiations in a wide range of situations, a number of guidelines have been formulated to make concessions effectively:

1. Never make concessions until you know all of the buyer's demands and opening position. Use probing to help reveal these.
2. Never make a concession unless you get one in return and don't feel guilty about receiving a concession.

3. Concessions should gradually decrease in size. At first you may be willing to offer "normal size" concessions. As time goes on, however, you should make much smaller ones; for example, use a pattern like the following: 300-245-220-205-201-200. This approach helps the prospect see that you are approaching your target position and are becoming much less willing to concede.
4. If a requested concession does not meet your objectives, don't be afraid to simply say, "No. I'm sorry, but I just can't do that."
5. All concessions you offer are tentative until the final agreement is reached and signed. Remember that you may have to take back one of your concessions if the situation changes.
6. Be confident and secure in your position and don't give concessions carelessly. If you don't follow this advice, your buyers may lose respect for your negotiating and business skills. Everyone wants to conduct business with someone who is sharp and who will be in business in the future. Don't give the impression that you are not and will not.
7. Don't accept the buyer's first attempt at a concession. Chances are the buyer has built in some leeway and is simply testing the water.
8. Help the buyer to see the value of any concessions you agree to. Don't assume the buyer will understand the total magnitude of your "generosity."
9. Start the negotiation without preconceived notions. Even though the buyers may have demanded certain concessions in the past, they may not do so in this negotiation meeting.
10. If, after making a concession, you realize you made some sort of mistake, tell the buyer and begin negotiating that issue again. For example, if you made a concession of delivery every two weeks instead of every four weeks but then realize that your fleet of trucks cannot make that route every two weeks, put the issue back on the table for renegotiation.
11. Don't automatically agree to a "let's just split the difference" offer by the buyers. Check out the offer to see how it compares to your target position.
12. If the customer says, "Tell us what your best price is, and we'll tell you whether we are interested," remain noncommittal. Respond, "In most cases, a price of $*X* is the best we can do. However, if you want to make a proposal, we'll see what we can do."[7]
13. Know when to stop. Don't keep trying to get more, even if you can.
14. Use silence effectively. Studies have shown cultural differences in the negotiator's ability to use silence. For example, Brazilians make more initial concessions (use less silence early) than North Americans, who make more than the Japanese.
15. Plan the session well. Know your **best alternative to a negotiated agreement (BATNA)**. What will be the result if you don't come to agreement? This is the standard or guide against which to evaluate the agreement you are trying to achieve. Sometimes it just makes sense to not come to an agreement rather than come to an agreement that makes the seller's team worse off. This concept is sometimes called **consequences of no agreement (CNA)**.

The granting and receiving of concessions is often very complex and can result in the negotiations taking months or years to complete. Setting the proper environment early in the meeting puts you well on the way to a successful negotiation. Remember to develop an agenda and be aware of win-lose strategies that buyers may use. Offer concessions strategically.

RECAP OF A SUCCESSFUL NEGOTIATION MEETING

This chapter discussed win-win and win-lose negotiation sessions. Seasoned veterans will note that in some situations, the session could more accurately be classified as **win-win not yet negotiating**. In win-win not yet negotiating, the buying team achieves its goals while the selling team doesn't. However, the sellers expect to achieve their goals in the near future, thanks to the results of that negotiation session.

When the session is over, be sure to get any negotiated agreements in writing. If no formal contract is possible, at least summarize the agreements reached. In most cases, legal staff will actually create the agreement. They will include a **Force Majeure clause**, which shields the selling company from the impact of events beyond their control such as acts of God (fires, explosions, earthquakes, drought, tidal waves and floods), wars, rebellions, riots, terrorism, and nuclear contamination.[8] Other clauses that firms add to the contract include triggers that change the terms of the contract like changes in labor costs, exchange rate changes, raw material price changes, and inflation changes. Finally, contracts usually include limits of liability for product failure (like only replacing the defective part we sold, but not the labor to replace it, and not paying the cost of the complete product that might have been damaged by my part's defect), and environmental impacts (like an oil spill that occurs because of a faulty part we sold).

thinking it through

How can the use of information technology help keep track of issues during a negotiation session and ensure that all agreements reached during a negotiation session are included in the final written agreement?

Don't forget to do postnegotiation evaluation and learn from your mistakes. Studies have shown that more cooperation exists if both sides expect future interactions.[9] Keep in mind that your goal is to develop a long-term partnership with your buyer (but this needs to be more than just lip service, as From the Buyer's Seat 12.1 illustrates). This process can be aided by being levelheaded, courteous, and, above all, honest. Also, do not try to get every concession possible out of your buyer. If you push too hard or too long, the buyer will get irritated and may even walk out. Never lose out on an agreement by being too greedy. Remember your goal: to reach a win-win settlement.

SELLING YOURSELF

Whether you realize it or not, you have been in negotiations your entire life. Think about the times you have discussed curfew with your parents, negotiated wages for a summer job, or bartered for your first car you picked up from the used car lot down the street. Some people love the thrill of creating a deal; others want to avoid the confrontation at all costs. Wherever you stand in that spectrum, the awareness of the mechanics of a negotiation will lead you to become a better and more consistent negotiator.

Even if you do not plan on entering the sales world anytime soon, the negotiation concepts discussed can help you in all aspects of life and set you apart from others in your organization. For example, you have just graduated college, accepted a new position at a leading manufacturing company in your area in quality control, and are eager to get started with your career. After the initial onboarding, you learn the ropes of your new job inspecting and testing the final product before it is shipped to the customer. A few weeks into the job, and as you get more comfortable with your duties, you have an idea that could potentially create efficiencies within the current manufacturing process and even reduce a workplace safety risk in your position.

From the **BUYER'S SEAT** 12.1

BEWARE SELLERS TOUTING THEIR "PARTNERSHIPS"

I've spent years in a unique position in terms of the sales process: much of the time I'm a sales rep, but I also spend time as a buyer. I managed a multimillion-dollar federal grant that spanned multiple years. During that time, I solicited bids for high-end equipment to be used for educational purposes. I worked extensively with a rep, let's call him Charlie, who worked for a local reseller of such equipment. Charlie continually stressed how his company valued "partnerships." But, to this day I don't understand what that means to him. For Charlie, it seemed to be just a [poor] negotiation tactic.

Case in point: We ordered a line of trainers totaling over $100,000. They're a particularly technical product with countless options, versions, models, and so on. Again, Charlie stressed both his and his company's focus on the "partnership" and that due to this "partnership," he would get us the best pricing and best service. Not only did I negotiate for a better price than his first one (which, according to him was *the* best he could do), but also Charlie sent the wrong products!

When we pressed Charlie to correct his error he said, "Well, you signed off on the order and it says the model name right there. But, since we value your partnership, we can work something out." To be fair, yes, the incorrect model number was stated on the quote. What Charlie refused to acknowledge was the model number varied from the intended product by *one number*. To further support my theory that Charlie does not value a "partnership," I have not heard a single thing from him since my grant funding ended last summer—despite having products that he committed to assembling sitting on my lab floor and questions on software still pending. This won't be the last grant we get, but this will be the last transaction with Charlie!

Source: Anonymous, names changed as requested.

Before strolling into your supervisor's office to convey your partially thought-out idea, think about the concepts involved in the negotiation process. Selling an idea within your organization is the same process as selling a product or service to a customer. First, define what you want to accomplish by speaking to your supervisor about the idea. Your target position might be to implement your idea within the next 90 days. Your minimum position might be to convey your idea thoroughly to your supervisor, regardless if the idea is used or not.

Next, prepare for the meeting by taking the time necessary to fully understand the current process, including how a change might affect other parts of the process as a whole, such as material sourcing or shipping. Refine your "sales pitch" so that the drawbacks of the current process and the benefits of the change are easily conveyed. Think about any hangups your supervisor might have about the idea and find ways around them. In addition, think about the tendencies of your supervisor and what his or her reactions might be. Customizing the "sale" of your idea to the "customer" will produce the best results. During the discussion, your supervisor might bring up some unexpected issues with your plan, so arriving at an idea that your supervisor is happy with might differ from your initial proposal. In the end, even if the idea is not implemented, you have shown your supervisor you are willing to offer ideas to better the company, and are professional in your approach to doing so.

A successful negotiation is a well-planned negotiation. With a little practice, you will be having successful win-win negotiations without even thinking about it. Selling yourself and your ideas is a rewarding process. Arm yourself with the knowledge of how to do so effectively.

Eric LaBelle, Senior National Account Manager, Vista Outdoor. Used with permission.

SUMMARY

This chapter described how to engage in win-win negotiating. It also described how buyers may engage in win-lose negotiating.

Almost anything can be negotiated. The areas of negotiation will depend on the needs of both parties and the extent of disagreement on major issues.

A successful salesperson is not necessarily a good negotiator. Important negotiator traits include patience and endurance, willingness to take risks, a tolerance for ambiguity, the ability to deal with conflict, and the ability to engage in negotiation without worrying that every person present will not be on one's side.

As in regular sales calls, careful planning counts. This step involves choosing the location, setting objectives, and developing and managing the negotiating team. The salesperson does not act alone in these tasks, but instead draws on the full resources of the firm.

Preliminaries are important in sales negotiation sessions. Friendly conversation and small talk can help reduce tensions and establish rapport. Agendas help set boundaries and keep the negotiation on track. Win-lose strategies that buyers use include a good guy-bad guy routine, lowballing, emotional outbursts, budget limitation, browbeating, and other tactics. As much as possible, the salesperson should respond to any win-lose maneuvers calmly and with the intent of bringing the other side back to a win-win stance.

Concessions, by definition, will occur in every negotiation. Many guidelines have been established to help negotiators avoid obvious problems. For example, no concession should be given unless the buyer gives a concession of equal value. Also, any concessions given are not formalized until the written agreement is signed; thus, all concessions are subject to removal if appropriate.

KEY TERMS

accommodating mode 328
adaptive planning 325
agenda 331
ambush negotiating 329
avoiding mode 328
best alternative to a negotiated agreement (BATNA) 337
brainstorming session 325
browbeating 335
budget bogey 334
budget limitation tactic 334
consequences of no agreement (CNA) 337
collaborating mode 329
competing mode 328
compromising mode 328
concession 336
emotional outburst tactic 334
face 332
Force Majeure Clause 338
good guy-bad guy routine 332
lowballing 333
minimum position 324
negotiation 320
negotiation jujitsu 336
nibbling 333
opening position 324
red herring 336
sneak attack 329
target position 324
trial balloon 336
win-lose negotiating 320
win-win negotiating 320
win-win not yet negotiating 338

ETHICS PROBLEMS

1. "If they are going to use win-lose negotiating, I will too. After all, I have to win!" Comment.
2. You have learned in this chapter that some members of the buying team might exhibit the accommodating mode. Are there any ethical ramifications if you know someone on the buying team is in that mode?

QUESTIONS AND PROBLEMS

1. Based on the situation described in From the Buyer's Seat 12.1, assume you are Charlie. Assume you really did mess up in all of the ways described in that story. Now, you really want to make amends and make things right with the buyer. Briefly explain exactly what you would do to mend fences and establish the start of a true partnership.
2. Suppose you're a salesperson of wholesale fresh fruits and vegetables, and you're negotiating with a large regional grocer over the number of deliveries you will make to its stores in a given week. Your maximum is seven times a week, your opening is four times a week, and your target is five times a week. After negotiating for some time, the grocer states, "Look, we're not willing to accept anything less than nine times a week, which includes two deliveries each on Saturday and Sunday, our busiest days." What do you do now?
3. Assume you're a salesperson who is a true collaborator in every sense of the word. Today you're supposed to engage in a negotiation with an important client. It's taken five months to set up this meeting, and your team of four, including your vice president, is assembled and ready to walk into the meeting. You are your team's designated leader. The cell phone of your vice president rings, and it's a relative, telling her that her son was just involved in a massive automobile accident. The vice president decides to leave the meeting and go to the hospital to be with her son. What do you do now?
4. In Sales Technology 12.1, you learned about new cloud-based software that can be used for online negotiations. What are some potential problems of negotiating totally online with a buying team (no face-to-face negotiating)?
5. According to the text, meeting in a neutral location is better than being on the turf of either the buyer or seller. What if the buyer requires that the session be held on its corporate campus?
6. Assume you are going to have your fourth and final job interview next Friday with Microsoft, to become a seller of cloud-based solutions. Knowledgeable friends have told you that because you passed the first two interviews, you will be offered the job during the upcoming interview. Also, you know that Microsoft likes to negotiate with its new hires.
   a. Think about your own needs and desires for your first job (such as salary, expense reimbursement, benefits, geographic location, and promotion cycle).
   b. For each need and desire listed, establish your target position, opening position, and minimum position.
   c. Microsoft has probably also developed positions for each of your needs and desires. Describe how you could discover these positions before next Friday's meeting.
7. Jillian Anderson, a salesperson for Hershey, is preparing for an important negotiation session with Kroger, a large national retail grocery chain, regarding an upcoming promotional campaign. Her boss has strongly suggested that he attend the meeting with her. The problem is that her boss is not a good negotiator: he tends to be moody, is hard to predict, and tries to resolve conflict by changing the subject. What should Jillian do?
8. "You are the worst possible person to have to negotiate for yourself. You care too much about the outcome. Always let someone else negotiate for you." State your reaction to this statement. What implications does it have in industrial sales negotiations?
9. During negotiation, buyers make all kinds of statements. What would be your response to the following, assuming each occurred early in the meeting?
   a. We refuse to pay more than $1,500 each. You owe us that price. Take it or leave it!
   b. For all the business we've given you over the years, I hope you're going to take care of us in this negotiation. I hope you remember how good of a customer we've been.
   c. Nothing is final until our lawyers say so.
   d. One of our important buyers can't make it here today. Sorry. But let's go ahead and see what progress we can make.
   e. Tell you what, we need free delivery. Period. Can you do that?
10. You come to the meeting with an agenda. But the buying team also comes with an agenda, and it's very different from yours, in terms of the order of negotiation of the various issues. What do you do now?

CASE PROBLEMS

case 12.1

DoubleTree Hotels

DoubleTree has more than 300 hotels in 23 different countries. The chain is owned by Hilton and strives to create what it terms CARE (Create A Rewarding Experience) for all of its guests. The CARE system starts with a warm chocolate chip cookie to welcome each guest. That is followed with stylish guest rooms, each including the Sweet Dreams® by DoubleTree Sleep Experience. Most guest rooms offer the higher-quality CITRON bath products by Crabtree & Evelyn. DoubleTree also offers Fitness Rooms for its guests.

Julie, a salesperson for Micros, was attempting to negotiate with DoubleTree with regard to Micros's OPERA Reservation System (ORS). ORS, a central reservation system, is a part of an enterprise-wide room inventory management system offered by Micros. ORS has many outstanding features, including the following: It supports multicurrency and multilanguage situations; it lets you set up rate structures for individual properties or groups of properties; it can easily handle complicated situations, such as shared reservations, frequent-flyer, and loyalty program memberships, negotiated rates, and rate discounts; and it conveniently searches for room availability across all of the properties.

Julie met with the DoubleTree buyers on eight different occasions before the formal negotiation meeting. She had created a win–win proposal that she was sure would meet the needs of DoubleTree and Micros. Her boss had even congratulated her on her hard work and the proposed solution. "You're going to get it, I'm sure!" she had said. "And then we can start talking about that raise you've been asking for!"

Everything was going great in the negotiation meeting until Julie was startled to hear Kevin Tarnoski, the key negotiator for DoubleTree, practically shout, "Listen, Julie! I can't believe you're asking that much for this little reservation system! The recession hit all of us in the hospitality industry very hard. Come to think of it, that's probably why you're trying to stick it to us with this price. Knock it off! Lower your price, or we'll go elsewhere!" He then proceeded to tell her how much he was willing to pay to lease her system.

Julie didn't know what to say. The price cut being requested by Kevin was 5 percent less than Micros's minimum price objective.

Questions

1. Evaluate the negotiation meeting to this point. How could Julie have better planned for the meeting?
2. What should Julie do now? Be explicit and give reasons for your answers. Make any necessary assumptions.

Sources: This is a fictitious scenario. Information about DoubleTree came from http://doubletree3.hilton.com/en/about/doubletree/index.html. Information about Micros came from www.micros.com/Solutions/ProductsNZ/OPERAReservationSystemORS.

case 12.2

Identifying Conflict-Handling Modes

Alexis is always looking to find a quick and fair solution to any conflicting situation. On more than one occasion she's suggested that "we just split the difference." To be honest, she really doesn't like conflict much at all.

Sofia is a very assertive person and isn't afraid to confront people in order to get her way. No one has ever called her "cooperative," although some like to have her on their team because they know they will probably get much more than their fair share in any dispute!

Ibrahim is a friendly, easygoing person whom everyone likes to be around. It's not uncommon for him to share things, even if it leaves him without enough for his own needs. In competitions he doesn't try to win. Instead he is always offering hopeful and encouraging comments to his competitors. In negotiations he can often be found to be a vocal advocate for the other side.

No one knows whom Alastair voted for in the last election, because he doesn't want to tell others for fear they might not like him. He doesn't assert himself in social situations. If someone suggests that a group he belongs to meet and talk about problems they are having, he won't say much. Instead he just won't show up to the meeting, finding some excuse to be somewhere else at that time.

Questions

1. Based on the information provided, what is the conflict-handling mode of each person?
2. What conflict-handling mode is not illustrated in the examples provided? Describe what that person is generally like.

ROLE PLAY CASE

Divide up into pairs; one person will serve as a buyer and the other as a Gartner salesperson. The buyer is the CIO for Logis. Logis is an international carrier that does overnight express package delivery, package delivery, and international shipping. It can ship anything anywhere.

Logis was a privately held company founded in 1995 to serve industrial service parts manufacturers, and blossomed into a full service company. The founder, though, became ill about 5 years ago and the company suffered. Recently, it was sold to a private investment company, which is going to make significant investments in the IT infrastructure. A CIO was brought in from another company owned by the same private investment company to build this new infrastructure. This CIO has worked with Gartner in the past, with good results.

As a rep or as a buyer, take a few minutes to determine your opening and target positions on such factors as price, training, service, and anything else you can think of. The buyer may also need to sketch out some key needs, which should be worked into opening positions. Given that the buyer and seller have worked together in the past, you can share a general idea of needs before you start. Both of you can use information about Gartner found in the role play section at the end of the book or on the Gartner Web site to determine your positions and negotiating strategies. In your planning, include the use of a win-lose tactic, but be willing to move back to win-win if the other person responds appropriately. No additional information will be provided by the instructor.

Note: For background information about these role plays, please see Chapter 1.

To the instructor: Additional information that will help you with this exercise is available in the Instructor's Manual.

ADDITIONAL REFERENCES

Calin-Ionel, Denes, and Valentin Grecu. *Essentials of Business Communication and Negotiation.* Saarbrücken, Germany: LAP LAMBERT Academic Publishing, 2016.

Chicksand, Daniel. "Partnerships: The Role That Power Plays in Shaping Collaborative Buyer–Supplier Exchanges." *Industrial Marketing Management* 48 (2015), pp. 121–39.

Gates, Steve. *The Negotiation Book: Your Definitive Guide to Successful Negotiating.* Hoboken, NJ: Wiley, 2016.

Holden, Reed K. *Negotiating with Backbone: Eight Sales Strategies to Defend Your Price and Value.* Old Tappan, NJ: Pearson Education, 2016.

Huemer, Lars. "Creating Cooperative Advantage: The Roles of Identification, Trust, and Time." *Industrial Marketing Management* 43, no. 4 (2014), pp. 564–72.

Schmitz, Tobias, Bastian Schweiger, and Jost Daft. "The Emergence of Dependence and Lock-In Effects in Buyer-Supplier Relationships–A Buyer Perspective." *Industrial Marketing Management* 55 (2016), pp. 22–34.

Shapiro, Daniel. *Negotiating the Nonnegotiable: How to Resolve Your Most Emotionally Charged Conflicts.* London: Penguin Books, 2017.

The Partnership Process

PART 2

©Thomas Barwick/Getty Images RF

chapter 13

BUILDING PARTNERING RELATIONSHIPS

SOME QUESTIONS ANSWERED IN THIS CHAPTER ARE

- What different types of relationships exist between buyers and sellers?
- When is each type of relationship appropriate?
- What are the characteristics of successful partnerships?
- What are the benefits and risks in partnering relationships?
- How do relationships develop over time?
- What are the responsibilities of salespeople in partnerships?

PROFILE

"Transforming a customer's need into a solution and seeing the benefits that come along with it for both parties is my motivation."

Ashley McNabb, AdAdapted Inc.

Courtesy of Ashley McNabb

PROFILE As a recent college graduate, I never thought sales was the job for me. I found myself listening to all the negative connotation that lingered around the word *sales*, but what I failed to realize was how rewarding a position in sales can really be. My current position as a sales consultant at AdAdapted Inc. has shown me the true side of sales and has taught me many skills I wouldn't have picked up so quickly in any other business-related position, my favorite being *customer relationship marketing.*

Customer relationship marketing, or relationship marketing, is creating a relationship between you and the customer that best fits the customer's needs. As you can imagine, there are many factors that go into building this relationship, and not all factors work the same with every customer. Just starting out as a sales consultant, I was faced with many different clients but was trained with only one sales pitch. I quickly realized that there was no universal sales pitch that would work with every client we had the opportunity to get on the phone with. This realization was when I began focusing on the client's needs and communicating to *listen*, not just give my 15-minute spiel in hopes of adding more digits to my paycheck.

Communication is one of the key factors to building and maintaining a successful relationship. When I am on the phone with new clients I like to first get an idea of who they are, their role in the company, what drives their company, and their needs and goals. This information helps me understand my customers and then decide how (or if) my company can help them. I tailor my message in a way that fits their needs and can be easily understood. When clients can sense that you are genuinely customer oriented, or put their needs first, they are more likely to trust you and pursue a relationship with you.

As much as I would like to say that sales is all about happy, successful relationships, there are times when this is not so. In my current position, I have experienced clients who have reached the commitment phase and then terminated the relationship; clients who have made it to the exploration phase and realized they weren't ready for what we had to offer; and I have even had clients who never moved past the awareness stage. There will be times when a customer isn't the right fit. Instead of trying to force a sale, especially when you know it will be no gain to the customer, be honest with them and end the interaction on good terms. Parting on good terms boosts your likability and rapport, potentially leading to future relationships down the road.

In business, and even in life, failure is inevitable. Of course, no one likes to be turned down or criticized, but in sales you learn to adapt to these unwanted outcomes. My failures in landing the deal with Johnson & Johnson, or locking in Dan Smith as a client (that super important CEO who would have made our profits go off the charts), or even the clients I lost at the various stages of relationships have taught me not to get down on myself and give up, but to persevere and change and grow. From these failures, I learned what needed to be improved and began to think more strategically about how I can create these long-term customer relationships.

Something I find intriguing about working in sales is the ambiguity of what the next client may bring. This uncertainty challenges me to always perform at the best of my ability and to really focus on understanding the customer, something I was unaware I had such a passion for. In taking on this sales role, I have learned a thing or two about myself. I have a very big heart for helping others. Transforming a customer's need into a solution and seeing the benefits that come along with it for both parties is my motivation. I am people oriented, so being able to understand someone on an intellectual level, as well as an emotional one, and then developing a relationship is something I find very rewarding. These are characteristics that all successful salespeople should carry and use to defy the standards of us being selfish or unkind.

Although the main focus in this chapter is building relationships between buyer and seller, internal relationships within your own company are just as important. With a big part of my job as a sales consultant consisting of maintaining current customer relationships and developing new ones, I also spend some of my time understanding my company as a whole and how working as a team is required in order to succeed. Without internal relationships, there is a lack of communication, dependability, knowledge, and motivation and salespeople couldn't deliver on promises to clients. If you can't put trust in each other, how do you expect customers to have trust in you?

Being new to the professional world can be scary. There are so many different job opportunities. What if I pick the wrong one? My advice is you won't. Even if you find yourself in a position that you don't like, building those internal relationships and external connections can go a long way and will be worth the temporary discomfort. If you are ever faced with an opportunity to work in sales, take it. Although you may not choose to stay in sales forever, you will learn that communicating to listen is much more effective than communicating to talk. You will learn that no matter how technologically advanced the world gets, human interaction will always be needed. Finally, you will learn that relationship building is important in every aspect of life.

Visit our Web site at: http://adadapted.com.

Ashley McNabb, sales consultant, AdAdapted Inc. Used with permission.

THE VALUE OF CUSTOMERS

Many people believe the emphasis in selling is on getting the initial sale. For most salespeople, however, sales increases from one year to the next are due to increasing the revenue from existing accounts, not just from getting new accounts. Even in industries where purchase decisions are made infrequently, salespeople gain a competitive advantage by maintaining strong relationships with their customers. Eventually, when buying decisions need to be made, those customers look to people they know and trust. Ashley McNabb, for example, discussed in the opening profile the importance of being trustworthy because people want to buy from people they know and trust.

Customers are, of course, the primary revenue source for companies. Some customers are worth more in terms of revenue than some salespeople recognize. For example, a car salesperson may think only of the immediate sale, but each customer is potentially worth hundreds of thousands of dollars in revenue over the salesperson's lifetime. Exhibit 13.1 illustrates the value of a small attorney's office over a 20-year period for just a few salespeople. For example, if an office equipment/supply salesperson sold all the copiers and office supplies needed during that 20-year period, total revenue would be almost $100,000! This is an example of **customer lifetime value (CLV)**, which is the combined total of all future sales

Exhibit 13.1
Selected Expenses for a Small Law Firm over a 20-Year Period

Item	Cost	Total
Computers	7 @ $2,000	$14,000
Printer/scanner/copier	7 @ $2,000	14,000
Copier/printer supplies	$70 per month	16,800
Telephone systems	3 @ $1,000	3,000
Other office supplies	$100 per month	24,000
Office furniture	$5,000	5,000
Total over 20 years		$76,800

(typically discounted back into current dollars). If the salesperson thinks in terms of just one sale, however, the customer is worth no more than $5,000.

thinking it through

How much do you spend on clothing each month? Now multiply that figure by 12. Assuming that you shop in the same places during the four years you will be in college, multiply that result by 4. The total is the amount of your clothing purchases over your college career. Does anyone treat you like a $1,000 customer, or are you treated like a $20 customer? What would you expect to be different in how you are treated if the store recognized your true value?

Research shows that successfully retaining customers is important to all companies. Using a consultative customer-oriented sales approach has been shown in several studies to improve both customer retention and firm profitability, even with commodity products.[1] Salespeople are critical to the process of keeping customers. Another study finds that the relationship quality between the salesperson and the buyer is one driver of financial performance. The better the relationship, the better the firm's performance.[2]

We have already discussed the importance of good service in generating referrals and of becoming a trusted member of the community in which your buyers operate so you can acquire more customers (see Chapter 6). The value of satisfied customers is so high that it makes good business sense to build the strongest possible relationships. Some sales experts believe that it takes, on average, seven visits to conclude an initial solo exchange, but only three to achieve the first reorder. Whether it is actually 7 + 3 in your business, or some other ratio, the reality is that the first sale is often merely a test. In fact, many companies now don't celebrate the first sale as much as they celebrate the first reorder! In this chapter we discuss the nature of relationships and the types of relationships that can be built, and we begin to explore how to build those relationships over time. In the next chapter we focus on strategies to build longer-term relationships.

RELATIONSHIPS AND SELLING

Buyers who are attitudinally loyal to Apple and its computers may also be behaviorally loyal, buying products like the iPad when they are introduced.

Many students may have heard of relationship marketing or customer relationship management (CRM) and wonder how these compare with building partnerships. *Relationship marketing* is a term with several meanings, but all reflect companies' attempts to develop stronger relationships with their customers. The premise is that loyal customers buy more, are willing to pay more, influence friends to also buy, and are willing to help develop new products.[3] Building a stronger relationship is accomplished through building loyalty. For example, Southwest Airlines may think of its Rapid Rewards frequent flyer program as the heart of relationship marketing; loyalty is rewarded with points that can be redeemed for free flights. But in professional selling, **relationship marketing** refers to creating the type of relationship that best suits the customer's need, which may or may not require a partnership.

There are two types of loyalty: behavioral and attitudinal.[4] **Behavioral loyalty** refers to the purchase of the same product from the same vendor over time. When someone purchases out of habit, for example, that pattern is behavioral loyalty. Recall that earlier we pointed out that buyers calculate profit by subtracting both price and shopping costs from the benefits received. Buying out of habit can reduce shopping costs and increase profit when past experience can indicate future satisfaction.

Attitudinal loyalty is an emotional attachment to a brand, company, or salesperson. For example, you may prefer Southwest Airlines to any other. That doesn't mean that you fly only Southwest; it's just that you like the company and its values.

Companies prefer buyers who are both attitudinally and behaviorally loyal; moreover, companies want loyal customers who buy regularly and stay customers forever. Companies want to receive as much of a customer's lifetime value, or CLV, as possible. Further, not every customer's CLV is the same. Recall the attorney firm in Exhibit 13.1—not every firm of that size will spend money on equipment the same way. Some firms will need more, others less. Thus, companies want loyal customers who are also bigger spenders. Lower lifetime value customers may not be as important to the company.

Customer lifetime value is influenced by more than just that customer's purchases, though. How much more might that attorney be worth as a customer to an office equipment dealer in terms of referrals, sales to the associates who leave and open their own offices, and additional repeat business if the dealership really kept the attorney as a customer for life? What about the value of a new product idea generated by the attorney? All these elements can add value to the company.

There are entire books written about loyalty; the important element to recognize here is that the emphasis in this book is on building long-term relationships, in part to capture as much CLV as possible. Salespeople with the longer-term view recognize the power of CLV and consider both behavioral and attitudinal loyalty as an objective sell in a different way than if focused only on making the next sale. There are, however, different types of relationships, as we discuss next.

TYPES OF RELATIONSHIPS

Each time a transaction occurs between a buyer and a seller, the buyer and the seller have a relationship. Some relationships may involve many transactions and last for years; others may exist only for the few minutes during which money is exchanged for goods.

This section describes two basic relationship types: market exchanges and partnerships.[5] There are two types of each, summarized in Exhibit 13.2.

MARKET EXCHANGES

A **market exchange** is a transaction between a buyer and a seller in which each party is concerned only about its own benefit. The seller is concerned only with making the sale, the buyer with getting the product at the lowest possible price. Most business transactions are market exchanges, and there are two types: solo exchanges and functional relationships.

Solo Exchanges

Suppose you are driving to the beach for spring break. A warning light on your car's dashboard comes on. You stop at the next gas station, and the service attendant says your car needs a new alternator. The alternator will cost $650, including

Exhibit 13.2
Types of Relationships between Buyers and Sellers

Factors Involved in the Relationship	Type of Relationship: Solo Market Transaction	Functional Relationship	Relational Partnership	Strategic Partnership
Time horizon	Short term	Long term	Long term	Long term
Concern for other party	Low	Low	Medium	High
Trust	Low	Low	High	High
Investments in the relationship	Low	Low	Low	High
Nature of the relationship	Conflict, bargaining	Cooperation	Accommodation	Coordination
Risk in relationship	Low	Medium	High	High
Potential benefits	Low	Medium	High	High

installation. At this point you might pay the quoted price, bargain with the service attendant for a lower price, or drive to another service station a block away and get a second opinion. After you select a service station, agree on a price, have the alternator replaced, and pay for the service, you have completed a one-shot market exchange. Neither you nor the service station attendant expects to engage in future transactions.

Because the parties in the transaction do not plan on doing business together again, both the buyer and the seller in a **solo exchange** pursue their own self-interests. In this example, you try to pay the lowest price for the alternator, and the service station tries to charge the highest price for it. The service station is not concerned about your welfare, just as you are not concerned about the service station's welfare. Or perhaps more accurately, the service station calculates profit from the relationship immediately after the transaction. The issue is not an ethical one; there is no intent to maliciously hurt the other party. At the same time, however, there is no future consideration to worry about in terms of whether the transaction was worthwhile.

Functional Relationships

Functional relationships are long-term market exchanges characterized by behavioral loyalty; the buyer purchases the same product out of habit or routine. Buyers in this type of relationship tend to have the same orientation as they do in solo exchanges, but the previous purchase influences the next purchase. As long as the buyer is satisfied and the product is available at a reasonable price and does what it is supposed to do, the buyer will continue to buy.

Sometimes firms buy from the same supplier for a long time because it is easier than searching for a new supplier every time they need an item. In functional relationships (as in any long-term buyer–seller relationship), customer satisfaction is very important. Without customer satisfaction, behavioral loyalty cannot develop. **Customer satisfaction** occurs when the buyer's expectations are met and needs are fulfilled (we discuss this in detail later in this chapter).[6] When satisfied, a buyer is less likely to shop around for the next purchase because less hassle means more value to the buyer.

For example, a buyer for your school purchases janitorial supplies—paper towels, soap, cleanser, and mops—for the cleaning crew. However, the buyer and the janitorial supply distributor have little interest in working closely together. The relationship between the buyer and the distributor's salesperson is not critical to the school's success as an educational institution. The buyer can decide to deal with another distributor if service is poor, the product fails to perform, or another distributor works harder to get the business–in other words, if the buyer becomes dissatisfied.

Another example is your grocery store. You shop there because it is convenient both in terms of how close it is to your home and in terms of how well you know the store and can find what you want easily. You go back, but you'd consider going elsewhere for a special sale or to find something you want. A relationship, if you can call it that, is simply functional: As long as they have what you want at a competitive price, you'll keep shopping there.

Even in these long-term market exchanges, both parties are interested primarily in their own profits and are unconcerned about the welfare of the other party. In market exchanges price may be the critical decision factor. It serves as a rapid means of communicating the basis for the exchange. Basically the buyer and the salesperson in a market exchange are always negotiating over how to "split up the pie," or how to make more in the transaction. Each calculates profit at the end of each transaction or at least on a frequent basis, usually reflective of the billing cycle. If the janitorial supply company invoices the university monthly, for example, then each side will calculate profit monthly. If the school's buyer gets an invoice that seems too large, it may cause the buyer to shop around next time because there was insufficient "profit" or value for the buyer.

On the positive side, market exchanges offer buyers and sellers a lot of flexibility. Buyers and sellers are not locked into a continuing relationship, thus buyers can switch from one supplier to another to make the best possible deal. However, these minimal relationships do not work well when buyers and sellers have an opportunity to increase the size of the pie by developing products and services tailored to their needs. These more complex transactions cannot be conducted solely on the basis of price. High levels of trust and commitment are needed to manage these types of relationships because buyers and sellers need to share sensitive information.[7]

PARTNERSHIPS

There are two types of partnerships: relational and strategic. In a partnership both parties are concerned about each other's welfare and about developing a **win-win relationship**. By working together, both parties benefit because the size of the pie increases.

Relational Partnerships

Many times the buyer and the salesperson have a close personal relationship that allows them to communicate effectively. These friendships create a cooperative climate between the salesperson and the customer. When both partners feel safe and stable in the relationship, open and honest communication takes place. Salesperson and buyer work together to solve important problems. The partners are not concerned about small details because they trust each other enough to know these will be worked out. These types of partnerships are not necessarily strategic to either organization, although they may be to the individuals involved, and are called **relational partnerships**.

How would you shop for a new car? If you knew someone in the car business, you'd probably go there first in order to work with someone you know and could trust. Now flip that relationship: If you bought cars regularly, you might want to build a friendship with a dealer's salesperson in order to rely on that friendship for protection against overly aggressive negotiating and other negative factors you

BUILDING Partnerships 13.1

TRUST TAKES TIME

Christina Harrod is a medical device sales representative at Applied Medical, selling to surgeons. Like many people who go into sales, she describes herself as a people person. "My job is most enjoyable during those critical times when I am building *true* relationships with my customers. Getting to know their families, why they chose their careers, the stresses of their day, and their current goals are all huge motivators to me. And here is the real kicker—I genuinely do care!"

As much as she enjoys building relationships with her customers, not all contacts are interested in building relationships beyond the basic transactions at the start. She's learned she has to earn their trust.

In addition, she's found that she has to adapt her sales approach to two completely different types of customers. "The first is the surgeon, who generally has very little time to talk during the day, let alone allowing a sales representative to build a professional friendship. The second customer group is hospital administrators. They usually have time to talk, listen to more complete product demonstrations, and can better communicate their own goals with sales representatives."

The challenge is that while it is easier to build a relationship with an administrator, often it is the surgeon who understands the true value of what she offers. "I find that the people with whom I often have a naturally easier time building relationships are also those who are willing to ultimately help me with the more difficult 'driver'-style customers. Even the customers who are initially the most difficult are frequently the ones who eventually warm up and exhibit significant trust. That is an ever-fascinating process."

Initially, she was discouraged that customers didn't recognize her ability to provide solutions. She was afraid that this reluctance would lead to failure to make her sales goals. "My colleagues and supervisors would point out that the business would come in time but that my customers first needed to see that they could trust me to provide a value-added solution. I continually called on account after account until some finally agreed that they needed something from me. Once they saw that I accomplished various tasks for them swiftly and correctly, I was given growing levels of trust. Throughout that process, I began a special niche relationship with my hard-to-reach driver customers. I find that these particular people have gone on to trust that I am able to truly help them meet or exceed their needs."

might be concerned about. You'd feel confident you were getting a good deal from a friend, and you'd be happy that she or he could make a sale.

The benefits of a relational partnership go beyond simple increased short-term profits. Although both partners are striving to make money in the relationship, they are also trying to build a working relationship that will last a long time. Kevin Clonch, account executive for Total Quality Logistics, says, "I have built long-lasting customer relationships, but I can honestly call many of my customers very good friends due to the relationships that we have built throughout the years." While Clonch sells a commodity (shipping services), Christina Harrod sells medical devices, and she has also found that relational partnerships take time, as she describes in Building Partnerships 13.1.

Relational partnerships can occur between a buyer and seller not only because of personal ties but also because each is important to the other professionally. For example, a trade show program may not be important enough to the organization to demand a strategic partner but is very important to the trade show manager. That manager may seek a relational partnership with a supplier, complete with personal investment of time and departmental resources, rather than a strategic organizational investment and commitment.

In Asian countries, the personal relationship is an important precursor to strategic partnerships. Several studies have found that social bonding and interpersonal commitment are necessary ingredients to any long-term partnership between Asian organizations.[8] In several studies examining relationships between buyers and sellers in China, interpersonal commitment was a precursor to organizational relationships; so without friendship, there was no partnership.[9]

In this chapter we talk about relationships between buyers and sellers, but these concepts also apply to personal relationships. A relational partnership is like a close friendship. In a close friendship you are not concerned with how the pie is split up each day because you are confident that, over the long run, each of you will get a fair share; further, the pie will be bigger because of your friendship. You trust your friend to care about you, and she or he trusts you in return.

Strategic Partnerships

Strategic partnerships are long-term business relationships in which the partner organizations make significant investments to improve the profitability of both parties. In these relationships the partners have gone beyond trusting each other to "putting their money where their mouths are." They take risks to expand the pie and to give the partnership a strategic advantage over other companies.

Strategic partnerships are created for the purpose of uncovering and exploiting joint opportunities. Members of strategic partnerships have a high level of dependence on and trust in each other, share goals and agree on how to accomplish those goals, and show a willingness to take risks, share confidential information, and make significant investments for the sake of the relationship.

One of the oldest strategic partnerships is that between HP and Disney, dating back to 1938, when Disney purchased test equipment for work on the movie *Fantasia*. Since then, the two companies have shared engineering resources to address needs that both have. Disney benefits from early advantages in engineering and HP from gaining customer insight that translates into new products.

Another example is Keyser Group and McDonald's. Think about what has to happen when McDonald's launches a new product–signs have to be changed in 37,000 stores all at the same time. That's Keyser's job: to make sure those signs are properly implemented all over the world, often on the same day. At the same time, Keyser works with McDonald's to test sign designs that help drive sales. Keyser, thanks to its work with McDonald's, has developed expertise in signage that few companies can claim, an expertise that others find valuable. McDonald's has also benefited with sales growth due to signage support. These two organizations have worked and grown together for decades.

Many salespeople are involved in both solo exchanges and functional relationships. Some customers buy once and are never heard from again. Others become loyal as long as everything goes smoothly. A few become friends, but strategic partnerships are rare. Exhibit 13.3 illustrates the differences in the nature of selling in market exchanges and long-term relationships.

Each type of relationship has its pluses and minuses. Companies cannot develop a strategic advantage from a market exchange, but they do get the flexibility to buy products from the supplier with the lowest cost when the order is placed. On the other hand, strategic partnerships create a win-win situation, but the companies are committed to each other and flexibility can be reduced. In the next section we talk about the characteristics of successful relationships–relationships that have the potential to develop into strategic partnerships.

Exhibit 13.3
Selling in Market Exchanges and Long-Term Relationships

Market Exchange Selling Goal: Making a Sale	Long-Term Relationship Selling Goal: Building Trust

Making Contact
• Find someone to listen.
• Make small talk.
• Ingratiate and build rapport.
Closing the Sale
• Deliver a sales pitch to
  • Get the prospect's attention.
  • Create interest.
  • Build desire.
  • Get the prospect to take action.
• Stay alert for closing signals.
• Use trial closes.
• Overcome objections.
• Close early and often.
Following Through
• Reestablish contact.
• Resell self, company, and products.
	Initiating the Relationship
	• Engage in strategic prospecting and qualifying.
	• Gather and study precall information.
	• Identify buying influences.
	• Plan the initial sales call.
	• Demonstrate an understanding of the customer's needs.
	• Identify opportunities to build a relationship.
	• Illustrate the value of a relationship with the customer.
	Developing the Relationship
	• Select an appropriate offering.
	• Customize the relationship.
	• Link the solution to the customer's needs.
	• Discuss customer concerns.
	• Summarize the solution to confirm benefits.
	• Secure commitment.
	Enhancing the Relationship
	• Assess customer satisfaction.
	• Take actions to ensure satisfaction.
	• Maintain open, two-way communication.
	• Expand collaborative involvement.
	• Work to add value and enhance mutual opportunities.

Source: Thomas Ingram, "Relationship Selling: Moving from Rhetoric to Reality," *Mid-American Journal of Business* 11 (1996), p. 6.

thinking it through

As a consumer, it is unlikely that you'll experience a strategic partnership, but you may experience the other relationship types. But put yourself in the place of a business buyer—what happens when the salesperson gets transferred? What are some of the factors that might influence how you answer this question?

MANAGING RELATIONSHIPS AND PARTNERING

Salespeople are usually responsible for determining the appropriate form of relationship and for making sure that their companies develop the appropriate types of relationships with customers. In other words, some customers want and need, a market exchange, others need a functional relationship, and still others need a strategic partnership. As salespeople identify customer needs for product benefits, they also identify needs for relationship benefits and select the appropriate strategy as a result. Salespeople are likely to manage a portfolio of relationships, some of which may be strategic and others functional.[10] With some accounts, a strategic partnership may be called for. With others, it may be a relational partnership or functional relationship. The salesperson must determine which relationship type is appropriate for optimizing the customer's lifetime value.

CHOOSING THE RIGHT RELATIONSHIP

As you can see from the discussion about what makes for a strategic relationship, at least one factor that influences a salesperson's choice of relationship is the type of relationship the customer desires. Becoming a strategic partner requires investment by both parties, and if the customer isn't willing to make that investment, then another type of relationship is called for. Even then, not every customer who wants a strategic partnership should become your strategic partner. Some of the factors to consider are size of the account, access and image in the market, and access to technology.

Size

Large accounts provide greater economies of scale which can often justify lower prices and higher investments. Size of the account, then, is one aspect to consider. But that doesn't mean that one should partner only with the largest accounts. In some cases, larger accounts are not necessarily the most profitable, particularly when the seller's investments are factored in.[11] For example, they may use their size to get better quantity discounts and more favorable terms, which can end up being greater than the savings realized if accounting systems are not good at capturing account-level costs. In other cases smaller accounts provide important benefits that larger accounts cannot, as we will discuss.

Size matters! Most strategic partnerships involve larger customers like Saks 5th Avenue (top) rather than Monsoon (bottom) because their size makes the investment in the partnership worthwhile.

(top): ©McGraw-Hill EducationAndrew Resek, photographer; (bottom): ©Charles Bowman/Alamy Stock Photo RF

Access and Image

A strategic partnership may be called for if an account can provide access to a specific, desired market or can enhance the image of the seller. For example, if you are new to a market you may want to sell at a loss to the most well-known client just to be able to claim you have that business. Your hope is that others will do business with you as a consequence.

You may recall the center-of-influence method from Chapter 6 on prospecting; this method of prospecting involves obtaining leads and referrals from people who are known in the community as experts or leaders. If you can identify these people, a strong relationship with them can be very important to obtaining opportunities to sell to others.

Access to Innovation

Some companies are called **lead users** because they face and resolve needs months or years ahead of the rest of the marketplace. These companies often develop innovations that the supplier can copy, either in the way it uses a product or by altering a product. Korcett, for example, needed to develop a site survey tool so that its technicians could more effectively manage inventory of Korcett equipment installed at customer locations. It teamed up with SRI (a custom software developer) to develop a solution that SRI can then sell to other companies. Korcett, in this situation, was a lead user.

Note that one important function salespeople provide is the ability to listen to customers and deliver that knowledge back to the company so better products can be developed.[12] That function is important in new product development, but does not necessarily

SALES Technology 13.1

MICRO-BURSTS OF PRODUCTIVITY

Companies spent over $26 billion on customer relationship management (CRM) software in 2016, an increase of greater than 12 percent from the previous year. But can technology really help manage relationships?

The answer is a resounding yes, according to Christopher Toppi, general manager, Compass Wire Cloth Corporation. But the answer really lies in improving service quality for the customer. "With the Microsoft Dynamics® CRM system, we have eliminated duplication of effort and streamlined our sales process with improved turnaround. And the system automatically creates the internal document we need to support our internal process and ISO (quallty) requirements. As a result, we are now more efficient, our sales team is more effective, and our customer satisfaction has increased considerably."

Research supports this enthusiastic review. One study found a 41 percent increase in productivity across salespeople while another found a 39 percent increase. Moreover, salespeople are five times more likely to reach sales targets if the CRM system is mobile versus those that aren't. In fact, CRM systems usage shows a 39 percent increase in customer retention.

While technology still can't replace people, it certainly can help salespeople be more productive while increasing customer satisfaction—and that has to be good for relationships.

Sources: "CRM Solution Reduces Manual Workload and Increases Efficiency by 99%," *RSM US*; "Gartner Says Customer Relationship Management Market Grew 12.3% in 2016," *Gartner*; "Ten Must-Know CRM Statistics and Trends," *Guides for CRM*, 2016.

require deep relationships. What lead users provide is more than information; they provide the opportunity to co-create innovations that can then be converted into products. Note also that this contributes to the customer lifetime value of such customers.

Other lead users may develop innovations in other areas of the business, such as logistics, that suppliers can copy. For example, H-E-B is a grocery chain covering Texas and Mexico that has led the development of radio frequency identification (RFID), a technology used in logistics. Several suppliers such as Campbells have spent time with H-E-B logistics engineers to learn how RFID can make logistics more efficient. Astute salespeople can identify such companies and develop strategic partnerships that lead to joint development of new products or technologies—important outcomes regardless of the size of the account.

USING TECHNOLOGY TO INCREASE EFFICIENCY

Companies are using technology to drive two key areas of salesperson performance. The first is the use of technology to help salespeople manage all the information required to be effective, a type of **knowledge management technology**. Such knowledge management technology might include product catalogs and all the detailed specifications of those products, but knowledge management technology also includes customer records and transaction/service histories.

The second is relational management technology, which can build on customer knowledge management systems to create models that can be used to develop strategy. Companies have struggled with such technologies, but as Sales Technology 13.1 shows, those struggles may be behind us.

Companies are also creating direct links with their customers and suppliers. Xerox and Baxter have developed electronic ordering mechanisms with their customers, and IBM uses private Web sites and Lotus Notes to enable suppliers to communicate with each other and with IBM buyers.

PHASES OF RELATIONSHIP DEVELOPMENT

Although not all relationships should become partnerships, strategic partnerships tend to go through several phases: (1) awareness, (2) exploration, (3) expansion, (4) commitment, and sometimes (5) dissolution.[13] Recent research indicates that the middle three stages are most important. Cultural differences may alter the way buyers and sellers move through these phases, but strategic partnerships go through these stages in most situations.

AWARENESS

In the **awareness** stage it is likely that no transaction has taken place. During the awareness phase salespeople locate and qualify prospects, while buyers identify various sources of supply. Buyers may see a booth at a trade show, an ad in a magazine, or some other form of marketing communication and seek additional information. Reputation and image in the marketplace can be very important for sellers at this point. One important trend is toward **supplier relationship management (SRM)**, which is the use of technology and statistics to identify important suppliers and opportunities for cost reduction, greater efficiency, and other benefits. Thus, awareness may result from analyzing current suppliers to identify those with whom a partnership may be possible.

Recognize, though, that relationships do not necessarily move from solo exchange to functional relationship to relational partnership to strategic partnership. Customers may actively seek partnerships for key areas of the firm's purchases, which may mean working to develop a strategic partnership with a new vendor. Or the relationship may develop over time and may involve one or more of the other forms of relationship. There is no requirement, however, that a partnership must start out as a solo exchange.

EXPLORATION

The **exploration** stage is a search and trial phase for both buyer and seller. Both parties may explore the potential benefits and costs of a partnership. At this point the buyer may make purchases, but these are likely in the form of market exchanges because neither side has committed to the relationship. Each purchase can be thought of as a test of the supplier's capability.

An important aspect during the exploration phase is the customer onboarding process. **Customer onboarding** is the process by which new customers are taught how to most effectively use what they just purchased in order to get the value they desire, as well as how to order service and/or supplies, what to expect in billing and payment, and other procedures that will enhance the customer experience. In some instances, a new product may require the customer to do things very differently and that may require a great deal of training at the start. For example, BizWiz is a marketing software program for contractors and home repair companies. To get the most out of it, customers have to redesign their marketing and sales processes significantly. BizWiz could sell more by lowering prices and doing less customer onboarding but the result would be few satisfied customers. Good onboarding is key for them to grow customer relationships beyond exploration.

Satisfaction is key for the relationship to move beyond exploration. We focus on satisfaction in Chapter 14; however, several points about satisfaction should be understood in the context of relationships. First, keep in mind that both satisfaction with the salesperson and satisfaction with the company and its products and services influence the development of the relationship.[14] Salesperson characteristics such as dependability and competence are tested in the exploration phase and improve satisfaction. Second, buyers will object during the exploration phase to characteristics of the salesperson's offer. How those objections are handled (the topic of Chapter 10) is an important factor in successfully negotiating the exploration stage.[15]

EXPANSION

At this point the supplier has passed enough tests to be considered for additional business. The **expansion** stage involves efforts by both parties to investigate the benefits of a long-term relationship. The relationship can still devolve into a functional relationship rather than a strategic partnership, but the intention of both parties is to develop the appropriate type of relationship. The buyer's dependence on the seller as a primary source of supply grows and may lead to the purchase of additional products. Further, both sides begin to probe regarding interest in a partnership; such probing is both internal and external. Remember that the decision for a strategic partnership requires credible commitments, so many in the selling organization may need to review the opportunity.

COMMITMENT

In the **commitment** stage the customer and seller have implicitly or explicitly pledged to continue the relationship for a period of time. Commitment represents the most advanced stage of the relationship. Investments are made in the relationship, especially in the form of sharing proprietary information, plans, goals, and the like.

In Chapter 11 we discussed obtaining commitment as a stage in the sales process. In that sense we are talking about asking the buyer to make a decision–a decision either to buy the product or to take the next step in the decision process. The commitment stage in a relationship involves promises by both buyer and seller to work together over many transactions, not just a single decision.

Note, too, that long relationships can occur without commitment. Companies may buy from the same vendors for a long time without really making a commitment to a relationship. Length of relationship is not the same as commitment.

DISSOLUTION

Dissolution can occur at any time in the relationship process, though it doesn't necessarily have to occur at all. Dissolution is the process of terminating the relationship and can occur because of poor performance, clash in culture, change in needs, and other factors. When dissolution occurs in latter stages of the relationship, the loss of investments made in the relationship can be significant and have an impact throughout both organizations.

CHARACTERISTICS OF SUCCESSFUL PARTNERSHIPS

Successful relationships involve cultivating mutual benefits as the partners learn to trust and depend on each other more and more. As trust develops, buyer and salesperson can resolve conflicts as they arise, settle differences, and compromise when necessary. Without trust there is no loyalty, and unhappy customers leave. While trust is important, other elements also characterize successful long-term relationships. The five foundational elements of strategic partnerships are (1) mutual trust, (2) open communication, (3) common goals, (4) commitment to mutual gain, and (5) organizational support (see Exhibit 13.4).

MUTUAL TRUST

The most important element in the development of successful long-term customer relationships is trust. **Trust** is a belief by one party that the other party will fulfill its obligations in a relationship. That trust has to be mutual, however. When salespeople and buyers trust each other, they are more willing to share relevant ideas, clarify goals and problems, and communicate more efficiently. Information shared between the parties becomes increasingly comprehensive, accurate, and timely. There is less need for salesperson and buyer to constantly monitor each other's actions because both believe the other party would not take advantage of them if given the opportunity.

Trust is an important building block for long-term relationships. A study of partnerships in both Latin America and Europe found trust to be the most important variable that contributes to the success of the relationship.[16] In cross-cultural situations, shared values is important to building trust.[17] Trust is a combination of five factors: dependability, competence, customer orientation, honesty, and likability. In this section we discuss these factors and how salespeople demonstrate their own trustworthiness.

Dependability

Dependability, the buyer's perception that the salesperson, and the product and company he or she represents, will live up to promises made, is not something a salesperson can demonstrate immediately. Promises must be made and then kept.

Exhibit 13.4
Foundations of Successful Relationships

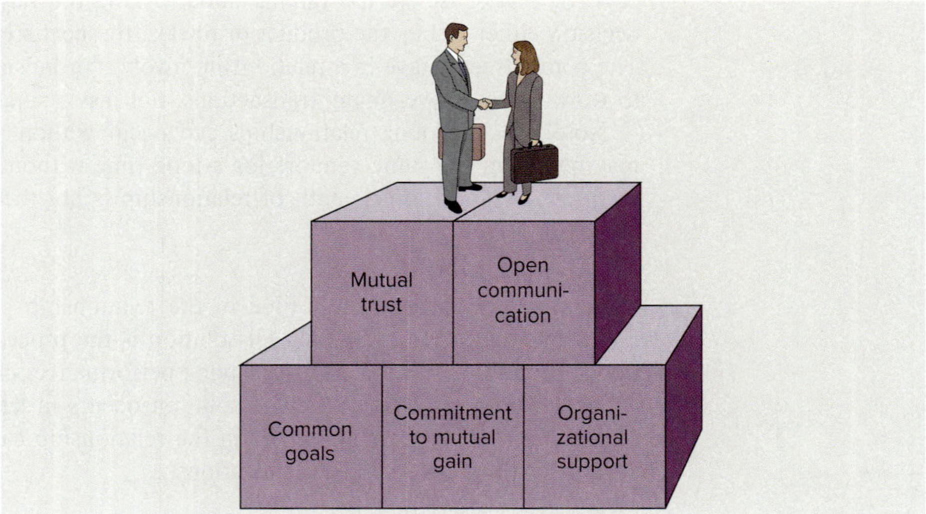

A tour of the manufacturing facility can be a sales tool to show dependability, as well as give prospective customers an opportunity to meet key manufacturing personnel.

Early in the selling process, a salesperson can demonstrate dependability by calling at times agreed to, showing up a few minutes early for appointments, and providing information as promised.

Third-party references can be useful in proving dependability, especially if the salesperson has not yet had an opportunity to prove it personally. If the seller can point to a similar situation and illustrate, through the words of another customer, how the situation was resolved, the buyer can verify the seller's dependability. Some companies also prepare case studies of how they solved a particular customer's problem to aid salespeople in proving the company's dependability.

Product demonstrations, plant tours, and other special types of presentations can also illustrate dependability. A product demonstration can show how the product will work, even under difficult conditions. A buyer for appliance component parts was concerned about one company's ability to produce the large volumes required. The salesperson offered a plant tour to prove that the company could live up to its promises of on-time delivery. When the buyer saw the size of the plant and the employees' dedication to making quality products, she was convinced.

The salesperson's prior experience and training can also be used to prove dependability. For a company (and a salesperson) to remain in business, there must be some level of dependability. Length of experience, however, is a weak substitute for proving dependability with action.

As time goes on and the relationship grows, the buyer assumes dependability. For example, a buyer may say, "Well, let's call Sue at Mega. We know we can depend on her." At this point the salesperson has developed a reputation within the account as dependable. But reputations can spread beyond that account through the buyer's community. A reputation for dependability, however, can be quickly lost if the salesperson fails to continue to deliver as promised.

Competence

Salespeople demonstrate **competence** when they can show that they know what they are talking about. Knowledge of the customer, the product, the industry, and the competition are all necessary to the success of the salesperson; in fact, recent research suggests that competence is a key component in developing trust.[18] Through the use of this knowledge, a salesperson demonstrates competence. For example, when a pharmaceutical representative can discuss the treatment of a disease in medical terms, the physician is more likely to believe that the rep is medically competent.

ethics

Salespeople recognize the need to appear competent. Unfortunately their recognition of the importance of competence may lead them to try to fake knowledge. Because buyers test the trustworthiness of a seller early in the relationship, they may ask questions just to see the salesperson's response. Salespeople should never make up a response to a tough question; if you don't know, say so but promise to get the answer quickly and then do it. At the same time, salespeople should try to present information objectively. Buyers can tell when salespeople are exaggerating the performance of their products.

Exhibit 13.5
Vistakon New Hire Training and Development

- Onboarding: 4 weeks
  - Week 1: District manager orientation and home study.
  - Week 2: Work with peer coach and home study.
  - Week 3: Work with field sales trainer in trainer's territory.
  - Week 4: Attend preceptorship and work with district manager to get certification.
- Primary sales school
  - Weeks 5 and 6: Attend primary sales school.
- Sales development
  - Week 7: Work with district manager in own territory.
  - Week 8: Field sales trainer works with rep in the rep's territory.
- Advanced sales development seminar
  - 2 weeks.

Product knowledge is the minimum; customers expect salespeople to know everything about their own products and their company. That's why company training is so important. Johnson and Johnson's Vistakon division, which serves the contact lens market, provides eight weeks of training to new salespeople, as you can see in Exhibit 13.5. One-fourth of that training is devoted to products, but a significant amount of additional training covers competitors, customers, and other market factors that salespeople need to know to be competent members of the industry. In addition to product competence, though, selling competence is also important. Much of the training focuses on increasing salespersons' selling competence so they can deliver the appropriate solutions to meet customers' needs. The result is a highly competent sales force that works in partnership with customers, helping them run their businesses more successfully.[19]

Customer Orientation

Customer orientation is the degree to which the salesperson puts the customer's needs first. Salespeople who think only of making sales are sales oriented rather than customer oriented. Buyers perceive salespeople as customer oriented when sellers stress benefits and solutions to problems over features. Stating pros and cons can also be perceived as being customer oriented because understanding the cons also indicates that the salesperson understands the buyer's needs.

Emphasizing the salesperson's availability and desire to provide service also indicates a customer orientation. For example, the statement "Call me anytime for anything that you need" indicates availability. Offering the numbers for toll-free hotlines, voice mail, and similar concrete information indicates a desire to respond promptly to the buyer and can serve as proof of a customer orientation. Ashley McNabb's customers, for example, have her cell number and expect to be able to call her whenever there is an issue.

Several studies show that customer orientation is vital to achieving sales performance and customer satisfaction, particularly for important purchases.[20] Multiple studies of salespeople across countries as varied as Macau and Finland showed customer orientation as a critical variable in predicting sales success;[21] similarly, several studies of buyers found that buyers are more loyal and more willing to tell others when their salesperson is customer oriented.[22]

Honesty

Honesty is both truthfulness and sincerity. While honesty is highly related to dependability ("We can count on you and your word because you are honest"), it is also related to how candid a salesperson is. For example, giving pros and cons can increase perceptions of honesty as well as a customer orientation.

From the BUYER'S SEAT 13.1

RED FLAGS

Buyers want to do business with people they can trust. But they quickly build up a repertoire of salesperson behaviors that signal a lack of trustworthiness.

For example, salespeople who feign interest in buyers are quickly spotted. Ed Braig, purchasing director for Central Texas Iron Works, says, "You are not my best friend. We do not share a common bond the day you notice I have a deer mount on my wall or you see I drink coffee from a Texas A&M mug. In fact, the deer could have been left here by my predecessor and the coffee mug handed me by the salesperson who just walked out as you walked in. It may not even be my office!"

Ed goes on to say, "My motto is make friends out of suppliers, not suppliers out of friends." His point is that you first have to earn his business and prove your worth. Then, and only then, is a friendship possible.

Kyle Beagle, deputy director for the Naval Facilities Engineering Command, says a low price is another red flag. "When their prices (are too low and) don't match the market, it shows they don't understand what we are trying to buy and we might get poor performance. We tend to ask for detailed cost breakdowns and have them show why their price is not within the average price range of competitors. If it looks too good to be true, it usually is."

Don Jones, founder of First Audit Group, watches eye contact. A red flag for him is when the salesperson looks away when asked a direct question. "They will look down or to the side until they've given me an answer. And usually the answer is vague or something to the effect of 'We can adjust for that.' Then they look back at me again."

As Ed says, "Never, ever lie! Lie once to me, and that's it."

Honesty is also related to competence. As we said earlier, salespeople must be willing to admit that they do not know something rather than trying to fake it; buyers consider salespeople who bluff to be dishonest.

ethics

The opposite, of course, is lying. Buyers figure out pretty quickly when they've been lied to, which is why one study determined honesty to be the most important component of trust for repurchase intentions.[23] In From the Buyer's Seat 13.1, purchasing professionals share some of their red flags that cause them to question a salesperson's honesty. As discussed in Chapter 2, lying will not just cost a salesperson business in the short term; the long-term damage can be quite serious to the success of the business and may bring on lawsuits or criminal charges.

Likability

According to research, likability may be the least important component of trust because most people can be nice, although in some countries other than the United States, likability is much more important.[24] **Likability** refers to behaving in a friendly manner and finding a common ground between buyer and seller. We noted earlier the importance of shared values, particularly in cross-cultural selling situations. Shared values are important for likability. Although likability is not as important as other dimensions, salespeople should still attempt to find a common ground or interest with all buyers. Buyers resent any attempts, though, of insincere rapport building. Do not feign interest if you truly aren't interested.

Likability can also be influenced with personal communications such as birthday cards, handwritten notes, and so forth. Many businesses send holiday cards and gifts to all customers, but personal touches make these gestures meaningful.

As you have probably noticed, the five dimensions of trust are tightly interrelated. Honesty affects customer orientation, which also influences dependability, for example. Salespeople should recognize the interdependence among these factors rather than simply focusing on one or two. For example, at one time many salespeople emphasized only likability. In today's market, professional salespeople must also be competent, dependable, honest, and customer oriented.

OPEN COMMUNICATION

Open and honest communication is a key building block for developing successful relationships. Buyers and salespeople in a relationship need to understand what is driving each other's business, their roles in the relationship, each firm's strategies, and any problems that arise over the course of the relationship. (Chapter 4 focuses on approaches for improving communication.) Such understanding comes through listening carefully to buyers. In fact, research shows that listening is important for building both trust and customer satisfaction.[25]

One difference between a relational partnership and a strategic partnership is the strength and number of lines of communication. In a relational partnership, most communication between the buyer and the selling organization goes through the salesperson. In a strategic partnership, there will be more direct communication ties between the buying organization and the selling organization. For example, the selling company's shipping department may talk directly with the buying organization's receiving department when a problem arises with a shipment.

When long-term relationships break up, there may be a triggering event that ends the relationship but the truth is, most relationships end due to multiple events that build over time.[26] Open communication should help reduce the effects of those little things that go wrong and end up creating bigger conflict. Suzanne Morgan, president of Print Buyers Online (a buying group for commercial printers), worries that concern for the other party may make customers reluctant to share their opinions when something goes wrong, especially if it seems like a little thing. Buyers, perhaps more so than sellers, may worry about hurting the salesperson's feelings and thus not be as open as the situation requires. She recommends, as does David Dennis of SBC Advertising, that salespeople make it as easy as possible for the buyer to speak up.[27]

Kaseya, a software company, was losing customers left and right, and nearly lost BTA, a London-based company. Darron Millar, BTA's technical director, said no one at his company had even met a Kaseya representative since the purchase, even though Kaseya had an office 20 minutes away. But that changed when Kaseya began a program of regular customer service calls, and Millar says, "We're now committed to Kaseya, which we would never have said before. We're now excited about Kaseya again, which, again, we're surprised to say."[28]

COMMON GOALS

Salespeople and customers must have common goals for a successful relationship to develop. Shared goals give both members of the relationship a strong incentive to pool their strengths and abilities. When goals are shared, the partners can focus on exploiting opportunities rather than arguing about who will benefit the most from the relationship.

Fujitsu recently released its "Technology and Service Vision," a statement of four key goals. This statement serves the dual purpose of communicating goals to customers and vendors alike.[29] The four serve as corporate level goals, and while individual buyers within Fujitsu will have more specific goals, the salesperson who can align account strategy to those goals will have a stronger sales opportunity.

Common goals can help when things go wrong. Customers and vendors are more likely to come together to solve challenges when they know they are both working toward the same objective.

Effective measuring of performance is particularly critical in the early stages of the partnership. The achievement of explicitly stated goals lays the groundwork for a history of shared success, which serves as a powerful motivation for continuing the relationship and working closely together into the future. Recall the concept of service level agreements, which is one way that performance is measured. Another way is the annual scorecard used by some companies to measure vendor performance. Main Industries, a company that paints ships for the U.S. Navy and others, has won many awards for its performance as a vendor based on such scorecards.

COMMITMENT TO MUTUAL GAIN

Members of successful partnerships actively work to create win-win relationships by making commitments to the relationship. For example, SRI provides scanning services to GRM, one of the largest box storage companies in the world. GRM then sells these services to its customers. SRI arranged free sales training for the GRM salespeople. While this training would increase sales of all of GRM's services, SRI also knew that more scanning services would get sold, too.

In a partnership, commitment to mutual gain means that one does not take advantage of the other. One party is always more powerful than the other party, but in a partnership, it does not exercise that power over the other. Mutual dependence creates a cooperative spirit. Both parties search for ways to expand the pie and minimize time spent on resolving conflicts over how to split it.

Mutual Investment

As a successful relationship develops, both parties make investments in the relationship. **Mutual investments** are tangible investments in the relationship by both parties. They go beyond merely making the hollow statement "I want to be a partner." Mutual investment may involve spending money to improve the products and services sold to the other party, though research says that sellers tend to invest more in relationships than buyers.[30] For example, a firm may hire or train employees, invest in equipment, and develop computer and communication systems to meet the needs of a specific customer. These investments signal the partner's commitment to the relationship in the long run and are important to securing loyalty, and are particularly important when made in the relationship by the larger partner.[31]

Thus, it is not enough to say that you are committed to the relationship; actions of commitment must follow to signal that the commitment is real. These actions make the commitment believable. Mutual investments are also called **relationship-specific assets**; in other words, these are resources specific to the relationship and cannot be easily transferred to another relationship.[32]

ORGANIZATIONAL SUPPORT

Another critical element in fostering good relationships is giving **boundary-spanning employees**—those employees who cross the organizational boundary and interact with customers or vendors—the necessary support. Some areas of support are training, rewards that support partnering behavior, and structure and culture. We start with structure and culture because these elements foster the others.

Structure and Culture

The organizational structure and management provide the necessary support for the salespeople and buyers in a partnering relationship. All employees in the firm need to "buy in"–in other words, accept the salesperson's and buyer's roles in developing the partnership. Partnerships created at headquarters should be recognized and treated as such by local offices, and vice versa. Without the support of the respective companies, the partnership is destined to fail.

The issue isn't just creating a culture among salespeople, however. The entire firm must have an orientation to building partnerships. Recall that strategic partnerships are characterized by direct, open communication between multiple members of both firms. If those nonselling members of the selling firm do not have a customer orientation, then the partnership may be doomed.

Training

Special training is required to sell effectively in a relationship-building environment. Salespeople need to be taught how to identify customer needs and work with customers to achieve better performance. UniFirst, a provider of uniforms and other textile services, has won several Stevie Awards for its sales training. "UniFirst continually strives to optimize our customer retention percentages as part of our 'Customers for Life' philosophy," said Jeff Brandli, UniFirst sales training specialist. "Our location managers are among the best in the industry and we wanted to further enhance existing strategies with new and improved ways to strengthen customer relationships. In our first year of deployment, we noticed a marked improvement in customer retention–a direct reflection of program's success."[33]

Rewards

Reward systems on both sides of the relationship should be coordinated to encourage supportive behaviors. In market exchanges buyers are rewarded for wringing out concessions from the salespeople, and salespeople are rewarded on the basis of sales volume. In a partnering relationship, rewarding short-term behaviors can be detrimental. For example, recent research regarding sales contests indicates that these short-term compensation events lead to short-term behaviors, such as getting sales at the expense of relationships.[34]

SELLING YOURSELF

Relationships are important in every area of life. As your faculty can tell you, some students want a transactional relationship (just come to class and get the grade) while others want a deeper relationship.

Faculty, though, are like customers in the sense that not all faculty members want to develop deeper relationships with students. When they do want deeper relationships, it is likely to be with students who show an interest in the class and who are worthy of the professor's trust. That means students who are dependable, competent, honest, and likable. A professor with a deeper relationship will understand your job interests more completely, offering introductions to potential employers, and provide access to job markets in the same way a customer may provide a salesperson with access to markets.

You may have an opportunity to develop a deeper relationship with a seasoned business executive, someone who might be willing to serve as a mentor. Bradley Richardson, a recent graduate, had the fortunate experience of a family friend who served as his mentor, even though the mentor works in a different field than Bradley wanted. But these relationships don't just happen–you have to make them happen.

While the concepts of this chapter are derived directly from research into business relationships, you can see how these concepts can apply now in your relationships with others.

SUMMARY

As we discussed in Chapter 1, many businesses are moving toward partnering strategies. A key premise is that long-term relationships can enable sellers to capture much, if not all, of a customer's lifetime value. Loyal buyers buy more and are willing to work more closely with sellers in mutually beneficial ways. However, most transactions between buyers and sellers will not be strategic partnerships. Many exchanges will continue to be market transactions and functional relationships.

Functional relationships and strategic partnerships are characterized by a mutual concern of each party for the long-run welfare of the other party. Both types of long-term relationships are based on mutual trust. However, strategic partnerships involve the greatest commitment because the parties are willing to make significant investments in the relationship.

Mutual trust, open communication, common goals, a commitment to mutual gain, and organizational support are key ingredients in successful relationships. These five factors form the foundation for win-win relationships between customers and salespeople.

Customers trust salespeople who are dependable, capable, and concerned about the customers' welfare. To build trust, salespeople need to be consistent in meeting the commitments they make to customers. Salespeople also need to demonstrate their concern for the well-being of customers.

KEY TERMS

attitudinal loyalty 348
awareness 356
behavioral loyalty 348
boundary-spanning employees 363
commitment 357
competence 359
customer lifetime value (CLV) 346
customer onboarding 356
customer orientation 360
customer satisfaction 349
dependability 358
dissolution 357
expansion 357
exploration 356
functional relationship 349
honesty 360
knowledge management technology 355
lead user 354
likability 361
market exchange 348
mutual investment 363
relational partnership 350
relationship marketing 347
relationship-specific assets 363
solo exchange 349
strategic partnership 352
supplier relationship management (SRM) 356
trust 358
win-win relationship 350

ETHICS PROBLEMS

1. If partnerships are win-win, does that mean that market exchanges are win-lose? Is there an ethical difference between win-win and win-lose? Does the customer's value equation [recall from Chapter 1 that Value = Benefits − (Selling price + Time and effort)] have to be equal in profit to the seller's profit equation for a transaction to be ethical?

2. A customer wants to buy one of your products but the price is just over the threshold she is allowed to spend and she knows that if she asks for permission, she'll be told to buy your competitor's product, which is just under the threshold. She asks you to divide the price in two and present her with two invoices—each under the threshold so she can buy. Is she asking you to do something unethical?

QUESTIONS AND PROBLEMS

1. When might relational partnerships become potentially dangerous for selling companies? Or should companies encourage salespeople to develop relational partnerships with all accounts? Why or why not?
2. Which is more important to the seller: attitudinal or behavioral loyalty? Why? What can a salesperson do to increase loyalty in buyers? How does loyalty relate to customer lifetime value?
3. Read From the Buyer's Seat 13.1. What are some of the red flags you consider when you think someone might not be telling you the truth or may not have your best interests at heart? Can you recall any such situations involving salespeople? How does this article influence how you will engage in rapport building with customers?
4. What company does the best job of building a relationship with you? Describe what they do to strengthen that relationship and why you like them so much. Identify five concepts from the chapter that are illustrated by your relationship with that company.
5. Which factors should a salesperson consider when deciding the type of relationship formed with a customer? How would these factors change when considering functional relationships versus strategic partnerships? What factors should the customer consider?
6. One executive once said that there are two types of people in the world: those who trust each person until proven untrustworthy, and those who trust no one until trust is earned. Which are you? How do you protect yourself as a buyer if you trust everyone first, and how do you avoid losing out on the benefits of relationships if you trust no one at first?
7. Ashley McNabb, in the opening profile, describes several factors in her business that seem to make deeper relationships between customers and vendors more important. What are they?
8. Read Sales Technology 13.1. Why is the software needed, and what other things could be done to increase sales and strengthen relationships with the information that these salespeople gather and put into the CRM software system?
9. There are five foundational elements to strategic partnerships. How do these differ for relational partnerships? Functional relationships? What if four of the five are strong—what type of relationship is that?

CASE PROBLEMS

case 13.1

Steve Retired!

When Steve White announced his retirement from Dollar Express, Jackie Morgan was concerned. After all, Steve had been one of her better customers and she was able to grow the business with Dollar Express by 50 percent over the past three years. Steve not only gave Jackie more business, he also recommended her to his friends, and Jackie was able to win at least two or three new accounts a year as a result. But Jackie really didn't know anyone else at Dollar Express, so she wasn't sure who would get this plum job.

Jackie's company, Heron Ridge, provides IT services to small- and medium-size businesses. Everything from accounting software to CRM software to Web site design and cyber security, Heron Ridge does it all. Steve headed up the Dollar Express online sales division, so he had responsibility for the company's Web site and digital promotions and social media strategy and execution.

When Jackie heard that Tom Oliver was named Steve's replacement, she quickly looked him up on LinkedIn. "Oh great," she groaned. According to his profile, he was coming from Franklin Five & Dime. While she didn't call on Franklin, she knew that its philosophy was to have multiple vendors with each getting small contracts and competing on price.

But she put her concern aside when Steve called to arrange a lunch meeting to introduce her to Tom.

"I really appreciate this opportunity to meet you, Tom," smiled Jackie.

"Yes, I appreciate it as well," Tom smiled back. "I've had a chance to review our business with you, and I see your company has done a great job for us. But my experience at Franklin suggests we may be overpaying." Steve squirmed, but didn't say anything. "But we'll do a deep account review with you, as we will with all of our larger vendors, so that I can get up to speed on everything. Do you think you could prepare a presentation on your company's performance for two weeks from now?"

Jackie nodded, and said she'd have it ready, as well as bring in the service manager for the account. She then asked Tom about his goals and objectives for the company's online sales division.

"A key issue for us," he replied, "is profitability." He went on to say that the CEO had mandated that Tom find ways to improve contribution margin of his department by 10 percent this year. "That's why we'll be taking such a close look at price."

Jackie knew she was in trouble. Her prices to Dollar Express were 5 to 10 percent higher than her competitors', and while she had been able to save Dollar Express money through streamlined operations, what she had done in the past wouldn't matter going forward.

As she drove back to the office after lunch, she thought about the Dollar Express account. She knew it was looking at some analytics solutions to support its online promotional campaigns and she had planned to bid on that. In fact, her quota for the year was based on increasing sales at Dollar Express, not decreasing!

Questions

1. Besides lowering price, what actions can Jackie propose to improve contribution margin?
2. What are some strategies she could take to defend the higher prices? What evidence or information would you need to support your ideas?
3. What type of relationship did she have with Steve? What did she do or fail to do that may make the future more difficult with Dollar Express, now that Tom is in charge?

case 13.2

Empire Safety Rental

Empire Safety Rental rents construction site safety fencing and related products, like those orange drums and traffic cones you see at highway construction sites. The company will also install safety fencing at a construction site, whether rented chain link or purchased plywood wall fencing. Laura Wohlers, Empire's owner, was faced with a dilemma.

Mike Caldwell, Empire's VP of sales, offered this information: "Laura, right now about 40 percent of our business, or $3 million, comes from three customers–Apex, Logan, and Eagle. The rest comes from 400 customers, of which 40 percent are one-time sales. That means 160 customers account for just over $1 million in sales every year but we'll never get business from them again."

"Yes, I know," she replied. Looking at her computer, she said, "And the margin on Apex, Eagle, and Logan is never more than 6 percent, while it can be as high as 15 percent on the midsize accounts and 30 percent on the small ones."

"That's because Apex, Eagle, and Logan always put everything out to bid. I keep telling them that there are hidden costs in that system–like the time and effort spent on bidding, managing multiple suppliers and their billing systems, and the like. I think we've got Logan convinced that if it gives us a margin of 10 percent for all of its business, we'll actually save the company money."

"Yes, but my question is really about the midsize accounts. Our business is based on price, reliability on delivery and installation, and safety. So how do we go about building a sales strategy with our midsize accounts so we can get away from commodity-based pricing and bidding wars on each project to contracts that span a year or two? We have to get our margins up–increases in health care and other types of insurance are killing us."

"Our salespeople know only two things: how to bid a job and where to take customers for lunch or for a cold beer. I don't know what else we could do."

Questions

1. What would you do? Assume that Empire has six salespeople calling on geographic territories and that Mike has responsibility for Apex, Logan, and Eagle. Be specific about the steps you would take.
2. Now assume that another salesperson has responsibility for Logan because it is in his geographic area. That person just told you he's going to quit to go to a competitor. What would you do, assuming that there is no noncompete clause that prevents him from selling to Logan for the competitor?

ROLE PLAY CASE

As with other role plays, you are a salesperson for Gartner. Additional information about Gartner can be found in the role play section at the end of the book or on the Gartner Web site, www.gartner.com/ncsc.

Cor-Plus is a manufacturer and distributor of packing materials, such as corrugated boxes, custom plastic packaging, bottles (both plastic and glass), and other products. It has three plants on the East Coast, with headquarters in Charlotte, North Carolina. You closed the first deal with this account nearly 10 months ago and have had some minor follow-on sales, but you know there is a lot more opportunity there. However, the CIO left about a month ago and a new CIO has come on board. Today you are calling on that person for the first time.

Seller: You would like to understand the new CIO's interest in relationship type (functional, transactional, etc.). Take a few minutes and prepare some questions that you think will help you determine which relationship will be appropriate. Then ask the buyer those questions as if part of a needs identification call. After you are finished, tell the buyer what relationship type (choose only one) you thought you were dealing with and why. See if you were right!

Buyer: When you play the buyer role, you should have prepared your questions for when you sell. So before the role play pick one of the relationship types and think about how you would answer the questions you developed. Also consider what your expectations would be in terms of after-sale service, pricing, and the like based on the relationship type you select.

Note: There is no additional information provided in the Instructor's Manual for this assignment. However, teaching notes are provided.

ADDITIONAL REFERENCES

Candi, Marina, and Kenneth B. Kahn. "Functional, Emotional, and Social Benefits of New B2B Services." *Industrial Marketing Management* 57 (August 2016), pp. 177–85.

Echchakoui, Said. "Salesperson Profitability in Relationship Marketing." *Journal of Modelling in Management* 9, no. 3 (2014), pp. 306–23.

Elsäßer, Marc, and Bernd W. Wirtz. "Rational and Emotional Factors of Customer Satisfaction and Brand Loyalty in Business-to-Business Setting." *Journal of Business and Industrial Marketing* 32, no. 1 (2017), pp. 138–52.

Ferro, Carlos, Carmen Padin, Göran Svensson, and Janice Payan. "Trust and Commitment as Mediators between Economic and Non-Economic Satisfaction in Manufacturer-Supplier Relationships." *Journal of Business and Industrial Marketing* 31, no. 1 (2016), pp. 13–23.

Hansen, John D., Donald J. Lund, and Thomas E. DeCarlo. "A Process Model of Buyer Responses to Salesperson Transgressions and Recovery Efforts: The Impact of Salesperson Orientation." *Journal of Personal Selling and Sales Management* 36, no. 1 (2016), pp. 59–69.

Joosten, Herm, Josée Bloemer, and Bas Hillebrand. "Is More Customer Control of Services Always Better?" *Journal of Service Management* 27, no. 2 (2016), pp. 218–46.

Nor Noor, Azila Mohd, and Kawsar Ahmad. "Investigating the Relationship between Key Account Management Performance and Repeat Orders: Does the Length of Relationship Matter?" *Asian Academy of Management Journal* 19, no. 2 (July 2014), pp. 23–42.

Nwamaka A. Anaza, and Brian Rutherford. "Increasing Business-to-Business Buyer Word-of-Mouth and Share-of-Purchase." *Journal of Business and Industrial Marketing* 29, no. 5 (2014), pp. 427–37.

Pérez, Lourdes, and Jesús Cambra-Fierro. "Value Generation in B2B Contexts: The SME's Perspective." *European Business Review* 27, no. 3 (2015), pp. 297–317.

Ponder, Nicole, Betsy Bugg Holloway, and John D. Hansen. "The Mediating Effects of Customers' Intimacy Perceptions on the Trust-Commitment Relationship." *Journal of Services Marketing* 30, no. 1 (2016), pp. 75–87.

Preikschas, Michael W., Pablo Cabanelas, Klaus Rüdiger, and Jesús F Lampón. "Value Co-Creation, Dynamic Capabilities, and Customer Retention in Industrial Markets." *Journal of Business and Industrial Marketing* 32, no. 3 (2017), pp. 409–20.

Rowe, William J., Cody Logan Chullen, and Jon F. Kirchoff. "The Impact of Customer Motivation on the Customer-Salesperson Relationship." *S.A.M. Advanced Management Journal* 81, no. 4 (Autumn 2016), pp. 23–36.

Strandberg, Christer, Olof Wahlberg, and Peter Öhman. "Effects of Commitment on Intentional Loyalty at the Person-to-Person and Person-to-Firm Levels." *Journal of Financial Services Marketing* 20, no. 3 (September 2015), pp. 191–207.

Tombs, Alastair G., Rebekah Russell-Bennett, and Neal M. Ashkanasy. "Recognising Emotional Expressions of Complaining Customers: A Cross-Cultural Study." *European Journal of Marketing* 48, no. 7/8 (2014), pp. 1354–74.

Tsu-Wei, Yu, and Tung Feng-Cheng. "Antecedents and Consequences of Insurer-Salesperson Relationships." *Marketing Intelligence & Planning* 32, no. 4 (2014), pp. 436–54.

Wang, Guocai, Shanliang Li, Xifeng Wang, Chunyu Lu, and Chen Lv. "Relationship-Specific Investment" *Social Behavior and Personality* 42, no. 7 (2014), pp. 1147–66.

©Monkey Business Images/Shutterstock.com RF

The Partnership Process

PART 2

chapter 14

BUILDING LONG-TERM PARTNERSHIPS

SOME QUESTIONS ANSWERED IN THIS CHAPTER ARE

- How important is service after the sale?
- How should salespeople stay in contact with customers?
- Which sales strategies stimulate repeat sales and new business in current accounts?
- Which techniques are important to use when handling complaints?

PROFILE

> *"To become successful in my position, it is essential for me to not only build new relationships with hotel owners, but also become a long-term partner with the hotel owners I work with."*
>
> Taylor Price, TravelClick

Courtesy of Taylor Price

PROFILE Success in my current role as a regional sales representative for TravelClick requires building true, long-term partnerships. TravelClick is the global provider of innovative, cloud-based and data-driven solutions for hotels to maximize revenue. Our suite of solutions includes Business Intelligence, Reservations & Booking Engine, Media, Web, Video, and Guest Management. As a seller for TravelClick, I work with and advise hotel partners on how to drive revenue and build their brand with these solutions. To become successful in my position, it is essential for me to not only build new relationships with hotel owners, but also become a long-term partner with the hotel owners I work with. Partnering is certainly not a quick or easy process, as trust must be earned.

A pivotal time in the buying process where trust is built is postsale. Many hotel owners I work with are purchasing complicated systems that they have no idea how to use. Although these systems drive revenue to the hotel, they don't come cheap. I find that postsale is the time when my hotel partners become most sensitive. I must stay as equally involved during postsale and the implementation process as I am in the other stages of the selling process. It is essential to their success with our products that I am there to answer questions, communicate implementation timelines, and occasionally reaffirm the value of TravelClick's programs if buyer's remorse starts to creep in. I've found the worst mistake I can make is to become unresponsive or unavailable during implementation.

After that initial postsale period, I stay in constant contact with my partners. My goal is to build more trust during this time. Many customers anticipate salespeople to disappear after a deal is signed, so maintaining the same level of communication and being there for my customers postsale really sets me apart from other salespeople or vendors they work with. After implementation, depending on the program purchased, I may set up training calls to walk them through their programs or set meetings to review any return on investment reporting. I find that each time I go the extra mile, I earn a little more trust from my customer and the closer I move toward my goal of becoming a long-term partner.

One great example of this is a hotel partner I work with that owns and manages multiple hotels in North and South Carolina. This particular hotel owner was struggling with driving corporate travelers to his hotel in Charlotte, North Carolina. After some discovery, we landed on a business intelligence program TravelClick offers that would help his sales team on-property contact corporate accounts booking local competitor hotels. He was excited about purchasing the program, but was also somewhat nervous because neither he nor any of his staff had ever used it before. This was also the first time he had partnered with TravelClick.

I knew that it would be extremely important that I continue to earn his trust postsale to ensure a partnership would be developed. After the purchase and implementation of our program, I set several training calls with the hotel owner and his staff. I also made sure his team routed any questions or concerns directly to me so they would have a timely response. After the training, I contacted the on-property team to set a strategy call, where I spent about an hour actually helping them decide which corporate accounts they would target.

Going the extra mile with the customer has solidified our long-term partnership. Not only is this partner extremely grateful, he boasts about TravelClick and our partnership at hospitality conferences and local Convention and Visitors Bureau (CVB) meetings. Solidifying this one partnership has produced many, many more partnerships.

Becoming a long-term partner is so important because it allows me to reach my sales goals with much more ease. I have hotel partners who reach out regularly with business challenges to find out what else TravelClick offers that can help. I also have many partners who refer me to other hotels when they see success with their solutions. Building a partnership with one hotel owner can result in many sales and many more partnerships.

Visit our Web site at: www.travelclick.com.

Taylor Price, regional sales representative, TravelClick. Used with permission

As we discussed in the previous chapter, relationships go through several stages, beginning with awareness and ending in dissolution. In this chapter we focus on the three stages between awareness and dissolution—exploration, expansion, and commitment—as illustrated in Exhibit 14.1. From the Buyer's Seat 14.1 describes these stages from the buyer's perspective and why supplier relationships are important. As you read the rest of the chapter, you will see strategies from the sales side to build and maintain relationships throughout the life of the partnership.

EXPLORATION

In the exploration stage, the relationship is defined through the development of expectations for each party. The buyer tests the seller's product, how the seller responds to requests, and other similar actions after the initial sale is made. A small percentage of the buyer's business is given to minimize the risk in case the vendor cannot perform. When the vendor performs well, trust is developed, as is a personal relationship.

Beginning the relationship properly is important if the relationship is going to last a long time. In the previous chapter, we noted the importance of customer onboarding processes. Here we dive deeper, focusing on the role of the salesperson. Beginning the relationship properly requires that the salesperson set the right expectations, monitor order processing, ensure proper use of the product, and assist in servicing the product.

Exhibit 14.1
Stages of Partnerships

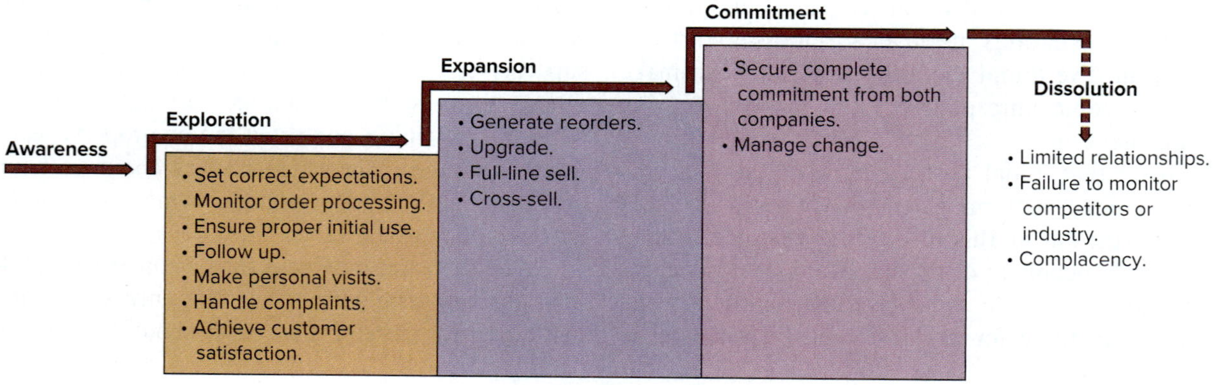

From the BUYER'S SEAT 14.1

STRATEGIC SUPPLIER RELATIONSHIPS

When a company saves money on a purchase, that savings drops straight to the bottom line. Cut a million in expenses and you add a million to profit.

There's much more to buying, though, than just trying to get the lowest price. Strategic supplier relationships are critical in nearly every business, and buyers work hard to strengthen those key relationships. According to a study in Finland, buyers consider strong relationships with important suppliers as a form of vertical integration but with less risk.

Early-supplier involvement in new product development demands strong supplier relationships. When relationships are stronger, suppliers are willing to invest more in co-engineering new products. In fact, research indicates that strong supplier relationships, such as the one shared by General Motors (GM) and Shanghai Automotive Industry Corporation (SAIC), are more likely to lead to radical innovations.

Anheuser-Busch InBev, brewers of Budweiser, developed strategic relationships with hops providers. These relationships led to better hops and more reliable supply. Conversely, Phones 4U pushed price concessions so hard that suppliers EE and Vodafone withdrew. Without suppliers, the company had to close.

Companies today compete for the best sources of supply. Managing supplier relationships strategically is one way to gain competitive advantage.

Sources: Priscila L. S. Miguel, Luiz A. L. Brito, Aline R. Fernandes, Fábio V. C. S. Tescari, and Guiherme S. Martins, "Relational Value Creation and Appropriation in Buyer-Supplier Relationships," *International Journal of Physical Distribution & Logistics Management* 44, no. 7 (2014), pp. 559–76; Milan Panchmatia, "Does SRM Represent the Last Source of Savings?," *Supply Management*, May 4, 2015; Khuram Shahzad, Ilkka Sillanpää, Elina Sillanpää, and Shpend Imeri, "Benchmarking Supplier Development: An Empirical Case Study Validating a Framework to Improve Buyer-Supplier Relationships," *Management and Production Engineering Review* 7, no. 1 (2016), pp. 56–70; Ruey-Jer Jean, Jyh-Shen Chiou, and Rudolf R. Sinkovics, "Interpartner Learning, Dependence, Asymmetry and Radical Innovation in Customer Supplier Relationships," *Journal of Business and Industrial Marketing* 31, no. 6 (2016), pp. 732–42.

SET THE RIGHT EXPECTATIONS

The best way to begin a relationship is for each party to be aware of what the other expects. To a large degree, customers base their expectations on sales presentations.

ethics

Salespeople should make sure customers have reasonable expectations of product performance. If the salesperson exaggerates the capabilities of the product or the company, the customer will be disappointed. Lisa Stassi, commercial real estate investor and manager, says this type of behavior is a one-time thing for her, meaning if salespeople set expectations too high, they don't get a second chance. Avoiding complaints by setting proper expectations is best. Long-term relationships are begun by making an honest presentation of the product's capabilities and eliminating any misconceptions before the order is placed.

MONITOR ORDER PROCESSING

Although many people may work on an order before it is shipped, the salesperson is ultimately responsible, at least in the eyes of the customer, for seeing that the product is received when promised. Purchase orders placed directly with a salesperson should be transmitted for entry into the system immediately. Also, progress on orders in process should be closely monitored. If problems arise in filling the order, the customer should be informed promptly; on the other hand, if the order can be filled sooner than promised, the customer should be notified so the proper arrangements can be made.

Fortunately computers have made the sales representatives' job easier. Salespeople can use pad computers to check inventory and order status. Progressive firms have introduced automated order systems that allow the customer to sign on the computer; the signature is sent to the company electronically, avoiding delays that might result if the contract were mailed.

Many firms, such as GE and Baxter, facilitate the automatic placement of orders by having their own computers talk to customers' computers. This technology is part of the **Internet of Things (IoT)**, the ability of devices and machines to talk to each other. For example, bars and pubs now have systems that monitor kegs of beer. When the kegs are nearly empty, notice is sent to the brewery by the computer, which then ships new kegs. That way, the bar never runs out. Such technology boosts the productivity of both the salespeople and the purchasing managers they call on. As a result, salespeople spend less time writing orders and more time solving problems; buyers save on ordering and inventory costs.

Monitoring order processing and other after-sale activities is critical to developing a partnership. Studies continually show that buyers are most often displeased with salespeople in this respect. Rossignol, the French ski and snowboard company, uses its CRM system to monitor order processing, ski shop inventories, and other data so salespeople can provide better after-sale service. Because skiing is a seasonal activity, sales are seasonal too. The company takes orders six months before shipping in order to plan ahead for the ski sale season, which is the early part of winter. But stores don't pay for the skis and snowboards until six months after shipping, or when orders are taken for the next year. Although it sounds like there is a lot of time to make sure things go smoothly, what is ordered for next year is a function of what is sold this year. The CRM system helps salespeople stay on top of how well their customers are doing in selling current inventory, so they can help sell that inventory out and make room for more. Thus, the partnership is created by helping both parties achieve their goals.[1]

This salesperson is training the customer in how to use the product properly. Getting customers off to the right start is essential to building long and satisfying relationships.

Courtesy of John Tanner

ENSURE PROPER INITIAL USE OF THE PRODUCT OR SERVICE

Customer dissatisfaction can occur just after delivery of a new product, especially if the product is technical or requires special installation. Customers unfamiliar with the product may have problems installing or using it. They may even damage the product through improper use. Many salespeople visit new customers right after initial deliveries to ensure correct use of the product. In this way they can also help the customer realize the full potential benefits of the product.

Some buyers may be knowledgeable about how to use the basic features of a product or service, but if it is not operating at maximum efficiency, the wise salesperson will show the buyer how to get more profitable use out of it. Many firms have staffed a customer service department to aid salespeople in this task. The salesperson is still responsible, however, to make sure the customer service department takes proper care of each new customer.

To be most effective, the salesperson should not wait until the user has trouble with the product. The fewer the difficulties allowed to occur, the greater will be the customer's confidence in the salesperson and the product.

FOLLOW UP

The first follow-up a salesperson should perform after the sale is a call to say thank you and to check to see that the product is working appropriately. Some salespeople use specialty advertising, or gifts imprinted with their company's name, to say thanks. These items are generally small enough to avoid concerns about bribery and can include desk clocks, pens, and the like. Chuck Gallagher, COO for American Funeral Financial, says the choice of a thank-you method is dependent on the buyer's social style. An analytical may prefer a concise e-mail message, whereas an expressive may enjoy a small gift. Justin Ferrell, salesperson for S&P Global, adds that it also depends on the stage of the relationship and your relationship goals. Tom Finlay of Reliable IT and Mary Wentworth, with Brazos Higher Ed, both agree that handwritten thank-you notes are appreciated, mainly because they are so rare. Tom adds that gifts are tricky because so many companies no longer allow employees to accept them. Bob Hall's company hosts a thank-you cookout for its customers, and more than half usually attend.[2]

Follow-up, though, doesn't stop with thank you. Salespeople should also follow up regularly with their accounts to identify any changing needs or possible problems. In fact, failing to follow up is a major complaint that buyers have about salespeople. One recent study indicated that 80 percent of sales executives believed their company provides great service, but only 8 percent of their customers agreed.[3] Why the mismatch in perceptions? Because salespeople all too often fail to follow up.

Recall, too, that different functional areas and members of the buying center had different needs to start with. Follow-up with only the users or those most directly involved with the product may result in other members of the buying center becoming dissatisfied. The nature of the follow-up should reflect their needs, which means, for example, that for a purchasing agent, follow-up should reflect the agent's concerns with the financial aspects, such as timely and accurate billing and return on investment.[4]

Personal visits can be the most expensive form of follow-up because of the time it takes to travel and because the sales call will last longer than one conducted through other means. A personal visit, though, can be extremely productive because the salesperson can check on inventories or the performance of the machine or other aspects that can be accomplished only at the customer's site. Plus, a customer may be more likely to disclose more information, such as a minor complaint or compliment, in a personal setting than over the phone. Regular personal visits can also build trust, a key component needed to move the relationship forward. But these visits aren't just niceties; they require planning and sales objectives as you prepare for the next sale.

Between personal visits, it is often a good idea to make contact via telephone. A salesperson can make 12 or more such calls within an hour, efficiently checking on clients. Telephone calls are two-way communication, giving the customer an opportunity to voice any concerns and minimizing intrusion. Contact management software, such as Microsoft Dynamics, can help salespeople schedule telephone follow-ups.

Few salespeople turn to the mail as a way to say thank you or follow up on a sale. Sometimes, though, sending a thank you by real mail (as opposed to e-mail) can set a salesperson apart. But for regular contact, e-mail may be sufficient. Aprimo and Marketo are two software offerings that automate e-mail follow-up, with e-mails triggered to follow up any number of events, such as a service call by a technician. The e-mails are signed by the salesperson and customized based on data from the CRM solution.

Following up with customers signals that the salesperson is dependable and customer oriented. Although the objective may be to create a functional relationship rather than a strategic partnership, such follow-up is still necessary to remind the customer that you are the salesperson with whom they want to do business.

HANDLE CUSTOMER COMPLAINTS

Handling complaints is critical to developing goodwill and maintaining partnerships. Complaints can occur at any time in the partnering process, not just during the exploration stage, but they may be more important in the early stages of a partnership. Attempts to establish partnerships often collapse because of shortsightedness in handling customer complaints. Some firms spend thousands of dollars on advertising but make the mistake of insulting customers who attempt to secure a satisfactory adjustment.

Complaints normally arise when the company and its products do not live up to the customer's expectations. Assuming the proper expectations were set, customers can be disappointed for any of the following reasons: (1) the product performs poorly, (2) it is being used improperly, or (3) the terms of the sales contract were not met. Although salespeople usually cannot change the product or terms, they can affect these sources of complaints, minimizing them by setting proper expectations and ensuring proper use.

We've long known that people tell more friends about bad experiences than they do good experiences. Studies repeatedly show that when a company fails in its dealings with a complainant, the latter will tell twice as many people as when the experience is good. For every dissatisfied person who complains, an estimated 50 more simply stop buying the product, but if the salesperson handles the situation well, and repurchase intentions increase.[5] One study found that half of those told about a bad experience refused to ever consider the offending vendor.[6] Worse, another study found that those who are centers of influence in a community are most likely to voice negative word of mouth after a bad experience.[7] In fact, a bad experience is far more likely to result in no future purchase than a good experience is to result in repurchase.[8] Companies that can improve customer satisfaction will see positive financial results and higher stock prices, mostly by avoiding negative experiences.[9]

Most progressive companies have learned that an excellent way to handle customer complaints is through personal visits by sales representatives. Thus, the salesperson may have total responsibility for this portion of the company's public relations. Salespeople who carry this burden must be prepared to do an effective job.

Complaints cannot be eliminated; they can only be reduced in frequency. The salesperson who knows complaints are inevitable can learn to handle them as a normal part of the job. The following discussion presents some techniques for responding to complaints; Exhibit 14.2 provides an overview.

Exhibit 14.2
Responding to Complaints

- Encourage buyers to tell their story.
- Determine the facts.
- Offer a solution.
- Follow through with action.

Source: Thomas Ingram, "Relationship Selling: Moving from Rhetoric to Reality," *Mid-American Journal of Business* 11 (1996), p. 6.

Encourage Buyers to Tell Their Story

Some customers can become angry over real or imaginary grievances. They welcome the salesperson's visit as an opportunity to voice complaints. Other buyers are less emotional in expressing complaints and give little evidence of irritation or anger, but the complaint is no less important. In either case customers need to tell their stories without interruption. Interruptions add to the irritation of emotionally upset buyers, making it almost impossible to arrive at a settlement that is fair to all parties.

Customers want a sympathetic reaction to their problems, whether real or imagined. They want their feelings to be acknowledged, their business to be recognized as important, and their grievances handled in a friendly manner. An antagonistic attitude or an attitude that implies the customer is trying to cheat the company seldom paves the way for a satisfactory adjustment. You can probably relate to this feeling if you have ever had to return a defective product or get some kind of adjustment made on a bill. Exhibit 14.3 suggests ways to handle irate customers.

Good salespeople show they are happy the grievance has been brought to their attention. After the customer describes the problem, the salesperson may express regret for any inconvenience. An attempt should then be made to talk about points of agreement. Agreeing with the customer as far as possible gets the process off to the right start.

Determine the Facts

It is easy to be influenced by a customer who is honestly making a claim for an adjustment. An inexperienced salesperson might forget that many customers make their case for a claim as strong as possible. Emphasizing the points most likely to strengthen one's case is human nature. Research shows that customers are more likely to exaggerate their claims when they perceive a weak interpersonal relationship with the salesperson or when they are uncertain of the seller's reliability or integrity.[10] But the salesperson has a responsibility to his or her company too. A satisfactory adjustment cannot be made until all the facts are known.

Whenever possible, the salesperson should examine, in the presence of the customer, the product claimed to be defective. Encouraging the customer to pinpoint the exact problem is a good idea. If the defect is evident, this step may be unnecessary. In other instances, make certain the complaint is understood. The purpose of getting the facts is to determine the cause of the problem so the proper solution can be provided.

Experienced salespeople soon learn that products may appear defective when actually nothing is wrong with them. For example, a buyer may complain that paint was applied exactly as directed but repainting became necessary in a short time;

Exhibit 14.3
Handling Rude or Irate Customers

1. Follow the Golden Rule—treat your customer the way you would like to be treated, no matter how difficult the client becomes.
2. Prove you listened—paraphrase the customer's concern, recognizing the customer's feelings along with the facts.
3. Don't justify, excuse, or blame others—be positive and thank the customer for bringing the problem to your attention so that you can resolve it.
4. Do the hard things first—the faster they get done, the more your customer will appreciate you and your efforts.
5. Call back if the customer hangs up.
6. Give the customer someone else to call, but only in case you are not available—don't pass the buck!

therefore, the paint was no good. However, the paint may have been spread too thin. Any good paint will cover just so much area. If the manufacturer recommends using a gallon of paint to cover 400 square feet with two coats and the user covers 600 square feet with two coats, the product is not at fault.

On the other hand, salespeople should not assume product or service failure is always the user's fault. They need an open mind to search for the facts in each case. In one instance, the paint spilled out of the bucket all over the buyer's truck while the customer took it back to Home Depot to register a complaint that the paint was too thin–like painting with milk. The Home Depot customer service representative refused to believe the buyer that the paint had spilled (even though the paint-covered truck was in the Home Depot parking lot), assuming the buyer used it and was trying to get it for free. The buyer agreed that it was reasonable to require him to take the claim up with the manufacturer, but the Home Depot clerk's assumption that the buyer lied about the missing paint cost Home Depot a $10,000 per year customer. Some companies have the policy that the customer is always right, in which case there is no need to establish responsibility. While there is still a need to determine what the cause was so the right solution can be offered, do not assume the customer is to blame.

In this phase of making an adjustment, salespeople must avoid giving the impression of stalling. The customer should know that the purpose of determining the facts is to permit a fair adjustment–that the inquiry is not being made to delay action or avoid resolution.

Offer a Solution

After the customer tells his or her story and the facts are determined, the next step is to offer a solution. At this time the company representative describes the process by which the company will resolve the complaint, and the rep should then gain agreement that the proposed solution is satisfactory. Recent research suggests that offering several solutions and allowing a customer to choose one is far more effective than telling the customer what the solution will be. Giving the customer a choice puts the customer in control, which increases satisfaction with how the complaint was handled.[11]

Company policies vary, but many assign the responsibility for settling claims to the salesperson. Other companies require the salesperson to investigate claims and recommend a settlement to the home office. Salespeople are in the best position to make adjustments fairly, promptly, and satisfactorily, especially if the customer and salesperson are geographically distant from the home office. Permitting salespeople to only recommend a course of action, though, assures the customer of attention from a higher level of management, increasing the likelihood that the customer will accept the action taken.

Whatever the company policy, the customer desires quick action and fair treatment and wants to know the reasons for the action. Most customers are satisfied if they quickly receive fair treatment. Customers are seldom convinced of the fairness of a solution that isn't exactly what they wanted unless the reasoning behind the decision is explained to them. Nothing discourages a customer more than having action postponed indefinitely or being offered vague promises. Although some decisions may take time, the salesperson should try to expedite action. The opportunity to develop a partnership may be lost if the time lapse is too great, even though action is taken in the customer's favor.

Some salespeople make disparaging remarks about their own companies or managers in an effort to shift the blame. Blaming someone else in the company is a poor practice because this behavior can cause the customer to lose faith in both the salesperson and the company. Moreover, if the customer does not like the proposed solution, the salesperson trusted to make an adjustment or recommendation should shoulder the responsibility. Any disagreement on the action taken should be ironed out between the salesperson and the home office staff. When reported to the customer, the action must be stated in a sound, convincing manner.

The action taken may vary with the circumstances. Some possible settlements when a product is unsatisfactory are the following:

1. Replace the product without cost to the customer.
2. Replace the product and share the costs with the customer.
3. Instruct the customer on how to proceed with a claim against a third party (for example, the paint manufacturer in the Home Depot situation).
4. Send the product to the factory for a decision.

Occasionally customers make claims they know are unfair. Although they realize the company is not at fault, they still try to get a settlement. Fortunately, relatively few customers do this.

To assume that a customer is willfully trying to cheat the company would be unwise. He or she may honestly see a claim as legitimate even though the salesperson can clearly tell that the company is not at fault. The salesperson does well, then, to proceed cautiously and, if any doubt exists, to treat the claim as legitimate.

A salesperson convinced that a claim is dishonest has two ways to take action. First, he or she can give the buyer an opportunity to save face by suggesting that a third party may be to blame. For example, if a machine appears not to have been oiled for a long time, a salesperson may suggest, "Is it possible that your maintenance crew neglected to oil this machine?" Second, the salesperson can unmask the fraudulent claim and appeal to the customer's sense of fair play. This procedure may cause the loss of a customer. In some cases, however, the company may be better off without that customer.

Answers to the following questions often affect the action to be taken:

- What is the dollar value of the claim? Many firms have established standard procedures for what they classify as small claims. For example, one moving and storage firm considers any claim under $200 to be too insignificant to investigate fully; thus, a refund check is issued automatically for a claim under this amount. Firms may also have a complete set of procedures and policies developed for every size of claim.
- How often has this customer made claims? If the buyer has instituted many claims in the past, the company may need to not only resolve the specific complaint but also conduct a more comprehensive investigation of all prior claims. Such a probe may reveal systematic flaws in the salesperson's company, product, or procedures. For example, Agria (a Swedish commercial insurance company) routinely examines customer complaints to determine if new services should be developed. One result is that Agria is one of the fastest-growing insurance companies in Europe.[12]
- How will the action taken affect other customers? The salesperson should assume that the action taken will be communicated to other prospects and customers. If the complaining customer is part of a buying community (discussed in Chapter 6), chances are good that others will learn about the resolution of the claim. Thus, the salesperson must take actions necessary to maintain a positive presence in that community, possibly even providing a more generous solution than the merits of the case dictate.

The solution that will be provided must be clearly communicated to the customer. The customer must perceive the settlement as being fair. When describing the settlement, the salesperson should carefully monitor all verbal and nonverbal cues to determine the customer's level of satisfaction. If the customer does not agree with the proposed course of action, the salesperson should seek ways to change the settlement or provide additional information about why the settlement is fair to all parties.

Follow Through with Action

A fair settlement made in the customer's favor helps resell the company and its products or services. The salesperson has the chance to prove what the customer has been told for a long time: that the company will devote time and effort to keeping customers satisfied.

The salesperson who has authority only to recommend an adjustment must take care to report the facts of the case promptly and accurately to the home or branch office. The salesperson has the responsibility to act as a buffer between the customer and the company. After the claim is filed, contact must be maintained with the customer to see that the customer secures the promised settlement.

The salesperson also has a responsibility to educate the customer to forestall future claims. After a claim has been settled to the customer's satisfaction is a fine time to make some suggestions. For example, the industrial sales representative may provide a new set of directions on how to oil and clean a machine.

Achieve Customer Satisfaction

Although complaints always signal customer dissatisfaction, their absence does not necessarily mean customers are happy. Customers probably voice only 1 in 20 of their concerns. They may speak out only when highly dissatisfied, or a big corporation's buyer may not be aware of problems until the product's users vent their frustration. Lower levels of dissatisfaction still hurt sales especially in today's high tech environment when a tweeted complaint can reach hundreds of followers. Salespeople should continuously monitor customers' levels of satisfaction and perceptions of product performance because customer satisfaction is the most important reason for reordering at this stage in the relationship.

When customers have complaints, they are likely to turn to the Internet to look for solutions. Many companies also monitor Facebook, even in B2B settings, as you can see in Sales Technology 14.1.

When the customer is satisfied, an opportunity for further business exists. Complaints and dissatisfaction can occur at any time during the relationship, but handling complaints well during the exploration stage is one way to prove that the salesperson is committed to keeping the customer's business. When customers sense such commitment, whether through the handling of a complaint or through other forms of special attention, they may be ready to move to the expansion stage.

EXPANSION

The next phase of the buyer–seller relationship is expansion. When a salesperson does a good job of identifying and satisfying needs and the beginnings of a partnership are in place, the opportunity is ripe for additional sales. As mentioned in the previous chapter, some companies celebrate the first reorder more than they do an initial purchase because the reorder signals a long and profitable relationship. With greater trust, the salesperson can focus on identifying additional needs and providing solutions. In this section we discuss how to increase sales from current

SALES Technology 14.1

FINDING SATISFACTION

Ken Madrigal, senior digital experience strategist for Verizon, has a difficult challenge. Because of its viral nature, the ability to call greater attention to customer issues, and the potential impact on brand perception, companies wrestle with the strategic and operational implications of enabling social media as a primary relationship channel and connection with customers.

"In today's competitive digital environment, customers, whether they are B2B or B2C, have high expectations for customized and unique engagements with a brand. Leveraging the personalized nature of consumers' social profile complemented with their company CRM profile is a powerful tool to build a strong connection with a customer."

Ken believes that vendors must consider investing in social listening and engagement platforms to understand what customer conversations in social media are driving brand perception. These platforms digest social media postings, then synthesize those into assessments of the market's satisfaction and attitudes. At some point, a company needs to choose if it is worth it to operationalize a process to engage with those conversations.

Ken adds, "In an age where referrals and the momentum of brand sentiment swing the decision of hundreds of thousands of customers, being an active participant in those social conversations can affect business." Ken recalled the United Airlines fiascos, including the viral video of a passenger being dragged off a flight. "Even in B2B settings, customer conversations in social media can affect other customers' positive or negative expectations."

Companies choosing to build a social engagement operation must go in with its eyes open and with an expectation that social listening is a long-term investment for return. Ken notes that 70 to 80 percent of Twitter is noise, but that 20 percent is powerful insight and Snapchat is where most millennials engage with one another, but no content is kept permanent.

But he points out that "customers talk to each other via social media. We can put our stuff on a Web site somewhere, but if we aren't part of the social media conversation, then we're missing a huge opportunity."

customers to expand the relationship. Keep in mind, however, that the activities of the exploration stage (monitoring order processing, handling complaints, and so on) still apply.

There are several ways to maximize the selling opportunity each account represents. These include generating reorders, upgrading, full-line selling, and cross-selling.

GENERATING REPEAT ORDERS

In some situations the most appropriate strategy is to generate repeat orders. For example, Cargill provides salt and other cooking ingredients to Kellogg's. The best strategy for the Cargill salesperson may be to ensure that Kellogg's continues to buy those ingredients from Cargill. Several methods can be used to improve the likelihood of reorders. We discuss each method in turn.

Be Present at Buying Time

One important method of ensuring reorders is to know how often and when the company makes decisions. Salesforce.com, Microsoft Dynamics, and other CRM software can provide order histories for accounts and give you a customer's buying cycle. For example, if you know that a particular customer reorders every 90 days, you can call on the 80th day with an offer and increase reorders.

Good service often involves following up on an installation just to make sure all is going as it should, as this technician is doing.

Buyers do not always have regular buying cycles, which can make it difficult for salespeople to be present at buying time. In these situations the seller still wants to be present in the buyer's mind. One way to remain in front of customers is with specialty advertising items, useful items that are imprinted with the company name. Pharmaceutical companies may give prescription pads to keep a drug's brand in front of the doctor, while a technology company may imprint a webcam with its name to go on top of the desktop screen. In both instances, the goal is to keep the brand name at the top of the buyer's mind so that when a purchase is made, that's the brand thought of first.

Help Service the Product

Most products need periodic maintenance and repair, and some mechanical and electronic products require routine adjustments. Such service requirements offer salespeople a chance to show buyers that the seller's interest did not end with the delivery of the product. Salespeople should be able to make minor adjustments or take care of minor repairs. If they cannot put the product back into working order, they must notify the proper company representative. They should then check to see that the repairs have been completed in a timely manner and to the customer's complete satisfaction.

As we discuss in Chapter 16, part of the salesperson's job is getting to know the company's maintenance and repair people. These repair people can act as the salesperson's eyes and ears when they make service calls. The same can be said in some settings with getting to know delivery people. At Gallery Furniture, delivery people look for empty rooms when delivering furniture because these rooms mean future sales. When a good relationship is established with service personnel, salespeople can learn of pending decisions or concerns and take the necessary action.

thinking it through

Some customers take advantage of salespeople by trying to have them perform almost all the routine maintenance on a product for free. What can you as a salesperson do to curb such requests? How do you know where to draw the line?

Provide Expert Guidance

An industrial buyer or purchasing agent may need help in choosing a proper grade of oil or in selecting a suitable floor cleaner. A buyer for a retail store may want help developing sales promotion ideas. For example, Morgen Fett, wine buyer for Whole Foods, bought more wine from one salesperson than any other. Why? Because he came up with novel ideas to help her sell more wine. What she found annoying were the salespeople who thought just being friendly was enough to earn increases in sales.

The salesperson usually prospers only if the buyer prospers. Obviously, unless buyers can use a product or service profitably or resell it at a profit, they have no need to continue buying from that product's seller. One expert suggests finding non-selling-related ideas to offer your customers. When you use your industry expertise to solve problems or develop opportunities for your clients that do not involve the sale of your product, you add value to the relationship, which can ultimately help you expand your business within the account.

Tim Simmons, of Teradata, relies heavily on experts who know not only their subject area but also their customers. When he was working with one retailer to develop a better business intelligence solution involving Teradata products, for example, he searched LinkedIn to find a consultant who was an expert in that area (as well as a former client). Through that consultant, he also found associates who were familiar with the account. He then built a team that successfully designed, sold, and implemented a solution.

Provide Special Assistance

Salespeople can find themselves in a position to chip in and help a buyer. Providing such special assistance is one hallmark of excellence in selling. Good relationships are built faster and made more solid by the salesperson who does a little something extra for a customer, performing services beyond his or her normal responsibilities.

Gail Walker, owner of the trade show and marketing company Marquis Communications, once worked in the booth of one of her customers at a trade show because a salesperson called in sick. JR Montalvo helped clean out a customer's closet so there would be room for the printer he had just sold them.

These little things can go a long way in building a relationship. While the tendency may be to rush off to the next sales call, sometimes you are better off just being helpful to the customer you already have.

UPGRADING

Similar to generating reorders is the concept of upgrading. **Upgrading**, also called *upselling,* is convincing the customer to use a higher-quality product or a newer product. In a modified rebuy, the salesperson seeks the upgrade because the new or better product serves the needs of the buyer more effectively than the old product did.

ethics

Another form of upgrading is when the salesperson attempts to add on or sell a premium version at the time of the close. For example, when you check in, the clerk at the hotel may suggest you upgrade to a suite for just a few dollars more. Pressure to engage in upgrading in consumer sales can lead to ethical concerns; issues have been raised regarding upgrading practices in industries as diverse as credit cards and funeral homes. These settings, particularly when salespeople are dealing with less educated consumers, can lend themselves to overselling, selling way beyond the buyers' needs. Professional salespeople sell to needs–no more, no less.

When your plan is to upgrade in a modified rebuy, emphasize that the initial decision was a good one during the initial call. Now, however, technology or needs have changed, and the newer product fits the customer's requirements better. Otherwise the buyer may believe that the seller is trying to take advantage of the relationship to foist a higher-priced product.

FULL-LINE SELLING

Full-line selling is selling an entire line of associated products. For example, an ESI salesperson may sell a Xerox printer but also wants to sell the dry ink and paper the printer uses, as well as a service contract. Or a Campbell Soup Company salesperson will ask a store to carry cream of potato soup as well as tomato soup.

The emphasis in full-line selling is on helping the buyer realize the synergy of owning or carrying all the products in that line. For example, the ESI salesperson may emphasize the security in using Xerox supplies, whereas the Campbell rep will point out that sales for all soups will increase if the assortment is broader.

CROSS-SELLING

Cross-selling is similar to full-line selling except the additional products sold are not directly associated with the initial products. For example, cross-selling occurs when the ESI salesperson attempts to sell IT network services to a printer customer or when a Campbell Soup Company rep sells spaghetti sauce to a soup buyer. Cross-selling involves leveraging the relationship with a buyer to identify needs for additional products; one reason is that it can cost much less to cross-sell to an existing client than to acquire a new client.[13] Again, trust in the selling organization and the salesperson already exists; therefore, the sale should not be as difficult as it would be with a new customer, provided the needs exist.

Cardinal Health has three major divisions: Medical Products, Pharmaceutical Products, and Services, but all three divisions are further broken down into specialties. As a result, some buyers may have as many as seven Cardinal salespeople calling on them. Cross-selling wasn't happening because the salespeople were too specialized–they didn't really know the other product areas. To take advantage of cross-selling opportunities, they first identified where such opportunities would be through analysis of data in their CRM system. They then developed training for salespeople to help create opportunities for cross-selling.

Training is not the only requirement for effective cross-selling, as illustrated in Exhibit 14.4. Some attempts at cross-selling, though, can resemble the initial sale because the buying center may change. For example, the medical equipment buyer may not be the same person who buys services. If that is the case, the salesperson will have to begin a relationship with the new buyer, building trust and credibility.

Convincing retailers to carry all of Nivea's skin care products is full-line selling; convincing them to carry shampoo or lip care or baby products is cross-selling. Both strategies leverage existing relationships to increase account share but cross-selling can also require moving into new buying centers.

©Deposit Photos/Glow Images RF

COMMITMENT

When the buyer–seller relationship has reached the commitment stage, there is a stated or implied pledge to continue the relationship, as we discussed in the last chapter. Formally this pledge may begin with the seller becoming a **preferred supplier**, which is a much greater level of commitment than the levels discussed in Chapter 11. Although preferred-supplier status may mean different things in different companies, in general it means that the supplier is assured of a large percentage of the buyer's business and will get the first opportunity to earn new business. For example, at John Deere, only preferred suppliers are eligible to bid on new product programs. Thus, preferred supplier is one term used for "partnership."

Chrysler, a division of Fiat Chrysler Automobiles (FCA), classifies its relationships with suppliers into four categories. The first is transactional, or what we called *solo exchange* in the previous chapter. The

Exhibit 14.4
Seven Tips for Effective Cross-Selling

1. *Product knowledge:* Salespeople have to know all their company's products. When companies introduce new cross-selling opportunities, training is needed to learn the new product lines.
2. *Cross-selling skills:* Salespeople must know how to identify the appropriate decision maker, how to leverage current relationships, and how to use other cross-selling skills. Cross-selling often requires additional training.
3. *Incentives:* Many salespeople are afraid of losing the first piece of business by asking for too much, so incentives can help make it worthwhile to ask.
4. *Reasonable quotas or goals:* The first goal when implementing a cross-selling strategy is to get salespeople to simply ask for the opportunity. Goals that are too tough encourage salespeople to force the cross-sale.
5. *Results tracking:* Effective organizations track results by individual and by sales team to identify cross-selling success. Many companies use contact management software like NetSuite or Salesforce.com for results tracking.
6. *Timing:* Creating a promotion campaign to support cross-selling efforts, particularly when seasonality is an issue, can make a cross-selling strategy successful. Timing also refers to making sure training occurs before the program starts.
7. *Performance appraisals:* Salespeople need feedback to identify where and how in the process to improve.

Sources: Vicki West, PhD, and Jan Minifie, PhD

second is coordinative, in which Chrysler may sign an annual contract. These two types of relationships are market exchanges. The next two are more strategic, with selective partnership being the first level. Suppliers are integrated into product development processes and work closely with Chrysler to develop effective interfaces. Alliances, or strategic partnerships, go even further, with integration of departments across the two companies, investment in joint assets, and joint concept development taking place. Such commitment is rare; few companies are strategic partners.

What does it take to become a preferred supplier? PPG Industries, as part of its Supplier Added Value Effort (SAVE) program, uses several criteria (listed in Exhibit 14.5). In some cases a PPG preferred supplier is a distributor, not a manufacturer. In these situations the supplier and PPG work in tandem to find the best manufacturers at the lowest prices, with the result being increased sales volume and better volume discounts. PPG gets the lowest price possible at the required service level, and the distributor makes more profit. Clearly this is a win–win opportunity.

Note that upgrading, full-line selling, cross-selling, and handling complaints will continue to occur during the commitment stage. Because a commitment has been made by both parties to the partnership, however, expectations are greater. Handling complaints properly, appropriately upgrading or cross-selling, and fulfilling new needs are even more important because of the high level of commitment made to the partner.

Many buyers evaluate suppliers on criteria similar to those used by PPG (see Exhibit 14.5). Although the salesperson may not be able to influence corporate culture, she or he plays an important role in managing the relationship and leading both sides into commitment.

SECURING COMMITMENT TO A PARTNERSHIP

When firms reach the commitment stage, elements in addition to trust become important. Along with the dimensions of trust such as competence and dependability and honesty (or ethics), there must be commitment to the partnership from the entire supplying organization, a culture that fits with the buyer's organizational culture, and channels of communication so open that the seller and buyer appear to be part of the same company.

Exhibit 14.5
Examples of Supplier Criteria to Sell to PPG

Hard Savings

- Payment terms, such as cash discounts.
- Improve process:
  Cycle time reduction (shorter order/delivery cycles, for example).
- Inventory management:
  Vendor inventory management.
- Quality and innovation:
  Variability reduction—no defects and no adjustments needed to make products fit our applications.
- Supply chain management:
  Optimum packaging—light packaging that reduces shipping costs while still protecting the product.

Soft Savings

- Commercial:
  Minority-owned vendors.
- Global initiatives:
  New markets—provide access to new markets, either by partnering into new markets or by adjusting products to fit needs of new markets.
- Improve process:
  Improve safety or environmental procedures.
- Quality and innovation:
  Training.
- Supply chain management:
  Bar coding—can reduce the time our employees take to process a shipment.

Source: PPG Industries

COMMITMENT MUST BE COMPLETE

Commitment to the relationship should permeate both organizations, from top management to the secretary who answers the phone. This level of commitment means devoting the resources necessary to satisfy the customer's needs and even anticipating needs before the buyer does.

The salesperson owns the responsibility to secure commitment from his or her own company. Senior management must be convinced of the benefits of partnering with a specific account and must be willing to allow the salesperson to direct the resources necessary to sustain the partnership. (Chapter 16 explores the process of building the internal partnerships the salesperson needs to coordinate those resources.)

Commitment also requires that all employees be empowered to handle the needs of the customer. For example, if the customer has a problem with a billing process, administration should be willing to work with the partner to develop a more satisfactory process. In a partnership the customer should not have to rely on only the salesperson to satisfy its needs. For Mike Power, sales manager for Lovejoy Inc., a big part of the equation is making sure that someone in the organization is always accessible to provide an answer or solve an opportunity. "Accessibility means that we can respond quickly to customer or distributor emergencies. For example, recently we received a call about a coupling breakdown at a steel mill at 1 a.m. From the time the mill's maintenance supervisor called the distributor's sales representative to the time we loaded the coupling on the truck for delivery, less than four hours had passed."[14] Accomplishing this feat took many more employees than just a salesperson.

COMMUNICATION

In the exploration stage, availability must be demonstrated (we already discussed the example of toll-free hotlines and voice mail to allow the seller's organization to respond quickly to customer calls). But in the commitment phase of a partnership, the seller must take a proactive communication stance. This approach means actively seeking opportunities to communicate at times other than when the salesperson has something to sell or the customer has a problem to resolve.

Partners are usually the first to learn about each other's new products, many times even codeveloping those products.[15] Part of the commitment between suppliers and their customer partners is the trust that such early knowledge will be kept confidential. Partners want to know what is coming out soon so they can make appropriate plans.

Salespeople should also encourage direct communication among similar functional areas. In previous stages the two firms communicated through the buyer and the salesperson. If multilevel selling occurred, it occurred at even levels—that is, vice presidents talking to one another. But when two firms commit to a partnership, the boundaries between them, at least in terms of communication, should blur, as illustrated in Exhibit 14.6.

The buyer's production department, for example, should be able to communicate directly with the seller's engineering department rather than going through the salesperson, if production needs to work on a change in the product design. Although the salesperson would want to be aware of a product design change and ensure that engineering responded promptly to the customer's concern, direct communication means more accurate communication and a better understanding of the customer's needs. A better solution is more likely to result when there is direct communication.

CORPORATE CULTURE

Corporate culture is the values and beliefs held by senior management. A company's culture shapes the attitudes and actions of employees and influences the development of policies and programs.[16] For example, consider the following scene. In a large room with concrete floors are a number of cubicles built from plywood. Each cubicle has a card table, two folding chairs, and a poster that says, "How low can you go?" Such is the scene in Bentonville, Arkansas, the corporate headquarters of Walmart, where salespeople meet their buyers for Sam's Club and Walmart. That room reflects Walmart's culture of the lowest possible price.

A similar culture of constantly seeking ways to drive down costs is necessary for a seller to develop a partnership with Walmart. A single salesperson will not change a company's corporate culture to secure a partnership with a buyer, but the salesperson must identify the type of culture both organizations hold and make an assessment of fit. Although a perfect match is not necessary, the salesperson must be ready to demonstrate that there is a fit. Offering lavish entertainment to a Walmart buyer, for example, would not demonstrate a fit. Telling the buyer that you are staying at a Circle 6 Motel might.

Companies have often sought international partners as a way to enter foreign markets. Walmart partnered with Cifra when the U.S. retailer entered the Mexican market. Cifra provides distribution services and products to Walmart for Sam's Club and Walmart stores located in Mexico City, Monterrey, and Guadalajara. When partnering with companies from other countries, country culture differences as well as corporate culture differences can cause difficulties.

Exhibit 14.6

Direct Communication between Partners

In traditional settings, companies communicate through a single buyer or purchasing agent and the salesperson. Partners, though, allow direct communication between members of the selling and buying companies.

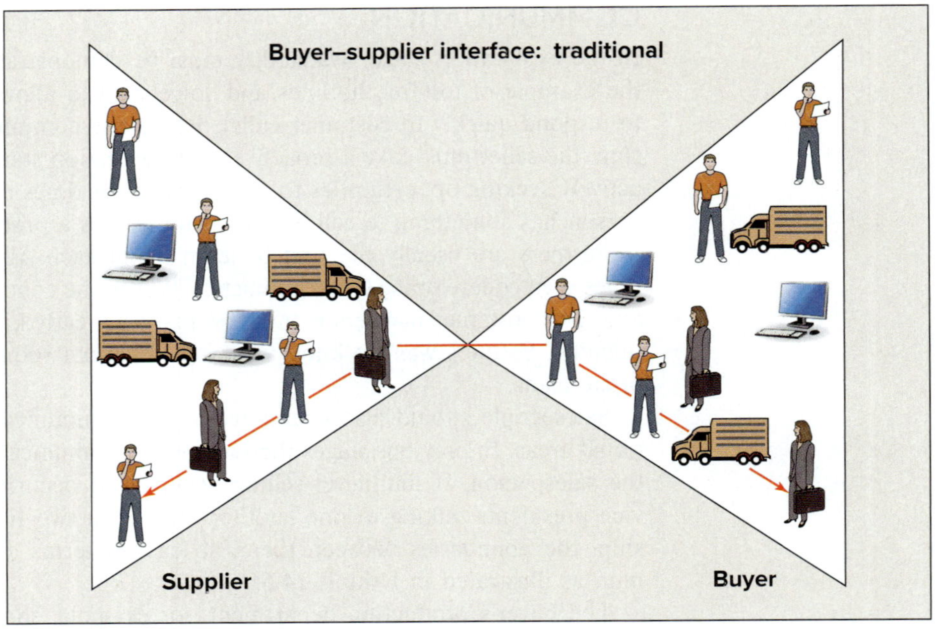

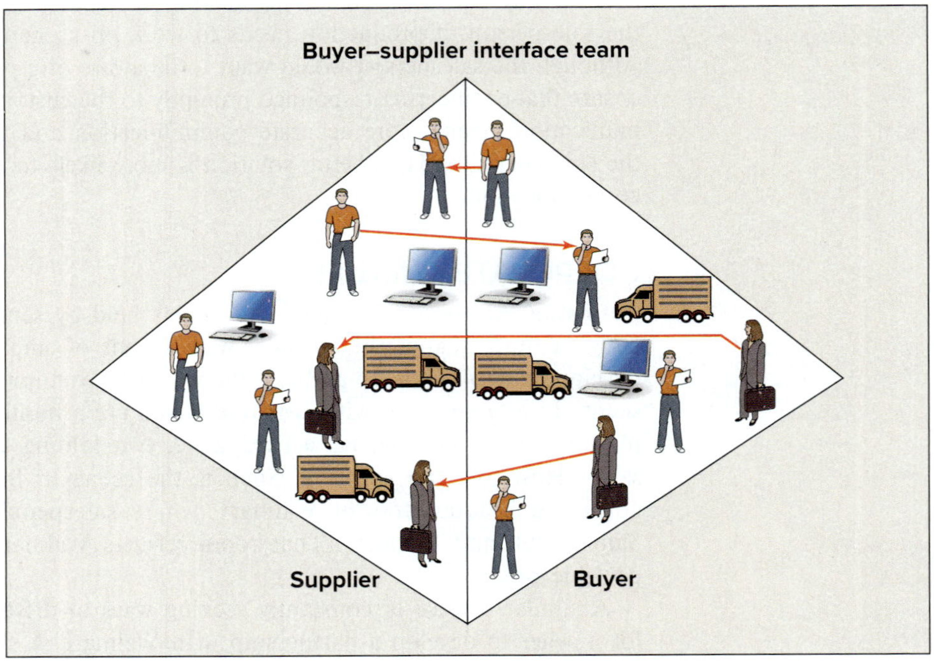

Though not attempting to change a company's culture, the salesperson who seeks a partnering relationship seeks change for both organizations. In the next section we discuss what types of changes salespeople manage and how they manage those changes.

THE SALESPERSON AS CHANGE AGENT

To achieve increasing revenue in an account over time, the salesperson acts as a **change agent,** or a cause of change in the organization. Each sale may involve some type of change—perhaps a change from a competitive product or simply a new version of the old one. Partnering, though, often requires changes in both the buying and selling organizations.

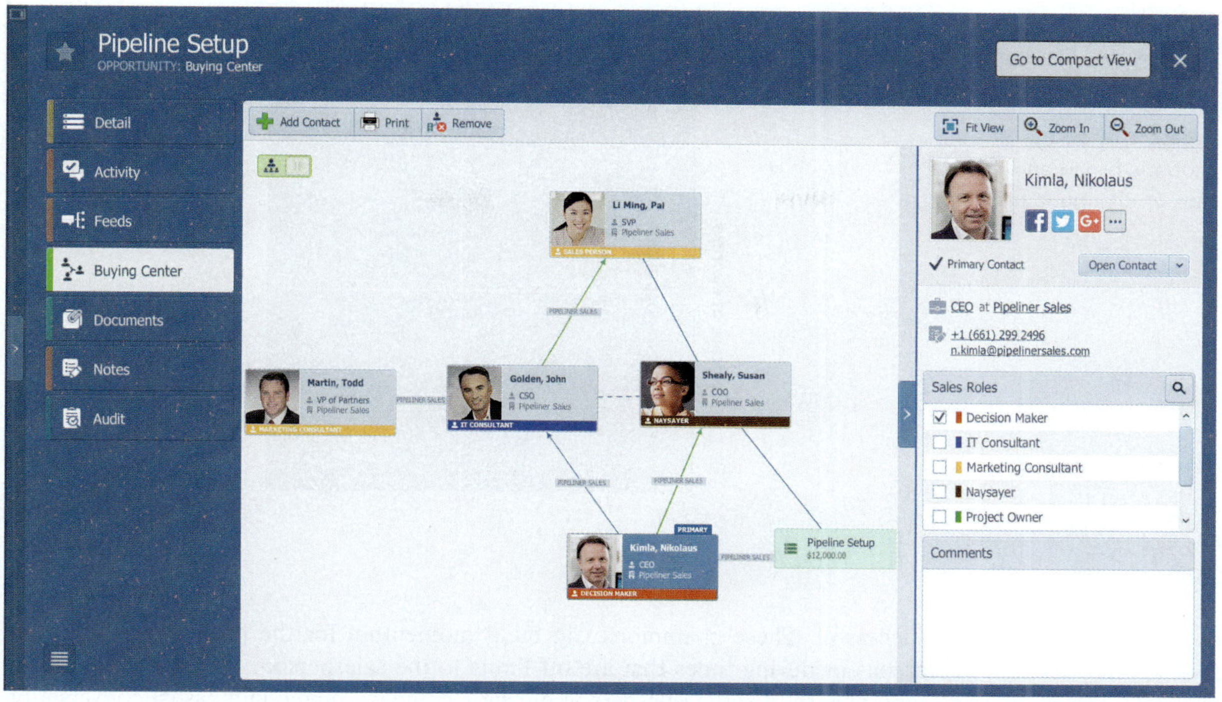

CRM systems like Pipeliner enable salespeople to map the buying center in their account. If you were selling to Pipeliner, this is what the buying center would look like.

Courtesy of Pipeliner

For example, American Distribution Systems (ADS), a pharmaceutical distributor, and Ciba-Geigy, a pharmaceutical manufacturer, took six months to implement a joint operating plan that integrated systems of both companies. ADS created a cross-functional team that re-created ADS systems to function as part of Ciba-Geigy. At the same time Ciba-Geigy had to share information and other resources to take full advantage of the benefits of the relationship. In this instance both buyer and seller had to change significantly for the partnership to work.

Change is not easy, even when it is obviously beneficial. The objective is to manage change, such as changing from steel to iron pipe, in the buyer's organization while giving the appearance of stability. Two critical elements to consider about change are its rate and scope. The **rate of change** refers to how quickly the change is made; the **scope of change** refers to the degree to which the change affects the organization. Broad changes affect many areas of the company, whereas narrow changes affect small areas. In general, the faster and broader the change, the more likely it will meet with resistance, as illustrated in Exhibit 14.7.[17]

To overcome resistance to change, the salesperson should consider several decisions. The first decision involves finding help in the buying organization for selling the proposal. Other important decisions are positioning the proposal, determining the necessary resources, and developing a time-based strategy.

Finding Champions

First, the choice of one or more champions must be made. **Champions,** also called *advocates* or *internal salespeople*, work for the buying firm in the areas most affected by the proposed change and work with the salesperson to make the proposal

Exhibit 14.7
Change and Resistance

Resistance to change is greatest when the scope is broad and the rate of change is fast.

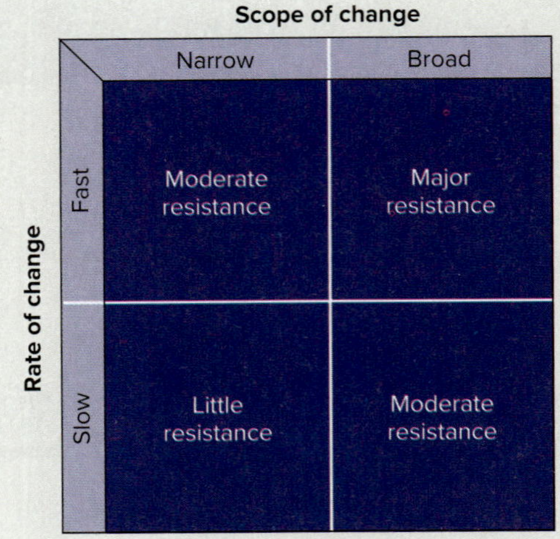

successful. These champions can build momentum for the proposal by selling in arenas or during times that are off limits to the salesperson. For example, a champion may sell for the salesperson during a company picnic in a casual conversation with a coworker.

Recognize that the change in status from preferred supplier to strategic partner may also require a champion. Champions not only help persuade the firm to change but also help implement the change once the decision has been made. Such was the case at Tyco when the company wanted to revamp how it purchased services and maintenance products. Not only did the situation call for a complete review of vendors, it also required changing how these products and services were purchased. Getting the changes through to all the departments required identifying champions who would lead the change.[18] Thus, champions are important to salespeople.

Salespeople can help potential champions by providing them with all the knowledge they will need. Knowledge builds confidence; champions will have the courage to speak up when they are certain they know what they are talking about. Salespeople can also motivate champions to participate fully in the decision process by showing how the decision meets their needs as well as the overall needs of the company.

Positioning the Change

Positioning a change is similar to positioning a product in mass marketing, as you may have learned in your principles of marketing course. In this case, however, the salesperson examines the specific needs and wants of the various constituencies in the account to position the change for the greatest likelihood of success.

Because salespeople are highly proactive in finding areas for improvement (or change) in their partners' organizations, positioning a change may determine who is involved in the decision. For example, suppose the Dell representative who calls on your school recognizes that the student computer labs are out-of-date. Is a proposal for new equipment primarily the domain of the computer services department, or is it the domain of faculty who teach computing classes? If the computer services department favors Dell but the users favor Apple, the Dell rep will be better served by positioning the change as the responsibility of the computer services department.

Positioning the proposed change appropriately may spell success or failure for the proposal.

Determining the Necessary Resources

The customer's needs may be beyond the salesperson's expertise. Recall that Tim Simmons, with Teradata, once brought in a consultant to help close and implement a deal with Hallmark. But Simmons often brings in teams of engineers, financial consultants, and others from within Teradata to make sure that the solution is configured properly and implemented in a way that brings the desired ROI.

The salesperson must assess the situation and determine what resources are needed to secure the buyer's commitment. Although the preceding example discusses allocation of personnel, salespeople must manage other resources as well, such as travel and entertainment budgets or sample supplies. (We discuss how to build internal partnerships to effectively coordinate company resources in Chapter 16.)

Developing a Time-Based Strategy

The salesperson must determine a strategy for the proposed change and set that strategy against a time line. This action accomplishes several objectives. First, the strategy is an outline of planned sales calls, with primary and minimum call objectives determined for each call. Second, the timeline estimates when each call should occur. Of course objectives and planned times will change depending on the results of each call, but this type of planning is necessary to give the salesperson guidance for each call, determine when resources are to be used, and make sure each call contributes to strategic account objectives.

For example, suppose Simmons would like to sell a system to Saks. He may determine that calls need to be made on five individuals at Saks. A time-based strategy would indicate which person should be visited first and what should be accomplished during that visit, as well as the order of visits to the remaining four members of the buying center. While the plan can be modified based on the prospect's responses, Exhibit 14.8 illustrates a simplified version of a timeline.

Exhibit 14.8

Timeline for Teradata/Saks

Month 1	Month 2	Month 3	Month 4	Month 5	Month 6
Visit CIO and CMO.	Visit director of cyber security—bring Teradata cyber analyst.	Visit director of marketing analytics with Teradata's chief analytics officer.	Arrange audit of analytics opportunity with ROI team.	Submit proposal to CIO, CMO, and CFO.	Sign agreement for new system.
Primary objective: Determine analytics and data needs.	Primary objective: Secure support in principle for on-premise system.	Primary objective: Specify objectives for new analytics plan and secure commitment in principle.	Primary objective: Document cost savings and revenue gains for ROI modeling.		
Minimum objective: Secure permission to see others in the IT area.					

DISSOLUTION

Too often salespeople believe that once a customer has committed to a partnership, less work is needed to maintain that relationship. That belief is untrue. Moreover, the recognition that everyone who touches the account has to continue to strengthen the account is important. Those who fail to strengthen the relationship may inadvertently weaken it.[19] Salespeople who subscribe to the belief that partnerships require less work fall victim to one or more common problems. As discussed in the previous chapter, the final stage for partnerships is dissolution, or breakup, but this stage can occur at any point, not just after commitment. Several potential problems, including maintaining few personal relationships, failing to monitor competitor actions or the industry, and falling into complacency, can lead to dissolution.

MAINTAINING FEW PERSONAL RELATIONSHIPS

Salespeople tend to call on buyers they like; it is natural to want to spend time with friends. The result is that relationships are cultivated with only a few individuals in the account. Unfortunately for such salespeople, buyers may leave the organization, transfer to an unrelated area, or simply not participate in some decisions. Truly effective salespeople attempt to develop multiple relationships within an account.

Darryl Lehnus, noted sales professional in the sports sales profession, advocates a *3-by-3 strategy*. What he means is make sure you have three personal relationships at three levels of the organization (at least nine relationships total). When you maintain a 3-by-3 strategy, the chances of getting surprised and losing an account are substantially reduced.[20]

FAILING TO MONITOR COMPETITOR ACTIONS

No matter how strong the partnership is, the competition will want a piece of the business. And no matter how good the salesperson is, there will still be times when the account is vulnerable to competitor action. Accounts are most vulnerable when a personnel change occurs (especially if the rep has developed relationships with a limited number of people in the account), when technology changes, or when major directional changes occur, such as a company starting a new division or entering a new market.

The successful salesperson, however, monitors competitor action even when the account seems invulnerable. For example, an insurance agency had all the insurance business at a state university in Texas for more than 10 years but failed to monitor competitor action at the state capital and lost the account when another insurance agency found a sympathetic buyer in Austin. The loss of this one account cut annual earnings by more than 70 percent.

Monitoring competitor action can be as simple as checking the visitor's log at the front desk to see who has dropped by or keeping up with competitor actions and asking buyers for their opinions. Frequently, developing relationships with the many potential influencers in an account will also keep salespeople informed about competitor actions. As each person is visited, questions and comments about competitors will arise, indicating the activity level of competition.

Monitoring competition also means thinking about the benefits competitors offer, what their products do, and what their selling strategies are. When salespeople understand what the competition offers, they can position their own company's unique capabilities more effectively. It is not enough to know where competitors have made calls; good salespeople also know what the competition is saying.

FAILING TO MONITOR THE INDUSTRY

Similar to failing to monitor competition is a failure to monitor the industry in which either the salesperson or the customer operates. Salespeople often assume that the responsibility of monitoring the industry lies with someone else—either higher-ups in their own company or the customer. But salespeople who fail to monitor both industries may miss opportunities that change creates. As an extreme example, what would happen to an advertising agency's account executive if the Internet were ignored?

How does a professional salesperson monitor the industry? By reading trade magazines, blogs, and e-newsletters and by attending trade shows and conferences. The Salesforce.com CRM software sales representative who handles the John Deere account has to read not only Paul Greenberg's blog to know what's going on in the CRM industry but also Beauchamp McSpadden's blog on agribusiness and farm insurance. It's not enough to know your company's industry; with strategic partners, you must also know their industry.

FALLING INTO COMPLACENCY

Perhaps the most common thief of good accounts is complacency. In sales terms, **complacency** is assuming that the business is yours and will always be yours. It is failing to continue to work as hard to keep the business as you did initially to earn the business. For example, Coca-Cola was the sole supplier to El Volcan, the stadium for the professional soccer team Los Tigres in Monterrey, Mexico. After many years the stadium's concessions manager began to become annoyed with Coca-Cola because service seemed lackadaisical. As a result, the contract was put out to bid; Pepsi responded with a significantly better offer and won the business.

Monty Covington, vice president of sales for Grocery Supply Co. (GSC), schedules annual account reviews with key accounts. In these reviews, he and the account manager ask the customer to evaluate GSC's performance and to identify strategies that can help both companies continue to grow. These annual reviews do not allow GSC to become complacent.

To avoid complacency, salespeople should regularly audit their own customer service. Some of the questions a salesperson may want to consider are these:

- Do I understand each individual's personal characteristics? Do I have these characteristics in my computer file on each account?
- Do I maintain a written or computerized record of promises made?
- Do I follow up on every customer request promptly, no matter how insignificant it may seem?
- Do I follow up on deliveries, make sure initial experiences are positive, and ensure that all paperwork is done correctly and quickly?
- Have I recently found something new that I can do better than the competition?

CONFLICT

Not all dissolution is the result of conflict, as you can see from the types of reasons that most often lead to dissolution. But conflict between buyer and seller can occur, and when it does, the issues can be much more complex than the "usual" complaint.

Customer–supplier conflict is sometimes the result of conflicting policies within the customer's organization and even conflict between parts of the organization. For example, members of a buying center may not agree on what is best; whoever doesn't get his or her way may then take it out on the salesperson. Or the conflict may be a long-standing dispute unrelated to the salesperson that results in poor purchasing policies. A salesperson can moderate such conflict by helping the customer develop appropriate policies; one salesperson even brought in her own purchasing VP to consult with one of her clients so the client could get some ideas on better purchasing policies.

Trust-destroying conflicts can be avoided with several steps. First, start with a clear product description. If the product is a component part or critical for other reasons and the potential for ambiguity exists, write out a clear description. Services providers are especially vulnerable to ambiguity in the sales process because services are intangible. Specifying those services as completely as possible helps avoid later conflict. Another important element is to define who has authority to do what–both for the customer and for the selling organization. For example, it has to be clearly understood who can authorize change orders if the product specs have to be modified. Both these ideas require clear documentation, but good documentation is critical should such a dispute reach the courts.

Recognize that complaints can be the beginning of major conflict. Pathology Associates Medical Laboratories (PAML) lost a million-dollar client simply because small complaints added up over time. There was no major problem, at least at the start: an error on a bill, a late shipment, or a lost product. But these escalated into major conflict and the loss of the account, in part because PAML was unable to track the complaints. It now uses Microsoft Dynamics (CRM software) to track complaints so it can both attack and solve any problems while also maintaining stronger customer relationships.[21] Similarly, Elavon used speech analytics to analyze customer complaint calls and learned that customers who want to terminate a relationship signal their displeasure with a serious complaint three phone calls before the termination call. Now Elavon uses the same speech analytics tool to identify causes of conflict so it can take preemptive action. It estimates that the system saved 600 accounts–about $1.7 million in revenue–in the first three months alone.[22]

We discussed complaint handling as part of the exploration stage, but keep in mind that poor handling of complaints leads to the dissolution stage! Complaints in later stages are likely to lead to full-blown conflict if trust is not carefully salvaged. To repair damage to trust in a conflict, one consultant recommends the following seven steps (compare to the complaint-handling process discussed earlier):

1. Observe and acknowledge what has happened to lead to the loss of trust.
2. Allow your feelings to surface but take responsibility for your actions.
3. Gain support–offer your peer a chance to save face and gain agreement on any mitigating circumstances.
4. Put the experience in the larger context to affirm your commitment to the relationship.
5. Shift the focus from assigning blame to problem solving.
6. Implement the solution.
7. Let go and move on.

Keep in mind that while the relationship may be between two organizations, even the deepest strategic partnership is ultimately the responsibility of two people.

Failing to monitor industry trends and changes is often a cause for losing a customer. One way to monitor the industry is to visit trade shows and see what the competition is offering.

Whatever the reason for dissolution, all is not necessarily lost. Customers who defect, or buy from other vendors, sometimes return. In fact, seeking to woo customers back is an important strategy for many companies. Sometimes, your only hope is to rebuild relationships with customers who left, as John Tanner describes in Building Partnerships 14.1.

SELLING YOURSELF

In the previous chapter we discussed how the concept of different types of relationships can also be applied to the relationships between students and professors and why you might want to work toward different relationships with different instructors. The focus is on how to build strong partnerships, which will apply to only certain situations.

One such situation is when you are involved in an organization on campus. Your organization will need to work with other organizations, both on campus and off. If you have big ideas you want to sell to others, the changes those will necessitate may also be big. That means identifying potential champions for change—people who will represent your ideas well to members in their own organizations or their departments of the school. Further, documenting decisions as part of the follow-up process will help avoid any conflict later, as well as demonstrate your professionalism and competence. Such follow-up will certainly set you apart!

Similarly, your organization may organize a fund-raising project or have T-shirt sales or some other sales transaction. How will you monitor orders (in the case of a T-shirt sale), how will you handle delivery, and will you engage in any postsale follow-up? If so, how?

In many different chapters in this book, you'll find references to the competitive advantage gained by having a personal reputation for integrity and competence. When opportunities for on-campus awards, scholarships, and postgraduation jobs arrive, your personal reputation will influence your ability to capitalize on those opportunities. In this chapter you've learned ways to demonstrate integrity and competence to satisfy and retain customers; apply those to your school environment, and you'll enjoy the type of personal reputation that leads to success.

BUILDING Partnerships 14.1

THE ONLY WAY IS UP!

Like many new salespeople, the first opportunity I got was in a territory that was underperforming, unable to meet sales goals. At Concentra, we provide occupational health care services, ranging from drug tests and employment physicals to physical therapy and injury care, for companies and their employees. Like most companies, Concentra wants to grow and has plans to grow the number of clinics substantially over the next few years. That growth was one reason why I joined because I knew there would be opportunity to grow my career.

But when I took over my territory, I quickly realized there were few new customers to be had. Worse yet—sales had declined significantly over the past few years. For me to be successful, I had to find out where the greatest leakage was and turn it around; that is, which accounts had reduced the most in how much business they gave us. Lost and current but shrinking accounts became my prospecting list. This strategy ran contrary to the company strategy of growth through new customers, but I knew that's where the biggest opportunity lay.

Service was the primary reason we were losing business. In fact, we're really a service business, so we have no choice but to deliver good service. For my accounts, though, service starts with me. When they realized they could count on me to follow up and do what I said I'd do, we began getting opportunities to win their business back. For example, it took nearly a year just to get in the door of one midsize account. In the course of talking with them before actually meeting them, I discovered that some of the prices my competitor was charging were as much as 30 percent less. Price, though, wasn't the issue—service was. When I finally got an appointment, I began by saying, "I can't touch some of the prices you are paying, but I can address your needs for better service." And, since I brought several staff members who actually deliver services with me, the client could see we were serious about it.

In spite of our higher prices, our commitment to outstanding service won us the account back. Our stronger reputation for patient satisfaction then enabled me to get into the large accounts where we never had the business.

My ability to serve my clients isn't just about the experience their employees have when they visit our clinic. My company also backed me up with research that I can use to prove to my clients how they can cut worker injuries with us and help them build a safer workplace. I work with my clients on a regular basis to review their injury and other occupational health history so that we can find ways to reduce health care expenses and improve the health of their employees. This type of service is unmatched in the industry. Knowing that I am improving the quality of life for workers in my community while helping their companies succeed motivates me to make sure I deliver the best service possible—and win back any lost customers.

Source: John R. Tanner

SUMMARY

Developing partnerships has become increasingly important for salespeople and their firms. Salespeople can develop partnerships and generate goodwill by servicing accounts properly and by strategically building relationships. Both salespeople and buyers benefit from partnering.

Many specific activities are necessary to ensure customer satisfaction and to develop a partnering relationship. The salesperson must maintain the proper perspective, remember the customer between calls, build perceptions of trust, monitor order processing, ensure the proper initial use of the product or service, help service the product, provide expert guidance and suggestions, and provide any necessary special assistance.

The best opportunities to develop goodwill are usually provided by the proper handling of customer complaints. Sales representatives should encourage unhappy customers to tell their stories completely, fully, and without interruption. A sympathetic attitude to a real or an imaginary product or service failure cannot be overemphasized. After determining the facts, the salesperson should implement the solution promptly and monitor it to ensure that proper action is taken.

The appropriate solution will depend on many factors, such as the seriousness of the problem, the dollar amount involved, and the value of the account. A routine should be developed to handle all complaints fairly and equitably.

In the expansion phase of the relationship, key sales activities are generating repeat orders, upgrading, cross-selling, and full-line selling. The goal is to achieve a partnership, in which case the seller is often designated a preferred supplier.

At this level of relationship, it is important that both organizations commit to the relationship from top to bottom and open communication directly between appropriate personnel in both organizations. At this point, salespeople become change agents as they work in both organizations to seamlessly integrate the partnership.

Sometimes relationships break up. When partnerships dissolve, usually there are multiple reasons for the breakup. For example, when a salesperson leans too heavily on a few personal relationships and those people leave or when the salesperson fails to monitor competitive actions, then the buying organization may feel less commitment to the relationship. Other reasons for dissolution include failing to monitor changes in the industry and becoming complacent. Winning a customer back is still a possibility and should be pursued when appropriate.

KEY TERMS

champion 389
change agent 388
complacency 393
corporate culture 387
cross-selling 384
full-line selling 383
Internet of Things (IoT) 374
preferred supplier 384
rate of change 389
scope of change 389
upgrading 383

ETHICS PROBLEMS

1. A customer is claiming you misrepresented a product in order to get the sale, so the contract should be voided. You know from other sources that the customer is in dire financial straits. You did not, at least in your mind, misrepresent the product. If your company agrees to cancel the contract, it is the same as saying you did misrepresent the product, and you could face termination or less drastic negative consequences. What should be done? (This is based on an actual event.)
2. The fairest solution to a customer's complaint is one that turns out to be against company policy, though certainly not against the law or unethical in any way. If you tried to do it, the chances are you could get away with it; but if caught, you would be terminated. What would you do? Would it matter if you knew that if caught, you would receive a mild reprimand? Or that others had done the same thing?
3. Some research suggests that fixing a customer's complaint can lead to an even stronger relationship. Should a company allow a minor problem with a product to continue, just to give reps that opportunity to solve the problem? Why or why not?

QUESTIONS AND PROBLEMS

1. Your company sells manufacturing equipment, and a new machine had a control problem that affected about 20 percent of customers. The problem was all over social media. How would you deal with this problem if a customer brought up that there were so many bad reviews on social media, though he's not had that problem—yet? How would you respond if a prospect brought it up? The problem turned out be a software glitch that could be fixed by downloading a patch from your company Web site, which could be done by customers. Once the patch was written, what would you do? Knowing that the patch was installed on all new systems, how would you deal with a prospect who brought it up?
2. Explain how active listening can be applied to a situation in which a customer makes a complaint. What can applying this art accomplish? What forms of active listening might actually cause *more* problems?
3. Read through From the Buyer's Seat 14.1 and Building Partnerships 14.1. These seem to be advocating opposite perspectives. How do you reconcile these two seemingly opposite positions?
4. The Miami Heat, like lots of sports teams, has a sales force that sells season tickets. Once someone is sold a season ticket package, the customer becomes someone else's responsibility. Every person in the office, no matter his or her regular job, has responsibility for a group of current customers; management believes this makes everyone more responsive to customer needs. But some customers complain; they would rather have the same salesperson who sold the tickets fix any problems. When should salespeople handle all complaints? When is it better to have everyone in the company take on some customer responsibility? When is it best to have one customer service department? Justify each response.
5. Reread Sales Technology 14.1. What role can salespeople play in avoiding the issues Ken Madrigal is facing?
6. What is your reaction to the statement "The customer is always right"? Is it a sound basis for making adjustments and satisfying complaints? Can it be followed literally? Why or why not?
7. In Building Partnerships 14.1, John Tanner says that service was essential to his strategy. Is that just because he's in a service business? In what types of situations involving products would service after the sale be a strategic sales factor?
8. How do you know when full-line selling, upgrading, or cross-selling strategies are appropriate?
9. What are the potential risks that a champion might face when advocating on your behalf? What are the various ways a salesperson can provide a potential champion with knowledge to build confidence? What types of knowledge will the champion need?

CASE PROBLEMS

case 14.1

McPherson & Co.

McPherson & Co. is a distributor of test equipment used in mining and oil applications. It represents a handful of different manufacturers who engineer solutions for wide-ranging environments. When Jasmine Harris, of Barsh Engineering, got the call from Eddie Schmidt at McPherson, she was excited. For over a year she worked to get McPherson to carry Barsh's geothermal test equipment, but there was no progress—until today, when Eddie asked if the Barsh Geo-Core Xcel would handle conditions in the North Sea oil fields.

"I don't know," Jasmine replied. "I've personally not had any customers drilling in that area, but I will ask our senior engineer and find out. What's the situation?"

"We've got a really good shot at landing some business from Royal Dutch Shell, but we've got some holes in our product line," Eddie replied. "I'm really thinking of making this an all-Barsh pitch, which would be about a $400,000 contract. Or I may give Shell two solutions, one all Barsh and one a mix of other products." He went into detail about the conditions in which the Geo-Core would have to work so Jasmine would know what questions to ask.

After the call, Jasmine called the senior engineer and asked if the product would work. Assured that it would, she went to work on a great proposal. Not only would a $400,000 sale represent a month's quota, she knew that McPherson was good for five times that in its other accounts. This opportunity was huge!

Eddie called Jasmine immediately when he got her e-mail with the proposal attached. "This looks great! I think the all-Barsh approach is best, so that's what we'll go with. I'll submit this to Shell tomorrow."

Two months later the first Geo-Cores were installed and operational. But within a week it was obvious that they weren't up to the demanding weather conditions of the North Sea. The machines were breaking down on average about every four hours. Eddie called Jasmine, quite upset with the results, particularly because Shell now wanted to cancel the entire agreement.

Questions

1. Assume you are Jasmine. What should you do?
2. Does the stage of the buyer–seller relationship matter? Which buyer is most important, Royal Dutch Shell or Barsh?
3. Your first call after hanging up with Eddie is with the senior engineer who gave you the wrong information. He claims there is a simple fix, but an engineer will have to make the trip there to do it, and that will be about a $5,000 trip. First, what would you say to your manager who has to sign off on that expense? Second, how do you handle the buyer?

case 14.2

Crisp Technology

As he drove to work, Rudy Gonzalez thought about CMA, his largest account. His company, Crisp Technology, provided components CMA used in the manufacturing of communications equipment used in ships and boats. But CMA's instrumentation division used none of Crisp's parts and has never tried them. Rudy knew, however, that his success in the coming year was dependent on growing sales at CMA. His increase in quota of 20 percent couldn't be achieved if he didn't double sales at CMA. Trouble was, he couldn't figure out how to get that done.

When he arrived at the office, he went straight to Sandra Holt's office. He knocked, and peered inside, saying, "Sandra, have you got a few minutes to talk account strategy with CMA?"

"Sure," she replied. "I've been meaning to bring that up. I went over the records and I've noticed a couple of things about CMA. First, we had half the number of engineering calls with the company this year than the year before. Second, I looked at CMA's sales figures for this year at Yahoo! Finance and I see that its sales are up 15 percent but our sales are flat. These two figures tell me we're not getting opportunities to design in our solutions into its new products, and we have a possibility of losing business there as it replaces older products with new ones." The way products get sold in this business is that they are often designed into CMA's products. Then the company that helped design the product has an exclusive agreement for two years–after that, it can be competitively bid but most of CMA's products are redesigned every two years anyway. That means that half of Rudy's business with CMA is at risk of being replaced every year. Sandra went on, "What do you estimate our share to be of CMA's business?"

Rudy gulped. He hadn't expected such tough grilling; in fact, he wasn't aware of either statistic. "In communications, we're at 25 percent, based on what I know of the company's total spend. Harbaugh has the same as us, while Primacore a little less but growing. The rest is split between five small companies. We don't have any of their business in instrumentation."

"What's the deal there?," she pushed. "Why not?"

"I've been introduced to Jenkins, director of the instrumentation design team, and he's nice enough. But he seems to be in pretty tight with Primacore. Seems he and the salesperson there are fishing buddies–they go to the Keys every year together. In fact, Jenkins is the one who introduced Primacore into communications."

Rudy went on to tell her that he had a solid relationship with Shawna Wick, director of communications engineering and Jenkins's peer. Further, Rick Bostwick, chief operating officer and Wick's and Jenkins's boss, was Rudy's original customer at CMA when he was director of engineering. But there's been a lot of turnover among the heads of the five communications product design teams who report to Wick and he doesn't know them as well. He explained that these are the people who call in suppliers for involvement in new product design. In instrumentation, there are only three design teams but instrumentation is equally as big as communications in total opportunity for Crisp.

Sandra stopped him and said, "Look, we're introducing a new design process next month that should reduce testing costs by 20 percent, with greater savings on instrumentation applications. We're also licensing two European technologies that will improve reliability of connectors substantially. These three introductions should really help you at CMA." She also told him that Bill Blake has been designated as the lead engineer for the new design process, while the European company is sending a sales engineer over to help train on the new products.

Questions

1. Sandra wants an account plan from Rudy that includes a list of the first five sales calls he'll make, to whom, and the objective. How should Rudy go about putting that plan together?
2. Assume its 90 days later. The new design process has been introduced to wide acclaim, both in the press and on social media. You were at a trade show in New York where you spoke with one of the design team leaders from instrumentation in the Crisp booth. She indicated that she really didn't think there was much aptitude for change, though she was impressed with the demonstration you gave her. "People like things the way they are," she said. You think she might be a possible advocate, but inertia is hard to overcome. How will you help her convince others that they need to change how they design new products?
3. What would you do if you learned that Jenkins doesn't pay anything for his annual fishing trip with the Primacore rep?

ROLE PLAY CASE

Today you will receive a telephone call from one of your accounts. The account is Fournier Equipment, a company that manufactures small construction equipment sold worldwide. There is one plant in St. Albans, Vermont; one in Montpellier, France; and one in Canberra, Australia. Fournier recently announced the acquisition of two small companies, one in Portland, Oregon, and another in Taiwan. The

CIO is concerned with how to integrate these new acquisitions IT infrastructure into Fournier's systems.

Each of you will take turns being the buyer and the seller. If divided into teams of three, the third person will observe. Your professor will give you a sheet to use when you are the buyer.

ADDITIONAL REFERENCES

Anaza, Nwamaka, and Brian Rutherford. "Increasing Business-to-Business Buyer Word-of-Mouth and Share-of-Purchase." *Journal of Business and Industrial Marketing* 29, no. 5 (2014), pp. 427–37.

Bemelmans, Jeroen, Hans Voordijk, Bart Vos, and Geert Dewulf. "Antecedents and Benefits of Obtaining Preferred Customer Status: Experiences from the Dutch Construction Industry." *International Journal of Operations & Production Management* 35, no. 2 (2015), pp. 178–200.

Briggs, Elten, Timothy D. Landry, and Patricia J. Daugherty. "A Framework of Satisfaction for Continually Delivered Business Services." *Journal of Business and Industrial Marketing* 31, no. 1 (2016), pp. 112–22.

Carter, Robert E., Conor M. Henderson, Inigo Arroniz, and Robert W. Palmatier. "Effect of Salespeople's Acquisition-Retention Trade-Off on Performance." *Journal of Personal Selling and Sales Management* 34, no. 2 (2014), pp. 91–107.

Chen, Chien-Chung, and Fernando Jaramillo. "The Double-Edged Effects of Emotional Intelligence on Adaptive Selling: Salesperson-Owned Loyalty Relationship." *Journal of Personal Selling and Sales Management* 34, no. 1 (2014), pp. 33–50.

Crosno, Jody L., Robert Dahlstrom, and Chris Manolis. "Comply or Defy? An Empirical Investigation of Change Requests in Buyer-Supplier Relationships." *Journal of Business and Industrial Marketing* 30, no. 5 (2015), pp. 688–99.

Ferro, Carlos, Carmen Padin, Göran Svensson, and Janice Payan. "Trust and Commitment as Mediators between Economic and Non-Economic Satisfaction in Manufacturer-Supplier Relationships." *Journal of Business and Industrial Marketing* 31, no. 1 (2016), pp. 13–23.

Graca, Sandra Simas, James M. Barry, and Patricia M. Doney. "Performance Outcomes of Behavioral Attributes in Buyer-Supplier Relationships."*Journal of Business and Industrial Marketing* 30, no. 7 (2015), pp. 805–16.

Jack, Eric P., and Thomas L. Powers. "Managing Strategic Supplier Relationships: Antecedents and Outcomes." *Journal of Business and Industrial Marketing* 30, no. 2 (2015), pp. 129–38.

Jahromi, Ali Tamaddoni, Stanislav Stakhovych, and Michael Ewing. "Managing B2B Customer Churn, Retention, and Profitability." *Industrial Marketing Management* 43, no. 7 (October 2014), pp. 1258–60.

Miguel, Priscila L. S., Luiz A. L. Brito, Aline R. Fernandes, Fábio V. C. S. Tescari, and Guiherme S. Martins. "Relational Value Creation and Appropriation in Buyer-Supplier Relationships." *International Journal of Physical Distribution & Logistics Management* 44, no. 7 (2014), pp. 559–76.

Mpinganjira, Mercy, Mornay Roberts-Lombard, and Göran Svensson. "Validating the Relationship between Trust, Commitment, Economic, and Non-Economic Satisfaction in South African Buyer-Supplier Relationships." *Journal of Business and Industrial Marketing*32, no. 3 (2017), pp. 421–31.

Mubarik, Shujaat, V. G. R. Chandran, and Evelyn S. Devadason. "Relational Capital Quality and Client Loyalty: Firm-Level Evidence from Pharmaceuticals, Pakistan." *Learning Organization* 23, no. 1 (2016), pp. 43–60.

Natti, Satu, Suvi Rahkolin, and Saila Saraniemi. "Crisis Communication in Key Account Relationships." *Corporate Communications* 19, no. 3 (2014), pp. 234–46.

Ruey-Jer Jean, Jyh-Shn Chiou, and Rudolf R. Sinkovics. "Interpartner Learning, Dependence, Asymmetry and Radical Innovation in Customer Supplier Relationships." *Journal of Business and Industrial Marketing* 31, no. 6 (2016), pp. 732–42.

Shahzad, Khuram, Ilkka Sillanpää, Elina Sillanpää, and Shpend Imeri. "Benchmarking Supplier Development: An Empirical Case Study Validating a Framework to Improve Buyer-Supplier Relationships." *Management and Production Engineering Review* 7, no. 1 (2016), pp. 56–70.

Sleep, Stefa, Sundar Bharadwaj, and Son K. Lam. "Walking a Tightrope: The Joint Impact of Customer and Within-Firm Boundary Spanning Activities on Perceived Customer Satisfaction and Team Performance." *Journal of Academy of Marketing Science* 43, no. 4 (July 2015), pp. 472–89.

Stock, Ruth M., and Marei Bednarek. "As They Sow, So Shall They Reap: Customers' Influence on Customer Satisfaction at the Customer Interface." *Journal Academy of Marketing Science* 42, no. 4 (July 2014), pp. 400–14.

PART 3

The Salesperson as Manager

©Andrey Burmakin/Shutterstock.com RF

chapter 15

MANAGING YOUR TIME AND TERRITORY

SOME QUESTIONS ANSWERED IN THIS CHAPTER ARE

- Why is time so valuable for salespeople?
- What can you do to “create” more selling time?
- What should you consider when devising a territory strategy?
- How does territory strategy relate to account strategy and building partnerships?
- How should you analyze your daily activities and sales calls?
- How can you evaluate your own performance so you can improve?

PROFILE

> *"Relationships are not forged in a ten-minute meeting at the back of the receiving dock, or even in a purchasing manager's office. They are built over time."*
>
> David Timmons, Fastenal

Courtesy of David Timmons

PROFILE There are only so many hours in the day. 24 to be exact.

When I first started looking for a job during college, managing those hours seemed impossible. Yes, I needed income, but how was I going to fit in school and homework? More importantly, how would it affect my freedom to play baseball? And so it was time, or the flexibility thereof, that contributed to me taking on my first role at Fastenal. With a variety of shift options, a position in warehouse support allowed me to work around class and baseball while earning enough cash to get by.

Fast-forward seven years, and time continues its dominating influence on what has become my career at that very same company. Fastenal is an industrial and construction supplier, operating retail stores that offer anything from nuts and bolts to safety equipment and janitorial products. Sales are primarily driven by an outside sales force who meet and interact with customers daily, which is somewhat unique in a time when online ordering and faceless interaction seem so prevalent. In my years here, I've held a number of sales roles, including sales support, outside sales, and general manager. With each position, I gained more understanding of our organization's value proposition, as well as the importance of managing my time and building customer relationships. Effectively managing time and consistently hitting performance goals eventually led me to a position as a national account sales specialist, a role that specifically caters to customers who have multiple facilities spread over a large geographic area, meaning they can be serviced by more than one of our conveniently located retail stores.

Managing over 25 customer relationships, in addition to a list of prospects (and an even longer list of contacts), necessitates that I both manage my time wisely, as well as keep a realistic sense of time as it relates to the sales process. If there is one thing I've learned, it's that relationship building is the key component to success in sales. In our business, people buy from people, not just out of catalogs or from a Web site. But relationships are not forged in a ten-minute meeting at the back of the receiving dock, or even in a purchasing manager's office. They are built over time.

When I took on this role, I was basically handed a set of neglected customers that had done business with us once upon a time, but who were now sporadic in their purchasing and largely nonresponsive to our outreach. One customer in particular stands out in my memory. I'd send the customer a monthly e-mail checking in. No response. I'd visit the local store to monitor activity and even stop at the customer site on occasion. Nothing. This went on for some time—not just a week or a month, but for seven months before the customer agreed to sit down and just meet with me.

Patience. Resilience. Follow-through. These are recurring lessons I have learned and will continue to learn as I build my book of business and grow relationships with my current and potential customers. And while I believe a bit of failure and some time in the field is the most effective teacher, there are a few pieces of advice I can share that relate to managing (and/or guarding) your time when in a sales role.

First, slow down. It seems counterintuitive, I know. But succumbing to the operational demands of a sales role, especially a traveling one with many accounts, will lead to burnout. Sales are made in the details. The difference is the personalized e-mail, the accurate quote, and the care you take to remember someone's name; these set you apart from the competition. Slow down. Do things right the first time, particularly the tasks that seem minor, for those are the ones that will spring up and cost you valuable time later when done incorrectly.

Second, step back and consider the long-game. The pressure of hitting today's sales targets make it easy to become shortsighted, especially if you're overwhelmed by the aforementioned operational demands. By stepping back and considering how your actions today will impact you months or even years down the road, you can proactively manage not only your time but your expectations. This is where that patience thing comes in again. I've gone to see customers and know I have the perfect solution for them, but if I come on too strong when they aren't ready, I'll be seen as just another pushy salesperson. Instead, I must consider how this phone call, this complex order, or this seemingly impossible delivery request is setting me up for an even bigger opportunity down the road, an opportunity to bring real value and solutions. Relationships are built over time. Step back. Imagine a future state. Take incremental steps to get it there.

My third piece of advice is to own your 24. There truly are only so many hours in the day, and even less in what many consider a "workday." As such, I implore you to use your resources to guard those hours and make them as effective as possible. Pull in the right people to help when needed. That's what they are there for. Use technology to streamline communication and to manage your routes and appointments. Organize your week and schedule routine tasks. Prioritize your time and allocate it to the customers and opportunities that contribute to the overall success of your book of business, and ultimately, the organization.

What we sell may change. How we sell it will evolve. But time is as constant as it is valuable. Use it wisely.

Visit our Web site at: www.fastenal.com.

THE VALUE OF TIME

The old axiom "Time is money" certainly applies to selling. If you work 8 hours a day for 240 days of a year, you will work 1,920 hours that year. If you earn $50,000, each of those hours will be worth $26.05. An hour of time would be worth $31.25 if your earnings climb to $60,000. Looking at your time another way, you would have to sell $260 worth of product per hour to earn $50,000 if you earned a 10 percent commission!

A recent study found that salespeople spend only 36 percent of their time with customers.[1] Where does the other 64 percent go? The other 1,200 hours are spent waiting, traveling, doing paperwork, or attending sales meetings. Thus, as a typical salesperson, you really have to be two to three times as good, selling $520 to $1,040 worth of products every hour to earn that $50,000 commission.

Salespeople have to carefully allocate resources such as time. Although every job will occasionally require burning the midnight oil, carefully planning one's time can make for a more balanced and enjoyable life.

©Dann Tardif/LWA/Blend Images RF

The lesson from this analysis is clear: Salespeople must make every hour count to be successful. Time is a resource that cannot be replaced if wasted. But time is just one resource, albeit a critical resource, at the salesperson's disposal.

Managing time and territory is often a question of how to allocate resources. Allocating resources such as time is a difficult management process, but when done well, it often spells the difference between stellar and average performance. Many times it is difficult to know what is really important and what only seems important. In this chapter we discuss how to manage your time. Building on what you have learned about the many activities of salespeople, we also provide strategies for allocating resources among accounts–that is, managing your territory.

Exhibit 15.1
The Self-Management Process

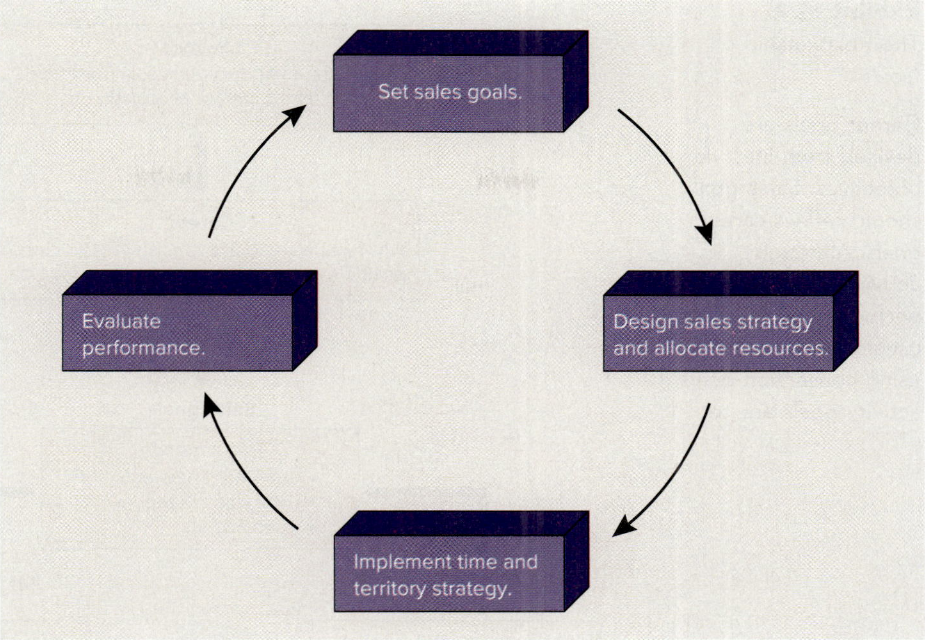

THE SELF-MANAGEMENT PROCESS

The self-management process in selling has four stages. The first stage is setting goals, or determining what is to be accomplished. The second stage is allocating resources and determining strategies to meet those goals. In the third stage the salesperson implements the time management strategies by making sales calls, sending e-mail or direct mail pieces, or executing whatever action the strategy calls for. In the fourth and final stage, the salesperson evaluates performance to determine whether the goals will be reached and the strategies are effective or whether the goals cannot be reached and the strategies must change. This process is illustrated in Exhibit 15.1 and will serve as an outline for this chapter.

SETTING GOALS

THE NEED FOR GOALS

The first step in managing any worthwhile endeavor is to consider what makes it worthwhile and what you want to accomplish. Salespeople need to examine their careers in the same way. Career goals and objectives should reflect personal ambitions and desires so the individual can create the desired lifestyle, as illustrated in Exhibit 15.2. When career goals reflect personal ambitions, the salesperson is more committed to achieving those goals.

The first step is to think about lifestyle and life ambitions. Greg Muzillo, founder of Proforma, believes these goals drive his salespeople more than any. "So we have a lot of folks that are at a half of a million (in annual sales revenue) or they're, whatever, $300,000, $500,000, $700,000, and they might say they'd like to make the Million Dollar Club, but they don't mean it in their heart and mind. I think there's some people who are happy to be comfortable in life, making $100,000, $200,000 whatever, and there are some people who are driven to create wealth."[2] He believes that this difference of what it takes to be comfortable in life is what separates those who make the Million Dollar Club at Proforma.

Exhibit 15.2
The Relationship of Goals

Career goals are devised from lifestyle objectives. Sales goals should reflect career goals. Although activities lead to sales, performance goals are usually set first. Then, using conversion goals, activity goals are set.

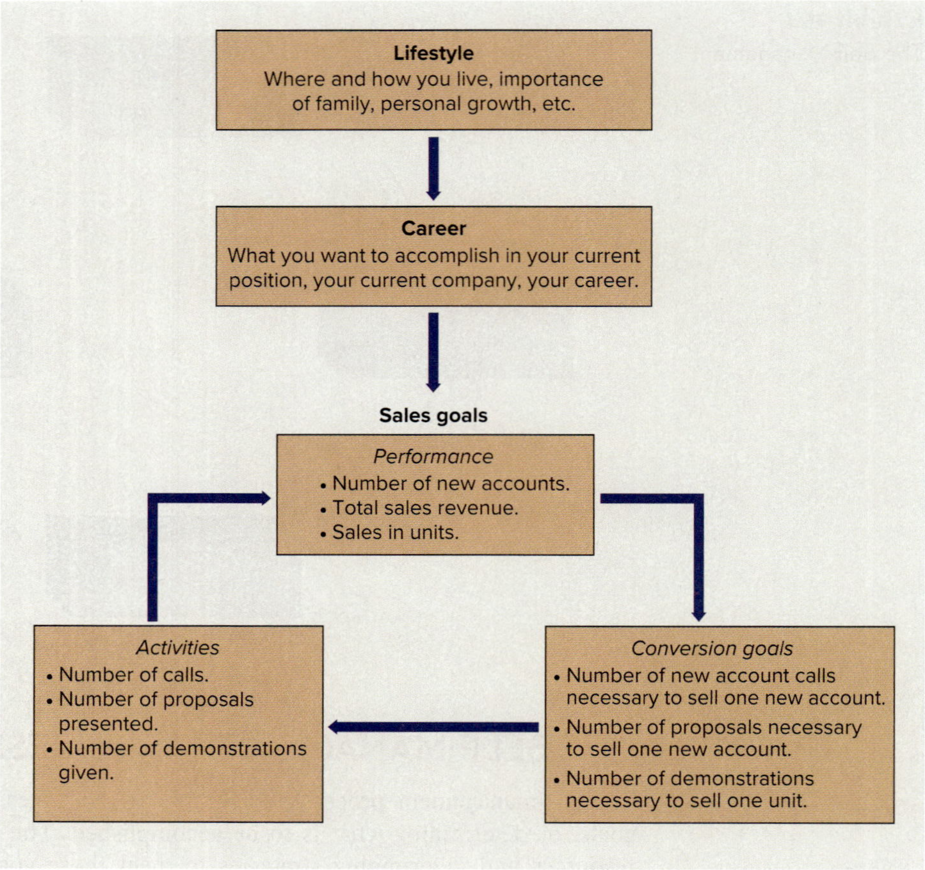

From lifestyle goals come career objectives. To achieve career objectives, salespeople must set sales goals. These sales goals provide some of the means for reaching personal objectives. Sales goals also guide the salesperson's decisions about which activities to perform, when to perform those activities, whom to see, and how to sell.

The salesperson lacking goals will drift around the territory, wasting time and energy. Sales calls will be unrelated to objectives and may be minimally productive or even harmful to the sales process. The result will be poor performance and, perhaps, the need to find another job. Cal Brown, a salesperson with Savant Capital Management, says, "If you don't know what you're doing, your high-impact activities will get crowded out, and you won't like where you end up!"[3]

In Chapter 7 you learned that salespeople should set call objectives so the activities performed during the call will bring them closer to those objectives. The same can be said for setting sales goals: When sales goals are set properly and adhered to, the salesperson has a guide to direct his or her activities.

THE NATURE OF GOALS

As you read in Chapter 7, goals should be specific and measurable, achievable yet realistic, and time based (SMART). Goals should be specific and measurable so the salesperson knows when they have been met. For example, setting a goal of making better presentations is laudable, but how would the salesperson know if the presentations

Some salespeople keep a reminder, like a photo of a new house, of their personal goals in front of them to help motivate themselves.

were better or worse? A more helpful goal would be to increase the number of sales resulting from those presentations. The best goal would be a specific increase, such as 10 percent. Then there would be no question about the achievement of the goal.

Goals should also be reachable yet challenging. One purpose of setting personal goals is to motivate oneself. If goals are reached too easily, little has been accomplished. Challenging goals, then, are more motivating. But if the goals are too challenging or if they are unreachable, the salesperson may give up.

Goals should be time based; that is, goals should have deadlines. Putting a deadline on a goal provides more guidance for the salesperson and creates a sense of urgency that can be motivating. Without a deadline, the goal is not specific enough and the salesperson may be able to drag on forever, never reaching the goal but thinking progress is being made. Imagine the motivational difference between setting a goal of a 10 percent increase in sales with no deadline and setting a goal of a 10 percent increase for the next month. The first instance lacks a sense of urgency, of needing to work toward that goal now. Without a deadline, the goal has little motivational value.

One problem some people have is periodically creating goals and then forgetting them. Goals should be written down and then posted. One strategy is to create a blank list with a line for each sale you need to make. If you need five sales to hit your target, you have five lines. Then when you sell one, you fill in the bottom, not the top, line. That way, the goal becomes four, and so forth, so for each sale made, you are reminded of how many are left to make. At Emora Ltd., a UK-based direct marketing agency, salespeople are encouraged to create their own sales goals and share them with their manager. While each salesperson can decide how to track their progress toward each goal, they also know that their sales manager will help them stay focused on achieving the goal.[4]

thinking it through

What types of goals have you set for yourself in your college career? For specific classes? How would these goals meet the criteria of specific and measurable, reachable yet challenging, and time based? How do you keep these goals in front of you? What would you do differently now?

TYPES OF SALES GOALS

Salespeople need to set three types of sales goals: performance, activity, and conversions (refer back to Exhibit 15.2). Although many salespeople focus only on how many sales they get, setting all three types of goals is necessary to achieve the highest possible success.

Performance Goals

Goals relating to outcomes are **performance goals**. In sales, outcomes such as the size of a commission or bonus check, the amount of sales revenue generated or number

Exhibit 15.3
Goal Calculations

Monthly earnings goal (performance goal):	$6,000
Commission per sale:	$750
$6,000 earnings ÷ $750 per sale = 8 sales	
Monthly sales goal (performance goal):	8
Closings goal (conversion goal):	10%
8 sales × 10 prospects per sale = 80 prospects	
Monthly prospects goal (performance goal):	80
Prospects per calls goal (conversion goal):	1 in 3
80 prospects × 3 calls per prospect = 240 calls	
Monthly sales calls goal (activity goal):	240
240 calls × 20 working days per month = 12 calls	
Daily sales calls goal (activity goal):	12

of sales generated, and the number of prospects identified are common performance goals. For example, the salesperson in Exhibit 15.3 set a performance goal of $6,000 in commissions and another performance goal of eight sales. Revenue quotas are an example of goals set by the company, but each salesperson should also consider setting personally relevant goals. For example, you may want to set higher goals so you can achieve higher earnings. People are more committed to achieving goals they set themselves; that commitment makes achieving them more likely. Performance goals should be set first because attaining certain performance levels is of primary importance to both the organization and the salesperson.

Personal development goals, such as improving presentation skills, are important to long-term professional growth and are a form of performance goals. Every person, whether in sales or other fields, should have some personal development goals. Reaching those goals will not only improve overall job performance but also increase personal satisfaction. Like all performance goals, however, these goals should meet the criteria of being specific, challenging, and time based. Further, it helps to make these goals measurable. For example, if you set improving presentation skills as a performance goal, some outcome such as increased sales or fewer objections should occur that you can measure to determine if your skills are truly improving.

Activity Goals

Salespeople also set activity goals. **Activity goals** are behavioral objectives: the number of calls made in a day, the number of demonstrations performed, and so on. Activity goals reflect how hard the salesperson wants to work. The company may set some activity goals for salespeople, such as a quota of sales calls to be made each week. Exhibit 15.3 lists two activity goals: 240 sales calls per month and 12 calls per day.

All activity goals are intermediate goals; that is, achieving them should ultimately translate into achievement of performance goals. As Teradata discovered by auditing sales performance, activity goals such as a specific number of telephone calls per day are needed for the salespeople to achieve the overall performance goals.[5] Activity goals help salespeople decide what to do each day, but those goals must ultimately be related to making sales.

However, activity goals and performance goals are not enough. For example, a salesperson may have goals of achieving 10 sales and making 150 calls in one month. The salesperson may get 10 sales but make 220 calls. That salesperson had to work much harder than someone who managed to get 10 sales in only 150 calls. What caused the difference? Answer that question and you, too, can work smarter rather than harder, but the answer presupposes that you first measured conversions and then set goals based on what should be achieved.

Conversion Goals

Conversion goals are measures of a salesperson's efficiency. Conversion goals reflect how efficiently the salesperson would like to work, or work smarter. Unlike performance goals, conversion goals express relative accomplishments, such as the number of sales relative to the number of calls made or the number of customers divided by the number of prospects. The higher the ratio, the more efficient the salesperson. Exhibit 15.3 lists two conversion goals: closing 10 percent of all prospects and finding one prospect for every three calls. In the preceding example, a rep earning 10 sales while making 150 calls could close 4 or 5 more sales by making 220 calls because that rep gains a sale every 15 calls.

Conversion goals are important because they reflect how efficiently the salesperson uses resources, such as time, to accomplish performance goals. For example, Freeman Exhibit Company builds custom trade show exhibits. Customers often ask for booth designs (called speculative designs) before making the purchase to evaluate the offerings of various competitors. Creating a custom booth design is a lot of work for a designer, and the cost can be high, but it does not guarantee a sale. If a salesperson has a low conversion rate for speculative designs, overall profits will be lower because the cost for the unsold designs must still be covered. If the rep can increase the conversion rate, the overall costs for unsold designs will be lower, hence increasing profits.

Working harder would show up as an increase in activity; working smarter should be reflected in conversion goals. For example, a salesperson may be performing at a conversion rate of 10 percent. Reaching a conversion goal of 12 percent (closing 1 out of 8 instead of 1 out of 10) would reflect some improvement in the way the salesperson operates–some method of working smarter.

Measuring conversions tells salespeople which activities work best. For example, suppose a salesperson has two sales strategies. If A generates 10 sales and B generates 8 sales, the salesperson may think A is the better strategy. But if A requires 30 sales calls and B only 20, the salesperson would be better off using strategy B. Thirty sales calls would have generated 12 sales with strategy B.

Comparing your performance with the best in your organization is a form of **benchmarking**.[6] Benchmarking can help you see where you are falling short. For example, if your conversion ratio of leads to appointments (the number of leads needed to get one appointment) is the same as that of the top seller but you are closing only half of your spec designs and that person is closing 80 percent, you know you are losing sales at the spec design stage. You can then examine what that person does to achieve the higher conversion ratio.

SETTING SALES GOALS

Performance and conversion goals are the basis for activity goals. Suppose a sale is worth $500 in commission. A person who wants to earn $4,000 per month (a performance goal) needs to make eight sales each month. If the salesperson sees closing 1 out of 10 prospects as a realistic conversion goal, a second performance goal results: The rep must identify 80 prospects to yield eight closings. If the rep can identify one prospect for every three sales calls (another conversion goal), 240 sales calls (an activity goal) must be made. Assuming 20 working days in a month, the rep must make 12 sales calls each day (another activity goal). Thus, activity goals need to be the last type of goals set because they will be determined by the desired level of performance at a certain rate of conversion.

Even though the conversion analysis results in a goal of 12 calls each day, that conversion rate is affected by the strategy the salesperson employs. A better strategy results in a higher conversion rate and better allocation of time, one of many important resources that must be allocated properly to achieve sales goals. We discuss how to allocate resources in the next section.

ALLOCATING RESOURCES

The second stage of the time and territory management process is to develop a strategy that allocates resources properly. These resources are allocated to different sales strategies used with different types of accounts with the purpose of achieving sales goals in the most effective and efficient manner possible.

RESOURCES TO BE ALLOCATED

Salespeople manage many resources. Some of these are physical resources, such as free samples, demonstration products, trial products, brochures, direct mail budgets, and other marketing resources. Each of these physical resources represents a cost to the company, but to the salesperson they are investments. Salespeople consider physical resources as investments because resources must be managed wisely to generate the best possible return. Whereas financial investments may return dividends or price increases, the salesperson's investments should yield sales.

A key resource that salespeople manage is time. Time is limited, and not all of a salesperson's work time can be spent making sales calls. Some time must be spent attending meetings, learning new products, preparing reports for management, traveling to sales calls, and handling other nonselling duties; in fact, nonselling activities can take up to 70 percent of a salesperson's time. Thus, being able to manage time wisely is important. As we discuss in the next chapter, salespeople also coordinate many of the company's other departments to serve customers well. Salespeople must learn how to allocate these resources in ways that generate the greatest level of sales.

WHERE TO ALLOCATE RESOURCES

For salespeople the allocation of resources is often a question of finding the customers or companies that are most likely to buy and then allocating selling resources to maximize the opportunities they offer. As you may have learned in your principles of marketing course, some market segments are more profitable than others. And just as the company's marketing executive tries to determine which segments are most profitable so that marketing plans can be directed toward those segments, salespeople examine their markets to allocate their selling resources.

Maximizing the opportunity means finding profitable ways to satisfy the greatest number of customers, but not necessarily everybody. One study of services to customers found that only 44 percent were profitable; the rest cost the company money.[7] In the following section we discuss how to analyze the market to identify potential customers that are most likely to buy so resources will be allocated properly.

ACCOUNT CLASSIFICATION AND RESOURCE ALLOCATION

Not all customers have the same buying potential, just as not all sales activities produce the same results. The salesperson has to concentrate on the most profitable customers and minimize effort spent with customers that offer little opportunity for profitable sales. The proportion of unprofitable accounts is usually greater than one would think. As a rule, 80 percent of the sales in a territory come from only 20 percent of the customers. Therefore, salespeople should classify customers on the basis of their sales potential to avoid spending too much time and other resources with low-potential accounts, thus helping to achieve sales goals.

Customer management is not just a time management issue. Managing customers includes allocating all the resources at the salesperson's disposal in the most productive manner. Time may be the most important of these resources, but salespeople also manage sample and demonstration inventories, entertainment and travel budgets, printed materials, and other resources.

ABC Analysis

The simplest classification scheme, called **ABC analysis**, ranks accounts by sales potential. The idea is that the accounts with the greatest sales potential deserve the most attention. Using the 80/20 rule, the salesperson identifies the 20 percent of accounts that (could) buy the most and calls those A accounts. The other 80 percent are B accounts, and noncustomers (or accounts with low potential for sales) are C accounts. Eli Lilly (a pharmaceuticals company) classifies physicians and SC Johnson Wax classifies retail stores this way. One use is planning sales calls; so for example, A accounts could be seen every two weeks, B accounts every six weeks, and C accounts only if there is nothing else to do. An example of an account analysis appears in Exhibit 15.4. As you can see, Sam Thompson has used estimated potential to classify accounts so he can allocate sales calls to accounts with the greatest potential.

ABC classification schemes work well only in industries that require regular contact with the same accounts, such as consumer packaged goods and pharmaceuticals. Some industries (plant equipment, medical equipment, and other capital

Exhibit 15.4
Account Classification

Salesperson: Sam Thompson A. Analysis of Call Pattern: 2016

Customer Type	Number of Customers Contacted	Number of Calls	Average Calls per Customer	Sales Volume	Average Sales per Call
A	15	121	8.1	$212,515	$1,756
B	21	154	7.3	115,451	756
C	32	226	7.0	78,010	345
D	59	320	5.4	53,882	168
Total	127	821		$460,859	561

B. Annual Territory Sales Plan (dollars in thousands)

	Actual Sales			2017 Estimated Potential Sales		Number of Calls Allocated	
Account	2014	2015	2016		Forecast		Classification
Allied Foods	$100	$110	$150	$250	$150	48	A
Pic N-Save	75	75	90	300	115	48	A
Wright Grocers	40	50	60	175	90	24	B
H.E.B.	20	30	30	150	30	24	B
Piggly Wiggly	10	10	25	100	55	18	C
Sal's Superstore	0	0	30	100	80	18	C
Buy-Rite	0	0	0	80	75	18	C
Tom Thumb	0	10	20	75	70	18	C
Apple Tree	0	5	12	60	60	12	D
Buy Lo	0	0	10	60	50	12	D
Whyte's Family Foods	10	8	9	50	40	12	D

Although Dr. Liu's practice may appear smaller than that of the clinic on the right, the astute salesperson would determine each business's sales potential before classifying either as an A, B, or C account.

(left): ©vm/Getty Images RF; (right):©UpperCut Images/SuperStock RF

products) may require numerous sales calls until the product is sold. After that sale, another sale may be unlikely for several years, and the number of sales calls may diminish. Then the A, B, and C classification may not be helpful.

Salespeople in some industries find grid and customer relationship analysis methods more useful than ABC analysis. They have learned that simply allocating sales activities on the basis of sales potential may lead to inefficiencies. For example, to maximize great potential, satisfied customers may need fewer calls than accounts of equal potential that are loyal to a competitor.

Grid Analysis

The **sales call allocation grid** classifies accounts on the basis of the company's competitive position with an account, along with the account's sales potential. As with ABC analysis, the purpose of classifying accounts through grid analysis is to determine which accounts should receive more resources. By this method, each account in a salesperson's territory falls into one of the four segments shown in Exhibit 15.5. The classification is determined by the salesperson's evaluation of the account on the following two dimensions.

First, the **account opportunity** dimension indicates how much the customer needs the product and whether the customer is able to buy the product. Some factors the salesperson can consider when determining account opportunity are the account's sales potential, growth rate, and financial condition. This rating is similar to the ABC analysis and is a measure of total sales potential. Again, the idea is that accounts with the greatest opportunity deserve the greatest resources.

Second, the **strength of position** dimension indicates how strong the salesperson and company are in selling the account. Some factors that determine strength of position are the present share of the account's purchases of the product, the attitude of the account toward the company and the salesperson, and the relationship between the salesperson and the key decision makers in the account. The strength of position helps the salesperson understand what level of sales is likely in the account. The account opportunity may be tremendous–say, $1 million. But if the account has always purchased another brand, the salesperson's strength of position is weak, and his or her real potential is something much less than $1 million.

Global accounts represent a difficult challenge in terms of determining potential and position. Position may be strong in one location and weak in another; potential

Exhibit 15.5
Sales Call Allocation Grid

Account Opportunity	Strength of Position: Strong	Strength of Position: Weak
High	*Segment 1* Attractiveness: Accounts are very attractive because they offer high opportunity, and the sales organization has a strong position. Sales call strategy: Accounts should receive a high level of sales calls because they are the sales organization's most attractive accounts.	*Segment 2* Attractiveness: Accounts are potentially attractive because they offer high opportunity, but the sales organization currently has a weak position with accounts. Sales call strategy: Accounts should receive a high level of sales calls to strengthen the sales organization's position.
Low	*Segment 3* Attractiveness: Accounts are somewhat attractive because the sales organization has a strong position, but future opportunity is limited. Sales call strategy: Accounts should receive a moderate level of sales calls to maintain the current strength of the sales organization's position.	*Segment 4* Attractiveness: Accounts are very unattractive because they offer low opportunity, and the sales organization has a weak position. Sales call strategy: Accounts should receive a minimal level of sales calls, and efforts should be made to selectively eliminate or replace personal sales calls with telephone sales calls, direct mail, etc.

Source: Raymond W. LaForge, Clifford E. Young, and B. Curtis Hamm, "Increasing Sales Productivity through Improved Sales Call Allocation Strategies," *Journal of Personal Selling and Sales Management*, November 1983, pp. 53–59.

may also vary. Marvin Wagner, an engineer with John Deere, has been working with Deere engineers and suppliers to Deere to standardize products globally. He's had to help suppliers negotiate with buying centers involving engineers in as many as four different countries, all with different expectations and preferences for different vendors. What may be preferred by engineers at the Arc-les-Gray plant in France may not even be considered by engineers in Ottumwa, Iowa.

The appropriate sales call strategy depends on the grid segment into which the account falls. Accounts with high potential and a strong position are very attractive because the salesperson should be able to sell large amounts relatively easily. Thus, these attractive accounts should receive the highest level of sales calls. For example, if you have an account that likes your product and has established a budget for it, and you know that the customer needs 300 units per year, you may consider that customer to be a segment 1 account (assuming 300 units is a high number) and plan to allocate more calls to that account. But if a competitor has a three-year contract with the account, you might be better off spending less time there. The account may buy 3,000 units per year, but you have little chance of getting any of that business. By classifying the account as a segment 2, you would recognize that the most appropriate strategy is to strengthen your position in the account. The sales call allocation grid, then, aids salespeople in determining where, by account, to spend time in order to meet sales goals.

The Grid and Current Customers

The sales call allocation grid is a great tool for analyzing current customers. Recall the value of a customer that was discussed in Chapter 13; many businesses

From the **BUYER'S SEAT** 15.1

MAKING THE LITTLE THINGS COUNT

Often it is the little things that count—in fact, most buyers will tell you that 3 of their top 10 peeves are salespeople failing to make or keep appointments, failure to follow up, and failure to keep promises.

Paul Tepfenhart, vice president of e-commerce for the grocer H-E-B, agrees. As one who has bought many technology solutions for H-E-B and formerly for Walmart.com, Paul has had a great deal of experience observing whether salespeople show up.

During the sales process, he emphasizes the importance of judging how a salesperson will take care of him after the sale by what happens during the sale. "Nothing damages credibility as a lack of dependability. Not showing up, being late, being unprepared are all symptoms of what might be poor execution later, something no buyer can afford. In sales, showing up, being prepared, optimistic, personable, and engaged is essential. It is the price of entry. It overcomes many other shortfalls. A successful start to a sales career begins with making an unwavering commitment to show up."

Mike Challoner, of Main Industries, agrees. "I need suppliers I can depend on. Our customers depend on us to deliver when we say we will, but for us to do that, our vendors have to show up when they say they will. And that means on time, but it also means living up to the promises they make."

Showing up on time, keeping promises—these seem simple. Yet, most buyers will tell you that if you do this, you'll separate yourself from the crowd.

Sources: Mike Challoner and Paul Tepfenheart, personal interviews; Anonymous, "Top 10 Things Salespeople Do That People Dislike," *Inner Circle*, Twin Cities, June 13, 2017.

experience little or no profit in the first year of a customer's life. But over time profit grows if the salesperson can increase sales in the account, find ways to reduce the cost to serve the account (for example, shipping more can lower shipping costs), and so on.

In a landmark study of the paper and plastics industry, the key to a company's profit was found to be customer share, not market share. **Customer share**, also called **account share**, is the average percentage of business received from a company's accounts in a particular category. A similar term is **share of wallet**, which is the same thing but usually for an individual consumer. Over 15 years ago, an analysis of companies in that industry indicated that even if a company was the dominant supplier to a group of buyers, another company could be more profitable if it served fewer customers but had all their business.[8] Since that study, numerous studies have found similar insights. As a result, many companies are looking for how to increase account share, rather than the number of accounts.[9]

INVESTING IN ACCOUNTS

Planning based on customer analysis should result in more effective use of the opportunities presented by accounts. This improvement relates to better use of time, which is allocated to the appropriate accounts (see From the Buyer's Seat 15.1). But developing good strategies entails more than developing good time use plans; strategies require the use of other resources as well.

Salespeople invest time, free samples or trials, customer training, displays, and other resources in their customers. Companies such as IBM use predictive modeling to determine which accounts are likely to be more productive. This knowledge helps salespeople determine where to invest resources–time, samples, displays, and so forth. Sales costs, or costs associated with the use of such resources, are not always costs in the traditional sense but rather are investments in the asset called customers. This asset generates nearly all of a firm's revenue. Viewed from this perspective, formulating a strategy to allocate resources to maintaining or developing customers becomes vitally important.

Salespeople must determine not only which customers require sales effort, but also what activities should occur. CRM software can assist through **pipeline analysis**: a process for identifying and managing sales opportunities, also known as *opportunity management*. Recall that in Chapter 6 we discussed how accounts can move through stages from lead to prospect to customer. NetSuite, for example, can complete a pipeline analysis, telling the salesperson how well she is moving accounts from one stage to the next. In addition to being useful in determining conversion ratios and ensuring that a salesperson is creating enough opportunities to reach sales goals, pipeline analysis requires identifying which stage an account is in. Recognizing the account's stage in the pipeline is useful to determine what steps are appropriate. You don't want to try to do a spec design with a prospect for whom you haven't finished identifying needs, for example.

IMPLEMENTING THE TIME MANAGEMENT STRATEGY

Time is a limited resource. Once spent, it cannot be regained. How salespeople choose to use their time often means the difference between superstar success and average performance. Susan Flaviano, a sales manager for Lonseal, offers the following tips for managing your time as a salesperson; keep these in mind as you read through this section:

- Start early. Get a jump start to the day before anyone else. Then you control the day without the day controlling you.
- Manage responsiveness. Although responsiveness is key to being successful, you cannot let customer calls, e-mail messages, and voice mail consume your day. We now have the ability to respond immediately, but it is important to choose specific times during the day to reply to correspondence so that you don't forget to meet your goals.
- Schedule in advance. I set most of my appointments one week in advance, which helps me stay on target. Usually, if there is not a set commitment, it is easy to justify staying in the office to get caught up on paperwork.
- Use downtime wisely. If you have a canceled appointment or extra time over lunch, or you arrive to an appointment early, use this time to plan or follow up. With our laptops and sophisticated project tracking tools, you can use this time anywhere and reduce the amount of time spent in your office or at home on Saturday catching up on paperwork![10]

Remember that your time is worth $30 to $40 an hour, but only if you use it to sell. Your company has invested a great deal to get prospects ready to see you but all of that goes for nought if no sales call is made. Use your time to hone a golf game or spruce up the yard, and opportunities to sell disappear. Although no manager really knows how a salesperson uses time, technology is giving managers a lot more information about time usage (see Sales Technology 15.1). But whether activities are closely or loosely monitored, when the results are posted, accurate conclusions can be drawn.

SALES Technology 15.1

WHOM DOES THE TECHNOLOGY SERVE?

Want to take off Tuesday afternoon and play golf? Don't take your company-provided cell phone with you. Some companies have an app called Xora which allows them to track where the cell phone is, even after hours.

Recently, Myrna Arias sued her company, Intermex, because she was fired for removing the app from her company-issued cell phone. She did so, she claims, because her manager confirmed that the company used the app to track her activities at night and on the weekends. In fact, he even bragged that he knew how fast she drove.

Ethical concerns over technology-based control of salespeople continue to mount, and not just because of questionable monitoring via cell phones. The requirement to use CRM technology to manage one's sales territory sounds reasonable, but much of the data that salespeople have to input benefit only the managers and not the salespeople. One salesperson, who asked to remain anonymous but who sells for a company that manufactures orthopedic products like replacement knees, says she spend 2 hours a day putting data into the company system—on top of the 8 hours she's expected to spend talking to doctors. The company uses that same data she enters to make sure she's making those calls.

She's not alone. Research shows one out of four salespeople spends 10 hours a week on their CRM system alone.

John Davis tossed out the standard CRM system and built his own system based on his needs as a salesperson—contact information, e-mail trails, and customer background information. Research backs him up. The real value to salespeople of CRM systems may be minimal, but where it is most useful is in time management.

So the system should help you create time for that golf game. Just don't take your cell phone with you.

Sources: Eugene Kim, "The Single Most Important Thing You Can Do to Be a Successful Salesperson," *Business Insider*, May 4, 2016, p. 5; Anonymous, "24/7 Monitoring on Company Cellphone Prompts Lawsuit," *Business Management Daily*, May 18, 2015; John Davis, "The CRM Struggle," *Agency Sales* 45, no. 6 (June 2015), pp. 10–15; Sergio Román and Rocío Rodríguez, "The Influence of Sales Force Technology Use on Outcome Performance," *Journal of Business & Industrial Marketing* 30, no. 6 (2015), pp. 771–83.

thinking it through

How do you plan your time now? Do you use a computer to help you manage your time? How much of your time is planned by others, and how much of it are you free to allocate? What do you do to make sure you use your time wisely?

DAILY ACTIVITY PLANNING

To be effective time planners, salespeople must have a good understanding of their own work habits. For example, some people tend to procrastinate in getting the day started, whereas others may want to knock off early. If you are a late riser, you may want to schedule early appointments to force yourself to get started. On the other hand, if your problem is heading for home too early, schedule late appointments so you work a full day.

Many salespeople have the opposite problem—they never seem to stop working. One study found that 81 percent of salespeople felt like they had to be available to their customers 24/7.[11] Pad computers and smartphones make the Internet and phone ubiquitous, but that is no excuse for failing to plan adequately. Susan Flaviano, now a sales manager for Lonseal, believed quantity of calls was the most important thing. But after a while, she realized she had no personal life and, more importantly, no more success

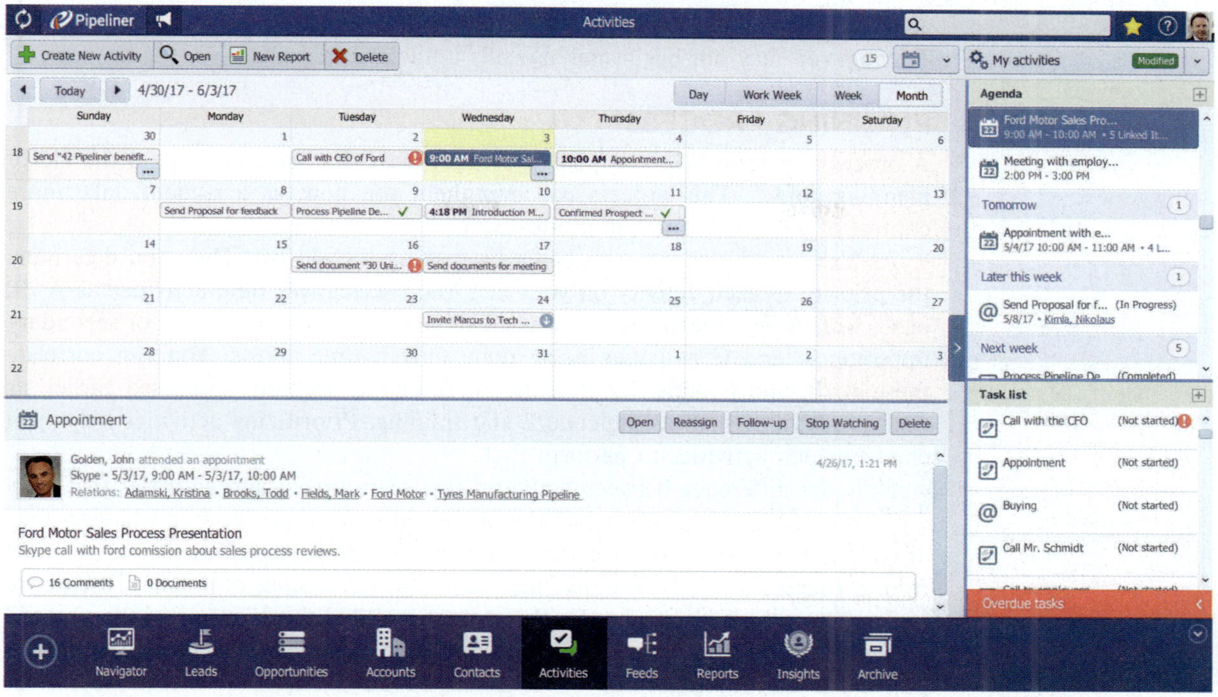

Salespeople lead busy lives. They use CRM software like Pipeliner to manage their time and accounts, and plan each day's activities.

Courtesy of Pipeliner

than anyone else. She backed off the quantity of calls and began to spend more time planning her activities; the result was an increase in both sales and personal time.[12]

GUIDELINES

Salespeople need to include time for prospecting and customer care in their daily activities. Some minimize the time for such activities because they think sales do not occur on such calls, but prospects and happy customers feed future sales. ESI, an office equipment sales division of Xerox, expects salespeople to handle customer care calls before 9 a.m. and after 4 p.m. and to schedule prospecting activities between 10 a.m. and noon and between 2 p.m. and 3 p.m. Scheduled appointments are worked in when customers require them. The company bases these guidelines on its experience with buyers and when they are available.

Such planning guides are designed to maximize **prime selling time**—the time of day at which a salesperson is most likely to see a buyer. One salesperson, Lee Brubaker with Sandler Systems, calls this "pay time."[13] Prime selling time depends on the buyer's industry. For example, a good time to call on bankers is late afternoon, after the bank has closed to customers. However, late afternoon is a bad time to call on physicians, who are then making rounds at the hospital or trying to catch up on a full day's schedule of patients. Prime selling time should be devoted to sales calls, with the rest of the day used for nonselling activities such as servicing accounts, doing paperwork, or getting information from the home office.

Prime selling time varies from country to country. In the United States prime selling time is usually 9 a.m. to 4 p.m. with the noon hour off for lunch. In Mexico lunch starts and ends later, generally from 12:30 to 2:00 p.m.; offices may not close until 7 p.m. or later. In Great Britain prime selling time starts later; a British Telecom rep may not begin making calls until 10 a.m.

PLANNING PROCESS

A process exists to help you plan your daily activities, with or without the aid of planning guides. This process can even help you now, as a student, take more control of your time and use it effectively.

As Exhibit 15.6 shows, you begin by making a to-do list. Then you determine the priority of each activity on your list. Many executives rank activities as A, B, or C, with A activities requiring immediate action, B activities being of secondary importance, and C activities being done only if time allows. You can correlate these A, B, and C activities with the A, B, and C accounts discussed earlier, as well as activities such as paperwork and training. Prioritizing activities helps you choose which activities to perform first.

Note the difference between activities that seem urgent and activities that truly are important. For example, when the phone rings, most people stop whatever they are doing to answer it. The ringing phone seems urgent. Activities such as requests from managers or even customers may have that same sense of urgency; the desire to drop everything else to handle the request is called the "tyranny of the urgent." And the "urgent" can get overwhelming: The average businessperson receives 274 personal e-mail messages and 304 business e-mail messages weekly, numbers that are growing over 6 percent per year.[14] Of course these statistics do not include telephone requests from customers. Yet, like most phone calls, even requests from customers may be less important than other tasks. Successful businesspeople learn to recognize what is truly urgent and prioritize those activities first.

The next step in the planning process is to estimate the time required for each activity. In sales, as we mentioned earlier, time must be set aside for customer care and prospecting. The amount of time depends on the activity goals set earlier and on how long each call should take. However, salespeople often have unique activities, such as special sales calls, demonstrations, customer training, and sales meetings, to plan for as well. Time must also be set aside for planning and paperwork.

Exhibit 15.6
Activities Planning Process

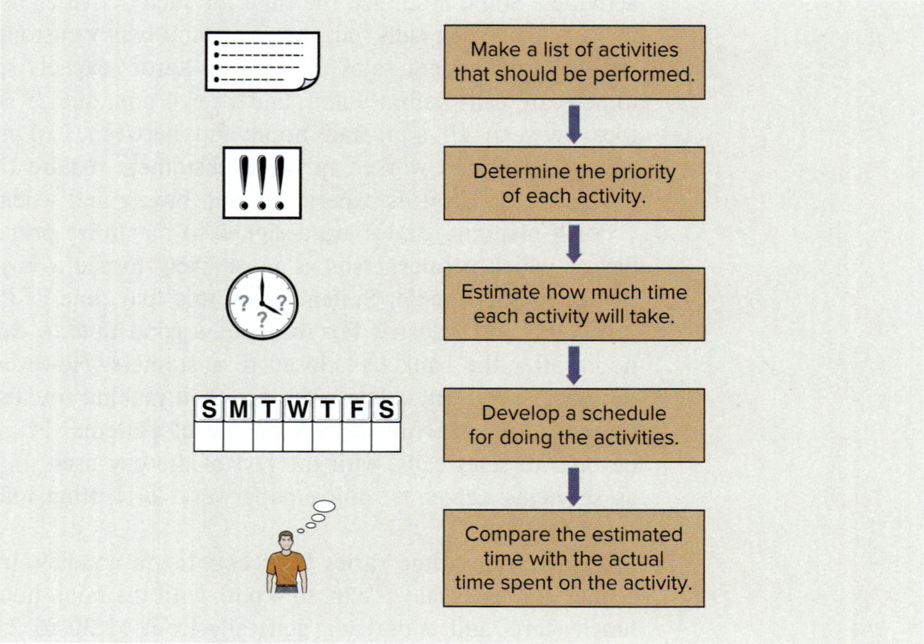

The next step, developing an effective schedule, requires estimating the amount of time such activities will require. As follow-up, be sure to compare how long an activity actually took with how long you thought it would take. Comparing actual time to planned time with the aid of calendaring tools in software systems like NetSuite can help you plan more accurately in the future.

Using the Computer for Planning

Many of the same CRM programs that salespeople use to identify and analyze accounts incorporate time-planning elements. This software can generate to-do lists and calendars through a tickler file or by listing certain customer types. A **tickler file** is a file or calendar that salespeople use to remember when to call specific accounts or take other actions.[15] For example, if customer A says to call back in 90 days, the computer will remind ("tickle") the salesperson in 90 days to call that customer. Or if the company just introduced a product that can knock out competitor B, the computer can generate a list of prospects with products from competitor B; the salesperson then has a list of prospects for the new product.

Need for Flexibility

Although working out a daily plan is important, occasions will arise when the plan should be laid aside. You cannot accurately judge the time needed for each sales call, and hastily concluding a sales presentation just to stick to a schedule would be foolish. If more time at one account will mean better sales results, the schedule should be revised.

To plan for the unexpected, your first visit of the day should be to a prime prospect (in the terms discussed earlier, this would be an A account or activity); then the next best potential customer should be visited (provided the travel time is reasonable); and so forth. If an emergency causes a change of plans, at least the calls most likely to result in sales will have been made.

MAKING MORE CALLS

Making daily plans and developing efficient routes are important steps toward better time use. But suppose you could make just one more call per day. Using our analysis from the beginning of this chapter and Exhibit 15.3, this change would mean 240 more calls per year, which is like adding one month to the year!

Some salespeople develop an "out Tuesday, back Friday" complex. They can offer many reasons why they need to be back in the office or at home on Monday and Friday afternoons. Such a behavior pattern means the salesperson makes 20 to 30 percent fewer calls than a salesperson who works a full week. John Plott, with DG Vault, got one large sale by working the full week. He was making cold calls on a Friday afternoon, trying to set up appointments for the following week, when he reached an attorney whose current vendor was unable to meet a deadline. The attorney said if he could get the software set up that afternoon, he could have the business. The result was a $30,000 account and $4,500 in commission.[16]

To get the most out of a territory, the sales representative must make full use of all available days. For example, the days before or after holidays are often seen as bad selling days. Hence, while the competition takes those extra days off, the salesperson can be working and making sales calls he or she would otherwise miss. The same reasoning applies to bad weather: Bad weather reduces competition and makes things easier for the salesperson who doesn't find excuses to take it easy. On the other hand, good weather can tempt the salesperson to go to the golf course, do yard work, or otherwise avoid the job. No matter the weather, the professional salesperson continues to work.

Salespeople who make calls in bad weather often find that their competition has taken the day off, leaving the field wide open for those who want to succeed.

Salespeople can use certain techniques to increase the time they spend in front of customers selling instead of traveling. These include routing and zoning.

Routing

Routing is a method of planning sales calls in a specific order to minimize travel time. Two types of sales call patterns, routine and variable, can be more efficient with effective routing. Using **routine call patterns**, a salesperson sees the same customers regularly. For example, Eli Lilly pharmaceutical salespeople's call plans enable them to see all important doctors in their territory at least once every six weeks. Some doctors (those who see large numbers of certain types of patients) are visited every two weeks. The salesperson repeats the pattern every six weeks, ensuring the proper call level.

Variable call patterns occur when the salesperson must call on accounts in an irregular order. In this situation the salesperson would not routinely call on each account within a specified period. Routing techniques are useful, but the salesperson may not repeat the call plan on a cyclical basis.

The four types of routing plans, **circular routing**, **leapfrog routing**, **straight-line routing**, and **cloverleaf routing**, are illustrated in Exhibit 15.7. If an Eli Lilly salesperson used the cloverleaf method (with six leaves instead of four) for a routine call pattern, every sixth Tuesday would find that salesperson in the same spot. But a salesperson with variable call patterns could use the cloverleaf method to plan sales calls for an upcoming week and then use the straight-line method the next week. The pattern would vary depending on the demands of the customers and the salesperson's ability to schedule calls at convenient times.

No matter the call pattern, routine or variable, software can be useful in mapping calls for efficiency. WorkWave Route Manager, for example, is one product that can plan routes for salespeople to minimize time in the car and maximize time with customers.

Zoning

Zoning means dividing the territory into zones, based on ease of travel and concentration of customers, to minimize travel time. First, the salesperson locates concentrations of accounts on a map. For example, an office supply salesperson may find that many accounts are located downtown, with other concentrations around the airport, in an industrial park, and in a part of town where two highways cross near a rail line. Each area is the center of a zone. The salesperson then plans to spend a day, for example, in each zone. In a territory zoned like the one in Exhibit 15.8, the salesperson might spend Monday in zone 1, Tuesday in zone 2, and so forth.

Zoning works best for compact territories or for situations in which salespeople do not call regularly on the same accounts. (In a large territory, such as the entire Midwest, a salesperson is more likely to use leapfrog routes, but the principle is similar.) Calling on customers that are in a relatively small area minimizes travel time between calls.

Salespeople can also combine zoning with routing, using a circular approach within a zone, for example. When zones are designed properly, travel time between accounts should be minimal.

Exhibit 15.7

Types of Routing Plans

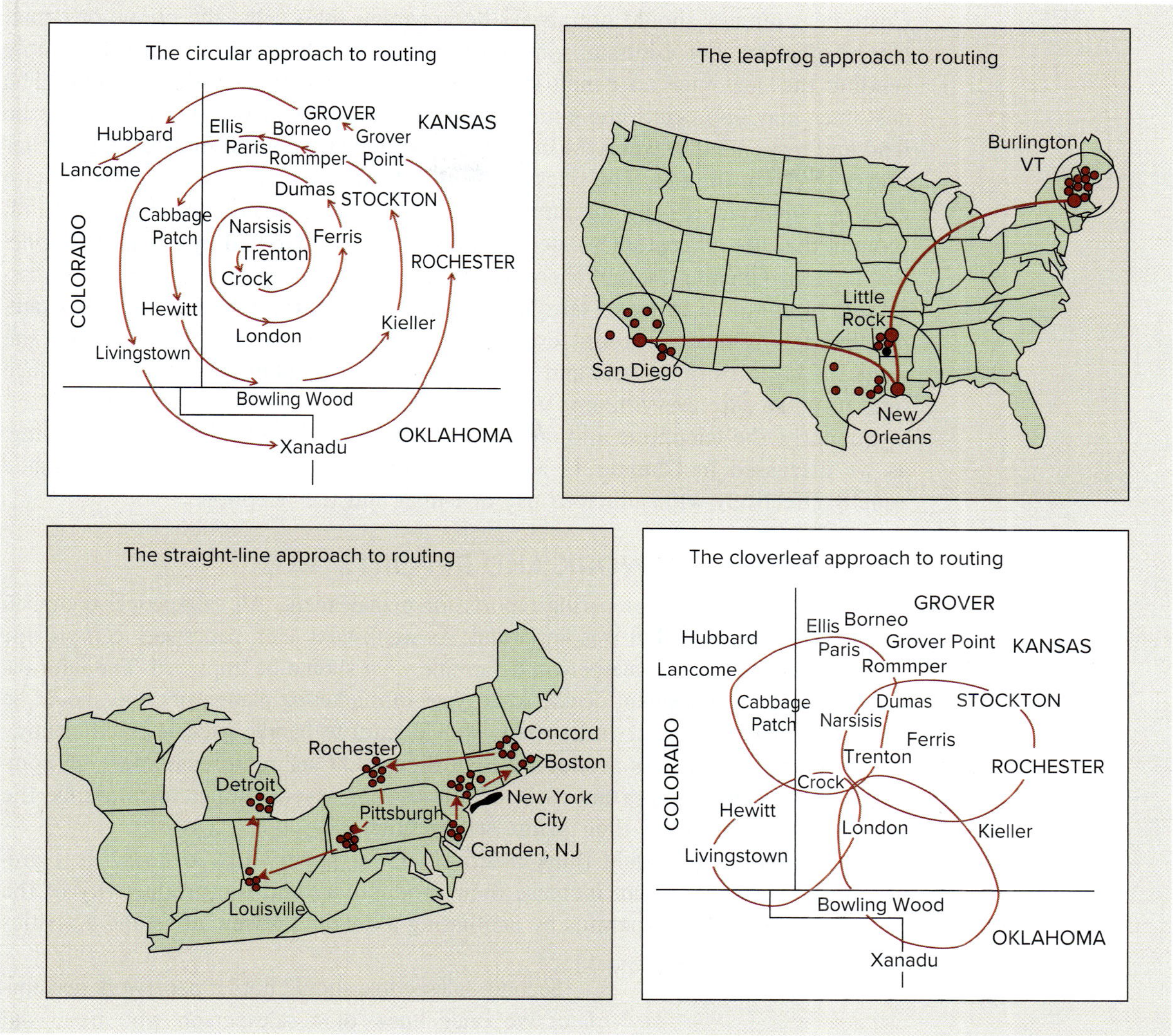

Exhibit 15.8

Zoning a Sales Territory. A salesperson may work in zone 1 on Monday, zone 2 on Tuesday, and so forth.

Source: *Waco Tribune Herald.*

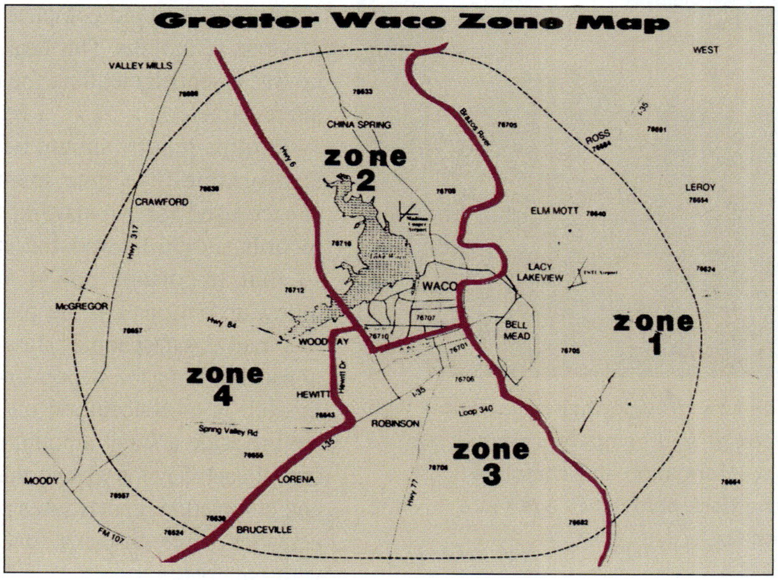

Using E-Mail and Telephone

Customer contacts should not always be in-person sales calls—the phone or e-mail can be effective. For example, some customer care calls can be handled by simply sending the customer an e-mail message asking whether everything is OK. The customer may appreciate the e-mail more than a personal visit because it can be read and responded to when the customer has time and doesn't interfere with other pressing responsibilities. The salesperson may be able to make more customer care calls by e-mail, increasing the number of contacts with customers. Keep in mind, though, that not all customer care activities should be handled by e-mail or phone. Recall from Chapter 14 that there are many reasons, such as reorders and cross-selling, to continue to make sales calls in person to current customers. For example, Sandra Kennedy, account executive for Spherion, has one account that she visits weekly. "It's my largest and most complicated account, and it just takes face time to make sure everything is going smoothly."[17]

Similarly, the telephone and direct mail can be used profitably for prospecting, as we discussed in Chapter 6. More calls, or customer contacts, can be made equally effectively with judicious use of e-mail and the telephone.

HANDLING PAPERWORK AND REPORTS

Every sales job requires preparing reports for management. All salespeople complain about such paperwork, but it is important. As we discuss later, paperwork can provide information that helps a salesperson determine what should be improved. The information also helps management decide what types of marketing plans work and should be used again. Therefore, every salesperson should learn to handle paperwork efficiently.

Paperwork time is less productive than time spent selling to customers, so completing it quickly is important. Salespeople can do several things to minimize the impact of paperwork on their prime selling time.

First, salespeople should think positively about paperwork. Although less productive than selling, it can increase their productivity and the productivity of the company's marketing programs by facilitating a detailed review of selling activities and marketing programs.

Second, salespeople should not let paperwork accumulate. We once knew of a salesperson who never did expense reports. He finally offered a summer intern 10 percent if she would complete his expense reports for the previous 12 months. This deal cost him $600; in addition, he was essentially lending the company $500 per month, interest free.

Many companies now provide their salespeople with wireless notebook or pad computers so they can access customer information and complete paperwork in the field, sometimes even in a customer's office.

Courtesy of John Tanner

Routine reports should be completed daily. Nonproductive time (like time spent waiting for a customer) can be used for paperwork. Call reports and account records should be updated immediately after the calls so that important points are remembered and any follow-up actions can be planned.

Finally, salespeople should set aside a block of nonselling time for paperwork. The quickest way to do this job is to concentrate on it and avoid interruptions. Setting aside a small amount of time at the beginning or end of each day for writing thank-you and follow-up notes and completing reports saves prime selling time for selling activities while ensuring that the salesperson keeps up with paperwork.

Using the Computer to Handle Paperwork and Communications

Many companies, such as McGraw-Hill, give their salespeople pad, laptop, or notebook computers. These computers can be linked with the company's network to access customer information and process other paperwork automatically. Salespeople who travel can thus complete their paperwork while in a coffee shop, hotel, an airport waiting area, and other places. Voice recognition systems enable salespeople to do paperwork without any paper; in fact, Amazon's Alexa product connects with CRM solutions so that salespeople can input data into their system at home each night.

Salespeople calling on overseas accounts can also file reports or check the status of orders, even though the home office in another time zone may be closed for the night. Computers can help international selling organizations operate smoothly by reducing communication barriers between the field and the home office. Computers and fax machines enable salespeople to communicate with colleagues and customers all around the world, despite significant time differences.

Some customer relationship management packages, like Pipeliner, include territory management capabilities. These packages allow salespeople to track their performance by calculating conversion rates, commissions, expenses, and other important figures. Such technology enables salespeople to file reports quickly. Larry Nichols, PK Companies, says Pipeliner reduced analysis and manager review time from 3 hours to less than 45 minutes. "It's all about next steps versus follow-ups. You multiply 6 hours a day times 15 people, and that is an incredible saving."[18]

To manage your time wisely, you must exploit a scarce resource in the most effective manner possible. Your objective is to make as many quality calls as possible by reserving prime selling time for selling activities. Routing, zoning, goal setting, and other methods of planning and scheduling time will help you maximize your prime selling time.

EVALUATING PERFORMANCE

Success in sales is a result of how hard and how smart a salesperson works. Unlike many other workers, salespeople have a great deal of control over both how hard and how smart they work. Evaluating performance is the component of self-management that provides direction for how hard the salesperson should be working as well as an opportunity to determine which strategies work best. Salespeople should evaluate each sales call individually but also look at which activity leads to desired outcomes and at what rate. Mike Rocker is a surgical products specialist for 3M, and covers the western half of the United States. He shares his perspective in Building Partnerships 15.1. Let's examine each component in more detail.

POSTCALL ANALYSIS

At the end of each call, many salespeople take a moment to write down what occurred and what needs to be done, perhaps using a printed form or entering the information into a territory management program such as NetSuite. Information such as the customer's purchase volume, key people in the decision process, and current vendors is important to have, but so is personal information such as the fact that the buyer's three children play soccer. The salesperson can use that information when preparing for the next call.

Remember the plan you made for each sales call? That plan included one or more objectives. Postcall analysis should include reflecting on whether those objectives were reached. The professional salesperson not only looks for specific areas to improve but also evaluates the success of the overall sales call.

BUILDING Partnerships 15.1

EVALUATING TIME: MIKE ROCKER

Currently, I am a surgery center specialist managing our relationship with a vendor partner and their sales team. I also work on internal cross-functional marketing, sales management, and sales learning and development teams. With this much responsibility, the way I manage my territory and time is critical to my effectiveness.

I usually like to travel with my vendor reps at least twice a year in their respective territories for at least two days a week. We meet with customers and distribution partners, creating plans for how to grow their business. We also travel to many industry and customer trade shows throughout the year around the country in their territories. With these sales expectations and customer interactions, one has to develop an effective plan and tactics to receive the most value for his or her time. I evaluate my performance in making the best use of my time. Here are a couple of my time and territory management tactics and tools I employ to be effective. I encourage you to develop your own tactics that are effective for you in your territory:

1. *You have to spend time on the opportunities that have the greatest potential.* We all have finite time in most instances with our customer. For example, when I make a trip to the western half of the United States to work with my sales team, I try to direct our efforts to our largest sales opportunities while I am in the territory. Of course, we do meet with our medium to small opportunities, but we just want to make sure we are maximizing our time in the field. Part of evaluating performance is how well we met that goal.
2. *Delegate items to your sales support team.* That team can include sales analyst, product specialist, contract specialist, and so on. These team players have specific skill sets and experience that will help you along the way in closing and completing the sales process. Even if you don't have specific resources assigned to you, finding people who can help you is important. Teaming and delegation is essential in any sales process, as it will free you to spend your time where it will pay off the most.
3. *Use digital tools such as e-mail, text messages, product webinars, and instant messaging wisely.* These tools have allowed me manage my territory virtually from anywhere. We most recently used a combination of webinars over three weeks to present a sterilization class to over 150 customers throughout the country. Because of these webinars, we were able to secure a nice amount of new business for Q3 without having to do as many individual presentations in someone's clinic or hospital.

I suspect these recommendations would apply in principle to many jobs, but you can see how you have to manage your territory as you embark on your sales career. The great thing about time and territory management is that you can personalize it to fit your and your customer's schedule. But like all aspects of your performance, you have to constantly get better at it!

ACTIVITY ANALYSIS

When planning their time, salespeople set certain activity goals. They use these goals not only as guidelines but also to evaluate their own performance. At the end of each day, week, and month, salespeople should review their activities in relation to the goals they set. Goals are written down or entered into Pipeliner when they are set—say, Sunday evening when planning the following week. Then, on Friday evening, the actual activities from each day would be tallied and totaled for the week and compared to the goals. The salesperson could then evaluate whether more calls of a certain type are needed in the following week.

All activity analysis can tell you is whether or not you made the call. Activity analysis is important—it helps you manage your efficiency and reduce wasted time. Activity analysis, though, doesn't tell you how well each call went.

PERFORMANCE ANALYSIS

Salespeople also need to evaluate performance relative to performance goals set earlier. For example, they often evaluate sales performance in terms of percentage of quota achieved. Of course a commission or a bonus check also tells the salesperson if the earnings goal was met.

An earnings goal can be an effective check for overall performance, but salespeople also need to evaluate sales by product type, as outlined in Exhibit 15.9. Salespeople who sell only part of the product line may be missing opportunities for cross-selling or full-line selling, which means they have to work harder to achieve the same level of sales as the salesperson who successfully integrates cross-selling and full-line selling in the sales strategy.

PRODUCTIVITY ANALYSIS

Salespeople also need to identify which strategies work. For example, if using a certain strategy improved the ratio of appointments to cold calls made, that approach should be continued. Otherwise the salesperson should change it or go back to a previous approach. Nathan Lockhart and Denver Prigmore, sales reps for Lockhart Industries, keep track of their sales call strategies and compare notes to determine which strategy works best and with which type of customer.

The **conversion ratio**, or number of sales per calls, is an important measure of effectiveness. Conversion ratios should also be calculated by account type; for example, a

Exhibit 15.9
Sales Evaluation Measures

Evaluation Measure	Calculation	How to Use It
Conversion rate For total performance By customer type By product type	Number of sales / Number of calls	Are your strategies effective? Do you need to improve by working smarter (i.e., a better strategy to improve your hit rate)? Compare yours to your company and/or industry average.
Sales achievement	\$ Actual sales / \$ Sales goal	Is your overall performance where you believe it should be? Are you meeting your goals? Your company's goals?
Commission	\$ Actual Commission / \$ Earnings goal	
Sales volume (in dollars)		
By customer type		Where are you most effective? Do you need help with a customer type?
By product category		Are you selling the whole line?
By market share		How are you doing relative to your competition?
By new customers		Are you building new business?
By old customers		Are you servicing your accounts properly?
Sales calls Prospecting calls Account calls Sales presentations Call frequency by customer type		Are your efforts in the right place?

This graphic illustrates sales performance by salesperson over time. The manager can pull this illustration out of data in a CRM system like Pipeliner.

Courtesy of Pipeliner

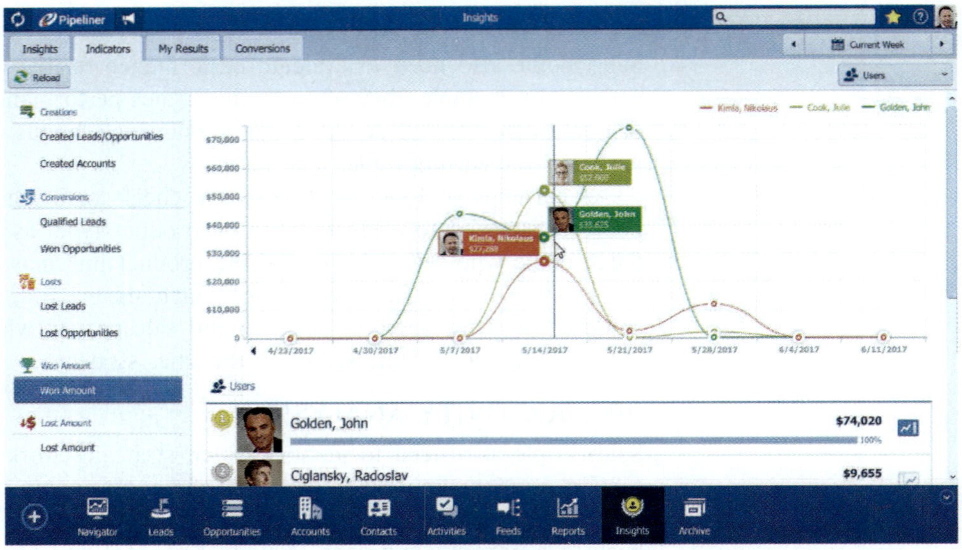

conversion ratio for type A accounts should be determined. Other conversion ratios can also pinpoint effective strategies and areas that need improvement.

Conversion ratios can also be calculated for each step of the sales cycle. Nathan and Denver, the two Lockhart salespeople, track outcomes for initial sales calls, needs identification calls, and closing calls, calculating conversion ratios for each step. Again, they compare notes to determine which approach works best.

SELLING YOURSELF

A theme for this chapter is self-analysis to improve performance. As a student, engaging in self-analysis is important so you repeat activities that are successful (lead to good grades) and avoid those that are not. Did pulling an all-nighter improve your exam performance? Or did you do better when you studied for shorter periods each day beginning a week ahead? (Research supports starting sooner and working during the day, rather than late into the night.)

Similarly, if you are in an organization and examine the organization's recruiting practices, you'll find that some methods work better than others. What method of finding leads worked best–posting a flyer in the dorms or posting an e-vite on Facebook? What events attracted the largest crowds, and which events provided the best prospective members? By applying what you've learned in this chapter to organizational recruiting (or fund-raising or other activities that mimic the sales process), you'll be able to improve your organization's performance.

But what about you? Do you set goals for your academic performance each semester? Do you track your progress toward those goals and keep the goals visible as a way to motivate yourself? Paul Lushin, a noted sales trainer based in Indianapolis, says, "Over the years, I've come to know myself very well: what makes me work harder and what I have to do to make myself do things I really don't want to do so that I can enjoy the performance I seek. I find that teaching this concept of knowing yourself is one of the most important things that can help salespeople succeed."[19] While he was talking about salespeople, the concept applies to students, too.

SUMMARY

A sales territory can be viewed as a small business. Territory salespeople have the freedom to establish programs and strategies. They manage a number of resources, including physical resources such as sample inventory, displays, demonstration equipment, and perhaps a company vehicle. More important, they manage their time, their customers, and their skills.

Managing a territory involves setting performance, activity, and conversion goals. Salespeople use these goals to allocate time to various activities and to manage customers.

To manage customers well, salespeople must analyze their potential. Accounts can be classified using the ABC method or the sales call allocation grid. These analyses tell how much effort should be put into each account. Some organizations use CRM software to conduct these analyses on the entire customer database, which helps identify patterns within a territory. Salespeople can use these patterns to develop account sales strategies.

More calls (working harder) can be accomplished by moving nonselling activities, such as paperwork, to nonselling time. Also, selling time can be used more efficiently (working smarter). For example, routing and zoning techniques enable salespeople to spend more prime selling time in front of customers instead of behind the steering wheel of a car.

Effective planning of the salesperson's day requires setting aside time for important activities such as prospecting and still making the appropriate number of sales appointments. Using the full workweek and employing technology such as telephones, computers, and fax machines can help the salesperson stay ahead of the competition.

Finally, salespeople must manage their skills. Managing skills involves choosing how to make sales calls and improving the way one sells. Improvement requires that salespeople first understand what they do well and what needs improvement. Evaluating their performance can provide them with that insight.

KEY TERMS

ABC analysis 411
account opportunity 412
account share 414
activity goals 408
benchmarking 409
circular routing 420
cloverleaf routing 420
conversion goals 408
conversion ratio 425
customer share 414
leapfrog routing 420
performance goals 407
pipeline analysis 415
prime selling time 417
routine call patterns 420
routing 420
sales call allocation grid 412
share of wallet 414
straight-line routing 420
strength of position 412
tickler file 419
variable call patterns 420
zoning 420

ETHICS PROBLEMS

1. A sales manager schedules all sales training and sales meetings on the weekend so salespeople lose no selling time. Is this ethical? Does your answer depend on how they get paid—straight salary, salary plus commission, or straight commission? What are other factors might influence your perception?

2. You have several major accounts that you are being asked to grow substantially in the new year. To do that, you have to ignore some of the needs of smaller and medium-sized accounts, accounts that are located in rural areas and farther away. Under what circumstances would this cause you ethical concern, if any? Would it matter what type of customer you served? Or if smaller companies actually paid prices with higher margins?

QUESTIONS AND PROBLEMS

1. Reread the chapter opening profile, From the Buyer's Seat 15.1, and Building Partnerships 15.1. What themes run through all three essays?
2. Mike Rocker, Susan Flaviano, and many other salespeople work out of their homes. Rocker and Flaviano both recognize how tempting it is to work longer and to put off paperwork until the weekends because it is so convenient. What problems might succumbing to such temptation cause? What safeguards can they put into place?
3. Mike Rocker and John Tanner both work in health care sales, but Rocker travels the western half of the United States and works out of his home, and Tanner manages a territory consisting of one small city and works out of the office. Compare and contrast the challenges they face in managing their business.
4. Shakespeare wrote, "To thine own self be true." How would you apply this statement to your planning and development activities?
5. Which factors are important for classifying customers? Why? How would these factors change depending on the industry?
6. Distinguish between routing and scheduling and between routing and zoning. Explain how routing and scheduling can interact to complement the planning of an efficient day's work.
7. Some companies talk about sales as being an opportunity to manage your own business. What, based on this chapter, would you say makes that perspective more accurate? Less accurate?
8. One sales manager said, "Sales is a numbers game. To make more sales, make more sales calls." Should sales managers encourage salespeople to continually increase the number of calls made each week? Explain your answer. Reread From the Buyer's Seat 15.1. How does this essay relate to your answer?
9. One recruiter told a class that students are used to getting feedback on how they are doing every couple of months, but salespeople do not get a "final grade" until a year has gone by. He claims that students have a hard time making that adjustment when they enter the work world. What do salespeople do to know where they stand at any given time? What do you do now that helps you know where you stand in your classes? Why is such knowledge important?
10. How would you use the sales call allocation grid or ABC analysis to determine a prospecting plan? Be specific, and number each step of the process you would use.

CASE PROBLEMS

case 15.1

Will Superion's Newest Salesperson Make It?

When Shelly Livesay-Jones took a position as a new salesperson for Superion, she wanted to be successful. She dutifully studied the product manuals and pricing information, read the case studies of customers who used Superion products, and read articles on competitors and their products. She memorized scripts on how to open a call and how to ask for the order.

After six weeks, though, she wasn't reaching even 70 percent of quota. She tried everything–making more phone calls to set up appointments, knocking on doors to meet potential buyers, and attending every networking event she could. But even when the marketing department gave her 25 leads one month, she couldn't even manage 5 first calls.

Superion sells equipment that can be sold with a service contract as well as supplies. In the following table, she could review what the other salespeople did in the previous 90 days. While the salespeople can prospect on their own, they are given leads by the marketing department. A service contract can be sold with the equipment or during the first 30 days following delivery at the same discounted price. In addition, a supply contract can also be closed with the initial product sale. Sales quotas are based on total revenue, so service and supply contracts can be very important, as the total cost is equivalent to 30 percent of the product sale.

	Equipment					Service		Supply
	Leads	Initial Calls	Proposals	Demos	Sales	With Initial Equipment Purchase	Sold Later	Contracts at Time of Equipment Purchase
Will Travis	66	60	52	26	24	10	3	4
Larry Davis	72	57	48	26	22	16	1	8
Sherry Gerard	54	51	45	28	23	7	9	7
Roger Freeman	57	49	40	19	19	9	8	9
Tasha Dawson	81	75	58	28	25	15	5	13
Fred Herman	66	60	54	25	22	18	0	14

Questions

1. Which salesperson should Shelly ask for help? And why?
2. If you were the sales manager, where would you focus your efforts for overall team improvement—generating better leads, writing better proposals, or doing better demos? And how do these activities seem to support closing service contracts at the time of the initial purchase?
3. Why would the company distinguish between service contracts sold with the equipment versus later?

case **15.2**

RipHeat

In January, Jane Bray took over the sales team at RipHeat, a division of a commercial real estate company that serves the cable TV industry. RipHeat, named for the two founders Riply and Heath, began by installing cable TV equipment in their own apartment buildings, then branched out into dorms and similar high-intensity multi-tenant dwellings, and now also provides technical support service to the tenants.

At lunch on Jane's first day, CEO Bob Riply said, "I want the division to expand significantly, but cash is tight, so hiring more salespeople isn't an option. But keep in mind we have a patented technology that our competitors can't match, so continuing our high growth rate seems likely."

"I think the first thing is to assess where we are with our top accounts," Jane replied. "We don't have 100 percent penetration with any account, do we?" Bob shook his head no, then said, "We've not been able to get an exclusive agreement except with ACH; they'll use us in all of their new projects and any refurbishing projects. But elsewhere, each new complex is determined by a bid process."

Bob began to tick off names and discuss the top accounts. "With the exclusive agreement, ACH will be our largest customer by the end of the year. Next will be The Orchard." The Orchard is a company that owns and operates apartments near colleges and universities across the country. There are currently 32 such complexes, with 20 on the books to be built in the coming year. Of those 32, 14 were acquired, and the rest were built by Orchard; half of those built are served by RipHeat and the others by two other vendors. Of the 14 acquired sites, all were served by various other vendors, but RipHeat has expressed an interest in upgrading to new equipment over the next two years. "How quickly they refurbish," said Bob, "will be determined by how well they are able to build the new units within budget, but I'd like to get an exclusive with them because of the growth. But they seem reluctant to put all their eggs in one basket."

Third on the list was Pinetree Properties, a company that owns 64 properties across the South. "They've got us in five of their newer complexes, all of which serve colleges and universities. Our systems are best suited to the high data demands students put on their Internet cable systems. The company has seven older university properties and plans to refurbish two each year. I think we'll win that, as they really see our benefits in that environment. Where we've struggled with them is in their family properties because they don't think it's worth the price premium to get the higher-quality product."

Young & Family was fourth. This family-owned business operates a dozen apartment complexes in Florida, with four in Miami. "Frank Young loves us. He's totally bought into our system of billing and will use us in any new properties they build. Right now, they're looking at two smallish complexes, both in Miami. They put us in the last three properties they built."

Last on the list of top five is The Franklin Group, which owns 32 properties in the Pacific Northwest. "Like Young, they like us a lot, but their growth rate has slowed. We're also in their last three properties, and our best shot there is probably refurbishing the older properties. They should be doing a complete makeover in the next five years, but getting them to make that investment has been tough," said Bob. Jane asked why, and Bob replied that the operations VP was in favor of it but the CFO was not. "Maybe we just need to find some new companies to work with."

Questions

1. Where would you place these accounts on the sales effort allocation grid? Justify your responses.
2. What is your sales strategy for each one? What is the order of priority?
3. If you were to look for new companies to work with, use the information from these descriptions and design the perfect prospect.

ROLE PLAY CASE

Six months ago, you went through your accounts and determined that how you've allocated your effort is not consistent with the potential of each account and your relative position. In one instance, National Steel, you've got a great relationship with the CIO and have called on National Steel once or twice a month. The company, however, isn't growing and there isn't anything new to offer to sell the customer. You decided that this is an account you no longer plan to visit in person but will check by phone.

Another account, Maguire Manufacturing, merited more calling. The company was taken over by a private equity firm about a year ago and much of the top management changed. In fact, a new CIO was just brought on board and it appears that there will be significant investment in the IT area. Because it continues to grow and has indicated that it may grow through acquisition of other companies, you've decided to visit it once or twice a month.

Grafton Gifts, a retailer and distributor of gifts and home decorating products, has been a tough account to understand. The CIO was brought in six months ago, and has confided that the sales and marketing systems are in disarray. While the VP of sales is happy, the VP of marketing wants a big data strategy and toolkit. The problem is that there seems to be no budget. Today you will visit the CIO and VP of marketing to determine whether you want to continue with this account.

Your professor will give you buyer sheets for your turn as a buyer.

ADDITIONAL REFERENCES

Borgh, Michel, Ad Jong, and Edwin J. Nijssen. "Alternative Mechanisms Guiding Salespersons' Ambidextrous Product Selling." *British Journal of Management* 28, no. 2 (April 2017), pp. 331-53.

Chen, Annie, Norman Peng, and Kuang-peng Hung. "Strategic Management of Salespeople When Promoting New Products: Moderating Effects of Sales-Related Organizational Psychological Climate." *European Journal of Marketing* 49, no. 9/10 (2015), pp. 1616-44.

Decarlo, Thomas E., and Son K. Lam. "Identifying Effective Hunters and Farmers in the Salesforce: A Dispositional-Situational Framework." *Journal of the Academy of Marketing Science* 44, no. 4 (July 2016), pp 415-39.

Dietz, Bart, Daan van Knippenberg, Giles Hirst, and Simon Lloyd D. Restubog. "Outperforming Whom? A Multilevel Study of Performance-Prove Goal Orientation, Performance, and the Moderating Role of Shared Team Identification." *Journal of Applied Psychology* 100, no. 6 (November 2015), pp. 1811-24.

Friend, Scott B., Jeff S. Johnson, Fred Luthans, and Ravipreet S. Sohi. "Positive Psychology in Sales: Integrating Psychological Capital." *Journal of Marketing Theory and Practice* 24, no. 3 (Summer 2016), pp. 306-27.

Gillespie, Erin Adamson, Stephanie M. Noble, and Son K. Lam. "Extrinsic versus Intrinsic Approaches to Managing a Multi-Brand Salesforce: When and How Do They Work?" *Journal of the Academy of Marketing Science* 44, no. 6 (November 2016), pp 707-25.

Ketchersid, Jeanne. "Goal Setting: Does It Help or Hurt Sales Performance?" *PR Newswire*, May 17, 2016.

Mallin, Michael L. "Developing Proactive Salespeople–A Study and Recommendations for Sales Management." *Development and Learning in Organizations* 30, no. 4 (2016), pp. 9-12.

Milovic, Alex, and Rebecca Dingus. "Everyone Loves a Winner . . . Or Do They? Introducing Envy into a Sales Contest to Increase Salesperson Motivation." *American Journal of Management* 14, no. 4 (November 2014), pp. 27-32.

Schrock, Wyatt A., Douglas E Hughes, Frank Q. Fu, Keith A. Richards, and Eli Jones. "Better Together: Trait Competitiveness and Competitive Psychological Climate as Antecedents of Salesperson Organizational Commitment and Sales Performance." *Marketing Letters* 27, no. 2 (June 2016), pp. 351-60.

©Monkey Business Images/123RF

The Salesperson as Manager

PART 3

chapter 16

MANAGING WITHIN YOUR COMPANY

SOME QUESTIONS ANSWERED IN THIS CHAPTER ARE

- Which areas of the company work with salespeople to satisfy customer needs?
- How do salespeople coordinate the efforts of various functional areas of the company?
- How do salespeople work with sales managers and sales executives?
- How do company policies, such as compensation plans, influence salespeople?
- How do salespeople work within the company to resolve ethical issues?
- What is the organizational structure, and how does it influence salesperson activities?

PROFILE

> *"In some ways, managing these relationships is a balancing act—to what extent do you sacrifice advocating for the customer and lean on the insight of your own team?"*
>
> *Sean Fulton, Bell Helicopter*

PROFILE From kindergarten all the way through college graduation, I took the approach that I could get the job done alone, whether that job be a group project or activity with an on-campus organization. My route of choice, acting a "lone wolf," was usually successful. This lone wolf approach is very common among those entering into sales; however, it is not common for those *lasting* in sales. I currently work in sales for Bell Helicopter, one of the world's largest helicopter manufacturers. I covered Latin America for two years, and my region has since shifted to the Middle East and Africa (MEA). I have the opportunity to work with customers in all hemispheres of the world, ranging from military leaders to oil and gas operators to VIPs who commute via helicopter. With such a diverse product and industry, global sales in the helicopter industry is one of the last places to take the lone wolf approach.

Courtesy of Sean Fulton

Starting my career at Bell Helicopter, I felt very confident that I would enjoy complete success right off the bat. I had the opportunity to study in one of the top sales programs in college; how different could it be?

I quickly learned the real world is vastly different; I could no longer take a lone wolf approach. Instead, I learned the critical skill of managing relationships within my organization. In some ways, managing these relationships is a balancing act—to what extent do you sacrifice advocating for the customer and lean on the insight of your own team? How do you manage your need for rapid support without alienating those helping you? How do you ensure the long-term stability of these critical relationships? Perfecting this process is critical in any sales role, but especially in one that is highly technical.

First, be humble. Accept that you do not know everything and cannot effectively execute a deal from start to finish by yourself. While you are on the front lines, there is an entire organization behind you. In any given sales opportunity, I rely on the following functions throughout the sales cycle: contracts, engineering, finance, legal, procurement, pricing, field reps, and program management. Every one of these groups can increase the chance of finding a win-win for your organization and the customer.

Covering MEA creates unique challenges. The customer profile, culture, regulations, time zones (8 to 10 hours from the United States), funding sources, and evolving global market all provide hurdles that no college education could thoroughly prepare me for. For example, I would like to think the contracts portion of my Business Law class would suffice for my contracts knowledge—that is far from the case. I regularly lean on Chris, my support in contracts, to help finalize contracts that both meet the customer's needs as well as the business goals of Bell Helicopter. I am not afraid to admit that I know a fraction of the contracts world compared to Chris and will often put him in direct contact with the customer. For example, he recently went to Nigeria to work through the complexities of a very intricate contract.

Second, learn new languages. Not a foreign language, but the language of each function you work with. Learning the basics not only increases your skill set, but also shows others you are interested in their field of expertise, increasing their willingness to assist you. If I am consistently going to Chris unable to differentiate between an FFP or ROM proposal, chances are he will grow less willing to help. Not only does speaking another function's language show that you have an interest, it makes the job of those support people easier as opposed to starting at step one every time.

Last, learn how to properly balance your customer's expectations versus the insight of your team. Obviously, all salespeople would like to say they fight to the end for every customer's needs and wants but in reality, that is not the case. Sales in MEA involve a different kind of risk than most other regions. Oftentimes, government entities require contract terms that are well outside Bell's typical terms and conditions. Given my responsibilities are sales driven, I would like to comply with all customer requests; however, I need to invite input from others to make sure I'm not creating problems for Bell or my colleagues. Customers have asked for very strange terms, which I take straight to Chris and ask "How would this impact Bell and you?" Showing consideration of the impact on the business as well as other individuals builds trust among your peers in other areas and shows that you are concerned with others, not just yourself. Chris often will find a way to make the situation work. However, there are times when the request creates too much risk for the organization and as a result, Chris will discourage it. While this may result in a lost deal or two, it will ensure the long-term success of our relationship and Bell. If I were to consistently ignore Chris's advice, I would quickly alienate him, creating a rift in that valuable relationship.

Sales is a unique role as you are the tip of the spear in your company. While your respective role is critical, the support you receive from the rest of your team is even more critical. The faster you can learn how to effectively collaborate with your team in a respectful, productive manner, the faster you will realize success.

Visit our Web site at: www.bellhelicopter.com.

Sean Fulton, sales representative, Bell Helicopter. Used with permission.

BUILDING INTERNAL PARTNERSHIPS

To effectively coordinate the efforts of various areas of a company, a salesperson must develop partnerships with the individuals in those areas. **Internal partnerships** are partnering relationships between a salesperson and another member of the same company. These partnerships should be dedicated to satisfying customer needs.

THE IMPORTANCE OF INTERNAL PARTNERSHIPS

By definition, a sales representative represents something. Students often think the title means that the salesperson represents only a company or a product, but at times the salesperson must represent the customer to the company. For example, the salesperson may have to convince the warehouse manager to ship a customer's product next to meet a special deadline. The salesperson does not have the authority to order the manager to ship the product, but he or she must use persuasion. Or the rep may have to negotiate with production to get a product manufactured to a customer's specifications. Sometimes success in landing a sale may depend on the salesperson's ability to manage such company efforts.

This ability to work with groups inside the company can directly affect the rep's pocketbook. One of the authors, while selling for a major corporation, had an opportunity to earn a large bonus by making 30 sales. He had 31 orders, but a sale didn't count until the product was delivered. Unfortunately 2 orders were delivered after the deadline, and he did not get the bonus. In tracking down the slow deliveries, the hapless salesperson learned that the order entry clerk had delayed processing the orders. A little probing uncovered the reason: She was upset with the way he prepared his paperwork! Her performance was evaluated on how quickly an order was delivered, but his sloppy paperwork always slowed her down and got her into trouble. Delaying work on his orders was her way of getting his attention.

It worked! For several months after that, he enlisted her help in filling out the paperwork properly before he turned it in. After that, she never had a problem with his orders. And when necessary to meet a customer's requirements, she would prioritize his orders.

THE ROLE OF SALES

Salespeople not only sell a company, its products, and its services to customers but also sell their customers' needs to their company so that their company will respond with a solution. Carrying the customer's voice across the organization is one of the most important functions of the sales force. Although many companies work to increase the customer contact time for support personnel so they will understand customers, often the only person who really understands what the customer needs and why is the salesperson. In fact, the ability to receive and act on customer knowledge brought back to the company by salespeople has been documented to positively influence market share, account share (or share of wallet), profit margins, and the customer's perceived value![1]

Nucor Fastener uses its CRM system to capture the voice of the customer. Salespeople's notes, along with a deep analysis of data from other systems such as financial records and shipping data, helped the company identify specific customer needs that required special treatment. For example, 50 percent of all rush orders were generated by only 12 customers. The account executives for those accounts were able to identify customer requirements that led to new service offerings, greater revenue, and higher customer satisfaction.[2]

Whether or not companies have a formal voice of the customer process, salespeople still have a responsibility to their customers to ensure that the company is responsive to their changing needs. Jim Keller, account executive for Teradata and mentioned in an earlier chapter, says, "You may not be able to directly alter a product's design right away. But I know my input, based on customer needs, has had an impact on when certain features were added and how certain functions were changed."

SELLING INTERNALLY

To service customers well, salespeople must often rely on personnel in other areas of the firm to do their respective jobs properly. Even in seemingly simple situations like selling shipping, it can take a lot of internal coordination, as described in Building Partnerships 16.1. But how well those other employees assist salespeople may be a function of the relationship the salesperson has already established with them. That relationship should be a partnership, just like the one the salesperson wants to establish with appropriate customers. To establish the appropriate partnership, the salesperson must invest time in understanding the customer's needs and then work to satisfy those needs.

thinking it through

Consider the impact electronic forms of communication have had on your life so far. How do such forms of communication help build internal partnerships, particularly when a salesperson is stationed far from company headquarters? How can such forms of communication hinder a salesperson's efforts to build internal partnerships?

As summarized in Exhibit 16.1, the first step of selling laterally is to recognize that it is the salesperson's responsibility to develop relationships with other departments. Rarely do other departments have an incentive to take the initiative. Salespeople who expect other workers to serve them are frustrated by the lack of support they receive. The better perspective is, How can I serve them so we can serve the customer better?

BUILDING Partnerships 16.1

SALES TAKES TEAMWORK

From the outside, sales sometimes looks like a tennis match—the lone salesperson taking on the business challenge. In reality, even businesses that seem like commodities require a team effort.

Phoenix International is a privately owned freight forwarder and customs broker that supports companies involved in international trade. As a sales executive at Phoenix International, Lillie Sanchez says her role extends beyond selling new business to making sure her client's needs and wants are met. "This may seem like an easy task, but it takes a solid relationship and strong management to be successful." Once she signs up a new client, she becomes his or her advocate within Phoenix. Sanchez's internal partnerships have to be strong because when something is delayed, the entire account could be lost. Sanchez offers this example: "Today I received a phone call from one of my clients, Jon. He was upset because his shipment was not going to arrive on the original estimated day due to a number of events. As I called his coordinator at Phoenix International to discuss various scenarios we could take to overcome the obstacle, the solution was simple and didn't take much time to resolve; with teamwork we were able to meet the customer's demands and make him happy."

Smithfield Foods sells ham to retailers. You would think that a salesperson could do that all by herself. Actually, you can sell pork and ham many different ways, some of which is more profitable than others. Smithfield's salespeople work closely with a product management team to develop innovative, customer-specific products that create value for the consumer and meet the needs of their retail customers. Says Rikki Ingram, "Not only do our salespeople work closely with the product management team, but they also work with R&D, operations, and marketing to ensure differentiation and value creation across all new product launches. Done correctly, both Smithfield and the retailer benefit."

These seem like commodities, but actually, the coordination and teamwork required to make these solutions happen can be what separates Phoenix and Smithfield from their competitors.

Exhibit 16.1
Seven Principles of Selling Internally

1. Understand that it's your problem. **Accept responsibility** for gaining the support of the internal staff.
2. **Appeal to a higher objective.** For example, show how what you are asking for meets an important company objective.
3. Probe to find out and **understand the personal and professional needs** of the internal customer. Use SPIN and active listening techniques.
4. Use arguments for support that adequately **address the internal customer's needs** as well as your own. Use your presentation skills.
5. Do not spend time or energy resenting the internal customer's inability to understand or accept your sense of urgency. Rather, spend this time fruitfully by trying to figure out how you can better communicate your needs in a manner that will **increase the internal customer's sense of urgency** to the level you need.
6. **Never personalize** any issues. Don't call names, blame the person in public, or hold a grudge.
7. Be prepared to **negotiate.**

Use questioning skills such as SPIN to understand the personal and professional needs of personnel in other departments. Salespeople should have excellent communication skills but sometimes fail to use these skills when dealing with internal customers and support groups. SPIN and active listening are just as important to understanding the needs of colleagues as they are to satisfying customer needs. For example:

SALESPERSON: What do you do with these credit applications? (*Situation*)

CREDIT REP: We key the information into the computer system, and then it is processed by a credit company each night. The next morning we get a report that shows who has been approved and who hasn't. That's why it is so important to have a clean copy.

SALESPERSON: So the quality of the copy we give you is a problem? (*Problem*)

CREDIT REP: That's right.

SALESPERSON: What happens when you can't read the copy we give you? (*Implication*)

CREDIT REP: We put in incorrect information, which can result in a customer's credit application being rejected when it should have been accepted.

SALESPERSON: What happens when that happens? (*Implication*)

CREDIT REP: That's when we call you. Then we get the right information and reenter it. But we get in trouble because the approval cycle was made longer, and you know that the goal is to have a customer's order shipped in three days. We can't meet that goal if we're still working on its credit application.

SALESPERSON: So you need legible applications–and probably e-mail would be better than handwritten, right? (*Needs payoff*)

CREDIT REP: Yes, that would help a lot.

Keep in mind too that the salesperson cannot simply order a colleague to do what the salesperson wants, such as approving a customer's credit application. But if a salesperson can show that doing what he or she wants will also meet the needs of the colleague, the salesperson is more likely to receive the desired aid. Just as when selling to an external customer, persuasion requires the salesperson to meet the other person's needs as well. For example, if a salesperson can show a plant manager how an expedited order will result in a higher profit margin, thereby more than covering the plant manager's higher costs and helping that manager make production targets, both the plant manager's needs and the customer's needs will be met.

People from other departments, except for billing and customer service, do not have direct contact with the customer. Therefore, they may not feel the same sense of urgency the customer or the salesperson feels. Successful internal sellers can communicate that sense of urgency by relating to the needs of the internal customer. Just as they do with external customers, salespeople need to communicate the need to act now when they sell internally. They need to secure commitment to the desired course of action. Also, just as with external customers, the salesperson should be sure to say thank you when someone agrees to provide the support requested.

Selling to internal customers also means keeping issues professional. Personal relationships can and should be developed. But when conflicts arise, focus on the issue, not the person. Personalizing conflict makes it seem bigger and harder to resolve. For example, rather than saying, "Why won't you do this?" ask, "If you can't do this, how can we resolve the customer's concern?" This type of statement focuses the other individual on resolving the real problem rather than arguing about company policy or personal competence.

Be prepared to negotiate. Remember from Chapter 12 that negotiation is a set of techniques to resolve conflict. Conflicts between salespeople and members of the firm representing other areas will occur, and negotiation skills can be used to respond to conflicts professionally.

Salespeople must work with many elements of their organization. In fact, few jobs require the boundary-spanning coordination and management skill that the sales job needs. In the next section we examine the many areas of the company with which the salesperson works, what their needs are, and how they partner with the salesperson to deliver customer satisfaction.

COMPANY AREAS IMPORTANT TO SALESPEOPLE

The sales force interacts with many areas of the firm. Salespeople work with manufacturing, sales administration, customer service, and human resources. In some industries requiring customization of products, engineering is an important department for salespeople. Finance can get into the picture as well when that department determines which customers receive credit and what price is charged. In addition, salespeople work with members of their own department and the marketing department.

GEICO, Hormel, Smithfield Foods, Federated Insurance, and a host of other companies offer training programs to new salespeople that include spending time working in all areas of the company. This training not only provides deep understanding of how each area works, it also helps build personal relationships that salespeople can rely on later.

MANUFACTURING

In general, manufacturing is concerned with producing product at the lowest possible cost. Thus, in most cases, manufacturing wants long production runs, little customization, and low inventories. Customers, however, want their purchases shipped immediately and custom-made to their exact specifications. Salespeople may have to negotiate compromises between manufacturing and the customer. Salespeople should also develop relationships with manufacturing so they can make accurate promises and guarantees to customers.

In addition, we've already discussed the importance of the salesperson in ensuring that customers' needs are heard and products designed that fit their needs. Research shows that close, collaborative relationships between salespeople and manufacturing yield better new product designs—better in the sense of greater market acceptance and sales volume.[3] Hose Master Inc., a manufacturer of industrial hoses, actually brings salespeople and customers together with manufacturing for training on products. Frank Caprio, major market specialist for Hose Master, says these training sessions always yield new ideas for products or product enhancements that manufacturing can implement quickly.[4]

ADMINISTRATION

The functions of order entry, billing, credit, and employee compensation require each company to have an administrative department. This department processes orders and sees that the salesperson gets paid for them. Employees in this area (as discussed earlier) are often evaluated on how quickly they process orders and how quickly the company receives customer payment. Salespeople can greatly influence both processes and realize substantial personal benefit for themselves.

Salespeople who develop internal partnerships with people in areas such as manufacturing and service can count on their internal partners for support.

©kupicoo/Getty Images RF

The credit department is an important part of administration. Understanding the needs of the credit department and assisting it in collecting payments can better position the salesperson to help customers receive credit later. A credit representative who knows that you will help collect a payment when a problem arises is more likely to grant credit to one of your customers. Some companies do not pay commission until after the customer has paid to ensure that salespeople sell to creditworthy accounts. These companies, such as General Electric, believe a close working relationship between sales and credit is critical to the financial health of the company. In fact, GE has a "Walk a Mile" program where salespeople spend a day in credit, and credit personnel spend a day in the field with salespeople. This program leads to greater understanding and communication that lasts long after the day of walking a mile in someone's shoes.[5]

SHIPPING AND INSTALLATION

The scheduling of product shipments may be part of sales administration or manufacturing, or it may be a separate department. Wherever shipping is located, salespeople need the help of the shipping department. When salespeople make special promises to expedite a delivery, they actually must depend on shipping to carry out the promise. Shipping managers focus on costs, and they often keep their costs under control by planning efficient shipping routes and moving products quickly through warehouses. Expedited or special-handling deliveries can interfere with plans for efficient shipping. Salespeople who make promises that shipping cannot or will not fulfill fail to meet their customer's needs. Even when the promise is made in good faith, there are times when shipping needs an extra hand; that's why many of the better salespeople have been known to help load a truck or even deliver products personally.

In some businesses, installation is part of the purchase. From the customer's perspective, the product doesn't deliver benefits until it is working to solve the problem. Some companies, such as those selling office equipment, the delivery team can set up the product and get it running. In other situations, another team has to install the product. Whichever is the case, the salesperson has to coordinate with the installation team and make sure that promises made are promises kept.

CUSTOMER SERVICE

Salespeople also need to interact with customer service. The need for this relationship should be obvious, but many salespeople arrogantly ignore the information obtained by customer service representatives. A technician who fixes the company's products often goes into more customers' offices or plants than the salesperson does. The technician often has early warning concerning a customer's switch to a competitor, a change in customer needs, or failure of a product to satisfy. For example, a Dell computer technician may be the first to spot a competitor's computer in the customer's office; the technician can ask what's going on and then warn the salesperson that the account is considering a competitive product. Close relationships and support of customer or technical service representatives mean not only better customer service but faster and more direct information flow to the salesperson. This information will help the salesperson gain and keep customers.

Salespeople, in turn, can help customer service by setting reasonable expectations for product performance with customers, training customers in the proper use of the product, and handling complaints promptly. Technicians are evaluated on the number of service calls they make each day and how long the product works between service calls, among other things. Salespeople can reduce some service calls by setting the right expectations for product performance. Salespeople can also extend the amount of time between calls by training customers in the proper use of the product and in preventive maintenance. An important by-product of such actions should be higher customer satisfaction.

MARKETING

Sales is part of marketing in some firms and separate from marketing in others. Marketing and sales should be highly coordinated because their functions are closely related. Both are concerned with providing the right product to the customer in the most efficient and effective manner. Sales acts as the eyes and ears of marketing, while marketing develops the promotions and products that salespeople sell.

Marketing not only generates leads for salespeople but also supports sales activities by sourcing products and preparing proposals. At Lawson Products, tighter sales and marketing collaboration has helped the company grow. One big win relates to a value added service Lawson offers around special order procurement, according to Liesl Abrahamson, VP of marketing and continuous improvement. "If there is something that is not in any of our warehouses, we can go and source that item for a customer on a special order basis," Abrahamson says. "We focused particularly in the quotation area of the process and were able to reduce the cycle time–how long it takes us to respond to the customer–by more than 50 percent. Concurrently, we now process upwards of seven percent more quotations every day." That translates to more business won because of faster response times to the customer and more quotes generated.[6]

Unfortunately not all marketing and sales departments just naturally get along. Several studies have shown that sales and marketing departments fail to communicate, don't trust each other, and even sabotage each other.[7] More recent studies, however, suggest that the differences run deeper than communication; the differences are driven by beliefs about what should be done and by whom, the perceived value of marketing versus sales, and other basic differences.[8] Proactive salespeople won't wait for marketing managers to make the first move. Rather than complain about poor marketing programs, proactive salespeople and sales managers prefer to participate in marketing decisions and keep communication lines open.

Gilbarco Veeder-Root provides fueling technology for retail and commercial fueling operations. The marketing department and sales organization worked together to create an integrated campaign that combined digital marketing with inside sales teams. The plan generated qualified leads then passed along to the salespeople. A key point, though, is that marketing agreed to delivering against metrics, such as the number of qualified leads, with qualified being defined by the sales organization. That's right–they set SLAs (service level agreements), with a result of closing a full year's worth of marketing-generated sales in only 90 days.[9] When sales and marketing work together, salespeople have better programs with which to sell.[10]

SALES

Within any sales force, there may be several types of salespeople. As you learned in earlier chapters, global account managers may work with the largest accounts while other representatives handle the rest of the customers, and the salesperson must interact with certain sales executives and sales managers. How these people work together is the subject of the next section.

PARTNERS IN THE SALES ORGANIZATION

The sales function may be organized in many different ways, but no matter how it is organized, it is rarely perfect. Usually some customer overlap exists among salespeople, meaning several salespeople have to work together to serve the needs of one account. Customer needs may require direct customer contact with the sales executive as well as the salesperson. At the same time, the salesperson must operate in an environment that is influenced by the policies and procedures created by that same sales executive and executed by the salesperson's immediate manager. In this section we examine how the activities of sales management affect salespeople.

SALES MANAGEMENT

Salespeople should understand the roles of both sales executives and field sales managers. Salespeople who are able to develop partnerships with their managers will have more resources available to perform at a higher level.

The Sales Executive

The sales executive, sometimes called chief sales officer or chief revenue officer, is the leader at the top of the sales force hierarchy. This person is a policy maker, making decisions about how the sales force will accomplish corporate objectives. Sales executives play a vital role in determining the company's strategies with respect to new products, new markets, sales forecasts, prices, and competition. The executives determine the size and organization of the sales force, develop annual and long-range plans, and monitor and control sales efforts. Sales executives also strive, or should strive, to create a corporate culture that supports appropriate behaviors by their sales managers and salespeople–behaviors that are both ethical and customer-oriented.[11] Duties of the sales executive include forecasting overall sales, budgeting, setting sales quotas, and designing compensation programs.

Size and Organization of the Sales Force

The sales executive determines how many salespeople are needed to achieve the company's sales and customer satisfaction targets. In addition, the sales executive must determine what types of salespeople are needed. For example, the sales executive determines whether global account management is needed. Many other types of salespeople can be selected, which we discuss later in this chapter. For now, keep in mind that the sales executive determines the level of customer satisfaction necessary to achieve sales objectives and then designs a sales force to achieve those goals. How that sales force is put together is important because salespeople often have to work together to deliver appropriate customer service and successfully accomplish sales goals.

Forecasting

Sales executives use a number of techniques to arrive at sales forecasts. One of the most widely used techniques is **bottom-up forecasting**, or simply adding each salesperson's own forecast into a forecast for total company sales. At each level of management, the forecast would normally be adjusted based on the manager's experience and broader perspective. This technique allows the information to come from the people closest to the market: the salespeople. Also, the forecast comes from the people with the responsibility for making those sales. But salespeople tend to be optimistic and may overestimate sales. Advertising sales managers at Yahoo! use the CRM system to call out salespeople who are too optimistic. "We're coaching managers to use this information to call people out," explains Patrick O'Leary, senior sales director. "If someone says, 'We've got another 500K coming in next week,' we can now say, 'You've been working on that deal 120 days when the average is thirty days. What conversation did you have that made you think that?'"[12]

ethics

Conversely, salespeople may underestimate future sales if they know their bonuses depend on exceeding forecasts or if they think their quotas will be raised. Wise managers should quickly realize when salespeople are underestimating forecasts, though the salespeople may be able to obtain significant earnings the first time. Such behavior, though, not only is unethical but also creates many problems for the organization, such as stockouts, which then cause lost sales.

Salespeople are especially important to the forecasting process when the executive is attempting to forecast international sales. Statistics provided by industry associations

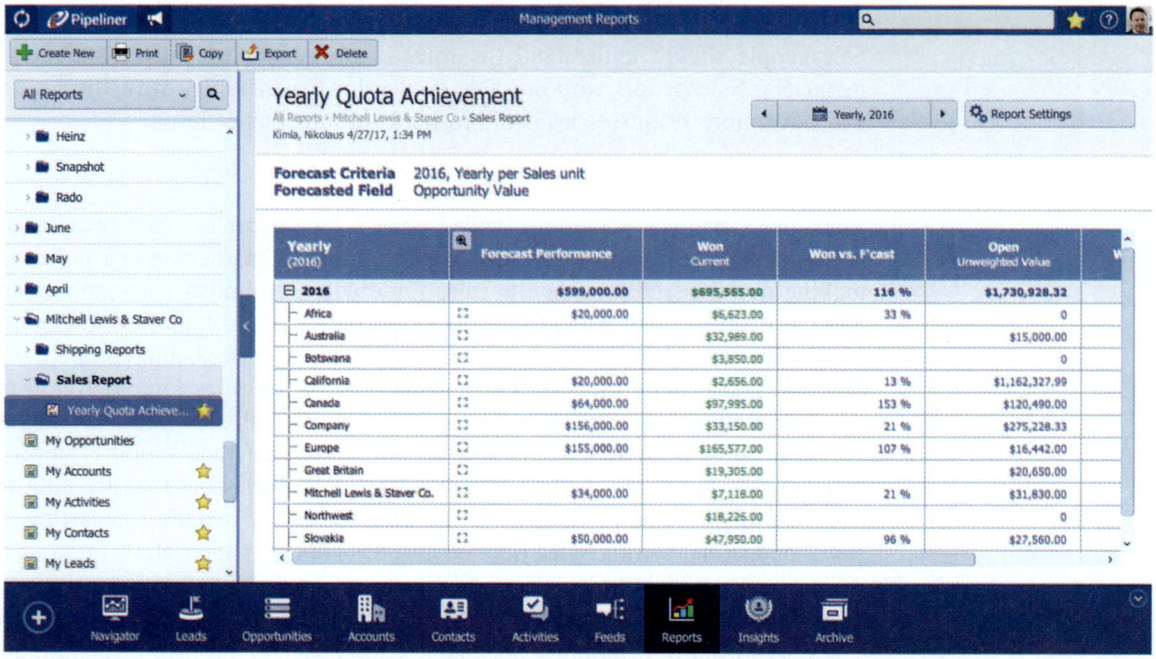

CRM systems, like Pipeliner, have built-in reporting so that managers and executives can pull up forecasts in real time, meaning they can see what salespeople are forecasting each day, based on where they are in the sales process

Courtesy of Pipeliner

or the government in the United States can be used to forecast sales, but are often not available in other countries or, if available, may be unreliable. Companies that operate in many different countries find that the only consistent numbers available may come from the sales force. In fact, one recent study of CFOs found that only 20 percent are "very confident" in their company sales forecasts.[13] Thus, accurate forecasts from salespeople can be very important in managing a company's inventory, manufacturing, capital investment, and other decisions.

Expense Budgets

Managers sometimes use expense budgets to control costs. An expense budget may be expressed in dollars (for example, the salesperson may be allowed to spend up to $500) or as a percentage of sales volume (such as expenses cannot exceed 10 percent of sales). A regional manager or salesperson may be awarded a bonus for spending less than the budget allocates. However, such a bonus may encourage the salesperson to underspend, which could hurt sales performance. For example, if a salesperson refuses to give out samples, customers may not be able to visualize how a product will work; thus, some may not buy. The salesperson has reduced expenses but hurt sales.

Although salespeople may have limited input into a budget, they do spend the money. Ultimately it is the salesperson's responsibility to manage the territorial budget. The salesperson not only has control over how much is spent and whether expenditures are over- or under budget but also, and more important, decides where to place resources. Recall from Chapter 15 that these resources, such as samples and trial units or trips to the customers' location, are investments in future sales. If they are used unwisely, the salesperson may still meet the expense budget but fail to meet his or her sales quota.

Control and Quota Setting

The sales executive faces the challenge of setting up a balanced control system that will encourage each sales manager and salesperson to maximize his or her individual results through effective self-control. As we have pointed out throughout this text, salespeople operate somewhat independently. However, the control system management can help salespeople manage themselves more effectively.

Quotas are a useful technique for controlling the sales force. A **quota** represents a quantitative minimum level of acceptable performance for a specific period. A **sales quota** is the minimum number of sales in units, and a **revenue quota** is the minimum sales revenue necessary for acceptable performance. Often sales quotas are simple breakdowns of the company's total sales forecast. Thus, the total of all sales quotas equals the sales forecast. Other types of quotas can also be used. Understanding quotas is important to the salesperson because performance relative to quota is evaluated by management.

Profit quotas or **gross margin quotas** are minimum levels of acceptable profit or gross margin performance. These quotas motivate the sales force to sell more profitable products or to sell to more profitable customers. Some companies assign points to each product based on the product's gross margin. More points are assigned to higher-margin products. The salesperson can then meet a point quota by selling either a lot of low-margin products or fewer high-margin products. For example, assume a company sells tools and test equipment. The profit margin (not including salesperson compensation) is 30 percent on tools but only 20 percent on test equipment. Tools may be worth three points each, whereas test equipment is worth two. If the salesperson's quota is 12 points, the quota can be reached by selling four tool orders, or six pieces of test equipment, or some combination of both.

One challenge sales managers face is recognizing that performance quotas can negatively influence a customer orientation as salespeople put the need to make quota ahead of their customers' needs.[14] One type of quota that can avoid this dilemma is an activity quota. **Activity quotas**, similar to the activity goals we discussed in the preceding chapter, are minimal expectations of activities for each salesperson. The company sets these quotas to control the activities of the sales force. This type of quota is important in situations where the sales cycle is long and sales are few because activities can be observed more frequently than sales. For example, for some medical equipment, the sales cycle is longer than one year, and a salesperson may sell only one or two units each quarter. Having a monthly sales target in this case would be inappropriate, but requiring a certain minimum number of calls to be made is reasonable. The assumption made by management is that if the salesperson is performing the proper activities, sales will follow with the customer's needs in mind. Activities for which quotas may be established include number of demonstrations, total customer calls, number of calls on prospects, or number of displays set up. Note that, in addition to a monthly activity target, there is also likely to be a quarterly or annual sales target.

Compensation and Evaluation

An important task of the sales executive is to establish the company's basic compensation and evaluation system. The compensation system must satisfy the needs of both the salespeople and the company. You, as a salesperson, need an equitable, stable, understandable system that motivates you to meet your objectives. The company needs a system that encourages you to sell products at a profitable price and in the right amounts.

Salespeople want a system that bases rewards on effort and results. Compensation must also be uniform within the company and in line with what competitors' salespeople receive. If competitors' salespeople earn more, you will want to leave and work for that competitor. But your company expects the compensation system to attract and keep good salespeople and to encourage you to do specific things. The system should reward outstanding performance while achieving the proper balance between sales results and costs.

Compensation often relates to quotas. As with quotas, salespeople who perceive the system as unfair may give up or leave the firm. A stable compensation system ensures that salespeople can reap the benefits of their efforts, whereas a constantly changing system may lead them to constantly change their activities but never make any money. A system that is not understandable will be ignored.

The sales executive decides how much income will be based on salary or incentive pay. The salesperson may receive a **salary**, which is a regular payment regardless of performance, or **incentive pay**, which is tied to some level of performance. There are two types of incentives: commission and bonus. A **commission** is incentive pay for an individual sale, whereas a **bonus** is incentive pay for overall performance in one or more areas. For example, a bonus may be paid for acquiring a certain number of new customers, reaching a specified level of total sales in units, or selling a certain amount of a new product.

Sales executives can choose to pay salespeople a straight salary, a straight commission, or some combination of salary, commission, and/or bonus. Most firms opt for some combination of salary and bonus or salary and commission. Fewer than 4 percent pay only commission, and slightly fewer than 5 percent pay only salary. Exhibit 16.2 illustrates how various types of compensation plans work.

Under the **straight salary** method, a salesperson receives a fixed amount of money for work during a specified time. The salesperson is assured of a steady income and can develop a sense of loyalty to customers. The company also has more control over the salesperson. Because income does not depend directly on results, the company can ask the salesperson to do things in the best interest of the company, even if those activities may not lead to immediate sales. Straight salary, however, provides little financial incentive for salespeople to sell more. For example, in Exhibit 16.2, the salesperson receives $3,500 per month no matter how much is sold.

Exhibit 16.2
How Different Types of Compensation Plans Pay

	Amount Paid to Salesperson				
Month	Sales Revenue	Straight Salary	Straight Commission*	Combination†	Point Plan‡
January	$50,000	$3,500	$5,000	$1,500 (salary)	$3,800
	6 tools			3,000 (commission)	
	10 testers			4,500 (total)	
February	$60,000	3,500	6,000	1,500 (salary)	4,800
	6 tools			3,600 (commission)	
	15 testers			5,100 (total)	
March	$20,000	3,500	2,000	1,500 (salary)	1,600
	2 tools			1,200 (commission)	
	5 testers			2,700 (total)	

*Commission plan pays 10 percent of sales revenue.

†Commission portion pays 6 percent of sales revenue.

‡Copiers are worth three points, faxes are worth two, and each point is worth $100 in commission.

Note: These commission rates are used only to illustrate how compensation schemes work. Point plans, for example, do not necessarily always yield the lowest compensation.

Many companies offer incentives, such as special awards, bonuses, and other rewards, for outstanding sales performance.

©Paul Bradbury/Caiaimage/Getty Images RF

Straight salary plans are used when sales require long periods of negotiation, when a team of salespeople is involved and individual results cannot be measured, or when other aspects of the marketing mix (such as advertising) are more important than the salesperson's efforts in generating sales (as in trade selling of consumer products). Most sales trainees also receive a straight salary.

A **straight commission** plan pays a certain amount per sale and includes a base and a rate but not a salary. The **commission base**, the item from which commission is determined, is often unit sales, dollar sales, or gross margin. The **commission rate**, which determines the amount paid, is expressed as a percentage of the base (such as 10 percent of sales or 8 percent of gross margin) or as a dollar amount (like $100 per sale). Exhibit 16.2 illustrates two straight commission plans: One pays 10 percent of sales revenue, and the other is a point plan that pays $100 per point (using the tools and testers example we discussed previously).

Commission plans often include a draw. A **draw** is money paid to the salesperson against future commissions–in essence a loan that guarantees a stable cash flow. For example, in Exhibit 16.3 the salesperson receives a draw of $3,000 per month. No commissions were earned during January, but the salesperson still received $3,000. In February the rep earned $5,000, but $2,000 went to pay back some of the draw from January, and the rep received only $3,000. In March the rep earned $4,500, of which $1,000 finished paying off the balance from January. Thus, the rep was given $1,500 in March.

Straight commission plans have the advantage of tying the salesperson's compensation directly to performance, thus providing more financial incentive for the salesperson to work hard. However, salespeople on straight commission have little company loyalty and certainly are less willing to perform activities, such as preparing reports, that do not directly lead to sales. Xerox experimented with such a plan but found that customer service suffered, as did company loyalty among salespeople.

Companies that do not emphasize service to customers or do not anticipate long-term customer relationships (like a company selling kitchen appliances directly to consumers) typically use commission plans. Such plans are also used when the sales force includes many part-timers because part-timers can earn more when their pay is tied to their performance. Also, part-timers may need the extra motivation straight commission can provide.

Under a bonus plan, salespeople receive a lump-sum payment for a certain level of performance over a specified time. Bonuses resemble commissions, but the amount paid depends on total performance, not on each individual sale. Bonuses, awarded monthly, quarterly, or annually, are always used with salary and/or commissions in **combination plans**. Combination plans, also called salary-plus-commission plans,

Exhibit 16.3
An Example of a Draw Compensation Plan

Month	Draw	Commission Earned	Payment to Salesperson	Balance Owed to Company
January	$3,000	$0	$3,000	$3,000
February	3,000	5,000	3,000	1,000
March	3,000	4,500	3,500	

provide salary and commission and offer the greatest flexibility for motivating and controlling the activities of salespeople. The plans can incorporate the advantages and avoid the disadvantages of using any of the basic plans alone.

The main disadvantage of combination plans lies in their complexity. Salespeople confused by this complexity could unknowingly perform the wrong activities, or sales managers could unintentionally design a program that rewards the wrong activities. Using the earlier office equipment example, if faxes and copiers were worth the same commission (for example, $100 per sale), the salesperson would sell whatever was easiest to sell. If faxes were easier to sell than copiers, the firm may make less money because salespeople would expend all of their effort selling a lower-profit product unless the volume sold made up for the lower margin. Even then, however, the firm may be stuck with a warehouse of unsold copiers.

thinking it through

As a buyer, under which plan would you prefer your salesperson to work? Which would you prefer if you were a salesperson? What conflicts might occur between buyer and seller because of the type of compensation plan?

FIELD SALES MANAGERS

Salespeople report directly not to a sales executive but to a **field sales manager**. Field sales managers hire salespeople, evaluate their performance, train them, and perform other important tasks. Salespeople find it useful to partner with their managers because the managers often represent the salespeople to other parts of the organization. Also, the salesperson often has to sell the manager first on any new idea before the idea can be pitched to others in management. Building a partnering relationship with managers can go a long way toward getting ideas accepted.[15]

Evaluating Performance

Field sales managers are responsible for evaluating the performance of their salespeople. The easiest method of evaluating performance is to simply add up the amount of sales that the salesperson makes. But sales managers must also rate their salespeople's customer service level, product knowledge, and other, less tangible qualities. Some companies, such as Federal Express, use customer satisfaction surveys to evaluate salespeople. In other companies, the manager rates each salesperson, using evaluation forms that list the desired aspects. (An example of an evaluation form appears in Exhibit 16.4.) Such evaluations help managers determine training needs, promotions, and pay raises.

The data salespeople input into the CRM system also play an important role in communicating their activities to the sales manager. The manager creates or pulls reports from the system to evaluate performance in a manner similar to the way the salesperson would. But these reports are not enough; sales managers should also make calls with salespeople to directly observe their performance. These observations can be the basis for recommendations for improving individual performance or for commending outstanding performance. Other information, such as customer response to a new strategy, can be gained by making calls. This information should be shared with upper management to improve strategies.

Training

The sales manager trains new hires and provides refresher training for experienced salespeople. To determine what refresher training they need, managers often use

Exhibit 16.4
Behavioral Observation Scale (BOS)

	Almost Never						Almost Always
1. Checks deliveries to see whether they have arrived on time.	1	2	3	4	5	6	7
2. Inputs data into CRM system on time.	1	2	3	4	5	6	7
3. Uses promotional brochures and correspondence with potential accounts.	1	2	3	4	5	6	7
4. Monitors competitors' activities.	1	2	3	4	5	6	7
5. Brushes up on selling techniques.	1	2	3	4	5	6	7
6. Reads marketing research reports.	1	2	3	4	5	6	7
7. Prospects for new accounts.	1	2	3	4	5	6	7
8. Makes service calls.	1	2	3	4	5	6	7
9. Rapidly answers customer inquiries.	1	2	3	4	5	6	7

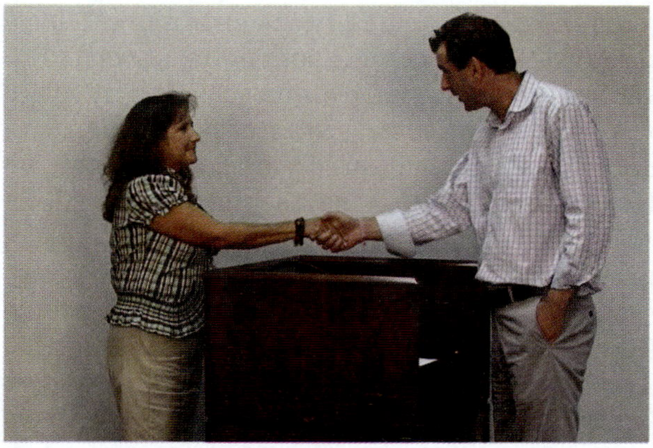

Professional salespeople constantly need to upgrade their skills; here, a salesperson for Frosty Acres Brands is practicing how to open a sales call when she calls on a restaurant.

Courtesy of John Tanner

information gathered while observing salespeople making sales calls. Content of training for new salespeople may be determined by a sales executive, but the field sales manager is often responsible for carrying out the training.

Most experienced salespeople welcome training when they perceive that it will improve their sales. Three out of four high-growth companies offer basic sales training, according to one recent study, while half also provide mentoring.[16] You should continue to welcome training, no matter how successful you are. It always offers the opportunity to improve your performance, or at least achieve the same level with less effort. Also, as you will see in Chapter 17, continuing to learn is important to the salesperson who is part of a learning organization.

MANAGING ETHICS IN SALES

Salespeople, particularly those within certain industries, have earned a reputation that is unfavorable. Most salespeople, though, want to act ethically. Because we have emphasized throughout this book methods of selling that help people solve problems and satisfy needs, we believe it is important to understand what companies do to encourage ethical behavior and how salespeople should work with their sales management partners to choose ethical options. First we discuss the sales executive's role in making ethics policy. Then we cover the roles of the field sales manager and the salesperson in implementing that policy.

ETHICS AND THE SALES EXECUTIVE

ethics

As mentioned earlier, sales executives should strive to create an ethical culture. While part of a sales executive's job is to determine corporate policy concerning what is considered ethical and what is not and how unethical behavior will be investigated and punished, it is also important that the sales executive support positive behaviors.[17] In addition, the sales executive must ensure that other policies, such as the performance measurement and compensation policies, support the ethics of the organization. Performance measurement and compensation policies that reward only outcomes may inadvertently encourage salespeople to act unethically because of pressure to achieve and a culture supporting the credo "the end justifies the means." But when behavioral performance measurement systems are in place, the compensation system can reward those who do things the right way. In addition, research shows that closer relationships with ethical managers support ethical behavior.[18] Although unethical behaviors may result in short-term gain (and therefore may accidentally be rewarded in an outcome-only compensation scheme), they can have serious long-term effects, such as loss of customers, unhappy salespeople who quit, and other negative outcomes.[19]

Sales executives must therefore develop a culture that creates behavioral norms regarding how things should be done and what behaviors will not be tolerated. Such a culture can be enhanced through the development of formal policy, training courses in ethics, ethics review boards, and an open-door policy. **Open-door policies** are general management techniques that allow subordinates to bypass immediate managers and take concerns straight to upper management when the subordinates perceive a lack of support from the immediate manager. Open-door policies enhance an ethical culture because salespeople can feel free to discuss troublesome issues that involve their managers with someone in a position to respond. Two versions are **ethics review boards** and ethics officers, both providing expert advice to salespeople who are unsure of the ethical consequences of an action. Ethics review boards may consist of experts inside and outside the company who are responsible for reviewing ethics policies, investigating allegations of unethical behavior, and acting as a sounding board for employees.

Salespeople also have the right to expect ethical treatment from their company. Fair treatment concerning compensation, promotion policies, territory allocation, and other actions should be delivered. Compensation is probably the area with the most common concerns, although problems can arise in all areas. Compensation problems can include slow payment, hidden caps, or compensation plan changes after the sale.

For example, IBM published a brochure for its salespeople that said that there was no **cap**, or limit, on earnings. Yet the brochure also had, in bold letters, the statement that IBM had the right to modify the program–even after the sale–until the commission was paid. When a salesperson sold one major account $24 million worth of software, the company changed his commission plan so he received less than $500,000 instead of the $2.6 million he expected. The salesperson filed suit, but IBM won in part because of the modification statement in the letter.[20] IBM had every legal right to take the action it did, and caps are not unethical; what was questionable was that the salesperson was not made aware of the cap prior to making the sale.

thinking it through

Should schools have ethics review boards? What advantages would such boards have for the student? For the teacher? Would salespeople reap the same types of benefits if their companies had ethics review boards?

Exhibit 16.5

Strategies for Handling Unethical Requests from a Manager

- Leave the organization or ask for a transfer.
- Negotiate an alternative course of action.
- Blow the whistle, internally or externally.
- Threaten to blow the whistle.
- Appeal to a higher authority, such as an ethics officer or ethics review board or a senior executive if ethics offices do not exist.
- Agree to the demand but fail to carry it out.
- Refuse to comply with the request.
- Ignore the request.

ETHICS AND THE FIELD SALES MANAGER

Salespeople often ask managers for direction on how to handle ethical problems, and the sales manager is usually the first person to investigate complaints of unethical behavior. Field sales managers can provide a role model for salespeople by demonstrating ethical behavior in role plays during training or when conducting sales calls in the field. Sales managers should also avoid teaching high-pressure techniques and manipulative methods of selling.

RESPONDING TO UNETHICAL REQUESTS

Salespeople may find themselves facing a sales manager who encourages them to engage in unethical behavior. When that situation occurs, a salesperson has several ways to avoid engaging in such behavior. Perhaps the most obvious option is to find another job, but that is not always the best solution. If the organizational culture supports the unethical request, however, finding another job may be the only choice. Exhibit 16.5 lists choices available to the salesperson.

Another way to handle unethical requests is to blow the whistle, or report the behavior, if the salesperson has adequate evidence (if adequate evidence is not available, sometimes simply threatening to blow the whistle may work). If this course of action is followed, the salesperson must be ready to accept a perception of disloyalty, retaliation by the manager, or other consequences. However, if senior management is sincere in efforts to promote ethical behavior, steps should be taken to minimize those negative outcomes. If an open-door policy or an ethics review board exists, the salesperson can take the concern to higher levels for review. For example, the salesperson could say, "I'm not sure that is appropriate. I'd like to get the opinion of the ethics review board." If the action is unethical, the sales manager may back down at that point. It is also possible that the manager will try to coerce the salesperson into not applying to the ethics review board; if that is the case, another course of action may prove to be a better choice.

Another strategy is to negotiate an alternative. This response requires the salesperson to identify an alternative course of action with a high probability of success. For example, if a sales manager tells the salesperson to offer a prospect a bribe, the salesperson should be prepared to prove that a price reduction would be just as effective. A similar tactic is simply to ignore the request. The salesperson may say to the manager that the request was carried out, when in fact it was not; the potential problem with this approach is that the salesperson has admitted to carrying out an unethical act (even though she or he did not), which can lead to future problems. Finally, the salesperson can simply deny the request. Denial can be a dangerous action in that it opens the salesperson to possible retaliation, particularly retaliation that is not obviously linked to the denial, such as denying access to training or reducing the size of the salesperson's territory.

thinking it through

Is it ethical to lie to your manager and say that you will engage in the unethical behavior that your manager demanded when you know you won't? Is all fair when you are combating a request to engage in unethical behavior?

The salesperson's choice of action will depend on how much proof is available, what alternative actions to the unethical action exist, and the type of relationship with the manager. Other factors to consider include the ethical climate of the organization and whether an open-door policy exists. The salesperson is always in control of his or her behavior and should never rationalize a behavior by placing responsibility on the sales manager.

SALESPEOPLE AS PARTNERS

Many types of salespeople exist, including telemarketing representatives, field salespeople, product specialists, and account specialists. Often there is some overlap in responsibilities; when overlap occurs, companies should have policies that facilitate serving the customer.

GEOGRAPHIC SALESPEOPLE

Most sales departments are organized geographically. A **geographic salesperson** is assigned a specific geographic territory in which to sell the company's products and services. Companies often combine geographic territories into larger branches, zones, or regions. For example, Eli Lilly has geographic regions that include 50 or more salespeople. Each Lilly salesperson has responsibility for a specific geographic area. For example, one rep may call on physicians in a portion of Dallas, using zip code boundaries to determine the territory; that rep may have all physicians in zip codes 75212, 75213, 75218, 75239, 75240, and 75252. Geographic salespeople may also work with account managers, product specialists, inside salespeople, and other members of the company's sales team.

ACCOUNT SALESPEOPLE

Companies may organize salespeople by account in several ways. The most extreme example is to give a salesperson the responsibility to sell to only one company but at every location of that company in the country or the world. In another common form of specialization, some salespeople develop new accounts while others maintain existing accounts. Developing new accounts requires skills different from maintaining an already sold account.

Similar customers often have similar needs, whereas different types of customers may have very different needs for the same product. In such cases salespeople may specialize in calling on only one or a few customer types, although they sell the same products. NCR has different sales forces for calling on manufacturing companies, retailers, and financial companies. Andritz, an international heavy machinery company, has salespeople who sell only to paper producers and other salespeople who sell only to wastewater treatment plants, even though the same product is being sold. Some Procter & Gamble salespeople call on central buying offices for grocery store chains; others call on food wholesalers.

Companies also divide their customers on the basis of size. Large customers, sometimes called **key accounts**, may have a salesperson assigned only to that account; in some cases a small sales force is assigned to one large account. In some firms one company executive coordinates all the salespeople who call on an account throughout the nation or the world. These executives are called **national account managers (NAMs)** or **strategic account managers (SAMs)**. These account managers are more than salespeople; they are business executives. Recent research questions the return on such account structures and notes that key accounts are often also less satisfied; according to another study, the reason may be that managing account

Exhibit 16.6
SAMs in the Sales Force

Although SAMs and geographic salespeople have different immediate managers, they still work together. SAMs coordinate the efforts of geographic reps within local buying offices of global accounts.

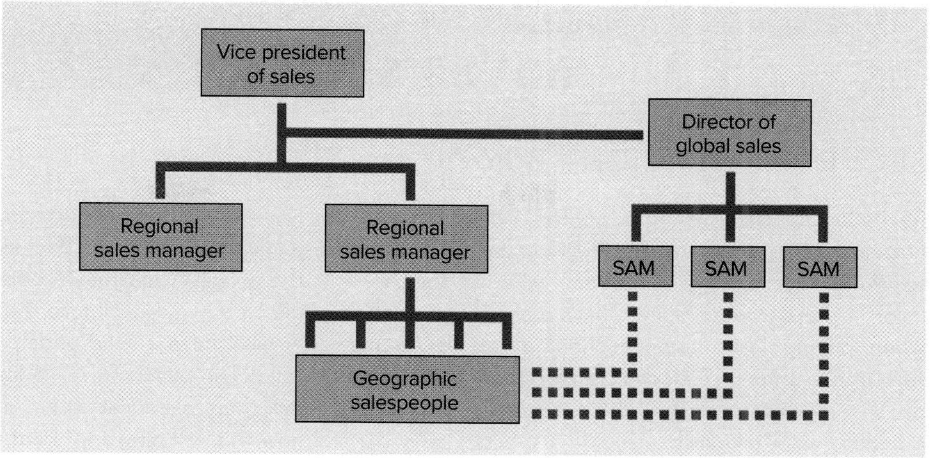

expectations is difficult, especially when the account knows it wields a lot of power.[21] However, some companies, such as PG&E, seem to get it right. This company's key accounts sales team won an industry award voted on by customers.[22]

Strategic account managers sometimes manage large teams of salespeople. Account strategy for a global account may be determined by this strategic account manager, who has to rely on local salespeople to implement the strategy at the local level. For example, Hershey's has a strategic account rep that calls on Walmart in Bentonville, Arkansas, but local salespeople work with individual stores and store managers. The local geographic rep's responsibility may involve coordinating with the local customer. This coordination may require customer training on the product (if the product is a machine or some other system) or working with a local store manager to set up displays, plan inventories, and so on. Local reps should also look for sales opportunities in the customer's location and provide this information to the SAM. They often become the eyes and ears of the SAM and provide early notice of opportunities or threats in the account, just as a service rep does for the geographic rep. SAMs often report directly to the vice president of sales or to a director of global sales, as illustrated in Exhibit 16.6, but work with geographic reps.

As described in Chapter 6, a **house account** is handled by a sales or marketing executive in addition to that executive's regular duties, and no commission is paid on any sales from that account. House accounts are often key accounts, but not all key accounts are house accounts. The main difference is that house accounts have no "true" salesperson. Walmart has negotiated to be a house account with some suppliers with the expectation that those suppliers will pass on to Walmart what they do not have to pay in commission or salary. General Dynamics attempted the same strategy when buying, but abandoned the plan upon realizing that lower costs also meant reduced service.

Somewhat different is the mega-account strategy used at Motorola. The top 20 international accounts are actually managed by Motorola's CEO, who works directly with the CEO in each account. These accounts are a form of house account, but the CEO has sales responsibility and sales goals to achieve.

PRODUCT SPECIALISTS

When companies have diverse products, their salespeople often specialize by types of products. Johnson & Johnson, which sells baby products, has two specialized sales forces: the disposable products sales force and the toiletries sales force. Cardinal Health has seven sales forces spread across three divisions: Medical

From the BUYER'S SEAT 16.1

SECURING THE RIGHT BUY-IN

Michelle Stewart, manager of HR Systems for the nuclear energy company Bruce Power, says, "You need to take time to engage your users," whether they are in IT or in the executive suite. That's a challenge, though, when buying information technology to run human resource systems. IT doesn't understand HR and HR doesn't understand IT. But both are needed to make the purchase work properly.

While working as a marketing manager for United Airlines, Ben Becker (now a consultant to several airlines) was tasked with selecting software to capture Web browsing data of customers when on the company's Web site. "This investment was well over a million dollars, not just for the software but also for the training and switch-over costs," notes Becker. For that reason, Becker adopted the "fail fast, fail cheap" approach. "I believe in pilots," says Becker, "not the pilots of our planes, although I believe in them too. No, I mean pilot tests." Among some of the leadership, the belief was that marketing doesn't influence demand—that if people want to fly, they will purchase it whether United markets to them or not. Says Becker, "If I sell my new tools on the premise that these tools will help us convince people to buy more, I'll lose the sale based on my premise. While I have a solid understanding of how these tools will help, not all of the leadership team does. Part of my job, then, is educating within the people I report to on how this will all work." Pilot tests do just that.

Joe Beery, SVP of Thermo Fischer Scientific, reminds us that "In IT, there is an infinite demand to what you bring to the table but a finite supply. We have to prioritize and recognize that not everybody is going to get what they want. Our mantra is . . . 'What can I do to help?' It's that perspective—that we're here to help—that drives positive conversations and eliminates friction. When you have a servant's heart, everyone gets a little more cooperative."

Sources: Aliah Wright, "HR and IT Must Work Together When Buying HR Technology," *HR News*, March 29, 2017; Anonymous, "Joseph P. (Joe) Beery," *Boardroom Insiders Profile*, September 14, 2015.

Equipment, Pharmaceuticals, and Services. Each sales force has its own regional, district, and area sales managers. Insuror's of Texas has salespeople who specialize in auto insurance, others who specialize in homeowner's insurance, and still others who specialize in medical and disability insurance. However, all of Insuror's salespeople operate under the same sales management structure. Regardless of the management structure, sometimes the technical knowledge requirements are so great that organizing territories by product makes sense.

In addition to having management responsibilities similar to those for geographic reps, product salespeople must coordinate their activities with those of salespeople from other divisions. Success can be greater for all involved when leads and customer information are shared. For example, a Cardinal Health equipment salesperson may have a customer who is also a prospect for services. Sharing that information with the services rep can help build a relationship that can pay off with leads for test instruments.

Sometimes the buying center doesn't naturally overlap from one decision to the next, even thought maybe it should. In From the Buyer's Seat 16.1, several decision makers describe how they worked to move decisions across divisions in their own company.

INSIDE VERSUS OUTSIDE

Our discussion to this point has focused on outside salespeople, called **field salespeople**—that is, salespeople who sell at the customer's location. **Inside salespeople** (first identified in Chapter 1) sell at their own company's location. Inside salespeople may handle walk-in customers or work entirely over the telephone and Internet, or they may handle both duties. For example, a plumbing supply distributor may sell entirely to plumbers and employ inside salespeople who sell to those plumbers who come into the distributorship to buy products. Ferguson, headquartered in Newport News, Virginia, manufactures plumbing products and has field salespeople, but it also has a contact center that includes inside salespeople.

As we discussed in Chapter 6, the job of some inside salespeople is to provide leads for field salespeople. Other types of inside salespeople include account managers, field support reps, and customer service reps. An inside salesperson who is an account manager has the same responsibilities and duties as a field salesperson except that all business is conducted over the phone. Ferguson, mentioned earlier, starts many of its new salespeople in inside sales, moving them into the field after a period of successful performance.

A **field support rep** works in a contact center in support of field salespeople and does more than prospect for leads. For example, field support reps at e-Rewards write proposals and price jobs, work directly with vendors to ensure satisfactory project completion, and interact with clients when needed. We discuss these representatives further when we address team selling strategies shortly.

Customer service reps (CSRs) are inbound salespeople who handle customer concerns. **Inbound** means they respond to telephone calls placed by customers, rather than **outbound**, which means the inside salesperson makes the phone call (prospectors, account managers, and field support representatives are outbound reps). For example, if you call the 800 telephone number on the back of a tube of Crest toothpaste, you will speak with an inbound customer service rep. Many companies are now using customer service reps to identify cross-selling and upselling opportunities, either by sending leads to field salespeople or closing the sales themselves. Suddenlink Communications, for example, has implemented a predictive model system that uses data from the CRM system to identify potential offers for customers who call about service. The customer service reps then make the sales pitch. Because the offers are more likely to be relevant to the buyer than a generic offer, customers don't seem to mind. In fact, they seem to like the approach—sales have increased over 20 percent since the launch of this system.[23]

Many companies use teams to work with large accounts. There may be members representing different functional areas of the company or, as in the case here, members of a global sales team meeting virtually.

SALES TEAMS

A growing number of companies are adopting a team approach to sales.[24] This concept is being used by companies that recognize they can best build partnerships by empowering one person, the account manager, to represent the organization. In **team selling** a group of salespeople support a single account. Each person on the team brings a different area of expertise or handles different responsibilities. As you see in Exhibit 16.7, each specialist can be called on to team up with the account managers.

Before adopting team selling, companies may have had one salesperson for each product line. Xerox, for example, once had separate copier, supplies, fax machine, printer, computer workstation,

Exhibit 16.7
Team Selling Organization

In team selling, product specialists work with account managers, who have total account responsibility. Product specialists are responsible for sales and service of only a limited portion of the product line and may work with several account managers.

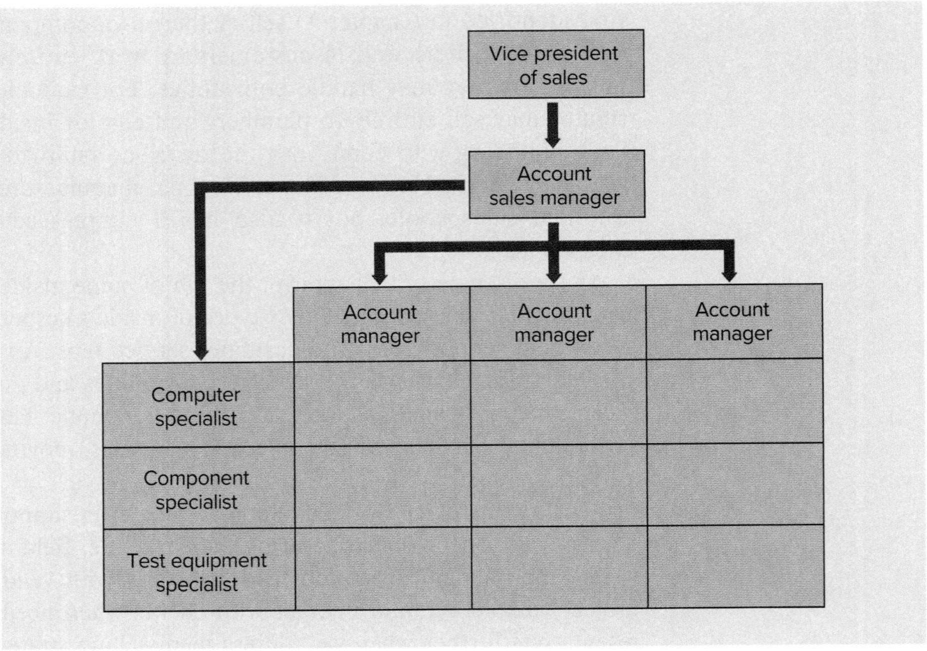

and communication network salespeople all calling on the same buyer. These reps would pass in customers' lobbies without recognizing one another. Customers grew tired of seeing as many as six salespeople from Xerox. Now one account manager calls on the buyer and brings in product specialists as needed.

Xerox uses permanent teams, whereas Teradata forms teams as needed. The data warehousing company will create a team that might include an expert in the vertical market in which the customer operates, a group of finance experts who can help develop the right financial measures for the decision, software engineers who make sure the Teradata product will work with the systems the customer already has in place, and the account manager.

In an extension of team selling, **multilevel selling**, members at various levels of the sales organization call on their counterparts in the buying organization. (As charted in Exhibit 16.8, for example, the vice president of sales calls on the vice president of purchasing.) Multilevel selling can take place without a formal multilevel sales team if the account representative requests upper-level management's involvement in the sale. For example, you may ask your company's vice president of sales to call on the vice president of operations at a prospect's company to secure top-level support for your proposal.

Another type of sales team is made up of the field rep and the field support rep (see Exhibit 16.9). Some companies use one field support rep (FSR) for each field salesperson, but most companies have several salespeople working with each FSR. The FSR performs as many selling tasks as possible over the telephone. But when a sales call is needed at the customer's location, the field support rep makes the appointment for the field rep. Such is the case with IBM.com, a division of IBM that provides software and technology consulting. Good communication and joint planning are necessary to avoid overbooking the field rep, as well as to prevent duplication of effort.

Technology has played a key role in promoting good communication and joint planning. Companies can use CRM systems, for example, to give every member

Exhibit 16.8
Forming Sales Teams for Multilevel Selling

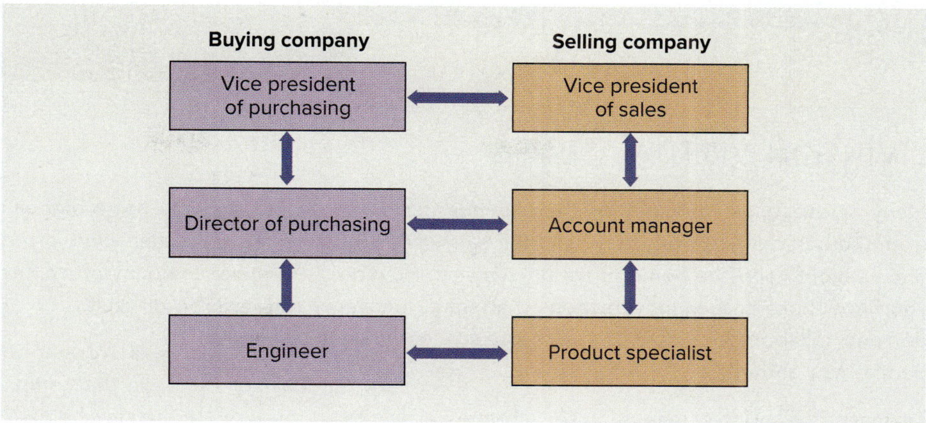

Exhibit 16.9
Inside–Outside Sales Team

Sometimes an inside rep or a field support rep works with accounts over the phone, and his or her partner, the field rep, makes calls at the customer's location.

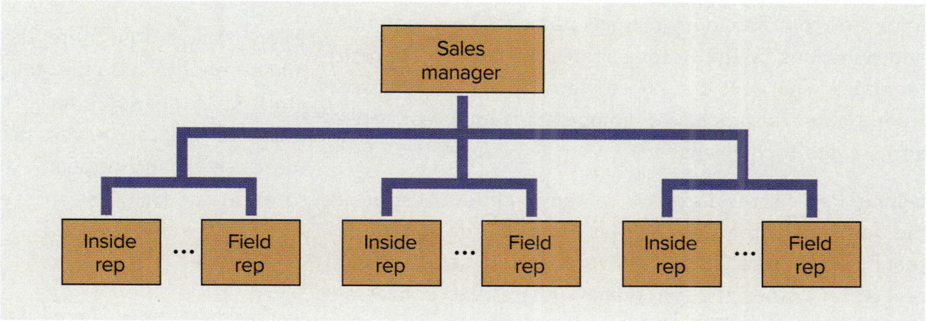

of the sales team access to all of the same customer records. This access means everyone knows what sales calls are planned and what happens as a function of the call. Another form of technology, represented by services like WebEx, enables someone to deliver a PowerPoint presentation to people scattered all over the world. Using WebEx, an account manager could present the account strategy, for example, to the sales team no matter where the members are located or present a proposal to a customer on another continent. See Sales Technology 16.1 for additional insight into the use of technology to promote good communication and joint planning.

SELLING YOURSELF

Many times students have to engage in team projects, sometimes without much instruction in what makes an effective team. Yet the quality of the team is much more than just the sum of the individuals who are team members. Just as in team selling, each member of the team has to understand what the overall objective is, what each individual's role is, and what activities have to be undertaken when. But simply understanding what to do is a small part of making the team successful. More importantly, each individual has to perform and complete each task on time.

In addition, each class has a compensation plan—how grades are distributed. Sometimes the grades are team-based, just as in sales. Sometimes grades are entirely individual, and sometimes the overall grade is a function of both team and individual evaluations. But other motivations can entice students to learn. Recognition, the opportunity to work on real business problems, recognition of the relevance of the material being covered, and even monetary awards in competitions

SALES Technology 16.1

LIVING IN VIRTUAL SPACE

Many salespeople work out of their homes, far away from the home office. They may see their sales manager once a month and the home office once a year. How do you have those casual conversations that spark innovation and collaboration? How do you create spaces where people can gather?

Lexmark, the printer manufacturer, created a "digital water cooler," or a place in the company's internal Web space that encouraged interaction. The project leader for a new product design team posted some sketches and questions by the water cooler in order to get some feedback. The next day, there were over 40 responses from 4 countries, including comments from salespeople and service technicians.

Dennis Pearce, the Lexmark system architect responsible for the water cooler, says that the design team reached people it wouldn't have ordinarily spoken to. A real water cooler, though, doesn't just create conversation about work. "The way you get them there is by having this ongoing water cooler where anything goes. That keeps a constant audience there for when you really need them for business purposes," he says.

Sales, though, has a bigger challenge—that of isolation. Working on their own, oftentimes in locations far away from any company office, feeling like a part of the company can be difficult.

Miriam Carey, a work-at-home business woman, says having friends in the company that you can text or IM throughout the day helps. "You don't have the built-in energy and dynamics of an office, so you need a system to help you feel connected."

Ellen Malloy does note that working from home has some benefits. "I do find that if it is a gorgeous morning, starting to answer emails from my front porch with a cup of coffee can be very productive and keeps me feeling positive and upbeat," she says. "So changing your location can be great and very helpful, but you have to find what works for you."

Sources: David Raths, "Knowledge Management: Persistence Pays Off in the Manufacturing Sector," *KM World* 26, no. 5 (May 2017), pp. 16–17, 32; Lynette Gil, "Best Practices for Salespeople Who Work at Home," *LifeHealthPro*, Part 1, May 13, 2016, and Part 2, May 20, 2016.

such as the National Collegiate Sales Competition can motivate different students to different levels of effort.

As you think about the courses you are taking, consider how you are compensated. Does the official compensation plan (grades, recognition, or the like) meet your motivational needs? In a group project, are your group members' needs being met? And are they living up to their responsibilities? These are real questions that plague professionals, whether they be salespeople or sales managers. Understanding how these questions apply to you now will help you select the right job later, as well as help you perform to your goals now.

SUMMARY

Successful salespeople manage resources and build internal partnerships with people in order entry, credit, billing, and shipping, as well as sales and marketing. These partnerships allow salespeople to keep the promises they make to customers when someone else must carry out those promises.

Salespeople in learning organizations also have a responsibility to carry the voice of the customer to other areas of the organization. Successful learning organizations are more adept at adapting to changing customer needs and developing successful products when salespeople fulfill their role of speaking for the customer.

In the sales organization salespeople work with and for a sales executive and a field sales manager. The sales executive determines policy and maintains financial control over the sales organization. Salespeople participate in the development of forecasts that the sales executive uses in the planning process.

Another policy decision involves the method of compensation for the sales force. The four basic methods are straight salary, straight commission, bonus, and a combination plan. Straight commission plans provide strong financial incentives for salespeople but give the company little control over their activities. Salary plans give greater control to the company but offer less incentive for salespeople to work hard.

Sales executives are also responsible for creating a culture that supports ethical activities. Policies (such as open-door policies) can encourage salespeople to act ethically. Ethical review boards are also useful in reviewing ethics policies, investigating potential ethics violations, and counseling salespeople who have concerns about the ethics of possible actions. Sometimes, however, salespeople face unethical requests from their managers. If that occurs, salespeople can choose from several courses of actions, such as blowing the whistle or appealing to an ethics review board.

Partnerships must be built within the sales force too. Some examples include team selling with product specialists, inside and outside teams, and multilevel selling.

KEY TERMS

activity quota 443
bonus 444
bottom-up forecasting 441
cap 448
combination plan 445
commission 444
commission base 445
commission rate 445
customer service rep (CSR) 453
draw 445
ethics review board 448
field sales manager 446
field salespeople 452
field support rep 453
geographic salesperson 450
gross margin quota 443
house accounts 451
inbound 453
incentive pay 444
inside salespeople 452
internal partnerships 434
key accounts 450
multilevel selling 454
national account manager (NAM) 450
open-door policy 448
outbound 453
profit quota 443
quota 443
revenue quota 443
salary 444
sales quota 443
straight commission 445
straight salary 444
strategic account manager (SAM) 450
team selling 453

ETHICS PROBLEMS

1. It took you four months to find a job, and you were almost out of money, when you finally landed your position. Today your boss asked you to do something you think is unethical, but she assures you that it is normal for this industry. You aren't sure what the corporate culture is yet because you are new at the company. You also aren't sure if she's telling you the truth or not. How do you respond?

2. Your company pays straight commission based on gross margin, and you have some ability to determine the price, thereby influencing gross margin. The product is standard, and changes are not made to it when it is sold. What should determine how much you charge someone?

QUESTIONS AND PROBLEMS

1. The director of sales took a call during a leadership meeting. He interrupted the meeting to say to the CFO that a client in Mobile, Alabama, wanted a rush order but that the credit department wouldn't allow it. The customer had a history for late payment and its last invoice would be late tomorrow. If this was your account, what would you do? Would it matter if the rush order was small or large?
2. Reread From the Buyer's Seat 16.1. How can you help your buyer get the right buy-in from executives above that person and users across the organization? The situations discussed there are primarily IT purchases. Why do those seem to require buy-in?
3. A company that rents office equipment to businesses pays its salespeople a commission equal to the first month's rent. However, if the customer cancels or fails to pay its bills, all of the commission is taken back, even if the customer cancels 10 months later. Is this policy fair? Why or why not? Why would the company have this plan?
4. Reread the chapter opening profile of Sean Fulton. Are you a lone wolf or a team player? Based on what you have seen in examples and profiles in the book, can you identify sales positions where a lone wolf approach would work and where it wouldn't? What is the difference?
5. What is the role of the geographic salesperson in a national or strategic account? Assume that you are a NAM. What would you do to ensure the support of geographic reps? How would that support differ if you were a product specialist and worked in a team situation, with different NAMs on different accounts? As a product specialist, how would you get the support of the account manager?
6. Consider your own experience in group work at school. What makes groups effective? How can you translate what you have learned about group work into working as part of a sales team?
7. Reread Sales Technology 16.1. Do you think new college graduates are better prepared for working in sales from their homes than were previous generations? Why or why not? How can you feel like your part of a company if you rarely see anyone else from that company?
8. A sales manager gets one too many complaints about pushy salespeople, poor follow-up after the sale, and a lack of customer care and wonders if the compensation plan is to blame. What can a manager do with compensation to promote greater customer service? What are other ways to motivate good customer service?
9. Many wise people say to worry about the things you can control and not to worry about the things you can't control. What does that mean for a salesperson, when so many promises a salesperson makes are actually fulfilled by someone else?
10. A sales exec recently shared that he was considering a pooled bonus for all field support reps. He felt that because someone could be dropped into a hot territory, sales and commissions could be very high; conversely, someone dropped into supporting a poor territory could work hard and not get a bonus. A pool bonus where everyone shares equally would protect that salesperson. Then an experienced FSR pushed back: "I don't like subsidizing poor performers. If you paid us straight commission, we'd know who could make it and who couldn't. Sure, it may take awhile to get rid of the deadwood, but after that, sales would skyrocket!" Explain why you agree or disagree with this statement. Would it matter if instead of a support rep (who don't actually close sales), the question focused on account execs (who do make sales)?
11. Salespeople are paid more than just about everyone in the company. This compensation difference can create jealousy, particularly among those who don't trust salespeople anyway and think salespeople just play golf and entertain their way to the big bucks. How can you combat these misperceptions? Does it really matter what others think about sales, or will the imperative to serve customers and thereby serve the company be enough?

CASE PROBLEMS

case **16.1**

Castleberry Controls

Castleberry Controls, a manufacturer of control systems for hydraulic systems, has the following compensation program. Reps are paid a $4,000 draw per month, with straight commission paid on a point system and a bonus based on quota performance. The FloMaster, Castleberry's newest product, does much the same thing as the older FlexFlow but 30 percent faster and with greater accuracy. The point system is shown in Table 1.

Table 1

Product	Points/Sale	Quota (units per month)
FloMaster	50	4
FlexFlow	40	5
MeterMax	35	6
Duplo	25	8
Aperio	5	45

Reps are paid $5 per point, or $5,165 plus a bonus of $500, if they sell quota for each product, for a total of $6,675. The total number of points to reach each month is 1,035, but reps have to reach quota for each product to get the bonus. Tables 2 through 4 show the performance of the district.

Table 2

Product	Quota	Number Sold
FloMaster	40	22
FlexFlow	50	78
MeterMax	60	63
Duplo	80	82
Aperio	450	479

Table 3

Name	FloMaster	FlexFlow	MeterMax	Duplo	Aperio	Total Points
Smith	3	11	7	9	52	1,320
Nguyen	5	6	7	9	53	1,255
Mills	2	9	7	11	46	1,210
Franklin	4	8	6	8	48	1,160
Ramamurthy	3	8	7	6	48	1,105
Gross	2	8	6	7	48	1,045
McDonough	1	8	6	8	48	1,020
Jackson	1	7	7	8	47	1,010
Tonga	1	7	5	8	45	930
Nair	0	6	5	8	44	835
Total	22	78	63	82	479	

Table 4
Total Sales Calls

Sales Call	FloMaster	FlexFlow	MeterMax	Duplo	Aperio	Total Calls
Quota	20	20	10	10	10	70
Mills	28	16	11	9	10	75
Gross	24	24	8	8	7	71
District average	27.2	18.6	9.5	10.4	9.7	75.4

Questions

1. Evaluate the district's sales performance. Draw conclusions ("Just where are we doing well? Doing poorly?") but don't fix anything yet. Justify your conclusions.
2. Compare the performance of Mills and Gross. What are some possible explanations for the poor FloMaster sales?
3. The VP of sales says the problem is a compensation plan problem. How would you fix it?
4. The company is planning to create a new position called product specialist. This salesperson will work with territory salespeople and will have a sales quota for FloMaster only. The product specialist salesperson will work with one sales team (8 to 12 salespeople), and once a territory rep has identified a FloMaster prospect, the rep will bring in the product specialist. How should the compensation plan be adjusted? Why?
5. The VP of sales managed to get the product specialist idea approved by the CEO, even though the CEO argued that the salespeople were just too lazy to make the effort to sell the FloMaster. "Lower the compensation on it to the territory reps, and everyone will sell the FlexFlow at its lower price," the CEO says. "The best way to get more FloMaster sales is to cut compensation on the FlexFlow to 20 points." What do you think should be done? Why?

case 16.2

TechArt

Jackson Carter, a salesperson at TechArt, looked up, surprised to see his manager standing next to him. He had just hung up the phone after talking with Tasha in the credit department. "Um, did I get a little too loud, Sara?" he asked his manager.

"Why don't you come in my office and let's talk over what just happened," she replied, grimly.

"Great," he thought to himself. "First, the Wisconsin Resources order gets delayed to the point where it wants to cancel it, then credit wants me to get another form filled out, and now, the boss wants to talk over what just happened. Well, what just happened was I lost my temper, but Tasha deserved it!" He sat down across the desk from Sara in her office, as she looked at him expectantly.

"I got a call this morning from Wisconsin Resources; you know, that's the 10-machine order I took two weeks ago." Sara nodded, so Jackson continued. "They were upset because nothing has been delivered yet, but I had told them lead times were only a week. Which is what I was told."

"Yes, they are a week. Why hasn't this shipped?" she asked.

"That's what I wanted to know. So I called Lou and asked him." Lou Wong is head of the warehouse in Milwaukee that serves all of Wisconsin, the Upper Peninsula of Michigan, and a few other areas. "Lou said the order was a credit hold. What you heard was my conversation with Tasha in credit. She tells me that it's on hold because a signature is missing on one of the forms. What gets me is no one called or e-mailed me about it. The credit department let it sit, and I had to call and ask about it. Sara, I'm tired of our credit department being a sales prevention department. It's as if the staff does everything they can to screw us up. Now Wisconsin Resources is threatening to cancel the order if I can't get a machine to the company by Friday, but I've got to call and say we missed a signature line and it will be a week after that before I can ship the first machine! Does TechArt want the business or what?"

Sara sat silently for a moment, then began to speak in a soft voice, trying to lower the tension in the room. But she knew Jackson wouldn't like what she had to say. "Sounds like you have a problem to me."

Jackson protested, "*I* have a problem? No, TechArt has a problem. It's just like trying to get paid. I can't get the company to pay the right commission. And service. Don't get me started on our so-called service department! The service staff never seem to want to fix my customers' machines!"

Sara said quietly, "Listen, we have 12 reps here in this office. Of the 12, I have only 1 that keeps having problems with people in corporate or at the distribution center or with the service department. So I've got two questions for you: How are you going to handle Wisconsin Resources? And how are you going to fix your problems with everyone else?"

Questions

1. Answer Sara's questions as if you were Jackson. To help you with your answer, consider that he and the service reps are in Milwaukee, distribution is in Chicago, and the corporate office (where credit, payroll, and other such functions are located) is in San Francisco.
2. Regarding Wisconsin Resources, would it matter to your answer if this were a new customer versus a long-time customer? Why or why not, and if so, how?
3. What should or could Sara do to help Jackson? Assume his sales performance is good, and she doesn't consider firing Jackson as an option.

ROLE PLAY CASE

You've just gotten back from Lambda Plumbing, the plumbing products manufacturer. Lambda actually is just one division of a conglomerate of 12 divisions, and you have the opportunity to sell to the entire company. But the company wants to know several things:

1. Can you create a custom tool that helps manage IT spend across all 12 divisions, even though they make purchase decisions independently?
2. Lambda would like the terms and conditions of the agreement altered so that it will receive an automatic 2 percent discount by paying automatically on the first of each month, and it wants the dispute resolution clause to reflect the laws of California, not Delaware as it currently states.
3. It wants permission to send a rep to your corporate headquarters to make a presentation to all the Gartner employees about Lambda Plumbing products for the do-it-yourself consumer. Employees who work in the field will be mailed a DVD presentation about Lambda Plumbing products.

Each student will take turns playing the salesperson. The first question has to be addressed by the chief engineer for the budget assessment tool. The second has to be addressed by the legal department. The final question has to be solved by the chief operations officer. If there are three people in a group, take turns observing. Your instructor will provide you with sheets for your role as one of the other Gartner managers.

ADDITIONAL REFERENCES

Brehmer, Per-Olof, and Jakob Rehme. "Proactive and Reactive: Drivers for Key Account Management Programmes." *European Journal of Marketing* 43, no. 7/8 (2009), pp. 961-84.

Guenzi, Paolo, Laurent Georges, and Catherine Pardo. "The Impact of Strategic Account Managers' Behaviors on Relational Outcomes: An Empirical Study." *Industrial Marketing Management* 38, no. 4 (2009), pp. 300-12.

Joshi, Ashwin W. "Salesperson Influence on Product Development: Insights from a Study of Small Manufacturing Organizations." *Journal of Marketing* 74, no. 1 (January 2010), pp. 94-108.

Le Meunier-FitzHugh, Kenneth, Jasmin Baumann, Roger Palmer, and Hugh Wilson. "The Implications of Service-Dominant Logic and Integrated Solutions on the Sales Function." *Journal of Marketing Theory and Practice* 19, no. 4 (Fall 2011), pp. 423-40.

Le Meunier-FitzHugh, Kenneth, and Nigel F. Piercy. "Improving the Relationship between Sales and Marketing." *European Business Review* 22, no. 3 (2010), pp. 287-305.

Malshe, Avinash. "An Exploration of Key Connections within Sales-Marketing Interface." *Journal of Business and Industrial Marketing* 26, no. 1 (2011), pp. 45-57.

Paparoidamis, Nicholas G., and Paolo Guenzi. "An Empirical Investigation into the Impact of Relationship Selling and LMX on Salespeople's Behaviours and Sales Effectiveness." *European Journal of Marketing* 43, no. 7/8 (2009), pp. 1053-61.

Piercy, Nigel F., David W. Cravens, and Nikala Lane. "Sales Manager Behavior-Based Control and Salesperson Performance: The Effects of Manager Control Competencies and Organizational Citizenship Behavior." *Journal of Marketing Theory and Practice* 20, no. 1 (Winter 2012), pp. 7-22.

Rouziès, Dominique, Anne T. Coughlan, Erin Anderson, and Dawn Iacobucci. "Determinants of Pay Levels and Structures in Sales Organization." *Journal of Marketing* 73, no. 6 (November 2009), pp. 92-104.

Schwepker, Charles H., Jr., and David J. Good. "Sales Quotas: Unintended Consequences on Trust in Organization, Customer-Oriented Selling, and Sales Performance." *Journal of Marketing Theory and Practice* 20, no. 4 (Fall 2012), pp. 437-52.

Shepherd, C. David, Geoffrey L. Gordon, Rick E. Ridnour, Dan C. Weilbaker, and Brian Lambert. "Sales Manager Training Practices in Small and Large Firms." *American Journal of Business* 26, no. 2 (2011), pp. 92-117.

Smith, Brent, Trina Larsen, and Bert Rosenbloom. "Understanding Cultural Frames in the Multicultural Sales Organization: Prospects and Problems for the Sales Manager." *Journal of Transnational Management* 14, no. 4 (October 2009), pp. 277-92.

Speakman, James I. F., and Lynette Ryals. "Key Account Management: The Inside Selling Job." *Journal of Business and Industrial Marketing* 27, no. 5 (2012), pp. 360-69.

Steward, Michelle D., Michael D. Hutt, Beth A. Walker, and Ajith Kumar. "Coordination Strategies of High-Performing Salespeople: Internal Working Relationships That Drive Success." *Journal of Academy of Marketing Science* 38, no. 5 (2010), pp. 550-66.

Steward, Michelle D., Michael D. Hutt, Beth A. Walker, and Ajith Kumar. "Role Identity and Attributions of High-Performing Salespeople." *Journal of Business and Industrial Marketing* 24, no. 7 (2009), pp. 463-76.

©Beau Lark/Corbis RF

The Salesperson as Manager

3

PART

chapter 17

MANAGING YOUR CAREER

SOME QUESTIONS ANSWERED IN THIS CHAPTER ARE

- Which entry-level jobs are available to new college graduates?
- Where do I find these jobs?
- How should I go about getting interviews, and what should I do when I have an interview?
- What selection procedures besides interviews might I go through?
- Which career paths are available in sales?
- How can I prepare myself for a promotion into management?

PROFILE

"For me it is the people and relationships you have the privilege to build with your customers, and if you do this right you will help one another grow your careers together."

Scott Thatcher, SAP

Courtesy of Scott Thatcher

PROFILE Like many college students, I didn't have a well-defined career path in mind as graduation approached. I knew I wanted to work in an interesting B2B company that would provide an opportunity to learn and develop professionally, but that's about as far out as I had imagined. Graduating in an economic downturn, I had to be patient and willing to take some interim steps in pursuing my career. Audit work with a temp accounting firm led to a full-time position with one of its customers, a small maritime agency in downtown. Although not a job I would have expected out of college, I worked directly with customers and business partners every day and learned the importance of customer service and building trusted relationships. I spent a little over a year working with a diverse group ranging from international sea captains and lawyers to longshoremen and tugboat crews. I found that I genuinely valued the business relationships I had made, and took a great deal of pride in our customer service.

A year into this role I received some great advice from a mentor, an alum of my university (Old Dominion University). He was a top performer at a commercial real estate developer. His advice was remarkably simple: Pick an industry and learn everything you can about it. I had been reading about the growing computer industry and thinking about potential career opportunities, so I began to research the companies, their business models, and the competitive landscape that made up the computer industry. To this day, I can vividly remember walking back into my college library a year and a half after graduating; it was definitely my best work in that library!

Working in a small market and not having the strongest academic record, I had to accept that I wasn't going to get a job with a leading technology employer like IBM. So I applied for a job with a local value-added reseller (VAR) for IBM, Microsoft, and HP, and landed my first sales position. I was paid a draw against the profit from my sales, so it was basically straight commission and not without risk. Within a year, however, my name was up on the wall as a top performer, and a year later I moved to a larger market and found increasingly better technology sales positions focusing on the federal government. In the end, it took me two years to find what has been a great career in technology sales. Without that mentor's advice, though, I may never have found my way to such a rewarding career. Make sure you are leveraging your school's industry relationships, and tap into the alumni network to seek advice from willing mentors who will help open doors for you.

I wasn't born a great salesperson any more than I was born a great student. I had to learn to have a long-term view on my career, and commit to a lifetime of learning from reading and on-the-job experience in order to truly master my craft. One of the most important takeaways from your college experience should be learning how to learn. You have to process so much information in today's technology-laden business climate, your ability to efficiently absorb, process, and interrelate information will determine your ability to compete in the workforce and advance your career. This is especially true for a career in sales where you regularly have to synthesize new product features with emerging market demand.

A few years ago, I reconnected with my first sales manager over LinkedIn because he was a consummate professional and great role model. It was rewarding to get his congratulations, having recently been promoted to general manager for Federal Civilian Government Sales at Microsoft, where I had responsibility for a $600M business. Currently, I am the chief operating officer for a business unit at SAP, a multinational ERP market leader. Sharing that success was also rewarding because a big part of my success at Microsoft, and now SAP, came from the skills I developed working in those first few jobs out of college.

Sales really boils down to three competencies: relationship building, critical thinking, and problem solving. Sales leaders in every industry are looking for a few key ingredients. For me, it is a sharp mind with a good balance of confidence and humility, a positive attitude, and a proven team player that is willing to own his or her mistakes. In today's business, sales is a team sport where matrixed organizations rely on role players to help drive revenue growth. In an interview, it is important to demonstrate these characteristics through real-life examples, not just say you have them. I run from candidates who exhibit a sense that the world owes them something; a successful career in sales requires you to invest an incredible amount up front to learn your craft. You also need to be in it for something more than the money. For me it is the people and relationships you have the privilege to build with your customers, and if you do this right you will help one another grow your careers together. As you set out on your journey, I hope you can find some valuable takeaways from my story, or maybe gain confidence in knowing it may take a few turns to get to the long road you are seeking.

Visit our Web site at: www.sap.com.

Scott Thatcher, chief operating officer for a business unit, SAP. Used with permission.

Landing that first career position is an exciting moment! However, the job search is just the first task in managing your career. Like the chess player who is thinking two or three moves ahead, you too must think about subsequent opportunities. Also like the chess player, you must maintain some flexibility so you do not checkmate your career if one strategy does not work.

Sales is a great place to begin a career. Just ask Mark Hurd, CEO of Oracle. Hurd started in sales with NCR and became president of the Teradata subsidiary and then president of NCR. From there, he took over Hewlett-Packard, leading a turnaround based on improving its sales force. At each step of the way, Hurd has grown each company by focusing attention on the sales function.

OPPORTUNITIES IN SELLING

Selling offers many opportunities. For some, the opportunity of selling is the money but surprisingly, perhaps, for many, sales is about serving others, finding creative solutions to problems, and getting to know lots of people.

Corporate executives clearly recognize the importance of selling experience in any career. Mark Hurd, CEO of one of the largest IT companies in the world, Oracle, got his start in sales, as have many other CEOs. As Mark says, "My first job after college was as a sales rep. I can't think of a better way for me to have started my career. Going into sales and working your way through sales and marketing is arguably the best way to get a solid understanding of your company, how it operates, what makes it successful, and–most importantly–its customers. There is absolutely no substitute for looking at an organization from the perspective of a customer. Those most successful in sales do exactly that." Many people have also found career satisfaction by staying in sales throughout their working lives.

There are more sales positions for new college graduates than any other type of position, according to a study in 2016.[1] But whether your career is sales or any other field, similar suggestions apply when searching for a job. In this chapter the focus is on the search for a sales position and how to land the first job. We examine how companies make hiring decisions and offer tips on how to build selling and management skills while managing a career.

Exhibit 17.1
A Good Match between Salesperson and Company

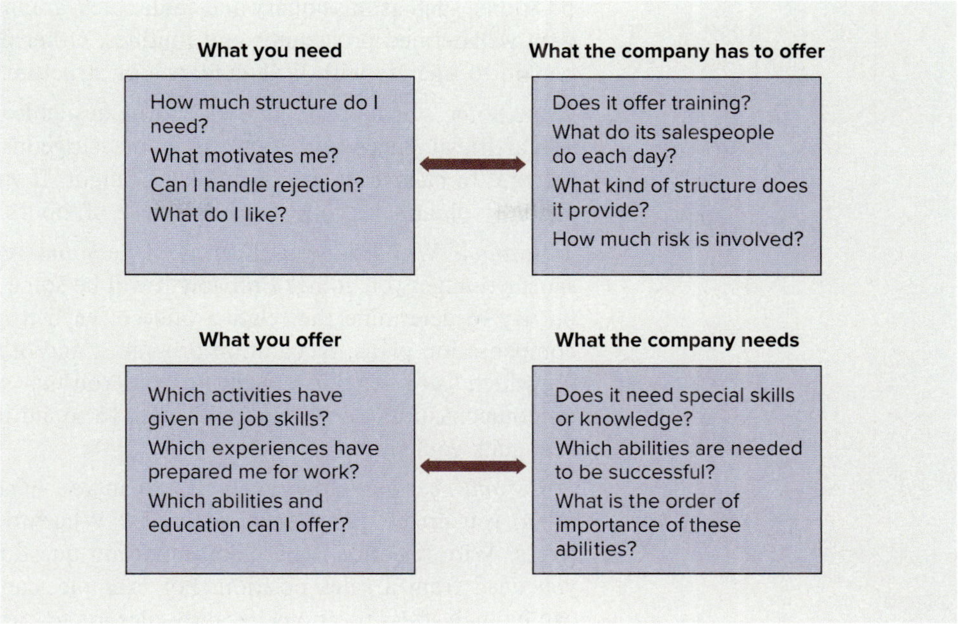

MAKING A GOOD MATCH

The keys to being successful and happy lie in finding a good match between what you need and desire in a position and the positions companies offer.[2] The first step, then, is to understand yourself, what you need, and what you have to offer. Then you must consider what each company needs and what each has to offer. As Exhibit 17.1 illustrates, a good match means your needs are satisfied by what the company offers and what you offer satisfies the company's needs.

UNDERSTANDING YOURSELF

Shakespeare said, "To thine own self be true," but to be true to yourself, you must know who you are, what you need, and what you can offer others.[3] Brandon Johnson, CTA, believes self-examination is an important first step in being a successful sales professional. As he says, "Know yourself, know your why, and know your stuff."[4] Knowing these things about yourself requires substantial self-examination. We will pose some questions that can help you follow Shakespeare's suggestion.

Many companies, such as Konica-Minolta, Oracle, IBM, and others, use exotic trips as a reward for top performers.

Understanding Your Needs

The first step in making a good match between what you have to offer and a company's position is to determine what you need. Important questions to consider include the following:

1. *Structure:* Can you work well when assignments are ambiguous, or do you need a lot of instruction? Do you need deadlines that others set, or do you set your own deadlines? If you are uncomfortable when left on your own, you may need structure in your work life. Many sales

positions, such as missionary and trade sales, are in a structured environment with well-defined procedures and routines. Other positions require the salesperson to operate with little guidance or structure.

2. *Time:* Some sales jobs require you to be available 24/7. For example, if you sell artificial knees and hips to trauma surgeons, you better be ready to respond to calls any time of the day or night. If you can't do that, then you should look at sales jobs that don't have off-hours demands.
3. *Motivation:* Will financial incentives, personal recognition, or simply job satisfaction get you going? Probably it will be some combination of the three, but try to determine the relative value of each to you. Then you can weigh compensation plans, recognition programs, and other factors when considering which sales position is right for you. You may want to review the section on compensation plan types in Chapter 16 to aid in determining which plan best suits your needs.
4. *Stress and rejection:* How much stress can you handle? Are you a risk taker, or do you prefer more secure activities? What do you do when faced with stress? With rejection? These are important questions in understanding what you need from a sales position. For example, capital equipment sales jobs can be high-stress positions because sales are few and far between. Other jobs may require you to wade through many rejections before landing a sale. If you thrive on that kind of challenge, the rewards can be gratifying. Some sales positions, though, involve working only with current customers, and salespeople incur little outright rejection. Every grocery store, for example, will carry at least some Procter & Gamble products so there is not the same stress placed on each individual sale.
5. *Interest:* What do you find interesting? Mechanical or technical topics? Merchandising? Art or fashion? You cannot sell something that bores you. You would just bore and annoy the customer.[5]

Understanding What You Have to Offer

Other resources that can help you understand the person you are may be available through your college's placement center. You must also take inventory of what you bring to the job:

1. *Skills:* What activities and experiences taught you certain skills? What did you learn from those experiences and your education that you can apply to a career? Keep in mind that it is not the activities in which you participated that matter to hiring companies; it is what you learned by participating that counts.
2. *Knowledge:* College has provided you with many areas of knowledge, but you have also probably learned much by participating in hobbies and other interests. For example, you may have special computer knowledge that would be useful in selling software, or you may have participated in a particular sport that makes you well suited to sell equipment to sporting goods stores. Kristen Scott found that her course in CRM and her experience in selling NetSuite at the National Collegiate Sales Competition enabled her to compete against other salespeople with years of experience and win a sales position with Oracle straight out of college.
3. *Qualities and traits:* Every person has a unique personality. What parts of your personality add value for your potential employer? Are you detail

Exhibit 17.2

Traits of Top Salespeople

1. Strong ego: able to handle rejection with healthy self-esteem.
2. Sense of urgency: getting it done now.
3. Ego driven: obsessive about being successful.
4. Assertive: being firm without being aggressive (see the discussion in Chapter 11).
5. Willing to take risks: willing to innovate.
6. Sociable: good at building relationships.
7. Abstract reasoner: able to handle complex selling situations and ideas.
8. Skeptical: a healthy bit of suspicion, not counting on commission until the sale is really a sale.
9. Creative: able to set oneself apart from the competition.
10. Empathic: able to place oneself in the buyer's shoes.

Source: Erika Rasmusson, "The Ten Traits of Top Salespeople," *Sales and Marketing Management*, August 1999, pp. 34-37.

oriented and systematic? Are you highly creative? In other words, what can you bring to the job that is uniquely you? Exhibit 17.2 lists traits of top salespeople, according to a study conducted for *Sales and Marketing Management* magazine nearly 20 years ago. Compare that to a more recent study (2015) that listed these characteristics: optimistic, emotionally stable, and extroverted.[6] One caveat in comparing the two studies is that the second did not ask the same questions. But note that neither list concludes that a top trait is "able to talk a lot."

Your answers to these questions will generate a list of what you have to offer companies. Then when you are in an interview, you can present features that make you a desirable candidate.

When to Ask These Questions

Unfortunately many students wait until just before graduation before seriously considering the type of career they desire. According to one career services director, students who start a search while in school will find a job three times faster than those who start after graduation. Although it is not always realistic to expect every student to map out a life plan prior to senior year, asking questions such as these as early as possible can guide a student to better course selection, better use of learning opportunities, and ultimately a better career decision. Then the student can begin actively searching for the job at the beginning of the senior year so that graduation signals the beginning of a career, not a career search.

UNDERSTANDING THE COMPANY

While developing a good feel for who you are and what you have to offer companies, you should also explore what is available and which companies offer positions that appeal to you. As you can see in Exhibit 17.3, numerous sources provide information about positions and growth opportunities in various industries and specific companies. Don't forget, though, that the best sources are personal; be

Exhibit 17.3

Sources of Job Information

Source	Example
Government	U.S. Industrial Outlook
Research services	Standard & Poor's Industry Surveys
Industry associations	Christian Booksellers' Association
Professional organizations	Sales and Marketing Executives International
General magazines	*Bloomberg Businessweek, Money*
Trade magazines	*Sales and Marketing Management, Selling Power*
Placement services	University placement office; nonfee private agencies such as Personnel One
Personal sources	Friends, relatives, industry association executives at trade shows, recruiters at career fairs
Web sites	marketingjobs.com, Glassdoor

sure to talk over job opportunities with your friends, friends of your parents, and your professors. Chat with speakers after class to learn more about their companies. Use term papers as an excuse to call professionals in a field that interests you. Join trade and professional associations now because these offer great networking opportunities. As someone who has studied sales, you should use your prospecting skills too. Next let's discuss how to evaluate what you learn about the companies and their positions.

What the Company Has to Offer

When you meet a salesperson or sales manager, you should ask about compensation and recognition programs, training, career opportunities, and other information to determine whether the company truly offers benefits to satisfy your needs. You should also explore daily activities of the salesperson, likes and dislikes about the job, and what that person thinks it takes to succeed. This information will help you determine whether a match exists.

For example, if you need structure, you should look for a sales position in which your day is structured for you. Any industry that relies on repeated sales calls to the same accounts is likely to be highly structured. Industries with a structured sales day include consumer packaged goods sales (Procter & Gamble, Quaker Oats, Smithfield Foods, and the like) and pharmaceutical sales (Cardinal Health, Eli Lilly Company, and so forth). Even these sales positions offer some flexibility and independence. Office and industrial equipment sales provide much less structure when the emphasis is on getting new accounts.

Knowing your comfort level with risk and your need for incentives should help you pick a company with a compensation program that is right for you. If you need the security of a salary, look for companies in trade sales, equipment sales, pharmaceuticals, or consumer packaged goods. But if you like the risk of straight commission, which can often be matched with greater financial rewards for success, explore careers in areas such as convention sales, financial services, and other straight commission jobs.

Other factors to consider include the size of the company and its promotion policies, particularly if the company is foreign. Many companies have a "promote from within" policy, which means that whenever possible they fill positions with people who already are employees. Such policies are very attractive if you seek career growth into management. A company that is foreign-owned, however, may prefer to staff certain positions with people from its home country.

Take advantage of interests you already have. If you are intrigued by medical science, seek a medical sales position. If merchandising excites you, a position selling to the trade would be appropriate. A bar of soap by itself is not exciting, but helping customers find ways to market that bar of soap is.

What the Company Needs

At this point in your job search, you may have narrowed your selection to a group of industries or companies. At a minimum you have a good picture of what a company should offer to land you as a salesperson. The next step is to find a company that needs you. Finding out what a company needs will require some research, but you will find this step fun and rewarding. From the Buyer's Seat 17.1 shares some tips on what sales recruiters look for when interviewing college students for sales positions.

From the BUYER'S SEAT 17.1

HOW SALES RECRUITERS EVALUATE CANDIDATES

A recruiter comes to campus and interviews 14 people per day, perhaps spending up to three days there. Then goes to the next campus and does the same thing—perhaps seeing over 100 students for each open sales position. So how can you stand out?

In general, act like a sales professional throughout the process.

Joe Merritt, sales manager with Federated, a commercial insurance company, says it starts and ends with impact. "Are they able to connect quickly and make people remember you?" As a salesperson would, he also wants to know, "Who is going to ask for the 'next step'—along those same lines I look for who sends me a note or email to follow up after an interview. You know why? Because no one does this! It makes you stand out." His expectation is that if you do these things in the interview process, you'll do them as a sales professional.

Dean Kyle, of Henry Schein, first considers whether they can ask questions to understand needs. "I role-play with each one of my candidates in the interview; I tell them exactly what will happen. Students will immediately be met by an objection. Every time the buyer will shake his head and gruffly state, 'Go away, we are already purchasing with company XYZ, we're happy, we don't need you.' What would you say?"

Dean continues, "After I present this scenario, I lean over the desk and ask them that exact question. Ninety percent of my candidates answer the same way. After a little stuttering, stammering, and fidgeting, they spit fact after fact at me and go into a long, well-rehearsed list of product superiority. Only 10 percent of students get it right—they probe! If I'm the buyer, I do not want to listen to a speech about product superiority; I want to be understood and heard. You accomplish this by asking questions. The 10 percent that impress me immediately calm their composure and ask probing questions. 'I've heard good things about Company XYZ. Can you tell me more?' When my candidates begin to ask questions and dig deeper, they find pain points and opportunities to build a successful presentation and ultimately a successful interview."

Sources: Aliah Wright, "HR and IT Must Work Together When Buying HR Technology," *HR News*, March 29, 2017; Anonymous, "Joseph P. (Joe) Beery," *Boardroom Insiders Profile*, September 14, 2015.

In general, companies look for three qualities in salespeople: good communication skills, self-motivation, and a positive and enthusiastic attitude. One sales consultant says these are reflections of the personality traits ego drive, ego strength, and empathy.[7] Recall from Exhibit 17.2 that other characteristics are important, such as a sense of urgency.

Companies in certain industries may also desire related technical skills or knowledge, such as medical knowledge for the field of pharmaceutical sales or insurance knowledge to enter that field. All companies need salespeople with computer skills because computers are increasingly being used to track and manage accounts, communicate internally, and perform other important activities. If you want to enter a field requiring specialized knowledge or skills, now is the time to begin acquiring that knowledge. Not only will you already have the knowledge when you begin to search for a position, but you will also have demonstrated self-motivation and the right kind of attitude by taking on the task of acquiring that knowledge and skill.

Career fairs, such as this one in the basketball arena on campus, can be a great opportunity to find internships or permanent sales positions.

Courtesy of Doug Gray, Old Dominion University

THE RECRUITING PROCESS

Early in this book we discussed the buying process so you would understand the purchase decision buyers make. Now we will look at the recruiting process so you will understand how companies will view you as a candidate for a sales job or any other position.

SELECTING SALESPEOPLE

In recent years companies have made considerable progress in screening and selecting salespeople. Most have discarded the myth that there is one single "sales type" who will be successful selling anything to anybody. Instead they seek people who match the requirements of a specific position, using various methods to gain information and determine whether a good match will be made.

APPLICANT INFORMATION SOURCES

To determine whether a match exists between the job requirements and the applicant's abilities, information about the applicant must be collected. Companies use five important sources of information: application forms, references, tests, personal interviews, and assessment centers. We describe these five sources from the perspective of the company so you can understand how they are used to make hiring decisions. We also explain how you should use these sources of information so you can present yourself accurately and positively.

The **application form** is an online or preprinted form that the candidate completes. You have probably already filled these out for part-time jobs you have had. The form should include factual questions concerning the profile the company established for the position. Responses on the form are also useful for structuring the personal interview. Résumés provide much of the same information application forms do but are often too individualized for easy comparison. For this and other reasons, companies must supplement résumés with an application form (we discuss résumés in greater detail later in this chapter).

Contacting **references**, or people who know the applicant, is a good way to validate information on the application form. References can also supplement the information with personal observations. The most frequently contacted references are former employers. Other references are coworkers, leaders of social or religious organizations, and professors. You should be aware that some organizations try to develop relationships with faculty so they can receive leads on excellent candidates before visiting the placement office. Professors recommend students who have demonstrated the qualities the recruiting companies desire.

When you select references, keep in mind that companies want references that can validate information about you. Choose references that provide different information, such as one character reference, one educational reference, and one work-related reference.

Experienced sales managers expect to hear favorable comments from an applicant's references. More useful information may be contained in unusual comments, gestures, faint praise, or hesitant responses that may indicate a problem. Before you offer someone's name as a reference, ask that person for permission. At that time you should be able to tell whether the person is willing to give you a good recommendation.

Intelligence, ability, personality, and interest **tests** provide information about a potential salesperson that cannot be obtained readily from other sources. Tests can also correct misjudgments made by sales managers who tend to act on "gut feelings." Although tests were widely criticized in the early 1980s for failing to predict success better than other sources did, recent studies indicate that assessment tests are growing in popularity once more, in part because of their improved predictive power. The new assessment tests, however, are more accurate when they are specifically related to sales and the situations potential salespeople may encounter.

Several types of tests may be given. H. R. Challey Inc. designs tests to determine a person's psychological aptitude for different sales situations. BSRP offers a test that measures a salesperson's call reluctance,[8] or fear of initiating contact. IBM requires sales candidates to demonstrate technical aptitude through a test, while Skyline (a company that sells exhibition equipment for trade shows and other displays) requires a test that indicates the individual's ability to handle details. Like many companies, KB Homes requires candidates to pass a math test because of the importance of calculating price correctly. Still other tests indicate a candidate's ethical nature. Companies may require candidates to take tests in all these categories.

The important point to remember about tests is to remain relaxed. If the test is a valid selection tool, you should be happy with the outcome no matter what it is. If you believe the test is not valid–that is, does not predict your ability to succeed in that job–you may want to present your feelings to the recruiter. Be prepared to back up your line of reasoning with facts and experiences that illustrate why you are a good candidate for the position.

Interviews, or personal interaction between recruiter and candidate, are an important source of information for recruiters. Companies now give more attention to conducting multiple interviews in the selection process because sometimes candidates show only slight differences. Multiple interviews can improve a recruiter's chances of observing the differences and selecting the best candidate. We cover interviews in more detail later in the chapter.

Companies sometimes evaluate candidates at centrally located **assessment centers**. In addition to being used for testing and personal interviews, these locations may simulate portions of the job. Simulating the job serves two purposes.

First, the simulation lets managers see candidates respond to a joblike situation. Second, candidates can experience the job and determine whether it fits them. For example, Merrill Lynch sometimes places broker candidates in an office and simulates two hours of customer telephone calls. As many as half the candidates may then decide that being a stockbroker is not right for them, and Merrill Lynch can also evaluate the candidates' abilities in a lifelike setting.

Companies use many sources of information in making a hiring decision, perhaps even asking for a copy of a videotaped presentation you may make for this class. These sources are actually selling opportunities for you. You can present yourself and learn about the job at the same time, continuing your evaluation of the match.

SELLING YOUR CAPABILITIES

With an understanding of the recruiting process from the company's point of view, you can create a presentation that sells your capabilities and proves you have the skills and knowledge the company wants. Preparing the résumé, gaining an interview, and presenting your capabilities in the interview are important activities that require sound planning to present yourself effectively.

PREPARING THE RÉSUMÉ

The résumé is the brochure in your marketing plan. As such, it needs to tell the recruiter why you should be hired. Tom Day, sales manager for Hormel, says he literally gets hundreds of résumés for sales positions, whether he has a position available or not. His company prefers to hire inexperienced salespeople right out of college, as do many companies, so don't let a lack of experience create anxiety or lead to misrepresentation on your résumé.[9] There are two broadly accepted formats for résumés: a conventional format and a functional style. In some career centers or if you choose to use an online résumé service, such as LiveCareer.com, you can choose from as many as 1,400 templates, but most follow the conventional style. Whether you choose the conventional style or the functional style of résumé, the purpose is to sell your skills and experience.

Conventional Résumés

Conventional résumés are a form of life history, organized by type of experience. The three categories of experience most often used are education, work, and activities/hobbies (see the example in Exhibit 17.4). Although it is easy to create conventional résumés, it is also easy to fail to emphasize important points. To avoid making this mistake, follow this simple procedure:

- List education, work experience, and activities.
- Write out what you gained in each experience that will help you prove you have the desired qualities.
- Emphasize what you learned and that you have the desired qualities under each heading.

For example, the résumé in Exhibit 17.4 is designed for a student interested in a sales career. Note how skills gained in this class are emphasized in addition to GPA and major. The candidate has also chosen to focus on customer service skills gained as a camp counselor, a job that a recruiter would otherwise overlook. Rather than just listing herself as a member of the soccer team, the candidate highlights the leadership skills she gained as captain.

Exhibit 17.4

Conventional Résumé Example

Cheryl McSwain

After June 1:
435 Wayward View, Apt. B
State College, PA 10303
203/555-1289

Present Address:
612 Homer
Aurora, CO 86475
804/555-9183

Career Objective: Sales in the telecommunications industry

Education:
Colorado University, Boulder, Colorado
Bachelor of Business Administration, June 2020
Marketing
GPA: 3.25 on 4.0 scale

Major Subjects:	Other Subjects:
Personal Selling	Microcomputing
Sales Management	Local Area Networks Management
Industrial Marketing	Telecommunications

Emphasized selling and sales management in computing and telecommunications. Learned SPIN, social styles, and other adaptive selling techniques. Studied LANWORKS and Novell network management.

Work Experience:
Sales representative, *The Lariat* (CU campus newspaper)
Practiced sales skills in making cold calls and selling advertising
Fall 2017 to present

Counselor, Camp Kanatcook
Learned customer service and leadership skills
Summers, 2017, 2018, 2019

Scholarships and Honors:
University Merit Scholar ($2,000/year, two years)
Top sales student, spring 2020
Dean's List, three semesters

Activities:
Member, Alpha Delta Pi Sorority
Rush chair, 2019
Motivated members to actively recruit; interviewed candidates for selection
Homecoming float chair, 2018
Managed float building; sorority awarded second in float competition

Women's soccer team, four years
Captain, 2019–2020
Led team to conference championship, fall 2019

Functional Résumés

Functional résumés reverse the content and titles of the conventional résumé, organizing by what the candidate can do or has learned rather than by types of experience. As you can see in Exhibit 17.5, an advantage of this type of résumé is that it highlights more forcefully what the candidate can do.

When preparing a functional résumé, begin by listing the qualities you have that you think will help you get the job. Narrow this list to three or four qualities and then list activities and experiences to prove that you have those skills and abilities. The qualities are the headings for the résumé; the activities and experiences show that you have those qualities. One difficulty with this type of résumé is that one past job may relate to several qualities. If that is the case, emphasize the activity within the job that gave you the experience for each specific quality.

GAINING THE INTERVIEW

Students should begin examining different industries as early as possible, as we suggested earlier. As graduation looms closer and the time for serious job hunting arrives, your knowledge of the industries and companies that interest you will put

Exhibit 17.5
Functional Résumé Example

Cheryl McSwain

After June 1:
435 Wayward View, Apt. B
State College, PA 10303
203/555-1289

Present Address:
612 Homer
Aurora, CO 86475
804/555-9183

Career Objective: Sales in the telecommunications industry

Sales and Customer Service Experience:

Studied SPIN and adaptive selling techniques in personal selling.
Sold advertising in *The Lariat*, campus newspaper. Responsibilities included making cold calls, presenting advertising strategies, and closing sales.
Performed customer service tasks as camp counselor at Camp Kanatcook. Served as the primary parent contact during drop-off and pick-up periods, answering parent queries, resolving parental concerns, and handling similar responsibilities.

Management and Leadership Experience:

Studied situational management in sales management.
Served as rush chair for sorority. Responsible for motivating members to recruit new members and developed and implemented a sales training seminar so members would present the sorority favorably within university guidelines.
Managed homecoming-float project. Sorority awarded second place in float competition.
Captained the women's varsity soccer team to a conference championship.

Telecommunications Skills and Experience:

Studied LANWORKS and Novell network management in telecommunications.
Designed, as a term project, a Novell-based LAN for a small manufacturing business.
Purchased and installed a six-computer network in a family-owned wholesaling business.

Scholarships and Honors:

University Merit Scholar ($2,000/year, two years)
Top sales student, spring 2020
Dean's List, three semesters

you a step ahead. You will also understand the process the company will go through in searching for a new salesperson.

Using Personal Contacts

More important, you have already begun to make personal contacts in those fields—contacts you can now use to gain interviews. The same salespeople and sales managers who gave you information before to help you with term projects will usually be happy to introduce you to the person in charge of recruiting. Contacts you made at job fairs and trade shows can also be helpful.

thinking it through

Many students feel uncomfortable asking for favors from people they barely know, such as asking an acquaintance to forward a résumé to a decision maker or set up an interview. How can you overcome such feelings of discomfort? Why would someone want to help you find places to interview? What obligations do you have to people who give you the names of job contacts?

Using Employment Postings

Responding to Web postings or newspaper advertisements can also lead to job interviews. You will need to carefully interpret employment postings and then respond effectively to them.

All ads are designed to sell, and employment ads are no exception. But what sounds great may not be wonderful in reality. Here are some phrases often found in such ads and interpretations of them:

Independent contractor: You will work on straight commission with no employee benefits. You will probably receive no training and little, if any, support. Some experienced salespeople prefer this type of position, but it is probably not the best place to start.

Earn up to $ (or *unlimited income* or *our top rep made $500,000 last year*)*:* You need to know what the average person makes and what the average first-year earnings are, not what the top rep made or the upper limit. The job could still be desirable, but you need to find out what reality is before accepting a position. Speak to someone who holds the position you are interviewing for and get the real scoop, and don't forget to check Glassdoor.com.

Sales manager trainee: This is another title for sales representative. Don't be put off or overly encouraged by high-sounding titles.

Bonuses paid weekly, daily commissions, or weekly commissions: These are high-pressure jobs and probably involve high-pressure sales.

Ten salespeople needed now! That's because everyone has quit. This company uses salespeople and then discards them.

You should look for two things in an ad: what the company needs and what it has to offer. The company should provide concrete information about training, compensation plan (although not necessarily the amount), amount of travel to expect, and type of product or service you will sell. You should also expect to find the qualifications the company desires, including experience and education. If this is a job you really want but you do not have the experience now, call and ask how to get it. Be specific: "What companies should I pursue that will give me the experience you are looking for?" If the ad requires e-mail response only, send an e-mail message and mention that you are a student. Many people are willing to help someone get started.

Responding to Postings

Many postings and ads will ask you to write or e-mail and may not list the company's name. A blind box number is given when the company name is not included in an ad; the box number is usually at the address of a website. For example, the ad may say to send a résumé to Job Posting 943 at Monster.com. Don't be put off by the lack of company name; the posting or ad may be placed by a company such as IBM that would otherwise receive a large number of unqualified applicants. Companies use blind postings and blind box numbers for many legitimate reasons.

Writing the Cover Letter

When you write in response to a posting, you are writing a sales letter—even if you send it by e-mail. Like any sales letter, it should focus on what you can do for the company, not what you expect from it. The letter should start with an attention getter. Here is one example:

> In today's economy, you need someone who can become productive quickly as a territory representative. Based on your posting at Monster.com, I believe that I am that person.

The Internet is a great source of leads for jobs; however, recruiters report receiving hundreds, and sometimes thousands, of résumés for every job they post. If you really want a job with a particular company, approach it like a sales opportunity and use your prospecting and relationship building skills.

Source: www.salesjobs.com

This attention getter is direct, focuses on a probable need, and refers to the posting. The attention getter tells why you should be considered. The probability of getting a response to this e-mail is far greater than if you simply said,

> Please consider me for the territory representative position you posted at Monster.com.

The body of the letter should center on two or three reasons why you should be hired. For example, if you have the qualities of self-motivation and leadership, devote two paragraphs relating each to the position. Use your résumé as proof. For example:

> A territory representative position often requires self-motivation. As you can see from the attached résumé, I demonstrated self-motivation as a sales representative for the campus newspaper, as a volunteer for the local food bank, and as a member of the Dean's Honor Roll during two of the last four semesters.

The letter should close with a request for action. Ask for an interview and suggest times you are available. For example:

> Please call me to arrange an interview. My schedule allows me to meet with you on Tuesday or Thursday afternoon.

An alternative is to state that you will call:

> I will call you early next week to discuss my potential as a salesperson for XYZ Corporation.

No response does not necessarily mean you have been rejected; follow up with a phone call if you do not hear anything within a week. One former student got a job because he called to verify that the sales manager had received his résumé. She had never seen it but was impressed enough with the student's phone call to arrange an appointment. Sometimes e-mail is lost or delayed, goes to a junk mail file and gets deleted, or simply is deleted accidentally—and you would not want a company to miss out on the opportunity to hire you because of a computer glitch!

THE INTERVIEW

Many students do not realize how much competition exists for the best entry-level sales positions, or perhaps they do not know what companies look for in new employees. Students often act as though they are shopping for a job. Job shoppers, however, are not seriously considered by recruiters, who are usually astute enough to quickly pick up on the student's lack of interest. If the job shopper does become interested, it is probably too late because the recruiter has already discounted this applicant. Like it or not, you are really competing for a job. As in any competition, success requires preparation and practice.

Preparing for the Interview

Students who know something about the company and its industry lead the competition. You have already looked for company and industry information in the library, in business reference books, and in periodicals. You visited its Web site. You have also interviewed the company's customers, salespeople, and sales managers. You can use this knowledge to demonstrate your self-motivation and positive attitude—two of the top three characteristics sales managers look for in sales candidates. You will find it easier to demonstrate the third top characteristic, communication skills, with the confidence you gain from proper preparation.

In addition to building knowledge of the "customer," you must plan your responses to the questions you will be asked. Exhibit 17.6 lists standard interview questions.

Exhibit 17.6

Frequently Asked Interview Questions

1. What are your long-range and short-range goals and objectives? When and why did you establish these goals, and how are you preparing yourself to achieve them?
2. What do you consider to be your greatest strengths and weaknesses?
3. Why did you choose the career for which you are preparing?
4. How do you think a friend or professor who knows you well would describe you?
5. Why should I hire you?
6. In what ways do you think you can make a contribution to our company?
7. Do you think your grades are a good indication of your academic achievement?
8. What major problem have you encountered, and how did you deal with it?
9. What do you know about our company? Why are you seeking a position with us?
10. If you were hiring a graduate for this position, what qualities would you look for?

Scenario questions are popular with recruiters. These questions ask what the candidate would do in a certain situation involving actions of competitors. (For example, what would you do if a customer told you something negative about your product that you knew to be untrue, and the customer's source of information was your competitor?) Such questions test ethics regarding competitors and the ability to handle a delicate situation. Scenario questions also test the candidate's response to rejection, ability to plan, and other characteristics. You can best prepare for these types of questions with this class and by placing yourself in the situations described in the cases and exercises in this book. You may also want to review the questions at the ends of the chapters.

The sales field has several unusual characteristics, such as travel, that influence the type of questions asked. For example, if significant travel is part of the position, you may be asked, "Travel is an important part of this job, and you may be away from home about three nights per week. Would you be able and willing to travel as the job requires?" However, some

Exhibit 17.7
Examples of Legal and Illegal Questions

Subject	Legal Questions	Illegal Questions
Name	Have you ever used another name?	What is your maiden name?
Residence	Where do you live?	Do you own or rent your home?
Birthplace or national origin	Can you, after employment, verify your right to work in the United States?	Where were you born? Where were your parents born?
Marital or family status	Statement of company policy regarding assignment of work of employees who are related. Statement of company policy concerning travel: Can you accept this policy?	With whom do you reside? Are you married? Do you plan a family?
Arrest or criminal record	Have you ever been convicted of a felony? (Such a question must be accompanied by a statement that a conviction will not necessarily disqualify the applicant.)	Have you ever been arrested?

Source: Baylor University Career Services Center.

questions are illegal, and you do not have to answer them, such as "What is your marital status? Do you plan to have a family? Will that affect your ability to travel?" Exhibit 17.7 lists some questions that are illegal, as well as legal questions that you may have to answer.

So what do you do when you are asked an illegal question? One thing you should do is report the incident to your school's career services personnel if the interview is taking place on campus or as a result of the campus career services center. But when actually faced with the question, you have several choices. One is to ask, "Why do you ask? Is that important?" You may find that it is a question asked by an interviewer out of personal curiosity, and the interviewer may not have realized the question was inappropriate. Another response is to simply reply, "I'm sorry, I would prefer not to answer that question." If probed, you can state that you believe the question is not legal, but you will check with career services later; if the question is legal, you will answer it later. If the interviewer is simply ignorant, you will probably get an apology, and then the interview will move on. Otherwise you've identified a company where you may not wish to work. Your final option is, of course, to go ahead and answer the question.

At some point during the interview, the recruiter will ask whether you have any questions. In addition to using the standard questions concerning pay, training, and benefits, you should prepare questions that are unlikely to have been answered already. For example, suppose your research has uncovered the fact that the company was recently awarded the Malcolm Baldrige Award for Quality; you might plan to ask what the company did to win that award.

You may also want to plan questions about the interviewer's career, how it got started, and what positions he or she has held. These questions work best when you are truly interested in the response; otherwise you might sound insincere. Answers to these questions can give you a personal insight into the company.

Also, you may often find yourself working for the interviewer, so the answers to your questions may help you decide whether you like and can work with this person.

Other important subjects to ask about are career advancement opportunities, typical first-year responsibilities, and corporate personality. You also need to know how financially stable the company is, but you can find this information for public firms in the library. If the firm is privately owned, ask about its financial stability.

Finally, it may seem trivial, but shine your shoes! You are interviewing for a professional position, so look professional. Recruiters have told us about students showing up for interviews dressed in cut off shorts and a T-shirt or looking hung over. Those interviews were over before they began. One interviewer even described how a student took a phone call from her mother during the interview. She told her mom that the interview was going great! Well, it was until she took the phone call. If you do not look the part now, an interviewer will not see you in the part.

During the Interview

The job interview is much like any other sales call. It includes an approach, needs identification, presentation, and gaining commitment. There are, however, several important differences because both parties are identifying needs and making presentations.

THE APPROACH Social amenities will begin the interview. You will not need the same type of attention getter that you would on a cold call. However, you may want to include an attention getter in your greeting. For example, use a compliment approach, such as "It must be very exciting to work for a Malcolm Baldrige award winner."

NEEDS IDENTIFICATION One difference between sales calls and job interviews is that both parties have needs they have individually defined before the meeting (in a sales call, SPIN helps you assist the buyer in defining needs). A question such as "Are you willing to relocate?" is used not to define needs so much as to determine whether the company's needs will be met. You should prepare questions that will help you learn whether the company's offer will meet your needs.

Take notes during the interview, especially when asking about the company, so you can evaluate whether your needs will be met. Carry a portfolio with extra résumés and blank paper and pens for note taking or use a pad computer, such as an iPad. You may want to ask, "Do you mind if I take notes? This information is important to me, and I don't want to forget anything."

Try to determine early whether your interviewer is a sales manager or a personnel manager. Personnel managers may have a difficult time telling you about the job itself, its daily activities, and so forth; they may be able to outline only things such as training and employee benefits. Sales managers can tell you a lot about the job, perhaps to the point of describing the actual territory you will work in.

Personnel managers do not like being asked about salary; you will find that many people will advise you not to ask about money on the first interview. On the other hand, you are making an important decision. Why waste your time or theirs if the salary is much lower than your other alternatives? Sales managers are less likely to object, but just in case, you may want to preface a question about earnings by saying, "Compensation is as important a consideration for me as training and other benefits when making a decision. Can you tell me the approximate earnings of a first-year salesperson?" You will probably get a range rather than a specific figure. You could also wait until a later meeting to ask about earnings.

People who prefer security desire compensation plans with an emphasis on salary. Other people like the potential rewards of straight commission. If either is important to you, ask about the type of compensation plan in the first meeting. For example, you should ask, "What type of compensation plan do you offer: salary, straight commission, or a combination of salary plus commission or bonus?"

PRESENTATION Features alone are not persuasive in interviews, just as features alone do not persuade buyers to purchase products. Recall the FEBA technique presented in Chapter 8, which stands for feature, evidence, benefit, agreement. Cheryl McSwain (see Exhibit 17.4) might say, "I was a camp counselor for two summers at Camp Kanatcook (*feature*), as you can see on my résumé (*evidence*). This experience taught me customer service skills that you will appreciate when I sell for you (*benefit*), don't you agree?"

If asked to describe yourself, use features to prove benefits. Recruiters will appreciate specific evidence that can back up your claims. For example, if you say you like people and that is why you think you would be a good salesperson, be prepared to demonstrate how your love of people has translated into action.

Many students carry portfolios into interviews. A **portfolio** is an organized collection of evidence of one's career.[10] For example, a portfolio might contain letters of reference, a résumé, thank-you letters from customers, a paper about an internship, a strategic plan created for a business policy class, or even photographs of the homecoming float for which you were chairperson. Some of our students offer videos of their sales calls from this class as part of their portfolios; these are often made available through YouTube to recruiters, along with digital portfolios that look like Web pages. Some universities use video software that allows recruiters to see role plays with the student's permission. Portfolios are one method of offering proof that you can deliver benefits.

thinking it through

How would you describe yourself in terms of features? What needs would be satisfied by those features so they could become benefits? What would go on your Web site or in your portfolio to prove your features? How could you use a Web site to market yourself?

Keep in mind that the interviewer also will be taking notes. Writing down answers takes the interviewer longer than it takes for you to speak. Once a question is answered sufficiently, stop and allow the interviewer time to write. Many applicants believe they should continue talking; the silence of waiting is too much to bear. Stay silent; otherwise, you may talk yourself out of a job (see Building Partnerships 17.1 on how to build your brand).

GAINING COMMITMENT Because sales positions usually require skill at gaining commitment, sales managers will want to see whether the candidate has that skill. Be prepared to close the interview with some form of gaining commitment: "I'm very excited about this opportunity. What is our next step?" Trent Weaver used this close, "Do you have any reservations about my candidacy for this position?" when he was interviewing. Now, years later, he owns two companies, and says he was surprised when a salesperson used that close on him recently! But he also said it was effective, because he shared with the candidate what his reservations were, the person overcame those objections, and got hired.

Be sure to learn when you can expect to hear from the company, confirm that deadline, and write it down. You may want to say, "So I'll receive a call or a letter within the next two weeks. Let's see, that would be the 21st, right?"

BUILDING Partnerships 17.1

BUILDING YOUR OWN BRAND

Everyone has a reputation, based on what they do and say. People know if they can trust you and believe you based on what you've done or said. So why do you need a personal brand?

The real reason, according to Jayson DeMers, is because "people want to do business with other people." A personal brand is your reputation plus a promise, made memorable. He claims that a personal brand helps you build an identity and a reputation. So what do you need for a personal brand?

1. **Decide what your brand will mean.** What is the professional reputation you want? In addition to words like *reliable* and *integrity*, Nickolaus Kimla, CEO of Pipeliner, wants his brand to include the phrase *thought leader*, or someone who is at the cutting edge of sales practice. Makes sense, since he sells sales software.
2. **Create a message.** Some call it an elevator speech, meaning you should be able to describe yourself and your brand in the time it takes to ride an elevator. Develop a one-sentence description of who you are and what you can do. If your brand promise is to create value in a particular field, then explain how in one sentence.
3. **Create hooks.** A hook is something that helps people remember who you are.
4. **Tie the hook to the purpose.** Wearing a pink bowtie as your hook may make you memorable, but give some thought as to how that will tie to the purpose. Kimla's hook is that his thought leadership is based on the Austrian School of Economics. Sounds impressive, and it is. (It helps that he's Austrian.) But that serves as the basis for his hook and is tied to his work as a thought leader.
5. **Perform.** Branding is about making a promise, so don't make a promise you can't or won't keep. In fact, Bo Hamrick, enterprise account executive for MRI Software, says that the first step to building a personal brand is to deliver value. Tim Simmons, director of strategic business solutions with Teradata, agrees. He says, "Solve clients' problems, be blunt, be truthful, and only provide solutions that work." Your brand performance should be obvious across all you do and say. (See Sales Technology 17.1 for how your social media presence should support your professional reputation.)

Zack Miller, CEO of Hatch, notes that a big part of building your brand is repeating the message at every opportunity. As he says, "Raise your hand!" Personal branding is something you can and should start now. While your own brand will morph over time as you develop new skills and interests, starting now will help you land that first position and give you time to hone your brand.

Sources: Jayson DeMers, "5 Steps to Building a Personal Brand (And Why You Need One)," *Fortune*, August 27, 2014; Nickolaus Kimla, Bo Hamrick, Zack Miller, and Tim Simmons, personal interviews.

Asking for commitment and confirming the information signal your professionalism and your organizational and selling skills.

SPECIAL TYPES OF INTERVIEWS

You can face many types of interviews: disguised interviews, stress interviews, and panel interviews, among others. **Disguised interviews**, or interviews in which the candidate is unaware that the interviewer is evaluating the candidate, are common at college placement offices. In the lobby you may meet a **greeter**, probably a recent graduate of your college, who will try to help you relax before a scheduled interview and offer you an opportunity to ask questions about the job and the company. Although you can obtain a lot of good information from a greeter, you may want to save some questions for the real interview. You may also want to repeat some questions in the interview to check for consistency. Keep in mind that the greeter is also interviewing you, even though the meeting seems like friendly conversation. Keep your enthusiasm high and your nerves low.

ethics

A **stress interview** is designed to place the candidate under severe stress to see how the candidate reacts. Stress interviews have been criticized as being unfair because the type of stress one experiences on a job interview often differs from the type of stress one would actually face on the job. Still, many reputable companies believe it is appropriate to try to determine how a candidate reacts to stress because stress is a real part of just about every sales position. One tactic is to ask three questions at once and see how the candidate answers; another is to ask, "How are you going to lose money for me?" (*translation:* What mistakes have you made in the past and what might you do in the future?) or other reversed versions of appropriate questions. Another strategy is to ask questions such as "What is 36 cubed?" or "What will the interest rates be on such and such a date (two years from now), to the exact one-hundredth please?"[11] While questionable in terms of measuring the appropriate form of stress, these methods are less questionable than the following: The interviewer asks the applicant to reveal something personal, such as a time when the person felt emotionally hurt. Once the situation has been described, the interviewer may mock the applicant, saying the situation wasn't that personal or that hurtful and surely the applicant can dig deeper. Another stress tactic is to ask the interviewee to sell something such as a pencil or a table; while this question is reasonable when used to observe selling style, being an unreasonable "customer" can turn the call into a stress interview.

Panel interviews require special tactics by the candidate to keep all interviewers involved. A focus on only the older gentleman may cost this young man a position.

You probably will not see stress interviews at a college placement office, but you could face one at some point in the job-hunting process. You may find it helpful to deal with a stress interview by treating it as a game (say to yourself, "She's just trying to stress me out; I wonder how far she will go if I don't react?"). Of course you may simply refuse to play the game, either by terminating the interview or by changing the subject. If you terminate the interview, you will probably not get the job.

In **panel interviews** you will encounter multiple interviewers. During a panel interview try to make eye contact with each interviewer. Focus on each person for at least three seconds at a time; anything less than that and you are simply sweeping the room. When asked a question, begin your answer by directing it to the questioner but then shift your attention to the group. By speaking to the group, you will keep all interviewers involved and avoid a two-person conversation. You may want to review how to sell to a group, described in Chapter 8.

Group interviews are similar to panel interviews, but they include several candidates as well as several interviewers. Group interviews may take place in a conference room or around a dinner table. If you find yourself in a group interview, avoid trying to top the stories of the other candidates. Distinguish yourself by asking interviewers about their careers and what they find it takes to be successful.

Treat social occasions during office or plant visits as interviews, and avoid alcohol or overeating. As with stress interviews, the key is to maintain your cool while being yourself. You cannot do that if you overindulge. Remember that companies are still evaluating you during these "social" events.

FOLLOW-UP

Regardless of the type of interview, you should send a thank-you note shortly afterward. Send one to the greeter, if possible (thus, you will probably want to get this person's business card). If you had a panel interview, find out who the contact person is and write to that person. If you send a thank-you card, you'll stand out. Most people who write a follow-up will send an e-mail, which is the least you should do. If you send a card, thank the person in the first paragraph, then summarize the interview. Focus your summary on the reasons why you should be hired. In the final paragraph reiterate your thanks and end with an assumptive statement, such as "I look forward to seeing you again." Whether you send a card or an e-mail, it should be short and to the point.

If you do not hear by the target date, contact the person. One former student got his first job simply because he followed up. Sales managers will appreciate the saleslike perseverance; personnel managers may not so you may want to send them an e-mail. Within another week, call the personnel manager also. Simply ask for the status of your application rather than whether you got the job. The process of deciding may have taken longer than expected, or other situations may have caused delays. You need to know where you stand, however, so you can take advantage of alternatives, if possible.

INTERVIEWING NEVER ENDS

Even if you spend your entire career with one company, your job interviewing days are not over after you land that first job; you will interview for promotions as well. Some companies even interview candidates for admission to management development programs. The same techniques apply in all these cases. You will still need to prepare properly, conduct the interview professionally, close for some level of commitment, and follow up.

MANAGING YOUR CAREER GOALS

An important aspect of career management is to set life-based objectives and then use them to determine your career objectives. Balance between family and work goals is necessary, or one of several negative consequences could occur, such as divorce or success without fulfillment. A recent study of 150 Glassdoor reviews left by salespeople found that work–life balance was one of the most important causes of job dissatisfaction and quitting.[12]

Balance, then, is important when setting career goals. Career decisions must be compatible with family and personal objectives. Keeping life goals in mind and remembering your reasons for setting those goals will help you map out a career with which you can be happy.

MAKING THE TRANSITION FROM COLLEGE TO CAREER

That first year after college is a unique and important time in anyone's life. How this transition is handled can have a big influence in whether you reach success or experience disappointment. Although a life's work is not created or ruined in the first months, a poor start can take years to overcome. It is not just a matter of giving up student attitudes and behaviors; making the transition also requires taking the time to understand and earn the rights, responsibilities, and credibility of being a sales professional. You will make mistakes during that transition; everyone does. But as many successful salespeople have learned, it isn't whether you make mistakes but rather whether you learn from them.

Many new hires want to make a great first impression, so they charge ahead and fail to recognize that the organization was there long before they were and has already developed its own way of doing things. The first thing to do is learn the organization's culture, its values, and the way things are done there.

Another important aspect of the first year is that you are under a microscope. Your activities are watched closely as management and your peers try to decide whether you are someone they can depend on. Demonstrate a mature willingness to learn, plus respect for those with experience. Part of this mature willingness to learn means you hold your expectations in check and keep your promotion hopes realistic. Remember that recruiters tend to engage in puffery when presenting the opportunities and benefits of a company. Although the recruiter said it may be possible to earn a promotion in six months, the average may be much longer.

Seek a partnership with your manager. Although partnership implies a peer-level relationship and you do not have the experience to be a true peer with your manager, use the same partnering skills with him or her that you would use with customers. Find out what your manager needs and wants and then do it. Every workday is a test day except that you sometimes write the questions. Just like your professor, your manager wants the answers, not the problems. Give your boss solutions, and you will be well on the way to a partnership.

DUAL CAREER PATH

When you start out in sales, many career options are open. Career paths can alternate between sales and marketing or follow a route entirely within sales or entirely within marketing. You may even wind up as chief executive officer of a major global corporation, like Mark Hurd at Oracle. Exemplifying how you might pursue various positions, Exhibit 17.8 depicts the various career paths for salespeople at Schneider Electric. In addition to sales management opportunities, many companies also have opportunities in marketing and product development that begin in sales.

CONTINUE TO DEVELOP YOUR KSAs

Knowledge, skills, and abilities, or **KSAs**, are the package that you offer your employer. You just spent four or five years and a lot of money developing a set of KSAs, but like any asset, your KSAs will begin to decay if you do not continue to

Exhibit 17.8

Sales Career Advancement at Schneider Electric

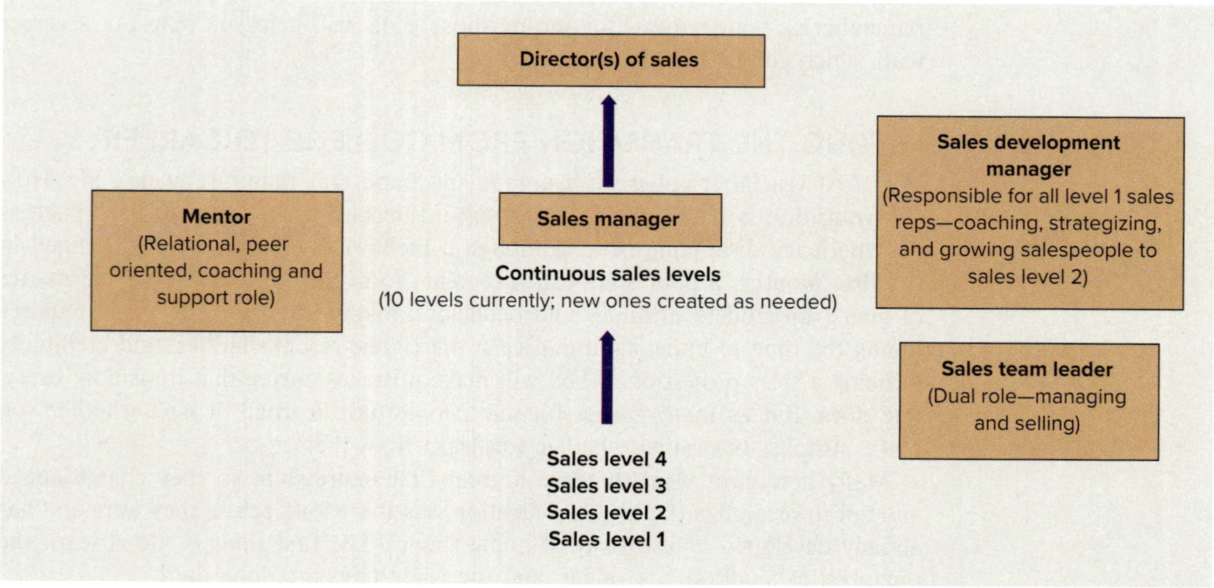

Exhibit 17.9

Soft Skills Developed at Oracle

- Negotiation
- Value messaging
- Competitive positioning
- Reference selling
- Working with partners
- Prospecting skills
- Best practices for how to lead a good sales cycle

invest in them. Because you are the person in your company to whom your career means the most, many companies, such as Cisco, have recognized that ownership of development belongs to the person, not to the company, and have turned training into self-directed development programs. In addition to self-directed training, much of the company's training has also gone virtual, meaning salespeople can access it online at any time.[13] Even if your company has not formalized development into a self-directed program or if the development program does not provide many options, take the time and effort to invest in yourself so you can grow in your career. As the philosopher Eric Hoffer said, "In times of change, the learners inherit the earth, while the learned find themselves beautifully equipped to handle a world that no longer exists."[14]

Research indicates that career development opportunities vary widely among companies, especially for salespeople. Look for programs that involve assessment of your skills, as well as direction and development of those skills. In Exhibit 17.9 Jeffrey Bailey summarizes soft KSAs developed in salespeople at Oracle. As he says, "We expect the reps to be able to spot challenges that our solutions can address and then be able to explain the value our solutions can deliver. We really don't try to train them on the products, only on understanding business issues and then being able to highlight the value we can bring. It is our sales consultants who get the real deep product training. There are just too many products to expect the reps to be deep in any of them."

Lifelong learning is important in today's learning organization. Although many companies have downsized, it is the versatile, well-educated employee who not only keeps a job but also develops a career.

Lifelong learning can be an important factor in not only improving your position but also enjoying what you do. Once you have a position within an organization, your objective will be to develop yourself to get a promotion and then to be successful in that promotion. (To get the promotion after that, you will need to do well in the job you are seeking.) You should take several significant actions in each position along the way. The first action is to understand your options because sales can often lead to various positions.

Sources of Improvement

Most companies continue to train their salespeople after basic sales training, but most training of experienced salespeople is product related rather than sales skills related. If you want to improve your selling skills, you may have to actively seek assistance.

The first place to start is with the field sales manager. When that person works with you in your territory, solicit feedback after each call. During these curbside conferences, you can learn a great deal about what you are doing from an objective observer. One warning, however: Make sure your manager observes only during the sales call and does not try to get into the act! As we discussed in the previous chapter, many sales managers are former salespeople who get excited in the heat of battle and may try to take over the sales call.

Peers provide another source. Who is successful in the company? When gathered together for a sales meeting, many successful salespeople pick one another's brains for new ideas and strategies. Offer to work with them in their territories for a day or so in order to learn from them. In most situations they will be flattered and helpful. Noncompeting salespeople in professional organizations such as Sales and Marketing Executives, an international organization of salespeople and

Learning doesn't end at graduation. This team of salespeople is learning about a new product.

©Hero Images/Getty Images RF

marketing managers, will also be flattered to share their tips with you.

Bookstores offer a wealth of material for developing sales skills. Many good books remind salespeople of the basics of selling and present advanced methods of selling and negotiating. Be sure to keep this book, too, because you will want to refer to it when you are in the field.

Sales seminars–in-person, online, or on DVDs and CDs–are also available. Seminars, such as those offered by Dale Carnegie and Tom Hopkins, can be very motivating. However, many experienced salespeople desire more than just motivation; they look for seminars that also teach new ways to present and gain commitment, as well as other sales skills such as accounting and finance. Some even learn to play golf because that's what their customers do.[15]

Another source of improvement is an industry association. Many industries and professions offer certification programs, which not only require that you improve and update your knowledge and skills but also offer proof to your customers that you have made that effort. Francisco Limas, sales representative with National Restaurant Supply in El Paso, sought certification in food safety and is now pursuing certification as a Foodservice Equipment Distributors Association Certified Salesperson. Though he's been recognized by the industry's top salespeople, he realizes that the certification provides both education and an assurance of quality to customers.[16] Certification was one measure of service quality that these buyers used when comparing suppliers.

Industry associations, though, can and do provide many training opportunities that may not lead to certification. For example, the National Association of Insurance and Financial Advisors (NAIFA) offers a number of professional development courses, including one called the NAIFA Sales System. The program is primarily delivered online, though it also includes a book and access to NAIFA mentors who will coach students through challenges that arise in their regular sales calls.[17]

In this course you have begun to develop your interpersonal persuasion, or selling, skills. Whether or not you plan a career in sales, you owe it to yourself to continue to develop these skills.

Learn Your Current Job

Learn all you can about the job you have now. Many people want promotions as fast as they can get them, regardless of their readiness. But consider that you will probably be managing the people who will be holding your current job. To be truly effective as their manager, you should learn all you can about the job of the people you hope to manage while in the best position to do so: while you are one of them.

Learn the Job You Want Next

A manager once said, "In order to become a manager, you must first be a manager." He meant that promoting someone is easier when that person already has the characteristics the position requires–that is, already acts like a manager–rather than having only potential.

Several ways exist for you to learn about the job you desire. First, solicit the help of people who hold the job now. Many companies expect managers to develop

SALES Technology 17.1

BUILDING YOUR ONLINE IDENTITY

Are you LinkedIn? Most students are on Instagram and Twitter but seem to be slow to get a profile on LinkedIn or to start using the Internet for professional purposes. Yet Jeffrey Bailey, sales manager for Oracle, stated that the company wouldn't even consider hiring a salesperson who hasn't used social media personally. "If a prospective salesperson isn't using LinkedIn professionally already, then they can't sell in today's environment," believes Bailey.

Begin your profile with a professional photo. Many universities now hold events with a photographer just so you can get a picture for your online use. Using a photo from a wedding reception or a selfie taken in your car might say that you're a fun-loving person but it doesn't scream "professional."

According to LinkedIn, the next step is to create a headline that describes who you are in 10 words. Yup, 10. Speak directly to the audience you want to attract, and consider adding keywords to make your profile show up in a search.

Describe your experience based on what you can do, not what you did. For example, if you were in charge of membership for a college organization, don't just say "Chair, Membership Committee." Rather, describe what you accomplished, such as "As Membership Chair, grew organization by 15 percent and increased member participation by 20 percent."

Be sure to post pictures and posts that support your experience. Photos of your organization in action, for example, document that what you say is true, and bring life to your profile.

And most importantly, don't be afraid to reach out. Liked a speaker in class? Find that person on LinkedIn and send an invitation, with a note saying how much you liked the presentation. Cat Knarr says that, while she was reluctant to reach out to one employer, not only did the person remember her but said he was looking for people like her and hired her.

Sources: Bernard Marr, "How to Create a Killer *LinkedIn* Profile That Will Get You Noticed, *LinkedIn*," June 19, 2017; Cat Knarr, "8 Secrets to Building a Stunning LinkedIn Profile," *Huffington Post*, April 5, 2014; Jeffrey Bailey, personal interview, November 8, 2012.

their people. Take advantage of that fact; ask for the help of such managers. Find out what they did to prepare themselves and what you should do.

Second, volunteer to take on special projects that will demonstrate your leadership and organizational abilities. Taking projects off the hands of your manager can also let you see the manager's responsibilities. Look for ways you can contribute to the overall sales team to show your commitment to the organization, your ability to lead and develop others, and your management skills.

In addition to improving your skills, many sales professionals also recommend building a personal brand—a professional reputation that is not only strong and positive but also widely recognized. Social media offer one outlet for building that brand, as discussed in Sales Technology 17.1.

MANAGING STRESS

Selling can be a stressful career. For example, with three days left in the month, Richard Langlotz, then a sales manager at Konica-Minolta but now a regional vice president, faced a sales team that lost $100,000 in business. One sale alone, worth $60,000, would have made the team's quota, but that account delayed its order for a few months. The other prospects decided to go with the competition. Suddenly it looked as though Langlotz was going to finish the month well below quota. To top it off, one of his salespeople quit. What did he do? "I took my sales team to a pizza place," Langlotz says. He thought about calling a meeting and getting tough with his team, but he realized they already had enough stress and didn't need any more from him. At the pizza parlor, without any prompting from him, each salesperson examined his or her prospect lists and determined how the team was going to move sales forecast for the next month into the current month. The team was successful, and Langlotz says he learned a valuable lesson. "When you have good people doing their best, they don't need more stress from their manager." Many salespeople liken sales to a roller-coaster ride, with great emotional highs when sales are good but emotional lows when sales are poor. Research shows that support from the sales manager, such as that offered by Langlotz, can go a long way to reduce stress among salespeople.[18]

For some people, coping with stress results in changing jobs. Changing jobs may be the right thing for some people to do. Others turn to less healthful releases, such as absenteeism, drugs, alcohol, and so forth.[19] All jobs have some stress; managing that stress is important to leading a happy and healthy life. However, managing stress does not always mean removing the cause of stress. Sometimes, as with the loss of a loved one, most people find they must manage stress because they cannot remove or change its cause. Two types of stress common to salespeople because of the unique nature of sales positions are situational stress and felt stress.

SITUATIONAL STRESS

Situational stress is short-term anxiety caused by a situational factor.[20] You may face situational stress when waiting to make a sales presentation for your class, for example. The best strategy to deal with situational stress is to leave the situation or remove the situational factor causing the stress, but that approach is not always possible. You cannot, for example, simply tell your instructor that you are too stressed to sell in class today, so you are leaving! One technique for managing situational stress is to imagine that the situational factor has been removed (see Exhibit 17.10 for more ideas). In class, imagine that you have already finished your role play. Mentally consider that feeling of relief you get when you know you have done a job well. Sometimes imaging success can reduce feelings of stress.

In sales, situational stress may be caused by impending presentations, deadlines for closing orders (as in Richard Langlotz's case), and similar situations. Situational stress can cause stage fright in even the most experienced salespeople. One

Exhibit 17.10
Coping with Situational Stress

Use imaging: Close your eyes and imagine yourself past the source of stress. Try to feel the actual sensation of what it will be like when the stress is gone.

Exercise: Exercise can moderate feelings of stress. When situational stress occurs over a period of time, set time aside for exercise breaks.

Take breaks: Take a walk, phone a friend, do something. If working on a stressful project, take regular stress breaks. Combine imaging techniques with breaks to increase the stress-reducing power of breaks.

Rest: In addition to breaks, be well rested when the situation arises. Research supports the need for a good night's sleep every night, not catching up on the weekend.

Prepare: If the situation involves future performance, prepare and practice. Prepare for every contingency, but don't let the tension build by thinking only of things going wrong.

Recover: Plan time for post-stress recovery before you charge into the next high-stress situation. Doing two major presentations in one day, for example, may not provide you with the recovery time you need to do well in the second presentation.

price of success is that situational stress will continue to occur, but successful salespeople learn to control their feelings of situational stress.

FELT STRESS

Felt stress lasts longer than situational stress because the causes are more enduring. **Felt stress** is psychological distress or anxiety brought about by job demands or constraints encountered in the work environment. For example, one study showed that when salespeople felt obliged to use coercive sales tactics, their levels of felt stress increased because they knew they were engaging in ethically questionable techniques.[21] Perhaps the most common form of felt stress is role stress, or feelings of stress caused by the salesperson's role.

Role stress is brought about by role conflict, role overload, and/or role ambiguity. **Role conflict** occurs when two partners demand incompatible actions of the salesperson. A common such occurrence is when the customer wants something that seems reasonable but the company won't allow it. Ted Howell represents a training company and was selling an e-learning training program. A customer wanted to see previous work, especially because he didn't like the demo version the company offered. Ted knew that the demo version didn't represent the client's solution, but his manager kept telling him that the demo should be sufficient. Ted's frustration level hit the boiling point in one call, to the point where his manager asked what was wrong. How do you tell your manager that he's the problem? Ted didn't, but he also gave the client another demo that was more in line with his needs. Seeing the right demo was all the client needed, and Ted got the sale.[22] Conflict occurred with the salesperson caught in the middle. **Role ambiguity** occurs when the salesperson is not sure what actions are required. The salesperson may not be sure what is expected, how to achieve it, or how performance will be evaluated and rewarded. **Role overload** is what happens when the role demands more than the person can perform. Asking a new salesperson to make the same types of presentations to high-level accounts that a veteran would make could cause role overload.

In general, the best way to handle role stress is to increase role accuracy (see Exhibit 17.11 for specific ideas). When the problem is role ambiguity, simply asking for further instruction or reviewing training materials may be helpful. Coaching and other management support can also be requested. Role conflict and role ambiguity require prioritizing activities. In the example of the salesperson who feels stress due to conflict between the customer's and the manager's demands, the salesperson must decide whose needs will be met. Once that decision is made, further stress can be avoided by refusing to dwell on the conflict. Note that the conflict is still there (both parties have conflicting demands), but the effect on the salesperson is minimized.

In either case a strong partnership with the sales manager can greatly aid in reducing stress. When a partnership is formed between a sales manager and a salesperson, the salesperson has a better understanding of the demands of the job, which activities should receive priority, and how the job should be performed. Partners also have access to more resources and more information, which can help remove some of the organizational constraints that can bring about stress.[23]

Exhibit 17.11

Reducing Role Stress

Prioritize: Set your own priorities so that when different people place conflicting expectations on you, your preset priorities determine where your actions will go.

Seek support: Enlist support of your priorities from your spouse, your manager, and other key people. By focusing on goals and priorities, you can reduce conflict over specific activities.

Reset expectations: By prioritizing and seeking support, you can reset expectations of various constituencies so that they are in harmony. Communicate and gain agreement on what you are capable of doing so that others' expectations of you are realistic.

Act and move on: Once you have made a decision to act, don't dwell on the conflict. Act and move on.

Strong sales skills can also reduce feelings of stress. Mastery of the job will reduce feelings of stress because the salesperson is in control of the situation.

SELLING YOURSELF

This entire chapter is about selling yourself throughout your career. Here we focus on some aspects specific to college students looking for a career.

College students may not realize the competition they face. That company is interviewing not only at your school, but also probably at three or four others. At each school it may talk to 15 students, or about 75 total, all for one position. In addition, recruiters get hundreds and sometimes thousand of résumés if they also post the job on the Internet. The key is to make yourself stand out and still be truthful.

Keeping the résumé simple is one way to get noticed. According to Eric Ruiz, CEO of SalesJobs.com, one mistake college students make is to put in too much detail. "All they want to know is if you can sell and what kind of numbers you've produced. For recent graduates, that's just a matter of putting the right spin on your part-time job at the local burger shack; instead of saying you 'worked the order window,' write that your shift had the highest sales numbers of any shift, or that you increased ice cream sales by 6 percent by suggesting a weekly 'buy one get one half-off' day."[24]

When responding to a posting on the Internet, don't just cut and paste your résumé into an online form. Special formatting may not come across properly when the recruiter looks at it online unless the file is saved as rich text. Similarly, don't use an uncommon software format that few recruiters may have. Your résumé may come across as dots, blocks, and zeroes.

Ruiz also suggests that you don't write a cover letter for each online posting. "Writing a cover letter does not help you in the sales industry. The people reading your résumé are HR professionals and sales recruiters; they're generally overworked, and find cover letters superfluous. Again, they're only interested in seeing hard data regarding what you've sold, whom you sold it to, and what numbers you produced. They are focused on your previous performance because being successful in sales requires such a specialized skill set," says Ruiz.

He suggests creating an individually tailored version of your résumé for each industry in which you're seeking employment, emphasizing knowledge and experience that would transfer to different industries. For example, if you're working in food and beverage sales but you want to get into medical equipment sales, write that you "have a large percentage of hospital accounts" and are "familiar with the purchasing staff at all the local hospitals" and that you've "sold to doctors before."

E-mail addresses like *myvixen* and *partystupid* may be fine in college but not when you're looking for a job. "E-mail addresses should be professional–first name, last name, and a number is fine," notes Ruiz. While Ruiz recognizes that many people apply for sales jobs, "It's the little things, like a follow-up e-mail address, that can help you get that dream job." Once you create a professional address, be sure to check it often, don't change it again (some companies report being unable to track down a good candidate), and don't let the mailbox fill up.

And clean up your Myspace and Facebook pages. Many companies regularly review these pages before making a hiring decision. Similarly, create a professional voice mail message. It's time to get professional!

SUMMARY

A sales career offers many opportunities for growth and personal development, but that career has to start somewhere. That is the purpose of the job search: to find a good match between what you need and have to offer and what a company needs and has to offer.

To achieve a match that results in mutual satisfaction, you must first understand who you are—specifically what you need and what you have to offer. You can ask yourself a number of questions to stimulate your thinking about the type of person you are and what you will need from a sales position. In addition, as you review your experiences in school, work, and other activities, you can identify the skills and characteristics that you have to offer.

Finding industries and companies with the characteristics you desire will require you to apply your marketing research skills. The library contains many sources of information that will help you. Personal sources can also be useful in providing information as well as leads for interviews, as can the Internet.

Sources for job interviews include the campus placement office, personal contacts, and advertisements. Résumés are personal brochures that help sell a candidate. Writing effective cover letters will help you get interviews off campus, while the interview itself is similar to a sales call. Plan questions that demonstrate your knowledge of and interest in the company. Also, plan to ask for information that will help you make your decision. Follow up after the interview to demonstrate your desire and perseverance.

You are the person in the company to whom your career means the most. Therefore, you must actively manage your own career. Set career goals that are compatible with family and personal objectives. Keeping the reasons for these career goals in front of you will enable you to make better decisions.

Learn the job you have now. You may someday manage people who have this job; the better you know it, the better you will be at managing it. To become a manager, you must first be a manager. Learn the manager's job as well and volunteer for activities and projects that will let you demonstrate your management ability.

Stress can occur in any job. Situational stress is short term, whereas felt stress is longer term. For many people, the key to managing stress is to reduce the influence of stressors because the causes of stress often cannot be eliminated.

Sales offers a challenging and exciting career. The opportunities are so varied that almost anyone can probably fit into some sales position. Even if you choose a career in another field, take advantage of the material in this chapter. You should find these job search and career management tips helpful in any field. Good luck!

KEY TERMS

application form 472
assessment center 473
conventional résumé 474
disguised interview 483
felt stress 491
functional résumé 475
greeter 483
group interview 484
interview 473
KSAs 486
panel interview 484
portfolio 482
references 473
role ambiguity 491
role conflict 491
role overload 491
role stress 491
situational stress 490
stress interview 484
tests 473

ETHICS PROBLEMS

1. You are interviewing for your dream job. Suddenly the interviewer notices your wedding ring and compliments you on it. But then he says, "You know, this job requires a lot of travel. What is your spouse going to say to that?" You answer the question, and he replies, "That's great, now, when you don't have kids. You don't have kids, do you? Because it is tough to be successful if you don't get the travel done." What do you do? What would you do if the interviewer said, "You know, handling conflict is an important part of this job. Describe a conflict you've had with your spouse and how you handled it."
2. Some people recommend signing up for as many interviews as possible, reasoning that the experience will be helpful when you find a company with a job you really want. (And who knows? You might find a job you like.) Is this practice ethical? Why or why not? If you answer that it depends, what does it depend on?

QUESTIONS AND PROBLEMS

1. What would you do differently if you were being interviewed by an amiable, a driver, an analytical, or an expressive? What about a panel interview with one driver and one amiable? One analytical and one expressive?
2. Reread the opening profile by Scott Thatcher. He didn't start out in sales. What was it about his jobs that led him to sales, and what is it about Scott that makes him successful? What is it about sales in general that gives someone like Scott a second chance for success? After all, he was not a stellar student.
3. Look at Exhibit 17.2. As the text says, this study is now about 20 years old, and it mentions another study. Rate yourself along those dimensions–which traits do you score high in? How would you prove that you have those traits? Based on the things you've learned about sales this semester, what are some behavioral patterns or behavioral characteristics that are also important for success in sales?
4. Looking at question 3 and reflecting on the opening profiles of all 17 chapters, which person do you think has a sales job you might want to do, and would do well? Why?
5. Some interviews are conducted over the phone or by videoconference. What do you think is important and different about these types of interviews compared to face-to-face interviews? Do you think these differences carry over into selling by phone versus videoconference versus in person?
6. Reread Building Partnerships 17.1. If a potential employer asked you today to describe your brand, what would it be? How do you make yourself memorable? What changes do you need to make to your social media presence to prepare for transitioning to a professional career and to build your personal brand?
7. Answer the questions in Exhibit 17.6 as you would in a sales job interview.
8. Your summer internship in a sales job was a bad experience. Your biggest complaint was that the sales manager seemed incompetent. Despite this negative experience, you like sales, so you are interviewing for a sales position. What would you say if asked why you do not seek full-time employment with the summer internship firm?
9. One recruiter called a professor to check on a student that the professor referred. The recruiter said, "You gave this student my name last Wednesday and now it is Tuesday. Does this delay signal a lack of interest?" How would you answer that if the recruiter was asking you the question and you were the student? Why would a recruiter comment on the time it took to call? (Note that this is based on an actual situation.)

10. You are in an interview, and you think this is your dream job. How would you secure commitment? What would you say different in the first interview if it is a screening interview on campus versus the fourth interview at company headquarters? Is securing commitment more or less important for sales positions than for other types of positions?

11. Most students who take this class are juniors or seniors. What things about school stress you out now? How do you deal with stress–both in healthy and maybe unhealthy ways? What would you say to a high school senior about to enter college to help manage stress in college?

CASE PROBLEMS

case 17.1

Sales Competition Time

On Monday, Dr. Zuber announced the Eastern Seaboard Sales Slam in class. "This competition has four sales programs in it, including us, and there will be five students competing from each school. Sponsors include Fastenal, ESI, State Farm, Cardinal Health, and Smithfield Foods. Each sponsor will have people there to recruit salespeople from the competitors; in fact, last year, all of our team members got job offers from the sponsors. The competition this year is in Norfolk, Virginia, at Old Dominion University. If you have an interest in competing, we have an organizational meeting this afternoon at four."

As they left the classroom, Jasmine said, "Is anyone going to try for the sales competition?"

Shelby replied, "Not me. I don't think I could do sales." "I don't think I could either go cold calling or try to call people on the phone I don't know and try to sell them something."

Jasmine said, "Yeah, but you're great at recruiting people into PSE." PSE is the student sales club on campus.

"That's different. People should belong," Shelby continued, "It's a great way to learn about jobs in marketing and sales."

"I think I'll compete, or at least check it out," replied Bill. "I just don't know what I want to sell. It has to be something I believe in." Murmurs of agreement followed. "And I want to have something different every day–I don't think I could sit behind a desk with the same old routine."

"I like the money," said Emily. "The opportunity to run it like your own business. I think I'd like that a lot. I'm definitely going to compete."

Dylan shook his head. "I don't know. I think I'd like to start in sales anyway. Maybe something where they come to me or I see the same people. I'm good with people once I get to know them. But the thought of a competition scares me."

"I've heard that a lot of companies start you out on the phones first," Roger noted. "Like IBM. You start out on the phones, and if you're good, then you get to go out into the field."

Questions

1. What kinds of jobs would Bill be suited for? Emily? Can Shelby's fears be overcome, or should she find a job that doesn't involve cold calling?
2. Using the Web, review the sponsors and see what their entry sales positions are like. Find a position for each student to apply for; you may have to look beyond the sponsors. Print the posting or listing and then on the same sheet (write on the back if you need to) justify your choice.
3. Pick one of the six positions you used in question 2 for yourself. Why is that a good fit for you? What makes you a good fit for the job?

case 17.2

Addie Spencer's Interview

At 8:45 a.m., Addie Spencer arrived at her campus placement center for a 9:00 interview. She was surprised to be greeted by Derrick Trujillo, whom she had known in a marketing class. This conversation followed:

DERRICK: Addie, good to see you! I see that you are interviewing with us today. [*shakes her hand and offers her a chair in the lobby*]

ADDIE: Derrick! Hi, how are you? I didn't know you were with HealthSouth. I've got the 9:00 spot.

DERRICK: Great! I started with HealthSouth right after graduation, and it has been a great six months. Tell me, are you interviewing with many medical firms or just with HealthSouth?

ADDIE: I'm very interested in pharmaceuticals, but I know that HealthSouth is doing real well. So I thought that I should consider all medical companies. One of the physicians at a sports medicine center recommended HealthSouth. She said that your company does a lot of the rehabilitation services for the NFL as well as here at the university.

DERRICK: That's right, we do! I'm glad to hear that others agree we are one of the best. [*leans a little closer*] Look, just relax in the interview. HealthSouth really likes to get people from State, and I'm sure you will do well. [*looks up at the entrance of an older woman*] Oh, here's Lauren Smith, my sales manager. She'll be interviewing you today. Lauren, here's an old friend of mine, Addie Spencer.

LAUREN: [*stepping forward and offering her hand*]: Addie, it's nice to meet you. Addie, that's a nice name.

ADDIE: [*shaking her hand firmly*]: It's short for Adelaide–my parents are Australian. It's nice to meet you, too, Ms. Smith. [*turning to Derrick*] Derrick, it was good to see you again. Perhaps we'll talk some more later. [*Addie and Lauren seat themselves in the interviewing room; Lauren has her Surface open with a small keyboard*]

LAUREN: Tell me about yourself, Addie.

ADDIE: I'm the oldest of three children, and we were raised in a small town in the eastern part of the state. As a kid, I was very interested in soccer and wanted to be an Olympic soccer player. But an ankle injury ended my soccer career. Still, I learned a lot about self-discipline and the importance of hard work to achieve success, and I am still involved in soccer as a coach for a youth team. In fact, I rehabbed my ankle at a HealthSouth center. Anyway, I chose State because it offers a strong marketing program. Marketing, and sales especially, seems to me to be a place where your success is directly related to your efforts. And I believe that more strongly now that I have taken the sales class here at State.

LAUREN [*types*]: I see. [*momentary silence as she finishes the notes, then looks up*] Tell me about a time when you were the leader of a group and things were not going your way. Perhaps it looked as if the group wasn't going to meet your objectives. What did you do?

ADDIE: Let's see. There was the time when we were working on a group project for my marketing research class. Understand, though, that we had not elected a formal leader or anything. But no one in the group really wanted to do the project; everyone thought that research was boring. So at a group meeting, I suggested we talk about what we liked to do in marketing. After all, we were all marketing majors. Each person talked about why he or she had chosen marketing. Then I framed the project around what they wanted out of marketing. When they looked at it as a marketing project instead of a research project, it became something they wanted to do.

LAUREN: Did you get an A?

ADDIE: No, we got a B+. But more important, we were the only group that had fun, and I think we learned more as a result.

LAUREN: I see. [*momentary silence as she types*] Tell me about your sales class–have you had any opportunity to use what you learned, and, if so, how'd you do?

ADDIE: You mean other than this interview? [*Lauren smiles*] I found that I use the questioning skills to learn about potential sorority members. These skills really helped me understand what they wanted in a sorority and whether we were a good fit. And the presentation skills I use with every in-class presentation, but I've not had a sales job, if that's what you mean.

The interview went on for nearly 30 minutes. Addie thought she had done fairly well. She stopped in the lobby to write down her impressions and record Lauren's answers to questions about the company. She smiled at Derrick, who was talking to another applicant.

Questions

1. What did Addie do right? Why was that right? What did she do wrong? Why was that wrong?
2. What was Derrick's purpose at the interview? What do you think Derrick could tell Lauren about Addie?
3. HealthSouth is a publicly traded company. What sources of information could Addie use to learn about the company? What information should she expect to get from those sources?

ROLE PLAY CASE

Congratulations, you just got promoted! Now you have to replace yourself by hiring a college graduate to take over your sales territory. Given everything you've learned about Gartner this semester and what you know about sales, take a few minutes to identify the three most important features a salesperson should bring to the job and the questions you'd ask to determine if the candidate had those features. Then take turns interviewing each other in your group. There is no candidate information to be provided–each student will portray himself or herself when playing the candidate role.

ADDITIONAL REFERENCES

Bande, Belén, Pilar Fernández-Ferrín, José A. Varela, and Fernando Jaramillo. "Emotions and Salesperson Propensity to Leave: The Effects of Emotional Intelligence and Resilience." *Industrial Marketing Management* 44 (January 2015), pp. 142–49.

Bush, Victoria, Alan J. Bush, Jared Oakley, and John E. Cicala. "The Sales Profession as Subculture: Implications for Ethical Decision Making." *Journal of Business Ethics* 142, no. 3 (May 2017), pp. 549–65.

Chan, Tat Y., Jia Li, and Lamar Pierce. "Compensation and Peer Effects in Competing Sales Teams." *Management Science* 60, no. 8 (August 2014), pp. 1965–84.

Chatterjee, Sayan, Venkat Narayanan, and William Malek. "How Strategy Execution Maps Guided Cisco System's Sales Incentive Compensation Plan." *Strategy & Leadership* 44, no. 6 (2016), pp. 25–34.

Cooper, Brett, and Mary Kate Naatus. "LinkedIn as a Learning Tool in Business Education." *American Journal of Business Education* 7, no. 4 (2014), pp. 299–311.

Decarlo, Thomas E., and Son K. Lam. "Identifying Effective Hunters and Farmers in the Salesforce: A Dispositional-Situational Framework." *Journal of theAcademy of Marketing Science* 44, no. 4 (July 2016), pp. 415–39.

DeCarlo, Thomas, Tirthankar Roy, and Michael Barone. "How Sales Manager Experience and Historical Data Trends Affect Decision Making." *European Journal of Marketing* 49. no. 9/10 (2015), pp. 1484–1504.

Gammoh, Bashar S., Michael L. Mallin, and Ellen Bolman Pullins. "The Impact of Salesperson-Brand Personality Congruence on Salesperson Brand Identification, Motivation and Performance Outcomes." *Journal of Product and Brand Management* 23, no. 7 (2014), pp. 543–53.

Gopalakrishna, Srinath, Jason Garrett, Murali K Mantrala, and Shrihari Sridhar. "Assessing Sales Contest Effectiveness: The Role of Salesperson and Sales District Characteristics." *Marketing Letters* 27, no. 3 (September 2016), pp. 589–602.

Guenzi, Paolo, and Federico Panzeri. "How Salespeople See Organizational Citizenship Behaviors: An Exploratory Study Using the Laddering Technique." *Journal of Business and Industrial Marketing* 30, no. 2 (2015), pp. 218–32.

Locander, David A., Frankie J. Weinberg, Jay P. Mulki, and William B. Locander. "Salesperson Lone Wolf Tendencies: The Roles of Social Comparisons and Mentoring in a Mediated Model of Performance." *Journal of Marketing Theory and Practice* 23, no. 4 (Fall 2015), pp. 351–69.

Madhani, Pankaj M. "Managing Sales Compensation: Career Life Cycle Approach." *SCMS Journal of Indian Management* 11, no. 3 (July–September 2014), pp. 5–15.

Mani, Sudha, Prabakar Kothandaraman, Rajiv Kashyap, and Bahar Ashnai. "Sales Role-Plays and Mock Interviews: An Investigation of Student Performance in Sales Competitions." *Journal of Marketing Education* 38, no. 3 (December 2016), pp. 183–98.

Mich, Claudia C., Susan E. Conners, and Lori Feldman. "The Impact of Experiential Learning on Student Perceptions of a Career in Sales." *Academy of Marketing Studies Journal* 18, no. 2 (2014), pp. 1–17.

Zide, Julie, Ben Elman, and Comila Shahani-Denning. "LinkedIn and Recruitment: How Profiles Differ across Occupations." *Employee Relations* 36, no. 5 (2014), pp. 583–604.

ROLE PLAY CASE 1

Instructor: See our book's Web site for buyer scenarios for this case.

PURINA ONE SMARTBLEND DOG FOOD[1]

For over 80 years, Purina has been making high-quality pet food, and has championed pet welfare. Purina works to help create safe havens for domestic violence survivors and their pets. Purina also treats its employees well, as evidenced by Purina being ranked number 3 on the Best Places to Work.

Purina is committed to offering the best dog food in the world. "We were the first brand in grocery and mass retail stores to offer pet food with real meat, poultry, or fish as the #1 ingredient, starting in 1987. We have continued as a leader through our development of targeted nutrition. Our team of more than 400 Purina researchers around the globe is dedicated to providing best-in-class nutrition for your pet," says Dan Chausow, of Purina Global Nutrition.[2] One of the highest-quality brands that Purina sells is its Purina ONE SmartBlend brand.

Some features of ONE SmartBlend brand include:

- Real meat, fish, or poultry is ALWAYS the number 1 ingredient
- Shredded meaty morsels (U.S. patent pending)
- Breakthrough use of botanical oils in senior formula
- Over 85 years of innovation in pet nutrition
- Only manufactured in company-owned facilities
- No added artificial flavors or preservatives

Current users overwhelmingly like the product, with over 93 percent indicating they would recommend Purina ONE to other dog owners.

Purina ONE SmartBlend comes in a variety of formulas (see its Web site for the most up-to-date list of products and prices, and information on each type):

- True Instinct Formula
  - With Real Turkey & Venison Dog Food
  - With Real Salmon & Tuna Dog Food
  - Grain-Free Formula With Real Chicken & Sweet Potato Dog Food
  - Grain-Free Formula With Beef & Sweet Potato Dog Food
- Puppy
  - Healthy Puppy Formula Premium Dog Food
  - Large Breed Puppy Formula Premium Dog Food
- Adult Premium
  - Lamb & Rice Formula Adult Premium Dog Food
  - Chicken & Rice Formula Adult Premium Dog Food
  - Small Bites Beef & Rice Formula Adult Premium Dog Food
  - Large Breed Adult Formula Premium Dog Food
  - Sensitive Systems Formula Adult Premium Dog Food
  - Healthy Weight Formula Adult Premium Dog Food
- Vibrant Maturity® 7+ Senior Formula Premium Dog Food

While prices can vary, we will assume these are the suggested retail prices, based on size of the bag:

Product	Size	Suggested Retail Price
True Instinct Formula (all varieties)	Small	$19.99
	Large	$29.99
Puppy (all varieties)	Small	$22.16
	Large	$34.18
Adult Premium (all varieties)	Small	$21.99
	Large	$33.59
Vibrant Maturity Senior Premium	Small	$22.00
	Large	$35.00

Purina offers the following noncumulative quantity discounts for resellers (the total number of bags can be based on mixed items; thus a reseller that buys 10 bags of True Instinct Formula With Real Turkey & Venison Dog Food and 31 bags of Large Breed Puppy Formula Premium Dog Food would get the 25 percent discount because it purchased 41 bags total in that single order):

Quantity Purchased	Discount Off Suggested Retail Price
Fewer than 40 bags	15 percent off
41-100 bags	25 percent off
Over 100 bags	40 percent off

Purina also offers a number of promotions for resellers. Resellers that set up an end-of-aisle display of at least 30 bags of a mix of sizes and flavors earn an extra 50 cents per bag discount on all bags purchased. For resellers that advertise Purina's products in the newspaper, there is a 50 percent co-op payment for the actual portion of the page cost of the advertisement. Thus if a grocery store runs a newspaper ad that includes one-eighth of a page for Purina's products, Purina will reimburse the grocery store for 50 percent of the cost of the ad.

There are a number of competitors in the premium dog food market that compete directly against the Purina ONE SmartBlend products, including IAMS ProActive Health and Rachael Ray Nutrish. There are also other premium dog foods such as Natural Balance, Canidae, and Premium Edge. Plus there are many private-label dog foods and other brands (ALPO, Wellness, Hills) that sometimes compete for the same customers. Even Purina Dog Chow, Purina's most popular brand, could perhaps be considered a competitor.

Sources: www.purinaone.com/dogs/why-switch, www.purinaone.com/dogs/products/dry-dog-food,

Situation 1: Animal Haven

Animal Haven, located in downtown New York City, is a nonprofit organization that finds homes for abandoned cats and dogs. When needed, and to improve the chances of adoption, Animal Haven also provides behavior intervention. Founded in 1967, it also provides a variety of programs that strengthen the bond between animals and people. For example, it hosts a Caring Kids program, which introduces children to basic animal care and animal welfare. Animal Haven has 10 full-time employees, with 4 part timers, plus many volunteers.

Fees charged for adoption range from $175 for a cat, to $375 for a puppy. The fee covers spay/neuter, vaccines, and a microchip. Animal Haven will not accept pets from people who want to relinquish their pet, nor will it accept animals that have a history of biting or aggression. Animal Haven will never euthanize for space or time. Animals that are adoptable can stay at Animal Haven for as long as it takes to get them adopted or placed in a more suitable rescue or foster situation. At any one time, Animal Haven has about 50 dogs that are ready to be adopted. (Source: www.animalhavenshelter.org.)

You are a salesperson for Purina. You are calling on the senior buyer at Animal Haven. You do not know what brand of dog food the shelter is currently using. Your goal is to sell at least 20 bags of assorted varieties of Purina ONE SmartBlend dog food.

Situation 2: PetSmart—Corporate Headquarters (Resell Situation)

PetSmart, Inc. is the largest specialty pet retailer with approximately 1,500 pet stores in the United States, Canada, and Puerto Rico and approximately 204 in-store PetSmart® PetsHotel® dog and cat boarding facilities. PetSmart has over 55,000 employees. The company offers a wide selection of competitively priced pet food and pet products and offers dog training, pet grooming, pet boarding, PetSmart Doggie Day Camp day care services, and pet adoption services in-store. (Source: www.PetSmart.com.)

You are a salesperson for Purina. You are calling on a corporate headquarters food buyer of PetSmart. Assume PetSmart has not carried Purina's ONE SmartBlend of dog foods in the past. Your goal is to have PetSmart's corporate headquarters approve the offering of at least some Purina ONE SmartBlend dog food in its stores and stock them in PetSmart's distribution warehouses. Assume the final decisions about which products will be offered in individual stores are up to the local store managers.

Situation 3: PetSmart—Local Store (Resell Situation)

PetSmart, Inc. is the largest specialty pet retailer with approximately 1,500 pet stores in the United States, Canada, and Puerto Rico and approximately 204 in-store PetSmart® PetsHotel® dog and cat boarding facilities. PetSmart has over 55,000 employees. The company offers a wide selection of competitively priced pet food and pet products and offers dog training, pet grooming, pet boarding, PetSmart Doggie Day Camp day care services, and pet adoption services in-store. (Source: www.PetSmart.com.)

You are a salesperson for Purina. You are calling on the grocery manager of a local PetSmart. Assume that PetSmart's corporate headquarters has approved the offering of Purina ONE SmartBlend dog food products and that PetSmart carries them in its distribution centers. However, this PetSmart has never carried Purina ONE SmartBlend dog food products in the past. Your goal is to have this store manager approve the offering of at least some products in her or his store. *Note:* If the store manager agrees to offer Purina ONE SmartBlend dog food, he or she will simply order the products from the PetSmart distribution center.

Situation 4: Kroger–Corporate Headquarters (Resell Situation)

Founded in 1883, Kroger is one of the largest retail stores in the world. Kroger operates 2,796 grocery retail stores in 35 states under nearly two dozen store names. The formats include supermarkets (including Kroger, Ralphs, Dillons, Smith's, King Soopers, Fry's, QFC, City Market, Owen's, Jay C, Pay Less, Baker's, Gerbes, Harris Teeter, Pick N' Save, Copps, Metro Market, and Mariano's), price-impact warehouse stores, and multi-department stores, which are similar to supercenters but offer an expanded variety of national brand apparel and general merchandise. Kroger is the only major U.S. supermarket company to operate its own three-tier distribution system. It also operates 38 food production/manufacturing facilities producing high-quality private-label products that provide special value for customers. (Source: www.kroger.com.)

You are a salesperson for Purina. You are calling on a corporate headquarters pet food buyer of Kroger. Assume Kroger has not carried Purina's ONE SmartBlend dog food in the past. Your goal is to have Kroger's corporate headquarters approve the offering of at least some Purina ONE SmartBlend dog food in its stores and stock them in Kroger's distribution warehouses. Assume the final decisions about which products will be offered in individual stores are up to the local store managers.

Situation 5: Kroger–Local Supermarket (Resell Situation)

Founded in 1883, Kroger is one of the largest retail stores in the world. Kroger operates 2,796 grocery retail stores in 35 states under nearly two dozen store names. The formats include supermarkets (including Kroger, Ralphs, Dillons, Smith's, King Soopers, Fry's, QFC, City Market, Owen's, Jay C, Pay Less, Baker's, Gerbes, Harris Teeter, Pick N' Save, Copps, Metro Market, and Mariano's), price-impact warehouse stores, and multi-department stores, which are similar to supercenters but offer an expanded variety of national brand apparel and general merchandise. Kroger is the only major U.S. supermarket company to operate its own three-tier distribution system. It also operates 38 food production/manufacturing facilities producing high-quality private-label products that provide special value for customers. (Source: www.kroger.com.)

You are a salesperson for Purina. You are calling on the grocery manager of a local Kroger. Assume that Kroger's corporate headquarters has approved the offering of Purina ONE SmartBlend dog food products and that Kroger carries them in its distribution centers. However, this Kroger has never carried Purina ONE SmartBlend dog food products in the past. Your goal is to have this store manager approve the offering of at least some products in her or his store. *Note:* If the store manager agrees to offer Purina ONE SmartBlend dog food, he or she will simply order the products from the Kroger distribution center.

Situation 6: Lowe's–Corporate Headquarters (Resell Situation)

Lowe's is an American retailer of home improvement and construction products and services. It operates over 2300 stores in the United States, Canada, and Mexico and has more than 17 million customers a week. Its more than 280,000 employees sell 13 product categories ranging from appliances and tools to paint, lumber, and nursery products. It also carries a limited assortment of food and pet food. (Source: www.lowes.com.)

You are a salesperson for Purina. You are calling on a corporate headquarters grocery and pet food buyer of Lowe's. Assume Lowe's has not carried Purina's ONE SmartBlend of dog foods in the past. Your goal is to have Lowe's corporate headquarters approve the offering of at least some Purina ONE SmartBlend dog food in its stores and stock them in Lowe's distribution warehouses. Assume the final decisions about which products will be offered in individual stores are up to the local store managers.

Situation 7: Lowe's–Individual Store (Resell Situation)

Lowe's is an American retailer of home improvement and construction products and services. It operates over 2300 stores in the United States, Canada, and

Mexico and has more than 17 million customers a week. Its more than 280,000 employees sell 13 product categories ranging from appliances and tools to paint, lumber, and nursery products. It also carries a limited assortment of food and pet food. (Source: www.lowes.com.)

You are a salesperson for Purina. You are calling on the outdoors department manager of a local Lowe's. Assume that Lowe's corporate headquarters has approved the offering of Purina ONE SmartBlend dog food products and that Lowe's carries them in its distribution centers. However, this Lowe's has never carried Purina ONE SmartBlend dog food products in the past. Your goal is to have this manager approve the offering of at least some products in her or his store. *Note:* If the store manager agrees to offer Purina ONE Smart Blend dog food, he or she will simply order the products from the Lowe's distribution center.

Situation 8: Camp Bow Wow (Franchise Headquarters)

Camp Bow Wow is "North America's largest and fastest growing pet care franchise and premier provider of fun, safe and individualized care." Today there are over 160 facilities across the United States. Some locations also offer in-home pet care and dog training services. The camps offer a number of benefits for the dogs: provides regular exercise to maintain a healthy weight; relieves boredom, separation anxiety, and destructive behavior at home; improves socialization with dogs and people; and enhances quality of life for the dog. Owners can rest assured their dog is in good hands:

- All Camp Counselors are extensively trained in dog behavior, pet first aid, and CPR.
- Each Camper is required to pass a socialization interview, be spayed or neutered, and be current on vaccinations.
- Live webcams are provided to check in on your dog from anywhere using a computer or mobile device.
- Facilities are monitored 24 hours a day, 7 days a week.

(Source: www.Campbowwow.com.)

You are a salesperson for Purina. You are calling on the food and nutrition specialist at the corporate headquarters of Camp Bow Wow. Assume the camp has never purchased your products before. Your goal is to have this specialist highly recommend Purina ONE SmartBlend dog food to franchise owners. *Note:* If the specialist agrees to recommend Purina ONE SmartBlend dog food, the individual franchise owners would purchase the product directly from Purina. Corporate headquarters does not warehouse or carry any food products.

Situation 9: Camp Bow Wow (Local Franchise Owner)

Camp Bow Wow is "North America's largest and fastest growing pet care franchise and premier provider of fun, safe and individualized care." Today there are over 160 facilities across the United States. Some locations also offer in-home pet care and dog training services. The camps offer a number of benefits for the dogs: provides regular exercise to maintain a healthy weight; relieves boredom, separation anxiety, and destructive behavior at home; improves socialization with dogs and people; and enhances quality of life for the dog. Owners can rest assured their dog is in good hands:

- All Camp Counselors are extensively trained in dog behavior, pet first aid, and CPR.
- Each Camper is required to pass a socialization interview, be spayed or neutered, and be current on vaccinations.
- Live webcams are provided to check in on your dog from anywhere using a computer or mobile device.
- Facilities are monitored 24 hours a day, 7 days a week.

(Source: www.Campbowwow.com.)

You are a salesperson for Purina. You are calling on a local franchise owner of a franchised Camp Bow Wow. Assume this camp has never purchased your products before. Your goal is to have this owner purchase at least twenty bags of Purina ONE SmartBlend dog food. *Note:* Corporate headquarters of Camp Bow Wow recommends Purina ONE SmartBlend dog food, but it is up to the individual franchise owners to make their own decisions. Any products purchased would be shipped from Purina's warehouses.

Situation 10: Dog Training Camp USA (DTC)

Dog Training Camp USA (DTC) is a group of dog training facilities located in the Raleigh/Durham/Chapel Hill, North Carolina, area. DTC is a member of the Association of Professional Dog Trainers, and strives to help dogs in the following areas: basic obedience; home manners; public manners; and aggression, anxiety, etc. Training can be specialized in the areas of social outings, trail walking, and search and rescue. DTC also offers private training in the dog's home, as well as workshops to help dog owners find more enjoyment with their pets. (Source: www.dogtrainingcampusa.com.)

You are a salesperson for Purina. You are calling on the senior buyer of DTC. Assume this camp has never purchased your products before. Your goal is to have this senior buyer purchase at least 20 bags of Purina ONE SmartBlend dog food. The dog food would be used while the dogs are in daily training. The trainers could also recommend the dog food when doing in-home training.

ROLE PLAY CASE 2

GARTNER

Gartner is a research and consultancy company. The company helps business leaders across all major functions in every industry and enterprise size with the objective insights they need to make the right decisions. Gartner's comprehensive suite of services delivers strategic advice and proven best practices to help clients succeed in their mission-critical priorities.

The typical Gartner buyer is the chief information officer (CIO), the person responsible for managing IT. Gartner clients use Gartner's services to help develop IT strategies, select IT products, implement IT solutions, and develop IT personnel. For example, Gartner has tools that help CIOs see how their budget stacks up against others in the same industry, which can aid in determining if they are overspending in some areas and underspending in others.

While Gartner services are actually quite complex and customized, these role plays will simplify things somewhat. The pricing is standardized at $50,000 for year 1 of a three-year contract, with an escalation to $51,500 and $53,100 in years 2 and 3. *Note:* This pricing is for role play purposes only and not reflective of actual pricing.

Three services are included in this fee. The first is access to Garner's research, supported by over 1,200 analysts covering 1,372 technology and business topics. This research ranges from reports on technology products and services (such as objective views regarding what products actually do and how well they work) to trends in IT spending. Think of it this way: If you invested heavily in videotapes, you'd own a lot of technology that is now obsolete. CIOs rely on Gartner to avoid such mistakes. In addition, Gartner's research can also help prevent companies from overspending, buying solutions that they really don't need.

The second is access to Gartner's cost optimization tool. This tool is an online assessment of the IT budget. The client enters the company's budget data (takes from 20 minutes to an hour or so) and gets back a standard comparison to similar companies of the same size and industry. Customized comparisons to specific peer groups can be purchased for an extra fee.

The third is access to a Gartner executive partner, an IT professional with years of experience who can help the CIO grow professionally. Note that more information on this service and the other two services is available on the Web site of the National Collegiate Sales Competition (NCSC). Students are encouraged to visit the NCSC site for more details.

In these scenarios, the companies are small to medium sized. Typically, overall corporate objectives are to grow revenue, reduce costs, and/or improve efficiency. How these objectives affect individual CIOs will vary depending on the importance of IT to the company's strategy.

Buyer Situations

TACTICAL GEAR Tactical Gear is a distributor and manufacturer of equipment and clothing used by the U.S. military and state and local first responders. The company is just over 10 years old, and what began as a side business for a young entrepreneur who was running a scuba diving shop selling equipment to Navy divers has grown to a $1.2 billion business with offices in San Diego and Virginia Beach (the two largest U.S. Navy locations). You met the CIO at an IT job fair and had a brief conversation, where you were told that the company has big growth plans, so you set up today's meeting.

PREMIERE MANUFACTURING Premiere is a maker of precision tools used in advanced manufacturing. From what you were able to glean from its Web site, the company is run by the second generation of the Torgerson family. You made an appointment with the CIO based on a referral from Community Bank & Trust's CIO, one of your clients, who mentioned that it could use some help but you don't really know much more than that.

THE 48 GROUP This company manufactures and distributes custom-designed packaging for the food industry, as well as other products made of plastic or paper (such as napkins and forks, but also products used when cooking food). You were calling on another client and had some time to kill so you decided to stop in and see if you could set up an appointment with the CIO. To your surprise, the CIO actually had time to see you now.

BANCMARK Today, you are calling on the information technology manager for BancMark, a national marketing consultancy that specializes in serving community banks. These are banks with fewer than 10 branches. You read a press release about the company, called, and got the appointment. On the phone call, you learned that BancMark manages marketing services for about 150 community banks, including Web site design and e-mail marketing. It also provides sales training for loan officers, although the banks prefer to use the term *business development* instead of *sales*, and it sells several personality profile tests to companies for use in selecting new loan officers as well as other sales consulting services. BancMark was named one of the fastest-growing companies in your area.

PORT GROUP Today, you are calling on the CIO of Port Group, a company with offices in New York, London, San Francisco, and your city. The company is a commercial real estate owner, property manager, and lender. Each year, the company creates an investment fund for qualified investors and then uses that to acquire commercial, industrial, or multi-family real estate, or to loan to others who want to buy real estate. The company owns just over 200 properties.

JAMES MANUFACTURING This company manufactures custom metal components that other companies design into their own products. Examples include the case used to make the milkshake machines used at McDonald's restaurants and the metal frames used in making airplane seating. The company serves a three-state area. It was just taken over by the third generation of the James family, and the new president wants to grow the business aggressively. You learned about the aggressive growth plans when reading a feature on the company, so you called the CIO and made an appointment, saying that you could help the business grow.

FUTURIS DESIGN Today, you are calling on the CIO of Futuris Design, who happens to be the older sibling of one of your college classmates. Futuris Design makes commercial display systems used in showrooms and trade shows. There are approximately 50 projects that are "live" at any particular time. These projects generally last between two weeks and three months, with shorter projects being trade show booth designs and longer projects going into commercial showrooms. The projects require several meetings with clients, suppliers, and sometimes municipal building inspectors. The president wishes to increase the number of projects that the company can handle without additional personnel. You met the president at a charity golf tournament about three weeks ago, who then introduced you to the CIO.

MORTAR Today, you are calling on the CIO of Mortar, an industrial services company. Jokingly, the company says it does everything, even mow the grass, but that's not far off. Mortar was your client until two years ago, when a new CIO came in and cancelled the contract. You saw in *Inside Business* that Mortar now has a new CIO, so you made an appointment. What you remember from when it was your client was how difficult its market is. Competition is stiff, and finding ways to be innovative to be worth premium prices is hard.

FINANCIAL RECOVERY ASSETS (FRA) Today, you are calling on the CIO for Financial Recovery Assets (FRA), a debt collection company with about 200 employees. The CIO called you after being told of your services by a friend. FRA enjoyed great growth for the first four years of existence, but growth has stalled recently. The economy has been good, so bad debt portfolios are harder to come by.

AVIDYNE AviDyne is a communications engineering company that manufactures custom communications systems for use in global shipping. Essentially, the company takes a ship and rebuilds the communications systems, as it specializes in refurbishing ships. The communications systems include onboard communications as well as ship-to-shore. The buyer has about 50 engineers employed. You met the CIO at a trade show in Brussels about two months ago and scheduled an appointment to discuss your product.

GLOSSARY

ABC analysis Evaluating the importance of an account. The most important is an A account, the second most important is a B account, and the least important is a C account.

accommodating mode Resolving conflict by being unassertive and highly cooperative. When using this approach, people often neglect their own needs and desires to satisfy the concerns of the other party.

account opportunity Another term for the sales potential dimensions of the *sales call allocation grid.*

account share See *customer share.*

acknowledge method Responding to an objection by letting the buyer talk, acknowledging that you heard the concern, and then moving on to another topic without trying to resolve the concern. Also called the *pass-up method.*

active listening Process in which the listener attempts to draw out as much information as possible by actively processing information received and stimulating the communication of additional information.

activity goals Behavioral objectives, such as the number of calls made in a day.

activity quota A type of quota that sets minimal behavioral expectations for a salesperson's activities. Used when the sales cycle is long and sales are few. Controls activities of salespeople.

adaptive planning The development of alternative paths to the same goal in a negotiation session.

adaptive selling Approach to personal selling in which selling behaviors and approaches are altered during a sales interaction or across customer interactions, based on information about the nature of the selling situation.

administrative law Law established by local, state, or federal regulatory agencies, such as the Federal Trade Commission or the Food and Drug Administration.

advantages Reasons why a feature would be important to someone.

agenda List of what will be discussed, and in what sequence, in a negotiation session.

agent Person who acts in place of his or her company. See also *manufacturers' agents.*

aggressive Sales style that controls the sales interaction but often does not gain commitment because it ignores the customer's needs and fails to probe for information.

always a share A buyer who will always allocate only a share to each vendor, never giving one vendor all of the business. See also *lost for good.*

ambush negotiating A win–lose tactic used by a buyer at the beginning of, or prior to, negotiations when the seller does not expect this approach. Also called *sneak attack.*

amiable Category in the social style matrix; describes people who like cooperation and close relationships. Amiables are low on assertiveness and high on responsiveness.

analogy Drawing a parallel between one thing and another.

analysis paralysis When a salesperson prefers to spend practically all his or her time analyzing the situation and gathering information instead of making sales calls.

analytical Category in the social style matrix; describes people who emphasize facts and logic. Analyticals are low on assertiveness and responsiveness.

annual spend The amount that is spent with each vendor and for what products.

application form Preprinted form completed by a job applicant.

articulation The production of recognizable speech.

assertive Sales manner that stresses responding to customer needs while being self-confident and positive.

assertiveness Dimension of the social style matrix that assesses the degree to which people have opinions on issues and publicly make their positions clear to others.

assessment center Central location for evaluating job candidates.

attitudinal loyalty An emotional attachment to a brand, company, or salesperson.

automatic replenishment (AR) A form of just-in-time inventory management where the vendor manages the customer's inventory, and automatically ships and stocks products at the customer's location based on mutually agreed-upon standards.

avoiding mode Resolving conflict in an unassertive and uncooperative manner. In this mode people make no attempt to resolve their own needs or the needs of others.

awareness The first phase in the development of a buyer-seller relationship, in which salespeople locate and qualify prospects and buyers consider various sources of supply.

backdoor selling Actions by one salesperson that go behind the back of a purchaser to directly contact other members of the buying center.

balance sheet method Attempts to obtain commitment by asking the buyer to think of the pros and cons of the various alternatives; often referred to as the *Ben Franklin method*.

balanced presentation Occurs when the salesperson shows all sides of the situation—that is, is totally honest.

barriers Buyer's subordinates who plan and schedule interviews for their superiors; also called *screens*.

behavioral loyalty The purchase of the same product from the same vendor over time.

benchmarking A process of comparing your activities and performance with those of the best organization or individual in order to improve.

benefit How a particular feature will help a particular buyer.

benefit opening Approach in which the salesperson focuses on the prospect's needs by stating a benefit of the product or service.

benefit summary method Obtaining commitment by simply reminding the prospect of the agreed-on benefits of the proposal.

best alternative to a negotiated agreement (BATNA) What will be the result if you don't come to negotiation agreement. This is a standard or guide against which to evaluate the agreement you are trying to achieve. Also called the *consequences of no agreement (CNA)*.

bird dog Individual who, for a fee, will provide the names of leads for the salesperson; also called a *spotter*.

blitz Canvassing method in which a large group of salespeople attempt to make calls on all prospective businesses in a given geographic territory on a specified day.

body language Nonverbal signals communicated through facial expressions, arms, hands, and legs.

bonus Lump-sum incentive payment based on performance.

boomerang method See *revisit method*.

bottom-up forecasting Forecast compiled by adding up each salesperson's forecast for total company sales.

boundary-spanning employees Employees who cross the organizational boundary and interact with customers or vendors.

brainstorming session Meeting in which people are allowed to creatively explore different methods of achieving goals.

bribes Payments made to buyers to influence their purchase decisions.

browbeating Negotiation strategy in which buyers attempt to alter the selling team's enthusiasm and self-respect by making unflattering comments.

budget bogey See *budget limitation tactic*.

budget limitation tactic Negotiation strategy in which one side claims that the budget does not allow for the solution proposed; also called *budget bogey*.

business defamation Making unfair or untrue statements to customers about a competitor, its products, or its salespeople.

buyer's remorse The insecurity a buyer feels about whether the choice was a wise one; also called *postpurchase dissonance*.

buying center Informal, cross-department group of people involved in a purchase decision.

buying community Small, informal group of people in similar positions who communicate regularly, often both socially and professionally.

buying signals Nonverbal cues given by the buyer that indicate the buyer may be ready to commit; also called *closing cues*.

CAN-SPAM Act Law intended to reduce deceptive e-mails and usually contains specifications, such as an opt-out process and complete contact information, that are allowable.

canned sales pitch A scripted sales pitch to follow without deviation.

cap A limit placed on a salesperson's earnings.

capital equipment Major purchases made by a business, such as computer systems, that are used by the business for several years in its operations or production process.

cash discount Price discount given for early payment in cash.

center-of-influence method Prospecting method wherein the salesperson cultivates well-known, influential people in the territory who are willing to supply lead information.

champion Person who works for the buying firm in the areas most affected by the proposed change and works with the salesperson for the success of the proposal; also called *advocate* or *internal salesperson*.

change agent Person who is a cause of change in an organization.

circular routing Method of scheduling sales calls that includes using circular patterns from the home base in order to cover the territory.

closed questions Questions that can be answered with a word or short phrase.

closing Common term for obtaining commitment, which usually refers only to asking for the buyer's business.

closing cues See *buying signals*.

cloverleaf routing Method of scheduling sales calls that involves using loops to cover different portions of the territory on different days or weeks; on a map it should resemble a cloverleaf.

coach Someone in a buying organization who can advise a salesperson.

cold call See *cold canvass method.*

cold canvass method Prospecting method in which a sales representative tries to generate leads for new business by calling on totally unfamiliar organizations; also called *cold calls.*

collaborating mode Resolving conflict by seeking to maximize the satisfaction of both parties and hence truly reach a win-win solution.

collateral Collection of documents that are designed to generate sales, and include such items as brochures, sales flyers and fact sheets, and short success stories.

collusion Agreement among competitors, made after contacting customers, concerning their relationships with customers.

combination plan Compensation plan that provides salary and commission; offers the greatest flexibility for motivating and controlling the activities of salespeople.

commission Incentive payment for an individual sale; often a percentage of the sale price.

commission base Unit of analysis used to determine commissions–for example, unit sales, dollar sales, or gross margin.

commission rate Percentage of base paid or the amount per base unit paid in a commission compensation plan–for example, a percentage of dollar sales or an amount per unit sold.

commitment The fourth stage in the development of a buyer-seller relationship in which the buyer and seller have implicitly or explicitly pledged to continue the relationship for an extended period.

common law Legal precedent that arises out of court decisions.

comparative cost-benefit analysis A comparison of the buyer's current situation's costs with the value of the seller's proposed solution. Can also be a comparison of the seller's product with a competitor's product.

compensation method Method used to respond helpfully to objections by agreeing that the objection is valid, but then proceeding to show any compensating advantages.

competence Whether the salesperson knows what he or she is talking about.

competing mode Resolving conflict in an assertive and noncooperative manner.

complacency The assumption that the business is yours and will always be yours.

compliment opening Approach in which the salesperson begins the sales call by complimenting the buyer in some fashion.

compromising mode Resolving conflict by being somewhat cooperative and somewhat assertive. People using this approach attempt to find a quick, mutually acceptable solution that partially satisfies both parties.

concession Agreement of one party in a negotiation meeting to change his or her position in some fashion.

consequences of no agreement (CNA) What will be the result if you don't come to negotiation agreement. This is a standard or guide against which to evaluate the agreement you are trying to achieve. Also called *best alternative to a negotiated agreement (BATNA).*

conspiracy Agreement among competitors, made prior to contacting customers, concerning their relationships with customers.

contract to sell Offer made by a salesperson that received an unqualified acceptance by a buyer.

conventional résumé Form of life history organized by type of work experience.

conversion goals Measures of salesperson efficiency.

conversion ratio Similar to a batting average; calculated by dividing performance results by activity results (for example, dividing the number of sales by the number of calls).

corporate culture The values and beliefs held by a company and expressed by senior management.

creativity The trait of having imagination and inventiveness and using it to come up with new solutions and ideas.

credibility The characteristic of being perceived by the buyer as believable and reliable.

credibility statement A description of the seller and his or her company, offered to buyers to show that the seller can meet their needs.

credulous person standard Canadian law stating that a company is liable to pay damages if advertising and sale presentation claims and statements about comparisons with competitive products could be misunderstood by a reasonable person.

creeping commitment Purchase decision process that arises when decisions made early in the process have significant influence on decisions made later in the process.

cross-selling Similar to full-line selling except that the additional products sold are not directly associated with the initial products.

cultural relativism A view that no culture's ethics are superior to those of another culture's.

cumulative discount Quantity discount for purchases over a period of time; the buyer is allowed to add up all the purchases to determine the total quantity and the total quantity discount.

customer benefit proposition Statement showing how a product addresses the buyer's specific needs.

customer lifetime value (CLV) The estimated value of the customer over the lifetime of the relationship between the organization and the customer.

customer onboarding The process of teaching a new customer how to use the new product, as well as how to order service and/or supplies, what to expect from billing, and other important procedures.

customer orientation Selling approach based on keeping the customer's interests paramount.

customer referral value (CRV) The monetary value of the referral as well as the costs to get and maintain the referral.

customer relationship management (CRM) A system to organize information about customers, their needs, company information, and sales information.

customer satisfaction Fulfillment of the buyer's expectations and needs.

customer service rep (CRP) Inbound salesperson who handles customer concerns.

customer share The percentage of business received from a company's accounts. Also called *account share* or *share of wallet.*

customer-centric Process of making the customer the center of everything that the selling firm does. See also *customer orientation.*

customer value proposition (CVP) The way in which a salesperson's product or service will meet the prospect's needs and how that is different from the offerings of competitors, especially the next-best-alternative.

customized presentation Presentation developed from a detailed and comprehensive analysis or survey of the prospect's needs that is not canned or memorized in any fashion.

data mining The use of artificial intelligence and statistical tools to discover hidden insights in the volumes of data in a database.

database Information about leads, prospects, and customers.

deception Unethical practice of withholding information or telling white lies.

decider Buying center member who makes the final selection of the product to purchase.

decoding Communication activity undertaken by a receiver interpreting the meaning of the received message.

dependability The act of the salesperson living up to promises made; is not something a salesperson can demonstrate immediately.

derived demand Situation in which the demand for a producer's goods is based on what its customers sell.

diagnostic feedback Information given to a salesperson indicating how he or she is performing.

digital collateral management system System that archives, catalogs, and retrieves digital media and text. Used by salespeople to create presentations.

direct denial method Method of answering objections in which the salesperson makes a relatively strong statement indicating the error the prospect has made.

direct request method Act of attaining commitment by simply asking for it in a straightforward statement.

disguised interview Discussion between an applicant and an interviewer in which the applicant is unaware that the interviewer is evaluating the applicant for the position.

dissolution The process of terminating the relationship; can occur because of poor performance, clash in culture, change in needs, and other factors.

distribution channel Set of people and organizations responsible for the flow of products and services from the producer to the ultimate user.

document camera Camera similar to a traditional overhead projector in its ability to display transparencies. However, because it is essentially a camera, it is also capable of displaying any three-dimensional object without the use of a transparency. Also called *visual presenter.*

Do-Not-Call Registry A federal registry that lists phone numbers consumers have asked to not be called by telemarketers of for-profit companies

draw Advance from the company to a salesperson made against future commissions.

driver Category in the social style matrix; describes task-oriented people who are high on assertiveness and low on responsiveness.

economic influencer Person who is concerned about the financial aspects of a purchase decision.

efficient consumer response (ECR) system Distribution system that drives inventory to the lowest possible levels, increases the frequency of shipping, and automates ordering and inventory control processes without the problems of stockouts and higher costs.

80–20 listening rule A guideline that suggests salespeople should listen 80 percent of the time and talk 20 percent of the time.

electronic data interchange (EDI) Computer-to-computer linkages between suppliers and buyers for information sharing about sales, production, shipment, and receipt of products.

electronic whiteboard A digital version of an easel.

e-missives Timely, useful information that a seller provides to a buyer. This information might have nothing to do with the seller or the seller's product. The goal is to help make friends with the buyer and cement the relationship.

emotional intelligence (EI) The ability to effectively understand and use your own emotions and those of people with whom you interact. Includes four aspects: (1) knowing your own feelings and emotions as they are happening, (2) controlling your emotions so you do not act impulsively, (3) recognizing your customer's emotions (called empathy), and (4) using your emotions to interact effectively with customers.

emotional labeling An active listening tool of discovering and naming the emotions behind the buyer's statements. For example, the salesperson might state, "It sounds like you are really frustrated."

emotional needs Organizational and/or personal needs that are associated with some type of personal reward and gratification for the person buying the product.

emotional outburst tactic Negotiation strategy in which one party attempts to gain concessions by resorting to a display of strong emotion.

encoding Communication activity undertaken by a sender translating his or her thought into a message.

end user Business that purchases goods and services to support its own production and operations.

endless-chain method Prospecting method whereby a sales representative attempts to get at least one additional lead from each person he or she interviews.

ethical imperialism The view that the ethical standards that apply locally or in one's home country should be applied to everyone's behavior around the world.

ethics Principles governing the behavior of an individual or a group.

ethics review board A group of experts inside and outside the company who are responsible for reviewing ethics policies, investigating allegations of unethical behavior, and acting as a sounding board for employees.

exclusive sales territories Method that uses a prospect's geographic location to determine whether a salesperson can sell to that prospect.

excuses Concerns expressed by the buyer that are intended to mask the buyer's true objections.

executive briefing center Presentation room set aside to highlight a company's products and capabilities.

executive summary In a written proposal, a summary of one page or less that briefly describes the total cost minus total savings, the problem to be solved, and the proposed solution.

expansion The third phase in the development of a relationship, in which it takes a significant effort to share information and further investigate the potential relationship benefits.

exploration The second phase in the development of a relationship, in which both buyers and sellers explore the potential benefits and costs associated with the relationship.

expressed warranty Warranty specified through oral or written communications.

expressive Category in the social style matrix; describes people who are both competitive and approachable. They are high on assertiveness and responsiveness.

extranet Secure Internet-based network connecting buyers and suppliers.

FAB When salespeople describe the features, advantages (why that feature is important), and benefits of their product or service.

face A person's desire for a positive identity or self-concept.

False Claims Act An 1863 law encouraging citizens to press claims against vendors that sell fraudulently.

feature (1) Quality or characteristic of the product or service. (2) Putting a product on sale with a special display and featuring the product in advertising.

feature dumping Talking about lots of features of little interest to the customer and wasting the buyer's time.

FEBA A method of describing a product or service where salespeople mention the feature, provide evidence that the feature actually does exist, explain the benefit (why that feature is important to the buyer), and then ask whether the buyer agrees with the value of the feature and benefit.

feedback Information given to a salesperson indicating how he or she is performing. Also called *diagnostic feedback.*

feel-felt-found method See *referral method.*

felt stress Persistent and enduring psychological distress brought about by job demands or constraints encountered in the work environment.

field sales manager First-level manager.

field salespeople Salespeople who spend considerable time in the customer's place of business, communicating with the customer face-to-face.

field support rep Telemarketer who works with field salespeople and does more than prospect for leads.

FOB destination The seller has title until the goods are received at the destination.

FOB factory The buyer has title when the goods leave the seller's facility.

focus of dissatisfaction The person in the organization who is most likely to perceive problems and dissatisfactions; leads to the focus of power.

focus of power The person in the organization who can approve, prevent, or influence action.

focus of receptivity The person in the organization who will listen receptively and provide a seller with valuable information; leads to the focus of dissatisfaction.

follow-up Activity that a salesperson performs after commitment is achieved.

Force Majeure clause A clause inserted into a negotiation contract which shields the selling company from the impact of events beyond their control such as acts of God (fires, explosions, earthquakes, drought, tidal waves, and floods), wars, rebellions, riots, terrorism, and nuclear contamination.

Foreign Corrupt Practices Act (FCPA) Law that governs the behavior of U.S. business in foreign countries; restricts the bribing of foreign officials.

forestall To resolve objections before buyers have a chance to raise them.

four A's The selling process, consisting of *a*cknowledge, *a*cquire, *a*dvise, and *a*ssure.

free on board (FOB) destination The seller has title until the goods are received at the destination.

friendly silent questioning stare (FSQS) The act of silently waiting to encourage buyers to elaborate or explain more fully what their concern is.

full-line selling Selling the entire line of associated products.

functional relationship Series of market exchanges between a buyer and a seller, linked together over time. These relationships are characterized as win-lose relationships.

functional résumé Life history that reverses the content and titles of a conventional résumé and is organized by what a candidate can do or has learned rather than by types of experience.

gatekeeper Buying center member who influences the buying process by controlling the flow of information and/or limiting the alternatives considered. Sometimes called *barrier* or *screen*.

geographic salesperson Salesperson assigned a specific geographic territory in which to sell all the company's products and services.

good guy–bad guy routine Negotiation strategy in which one team member acts as the "good guy" while another team member acts as the "bad guy." The goal of the strategy is to have the opposing team accept the good guy's proposal to avoid the consequences of the bad guy's proposal.

go-to-market strategies The various options that firms have to sell their products. Examples include the Internet, franchises, telemarketers, agents, value-added resellers, field salespeople, and so on.

greeter Interviewer who greets the applicant and may conduct a disguised interview.

gross margin quota Minimum levels of acceptable profit or gross margin performance.

group interview Similar to panel interview but includes several candidates as well as several interviewers.

halo effect How one does in one thing changes a person's perceptions about other things one does.

handouts Written documents provided to buyers before, during, or after a meeting to help them remember what was said.

honesty Combination of truthfulness and sincerity; highly related to dependability.

house accounts Accounts assigned to a sales executive rather than to the specific salesperson responsible for the territory containing the account.

implication questions Questions that logically follow one or more problem questions (in SPIN); designed to help the prospect recognize the true ramifications of the problem.

implied warranty Warranty that is not expressly stated through oral or written communication but is still an obligation defined by law.

impression management Activities in which salespeople engage to affect and manage the buyer's impression of them.

inbound Salespeople or customer service reps who respond to calls placed to the firm by customers rather than placing calls out to customers.

incentive pay Compensation based on performance.

indirect denial method Method used to respond to objections in which the salesperson denies the objection but attempts to soften the response by first agreeing with the prospect that the objection is an important one.

inflection Tone of voice.

influencer Buying center member inside or outside an organization who directly or indirectly influences the buying process.

influential adversaries Individuals in the buyer's organization who carry great influence and are opposed to the salesperson's product or service.

initiator The person who starts the buying process.

inside salespeople Salespeople who work at their employer's location and interact with customers by telephone or computer.

insight selling A prospecting method whereby salespeople evaluate prospects who do not necessarily have a clear understanding of what they need but who are in a state of flux and have been shown to be quite agile in making changes (that is, they are able and willing to act quickly when a compelling case is made to them).

integrated marketing communications Coordinated communications programs that exploit the strengths of various communication vehicles to maximize the total impact on customers.

internal partnerships Partnering relationships between a salesperson and another member of the same company for the purpose of satisfying customer needs.

Internet of Things (IoT) The ability of devices and machines to talk to each other.

interview Personal interaction between candidates and job recruiters for the purpose of evaluating job candidates.

intimate zone That physical space around a buyer that is reserved primarily for a person's closest relationships. See also *social zone, public zone,* and *personal zone.*

introduction opening Approach method in which salespeople simply state their names and the names of their companies.

inventory turnover Measure of how efficiently a retailer manages inventory; calculated by dividing net sales by inventory.

invitation to negotiate The initiation of an interaction, usually a sales presentation, that results in an offer.

just-in-time (JIT) inventory control Planning system for reducing inventory by having frequent deliveries planned just in time for the delivered products to be assembled into the final product.

key accounts Large accounts, usually generating more than a specified amount in revenue per year, that receive special treatment.

kickbacks Payments made to buyers based on the amount of orders they place for a salesperson's products or services.

knowledge management technology Information technology that captures knowledge from people, organizes that knowledge, and makes it available to others.

KSAs Acronym for knowledge, skills, and abilities; the package that a candidate offers an employer.

LAARC method Method to respond to objections: Listen, Acknowledge, Assess (the validity of the objection), Respond, Confirm (that the objection has been answered).

lead A potential prospect; a person or organization that may have the characteristics of a true prospect.

lead management system The part of the lead process in which salespeople carefully analyze the relative value of each lead.

lead qualification system A process for qualifying leads.

lead user Company that faces and resolves needs months or years ahead of the rest of the marketplace.

leapfrog routing Method of scheduling calls that requires the identification of clusters of customers; visiting these clusters and "leaping" over single, sparsely located accounts should minimize travel time from the sales office to customers.

life-cycle costing Method for determining the cost of equipment or supplies over their useful life.

likability Behaving in a friendly manner and finding a common ground between the buyer and seller.

lost for good A buyer who gives all business to one vendor is considered lost for good for all of the out-suppliers because the buyer has cemented this relationship for a long period of time. See also *always a share.*

loudness Speech characterized by high volume and intensity.

lowballing Negotiation strategy in which one party voices agreement and then raises the cost of that agreement in some way.

lubrication Small sums of money or gifts, typically paid to officials in foreign countries, to get the officials to do their jobs more rapidly.

major sale Sale that involves a long selling cycle, a large customer commitment, an ongoing relationship, and large risks for the buyer if a bad decision is made.

manipulation Practice by a salesperson to eliminate or reduce the buyer's choice unfairly.

manufacturer Firm that buys goods and services to manufacture and sell other goods and services to its customers.

manufacturers' agents Independent businesspeople who are paid a commission by a manufacturer for all products and services the agents sell.

market exchange Relationship that involves a short-term transaction between a buyer and a seller that do not expect to be involved in future transactions with each other.

material requirements planning (MRP) Planning system for reducing inventory levels by forecasting sales, developing a production schedule, and ordering parts and raw materials with specific delivery dates.

merchandise market A form of exhibition or trade show used in fashion industries for manufacturers to sell products to retailers.

minimum call objective The minimum that a salesperson hopes to accomplish in an upcoming sales call.

minimum position Negotiation objective that states the absolute minimum level the team is willing to accept.

mirroring Where one person copies the nonverbals of another.

missionary salespeople Salespeople who work for a manufacturer and promote the manufacturer's products to other firms. Those firms buy products from distributors or other manufacturers, not directly from the salesperson's firm.

modified rebuy Purchase decision process associated with a customer who has purchased the product or service in the past but is interested in obtaining additional information.

MRO supplies Minor purchases made by businesses for maintenance and repairs, such as towels and pencils.

multichannel strategy The process of a firm using various go-to-market strategies at the same time.

multilevel selling Strategy that involves using multiple levels of company employees to call on similar levels in an account; for example, the VP of sales might call on the VP of purchasing.

multiple-sense appeals Method of attracting as many of the senses (hearing, sight, touch, taste, and smell) as possible.

mutual investment Tangible investments in the relationship by both parties (seller and buyer).

national account manager (NAM) Sales executive responsible for managing and coordinating sales efforts on a single account nationwide.

need payoff questions Questions that ask about the usefulness of solving the problem.

negative referral A customer who tells others about how poorly you or your product performed.

negotiation Decision-making process through which buyers and sellers resolve areas of conflict and arrive at agreements.

negotiation jujitsu Negotiation response in which the attacked person or team steps away from the opponent's attack and then directs the opponent back to the issues being discussed.

net present value (NPV) The investment minus the net value today of future cash inflows (discounted back to their present value today at the firm's cost of capital).

networking Establishing connections to other people and then using those networks to generate leads, gather information, generate sales, and so on.

new task Purchase decision process associated with the initial purchase of a product or service.

nibbling Negotiation strategy in which the buyer requests a small extra or add-on after the deal has been closed. Compared with *lowballing,* a nibble is a much smaller request.

noises Sounds unrelated to the message being exchanged between a salesperson and a customer.

noncompete clause A clause in a contract that limits one party, in this case the salesperson, from working for a competitor.

nondisclosure agreement (NDA) A contract that specifies what information is owned by whom and the conditions under which that information can be shared or used.

nonverbal communication Nonspoken forms of expression—body language, space, and appearance—that communicate thoughts and emotions.

North American Industry Classification System (NAICS) A uniform classification system for all businesses for all countries in North America.

objection Concern or question raised by the buyer.

offer Specific statement by a seller outlining what the seller will provide and what is expected from the buyer.

office scanning Activity in which the salesperson looks around the prospect's environment for relevant topics to talk about.

omnichannel buyer Customer who uses multiple channels or sources for gathering information.

open questions Questions for which there are no simple yes–no answers.

open-door policy General management technique that allows subordinates to bypass immediate managers and take concerns straight to upper management when the subordinates feel a lack of support from the immediate manager.

opening A method designed to get the prospect's attention and interest quickly and make a smooth transition into the next part of the presentation. Examples include introduction, product, question, referral, and so on.

opening position The initial proposal of a negotiating session.

opportunity cost The return a buyer would have earned from a different use of the same investment capital.

optimistic call objective The most optimistic outcome the salesperson thinks could occur in a given sales call.

order Written order that becomes a contract when signed by an authorized representative of a salesperson's company.

original equipment manufacturer (OEM) Business that purchases goods (components, subassemblies, raw and processed materials) to incorporate into products it manufactures.

outbound Salespeople, customer service reps, prospectors, account managers, and field support telemarketers who place phone calls out to customers.

outlined presentation Systematically arranged presentation that outlines the most important sales points. Often includes the necessary steps for determining the prospect's needs and for building goodwill at the close of the sale.

panel interview Job interview conducted by more than one person.

pass-up method See *acknowledge method.*

payback period Length of time it takes for the investment cash outflows to be returned in the form of cash inflows or savings.

performance feedback A type of feedback that salespeople often get from their supervisors that focuses on the seller's actual performance during a sales call.

performance goals Goals relating to outcomes, such as revenue.

personal selling Interpersonal communication process in which a seller uncovers and satisfies the needs of a buyer to the mutual, long-term benefit of both parties.

personal zone That physical space around a buyer that is reserved for close friends and those who share special interests. See also *public zone, social zone,* and *intimate zone.*

persuading Influencing someone to do something through reasoning or argument.

persuasion Practice by a salesperson designed to influence the buyer's decision, not manipulate it. See also *manipulation.*

pioneer selling Selling a new and different product, service, or idea. In these situations the salesperson usually has difficulty establishing a need in the buyer's mind.

pipeline analysis A process for identifying and managing sales opportunities; also called opportunity management. See also *sales funnel.*

poaching The unethical act of stealing a prospect from a salesperson in the same company.

portfolio Collection of visual aids that can be used to enhance communication during a sales call.

postpone method Objection response technique in which the salesperson asks permission to answer the question at a later time.

postpurchase dissonance See *buyer's remorse.*

preferred supplier Supplier that is assured a large percentage of the buyer's business and will get the first opportunity to earn new business.

prequalification Determination by firms whether leads are qualified before turning them over to the field sales force.

price discrimination Situation in which a seller gives unjustified special prices, discounts, or special services to some customers and not to others.

primary call objective Actual goal the salesperson hopes to achieve in an upcoming sales call.

prime selling time Time of day at which a salesperson is most likely to be able to see a customer.

privacy law Law that limits the amount of information that a firm can obtain about a consumer and specify how that information can be used or shared.

probing method Method to obtain commitment in which the salesperson initially uses the direct request method and, if unsuccessful, uses a series of probing questions designed to discover the reason for the hesitation.

problem questions Questions about specific difficulties, problems, or dissatisfactions that the prospect has.

product opening Approach in which the salesperson actually demonstrates the product features and benefits as soon as he or she walks up to the prospect.

profit margin The net profit the reseller makes, expressed as a percentage of sales. Also called *margin.*

profit quota Minimum levels of acceptable profit or gross margin performance.

promoter Your most loyal customer who not only keeps buying from you but also urges friends and associates to do the same.

prospect A lead that is a good candidate for buying what the salesperson is selling.

prospecting The process of locating potential customers for a product or service.

public zone That physical space around a person in which listening to speeches and interacting with passersby is comfortable for that person. See also *personal zone, intimate zone,* and *social zone.*

push money See *spiffs.*

qualifying a lead The process of determining whether a lead is in fact a prospect.

quantifying the solution Showing the prospect that the cost of the proposal is offset by added value. See also *value analysis.*

question opening Beginning the conversation with a question or stating an interesting fact in the form of a question.

quick-response (QR) system System of minimizing order quantities to the lowest level possible while increasing the speed of delivery to drive inventory turnover; accomplished by prepackaging certain combinations of products.

quota Quantitative level of performance for a specific time period.

rapport Close, harmonious relationship founded on mutual trust.

rate of change The speed at which change is occurring; a critical element to consider about change.

rational needs Organizational and/or personal needs that are directly related to product performance.

reciprocity Special relationship in which two companies agree to buy products from each other.

red herring A minor point brought up to distract the other side from the main issue being negotiated.

references People who know an applicant for a position and can provide information about that applicant to the hiring company.

referral event Gathering designed to allow current customers to introduce prospects to the salesperson in order to generate leads.

referral method Method of helpfully responding to objections in which the salesperson shows how others held similar views before trying the product or service. Also called the *feel–felt–found method.*

referral opening Approach in which the name of a satisfied customer or friend of the prospect is used at the beginning of a sales call.

referred lead Name of a lead provided by either a customer or a prospect of the salesperson.

relational partnership Long-term business relationship in which the buyer and seller have a close, trusting relationship but have not made significant investments in the relationship. These relationships are characterized as win–win relationships.

relationship marketing Marketing that seeks to win customers by building the right type of relationship desired by those customers.

relationship-specific assets Resources that are specific to a relationship and cannot easily be transferred to another one.

request for proposal (RFP) Statement issued by a potential buyer desiring bids from several potential vendors for a product. RFPs often include specifications for the product, desired payment terms, and other information helpful to the bidder. Also called *request for bids* or *request for quotes*.

requirements Conditions that must be satisfied before a purchase can take place.

resale price maintenance Contractual term in which a producer establishes a minimum price below which distributors or retailers cannot sell their products.

reseller Business, typically a distributor or retailer, that purchases products for resale.

response time The time between sending a message and getting a response to it.

responsiveness The degree to which people react emotionally when they are in social situations. One of the two dimensions in the social style matrix.

return on investment (ROI) Net profits (or savings) expected from a given investment, expressed as a percentage of the investment.

revenue quota The minimum amount of sales revenue necessary for acceptable performance.

reverse auction An auction, but instead of a seller offering a product and buyers bidding, a buyer offers a contract and sellers bid; prices fall as sellers compete to win the sale.

revisit method Process of responding to objections by turning the objection into a reason for acting now. Also called the *boomerang method*.

role ambiguity The degree to which a salesperson is not sure about the actions required in the sales role.

role conflict The extent to which the salesperson faces incompatible demands from two or more constituencies that he or she serves.

role overload A role (or job) demanding more than the person can perform.

role stress The psychological distress that may be a consequence of a salesperson's lack of role accuracy.

routine call patterns Method of scheduling calls used when the same customers are seen regularly.

routing Method of scheduling sales calls to minimize travel time.

salary Compensation paid periodically to an employee independently of performance.

sale The transfer of title to goods and services by the seller to the buyer in exchange for money.

sales asset management system System that archives, catalogs, and retrieves digital media and text. Used by salespeople to create presentations.

sales call allocation grid Grid used to determine account strategy; the dimensions are the strength of the company's position with the account and the account's sales potential.

sales force–intensive organization Firm whose go-to-market strategy relies heavily on salespeople.

sales funnel A prospecting term that reflects that some leads do not become prospects and that some prospects do not become customers. One thousand leads might be needed, for example, to generate 200 prospects, of which only 15 might become customers. This funnel of smaller and smaller numbers is called the sales funnel.

sales portals Online databases that include in one place many sources of information that the salesperson might need. Includes items such as account data, competitor intelligence, and news about the industry, the company, and the economy.

sales puffery Exaggerated statements about the performance of products or services.

sales quota The minimum number of sales in units.

scope of change The extent or degree to which change affects an organization; a critical element to consider about change.

screens See *barriers*.

secondary call objectives Goals a salesperson hopes to achieve during a sales call that have somewhat less priority than the primary call objective.

seeding Sending the customer information that could be useful to the customer, but this does not include sales related information like pricing, brochures, and so on.

selective perception The act of hearing what we want to hear, not necessarily what the other person is saying.

selling analytics An attempt to gain insights into customers by using sophisticated data mining and analytic techniques.

selling center A team that consists of all people in the selling organization who participate in a selling opportunity.

selling deeper Selling more to existing customers.

service level agreement A component in a contract that specifies objective measures and minimum standards for service delivery

services End-user purchases such as Internet and telephone connections, employment agencies, consultants, and transportation.

sexual harassment Unwelcome sexual advances, requests for sexual favors, and other similar verbal (such as jokes) and nonverbal (such as graffiti) behaviors.

share of wallet See *customer share.*

simple cost-benefit analysis Simple listing of the costs and savings that a buyer can expect from an investment.

situation questions General data-gathering questions about background and current facts that are very broad in nature.

situational stress Short-term anxiety caused by a situational factor.

six sigma selling programs Programs designed to reduce errors introduced by the selling system.

small talk Talk about current news, hobbies, and the like that usually breaks the ice for the actual presentation.

sneak attack See *ambush negotiating.*

social media The technological component of the communication, transaction, and relationship-building functions of a business that leverages the network of customers and prospects to promote value cocreation.

social networking Using Web sites to interact.

social style matrix Method for classifying customers based on their preferred communication style. The two dimensions used to classify customers are assertiveness and responsiveness.

social zone The physical space around a person in which business transactions and other impersonal relationships are comfortable for the person. See also *public zone, intimate zone,* and *personal zone.*

solo exchange Both the buyer and the seller pursue their own self-interests because they do not plan on doing business together again.

speaking-listening differential The difference between the 120-to-160-words-per-minute rate of speaking versus the 800-words-per-minute rate of listening.

spiffs (push money) Payments made by a producer to a reseller's salespeople to motivate the salespeople to sell the producer's products or services.

SPIN Logical sequence of questions in which a prospect's needs are identified. The sequence is situation questions, problem questions, implication questions, and need payoff questions.

spotter See *bird dog.*

Standard Industrial Classification (SIC) A uniform classification system for an industry. The SIC system is being replaced by the new *North American Industry Classification System (NAICS).*

standard memorized presentation Carefully prepared sales story that includes all the key selling points arranged in the most effective order; often called a canned sales presentation.

statutory law Law based on legislation passed by either state legislatures or Congress.

straight commission Compensation method of a certain amount per sale; plan includes a base and a rate but not a salary.

straight rebuy Purchase decision process involving a customer with considerable knowledge gained from having purchased the product or service a number of times.

straight salary Compensation method that pays a fixed amount of money for working a specified amount of time.

straight-line routing Method of scheduling sales calls involving straight-line patterns from the home base in order to cover the sales territory.

strategic account manager (SAM) A company executive who coordinates all the salespeople who call on an account throughout the nation or the world. Also called *national account manager (NAM).*

strategic partnership Long-term business relationship in which the buyer and seller have made significant investments to improve the profitability of both parties in the relationship. These relationships are characterized as win–win relationships.

strength of position Dimension of the sales call allocation grid that considers the seller's strength in landing sales at an account.

stress interview Any interview that subjects an applicant to significant stress; the purpose is to determine how the applicant handles stress.

style flexing Adjusting your behavior to mirror or match that of your customer.

submissive Selling style of salespeople who are often excellent socializers and like to spend a lot of time talking about nonbusiness activities. These people are usually reluctant to attempt to obtain commitment.

subordination Payment of large sums of money to officials to get them to do something that is illegal.

superior benefit method Type of compensation method of responding to an objection during a sales presentation that uses a high score on one attribute to compensate for a low score on another attribute.

supplier relationship management (SRM) The use of technology and statistics to identify important suppliers and opportunities for cost reduction, greater efficiency, and other benefits.

supply chain logistics The management of the supply chain.

supply chain management (SCM) Set of programs undertaken to increase the efficiency of the distribution and inventory management system that moves products all the way from suppliers to the producer's facilities and then to the end user.

systems integrator Outside vendor who has been delegated the responsibility for purchasing; has the authority to buy products and services from others.

target position Negotiation objective that states what the team hopes to achieve by the time the session is completed.

team selling Type of selling in which employees with varying areas of expertise within the firm work together to sell to the same account(s).

technical influencer Person who makes sure that a purchase meets technical requirements.

testimonial Statement, usually in the form of a letter, written by a satisfied customer about a product or service.

tests Personality or skills assessments used in assessing the match between a position's requirements and an applicant's personality or skills.

third-party-testimony method Method of responding to an objection during a sales presentation that uses a testimonial letter from a third party to corroborate a salesperson's assertions.

tickler file File or calendar used by salespeople to remind them when to call on specific accounts.

trade fair The European term for *trade show.*

trade salespeople Salespeople who sell to firms that resell the products rather than using them within their own firms.

trade secrets Information owned by a company that gives it a competitive advantage.

trade show Short exhibition of products by manufacturers and distributors.

trial balloon An idea floated without being actually offered.

trial close Questions the salesperson asks to take the pulse of the situation throughout a presentation.

trial order A small order placed by a buyer in order to test the product or the vendor. Not to be confused with trial close.

trust Firm belief or confidence in the honesty, integrity, and reliability of another person.

turnover (TO) How quickly a product sells, given a level of effort to sell it.

24/7 service A phrase that highlights the fact that customers expect a selling firm to be available 24 hours a day, 7 days a week.

two-way communication Interpersonal communication in which both parties act as senders and receivers. Salespeople send messages to customers and receive feedback from them; customers send messages to salespeople and receive responses.

tying agreement Agreement between a buyer and a seller in which the buyer is required to purchase one product to get another.

Uniform Commercial Code (UCC) Legal guide to commercial practice in the United States.

upgrading Convincing the customer to use a higher-quality product or a newer product. Also called *upselling.*

user Member of a buying center who ultimately will use the product purchased.

value The total benefit that the seller's products and services provide to the buyer. Also, the customer's perceived benefit received minus the selling price and minus the costs and hassles of buying.

value analysis Problem-solving approach for reducing the cost of a product while providing the same level of performance. See also *quantifying the solution.*

variable call patterns A nonsystematic method that a salesperson occasionally uses for calling on accounts.

vendor analysis A formal method used by organizational buyers to summarize the benefits and needs satisfied by a supplier.

vendor loyalty Commitment of a buyer to a specific supplier because of the supplier's superior performance.

versatility A characteristic, associated with the social style matrix, of people who increase the productivity of social relationships by adjusting to the needs of the other party.

videoconferencing Meetings in which people are not physically present in one location but are connected via voice and video.

virtual sales call See *Webcasting.*

visual presenter See *document camera.*

voice characteristics The rate of speech, loudness, pitch, quality, and articulation of a person's voice.

warranty Assurance by the seller that the goods will perform as represented.

Webcasting Videoconferencing in which the meeting is broadcast over the Internet.

webinar Online seminar.

win–lose negotiating Negotiating philosophy in which the negotiator attempts to win all the important concessions and thus triumph over his or her opponent.

win–win negotiating Negotiating philosophy in which the negotiator attempts to secure an agreement that completely satisfies both parties.

win–win not yet negotiating A negotiation session in which the buying team achieves its goals while the selling team does not. However, the sellers expect to achieve their goals in the near future, thanks to the results of that negotiation session.

win–win relationship Type of relationship in which firms make significant investments that can improve profitability for both partners because their partnership has given them some strategic advantage over their competitors.

word picture Story or scenario designed to help the buyer visualize a point.

zoning Method of scheduling calls that divides a territory into zones. Calls are made in a zone for a specified length of time and then made in another zone for the same amount of time.

ENDNOTES

CHAPTER 1

1. Wendell Berry, *The Unsettling of America*, 3rd ed. (San Francisco: Sierra Club Books, 1996).
2. Andrea L. Dixon and John F. Tanner, "Transforming Selling: Why It Is Time to Think Differently about Sales Research," *Journal of Personal Selling and Sales Management* 32, no. 1 (Winter 2012), pp. 9–14.
3. Pekka Töytäri and Risto Rajala, "Value-Based Selling: An Organizational Capability Perspective," *Industrial Marketing Management* 45 (2015), pp. 101–12; Adrian Payne and Pennie Frow, "Developing Superior Value Propositions: A Strategic Marketing Imperative," *Journal of Service Management* 25, no. 2 (2014), pp. 213–27.
4. Jerry Mclaughlin, "The Loyalty Myth and Other Misunderstandings," *Brandweek* 52, no. 1 (January 10, 2011), p. 22.
5. V. Kumar, Sarang Sunder, and Robert P. Leone, "Measuring and Managing a Salesperson's Future Value to the Firm," Journal of Marketing Research 51, no. 5 (2014), pp. 591–608.
6. Balboni, Bernardo, and Harri Terho. "Outward-looking and future-oriented customer value potential management: The sales force value appropriation role." *Industrial Marketing Management* 53 (2016), pp. 181–193; Koosha, Hamidreza, and Amir Albadvi. "Customer lifetime valuation using real options analysis." *Journal of Marketing Analytics* 3, no. 3 (2015), pp. 122–134; Valenzuela, Leslier, Eduardo Torres, Pedro Hidalgo, and Pablo Farías. "Salesperson CLV orientation's effect on performance." *Journal of Business Research* 67, no. 4 (2014), pp. 550–557.
7. Cindy B. Rippé, Suri Weisfeld-Spolter, Yuliya Yurova, Dena Hale, and Fiona Sussan, "Guiding When the Consumer Is in Control: The Moderating Effect of Adaptive Selling on the Purchase Intention of the Multichannel Consumer," *Journal of Consumer Marketing* 33, no. 6 (2016), pp. 469–78; Sarah Sluis, "4 Ways to Master Omnichannel Selling," *CRM Magazine* 18, no. 7 (2014), pp. 48–51.
8. Firms that do this are often said to exhibit service-dominant logic.
9. Vida Siahtiri, Aron O'Cass, and Liem Viet Ngo, "Exploring the Roles of Marketing and Selling Capabilities in Delivering Critical Customer Centric Performance and Brand Performance Outcomes for B2B Firms," *Journal of Strategic Marketing* 22, no. 5 (2014), pp. 379–95; Douglas Hughes, Joël Bon, and Adam Rapp, "Gaining and Leveraging Customer-Based Competitive Intelligence: The Pivotal Role of Social Capital and Salesperson Adaptive Selling Skills," *Journal of the Academy of Marketing Science* 41, no. 1 (2013), pp. 91–110; Lalit Manral, "The Customer-Centric Logic of Multi-product Corporations," *Journal of Strategy and Management* 9, no. 1 (2016), pp.74–92.
10. From a presentation by a senior vice president of Florida Power and Light, April 2017.
11. Excerpts from communication by Glenn R. Price; used by permission.
12. This is important because salespeople can be instrumental in breaking down functional silos.
13. The newer the product, the more salespeople might be needed to explain the benefits.
14. "20% of US B2B Sales Jobs to Go by 2020: Only 'Consultants' to Thrive," *International Journal of Sales Transformation*, no. 1.2 (July 2015), pp. 58–59.
15. Many companies are looking for salespeople who are relationship builders more so that "product-pushers." See for example: Brian de Haaff "Why This CEO Will Never Hire Another Salesperson," January 21, 2015, www.linkedin.com/pulse/why-ceo-never-hire-another-salesperson-brian-de-haaff, accessed February 25, 2017.
16. Charles H. Schwepker, "Influencing the Salesforce through Perceived Ethical Leadership: The Role of Salesforce Socialization and Person–Organization Fit on Salesperson Ethics and Performance," *Journal of Personal Selling and Sales Management* 35, no. 4 (2015), pp. 292-313; Emily C. Tanner, John F. Tanner, and Kirk Wakefield, "Panacea or Paradox? The Moderating Role of Ethical Climate," *Journal of Personal Selling and Sales Management* 35, no. 2 (2015), pp. 175-90.
17. Gisela I. Gerlach, Kai Rödiger, Ruth Maria Stock, and Nicolas A. Zacharias, "Salespersons' Empathy as a Missing Link in the Customer Orientation–Loyalty Chain: An Investigation of Drivers and Age Differences as a Contingency," *Journal of Personal Selling and Sales Management* 36, no. 3 (2016), pp. 221–39; Douglas B. Grisaffe, Rebecca VanMeter, and Lawrence B. Chonko, "Serving First for the

Benefit of Others: Preliminary Evidence for a Hierarchical Conceptualization of Servant Leadership," *Journal of Personal Selling and Sales Management* 36, no. 1 (2016), pp. 40–58.

18. See Belén Bande, Pilar Fernández-Ferrín, José A. Varela, and Fernando Jaramillo, "Emotions and Salesperson Propensity to Leave: The Effects of Emotional Intelligence and Resilience," *Industrial Marketing Management* 44 (2015), pp. 142–53; Selma Kadic-Maglajlic, Irena Vida, Claude Obadia, and Richard Plank, "Clarifying the Influence of Emotional Intelligence on Salesperson Performance," *Journal of Business and Industrial Marketing* 31, no. 7 (2016), pp. 877–88; Richard McFarland, Joseph Rode, and Tasadduq Shervani, "A Contingency Model of Emotional Intelligence in Professional Selling," *Journal of the Academy of Marketing Science* 44, no. 1 (2016), pp. 108–18; Zazli Lily Wisker and Athanasios Poulis, "Emotional Intelligence and Sales Performance: A Myth or Reality?," *International Journal of Business and Society* 16, no. 2 (2015), pp. 185–200; Chien-Chung Chen and Fernando Jaramillo, "The Double-Edged Effects of Emotional Intelligence on the Adaptive Selling–Salesperson-Owned Loyalty Relationship," *Journal of Personal Selling and Sales Management* 34, no. 1 (2014), pp. 33–50; Susanne Wiatr Borg and Wesley J. Johnston, "The IPS-EQ Model: Interpersonal Skills and Emotional Intelligence in a Sales Process," *Journal of Personal Selling and Sales Management* 33, no. 1 (2013), pp. 39–52; Felicia G. Lassk and C. David Shepherd, "Exploring the Relationship between Emotional Intelligence and Salesperson Creativity," *Journal of Personal Selling and Sales Management* 33, no. 1 (2013), pp. 25–38.
19. See Clifford Nass, "The Keyboard and the Damage Done," *Pacific Standard*, May–June 2012, pp. 22–25.
20. Adam Grant, "Emotional Intelligence Is Overrated," 2014, www.linkedin.com/pulse/20140930125543-69244073-emotional-intelligence-is-overrated-amp%3BmidToken=AQGT0abSxkbTlg&%3BfromEmail=fromEmail&trk=eml-b2_content_ecosystem_digest-recommended_articles-67-null&%3But=2BN16X7JhQiSs1, accessed February 25, 2017.
21. Corrine A. Novell, Karen A. Machleit, and Jane Ziegler Sojka, "Are Good Salespeople Born or Made? A New Perspective on an Age-Old Question: Implicit Theories of Selling Ability," *Journal of Personal Selling and Sales Management* 36, no. 4 (2016), pp. 309–20.
22. Fahri Karakaya, Charles Quigley, Frank Bingham, Juerg Hari, and Aslihan Nasir, "Business Students' Perception of Sales Careers: Differences between Students in Switzerland, Turkey, and the United States," *Journal of Education for Business* 89, no. 1 (2014), pp. 13–19.

CHAPTER 2

1. Alex Milovic and Rebecca Dingus, "Everyone Loves a Winner . . . Or Do They? Introducing Envy into a Sales Contest to Increase Salesperson Motivation," *American Journal of Management* 14, no. 4 (November 2014), pp. 27–32; Douglas B. Grisaffe and Fernando Jaramillo, "Toward Higher Levels of Ethics: Preliminary Evidence of Positive Outcomes," *Journal of Personal Selling and Sales Management* 27, no. 4 (2007), pp. 355–71; F. Juliet Poujol and John F. Tanner Jr., "The Impact of Sales Contests on Salesperson Customer Orientation," *Journal of Personal Selling and Sales Management* 30, no. 1 (2010), pp. 33–46.
2. M. Karami, O. Olfati, and A. J. Dubinsky, "Influence of Religiosity on Retail Salespeople's Ethical Perceptions: The Case in Iran," *Journal of Islamic Marketing* 5, no. 1 (2014), pp. 144–72; J. Tsalikis and Walfried Lassar, "Measuring Consumer Perceptions of Business Ethical Behavior in Two Muslim Countries," *Journal of Business Ethics* 89 (2009), pp. 91–98.
3. Thomas Wotruba, "The Evolution of Personal Selling," *Journal of Personal Selling and Sales Management* (Summer 1991), pp. 1–12; William C. Moncrief and Greg W. Marshall, "The Evolution of the Seven Steps of Selling," *Industrial Marketing Management* 34 (January 2005), pp. 13–22; Mike French, "Slowly Becoming Sales Promotion Men? Negotiating the Career of the Sales Representative in Britain, 1920s to 1970s," *Enterprise & Society* 17, no. 1 (March 2016), pp. 39–79.
4. George W. Dudley and John F. Tanner Jr., *The Hard Truth about Soft Selling* (Dallas, TX: Behavioral Science Research Press, 2005).
5. Wei-Ming Ou, Chia-Mei Shih, and Chin-Yuan Chen, "Effects of Ethical Sales Behavior on Satisfaction, Trust, Commitment Retention, and Word-of-Mouth," *International Journal of Commerce and Management* 25, no. 4 (2015), pp. 673–86; Sergio Roman and Salvador Ruiz, "Relationship Outcomes of Perceived Ethical Sales Behavior: The Customer's Perspective," *Journal of Business Research* 58 (April 2005), pp. 439–51.
6. Baiyun Gong, Xin He, and Huei-Min Hsu, "Guanxi and Trust in Strategic Alliances," *Journal of Management History* 19, no. 3 (2013), pp. 362–76; John D. Hansen and Robert J. Riggle, "Ethical Salesperson Behavior in Sales Relationships," *Journal of Personal Selling and Sales Management* 29, no. 2 (2009), pp. 151–66.

7. Jay P. Mulki, Jorge Fernando Jaramillo, and William B. Locander, "Critical Role of Leadership on Ethical Climate and Salesperson Behaviors," *Journal of Business Ethics* 86 (2009), pp. 125–41; John W. Cadogan, Nick Lee, Anssi Tarkainen, and Sanna Sundqvist, "Sales Manager and Sales Team Determinants of Salesperson Ethical Behaviour," *European Journal of Marketing* 43 (2009), pp. 907–37; Charles Schwepker and Robert J. Schwartz, "The Influence of Ethical Servant Leader and Ethical Climate on Customer Value Enhancing Sales Performance," *Journal of Personal Selling and Sales Management* 35, no. 2 (2015), pp. 93–104.
8. Ashley Kieler, "Wells Fargo New Account Openings Down 30% after Fake Account Fiasco," *The Consumerist,* February 17, 2017, https://consumerist.com/2017/02/17/wells-fargos-new-account-openings-down-30-after-fake-account-fiasco/, accessed May 15, 2017.
9. Jacklyn Martin, "Ethical Communication in a Retail Banking Call Center Sales Situation," *Journal of Internet Banking and Commerce* 22, no. S7 (January 2017), pp. 1–8.
10. Christophe Fournier, John F. Tanner Jr., Lawrence B. Chonko, and Chris Manolis, "Revisiting Antecedents of Salesperson Propensity to Leave: The Moderating Role of Ethical Climate," *Journal of Personal Selling and Sales Management* (2009), pp. 7–22; Fernando Jaramillo, Beln Bande, and Jose Varela, "Servant Leadership and Ethics: A Dyadic Examination of Supervisor Behaviors and Salesperson Perception," *Journal of Personal Selling and Sales Management* 35, no. 2 (2015), pp. 108–20.
11. James DeConinck and Mary Beth DeConinck, "The Relationship among Ethical Leadership, Ethical Climate, Supervisory Trust, and Moral Judgment," *Academy of Marketing Studies Journal* 20, no. 3 (2016), pp. 89–99.
12. C. H. Schwepker and T. N. Ingram, "Ethical Leadership in the Salesforce: Effects on Salesperson Customer Orientation, Commitment to Customer Value and Job Stress," *Journal of Business and Industrial Marketing* 31, no. 7 (2016), pp. 914–27; V. Badrinarayanan, A. Dixon, V. L. West, and G. M. Zank, "Professional Sales Coaching: An Integrative Review and Research Agenda," *European Journal of Marketing* 49, no. 7/8 (2015), pp. 1087–113.
13. Charles H. Schwepker and R. J. Schultz, "The Impact of Trust in Manager on Unethical Intention and Customer-Oriented Selling," *Journal of Business and Industrial Marketing* 28, no. 4 (2013), pp. 347–56; Fernando Jaramillo, Belen Bande, and Jose Varela, "Servant Leadership and Ethics: A Dyadica Examination of Supervisor Behaviors and Salesperson Perceptions," *Journal of Personal Selling and Sales Management* 35, no. 2 (2015), pp. 108–20.
14. Dennis N. Bristow, Rajesh Gulati, Douglas Amyx, and Jennifer Slack, "An Empirical Look at Professional Selling from a Student Perspective," *Journal of Education for Business* 81, no. 5 (May–June 2006), pp. 242–49; Alan Bush, Victoria Bush, Jared Oakley, and John Cicala, "Formulating Undergraduate Student Expectations for Better Career Development in Sales: A Socialization Perspective," *Journal of Marketing Education* 36, no. 2 (2014), pp. 120–29.
15. Shirley Hunter, personal correspondence. Used with permission.
16. William Bearden, Thomas Ingram, and Raymond LaForge, *Marketing: Principles and Perspectives* (New York: McGraw-Hill/Irwin, 2004).
17. John Palley, quoted in Hampton Roads Chamber of Commerce MemberMail, May 15, 2017, and listed "as seen in Forbes.com."
18. Rich Kraus, Exclusive IOMA Survey: "How Employers Address Sexual Harassment," *HR Focus* 78, no. 12 (2007), pp. 3–5. personal correspondence. Used with permission.
19. John F. Riggs, Scott Widmier, and Richard E. Plank, "The Impact of Pharmaceutical Industry Salesperson Regulations, Guidance Statements, and Laws on Their Sales Behaviors: A Taxonomy with Managerial Insights," *International Journal of Pharmaceutical and Healthcare Marketing* 10, no. 2 (2016), pp. 161–91.
20. Tara J. Radin and Carolyn E. Predmore, "The Myth of the Salesperson: Intended and Unintended Consequences of Product-Specific Sales Incentives," *Journal of Business Ethics* 36 (2002), pp. 79–92.
21. Andres Zoltners, Prakesh Sinha, and S. Lorimer, "Breaking the Sales Force Incentive Addiction: A Balanced Approach to Sales Force Effectiveness," *Journal of Personal Selling and Sales Management* 32, no. 2 (2012), pp. 171–86.
22. David Friend, "Rogers Ponies Up $200,000 Fine under Anti-Spam Law," *TheStar.com,* November 20, 2015, www.thestar.com/business/2015/11/20/rogers-ponies-up-200000-fine-under-anti-spam-law.html, accessed June 20, 2017; Anonymous, "Largest CAN-Spam Fine to Be Paid," *Virus Bulletin,* April 1, 2006, www.virusbulletin.com/blog/2006/04/largest-can-spam-fine-be-paid, accessed June 20, 2017.
23. Halliburton, "Sensitive Transactions," www.halliburton.com/AboutUs/default.aspx?pageid=2326, accessed May 17, 2017. If you go to the Halliburton main page and search "sensitive transactions," you'll find the same document in other languages.
24. Meryl Davids, "Global Standards, Local Problems," *Journal of Business Strategy,* January–February 1999,

pp. 22–35; James Murphy, "The Morality of Bargaining: Insights from 'Caritas in Veritate,'" *Journal of Business Ethics*, Supplement 100 (2011), pp. 79–88; Susanna Ripken, "Corporations Are People Too: A Multi-Dimensional Approach to the Corporate Personhood Puzzle," *Fordham Journal of Corporate and Financial Law* 15, no. 1 (2009), pp. 97–177. Check out all three of these; they are very different types of articles dealing with the ethical and philosophical issues of subordination, bribery, and culture.

25. John F. Riggs, Scott Widmier, and Richard E. Plank, "The Impact of Pharmaceutical Industry Salesperson Regulations, Guidance Statements, and Laws: A Taxonomy with Managerial Insights," *International Journal of Pharmaceutical and Healthcare Marketing* 10, no. 2 (2016), pp. 161–91.
26. Kanga Kong and Jungah Lee, "Samsung Heir, Jay Y. Lee, Arrested on Bribery Allegations," *Bloomberg Technology,* February 17, 2017, www.bloomberg.com/news/articles/2017-02-16/south-korea-court-approves-arrest-of-samsung-heir-jay-y-lee, accessed May 17, 2017.
27. Nick Fletcher, "GlaxoSmithKline to Pay L297m Fine over China Bribery Network," *The Guardian,* September 9, 2014, www.theguardian.com/business/2014/sep/19/glaxosmithkline-pays-297m-fine-china-bribery, accessed May 17, 2017; Anonymous, "Brazilian Construction Company Pays Record Fine in Bribery Case," *The Nation,* December 22, 2017, http://hamariweb.com/finance/news/brazilian_construction_company_pays_record_fine_in_bribery_case_nid1903190.aspx, accessed March 17, 2017.

CHAPTER 3

1. Organization for Economic Cooperation and Development, "Size of Public Procurement Market," in *Government at a Glance 2011*, OECD Publishing, 2011, http://dx.doi.org/10.1787/gov_glance-2011-46-en, accessed September 27, 2012.
2. James A. Cooke, "From Many, One IBM's Unified Supply Chain," *Supply Chain Quarterly*, www.supplychainquarterly.com/topics/Procurement/20121217-from-many-one-ibmsunified-supply-chain/, accessed May 24, 2017.
3. Golino Ruggeri and Matteo Kalchschmidt, "Designing an Expert System to Support Competitiveness through Global Sourcing," *International Journal of Production Research* 53, no. 13 (2015), pp. 383–86.
4. Seth McNew, "Top Apple Suppliers to Buy in 2017," *The Motley Fool,* April 1, 2017, www.fool.com/investing/2017/ 04/01/3-best-apple-suppliers-to-invest-in-2017.aspx, accessed May 22, 2017.
5. Christopher Ryan, "The Evolving Journey of the B2B Buyer," January 26, 2016, www.business2community.com/sales-management/evolving-journey-b2b-buyer-01433392#qiW7vq8LVYMYHu4h.97, accessed May 22, 2017; statistic cited is from a presentation citing Forester Research.
6. Anni-KaisaKähkönen, Katrina Lintukangas, and Jukka Hallikas, "Buyer's Dependence in Value-Creating Supplier Relationships," *Supply Chain Management* 20, no. 2 (2015), pp. 151–62; Maarten Sjoerdsma and Arjan J. van Weele, "Managing Supplier Relationships in a New Product Development Context," *Journal of Purchasing and Supply Management* 21, no. 3 (September 2015), pp. 192–99.
7. www.evcoplastics.com/engineering/early-supplier-involvement, accessed May 27, 2017.
8. Robert Dwyer and John F. Tanner Jr., *Business Marketing: Connecting Strategy, Relationships, and Learning,* 4th ed. (New York: McGraw-Hill/Irwin, 2009).
9. Goutam Chakraborty, Prashant Srivastava, and Fred Marshall, "Are Drivers of Customer Satisfaction Different for Buyers/Users from Different Functional Areas?," *Journal of Business & Industrial Marketing* 22, no. 1 (2007), pp. 20–39.
10. Scott Friend, Carolyn Curasi, James Boles, and Danny Bellenger, "Why Are You Really Losing Sales Opportunities? A Buyers' Perspective on the Determinants of Key Account Sales Failures," *Industrial Marketing Management* 43, no. 7 (October 2014), pp. 1124–28.
11. Peter Bendor-Samuel, "The Problem with End-User Computing Environment," *CIO*, www.cio.com/article/3177373/it-industry/the-problem-with-the-end-user-computing-environment.html, accessed May 23, 2017.
12. This section is based on the classic Robert Miller and Steve Heiman book, *Successful Large Account Management* (New York: Warner Books, 1985, updated 2005).
13. *SRM Insights Report*, Source One Management Services LLC, 2017, www.sourceoneinc.com/wp-content/uploads/2015/08/SRM-Insights-Report.pdf, accessed May 24, 2017.
14. Marc Elsäßer and Bernd W. Wirtz, "Rational and Emotional Factors of Customer Satisfaction and Brand Loyalty in a Business-to-Business Setting," *Journal of Business & Industrial Marketing* 32, no. 1 (2017), pp. 138–52.
15. Javad Seif and Masoud Rabbani, "Component Based Life Cycle Costing in Replacement Decisions, "*Journal of Quality in Maintenance Engineering* 20, no. 4 (2014), pp. 436–52.
16. Anthony Higham, Chris Fortune, and Howard James, "Life Cycle Costing: Evaluating Its Use in

UK Practice," *Structural Survey* 33, no. 1 (2015), pp. 73-87.

17. Matias Bronnenmayer, Bernd W. Wirtz, and Vincent Göttel, "Success Factors of Management Consulting," *Review of Managerial Science* 10, no. 1 (January 2016), pp. 1-34.
18. Thomas L. Zeller, Brian B. Stanko and Andrew D. Tressler, "How Risky Are Your Lease vs. Buy Decisions," *Management Accounting Quarterly* 17, no. 1 (Fall 2015), pp. 9-18.
19. Roberto Grandinetti, "Exploring the Dark Side of Cooperative Buyer- Seller Relationships," *Journal of Business & Industrial Marketing* 32, no. 2 (2017), pp. 326-36.
20. Mariana Gomes, Teresa Fernandes, and Amelia Brandão, "Determinants of Brand Relevance in a B2B Service Purchasing Context," *Journal of Business & Industrial Marketing* 31, no. 2 (2016), pp. 193-204; see also Elsäßer and Wirtz, "Rational and Emotional Factors of Customer Satisfaction and Brand Loyalty."
21. Pejvak Oghazi, Fakhreddin F. Rad, Ghasem Zaefarian, Hooshang M. Beheshti, and Sina Mortazavi, "Unity in Strength: A Study of Supplier Relationship Management Integration," *Journal of Business Research* 69, no. 11 (November 2016), pp. 480-84.
22. Tom Stundza, "One Way to Get a Raise: Take a Course," *Purchasing* 138 (December 2009), p. 50.
23. John Belz Snyder, "GM Commits to Sustainable Natural Rubber for Tires," *Autoblog,* May 18, 2017, www.autoblog.com/ 2017/05/16/gm-commits-sustainable-natural-rubber-tires/, accessed June 12, 2017.
24. William Ho, Xiaowei Xu, and Prasanta Dey, "Multi-Criteria Decision Making Approaches for Supplier Evaluation and Selection: A Literature Review," *European Journal of Operational Research* 202 (April 2010), pp. 16-31.

CHAPTER 4

1. "Global Gaps in Core Sales Skills," *International Journal of Sales Transformation,* no. 1.2 (July 2015), pp. 60-61.
2. Grant Cardone, "The 50 Best Qualities of Great Salespeople," *Proofs* 95, no. 3 (June 2012), pp. 15-16. Recent research shows that active listening is the weakest skill among U.S. salespeople: "Global Gaps in Core Sales Skills," *International Journal of Sales Transformation*, no. 1.2 (July 2015), pp. 60-61. See also Kuang-Peng Hung and Chung-Kuang Lin, "More Communication Is Not Always Better? The Interplay between Effective Communication and Interpersonal Conflict in Influencing Satisfaction," *Industrial Marketing Management* 42, no. 8 (2013), pp. 1223-32.
3. See for example: Stacy Oderstrom, "Great Salespeople Listen and Learn to Leverage Established and New Brands." Franchising World (2015), pp. 74-75. Rick Rummage, "Listen and Learn if You Want to Sell." Bank Investment Consultant 22, no. 4 (May 2014), pp. 36-38. Pryor, Susie, Avinash Malshe, and Kyle Paradise. "Salesperson Listening in the Extended Sales Relationship: An Exploration of Cognitive, Affective, and Temporal Dimensions." Journal of Personal Selling & Sales Management 33, no. 2 (2013), pp. 185-196. Drollinger, Tanya, and Lucette B. Comer. "Salesperson's listening ability as an antecedent to relationship selling." Journal of Business & Industrial Marketing 28, no. 1 (2013), pp. 50-59.
4. See, for example, Penny Herscher, "Make Every Second of Silence Count," *Executive Leadership* 31, no. 12 (December 2016).
5. Yam B. Limbu, C. Jayachandran, Barry J. Babin, and Robin T. Peterson, "Empathy, Nonverbal Immediacy, and Salesperson Performance: The Mediating Role of Adaptive Selling Behavior," *Journal of Business and Industrial Marketing* 31, no. 5 (2016), pp. 654-67; Raj Agnihotri, Valter Afonso Vieira, Karin Borges Senra, and Colin B. Gabler, "Examining the Impact of Salesperson Interpersonal Mentalizing Skills on Performance: The Role of Attachment Anxiety and Subjective Happiness," *Journal of Personal Selling and Sales Management* 36, no. 2 (2016), pp. 174-89; Vanessa Van Edwards, "Supercharging Your Sales with Body Language," *Brand Quarterly* no. 13 (2014), pp. 8-11.
6. Owen Hargie, *The Handbook of Communication Skills*, 2nd ed. (London: Routledge, 1997).
7. John Perry, "Palm Power in the Workplace," *The American Salesman* 46 (October 2001), p. 22.
8. R. J. Zimmerman, team leader of ticket sales, The Aspire Group, personal correspondence, used with permission.
9. Marianne LaFrance, *Why Smile: The Science behind Facial Expressions* (New York: Norton, 2013).
10. Dale Carnegie, a noted sales training consultant, would disagree with this advice. He suggests that not offering a handshake shows a lack of assertiveness.
11. "Britons Waving Goodbye to Humble Handshake," www.indianexpress.com/news/britons-wavinggoodbye-to-humble-handshake/572050, accessed August 30, 2012.
12. All material presented in the five principles was written by Vicki L. West; used by permission.
13. Maura Schreier-Fleming, "Breaking Out of Phone Mail Jail," *American Salesman* 58, no. 8 (2013), pp. 25-27.

14. Jennifer L. Dapko and Andrew B. Artis, "Less Is More: An Exploratory Analysis of Optimal Visual Appeal and Linguistic Style Combinations in a Salesperson's Initial-Contact E-Mail to Millennial Buyers within Marketing Channels," *Journal of Marketing Channels* 21, no. 4 (2014), pp. 254–67.
15. For other good suggestions, see Emma Snyder, "20 Sales Email Opening Lines That Put 'Hi, My Name Is' to Shame," February 27, 2017, http://blog.hubspot.com/sales/sales-email-opening-lines?utm_campaign=blog-rss-emails&utm_source=hs_email&utm_medium=e-mail&utm_content=20851367, accessed March 18, 2017.
16. Joel Whalen, personal correspondence.
17. See Nick Churick, "9 Actionable Ways to Find Anyone's Email Address (8 of Them Are FREE)," December 1, 2016, https://ahrefs.com/blog/find-email-address/, accessed March 18, 2017.
18. For additional information, see the following: Anup Soans, "Selling across Cultures," February 24, 2014, www.td.org/Publications/Blogs/Sales-Enablement-Blog/2014/02/Selling-Across-Cultures, accessed March 11, 2017; Tom Hopkins, "Selling to Other Cultures," *Entrepreneur*, 2017, www.entrepreneur.com/article/83782, accessed March 11, 2017.
19. For additional insights, see the following: Tom Hopkins (2017), "Selling to Other Cultures," Entrepreneur, as viewed March 11, 2017 at https://www.entrepreneur.com/article/83782.
20. For important differences to consider when translating into other languages, see www.transperfect.com.

CHAPTER 5

1. A. Aidla, L. Kõiv, and D. Reinumägi, "Improving Personal Sales Performance by Considering Customer Personality Traits," *GSTF Business Review* 4, no. 4 (2016), pp. 39–46.
2. Paolo Guenzi, Luigi M. De Luca, and Rosann Spiro, "The Combined Effect of Customer Perceptions about a Salesperson's Adaptive Selling and Selling Orientation on Customer Trust in the Salesperson: A Contingency Perspective," *Journal of Business & Industrial Marketing* 31, no. 4 (2016), pp. 553–64.
3. Richard A. Rocco and D. Joel Whalen, "Teaching Yes, and . . . Improv in Sales Classes: Enhancing Student Adaptive Selling Skills, Sales Performance, and Teaching Evaluations," *Journal of Marketing Education* 36, no. 2 (2014), pp. 197–208.
4. Erdener Kaynak, Ali Kara, Clement S. F. Chow, and Tommi Laukkanen, "Role of Adaptive Selling and Customer Orientation on Salesperson Performance: Evidence from Two Distinct Markets of Europe and Asia," *Journal of Transnational Management* 21, no. 2 (2016), pp. 62–83.
5. Thomas W. Leigh, Thomas E. DeCarlo, David Allbright, and James Lollar," Salesperson Knowledge Distinctions and Sales Performance," *Journal of Personal Selling and Sales Management* 34, no. 2 (2014), pp. 123–40.
6. Matthew Dixon and Brent Adamson, *The Challenger Sale: Taking Control of the Customer Conversation* (New York: Portfolio/Penguin, 2011).
7. Wouter E. Berg, Willem Verbeke, Richard P. Bagozzi, Loek Worm, Ad (Addy) Jong, and Ed Nijssen, "Salespersons as Internal Knowledge Brokers and New Products Selling: Discovering the Link to Genetic Makeup," *Journal of Product Innovation Management* 31, no. 4 (2014), pp. 695–709.
8. Name of company changed as required.
9. See Kimiz Dalkir and Jay Liebowitz, *Knowledge Management in Theory and Practice*, 2nd ed. (Cambridge, MA: MIT Press, 2011); David A. Locander, Jay P. Mulki, and Frankie J. Weinberg, "How Do Salespeople Make Decisions? The Role of Emotions and Deliberation on Adaptive Selling, and the Moderating Role of Intuition," *Psychology & Marketing* 31, no. 6 (2014), pp. 387–403; Gregorio Martín-de Castro, "Knowledge Management and Innovation in Knowledge-Based and High-Tech Industrial Markets: The Role of Openness and Absorptive Capacity," *Industrial Marketing Management* 47 (2015), pp. 143–46.
10. For more information see Accenture, www.accenture.com/us-en/service-sales-strategy-transformation; Miller Heiman, www.millerheimangroup.com/wp-content/uploads/sites/7/2016/09/Professional-Selling-Skills-Product-Sheet.pdf. See also Robert B. Miller, Stephen E. Heiman, Tad Tuleja, and J. W. Marriott, *New Strategic Selling: The Unique Sales System Proven Successful by the World's Best Companies* (New York: Grand Central Publishing, 2005).
11. Douglas Hughes, Joël Bon, and Adam Rapp, "Gaining and Leveraging Customer-Based Competitive Intelligence: The Pivotal Role of Social Capital and Salesperson Adaptive Selling Skills," *Journal of the Academy of Marketing Science* 41, no. 1 (2013), pp. 91–110.
12. Michael Leimbach, "Sales Versatility: Connecting with Customers Everytime," *American Salesman* 61, no. 8 (2016), pp. 21–25.
13. David Merrill and Roger Reid, *Personal Styles and Effective Performance* (Radnor, PA: Chilton, 1981).
14. For details, see www.wilsonlearning.com/wlw/products/brv.
15. Leimbach, "Sales Versatility: Connecting with Customers Everytime."

CHAPTER 6

1. It is even important for nonprofit organizations.
2. Some organizations refer to their salespeople as hunters and farmers. Hunters go out and locate

potential leads. Farmers are the ones who develop the leads into prospects and customers.

3. Paolo Guenzi and Kaj Storbacka. "The Organizational Implications of Key Account Management: A Case-Based Examination," *Industrial Marketing Management* 45 (2015), pp. 84–97; Iain A. Davies and Lynette J. Ryals, "Attitudes and Behaviours of Key Account Managers: Are They Really Any Different to Senior Sales Professionals?," *Industrial Marketing Management* 42, no. 6 (2013), pp. 919–31.
4. Brent Adamson, Matthew Dixon, and Nicholas Toman, "The End of Solution Sales," *Harvard Business Review* 90, no. 7/8 (July 2012), pp. 60–68.
5. Mahima Hada, Rajdeep Grewal, and Gary L. Lilien, "Supplier-Selected Referrals," *Journal of Marketing* 78, no. 2 (2014), pp. 34–51.
6. Phil Birt, personal correspondence; used by permission.
7. Anthony Urbaniak, "Prospecting Systems That Work," *American Salesman* 61, no. 1 (2016), pp. 27–30.
8. Nikoletta-Theofania Siamagka, George Christodoulides, Nina Michaelidou, and Aikaterini Valvi, "Determinants of Social Media Adoption by B2B Organizations," *Industrial Marketing Management* 51 (2015), pp. 89–99.
9. Tony J. Hughes, "Is Social Media a Complete Waste of Time?," 2016, www.linkedin.com/pulse/social-media-complete-waste-time-tony-j-hughes, accessed December 20, 2016.
10. See, for example, Matt Bryom, "Say Hello to Vlogging: Why You Should Be Video Blogging," February 22, 2017, www.business.com/articles/say-hello-to-vlogging-why-you-should-be-video-blogging/, accessed Marcy 13, 2017.
11. Bang Nguyen, Xiaoyu Yu, T. C. Melewar, and Junsong Chen, "Brand Innovation and Social Media: Knowledge Acquisition from Social Media, Market Orientation, and the Moderating Role of Social Media Strategic Capability," *Industrial Marketing Management* 51 (2015), pp. 11–25; Sylvie Lacoste, "Perspectives on Social Media and Its Use by Key Account Managers," *Industrial Marketing Management* 54 (2016), pp. 33–43.
12. Sarah Quinton and Damien Wilson, "Tensions and Ties in Social Media Networks: Towards a Model of Understanding Business Relationship Development and Business Performance Enhancement through the Use of LinkedIn," *Industrial Marketing Management* 54 (2016), pp. 15–24.
13. Tony J. Hughes, "How to Apply Advanced Strategic Social Selling in the Enterprise," January 31, 2016, www.linkedin.com/pulse/how-sap-applies-advanced-strategic-social-selling-tony-j-hughes?midToken=AQGT0abSxkbTlg&trk=eml-b2_content_ecosystem_digest-network_publishes-270-,null&fromEmail=fromEmail&ut=2Xx1kr8q3UmA1, accessed March 18, 2017.
14. Kunal Swani, Brian P. Brown, and George R. Milne, "Should Tweets Differ for B2B and B2C? An Analysis of Fortune 500 Companies' Twitter Communications," *Industrial Marketing Management* 43, no. 5 (2014), pp. 873–81.
15. Barbara A. Schuldt and Jeff W. Totten, "Application of Social Media Types in the Sales Process," *Academy of Marketing Studies Journal* 19, no. 3 (2015), pp. ccxxx–ccxlii.
16. See Jennifer Lai, "5 Twitter Trips for Your Company," CNN *Money.com*, July 22, 2009, http://brainstormtech.blogs.fortune.cnn.com/2009/07/22/5-twitter-tips-for-yourcompany, accessed February 12, 2010.
17. Agnihotri et al., "Bringing 'Social' into Sales," p. 333.
18. Gaurav Sabnis, Sharmila C. Chatterjee, Rajdeep Grewal, and Gary L. Lilien, "The Sales Lead Black Hole: On Sales Reps' Follow-Up of Marketing Leads," *Journal of Marketing* 77, no. 1 (2013), pp. 52–67.
19. Eddie B. Allen Jr., "Sheer Brilliance," *Deliver Magazine*, February 2012, pp. 20–21.
20. Maria Sarmento, Cláudia Simões, and Minoo Farhangmehr, "Applying a Relationship Marketing Perspective to B2B Trade Fairs: The Role of Socialization Episodes," *Industrial Marketing Management* 44 (2015), pp. 131–41.
21. Mark Hunter, "What's the Value of Cold Calling in Sales?," 2017, www.linkedin.com/pulse/its-2017-whats-value-cold-calling-sales-mark-hunter, accessed February 14, 2017.
22. See, for example, Sandra Beckwith, "Going Deeper," *Deliver Magazine*, December 2009, pp. 13–17.
23. Jeff Haden, "Incorrectly Used Words That Can Make You Look Dumb," December 3, 2014, www.linkedin.com/pulse/article/20141203134446-20017018-40-incorrectly-used-words-that-can-make-you-look-dumb, accessed March 18, 2017.
24. This is found in many places on the Web, including www.answerology.com/index.aspx/question/2674611_icdnuolt-blveiee-taht-I-cluod-aulaclty-uesdnatnrd-waht-Iwas-rdanieg-The-phaonmneal-pweor-of-the-.html, accessed September 9, 2012.
25. This poem is found in many places on the Web.
26. British Admiralty instruction dealing with the storage of warheads and torpedoes: Carl C. Gaither and Alma E. Cavazos-Gaither, *Practically Speaking: A Dictionary of Quotations on Engineering, Technology and Architecture,* Taylor & Francis, 1998.
27. For more information, see Gaurav Sabnis, Sharmila C. Chatterjee, Rajdeep Grewal, and Gary L. Lilien,

"The Sales Lead Black Hole: On Sales Reps' Follow-Up of Marketing Leads," *Journal of Marketing* 77, no. 1 (2013), pp. 52–67; Aaron D. Arndt and Jason Harkins, "A Framework for Configuring Sales Support Structure," *Journal of Business and Industrial Marketing* 28, no. 5 (2013), pp. 432–43.
28. See www.salesleadmgmtassn.com.

CHAPTER 7

1. See Alex Stein and Michael Smith, "CRM Systems and Organizational Learning: An Exploration of the Relationship between CRM Effectiveness and the Customer Information Orientation of the Firm in Industrial Markets," *Industrial Marketing Management* 38, no. 2 (2009), pp. 198–206.
2. Dawn Hedges, personal correspondence; names changed to protect confidentiality.
3. See, for example, Chip Eichelberger, "Go from Good to Great: How to Boost Your Sales Career," *American Salesman* 60, no. 4 (2015), pp. 3–7; Jim Holden "Elevating the Sales Profession: What Sellers Crave and Sales Managers Need for Success," *Industrial and Commercial Training* 48 no. 4 (2016), pp. 194–98.
4. Neil Rackham, *Major Account Sales Strategy* (New York: McGraw-Hill, 1989), p. 39.
5. For their latest book on the topic, see Robert B. Miller, Stephen E. Heiman, Diane Sanchez, and Tad Tuleja, *The New Conceptual Selling: The Most Effective and Proven Method for Face-to-Face Sales Planning* (New York: Warner Business, 2005).
6. Jim Hersma, personal correspondence; used with permission.
7. Special thanks to Karl Sooder for sharing this information.
8. Rackham, *Major Account Sales Strategy.*
9. Ibid., p. 30.
10. Brent Adamson, Matthew Dixon, and Nicholas Toman, "The End of Solution Sales," *Harvard Business Review* 61 (July–August 2012), pp. 60–68.
11. See Emma Brudner, "The Best Day to Prospect and 14 More Need-to-Know Sales Stats," July 6, 2015, https://blog.hubspot.com/sales/the-best-day-to-prospect-and-14-more-need-to-know-sales-stats?utm_campaign=blog-rss-emails&utm_source=hs_email&utm_medium=email&utm_content=20395210#sm.000006ak0j0ca2f6vu92j8cbnk3xz, accessed March 18, 2017.
12. For more insights into Webcasting, see Rod McColl and Yann Truong, "The Effects of Facial Attractiveness and Gender on Customer Evaluations during a Web-Video Sales Encounter," *Journal of Personal Selling and Sales Management* 33, no. 1 (2013), pp. 117–28; Cheng Yi, Zhenhui (Jack) Jiang, and Izak Benbasat, "Enticing and Engaging Consumers via Online Product Presentations: The Effects of Restricted Interaction Design," *Journal of Management Information Systems* 31, no. 4 (2015), pp. 213–42.

CHAPTER 8

1. Building partnerships and strong relationships is a process that starts when a lead is identified and continues throughout all postsale service and future calls.
2. Based on personal correspondence with Karl Sooder; used with permission.
3. Of course, many aspects of first impressions, such as race and gender, are outside the control of the salesperson.
4. For more about the importance of starting right, see Zachary R. Hall, Michael Ahearne, and Harish Sujan, "The Importance of Starting Right: The Influence of Accurate Intuition on Performance in Salesperson-Customer Interactions," *Journal of Marketing* 79, no. 3 (2015), pp. 91–109.
5. Matt Leaf, personal correspondence; used with permission.
6. For more information, see Christopher R. Plouffe, Willy Bolander, and Joseph A. Cote, "Which Influence Tactics Lead to Sales Performance? It Is a Matter of Style," *Journal of Personal Selling and Sales Management* 34, no. 2 (2014), pp. 141–59; Subhra Chakrabarty, Robert E. Widing, and Gene Brown, "Selling Behaviours and Sales Performance: The Moderating and Mediating Effects of Interpersonal Mentalizing," *Journal of Personal Selling and Sales Management* 34, no. 2, (2014), pp. 112–22; Anthony J. Urbaniak, "Beginning Your Sales Presentation," *American Salesman* 59, no. 1 (2014), pp. 22–25.
7. Dan Seidman, "Hilarious Selling Mistakes," www.sellingpower.com/content/video, accessed March 16, 2010.
8. This example is adapted from one provided in *The Little Blue Book of Customer Service* (Winona, MN: Fastenal Books, 2016), p. 39. The same general story is found in many sales training modules as well as at multiple locations on the Web.
9. Angie Main; used with permission.
10. Neil Rackham, *SPIN Selling* (New York: McGraw-Hill, 1988).
11. *The Little Blue Book of Customer Service*, p. 42.
12. Neil Rackham, "Sales Strategies to Capture Market Share in a Down Economy," 2009, www.thefreelibrary.com/Sales+strategies+to+capture+market+share+in+a+down+economy%3A+selling...-a0206465342, accessed May 17, 2013.
13. Ray Hanson, personal correspondence; used by permission.

14. This can be found at many places on the Web, including www.davidpbrown.co.uk/psychology/smart-test.html, accessed October 16, 2012.
15. Credibility is important. See John R. Graham, "Talking Our Way out of Sales," *American Salesman* 61, no. 10 (2016), pp. 26–30; Aaron Arndt, Kenneth Evans, Timothy D. Landry, Sarah Mady, and Chatdanai Pongpatipat, "The Impact of Salesperson Credibility-Building Statements on Later Stages of the Sales Encounter," *Journal of Personal Selling and Sales Management* 34, no. 1 (2014), pp. 19–32.
16. Cara Hale Alter, *The Credibility Code: How to Project Confidence and Competence When It Matters Most* (Meritus Books, 2012); Harry Labana, "Building Credibility on All Sides," *Bloomberg Businessweek*, www.businessweek.com/managing/content/oct2010/ca20101029_327671.htm?campaign_id=yhoo, accessed October 14, 2012.
17. Jim Hersma, personal correspondence; used with permission.
18. Todd Graf, personal correspondence; used with permission.
19. Tracey Brill, personal correspondence; used with permission.

CHAPTER 9

1. Gordon Hester, "The Neuroscience behind Stories," *Direct Selling News*, October 2010, pp. 60–64.
2. David A. Gilliam and Karen E. Flaherty, "Storytelling by the Sales Force and Its Effect on Buyer–Seller Exchange," *Industrial Marketing Management* 46 (2015), pp. 132–42.
3. A highly recommended source is David O'Neil, Steve Gerst, and Sharyl Prom, *Business Insights: How to Find and Effectively Communicate Golden Nuggets in Retail Data* (Brooklyn, NY: Delta Publishing Group, 2014).
4. "Points of Hue," https://delivermagazine.com/2010/02/points-of-hue/, accessed March 2010, p. 4.
5. Patricia Fripp, "9 Timely Tips for Pre-Presentation Preparation," *American Salesman* 61, no. 4 (2016), pp. 27–30; Darrin Fleming, "When Demos Sabotage the Sale," *Sales & Service Excellence Essentials* 13, no. 12 (2014), p. 7.
6. Personal correspondence.
7. Jeff S. Johnson, Scott B. Friend, and Avinash Malshe, "Mixed Interpretations of Sales Proposal Signals," *Journal of Personal Selling and Sales Management* 36, no. 3 (2016), pp. 264–80.
8. See, for example, www.qvidian.com.
9. Karl Sooder, "The Value Presentation," used with permission; Töytäri, Pekka and Risto Rajala, "Value-Based Selling: An Organizational Capability Perspective," *Industrial Marketing Management* 45 (2015), pp. 101–12; Marc Wouters and Markus A. Kirchberger, "Customer Value Propositions as Interorganizational Management Accounting to Support Customer Collaboration," *Industrial Marketing Management* 46 (2015), pp. 54–67.
10. The first example is adapted from Nicholas A. C. Read and Stephen J. Bistritz, *Selling to the C-Suite: What Every Executive Wants You to Know about Successfully Selling to the Top* (New York: McGraw-Hill,2009), p. 135. The second example is provided by Karl Sooder.

CHAPTER 10

1. Anthony Urbaniak, "Objections: A Natural Part of the Sales Process," *American Salesman* 60, no. 2 (2015), pp. 13–16.
2. "LAARC Sales Resistance Mitigation Tactic," www.provenmodels.com/555/laarc-sales-resistance-mitigation-tactic, accessed October 25, 2012.
3. Salespeople can forestall known concerns but shouldn't bring up issues that aren't even a problem with a particular prospect. Thus the need for good precall information gathering becomes obvious.
4. Mike Rockwood, "Desperately Seeking Objections," *Electrical Wholesaling* 97, no. 5 (2016), pp. 25–26.
5. Proverbs 18:13.
6. Howard Feiertag, "Clarify Client's Objection by Asking Questions," *Hotel Management* 227, no. 10 (August 2012), p. 12.
7. Ron Karr, "Do You Give Up Too Easily on Tough-to-Sell Prospects?," *American Salesman* 60, no. 4 (2015), pp. 8–14.
8. Personal correspondence; name of firm and industry withheld by request.
9. Emma Snider "28 Responses to the Dreaded Sales Objection 'It Costs Too Much,'" March 14, 2017, https://blog.hubspot.com/sales/price-objection-responses#sm.000006ak0j0ca2f6vu92j8cbnk3xz, accessed March 25, 2017.
10. James C. Anderson, Normalya Kumar, and James A. Narus (2008), "Become a Value Merchant," *Sales and Marketing Management*, May–June 2008, p. 21.
11. Tracey Brill, personal correspondence; used with permission.
12. Anthony J. Urbaniak, "Ways to Turn Today's No into a Sale Down the Road," *American Salesman* 58, no. 5 (2013), pp. 22–26.

CHAPTER 11

1. James Zboia, Ronald A. Clark, and Diana L. Haytko, "An Offer You Can't Refuse: Consumer Perceptions of Sales Pressure," *Journal of the Academy of Marketing Science* 44, no. 6 (November 2016), pp. 806–21.

2. Neil Rackham, *SPIN Selling* (New York: McGraw-Hill, 1988), pp. 19-51.
3. Rakesh Singh and Pingali Venugopali, "The Impact of Salesperson Customer Orientation on Sales Performance via Mediating Mechanism," *Journal of Business and Industrial Marketing* 30, no. 5 (2015), pp. 594-607.
4. Scott Blakely and Paul Calahan, "Take Back Your Credit with Long-Term Contracts in the Face of Customers' TPS," *Business Credit* 117, no. 1 (January 2015), pp. 42-47.
5. Tasha Anderson, "Fleet Services," *Alaska Business Monthly* 33, no. 5 (May 2017), pp. 44-49.
6. Bruce Culbert, personal correspondence, February 20, 2008; used with permission.
7. Nawar N. Chaker, David W. Schumann, Alex Zablah, and Daniel J. Flint, "Exploring the State of Salesperson Insecurity: How It Emerges and Why It Matters," *Journal of Marketing Theory and Practice* 24, no. 3 (2016), pp. 344-64.
8. Mark Hunter, "Passion as a Sales Tool," *Agency Sales* 46, no. 4 (April 2016), pp. 26-29.
9. Marvin A. Jolson, "Selling Assertively," *Business Horizons,* September-October 1984, pp. 71-77.
10. www.reddit.com/r/sysadmin/comments/2q6xyh/overlyaggressivesalespeople/, accessed June 1, 2017, posted in 2015.
11. Nawar N. Chaker, David W. Schumann, Alex Zablah, and Daniel J. Flint, "Exploring the State of Salesperson Insecurity: How It Emerges and Why It Matters," *Journal of Marketing Theory and Practice* 24, no. 3 (Summer 2016), pp. 344-64.
12. Maryse Koehl, Juliet F. Poujol, and John F. Tanner Jr., "The Impact of Sales Contests on Customer Listening: An Empirical Study in a Telesales Context," *Journal of Personal Selling and Sales Management* 36, no. 3 (2016), pp. 281-92.
13. Houjeir, Roudaina and Ross Brennan, "The influence of culture on trust in B2B banking relationships." *The International Journal of Bank Marketing* 35, no. 3 (2017), pp. 495-515.
14. John Branton, "Closing Sales the Right Way," *National Underwriter, Life & Health* 113, no. 5 (March 2, 2009), p. 31.
15. Eleanor Brownell, "How to Make Yourself Memorable," *American Salesman* 55, no. 3 (March 2010), pp. 24-28.
16. Examples from Jackson Keyes and Yusef Trowell given via personal correspondence, June 2, 2017, used with permission.
17. Nwamaka A. Anaza and Brian Rutherford, "Increasing Business-to-Business Buyer Word-of-Mouth and Share-of-Purchase," *Journal of Business and Industrial Marketing* 29, no. 5 (2014), pp. 427-437.
18. Aniefre Eddie Inyang. "The Buffering Effects of Salesperson Service Behaviors on Customer Loyalty after Service Failure and Recovery," *Journal of Managerial Issues* 27, no. 1-4 (2015), pp. 102-19.
19. Jasmin Bergeron and Michel Laroche, "The Effects of Perceived Salesperson Listening Effectiveness in the Financial Industry," *Journal of Financial Services Marketing* 14, no. 1 (June 2009), pp. 6-25; Yosra Missaoui. "Non-verbal Communication Barriers When Dealing with Saudi Sellers," *International Journal of Organizational Leadership* 4, no. 4 (2015), pp. 392-402.
20. Dave Alexander, personal correspondence, May 15, 2017.
21. Raj Agnihotri, Adam Rapp, and Kevin Trainor, "Understanding the Role of Information Communication in the Buyer-Seller Exchange Process: Antecedents and Outcomes," *Journal of Business and Industrial Marketing* 24, no. 7 (2009), pp. 474-99.
22. Dave Stein, "Smart Sales: Let's Role the Videotape," *Sales and Marketing Management* 160, no. 3 (May-June 2008), p. 8.

CHAPTER 12

1. Uchenna Uzo and Jude O. Adigwe, "Cultural Norms and Cultural Agents in Buyer-Seller Negotiation Processes and Outcomes," *Journal of Personal Selling and Sales Management* 36, no. 2 (2016), pp. 126-43.
2. The information in this section was developed from Kenneth Thomas, "Conflict and Conflict Management," in *The Handbook of Industrial and Organizational Psychology*, ed. Marvin Dunnette (Skokie, IL: Rand McNally, 1976).
3. "Fractured English," *Have a Good Day*, January 1997, pp. 1-2.
4. See "Good Guy/Bad Guy," http://changingminds.org/disciplines/negotiation/tactics/good-bad_guy.htm, accessed October 28, 2012.
5. John Patrick Dolan, "How to Overcome the Top Ten Negotiating Tactics," www.myarticlearchive.com/articles/5/025.htm, accessed March 25, 2017.
6. Rhona E. Johnsen and Sylvie Lacoste, "An Exploration of the 'Dark Side' Associations of Conflict, Power and Dependence in Customer-Supplier Relationships," *Industrial Marketing Management* 59 (2016), pp. 76-95; Roger Fisher and William Ury, *Getting to Yes: Negotiating Agreement without Giving In*, 2nd ed. (Boston: Houghton Mifflin, 1991).
7. James C. Anderson, James A. Narus, and Marc Wouters, "Tiebreaker Selling," *Harvard Business Review* 92, no. 3 (2014), pp. 90-96.

8. For more information, see https://ppp.worldbank.org/public-private-partnership/ppp-overview/practical-tools/checklists-and-risk-matrices/force-majeure-checklist/sample-clauses, accessed March 26, 2017.
9. Stephanie P. Thomas, Karl B. Manrodt, and Jacqueline K. Eastman, "The Impact of Relationship History on Negotiation Strategy Expecations: A Theoretical Framework," *International Journal of Physical Distribution & Logistics Management* 45, no. 8 (2015), pp. 794–813.

CHAPTER 13

1. Alfred Pelham, "Do Consulting-Oriented Sales Management Programs Impact Salesforce Performance and Profit?," *Journal of Business and Industrial Marketing* 21, no. 3 (2006), pp. 175–86; Thomas E. Decarlo and Son K. Lam, "Identifying Successful Hunters and Farmers in the Sales Force: A Dispositional/Situational Framework," *Journal of the Academy of Marketing Science* 44, no. 4 (July 2016), pp. 415–29.
2. Robert W. Palmatier, Lisa K. Scheer, Mark B. Houston, Kenneth R. Evans, and Srinath Gopalakrishna, "Use of Relationship Marketing Programs in Building Customer–Salesperson and Customer–Firm Relationships: Differential Influences on Financial Outcomes," *International Journal of Research in Marketing* 24, no. 3 (2007), pp. 210–24.
3. V. Kumar and Denish Sha, "Can Marketing Lift Stock Prices?," *Sloan Management Review* 52, no. 4 (2011), pp. 24–26; Petr Suchánek, Jiri Richter, and Maria Králová, "Customer Satisfaction, Product Quality and Performance of Companies," *Review of Economic Perspectives* (2014), pp. 329–44.
4. John F. Tanner Jr., *Analytics & Dynamic Customer Strategy* (New York: Wiley, 2014).
5. Robert Dwyer, Paul Schurr, and Sejo Oh, "Developing Buyer–Seller Relationships," *Journal of Marketing* (April 1987), pp. 11–27. This is the paper that really started the academic field of relationship marketing.
6. Raj Agnihotri, Rebecca Dingus, Michael Y Hu, and Michael T. Krush, "Social Media: Influencing Customer Satisfaction," *Industrial Marketing Management* 53 (February 2016), pp. 172–80.
7. Tai Yi-Ming and Ho Chin-Fu, "Effects of Information Sharing on Customer Relationship Intention," *Industrial Management and Data Systems* 110, no. 9 (2010), pp. 1385–1401; Po-Yuan Chen, Kuan-Yang Chen, and Lei-Yu Wu, "The Impact of Trust and Commitment on Value Creation in Asymmetric Buyer-Seller Relationships: The Mediation Effect of Specific Asset Investments," *Journal of Business and Industrial Marketing* 32, no. 3 (2017), pp. 457–71.
8. Y. H. Wong, Humphry Hung, and Wing-ki Chow, "Mediating Effects of Relationship Quality on Customer Relationships: An Empirical Study in Hong Kong," *Marketing Intelligence and Planning* 25, no. 6 (2007), pp. 581–99; Brian Crombie, "Is Guanxi Social Capital?," *The ISM Journal of International Business* 1, no. 2 (2011), pp. 1–28; Zohaib Razzaq, Salman Yousaf, and Zhao Hong, "The Moderating Impact of Emotions on Customer Equity Drivers and Loyalty Intentions: Evidence of within Sector Differences," *Asia Pacific Journal of Marketing and Logistics* 29, no. 2 (2017), pp. 239–64.
9. Wen-Hung Wang, Chiung-Ju Liang, and Yung-De Wu, "Relationship Bonding Tactics, Relationship Quality, and Customer Behavioral Loyalty–Behavioral Sequence in Taiwan's Information Services Industry," *Journal of Services Research* 6, no. 1 (2006), pp. 31–57; Michael Trimarchi, Peter W. Liesch, and Rick Tamaschke, "A Study of Compatibility Variation across Chinese Buyer–Seller Relationships," *European Journal of Marketing* 44, no. 1–2 (2010), pp. 87–113; Guocai Wang, Shanliang Li, Xifeng Wang, Chunyu Lu, and Chen Lv, "Relationship Specific Investment, Guanxi Behavior, and Salesperson-Owned Customer Loyalty," *Social Behavior and Personality* 42, no. 7 (2014), pp. 1147–66.
10. Michael D. Johnson and Fred Selnes, "Customer Portfolio Management: toward a Dynamic Theory of Relationships," *Journal of Marketing* 68, no. 2 (2004), pp. 1–17; Robert C. Dudley and Das Narayandas, "A Portfolio Approach to Sales," *Harvard Business Review* 84 (July–August 2006), pp. 16–24; Said Echchakoui, "Salesperson Profitability in Relationship Marketing," *Journal of Modelling in Management* 9, no. 3 (2014), pp. 306–23.
11. Dennis Campbell and Frances Frei, "The Persistence of Customer Profitability: Empirical Evidence and Implications from a Financial Services Firm," *Journal of Service Research* 7, no. 2 (2004), pp. 107–124; Morten Holm, V. Kumar, and Carsten Rohde, "Measuring Customer Profitability in Complex Environments: An Interdisciplinary Contingency Framework," *Journal of the Academy of Marketing Science* 40, no. 3 (2012), pp. 387–401.
12. Glen L. Urban and John R. Hauser, "Listening In to Find and Explore New Combinations of Customer Needs," *Journal of Marketing* 68, no. 2 (2004), pp. 72–87; Wadie Nasri and Lanouar Charfeddine, "Motivating Salespeople to Contribute to Marketing Intelligence Activities: An Expectancy Theory

Approach," *International Journal of Marketing Studies* 4, no. 1 (2012), pp. 168–75.
13. Dwyer et al., "Developing Buyer-Seller Relationships."
14. Paolo Guenzi and Laurent Georges, "Interpersonal Trust in Commercial Relationships: Antecedents and Consequences of Customer Trust in the Salesperson," *European Journal of Marketing* 44, no. 1-2 (2010), pp. 114-28; Marc Elsäßer and Bernd W. Wirtz, "Rational and Emotional Factors of Customer Satisfaction and Brand Loyalty in a Business-to-Business Setting," *Journal of Business and Industrial Marketing* 32, no. 1 (2017), pp. 138-52.
15. Kim Sydow Campbell, Lenita Davis, and Lauren Skinner, "Rapport Management during the Exploration Phase of the Salesperson-Customer Relationship," *Journal of Personal Selling and Sales Management* 26, no. 4 (2006), pp. 359-70; Anja Geigenmuller and Larissa Greschuchna, "How to Establish Trustworthiness in Initial Service Encounters," *Journal of Marketing Theory and Practice* 19, no. 4 (Fall 2011), pp. 391-405.
16. Constanza Bianchi and Abu Saleh, "On Importer Trust and Commitment: A Comparative Study of Two Developing Countries," *International Marketing Review* 27, no. 1 (2010), pp. 55-70.
17. Roudaina Houjeir and Ross Brennan, "Trust in Cross-Cultural B2B Financial Services Relationships," *Journal of Financial Services Marketing* 21, no. 2 (June 2016), pp. 90-102.
18. Guenzi and Georges, "Interpersonal Trust in Commercial Relationships."
19. Alfred Pelham, "The Impact of Industry and Training Influences on Salesforce Consulting Time and Consulting Effectiveness," *Journal of Business and Industrial Marketing* 24, no. 8 (2009), pp. 575-84.
20. Paolo Guenzi, Luigi M. De Luca, and Rosann Spiro, "The Combined Effect of Customer Perceptions about a Salesperson's Adaptive Selling and Selling Orientation on Customer Trust in the Salesperson: A Contingency Perspective," *Journal of Business and Industrial Marketing* 31, no. 4 (2016), pp. 553-64.
21. Mark E. Cross, Thomas G. Brashear, Edward E. Rigdon, and Danny N. Bellenger, "Customer Orientation and Salesperson Performance," *European Journal of Marketing* 33, 41, no. 7-8 (2007), pp. 821-39; Emily A. Goad and Fernando Jaramillo, "The Good, the Bad, and the Effective: A Meta-Analytic Examination of Selling Orientation and Customer Orientation on Sales Performance," *Journal of Personal Selling and Sales Management* 34, no. 4 (2014), pp. 285-95; Ernener Kaynak, Ali Kara, Clement S. F. Chow, and Tommi Laukkanen, "Role of Adaptive Selling and Customer Orientation on Salesperson Performance: Evidence from Two Distinct Markets of Europe and Asia," *Journal of Transnational Management* 21, no. 2 (April-June 2016), pp. 62-83.
22. Gerrard Macintosh, "Customer Orientation, Relationship Quality, and Relational Benefits to the Firm," *Journal of Services Marketing* 21, no. 3 (2007), pp. 150-68; Jon C. Carr and Tara B. Lopez, "Examining Market Orientation as Both Culture and Conduct: Modeling the Relationship between Market Orientation and Employee Responses," *Journal of Marketing Theory and Practice* 15, no. 2 (2007), pp. 113-27.
23. Patrick Poon, Gerald Albaum, and Cheng-Yue Yin, "Exploring Risks, Advantages, and Inter-Personal Trust in Buyer-Salesperson Relationships in Direct Selling in a Non-Western Country," *International Journal of Retail and Distribution Management* 45, no. 3 (2017), pp. 328-42.
24. John M. Hawes, Kenneth Mast, and John E. Swan, "Trust Earning Perceptions of Sellers and Buyers," *Journal of Personal Selling and Sales Management* (Spring 1989), pp. 1-8; J. Tsalikis and Walfried Lassar, "Measuring Consumer Perceptions of Business Ethical Behavior in Two Muslim Countries," *Journal of Business Ethics* 89 (2009), pp. 91-98.
25. Jasmin Bergeron and Michel Laroche, "The Effects of Perceived Salesperson Listening Effectiveness in the Financial Industry," *Journal of Financial Services Marketing* 14, no. 8 (June 2009), pp. 6-25; Omar S. Itani and Eddie Aniefre Inyang, "The Effects of Empathy and Listening of Salespeople on Relationship Quality in the Retail Banking Industry," *International Journal of Bank Marketing* 33, no. 6 (2015), pp. 692-716.
26. Thomas Hollmann, Cheryl Burke Jarvis, and Mary Jo Bitner, "Reaching the Breaking Point: A Dynamic Process Theory of Business-to-Business Customer Defection," *Journal of the Academy of Marketing Science* 43, no. 2 (March 2015), pp. 25-78.
27. Lisa Cross, "Establishing Customer Loyalty," *Graphic Arts Monthly* 76, no. 9 (2004), pp. 39-42; Kimberly Scher, "Breaking Up Is Hard to Do: Knowing When a Customer Relationship Is Worth Keeping," *Catalyst,* September-October 2008, pp. 26-29.
28. Christine Horton, "Kaseya Turnaround Focuses on Customer Relationships," *Channel Pro,* May 10, 2016, p. 4.
29. "Fujitsu Sets Out 'Fujitsu Technology and Service Vision 2017,'" *ICT Monitor Worldwide*, April 18, 2017.
30. Gilbert N. Nyaga, Judith M. Whipple, and Daniel F. Lynch, "Examining Supply Chain Relationships: Do Buyer and Supplier Perspectives on Collaborative

Relationships Differ?," *Journal of Operations Management* 28, no. 2 (March 2010), pp. 101–15.

31. Constanza Bianchi and Abu Saleh, "On Importer Trust and Commitment: A Comparative Study of Two Developing Countries," *International Marketing Review* 27, no. 1 (2010), pp. 55–70; Po-Yuan Chen, Kuan-Yang Chen, and Lei-Yu Wu, "The Impact of Trust and Commitment on Value Creation in Asymmetric Buyer-Seller Relationships: The Mediation Effect of Specific Asset Investments," *Journal of Business and Industrial Marketing* 32, no. 3 (2017), pp. 457–71.
32. Lisa K. Scheer, Fred C. Miao, and Robert W. Palmatier, "Dependence and Interdependence in Marketing Relationships: Meta-Analytic Insights," *Journal of the Academy of Marketing Science* 43, no. 6 (November 2015), pp. 694–712.
33. Anonymous, "UniFirst Wins Two Stevie Awards," March 1, 2017, www.unifirst.com/company/press-releases/unifirst-wins-two-stevie-awards-for-sales-training/, accessed June 9, 2017.
34. F. Juliet Poujol and John F. Tanner Jr., "The Impact of Contests on Salespeople's Customer Orientation: An Application of Tournament Theory," *Journal of Personal Selling and Sales Management* 30, no. 1 (Winter 2010), pp. 33–46.

CHAPTER 14

1. Dough Henschen, "SaaS-Based BI Tracks Rossignol Ski and Snowboard Sales," *Intelligent Enterprise Online,* January 5, 2010, http://intelligent-enterprise.informationweek.com/showArticle.jhtml;jsessionid=14FHIGTREQRNLQE1GHRSKH4ATMY32JVN?articleID=222200361, accessed March 24, 2010.
2. Bob Hall, "Saying Thanks," *Quick Printing* 33, no. 1 (October 2009), p. 6.
3. Samuel Greengard, "Keeping the Customer Satisfied," *CIO Insight* 109 (November 2009), pp. 32–35.
4. Goutam Chakraborty, Prashant Srivastava, and Fred Marshall, "Are Drivers of Customer Satisfaction Different for Buyers/Users from Different Functional Areas?" *Journal of Business and Industrial Marketing* 22, no. 1 (2007), pp. 20–32; Kenneth R. Lord and Pola Gupta, "Response of Buying-Center Participants to B2B Product Placements," *Journal of Business and Industrial Marketing* 25, no. 3 (2010), pp. 188–95.
5. Celso Augusto de Matos, Carlos A.V. Rossi, Ricardo T. Veiga, and Valter A. Vieira, "Consumer Reaction to Service Failure and Recovery: The Moderating Role of Attitude toward Complaining," *Journal of Services Marketing* 23, no. 7 (2009), pp. 462–75; Constantine Lymperopoulos and Ioannis E. Chaniotakis, "Price Satisfaction and Personnel Efficiency as Antecedents of Overall Satisfaction from Consumer Credit Products and Positive Word of Mouth," *Journal of Financial Services* 13, no. 1 (2008), pp. 63–71.
6. Rob Gerlsbeck, "Bad Reputation Can't Be Beat," *Marketing* 111, no. 14 (2006), p. 6.
7. K. R. Jayasimha, Harish Chaudhary, and Anurag Chauhan, "Investigating Consumer Advocacy, Community Usefulness and Brand Avoidance," *Marketing Intelligence & Planning* 35, no. 4 (2017), pp. 488–509.
8. Chih-Cheng Volvic Chen and Chih-Jou Chen, "The Role of Customer Participation for Enhancing Repurchase Intention," *Management Decision* 55, no. 3 (2017), pp. 547–62.
9. Claes Fornell, Forrest V. Morgeson III, and G. Tomas M. Hult, "Stock Returns on Customer Satisfaction Do Beat the Marketing: Gauging the Effect of Marketing Intangibles," *Journal of Marketing* 80, no. 5 (September 2016), pp. 1–18.
10. Lloyd C. Harris, Raymond P. Fisk, and Hana Sysalova, "Exposing Pinocchio Customers: Investigating Exaggerated Service Stories," *Journal of Service Management* 27, no. 2 (2016), pp. 63–90.
11. Chia-Chi Chang, "When Service Fails: The Role of the Salesperson and the Customer," *Psychology & Marketing* 23, no. 3 (2006), pp. 203–14; Concepción Varela-Neira, Rodolfo Vázquez-Casielles, and Víctor Iglesias, "Explaining Customer Satisfaction with Complaint Handling," *International Journal of Bank Marketing* 28, no. 2 (2010), pp. 88–112.
12. "Ikea: Not Sweden's Only Quality Company," *Strategic Direction* 22, no. 5 (2006), pp. 5–7.
13. James J. Zboja and Michael D. Hartline, "An Examination of High-Frequency Cross-Selling," *Journal of Relationship Marketing* 11, no. 1 (2012), 41–56.
14. Mike Power, "Accessibility Is Top Priority," *Industrial Distribution* 94, no. 10 (2005), p. 56.
15. Dwyer and Tanner, *Business Marketing.*
16. John W. Barnes, Donald W. Jackson Jr., Michael D. Hutt, and Ajith Kumar, "The Role of Culture Strength in Shaping Sales Force Outcomes," *Journal of Personal Selling and Sales Management* 26, no. 3 (2006), pp. 255–70; Hassan Ghorbani, Seyedeh Masoomeh, Abdollahi Demneh, and Arezoo Khorsandnejad, "An Empirical Investigation of the Relationship between Organizational Culture and Customer Orientation: The Mediating Effect of Knowledge Management (An Empirical Study in the Household Appliance Industry in Iran)," *International Journal of Marketing Studies* 4, no. 3 (June 2012), pp. 58–67.
17. John F. Tanner Jr., Jorge Wise, Christophe Fournier, and Sandrine Hollet, "Executives' Perspectives of the

Changing Role of the Sales Profession: Views from France, the United States, and Mexico," *Journal of Business and Industrial Marketing* 23, no. 3 (2008), pp. 193-202.

18. Paul Teague, "Congratulations to Tyco International," *Purchasing* 138, no. 9 (September 17, 2009), p. 11.
19. J. Garry Smith and Donald P. Roy, "A Framework for Developing Customer Orientation in Ticket Sales Organizations," *Sport Marketing Quarterly, Suppl. Special Issue: Sales Force Management in Sport* 20, no. 2 (June 2011), pp. 93-102.
20. Darryl Lehnus, "Building the 333 Relationship Strategy," *Baylor University S3 Newsletter*, October 15, 2012.
21. Jessica Sebor, "CRM Gets Serious," *Customer Relationship Management,* February 2008, pp. 23-26.
22. Anonymous, "Impact 360 Success Story: Elavon," www.verint.com/assets/verint/documents/case-studies/contact-center/elavon_cs_us.pdf, accessed June 14, 2017.

CHAPTER 15

1. Justina Gnyp, "Productivity Initiatives Distracting Sales Teams and Stifling Business Performance, Accenture Study Finds," *Business Wire,* September 27, 2016, http://search.proquest.com.ezproxy.baylor.edu/docview/1823408327/C8584A2EE92B4B0FPQ/6?accountid=7014, accessed June 15, 2017.
2. Michael Cornnell, "My Trip to the Million-Dollar Club," *Print + Promo* 53, no. 6 (June 2015), pp. 44-46
3. Cal Brown, personal interview.
4. Lauren Harrison, "Emora Ltd. Reveals the Secrets to Goal Setting," PRWeb (February 23, 2017), www.prweb.com/releases/emora/goalsettingsecrets/prweb14086128.htm, accessed June 12, 2017.
5. Leigh Anne Pearson, "Sales Performance at Teradata," Baylor University Center for Professional Selling Report, May 15, 2011.
6. Michael J. Barone and Thomas E. DeCarlo, "Performance Trends and Salesperson Evaluations: The Moderating Roles of Evaluation Task, Managerial Risk Propensity, and Firm Strategic Orientation," *Journal of Personal Selling and Sales Management* 32, no. 2 (Spring 2012), pp. 207-12; Tracy Gonzalez-Padron, M Billur Akdeniz, and Roger J Calantone, "Benchmarking Sales Staffing Efficiency in Dealerships using Extended Data Envelope Analysis," *Journal of Business Research* 67, no. 9 (September 2014), pp. 1904-11.
7. Lawrence Ang and Ben Taylor, "Managing Customer Profitability Using Portfolio Matrices," *Journal of Database Marketing & Customer Strategy Management* 12, no. 4 (2005), pp. 298-304.
8. Adel El-Ansary and Waleed A. El-Ansary, *Winning Customers, Building Accounts: Some Do It Better Than Others* (Jacksonville, FL: Paper and Plastics Education and Research Foundation, 1994).
9. Douglas Hughes, Joel LeBon, and Adam Rapp, "Gaining and Leveraging Customer-Based Competitive Intelligence: The Pivotal Role of Social Capital and Salesperson Adaptive Selling Skills," *Journal of the Academy of Marketing Science* 41, no. 1 (January 2013), pp. 91-110; Wagner Kamakura, "Cross-Selling: Offering the Right Product to the Right Customer at the Right Time," *Journal of Relationship Marketing* 6, no. 3/4 (January 2008), pp. 41-54.
10. Susan Flaviano, personal correspondence; used with permission.
11. "Survey Says Employees Feel Obligated 24/7," *Manufacturing Business Technology* 24, no. 9 (2006), p. 9.
12. Flaviano, personal correspondence.
13. Lee Brubaker, "Make Sure Pay Time Pays," *American Salesman* 51, no. 8 (2006), pp. 27-29.
14. Sara Radicati, "Email Statistics Report: 2014-2018," www.radicati.com/wp/wp-content/uploads/2014/01/Email-Statistics-Report-2014-2018-Executive-Summary.pdf, accessed June 13, 2017.
15. Tom Reilly, "How Good Is Your Sales Follow-Up?" *Industrial Distribution* (October 2016), p. 5.
16. John Plott, personal correspondence, March 1, 2008; used with permission.
17. Sandra Kennedy, personal correspondence, January 2, 2013; used with permission.
18. Anonymous, PK Companies, www.pipelinersales.com/case-studies-testimonials/, accessed June 13, 2017.
19. Paul Lushin, personal correspondence, September 7, 2013; used with permission.

CHAPTER 16

1. Douglas E. Hughes, Joël Le Bon, and Adam Rapp, "Gaining and Leveraging Customer-Based Competitive Intelligence: The Pivotal Role of Social Capital and Salesperson Adaptive Selling Skills," *Journal of the Academy of Marketing Science* 41, no. 1 (January 2013), pp. 91-110.
2. Neville May, "Communication Breakdown," *Sales & Marketing Management* 160, no. 4 (July-August 2009), pp. 12-13.
3. Ashwin W. Joshi, "Salesperson Influence on Product Development: Insights from a Study of Small Manufacturing Organizations," *Journal of Marketing* 74, no. 1 (January 2010), pp. 94-108.

4. Frank Caprio, "There Is Power in a Self-Assured Salesperson," *Industrial Distribution* 98, no. 6 (November 2009), p. 55.
5. Matthew Carr, "Stepping in Time: Unifying Cross-functional Relationships to Mitigate Risk and Improve Cash Flow," *Business Credit* 111, no. 5 (May 2009), pp. 56–58.
6. Anna Wells, "Lawson Products Take Business to the Next Level," *Industrial Maintenance & Plant Operations* (March 17, 2015), p. 1.
7. Kenneth Le Meunier-FitzHugh and Nigel F. Piercy, "Improving the Relationship between Sales and Marketing," *European Business Review* 22, no. 3 (2010), pp. 287–305; Robert Dwyer and John F. Tanner Jr., *Business Marketing: Connecting Strategy, Relationships, and Learning,* 4th ed. (Burr Ridge, IL: McGraw-Hill/Irwin, 2009).
8. Douglas E. Hughes, Joël Le Bon, and Avinash Malshe, "The Marketing–Sales Interface at the Interface: Creating Market-Based Capabilities through Organizational Synergy," *Journal of Personal Selling and Sales Management* 32, no. 1 (Winter 2012), pp. 57–69; Avish Malshe, "How Is Marketers' Credibility Construed within the Sales-Marketing Interface?," *Journal of Business Research* 63 (January 2010), pp. 13–19; Michael Beverland, Marion Steel, and G. Peter Dapiran, "Cultural Frames That Drive Sales and Marketing Apart: An Exploratory Study," *Journal of Business and Industrial Marketing* 21, no. 6 (2006), pp. 386–402.
9. Anonymous, "Gilbarco Veeder-Root: A Case Study," http://revmarketer.pedowitzgroup.com/rs/042-VGP-319/images/Gilbarco_Case_Study_v1r1.pdf, accessed June 14, 2017.
10. Avinash Malshe, "An Exploration of Key Connections within Sales-Marketing Interface," *Journal of Business and Industrial Marketing* 26, no. 1 (2011), pp. 45–57; Pankai M. Madhani, "Sales and Marketing: Integration," *Journal of Indian Management* 12, no. 2 (April–June 2015), pp. 17–28.
11. James B. DeConinck, Mary Beth DeConinck, and Hollye K. Moss, "The Relationship among Ethical Leadership, Ethical Climate, Supervisory Trust, and Moral Judgment," *Academy of Marketing Studies Journal* 20, no. 3 (2016), pp. 89–99;Charles H. Schwepker and Thomas N. Ingram, "Ethical Leadership in the Salesforce: Effects on Salesperson Customer Orientation, Commitment to Customer Value and Job Stress," *Journal of Business and Industrial Marketing* 31, no. 7 (2016), pp. 914–27.
12. Sarah Sluis, "Yahoo Sees Crystal Clear Forecasts with C9 Analytics," *Customer Relationship Management* 18, no. 9 (September 2014), p. 49.
13. Anonymous, "ClearSlide and Aberdeen Group Present Webinar on Transforming the Business of Selling," PR Newswire (September 20, 2016), www.prnewswire.com/news-releases/clearslide-and-aberdeen-group-present-webinar-on-transforming-the-business-of-selling-300206720.html, accessed June 15, 2017.
14. Charles H. Schwepker Jr. and David J. Good, "Sales Quotas: Unintended Consequences on Trust in Organization, Customer-Oriented Selling and Sales Performance," *Journal of Marketing Theory and Practice* 20, no. 4 (Fall 2012), pp. 437–52; F. Juliet Poujol and John F. Tanner Jr., "The Impact of Sales Contests on Salespeople's Customer Orientation: An Application of Tournament Theory," *Journal of Personal Selling and Sales Management* 30 (Winter 2010), pp. 33–46.
15. Michael L. Mallin, Edward O'Donnell, and Michael Y. Hu, "The Role of Uncertainty and Sales Control in the Development of Sales Manager Trust," *The Journal of Business & Industrial Marketing* 25, no. 1 (2010), pp. 30–44; Thomas G. Brashear, Chris Manolis, and Charles M. Brooks, "The Effects of Control, Trust, and Justice on Salesperson Turnover," *Journal of Business Research* 58 (March 2005), pp. 241–57.
16. Anonymous, "New Study Sales Force Practices of Middle Market Companies," National Center for the Middle Market, www.thestreet.com/story/13530893/3/new-study-reveals-sales-force-practices-of-middle-market-companies.html, accessed June 15, 2017.
17. Jay P. Mulki, Jorge Fernando Jaramillo, and William B Locander, "Critical Role of Leadership on Ethical Climate and Salesperson Behaviors," *Journal of Business Ethics* 86, no. 2 (May 2009), pp. 126–51; Charles Schwepker and Roberta J. Schultz, "Influence of the Ethical Servant Leader and Ethical Climate on Customer Value Enhancing Sales Performance," *Journal of Personal Selling and Sales Management* 35, no. 2 (2015), p. 93.
18. Craig A. Martin, "An Empirical Examination of the Antecedents of Ethical Intentions in Professional Selling," *Journal of Leadership, Accountability and Ethics* 9, no. 1 (February 2012), pp. 19–26; Raj Agnihotri and Michael T Krush, "Salesperson Empathy, Ethical Behaviors, and Sales Performance: The Moderating Role of Trust in One's Manager," *Journal of Personal Selling and Sales Management* 35, no. 2 (2015), pp. 164–72.
19. Poujol and Tanner, "The Impact of Sales Contests on Salespeople's Customer Orientation"; Sean Valentine and Gary Fleischman, "Ethics Training and Businesspersons' Perceptions of Organizational Ethics," *Journal of Business Ethics* 52 (July 2004), pp. 391–409.

20. Norman L. Tolle, "Brochure Setting Forth Sales Incentive Plan Did Not Create Binding Contract," *Employee Benefit Plan Review* 61, no. 5 (2006), pp. 26–27.
21. Dominique Rouziès, John Hulland, and Donald W. Barclay, "Does Marketing and Sales Integration Always Pay Off? Evidence from a Social Capital Perspective," *Journal of the Academy of Marketing Science* 42, no. 5 (September 2014), pp. 511–27; Arun Sharma and Heiner Evanschitzky, "Returns on Key Accounts: Do the Results Justify the Expenditures?" *Journal of Business & Industrial Marketing* 31, no. 2 (2016), pp. 174–82.
22. Anonymous, "PG&E Recognized by the Edison Electricity Institute and Key Account Customers for Outstanding Customer Service," *Energy Weekly News* (April 28, 2017), p. 120.
23. Heather Fletcher, "Suddenlink Calls for Change," *Target Marketing* 33, no. 2 (February 2010), p. 10.
24. Eli Jones, Andrea L. Dixon, Lawrence B. Chonko, and Joseph P. Cannon, "Key Accounts and Team Selling: A Review, Framework, and Research Agenda," *Journal of Personal Selling & Sales Management* 25, no. 2 (2005), pp. 181–98.

CHAPTER 17

1. Pontoon; Sales Positions Top List of Most Available Jobs for College Graduates in the U.S. Anonymous, "Sales Positions Top List of Most Available Job for College Graduates in the US," *Economics Week* (Aug 12, 2016), pp. 270.
2. Patricia V. Rivera, "The Birth of a Salesman," *Atlanta-Journal and Constitution,* August 12, 2007, p. 1D.
3. Thomas Phelps, "Things You Should Look for in a Sales Job," *the balance* (March 1, 2017), www.thebalance.com/top-things-you-should-look-for-in-a-sales-job-2918401, accessed June 16, 2017.
4. Brandon Johnson, personal correspondence, June 15, used with permission.
5. Leo Tenenblat, "10 Things You Should Know before Taking a Job in Sales," *AppMesh Blog,* September 3, 2015, http://blog.appme.sh/2015/09/10-things-you-should-know-before-sales.html, accessed June 16, 2017.
6. James M. Loveland, John W. Lounsbury, Soon-Hee Park, and Donald W. Jackson, "Are Salespeople Born or Made? Biology, Personality, and the Career Satisfaction of Salespeople," *Journal of Business and Industrial Marketing* 30, no. 2 (2015), pp. 233–40.
7. Deborah Aarts, "The 3 Inherent Traits of Great Salespeople," *Profit* 29, no. 5 (November 2010), p. 38.
8. George W. Dudley and Shannon L. Goodson, *Earning What You're Worth? The Psychology of Sales Call Reluctance,* 2nd ed. (Dallas: Behavioral Science Research Press, 2008).
9. Tom Day, personal interview.
10. Ti Yu, "E-Portfolio, a Valuable Job Search Tool for College Students," *Campus-Wide Information Systems* 29, no. 1 (2012), pp. 70–76; Lucy Aitken, "Me and My Portfolio," *Campaign,* May 14, 2004, pp. 36–37; Denny E. McCorkle, Joe E. Alexander, James Reardon, and Nathan D. Kling, "Developing Self-Marketing Skills: Are Marketing Students Prepared for the Job Search?," *Journal of Marketing Education* 25 (December 2003), pp. 196–207.
11. Katie Carano, "Successful Interview and Negotiation Strategies: A Review," *Career Planning and Adult Development Journal* 26, no. 4 (Winter 2010/2011), pp. 28–44; Laura Huag, "Intimidation and Stress: All in a Day's Interview," *Financial Times,* November 28, 2005, p. 14.
12. John F. Tanner Jr., Juliet Poujol, and Christophe Fournier, "Building a Brand: Salespersons' Perceptions of the Companies They Worked For," forthcoming.
13. Susan Denny, personal interview.
14. Diane McGrath, "Continuous Learning," *Update,* Fourth Quarter 1998, p. 8.
15. Stefanie L. Boyer and Brian Lambert, "Take the Handcuffs off Sales Team Development with Self-Directed Learning," *T&D* 62, no. 11 (November 2008), pp. 62–67.
16. Lisa White, "Francisco Limas," *Foodservice Equipment & Supplies* 60, no. 7 (2007), p. 49.
17. Diane Powers, "Achieving Professional Sales Growth," *Advisor Today* 104, no. 5 (May 2009), p. 53.
18. Jay Prakash Mulki, Fernando Jaramillo, Shavin Malhotra, and William B. Locander, "Reluctant Employees and Felt Stress: The Moderating Impact of Manager Decisiveness," *Journal of Business Research* 65, no. 1 (January 2012), p. 77; Jeffrey E. Lewin and Jeffrey K. Sager, "Salesperson Burnout: A Test of the Coping-Mediational Model of Social Support," *Journal of Personal Selling and Sales Management* 28, no. 3 (Summer 2008), pp. 233–46.
19. Songqi Liu, Mo Wang, Yujie Zhan, and Junqi Shi, "Daily Work Stress and Alcohol Use: Testing Cross-Level Moderation Effects of Neuroticism and Job Involvement," *Personnel Psychology* 62, no. 3 (Autumn 2009), pp. 575–97; Anthony Urbaniak, "Managing Stress," *SuperVision* 67, no. 8 (2006), pp. 7–9.
20. Mulki et al., "Reluctant Employees and Felt Stress"; Neil McAdam, "Situational Stress and Restriction of Stylistic Repertoire in High Potential Managerial Aspirants: Implications for the Implementation of the 'New Organization,'" *Journal of Management and Organization* 12, no. 1 (2006), pp. 40–67.

21. Richard G. McFarland, "Crisis of Conscience: The Use of Coercive Sales Tactics and Resultant Felt Stress in the Salesperson," *Journal of Personal Selling & Sales Management* 23, no. 4 (2003), pp. 311–31.
22. Ted Howell, personal correspondence, March 4, 2008; used with permission.
23. Lewin and Sager, "Salesperson Burnout"; Praveen Aggarwal, John F. Tanner Jr., and Stephen B. Castleberry, "Factors Associated with Propensity to Leave the Organization: A Study of Salespeople," *Marketing Management Journal* 14, no. 1 (2004), pp. 90–102.
24. Eric Ruiz, personal interview; used with permission.

ROLE PLAY CASE

1. Some of the descriptions in this case came directly from the company's Web sites.
2. www.purinaone.com/?utm_campaign=always+on&utm_medium=cpc&utm_source=-google&utm_content=pet-purina+one-Google%7C-Branded%7CGeneral&utm_term=purina+one, accessed March 26, 2017.

COMPANY INDEX

Accenture, 132
Achieve Global, 208
ACME Tools, 253
Acme Transfer, 245
AdAdapted Inc., 345–346
ADS. *See* American Distribution Systems (ADS)
Adult Swim, 158
Aetna, 239
Agria, 379
Air Canada, 237
Ajax Corporation, 301
AK Steel, 259
Alcatel-Lucent, 314
Alken-Murray, 261
Allied Signal, 314
Amazon, 228, 423
American Distribution Systems (ADS), 389
American Funeral Financial, 375
Andritz, 450
Apple, 65, 347, 390
Applied Medical, 351
Aptos, 116
Arkos, 291
Arrow Electronics, 13
Asset Recovery Management (ARM), 90, 196, 226, 255, 316
AT&T, 63, 131, 161, 205

Ballard Medical Products, 10
BancVue, 196
Barton Hargrave, 55
Baxter, 69–70, 356, 374
Bell Helicopter, 433–434
Bell Micro, 152
Black & Decker, 13
Blackhawks Corporate Hospitality, 25, 26
Blue Company, 260
Boeing, 10
Brazos Valley Equipment, 61
Bridgestone, 209
Bristol-Myers Squibb, 159
Business Network International (BNI), 154

Cabela, 297
Campbell Soup Company, 10, 384
Cardinal Health, 384, 451–452, 470, 495
Cargill, 381
Cartoon Network, 158
Castleberry Controls, 459
Central Texas Iron Works, 361
Chicago Blackhawks, 25
Chicago Marriott Downtown Magnificent Mile, 171
Chrysler, 384–385
Ciba-Geigy, 389
Cifra, 387
Cisco, 112, 487
Citation Box & Paper Company, 150
ClearScan, 314
CLS Partners, 259
CNN, 158
Coca-Cola, 301, 393
Colgate-Palmolive, 130, 270, 324
Computer Specialists Inc., 165
Concentra, 396
Cor-Plus, 368
Corporate Executive Board, 150, 166
Crisp Technology, 399
Cub Foods, 250, 321

Dealer's Electric, 61
DEI Management Group, 150
Dell, 60, 62, 309, 390, 439
Delta Air Lines, 180
DG Vault, 419
DIMIS, 90
DiscoverOrg, 180
Disney, 21, 226, 352
Dollar Express, 366–367
DoubleTree Hotels, 342
Dow Chemical, 13
Driltek, 13
Duluth Transit Authority (DTA), 128
Dun & Bradstreet, 149, 288
Du Pont, 13, 16
Duravent, 129

Eagle Equipment, 160
Eli Lilly, 411, 420, 450, 470
El Volcan, 393
Emora Ltd., 407
Empire Safety Rental, 367
emWare, Inc., 189
ESI, 287, 383–384, 417, 495
EVCO, 68

Fastenal, 79, 212, 216, 403–404, 495
Federal Aviation Administration, 63
Federal Express, 21, 446
Federal Trade Commission (FTC), 44, 48
Federated Insurance, 438
FedEx, 32
Fiat Chrysler Automobiles, 384
First Group Inc., 128
First National Bank of Shreveport, Louisiana, 163
Fiskars, 158
Forester, 67
Fortune 500, 181, 229, 298, 329
Fournier Equipment, 400
Franklin Group, 430
Freeman Exhibit Company, 409
Frito-Lay, 14, 68
Frosty Acres Brands, 63, 447
FSS, 91, 196, 226, 255, 316
FTC. *See* Federal Trade Commission (FTC)
Fujitsu, 362

Gallery Furniture, 382
Gallovidian Fresh Foods, 324
Gartner, 27, 144–145, 343

GDP Technologies, 147
GE. *See* General Electric (GE)
GEICO, 438
GelTech, 196
General Dynamics, 451
General Electric (GE), 8, 21, 176, 374, 438–439
General Motors (GM), 81, 373
Georgia-Pacific, 8
Goodyear, 261
Grafton Gifts, 431
GRM, 363
Grocery Supply Co. (GSC), 393
Gryphon Networks, 206
GSC. *See* Grocery Supply Co. (GSC)

Haiku, 171
Halliburton, 51
Harris Corporation, 63
H-E-B, 355, 414
Henry Schein, 471
Heron Ridge, 366
Hershey's, 451
Hewlett-Packard (HP), 35, 299, 352, 466
HighPoint Solutions, 196
Home Depot, 13, 21, 378, 379
Honeywell, 244
Hoover's, 182
Hormel, 7, 14, 17, 61, 63, 76, 128, 321, 438, 474
HP. *See* Hewlett-Packard (HP)
H.R. Challey Inc., 473
Hudgins ChemSupply, 56

IBM, 39, 65, 156, 166, 356, 414, 448, 454, 465, 467, 473, 477, 495
Ingersoll Rand, 150
InsideSales.com, 189
InsideView, 180
Insurors of Texas, 487
Intel, 13, 60
Intermex, 416
International Flavors and Fragrances (IFF), 64

John Deere, 61, 65, 156, 384, 393, 413
Johnson Electronics, 186
Johnson & Johnson, 345, 360, 451
Justice Department, 48

Kaseya, 362
KB Homes, 473
Kellogg's, 381
Keyser Group, 352
Kia Motors, 183
Kohler, 127, 240
Konica-Minolta, 467, 489
Korcett, 290, 354

Lambda Plumbing, 461
Lands' End, 31
Lawson Products, 440
Lexmark, 456
Linz Jewelers, 249, 250
Lockheed Martin, 148, 149
Logis, 343
Lonseal, 415, 416
Lotus Notes, 356
Lovejoy Inc., 386
Lynch Landscaping, 120

Maguire Manufacturing, 430
Main Industries, 363, 414
Makita, 17
The Marine Corps, 180
Marriott Hotels, 150
McDonald's, 352
McGraw-Hill, 423
McKesson Corporation, 61, 125
McKinsey & Company, 114
McPherson & Co., 398–399
Merck, 8, 13, 239
Merrill Lynch, 182, 474
MetLife, 17
Micros, 342
Microsoft, 17, 238, 465–466
Miller Heiman Group, 132, 208
Minnesota Sports Facilities Authority (MSFA), 195
Mizzen Industries, 91, 196, 226, 255, 316
Moody's, 182
Motion Industries, 235
Motorola, 35, 162, 451
MoxyChem, 56
Mul-T-Lock, 235

Nabisco, 64
NAIFA. *See* National Association of Insurance and Financial Advisors (NAIFA)
National Adhesives, 301
National Association of Insurance and Financial Advisors (NAIFA), 488
National Association of State Purchasing Officials, 63
National Steel, 430
NCR, 31, 450, 466
Nestlé, 185
Nielsen, 13
Nokia, 63
Northwestern Mutual, 10
Novartis, 184
Nucor Fastener, 435

Office Depot, 163
OfficeMax, 15
Oracle, 306, 310, 466–467, 486–487, 489
The Orchard, 429
Ortho-Clinical Diagnostics, 8

PAML. *See* Pathology Associates Medical Laboratories (PAML)
Passport Health, 254
Pathology Associates Medical Laboratories (PAML), 394
Pedowitz Group, 38, 78, 293, 310
Personal Medicine, 156
Pfizer, 17
PG&E, 451
Phoenix International, 436
Pinetree Properties, 430
Pioneer, 160
Pipl.com, 180
PPG Industries, 385
Premiere, 172
Presidential Aviation, 195, 225
Print Buyers Online, 362
Procter & Gamble (P&G), 7, 14, 80, 239, 450, 468, 470
Prodio, 315
Programmable UV Sanitizing Wand, 254, 284

Quaker Oats, 470

Ralph Lauren, 250
Regent Seven Seas Cruises, 195, 225
Revlon, 13
Reynolds Metal Company, 10
Riddell Helmets, 159
RipHeat, 429–430
Rossignol, 374
Royal Dutch Shell, 398

Safe Harbor Financial, 305
Saks, 391

SalesJobs.com, 41–42, 140, 294, 308, 381, 393
Sam's Club, 387
Samsung, 52, 186
Sandler Systems, 417
SBC Advertising, 362
Schneider Electric, 486
SC Johnson, 209, 299
SGA, Inc., 308
Shanghai Automotive Industry Corporation (SAIC), 373
Shimadzu Scientific Instruments, 291
Silicon Optronics, 187
Singer Sewing Machines, 31
Small Business Administration, 63
Smithfield Foods, 62, 436, 438, 470, 495
Smith & Nephew, 109
Sony, 98
Southwest Airlines, 311, 347–348
Spiegel, 31
Sprint, 163
SRI, 354, 363
SSI-India, 290
Standard & Poor's, 182
State Farm Insurance, 13
SuddenLink Communications, 453
Superion, 428
Synesis Corporation, 161
Sysco, 63

Target Corporation, 110, 250, 261, 284
Taylor Communications, 8, 17, 327
TechArt, 460–461
Teradata, 32, 43, 66, 292, 297, 383, 391, 408, 435, 454
The Orchard, 429
3M, 59, 191, 199, 423
T-Mobile, 130
Tom James Company, 3
Tommy Hilfiger, 250
Total Quality Logistics, 351
Toyota, 97, 98
TravelClick, 371–372
truTV, 158
Turner Broadcasting, 158
Tyco, 390
Tymco, 307

UCC. *See* Uniform Commercial Code (UCC)
UniFirst, 364
Uniform Commercial Code (UCC), 44, 45-46, 54
Union Pacific, 115
United Airlines, 381, 452
U.S. Commercial Service, 182
U.S. Department of Labor, 20
U.S. Steel, 13

Verizon, 63, 78, 381
Vista Outdoor, 319
Vistakon, 360
Volvo, 50

Walker Muffler, 261
Walmart, 13, 14, 39, 202, 249–250, 321, 387, 451
Walt Disney Studios, 226
Wells Fargo, 30, 34
WestRock, 158
Wilson Learning, 208

Xerox, 155, 176, 190, 356, 383, 384, 417, 445, 453–454

Yellow Book USA, 120
Young & Family, 430
YouTube, 156, 482
Yummy Earth Organic, 217

Zadro Inc., 254, 284
Zimmer, 144, 181
ZoomInfo, 180

SUBJECT INDEX

Aarts, Deborah, EN-16
ABC analysis, 411-412
Ability to pay, 149
Abosag, Ibrahim, 27
Abrahamson, Liesl, 440
Accommodating mode, 328
Account classification, 410-414
Account opportunity dimension, 412
Accounts
expense, 41
house, 451
investing in, 414-415
key, 450
Account salespeople, 450-451
Account share, 414
Account team managers, 10
Acknowledge method, 274
Active listening
explanation, 98, 100
on the phone, 112
suggestions for, 100-103
testing your skills in, 101
Activity analysis, 424
Activity goals, 408
Activity quotas, 443
Adamson, Brent, EN-6, EN-7
Adaptation, 99
Adaptive planning, 325
Adaptive selling
buyer's perspective on, 127
explanation of, 127-130
knowledge and, 130-132
presentation types, 126-127
reasons for using, 127-130
social style matrix, 132-140
systems for developing, 140-141
Adigwe, Jude O., EN-10
Administration, 438-439
Administrative laws, 44
Advantages, relating features to, 216
Advertising
function of, 7
marketing communications program, 6
Advocates (champions), 389
Agency, 45
Agenda, negotiation session, 331
Agent, 45
Aggressive salespeople, 298
Agnihotri, Raj, 57, EN-5, EN-7, EN-10
Ahearne, Michael, EN-8
Ahmad, Kawsar, 369
Aidla, A., EN-6
Aitken, Lucy, EN-16
Akdeniz, M Billur, EN-14
Alavi, Sascha, 317
Albadvi, Amir, EN-1
Albaum, Gerald, EN-12
Alexander, Joe E., EN-16
Allbright, David, EN-6
Allen, Eddie B. Jr., EN-7
Alter, Cara Hale, EN-9
Alvarez, Mark, 21
"Always a share" strategy, 78
Ambush negotiation, 329
Amiables, 135, 136
Amyx, Douglas, EN-3
Analogy, 97
Analysis paralysis, 180
Analyticals, 135-136
Analytical skills, 18
Anaza, Nwamaka A., 91, 401, EN-10
Andaleeb, Syed Saad, 145
Anders, Abram, 123
Anderson, James C., EN-9, EN-10
Anderson, Tasha, EN-10
André, Jean-marc, 91
Ang, Lawrence, EN-14
Anić, Ivan-Damir, 91
Annual spend, 80
Appearance. *See* Physical appearance
Application form, 472
Appointments. *See* Sales appointments
Appreciation, customer, 306
Arias, Myrna, 416
Arm movements, nonverbal communication through, 104
Arndt, Aaron D., 27, 145, 285, 317, EN-8
Arroniz, Inigo, 401
Articulation, 97
Artis, Andrew B., 172, EN-6
Ashkanasy, Neal M., 369
Ashnai, Bahar, 498
Assertiveness
explanation of, 133
indicators of, 133
salespeople, 299
in social style matrix, 133, 137, 139
Assessment centers, 473
Assumptive close, 304
Athanasopoulou, Pinelopi, 91
Atkinson, William, 196
Attitudes
ethical behavior of salespeople, 35
positive, 296-297
Attitudinal loyalty, 81, 348
Authority to buy, leads and, 149
Automatic replenishment (AR), 79, 250
Automation systems, 11
Autry, Chad W., 91
Avoiding mode, 328
Awareness stage of relationship development, 356

Babin, Barry J., 317, EN-5
Backdoor selling, 40-41
Background noise, 95
Badrinarayanan, V., EN-3
Bagozzi, Richard P., EN-6
Bailey, Jeffrey, 306, 489
Balanced presentation, 220
Balance sheet method, 301-302
Balboni, Bernardo, EN-1

Baldauf, Artur, 145
Baldwin, Alec, 287
Bande, Belén, 57, 497, EN-2, EN-3
Barclay, Donald W., EN-16
Barnes, John W., EN-13
Barone, Michael J., 498, EN-14
Barrett, Deborah J., 123
Barriers, sales calls and, 189
Barry, James M., 401
Bartlett, Katharine T., 57
Bateman, Connie, 57
BATNA (Best alternative to a negotiated agreement), 337
Baumann, Jasmin, 462
Baxter, Roger, 227
Beagle, Kyle, 361
Bearden, William, EN-3
Beatty, Sharon E., 91
Becker, Ben, 452
Beckwith, Sandra, EN-7
Bednarek, Marei, 401
Beery, Joseph P. (Joe), 452, 471
Behavioral loyalty, 81, 348
Behavioral observation scale (BOS), 447
Behavior patterns, in negotiation session, 327-329
Beheshti, Hooshang M., EN-5
Belew, Shannon, 172
Bellenger, Danny N., 145, 255, EN-4, EN-12
Bello, Daniel C., 91
Bemelmans, Jeroen, 401
Benbasat, Izak, EN-8
Benchmarking, 409
Bendor-Samuel, Peter, EN-4
Benefit-in-reserve close, 304
Benefit opening, 203
Benefits
  definition of, 215
  example of, 215
  relating features to, 215-217
  relationship with costs, 264
Benefit statements, 295
Benefit summary method, 300
Ben Franklin method, 301
Benoit (née Moeller), Sabine, 255
Bergeron, Jasmin, EN-10, EN-12
Berg, Wouter E., EN-6
Berry, Wendell, EN-1
Best alternative to a negotiated agreement (BATNA), 337
Beverland, Michael, EN-15
Bharadwaj, Sundar, 401
Bianchi, Constanza, EN-12
Bible, Amy, 288
Big Data, prospecting through, 161
Bingham, Frank, EN-2
Bird dogs, 161
Birt, Phil, 152, EN-7
Bistritz, Stephen J., EN-9
Bitner, Mary Jo, 91, EN-12
Blake, Bill, 400
Blakely, Scott, EN-10
Blankenship, John, 316
Bleiler, Seth, 199, 223
Blink rate, 104
Blitz, 160
Bloemer, Josée, 369
Blogs, 163
Blount, Jeb, 27, 172
Body angle and movements, 104
Body language
  arms and, 104
  body angle and, 104
  explanation of, 103
  face and, 104
  hands and, 105
  legs and, 105
  patterns of signals during sales presentation, 105-106
  sending messages with, 106-111
Bogner, Chareen, 125
Bolander, Willy, 145, 317, EN-8
Boles, James S., 145, 255, EN-4
Bon, Joël, EN-1, EN-6
Bonney, Leff, 57
Bonus, 444
Booher, Dianna Daniels, 227
Boomerang method, 273
Borcherds, M. M, 145
Borders, Leila, 257
Borgh, Michel, 431
Borg, Susanne Wiatr, EN-2
Boso, Nathaniel, 145
Bostwick, Rick, 400
Bottom-up forecasting, 441
Boundary-spanning employees, 363
Boyer, Stefanie L., EN-16
Boyle, Alex, 172
Braig, Ed, 361
Brainstorming session, 325
Brandão, Amelia, EN-5
Branding, personal, 485
Brandli, Jeff, 364
Branton, John, EN-10
Brashear, Thomas G., EN-12, EN-15
Bray, Jane, 429
Brehmer, Per-Olof, 462
Brennan, Ross, EN-10
Bribes
  cultural differences on, 52
  explanation of, 38
  subordination and, 51
Briggs, Elten, 401
Brill, Tracey, EN-9
Bristol-Myers Squibb, 159
Bristow, Dennis N., EN-3
Brito, Luiz A. L., 373, 401
Brochures, in sales presentation, 236
Brock, Shelby Hughes, 172
Brody, Gerard, 57
Bronnenmayer, Matias, EN-5
Brooks, Brendan, 157
Brooks, Charles M., EN-15
Browbeating, 335-336
Brown, Brian P., EN-7
Brown, Cal, EN-14
Brown, Christopher, 27
Brownell, Eleanor, 306, EN-10
Brown, Gene, 145, EN-6
Brown, Linden, 27
Brubaker, Lee, 417, EN-14
Brudner, Emma, EN-8
Bruns, Travis, 89
Bryom, Matt, EN-7
Budget bogey, 334
Budget limitation tactic, during negotiation, 334
Building Partnership Model, 20-21
Buran, Lindsey, 176
Burgoon, Judee K., 123
Bush, Alan J., 57, 145, 497, EN-3
Bush, Victoria, 57, 497, EN-3
Business defamation, 48
Business-to-business channels, 13
Buyer comments
  benefit statements, 295
  buyer questions, 295
  explanation of, 294-295
  requirements, 295
  trial close responses, 295-296
Buyer questions, 295
Buyers. *See* Customers; Prospects
Buyer-seller relationship, 14. *See also* Partnerships; Relationships
Buyer's perspective
  on adaptive selling, 128
  buying behavior and process, 81
  commitment, 288
  in communication, 99
  ethics and legal issues, 32
  on negotiation, 339
  on objections, 266
  on prospects, 162

on recruiters, 471
on relationships, 361, 373
on sales and sales team, 452
on sales call, 176, 220
on salesperson, 9
on sales presentations, 246
on time and territory management, 414
of unethical sales behavior, 41
Buyer's remorse, 305
Buying centers. *See also* Organizational buying decisions; Purchasing
explained, 70
importance of knowing people in, 70–72
individual needs of members in, 76–78
multiattribute model used by, 82–86
Buying community, 155
Buying decisions. *See also* Organizational buying decisions
modified rebuys, 70
new tasks, 68–69
straight rebuys, 69–70
Buying signals, 294

Cabanelas, Pablo, 369
Cabiddub, Francesca, 255
Cabuk, Serap, 145
Cadogan, John W., EN-3
Calahan, Paul, EN-10
Calantone, Roger J, EN-14
Calderwood, Shaun, 42
Caldwell, Mike, 367
Calin-Ionel, Denes, 343
Call tracking software, 181
Cambra-Fierro, Jesús, 369
Campbell, Dennis, EN-11
Campbell, Kim Sydow, EN-12
Candi, Marina, 368
Caniato, Federico, 197
Canned presentation, 126
Canned sales pitches, 31
Cannon, Joseph P., EN-16
CAN-SPAM Act, 51
Cap, 448
Capital equipment, 61
Caprio, Frank, 438, EN-15
Carano, Katie, EN-16
Cardone, Grant, EN-5
Cardon, Peter W., 145, 227
Careers. *See* Sales careers
Carey, Miriam, 456
Carnegie, Dale, 202, EN-5
Carr, Jon C., EN-12
Carr, Matthew, EN-15
Carter, Jackson, 460
Carter, Justin, 229, 252
Carter, Robert E., 401
Cash discounts, 291
Castleberry, Stephen B., 123, 319, EN-17
Catalogs, in sales presentation, 236
Cavazos-Gaither, Alma E., EN-7
Center-of-influence method, 154
Chaker, Nawar N., EN-10
Chakrabarty, Subhra, 145, EN-8
Chakraborty, Goutam, EN-4, EN-13
Challoner, Mike, 414
Champions, 389
Chandran, V. G. R., 401
Chang, Chia-Chi, EN-13
Change
champions of, 389–390
positioning for, 390–391
rate of, 389
resources for, 391
scope of, 389
time-based strategy for, 391
Change agents, 388–391
Chaniotakis, Ioannis E., EN-13
Channel manager, 10
Chan, Tat Y., 497
Charfeddine, Lanouar, EN-11
Chatterjee, Sayan, 498
Chatterjee, Sharmila C., EN-7
Chaudhary, Harish, EN-13
Chauhan, Anurag, EN-13
Chawla, Vaibhav, 57
Chen, Annie, 431
Chen, Chien-Chung, 401, EN-2
Chen, Chih-Cheng Volvic, EN-13
Chen, Chih-Jou, EN-13
Chen, Chin-Yuan, EN-2
Chen, Junsong, 172, EN-7
Chen, Kuan-Yang, EN-11, EN-13
Chen, Po-Yuan, EN-11, EN-13
Chicksand, Daniel, 343
Chin-Fu, Ho, EN-11
Chiou, Jyh-Shen, 373, 401
Chonko, Lawrence B., EN-1, EN-3, EN-16
Chow, Clement S. F., EN-6, EN-12
Chow, Wing-ki, EN-11
Chressanthis, George A., 57
Christodoulides, George, EN-7
Chuah, Stephanie Hui-Wen, 91
Chullen, Cody Logan, 369
Churick, Nick, EN-6
Cicala, John E., 57, 497, EN-3
Circular routing, 420
Claiborne, Liz, 13
Clarifying information, 101–102
Clark, Melissa, 57
Clark, Rebecca, 93, 118
Clark, Ronald A., 317, EN-9
Clayton Act (1914), 48
Client relationship managers, 8
Clonch, Kevin, 351
Closed questions, 208, 209
Closing. *See also* Commitment
explanation of, 288
importance of securing, 289–290
Closing cues
explanation of, 294
nonverbal, 296
Cloud-based negotiating software, 324
Cloverleaf routing, 420
CLV (Customer lifetime value), 6, 346
CNA (Consequences of no agreement), 337
Coach, 72
Cobell, James, 311
Code of ethics, 35–37
Cold calling, 160–161
Cold canvass method, 160–161
Coleman, Joshua T., 123
Collaborating mode, 329
Collateral, 239
Colleagues, ethical behavior with, 43–44
Collusion, 49
Columbus, Louis, 161
Combination plans, 445–446
Comer, Lucette B., EN-5
Commerce Business Daily, 63
Commission, 444
performance analysis and, 425
sales goals, 407–408
Commission base, 445
Commission rate, 445
Commitment
adaptive selling and, 297–298
assertiveness of salesperson and, 298–299
attempting to obtain, 293–296
buyer's perspective on, 288
closing sales call, 310

creeping, 288
examples of, 289
failure to obtain, 307-310
to financial terms and conditions, 290-293
importance of securing, 288-290
to mutual gain for, 363
positive attitude, 296-297
principles for successfully obtaining, 296-299
right product sold in the right amount and, 299
salesperson's responsibilities, 305-306
stage of relationship development, 357
traditional methods, 304
when to obtain, 293-296
Commitment methods
alternative choice, 303
balance sheet method, 301-302
benefit summary, 300
direct request, 300
overview, 299-300
probing, 302-303
trial offers, 303-304
Commitment stage of relationships, 384-391
communication in, 387
corporate culture, 387-388
explanation of, 384-385
salesperson as change agent in, 388-391
securing, 385
Common law, 44
Communication. *See also* Nonverbal communication; Telephone communication
active listening, 98-103
breakdowns in, 94-95
buyer's perspective of, 99
comparisons of various methods of, 111
cultural differences and, 115-118
face-to-face, 111
keeping open lines of, 98
process of two-way, 94-95
social media, 114-115
stories used for, 97-98
through technology, 111-118
verbal messages, 96-98
voice characteristics, 96-97
word choice and, 96
word-of-mouth, 77
Communication tools, 279-280
Companies. *See also* Corporate culture
finding a good match between salesperson and, 469-471
policies of, and ethical behavior of salespeople, 34, 35
salesperson's understanding, 438-440
Company knowledge, adaptive selling and, 130
Comparative cost-benefit analysis, 247
Compensation method, 272-273
Compensation plans, 443-446
Competence, 359-360
Competing mode, 328
Competitors
ethical behavior with, 44
failing to monitor actions of, 392-393
interference with, 49
Complacency, 393
Complaints, customer, 376-380
Compliment opening, 203
Compromising mode, 328
Computers
to handle paperwork and communications, 423
used in sales presentations, 239-240
Concessions, during negotiations, 336-337
Confente, Ilenia, 91
Confidence, in salespeople, 19
Confidential information, ethical behavior and, 40
Configure price quote (CPQ) software, 181
Conflict
in buyer-seller relationships, 393-395
personalizing, 437
Conflict-handling behavior modes, 327-329
Conlow, Rick, 227
Conners, Susan E., 498
Consequences of no agreement (CNA), 337
Conspiracy, 49
Consumer channels, 13-14
Consumers, 63-64
Continuous yes close, 304
Contract to sell, 45
Conventional résumés, 474-475
Conversation, summarizing, 102-103
Conversion goals, 408-409
Conversion ratio, 425-426
Cooke, James A., EN-4
Cooper, Brett, 498
Cornnell, Michael, EN-14
Corporate culture
appearance choices and, 110
explanation, 387-388
partnerships and, 363-364
Cortina, Christine, 175
Cost-benefit analysis, 246-247
Costs, shipping, 292-293
Cote, Joseph A., 317, EN-8
Coughlan, Anne T., 462
Cover letters, 477-479
Cravens, David W., 462
Creativity, 19
Credibility, 219
Credibility statement, 219
Credit terms, 291-292
Credulous person standard, 47
Creeping commitment, 67-68
Crombie, Brian, EN-11
Crosno, Jody L., 401
Cross, Lisa, EN-12
Cross, Mark E., EN-12
Cross-selling, 384
CRV (Customer referral value), 151
Cuevas, Javier Marcos, 27
Culbert, Bruce, 38, 293, 310, EN-10
Cultural differences
body movement and, 108
in commitment stage, 387-388
in communication style, 115-118
handshaking and, 108
in negotiations, 322, 326, 331
probing method, 303
Cultural relativism, 52
Curasi, Carolyn F., 145, 255, EN-4
Customer benefit proposition, 215
Customer-centric, 8
Customer lifetime value (CLV), 6, 346
Customer onboarding, 356
Customer orientation, 360
Customer referral value (CRV), 151
Customer relationship management (CRM)
adaptive selling, 131-132
explanation of, 11
inside salespeople, 140
Customer relationship management (CRM) software, 41-42
Customer relationship marketing, 345

Customers
accurate data, 167
appearance choices and, 110
confirming choice, 305
expectations on social styles, 138
getting attention of, during sales call, 202-203
getting signature of, 305-306
handling complaints from, 376-380
identifying social styles, 136-137
knowledge of, 18, 130-131
market and, 15
obtaining precall information about, 189
satisfied, as source for leads, 151-152
setting the pace, 297-298
sexual harassment, 43
types of, 60-64
value of, 346-347
Customer satisfaction, 349
Customer service, 439
Customer service reps (CSRs), 453
Customer share, 414
Customer-supplier conflict, 394
Customer value proposition (CVP), 4, 187
Customized sales presentations, 126-127
Custom marketing messages, 116

Daft, Jost, 343
Dahlstrom, Robert, 401
Daily activity planning, 416-417
Dalkir, Kimiz, EN-6
Daniels, Ellen, 229
Dant, Rajiv P., 196, 255
Dapiran, G. Peter, EN-15
Dapko, Jennifer L., 172, EN-6
Das, Gopal, 145
Databases, prospect information in, 160
Data mining, 160
Daugherty, Patricia J., 401
Davids, Meryl, EN-3
Davies, Iain A., EN-7
Davis, Jesse, 181
Davis, John, 416
Davis, Lenita, EN-12
Day, Tom, EN-16
DeCarlo, Thomas E., 57, 369, 431, 498, EN-6, EN-11, EN-14
Deception, 37
Deciders, 72
Decoding, 94
DeConinck, James B., 57, EN-3, EN-15
DeConinck, Mary Beth, 57, EN-3, EN-15
DeGroot, Robert P., 285
Deitz, George D., 57
De Luca, Luigi M., 227, 317, EN-6, EN-12
De Matos, Celso Augusto, EN-13
DeMers, Jayson, 485
Demneh, Abdollahi, EN-13
Dennis, David, 362
Denny, Sunny, EN-16
Dependability, 358-359
Derived demand, 65
Dessein, Wouter, 57
Devadason, Evelyn S., 401
Dey, Prasanta, EN-5
Diagnostic feedback, 131
Dietz, Bart, 431
Digital collateral management systems, 239
Digital easels, 240
Digital marketing, power of, 78
Dingus, Rebecca, 57, 431, EN-2, EN-11
Direct demand, 65
Direct denial method, 270-271
Directories, prospects developed from, 159-160
Direct request method, 300
Discounting the cash flow, 248
Discounts
cash, 291
cumulative, 291
quantity, 290-291
single-order, 290-291
Disguised interview, 483
Dissolution stage of relationships
complacency in, 393
conflict in, 393-395
explanation of, 357, 392
limited personal relationships and, 392
monitoring competitor actions and, 392-393
monitoring the industry and, 393
Distance zones, 109
Distribution channels
sales jobs and, 13
selling and, 11-14
Dixon, A., EN-3
Dixon, Andrea L., EN-1, EN-16
Dixon, Matthew, EN-6, EN-7, EN-8
Dixon, Taylor, 59
Document cameras, 240
Dolan, John Patrick, EN-10
Doney, Patricia M., 401
Do-Not-Call Registry, 50
Donovan, J., 227
Donthu, Naveen, 91
Dossey, Les, 297
Dowell, David, 27
Draw, 445
Dress code, 110
Drivers, 135, 136
Drollinger, Tanya, EN-5
Drumm, Kimberly, 287, 288
Dual career path, 486
Dubinsky, A. J., 145, EN-2
Dudley, George W., EN-2, EN-16
Dudley, Robert C., EN-11
Dunne, Bill, 64, 67, 70
Dunnette, Marvin, EN-10
Dwyer, Robert, EN-4, EN-11, EN-12, EN-13, EN-15

Early procurement involvement, 68
Early supplier involvement, 68
Earnings, salespeople, 425
Echchakoui, Said, 368
Economic influencer, 72
Efficient consumer response (ECR) systems, 79, 250
Eichelberger, Chip, EN-8
80-20 listening rule, 98
El-Ansary, Adel, EN-14
El-Ansary, Waleed A., EN-14
Electronic data interchange (EDI), 79-80, 250
Electronic whiteboards, 240
Elevator speech, 154
Eligibility to buy, leads and, 150
Elman, Ben, 498
Elsäßer, Marc, 369, EN-4, EN-5, EN-12
El-Sayed Mansour, Samira A., 27
E-mail
managing time by making more, 422
suggestions for communicating via, 112-113
tracking software, 181
Emotional close, 304
Emotional intelligence (EI), 19-20
Emotional needs, 73
Emotional outburst tactic, during negotiations, 334
Employment postings, 477

Encoding, 94
Endless-chain method, 152-153
End users, 61
Engle, Chad, 213
Entertainment gifts, 38-39
Environment, communication breakdowns and, 97
Esper, Terry L., 145
Ethical behavior. *See also* Legal issues
buyers' view of unethical behaviors, 41
with colleagues, 43-44
with competitors, 44
with customers, 37-41
definition of, 30
factors influencing, 33-37
salesperson profile, 29-30
with salesperson's company, 41-43
Ethical decision making checklist, 36
Ethical imperialism, 52
Ethics
codes of, 35-37
definition of, 30
international issues related to, 51-52
managing, 447-450
partnering relationships and, 32-33
Ethics review boards, 448
Evaluation. *See also* Performance evaluation
multiattribute model of product, 82-86
of product performance, 67
Evanschitzky, Heiner, EN-16
Evans, Kenneth R., 285, 317, EN-9, EN-11
Ewing, Michael, 401
Exclusive sales territories, 150
Excuses, 268
Executive briefing centers, 240-241
Executive summary, 243
Expansion stage of relationships
cross-selling, 384
explanation of, 357, 380-381
full-line selling, 383-384
generating repeat orders, 381-383
upgrading and, 383
Expectations, in partnerships, 373
Expense accounts, 41
Expense budgets, 442
Exploration stage of relationships
customer complaints handled in, 376-380
definition of, 356-357
ensuring proper use of product/service, 374-375
explanation of, 372
follow-up in, 375-376
order processing monitored in, 373-374
setting expectations in, 373
Expressed warranty, 46
Expressives, 135, 136
Extranets, 158
Eye contact, 107, 117-118

FAB (features, advantages, and benefits), 216
Face, 332
Face, body language and, 104
Facebook, 114-115, 121, 132, 155, 156, 180
Face-to-face communication, 111
Facial muscles, 107
False Claims Act, 47
Farhangmehr, Minoo, EN-7
Farías, Pablo, EN-1
Feature dumping, 214
Features
definition of, 215
example of, 215
related to benefits, 215-217
FEBA (features, evidence, benefits, agreement), 216
Federal Trade Commission Act (1914), 48
Feedback
communication process, 94
diagnostic, 131
performance, 131
Feel-felt-found method, 273
Feiertag, Howard, EN-9
Feldman, Lori, 498
Feller, Bryan, 145
Fellingham, Charles, 172
Feng-Cheng, Tung, 369
Fernandes, Aline R., 373, 401
Fernandes, Teresa, EN-5
Fernández-Ferrín, Pilar, 497, EN-2
Ferrell, Justin, 375
Ferris, Gerald R., 145
Ferro, Carlos, 369, 401
Fett, Morgen, 382
Field sales managers
definition of, 446
ethics and, 449
evaluation of performance by, 446
training by, 446-447
Field salespeople, 15, 452
Field support rep, 453
Financial rewards, 20
Financial terms
credit terms and, 291-292
discounts and, 290-291
presenting price, 293
shipping costs and, 292-293
Finlay, Tom, 375
First impressions, 201-202
Fisk, Raymond P., EN-10
Flaherty, Karen E., EN-7
Flaviano, Susan, 416, EN-14
Fleischman, Gary, EN-15
Fleming, Darrin, EN-9
Fletcher, Heather, EN-16
Fletcher, Nick, EN-4
Flint, Daniel J., EN-10
Floyd, Kory, 123
FOB destination, 45
FOB factory, 46
FOB installed, 292
Focus of dissatisfaction, 188
Focus of power, 188
Focus of receptivity, 188
Follow-up, 306
after interview, 484
procedures for, 375-376
Food and Drug Administration, 44
Force Majeure Clause, 338
Ford, Sarah, 314
Foreign Corrupt Practices Act (FCPA), 52
Foreman, Jeff, 91
Forestall, 265-266
Fornell, Claes, EN-13
Fortune, Chris, EN-4
Four A's, 200
Fournier, Christophe, EN-3, EN-13, EN-16
Free on board (FOB), 292
Free on board (FOB) destination, 45
Freese, Thomas A., 227
Frei, Frances, EN-11
French, Mike, EN-2
Frey, Robert S., 255
Friend, David, EN-3
Friendly silent questioning stare (FSQS), 269
Friend, Scott B., 145, 255, 317, 431, EN-2, EN-4, EN-9

Fripp, Patricia, EN-9
Frow, Pennie, EN-1
FSQS. *See* Friendly silent questioning stare
Fu, Frank Q., 431
Full-line selling, 383-384
Fulton, Sean, 433-434
Functional relationships, 349-350
Functional résumés, 475-476

Gabler, Colin B., EN-5
Gabrielsson, Mika, 27
Gaither, Carl C., EN-7
Gallagher, Chuck, 375
Gammoh, Bashar S., 498
Gardner, Lenann McGookey, 123
Gardner, Sean, 314
Garrett, Jason, 498
Gatekeepers, 72
Gates, Steve, 343
Gautier, Laurence, 91
Geigenmuller, Anja, EN-12
Genius management, 132
Geographic salesperson, 450
Georges, Laurent, 462, EN-12
Gerlach, Gisela I., EN-1
Gerlsbeck, Rob, EN-13
Gerst, Steve, EN-9
Gestures
  in active listening, 100
  hand, 105
  handshaking and, 107-108
Ghosh, Mrinal, 57
Gifts
  ethical behavior with customers and, 38-39
  used in sales presentation, 235-236
Gilleland, Molly, 257
Gillespie, Erin Adamson, 431
Gilliam, David A., EN-9
Gil, Lynette, 456
Giovanis, Apostolos, 91
Girard, Joe, 148
Gligor, David M., 91
Glynn, Mark S., 227
Gnyp, Justina, EN-14
Goad, Emily A., EN-12
Goals
  activity, 408
  activity analysis of, 424
  calculations, 408
  career, 406, 484-489
  conversion, 408-409
  nature of, 406-407
  need for, 405-406
  performance, 407-408
  relationship of, 406
  setting sales, 409
  types of sales, 407-409
Gomes, Mariana, EN-5
Gong, Baiyun, EN-2
Gonzalez-Padron, Tracy, EN-14
Gonzalez, Rudy, 399
Good, David J., 462, EN-15
Good-guy-bad-guy routine, 332-333
Goodson, Shannon L., EN-16
Gopalakrishna, Srinath, 498, EN-11
Gordon, Geoffrey L., 462
Gordon, Nancy, 315
Goss, Zachary, 3
Go-to-market strategies, 6
Göttel, Vincent, EN-5
Gould, A. Noel, 91
Government agencies
  lead information from, 166
  as type of customer, 62-63
Graca, Sandra Simas, 401
Graf, Todd, EN-9
Graham, Greg, 229
Graham, John R., EN-9
Gramm-Leach-Bliley Act (1999), 50
Grandinetti, Roberto, EN-5
Grant, Adam, EN-2
Grant, Terri, 145
Graphics, in sales presentation, 234-235
Grecu, Valentin, 343
Greengard, Samuel, EN-13
Greeter, 483
Greschuchna, Larissa, EN-12
Grewal, Dhruv, 196
Grewal, Rajdeep, EN-7
Grid analysis, 412-414
Grisaffe, Douglas B., EN-1, EN-2
Gross margin quotas, 443
Group interviews, 483
Groups
  objections when selling to, 277
  selling to, 221-222
Guarantee, 46
Guba, Jan H., 317
Guenzi, Paolo, 145, 227, 317, 462, 498, EN-6, EN-7, EN-12
Guerrero, Laura K., 123
Gulati, Mitu, 57
Gulati, Rajesh, EN-3
Gupta, Pola, EN-13
Gustafsson, Magnus, 255
Guzzo, Sheena, 99
Hada, Mahima, EN-7
Haden, Jeff, EN-7
Haiku Deck, PowerPoint presentations, 238
Hajli, Nick, 145
Hale, Dena, EN-1
Hall, Bob, EN-13
Hallikas, Jukka, EN-4
Hall, Judith A., 123
Hall, Zachary R., EN-8
Halo effect, 203
Hamaski, Akimi, 195
Hamm, B. Curtis, 413
Hamrick, Bo, 485
Hamwi, G. Alexander, EN-2
Hand gestures, 105
Handouts, 242
Handshaking, 107-108
Hands, nonverbal communication through, 105
Handwritten notes, 306
Hansen, John D., 57, 369, EN-3
Hanson, Ray, 216, EN-8
Hargie, Owen, EN-5
Hargrave, Barton, 55
Hari, Juerg, EN-2
Harkins, Jason, EN-8
Harris, Jasmine, 398
Harris, Lloyd C., EN-13
Harrison, Lauren, EN-14
Harrod, Christina, 351
Hartline, Michael D., EN-13
Harvey, Rob, 32
Hassan, Ghorbani, EN-13
Hauser, John R., EN-11
Hawes, John M., EN-12
Haytko, Diana L., 317, EN-9
Hazeldine, Simon, 123
Hearing, 100
Hedges, Dawn, 181, EN-8
Heffernan, Troy, 27
Heiman, Miller, EN-6
Heiman, Stephen E., EN-6, EN-8
Henderson, Conor M., 401
Henschen, Dough, EN-13
Herman, Gary, 90
Herscher, Penny, EN-5
Hersma, Jim, EN-8, EN-9
Hester, Gordon, EN-9
He, Xin, EN-2
Hidalgo, Pedro, EN-1
Higham, Anthony, EN-4
Hightower, Emily, 25
Hillebrand, Bas, 369
Hill, Ronald Paul, 57

Hingley, Martin, 91
Hirst, Giles, 431
Hochstein, Bryan W., 57
Hoeppner, Sven, 57
Hoffeld, David, 285
Holden, Jim, EN-8
Holden, Reed K., 343
Holder, Dick, 10
Hollet, Sandrine, EN-13
Hollmann, Thomas, 91, EN-12
Holloway, Betsy Bugg, 91, 369
Holm, Morten, EN-11
Holopainen, Mari, 123
Honest communication, 362
Honesty, 360-361
Hong, Zhao, EN-11
Hopkins, Tom, EN-6
Horgan, Terrence G., 123
Horton, Christine, EN-12
Houjeir, Roudaina, EN-10
House accounts, 150, 451
Houston, Mark B., 196, EN-11
Howell, Ted, EN-17
Ho, William, EN-5
Hsiao, Shih-Hui, 145
Hsieh, Julie, 26
Hsu, Huei-Min, EN-2
Huag, Laura, EN-16
Huang, Chih-Yun, 317
Huemer, Lars, 343
Hughes, Douglas E., 145, 431, EN-1, EN-6, EN-14, EN-15
Hughes, Jesse, 172
Hughes, Paul, 145
Hughes, Tim, 172
Hughes, Tony J., EN-7
Hulland, John, EN-16
Hult, M., EN-13
Hultman, Magnus, 145
Hult, Tomas, M., 91
Hu, Michael Y., EN-11, EN-15
Humor, in sales presentation, 234
Hung, Humphry, EN-10
Hung, Kuang-Peng, 431, EN-5
Hunter, Mark, 172, 297, EN-7, EN-10
Hunter, Shirley, EN-3
Hurd, Mark, 466
Hurmerinta, Anna, 255
Husser, Jocelyn, 91
Hutt, Michael D., 462, EN-13

Iglesias, Víctor, EN-13
Ikuine, Fumihiko, 317
Illustrations, 237
Imeri, Shpend, 373, 401
Implication questions, 211
Implied warranty, 46
Impression management
  blunders and, 205
  explanation of, 200
  first impressions, 201-202
  getting customer's attention, 202-203
  rapport and, 204-205
  selecting a seat and, 202
  small talk and, 204
  waiting for prospect and, 200-201
Inamizu, Nobuyuki, 317
Inbound salespeople, 453
Incentive pay, 444
Indirect denial method, 271-272
Industrial Revolution, 31
Inflection, 96-97
Influencers, 71-72
Influential adversaries, 179
Information
  clarifying, 101-102
  repeating, 100
  restating or rephrasing, 101
  up-to-date, 277
  within your company, 180
Information control, 329
Information sources
  Internet, 180
  noncompeting salespeople, 182
  from the prospect, 182
  secretaries and receptionists, 181
  traditional secondary sources, 182
  within your company, 180
Information technology, ability to use, 18
Ingram, Rikki, 62, 436
Ingram, Thomas N., 353, 377, EN-3, EN-15
Initiators, 71
Inside salespeople, 15, 162-163, 452
Insight selling, 150
Institutions, as customers, 63
In-suppliers, 70
Integrated marketing communications, 7
Integrity, 18
Interactive whiteboards, 240
Internal partnerships
  definition of, 434
  importance of, 434
  sales role in, 435
  selling internally, 435-437
Internal salespeople (champions), 389
Internal selling, 435-437
  principles of, 436
International markets. *See also* Cultural differences
  ethical and legal issues, 51-52
  government agencies and, 63
  precall information and, 182
Internet. *See also* Social media; Social networking
  impact on selling/salespeople, 6-7
  prospect information found on, 180
  purchases from, 60
  as source for prospects, 156, 158
  word-of-mouth information, 77
Internet of Things (IoT), 374
Interviews (employment)
  case example, 480
  disguised, 483
  explanation of, 473
  frequently asked questions, 479
  gaining commitment in, 482-483
  group, 483-484
  needs identification in, 481-482
  panel, 483
  preparing for, 479-481
  presentation in, 482
  stress, 483
Intimate zone, 108
Introduction opening, 203
Inventory turnover, 249-250
Invitation to negotiate, 45
Inyang, Eddie Aniefre, EN-10, EN-12
IoT (Internet of Things), 374
Itani, Omar S., EN-12
Ivanova-Gongne, Maria, 255

Jack, Eric P., 401
Jackson, Donald W. Jr., EN-13, EN-16
Jacqueline K. Eastman, EN-11
Jahromi, Ali Tamaddoni, 401
Jain, Nitin, 57
James, Howard, EN-4
Jaques, Emma, 255
Jaramillo, Fernando, 57, 401, 497, EN-2, EN-3, EN-12, EN-15, EN-16
Jarvis, Cheryl Burke, 91, EN-12
Jayachandran, C., EN-5
Jayasimha, K. R., EN-13
Jaychandran, C., 317

Jay, Joelle, 145
Jeanetta, Beth, 231-232
Jean, Ruey-Jer, 373, 401
Jelinek, Ronald, 317
Jiang, Zhenhui (Jack), EN-8
Job information, sources of, 469
Job search. *See also* Sales careers
  applicant information sources and, 472-474
  follow-up after interview, 484
  gaining interviews in, 475-479
  interviews, 479-484
  personal branding and, 485
  résumé preparation, 474-475
  sources of job information for, 469
Johnsen, Rhona E., EN-10
Johnson, Brandon, 467, EN-16
Johnson, Jeff S., 317, 431, EN-9
Johnson, Michael D., EN-11
Johnston, Wesley J., EN-2
Jolson, Marvin A., EN-10
Jones, Don, 361
Jones, Edward, 149
Jones, Eli, 431, EN-16
Jong, Ad (Addy), 431, EN-6
Joosten, Herm, 369
Joshi, Ashwin W., 462, EN-14
Julkunen, Saara, 27
Just-in-time (JIT) inventory control, 79, 250

Kadic-Maglajlic, Selma, 317, EN-2
Kähkönen, Anni-Kaisa, EN-4
Kahn, Kenneth B., 368
Kalchschmidt, Matteo, EN-4
Kamakura, Wagner, EN-14
Kane, Nick, 227
Kara, Ali, 145, EN-6, EN-12
Karakaya, Fahri, EN-2
Karami, M., EN-2
Karr, Ron, EN-9
Kasabov, Edward, 57
Kashyap, Rajiv, 498
Kaski, Timo, 123
Kato, Junichi, 196
Kaynak, Erdener, EN-6, EN-12
Keinänen, Hanna, 91
Kekec, Pinar, 91
Keller, Jim, 32, 43, 435
Kennedy, Sandra, 422, EN-14
Kershaw, Clayton, 335
Ketchersid, Jeanne, 431
Kevin, Trainor, EN-10
Key accounts, 450
Keyes, Jackson, 306, EN-10
Khedkar, Pratap, 57
Khorsandnejad, Arezoo, EN-13
Kickbacks, 38
Kieler, Ashley, EN-3
Kim, Eugene, 416
Kimla, Nickolaus, 485
Kirchberger, Markus A., EN-9
Kirchoff, Jon F., 369
Kleinaltenkamp, Michael, 255
Kling, Nathan D., EN-16
Knapp, Mark L., 123
Knarr, Cat, 489
Knowledge
  about sales situations, 130-131
  and adaptive selling, 130-132
  company, 130
  creating, 131
  of customer, 130-131
  product, 130
  retrieved from knowledge management system, 131-132
  role in adapting, 140
Knowledge management software, 130-131
Knowledge management technology, 355
Knutson, Andrew, 246
Koehl, Maryse, 123, EN-10
Kõiv, L., EN-6
Kong, Kanga, EN-4
Konrath, Jill, 145
Koosha, Hamidreza, EN-1
Kothandaraman, Prabakar, 498
Kozlenkova, Irina V. G., 91
Králová, Maria, EN-11
Kraus, Rich, 47, EN-3
Krush, Michael T., 57, EN-11, EN-15
KSAs (knowledge, skills, and abilities), 486-489
Kuhnke, Elizabeth, 123
Ku, Hsuan-Hsuan, 317
Kuivalainen, Olli, 91
Kumar, Ajith, 462, EN-13
Kumar, Normalya, EN-9
Kumar, V., 172, 227, 255, EN-1, EN-11
Kurnoga, Natasa, 91
Kyle, Dean, 471

LAARC method, 265
Labana, Harry, EN-9
LaBelle, Eric, 319
Lacoste, Sylvie, EN-7, EN-10
Lafontaine, Francine, 57
LaForge, Raymond W., 413, EN-3
LaFrance, Marianne, EN-5
Lai, Jennifer, EN-7
Lambert, Brian, 462, EN-16
Lampón, Jesus F., 369
Lam, Son K., 401, 431, 498, EN-11
Landry, Timothy D., 285, 317, 401, EN-9
Lane, Nikala, 462
Langlotz, Richard, 489
Laroche, Michel, EN-10, EN-12
Larsen, Trina, 462
Lassar, Walfried, EN-2, EN-12
Lassk, Felicia G., EN-2
Laukkanen, Tommi, EN-6, EN-12
Laws. *See* Legal issues
Lead management system, 166
Lead prioritization software, 181
Lead qualification system, 166
Leads, 148. *See also* Prospects
  ability to pay, 149
  accessibility of, 149
  authority to buy, 149
  criteria for, 150
  eligibility to buy, 150
  generating through social media, 155
  prequalification of, 166
  qualifying, 148
  reasons for needs, 149
  referred, 152
  sources of, 151
Lead users, 354
Leaf, Matt, EN-8
Leapfrog routing, 420
Le Bon, Joël, EN-14, EN-15
Lee, Jay Y., 52
Lee, Jungah, EN-4
Lee, Nick, EN-3
Legal issues. *See also* Ethical behavior
  bribery and, 52
  business defamation, 48
  collusion, 49
  conspiracy, 49
  illegal business practices, 48-51
  interference with competitors, 49
  international, 51-52
  laws influencing ethical behavior of salespeople, 35
  misrepresentation, 46-48
  price discrimination, 49-50
  privacy laws, 50
  reciprocity, 48

restriction on resellers, 49
sales puffery, 46-48
tying agreements, 48-49
Uniform Commercial Code (UCC), 45-46
Legs, nonverbal communication through, 105
Lehnus, Darryl, 392, EN-14
Lehrer, Jessica, 29, 32, 47
Leigh, Thomas W., EN-6
Leimbach, Michael, EN-6
Le Meunier-FitzHugh, Kenneth, 462, EN-15
Lenling, David, 76
Leone, Robert P., 172, EN-1
Lespinet-najib, Véronique, 91
Letters
in response to job postings, 477-479
sales, 163-165
thank-you, 310
Lewin, Jeffrey E., EN-16
Li, Connie, 227
Li, Jia, 498
Li, Shanliang, 369, EN-11
Li, Sze Sze, 227
Liang, Chiung-Ju, EN-11
Liebowitz, Jay, EN-6
Liesch, Peter W., EN-11
Life-cycle costing, 75
Liinamaa, Johanna, 255
Likability, 361-362
Lilien, Gary L., EN-7
Limbu, Yam B., 317, EN-5
Lin, Chung-Kuang, EN-5
Lindgreen, Adam, 91
LinkedIn, 114-115, 122, 132, 155, 156, 180
Lintukangas, Katrina, EN-3
Lists, prospects developed from, 159-160
Liu, Annie H., 91
Liu, Songqi, EN-12
Livesay-Jones, Shelly, 428
Locander, David A., 498, EN-6
Locander, William B., 498, EN-3, EN-15, EN-16
Lockhart, Nathan, 425
Lockheed Martin 148, 149
Lo, Desmond Ho-Fu, 57
Loe, Terry, 257
Lollar, James, EN-6
Lombardoa, Sebastiano, 255
Long-term relationships, 353. *See also* Partnerships; Relationships
Lopez, Carmen, 316
Lopez, Miguel, 195, 225
Lopez, Tara B., EN-12
Lord, Kenneth R., EN-13
Lorimer, S., EN-3
Lost for good, 77
Loudness, 96
Lounsbury, John W., EN-16
Loveland, James M., EN-16
Lowballing, 333-334
Loyalty
attitudinal, 348
behavioral, 348
value of, 81
Lubrication, 51
Lu, Chunyu, 369, EN-11
Lund, Donald J., 57, 91, 369
Luotola, Hanna, 255
Lushin, Paul, EN-14
Luthans, Fred, 431
Luzzini, Davide, 197
Lv, Chen, 369, EN-11
Lymperopoulos, Constantine, EN-13
Lynch, Daniel F., EN-12

Macalincag, Karl, 147
Macdonald, Emma K., 255
Machleit, Karen A., 27, EN-2
Macintosh, Gerrard, EN-12
Madden, John, 205
Madhani, Pankaj M., 498, EN-15
Madrigal, Ken, 78, 381
Mady, Sarah, 285, 317, EN-9
Magyar, Mária, 196
Maintenance, repair, and overhaul (MRO) supplies, 61
Major sale, 209
Makhitha, K. M., 91
Malek, William, 498
Malhotra, Shavin, EN-16
Mallin, Michael L., 431, 498, EN-15
Malloy, Ellen, 456
Malshe, Avinash, 317, 462, EN-5, EN-9, EN-15
Malshe, Avish, EN-15
Mandják, Tibor, 196
Manipulation, ethical selling and, 33
Mani, Sudha, 498
Manolis, Chris, 401, EN-3, EN-15
Manral, Lalit, EN-1
Manrodt, Karl B., EN-11
Mantrala, Murali K, 498
Manufacturers, 60-61
Manufacturers' agents, 13-14
Manufacturing, 438
Maps, 237
Marimuthu, Malliga, 91
Market exchanges
definition of, 348
functional relationships, 349-350
selling goals, 353
solo exchanges, 348-349
Marketing communication, integrated, 7
Marketing department, 158, 439-440
Marr, Bernard, 489
Marriott, J. W., EN-6
Marshall, Fred, EN-4, EN-13
Marshall, Greg W., EN-2
Martin, Craig A., EN-15
Martín-de Castro, Gregorio, EN-6
Martinez, Sabrina, 81
Martin, Jacklyn, EN-2
Martín, Pedro Juan, 145
Martins, Guiherme S., 373, 401
Maryse, K., 123
Masoomeh, Seyedeh, EN-13
Mast, Kenneth, EN-12
May, Neville, EN-14
McAdam, Neil, EN-16
McColl, Rod, EN-8
McCorkle, Denny E., EN-16
McFarland, Richard G., 317, EN-2, EN-17
McGrath, Diane, EN-16
Mclaughlin, Jerry, EN-1
McNabb, Ashley, 345-346
McNew, Seth, EN-4
McNichols, Barry, 55
Media, used to display visuals, 237-240
Medical sales prospecting, 157
Melewar, T. C., 172, EN-7
Mena, Jeannette A., 91
Merchandise markets, 159
Merrill, David, 132, EN-6
Merritt, Joe, 471
Meyer, Bob, 10
Miao, Fred C., 91, EN-13
Michaelidou, Nina, EN-7
Mich, Claudia C., 498
Miguel, Priscila L. S., 373, 401
Millar, Darron, 362
Miller, Robert B., EN-6, EN-8
Miller, Zack, 485
Milne, George R., EN-7

Milovic, Alex, 57, 431, EN-2
Minimum call objective, 185
Minimum position, 324
Minor-point close, 304
Mirroring, 107
Misrepresentation, 46-48
Missaoui, Yosra, 317, EN-10
Missionary salespeople, 13
Mobilizers, 188
Models, as visual selling aid, 235-236
Modified rebuys, 70
Mogre, Riccardo, 91
Moncrief, William C., 145, EN-2
Morales, Jorge, 195, 225
Morgan, Jackie, 366
Morgan, Suzanne, 362
Morgeson III, Forrest V., EN-13
Morrison, Mark, 27
Mortazavi, Sina, EN-5
Moss, Hollye K., 57, EN-15
Mpinganjira, Mercy, 401
Mubarik, Shujaat, 401
Mulki, Jay P., 498, EN-3, EN-6, EN-15, EN-16
Multiattribute model
  explanation of, 82
  implications for salespeople, 85-86
  importance weights and, 83-84
  overall evaluation and, 84
  performance evaluation of characteristics and, 82-83
  supplier selection and, 84-85
  value offered and, 84
Multichannel strategy, 6
Multilevel selling, 454-455
Multiple-sense appeals, 230
Mutual investments, 363
Mutual trust, 358-362
Muzillo, Greg, 405

Naatus, Mary Kate, 498
Narayanan, Venkat, 498
Narayandas, Das, EN-11
Narus, James A., EN-9, EN-10
Nasir, Aslihan, EN-2
Nasri, Wadie, EN-11
Natarajan, Santosh, 290
National account managers (NAMs), 450
Natti, Satu, 401
Naudé, Peter, 27
Need payoff questions, 211-212
Needs
  of buying center individuals, 76-78
  emotional, 73
  for goals, 405-406
  identifying prospect's, 206-214
  objections related to, 261-262
  organizational, 74-76
  rational, 73
  reiterated during sales call, 212
  root cause of, 207
Negative referral, 152
Negotiation
  agenda, 331
  ambush, 329
  buyer's perspective on, 339
  buyers *vs.* sellers, 321
  concessions made during, 336-337
  conflict-handling behavior modes for, 327-329
  definition of, 320
  general guidelines for, 331-332
  information control during, 329
  items/topics open for, 321
  location for, 323
  meeting, 329-338
  nature of, 320-323
  nonnegotiation selling *vs.*, 320-321
  planning for, 323-329
  self-inventory, 322
  setting objectives for, 323-326
  team selection and management for, 326-327
  time allotment for, 323
  traits for successful, 321-323
  win-lose, 320
  win-win, 320
  win-win not yet, 338
Negotiation jujitsu, 336
Nelson, Michael, 189
Nemkova, Ekaterina, 145
Net present value (NPV), 248
NetSuite, 140, 385, 415, 468
Networking, leads found through, 153-155. *See also* Social networking
Neumann-Bódi, Edit, 196
New tasks situations, 68-69
Ngo, Liem Viet, EN-1
Nguyen, Bang, 91, 172, EN-7
Nibbling, 333
Nichols, Larry, 423
Nickell, David, 91
Nijssen, Ed, EN-6
Nijssen, Edwin J., 431
Noble, Stephanie M., 431
Noises, 95
Noncompete clause, 42
Nondisclosure agreement (NDA), 40
Nonnegotiation selling *vs.* negotiation, 320-321
Nonsalespeople, personal selling by, 5-6
Nonverbal communication
  appearance and, 109-111
  arms and, 104
  body angle and, 104
  body language patterns and, 105-106
  distance zones and, 109
  explanation, 103
  face and, 104
  hands and, 105
  legs and, 105
  physical contact and, 108-109
  sending messages with, 106-111
  space/physical contact and, 108-109
Nonverbal cues
  assessing prospects' reactions by, 217-218
  body language patterns, 105-106
Nonverbal probing, 269
Nor Noor, Azila Mohd, 369
North America industry classification system (NAICS) code, 160
Novell, Corinne, 27
Novell, Corrine A., EN-2
Nwamaka A. Anaza, 369
Nyaga, Gilbert N., EN-12

Oakley, Jared, 57, 497, EN-3
Obadia, Claude, 317, EN-2
Objection response methods
  acknowledgment as, 274
  compensation as, 272-273
  direct denial as, 270-271
  indirect denial as, 271-272
  postpone method, 274-275
  probing as, 269
  referral as, 273
  revisit as, 273-274
  third-party-testimony, 273
  with tough customers, 280-281
  using, 275-276
  when commitment is not obtained, 307-310

Objections
anticipation of, 265
buyer's perspectives on, 266
confirming answers to, 276
definition of, 258
evaluation of, 268
five major types of, 261
forestalling known concerns about, 265-266
listening to, 267-268
price, 277-280
probing in order to understand, 269
related to needs, 261-262
related to the price, 263-264
related to the product, 262
related to the source, 262-263
related to the time, 264
selling to group of buyers, 277
truthfulness in dealing with, 268-269
when buyers raise, 258-259
when commitment is not obtained, 307-310
Objectives
negotiation, 323-326
sales call, 182-187
Obligations, 46
O'Cass, Aron, EN-1
O'Donnell, Edward, EN-15
OEM purchasers, 60-61
Offenberger, Brian, 196
Offer, 45
Office scanning, 204
Oghazi, Pejvak, EN-5
Oh, Joon-hee, 57
Öhman, Peter, 369
Oh, Sejo, EN-11
O'Leary, Patrick, 441
Olfati, O., EN-2
Oliver, Tom, 366
Omnichannel buyers, 5
O'Neil, David, EN-9
Open communication
relationship development, 362
sending verbal messages, 98
Open-door policies, 448
Opening, 203
Opening position, 324
Open questions, 208, 209
Opportunity cost, 248-249
Opportunity management, 415
Optimism, 19
Optimistic call objective, 185
Oral agreements, written agreements *vs.*, 46
Orders
explanation of, 45
monitoring processing of, 373-374
trial, 299
Organizational buying decisions
complexity of, 64-65
creeping commitment in, 67-68
importance of understanding, 64
multiattribute model of product evaluation and choice for, 82-86
steps in, 65-67
supplier evaluation and choice and, 73-78
types of, 68-70
Organizational needs and criteria
economic, 74-75
quality criteria, 75
service criteria, 75-76
Organizational support, 363-364
Organizations. *See* Companies
Original equipment manufacturers (OEMs), 60-61
Outbound salespeople, 453
Outlined presentations, 126, 127
Out-suppliers, 70
Ou, Wei-Ming, EN-2

Padin, Carmen, 369, 401
Palley, John, 40, EN-3
Palmatier, Robert W., 91, 196, 255, 401, EN-11, EN-13
Palmer, Roger, 462
Panagopoulos, Nikolaos G., 145
Panchmatia, Milan, 373
Panel interviews, 483
Panzeri, Federico, 498
Paparoidamis, Nicholas G., 462
Paperwork, 422-423
Paradise, Kyle, EN-5
Pardo, Catherine, 462
Park, Jungkun, 57
Park, Soon-Hee, EN-16
Partnering-oriented selling, 31
Partnerships
adaptive selling and, 129
branding and, 485
Building Partnership Model, 20-21
building relationships and, 351
buyer behavior and, 74
commitment and, 294
commitment to mutual gain in, 362
common goals in, 362-363
communication principles and, 116
customer lifetime value and, 116
ethics and, 32-33, 38
mutual trust in, 358-362
negotiations and, 335
objections and, 260
open communication for, 362
organizational support for, 363-364
prospecting and, 157
relational, 350-352
relational *vs.* strategic, 362
sales calls and, 191, 213
sales presentations and, 231
sales teamwork, 436
selling and salespeople, 15
stages of, 372
strategic, 352-353
Partnership stages
awareness, 356
commitment, 357, 384-391
dissolution, 357, 392-395
expansion, 357, 380-384
exploration, 356-357, 372-380
Passive listening, 100
Pass-up method, 274
Paterson, Jeannie Mari, 57
Pavlovich, Tim, 60, 309
Payan, Janice, 369, 401
Payback period, 247-248
Payne, Adrian, EN-1
Pearce, Dennis, 456
Pearson, LeeAnne, 294
Pearson, Leigh Anne, EN-14
Pelham, Alfred, EN-11, EN-12
Peng, Norman, 431
Peredo, Juan Guillermo, 260
Pérez, Lourdes, 369
Performance, 46
Performance analysis, 425
Performance appraisal, 385
Performance evaluation
activity analysis, 424
performance analysis, 425
postcall analysis, 423
productivity analysis, 425-426
Performance feedback, 131
Performance goals, 407-408
Perry, John, EN-5
Personal attire, 109-111
Personal branding, 485

Personal code of ethics, 35-37
Personal contacts, 476
Personal development goals, 408
Personal selling. *See also* Adaptive selling; Selling
definition of, 4
emphasis placed on, *vs.* advertising, 6-7
evolution of, 31
reasons to learn about, 4-6
role of salespeople and, 6-7
Personal space, 108-109
Personal zone, 108
Persuasion
ethical selling and, 33
explanation of, 96
Petersen, J. Andrew, 172
Peterson, Robert, 125, 175
Peterson, Robin T., 317, EN-5
Phelps, Thomas, EN-16
Phone calls. *See* Telephone communication
Photographs, 237
Physical appearance
attire, 109-111
first impressions and, 201
Physical contact, 108-109
Pierce, Lamar, 498
Piercy, Nigel F., 462, EN-15
Pinterest, 114-115
Pioneer selling, 261
Pipeline analysis, 415
Plank, Richard E., 57, 317, EN-2, EN-3, EN-4
Plott, John, EN-14
Plouffe, Christopher R., 317, EN-8
Poaching, 44
Poddar, Amit, 91
Poddar, Prashant, 57
Ponder, Nicole, 369
Pongpatipat, Chatdanai, 285, 317, EN-9
Poon, Patrick, EN-12
Portfolio, 237, 482
Postcall analysis, 423
Postings, employment, 477
Postpone method, 274-275
Postpurchase dissonance, 305
Posture, 108
Poujol, F. Juliet, 123, EN-2, EN-10, EN-13, EN-15, EN-16
Poulis, Athanasios, 317, EN-2
Power, Mike, EN-13
PowerPoint presentations, 238
Powers, Diane, EN-16
Powers, Thomas L., 401
Predictive analytics software, 181
Predmore, Carolyn E., EN-3
Preferred supplier, 384
Preikschas, Michael W., 369
Prendergast, Gerard Paul, 227
Prequalification of leads, 166
Presale-commitments, 289
Presentations. *See* Sales presentations
Prezi, PowerPoint presentations, 238
Price
discrimination, 49-50
objections related to, 263-264
presenting, 293
Price, Betsy, 90
Price, Glenn R., 10, EN-1
Price objections, 277-280
establishing value of the product, 277-279
up-to-date information, 277
using communication tools, 279-280
Price, Shirley, 316
Price, Talyor, 371
Prigmore, Denver, 425
Primary call objective, 185
Prime selling time, 417-418
Prior, Daniel D., 255
Privacy laws, 50
Probing method, 269
in commitment, 302-303
verbal, 218
Problem questions, 210-211
Problem/solution model, 217
Product
demonstrations, 240-242
ensuring proper use of, 374-375
objections related to, 262
Productivity analysis, 425-426
Product knowledge
adaptive selling and, 130
cross-selling and, 385
by salespeople, 18
Product opening, 203
Product specialists, 451-452
Profit margin, 61-62, 249
Profit of sellers *vs.* buyers, 5
Profit quotas, 443
Promoters, 151
Prom, Sharyl, EN-9
Proposals. *See also* Request for proposal (RFP)
presenting, 243-244
request for proposal (RFP), 243
written, 243-244
Prospecting
definition of, 148
importance of, 148
lead qualification system for, 166-167
overcoming reluctance for, 167-168
qualifying the lead, 148
Prospects
assessing reactions of, 217-219
characteristics of good, 148-150
identifying needs of, 206-214
learning information about, prior to sales call, 177-179
obtaining information directly from, 177-178
responding to objections from, 190
waiting for sales call with, 200-201
Prospects, methods and sources for obtaining, 150-151
cold calling, 160-161
company web sites, 156
databases and data mining, 160
endless-chain method, 152-153
expertise, 163
government agencies, 166
inside salespeople, 162-163
lists and directories, 159-160
marketing department, 158
merchandise markets, 159
networking, 153-155
publications, 160, 163
sales letters, 163-165
satisfied customers, 151-152
social media, 155-156
spotters, 161-162
trade fairs, 158
trade shows, 158
webinars and seminars, 159
Pryor, Susie, EN-5
Public zone, 109
Pullins, Ellen Bolman, 123, 498
Purchasing. *See also* Buying centers; Organizational buying decisions
importance of, 14-15
steps in, 65-67
Push money, 49

Qualifying the lead, 148
Quantifying the solution, 244. *See also* Value analysis
Quantity discounts, 290-291

Question opening, 203
Questions
about buyer's needs, 214-219
closed, 208-209
frequently asked, 479
implications, 211
need payoff, 211-212
open, 208-209
problem, 210-211
situation, 210
Quick-response (QR) systems, 79, 250
Quigley, Charles, EN-2
Quinton, Sarah, EN-7
Quota, 443

Rabbani, Masoud, EN-4
Rackham, Neil, 183, 188, 216, EN-8, EN-10
Rad, Fakhreddin F., EN-5
Radicati, Sara, EN-14
Radin, Tara J., EN-3
Rahkolin, Suvi, 401
Rajala, Risto, 197, EN-1, EN-9
Rajh, Edo, 91
Rajh, Sunèana Piri, 91
Rapp, Adam, EN-1, EN-6, EN-10, EN-14
Rapp, Justine M., 57
Rapport, 204-205
Rasmusson, Erika, 469
Rate of change, 389
Raths, David, 456
Rational needs, 73
Rauschnabel, Philipp A., 91
Razzaq, Zohaib, EN-8
Read, Nicholas A. C., 172, EN-9
Reardon, James, EN-16
Receptionists, prospect information from, 181
Reciprocity, 48
Recruitment process, 472-474
Red herring, 336
References, 473
Referral events, 152
Referral method, 273
Referral opening, 203
Referred lead, 152
Rehme, Jakob, 462
Reid, Roger, 132, EN-6
Reilly, Tom, EN-14
Reinartz, Werner, 227, 255
Reinumägi, D., EN-6
Relational management technology, 355
Relational partnerships, 350-352
Relationship development
commitment to mutual gain for, 363
common goals for, 362-363
mutual trust in, 358-362
open communication for, 362
organizational support for, 363-364
Relationship marketing, 347-348
Relationships
building custom marketing messages, 116
built through two-way communication, 94-95
buyer's perspectives on, 361, 373
choosing the right, 354-355
functional, 349-350
goal of building, 258
goals, 362-363
long-term, 353
management of, 355
market exchanges, 348-350
solo exchanges, 348-349
stages in, 356-357
types of, 348-353
win-win, 350
Relationship-specific assets, 363
Repeating information, 100
Repeat orders, generating, 381-383
Rephrasing information, 101
Reports, 422-423
Request for proposal (RFP), 243
Resale price maintenance, 49
Resellers
explanation of, 61-62
restriction on, 49
selling value to, 249-250
Resource allocation
account classification and, 410-414
explanation of, 410
finding profitable customers and, 410
investing in accounts and, 414-415
types of resources for, 410
Response time, 111
Responsiveness
explanation of, 133
indicators of, 134
in social style matrix, 134, 137, 139
Restating information, 101
Restubog, Simon Lloyd D., 431
Résumés
conventional, 474-475
explanation of, 474
functional, 475-476
individually tailored, 492
Return on investment (ROI), 61-62, 247
Return on space, 250
Revenue quotas, 443
Revisit method, 273-274
Reward systems, relationship development and, 364
Reynolds, Matt, 172
RFP. *See* Request for proposal
Richards, Keith A., 431
Richards, Skylyn, 284
Richter, Jiri, EN-11
Rick, Tamaschke, EN-11
Ridnour, Rick E., 125, 462
Rigdon, Edward E., EN-12
Riggle, Robert J., EN-3
Riggs, John F., 57, EN-3, EN-4
Ripken, Susanna, EN-4
Rippé, Cindy B., 27, 145, EN-1
Risk, of loss, 45-46
Risk reduction, 77-78
Rivera, Patricia V., EN-16
Roberts-Lombard, Mornay, 401
Robinson-Patman Act (1934), 48
Rocco, Richard A., EN-6
Rocker, Mike, 423, 424
Rockwood, Mike, EN-9
Rode, Joseph, 317, EN-2
Rödiger, Kai, EN-1
Rodríguez, Rocío, 416
Rogers, D. L., 27
Rohde, Carsten, EN-11
Role ambiguity, 491
Role conflict, 491
Role overload, 491
Role Play cases, 27, 57, 90-91, 122, 144-145, 172, 196, 226-227, 251-252, 285, 316-317, 343, 368, 400-401, 430-431, 461-462, 497
Role stress, 491
Rollins, Minna, 91
Román, Sergio, 145, 416, EN-2
Ronchi, Stefano, 197
Rosenbloom, Bert, 462
Rossi, Carlos A.V., EN-13
Rourke, John, 42
Routine call patterns, 420
Routing, 420
Routing plans, 420-421

Rouziès, Dominique, 462, EN-16
Rowe, William J., 285, 369
Roy, Donald P., EN-14
Roy, Tirthankar, 498
Rüdiger, Klaus, 369
Ruggeri, Golino, EN-4
Ruiz, Eric, EN-17
Ruiz, Salvador, EN-2
Russell-Bennett, Rebekah, 369
Russo, Ivan, 91
Rutherford, Brian N., 57, 91, 369, 401, EN-2, EN-10
Ryals, Lynette J., 462, EN-7
Ryan, Christopher, EN-4

Sabnis, Gaurav, EN-7
Sager, Jeffrey K., EN-16
Salary, 444
Sale
  contract to sell *vs.*, 45
  Uniform Commercial Code, 45
Saleh, Abu, EN-12
Sales acceleration technology, 181
Sales appointments
  objections to setting up, 259
  responses to objections concerning, 190
  telephoning for, 190
Sales asset management systems, 239
Sales call allocation grid, 412-413
Sales calls. *See also* Sales presentations
  appointment for, 188-190
  asking questions, 206-214
  assessing reactions of, 217-219
  building credibility during, 219-221
  buyer's perspective on, 176, 220
  cultivating relationships, 189-190
  elements of, 200
  impression management for, 200-205
  information obtained prior to, 177-179
  information sources for, 180-182
  making an appointment for, 188-190
  objectives for, 182-187
  offering value during, 214-219
  planning for, 176-177, 191-192
  process diagram, 177
  right person for, 188
  right place for, 189
  right time for, 189
  selling to groups and, 221-222
  selling yourself and, 192, 222-223
  SPIN® technique for, 209-212
  with subordinates, 189-190
  telephoning for an appointment, 190
  virtual, 189
Sales careers. *See also* Job search
  college to career transition, 484-486
  developing your KSAs (knowledge, skills, and abilities), 486-489
  dual career path and, 486
  match between salesperson and company for, 467-471
  opportunities in, 466
  recruitment process for, 472-473
  resume preparation, 474-475
  stress management in, 489-492
Sales content management software, 181
Sales department, 440
Sales executives
  compensation and evaluation decisions by, 443-446
  control and quota setting by, 443
  duties of, 441-446
  ethics and, 447-450
  expense budget decisions by, 442
  forecasting by, 441-442
  size and organization of sales force decisions by, 441
Sales force automation (SAF) systems, 11
Sales force-intensive organizations, 6
Sales force, size and organization of, 441
Sales forecasting, 441-442
Sales funnel, 148
Sales jobs. *See also* Job search
  continuum, 16
  creativity level of, 16
  describing, 14-16
  and distribution channel, 13
  examples of, 17
  management opportunities in, 21
Sales letters, 163-165
Sales management
  ethics and, 447-450
  field, 446-447
  sales executive duties, 441-446
Salespeople
  ability to use information technology, 18
  account, 450-451
  as account team managers, 10
  after-sale support by, 67
  aggressive, 298
  analytical skills, 18
  assertive, 299
  attitudes of, 296-297
  behaviors of successful, 265-269
  business defamation by, 48
  as change agent, 388-391
  changing roles of, 42-43
  characteristics of successful, 17-20
  as client relationship managers, 8
  communication skills, 19
  company areas important to, 438-440
  compensation plans for, 444-445
  confidence in, 19
  creativity, 19
  emotional intelligence, 19-20
  ethical behavior of, 18, 33-37
  field, 15, 446-447
  flexibility and agility, 19
  geographic, 450
  importance of knowing people in buying center, 70-72
  inbound, 453
  as information providers, 10-11
  inside, 15
  inside *vs.* outside, 452-453
  integrity, 18
  as made *vs.* born, 20
  missionary, 13
  multiattribute model used by, 85-86
  objections related to, 258
  optimism, 19
  orientation of, 31
  outbound, 453
  as partners, 450-455
  product specialists, 451-452
  profiles of, 3, 29, 59, 93, 125, 147, 175, 199, 229, 257, 287, 319, 345-346, 371-372, 403-404, 433-434, 465-466
  responding to unethical requests, 449-450
  role in a business, 6-7
  roles of, 8-11
  self-motivated, 18

submissive, 298
supply chain logistics/channel manager role of, 10
trade, 13
traits of top, 469
types of, 11-17
understanding oneself, 455-456
versatility of, 139
Sales portals, 180
Sales presentations
addressing needs of buyer in, 233
buyer's perspective on, 246
characteristics of strong, 230-233
customized, 126-127
handouts used for, 242
methods of strengthening, 233-250
objections offered during, 259
outlined, 126, 127
product demonstrations for, 240-242
reducing jitters for, 251
selling yourself and, 251-252
social styles and, 137-138
standard memorized, 126
value analysis for, 244-250
verbal tools for, 233-234
visual tools for, 234-240
written proposals, 243-244
Sales puffery, 46-47
Sales quotas, 443
Sales software, compliance and, 42
Sales team
buyer's perspectives on, 452
inside-outside, 455
multilevel selling, 454-455
overview of, 453-454
Samples, used in sales presentation, 235-236
Sanchez, Diane, EN-8
Sanchez, Lillie, 436
Sanders, T., 197
Sandler, Camille, 74
Saraniemi, Saila, 401
Sarmento, Maria, EN-7
Sasaki, Karen, 291
Satisfied customers, as source for leads, 151-152
Sato, Hidenori, 317
Satornino, Cinthia B., 145
SAVO digital collateral management system, 239
Scheer, Lisa K., 91, EN-11, EN-13
Schelenz, Robyn, 238
Scher, Kimberly, EN-12
Schlesinger, Steve, 294
Schmidt, Eddie, 398
Schmitz, Tobias, 343
Schoenberg, Richard, 196
Schons, Laura, 227
Schreier-Fleming, Maura, EN-5
Schrock, Wyatt A., 431
Schuldt, Barbara A., EN-7
Schultz, Roberta J., 57, EN-3, EN-15
Schumann, David W., EN-10
Schurr, Paul, EN-11
Schwartz, Robert J., EN-3
Schweiger, Bastian, 343
Schwepker, Charles H., 57, 462, EN-1, EN-3, EN-15
Scope of change, 389
Screens, sales calls and, 189
Sebor, Jessica, EN-14
Secondary call objective, 185
Secretaries
prospect information from, 181
responding to objections from, 190
Securities and Exchange Commission, 44
Seeding, 192
Seidman, Dan, EN-8
Seif, Javad, EN-4
Selden, Gary, 257
Selective perception, 218
Self-assessment, of social styles, 137
Self-management process
account classification in, 410-414
explanation of, 405
goal setting in, 405-409
implementing time management strategies in, 415-423
investments in accounts, 414-415
performance evaluation in, 423-426
resource allocation in, 410-415
Self-touching gestures, 105
Selling. *See also* Adaptive selling; Personal selling
automation systems and, 11
backdoor, 40-41
cross-, 384
distribution channels and, 11-14
ethics and, 30-37
evolution of, 31-32
internal, 435-437
multilevel, 454-455
by nonsalespeople, 5-6
rewards in, 20-21
team, 453
Selling analytics, 18
Selling center, 180
Selling deeper, 152
Selling yourself, 22-23, 53, 86, 118, 141, 168-169, 192, 222-223, 251-252, 281, 311, 338-339, 364, 395, 426, 455-456
Selnes, Fred, EN-11
Senra, Karin Borges, EN-5
Serkedakis, Michael, 257
Service demonstration, 240
Service level agreements (SLAs), 38, 76
Services
ensuring proper use of, 374-375
examples of end user, 61
Sexual harassment, 43-44
Sfekas, Andrew, 57
Sha, Denish, EN-11
Shahani-Denning, Comila, 498
Shahzad, Khuram, 373, 401
Shaking hands, 107-108
Shannahan, Kirby L. J., 145
Shannahan, Rachelle J., 145
Shapiro, Daniel, 343
Share of wallet, 414
Sharkur, Deyan, 81
Sharma, Arun, EN-16
Shepherd, C. David, 462, EN-2
Sheridan, Matt, 255
Sherman Antitrust Act (1890), 48
Sherrell, Daniel L., 57
Shervani, Tasadduq A., 317, EN-2
Shih, Chia-Mei, EN-2
Shi, Junqi, EN-16
Shipping costs, 292-293
Shipping department, 439
Siahtiri, Vida, EN-1
Siamagka, Nikoletta-Theofania, EN-7
Signature, customers, 305-306
Significant others, influencing ethical behavior of salespeople, 35
Silence, in conversations, 103
Sillanpää, Elina, 373, 401
Sillanpää, Ilkka, 373, 401
Simmons, Tim, 66, 297, 485
Simões, Cláudia, EN-7
Simon, Judit, 196
Simple cost-benefit analysis, 246
Sinčić Ćorić, D., 91
Singh, Rakesh, 317, EN-10
Singh, Ramendra, 145
Single-order discount, 290-291

Sinha, Prakesh, EN-3
Sinkovics, Rudolf R., 373, 401
Situation questions, 210
Six sigma selling programs, 8
Sjoerdsma, Maarten, EN-4
Skin color/tautness, as facial cue, 104
Skinner, Lauren, EN-12
Skinner, Steven J., 285
Slack, Jennifer, EN-3
Sleep, Stefa, 401
SlideShark, PowerPoint presentations, 238
Sluis, Sarah, EN-1, EN-15
Small talk, 204
SMART, 184, 406
SMART boards, 240
Smilansky, Oren, 172
Smith, Brent, 462
Smith, Dan, 345
Smith, J. Garry, EN-14
Smith, Michael, EN-8
Sneak attack, 329
Snider, Emma, EN-9
Snyder, John Belz, EN-5
Soans, Anup, EN-6
Sobczak, Art, 123
Social media. *See also* Social networking
  in communication, 114-115
  generating leads through, 155-156
  information found in, 180
  resolving objections using, 271
  selling through, 114
Social networking
  knowledge retrieval from, 132
  Twitter, 114-115, 155-156
Social style matrix
  explanation of, 132-133
  identification of customers' social styles and, 136-137
  role of knowledge and, 140
  sales presentations and, 137-138
  social style categories in, 133-136
  social style dimensions in, 133
  versatility and, 139
Social styles
  adjusting, 139
  categories of, 133-136
  customer expectations based on, 138
  dimensions of, 133
  identifying customers', 136-137
  self-assessment of, 137
Social zone, 108
Sodomka, Jim, 167
Software. *See also* Customer relationship management (CRM) software
  contact management, 375
  knowledge management, 131
  for pipeline analysis, 415
Sohi, Ravipreet S., 431
Sojka, Jane Ziegler, 27, EN-2
Solo exchanges, 348-349
Solomon, Denise H., 123
Sooder, Karl, EN-8, EN-9
Souchon, Anne L., 145
Sources, objections related to, 262-263
Space
  personal, 108-109
  return on, 250
Speaking-listening differential, 98
Speakman, James I. F., 462
Special treatment, ethical behavior with customers and, 39-40
Spencer, Addie, 496
Spiffs, 49
Spina, Gianluca, 197
SPIN® technique, 209-212
Spiro, Rosann, 227, 317, EN-6, EN-12
Spotters, 161-162
Sridhar, Shrihari, 498
Srivastava, Prashant, EN-4, EN-13
SRM (Supplier relationship management), 356
Stakhovych, Stanislav, 401
Standard industrial classification (SIC) code, 160
Standing-room-only close, 304
Stanko, Brian B., EN-5
Stanley, Colleen, 27
Starr, Bob, 315
Stassi, Lisa, 373
Statutory law, 44
Steel, Marion, EN-15
Stein, Alex, EN-8
Stein, Dave, 308, EN-10
Stemper, Chase, 121
Steward, Michelle D., 462
Stewart, Michelle, 452
Stock, Ruth Maria, 401, EN-1
Storbacka, Kaj, EN-7
Stories, 97-98
Storytelling, 233-234
Straight commission, 445
Straight-line routing, 420
Straight rebuys, 69-70
Straight salary method, 444
Strandberg, Christer, 369
Strategic account managers (SAMs), 450
Strategic partnerships, 352-353
Stratten, Scott, 172
Strength of position dimension, 412
Stress
  felt, 491-492
  role, 491
  in sales jobs, 489-492
  situational, 490-491
Stress interviews, 483
Stress management, 489-492
Stundza, Tom, EN-5
Style flexing, 133
Submissive salespeople, 298
Subordination, 51
Suchánek, Petr, EN-11
Sujan, Harish, EN-8
Sunder, Sarang, EN-1
Sundqvist, Sanna, EN-3
Superior benefit method, 272
Supplier Added Value Effort (SAVE) program, 385
Supplier relationship management (SRM), 80, 356
Suppliers
  creeping commitment and, 68
  evaluation and choice of, 73-78
  modified rebuys and, 70
  risk reduction and, 77-78
  searching for qualified, 66-67
  selecting, 84-85
  service criteria and, 76
Supplier selection, in multiattribute model, 84-85
Supply chain logistics, 10
Supply chain management (SCM), 79-81
Sussan, Fiona, 27, EN-1
Sustainability, 81
Svensson, Göran, 369, 401
Swani, Kunal, EN-7
Swan, John E., EN-12
Swanson, Mark, 90
Sysalova, Hana, EN-13
Systems integrators, 149
Szalkai, Zsuzsanna, 196

Tagging, 132
Tanner, Emily C., 57, EN-1

Tanner, John F. Jr., 57, 123, 172, 311, 396, EN-1, EN-2, EN-3, EN-4, EN-10, EN-11, EN-13, EN-15, EN-16, EN-17
Target position, 324
Tarkainen, Anssi, EN-3
Tarnoski, Kevin, 342
Taylor, Ben, EN-14
Teague, Paul, EN-14
Team
- negotiation, 326-327
- sales, 453-455

Team selling, 453
Team selling organization, 454
Technical influencer, 72
Technology. *See also* Computers; Internet
- cloud-based negotiating software, 324
- communication via, 111-118
- compliance and sales software, 42
- to create sale territories, 416
- digital marketing, 78
- finding satisfaction, 381
- increasing adaptability by inside salespeople, 140
- micro-bursts of productivity, 355
- objections using social media, 271
- PowerPoint presentations, 238
- pricing solutions, 291
- prospecting through Big Data, 161
- sales acceleration technology, 181
- sales force automation systems, 11
- selling through social media, 114
- tech-powered selling, 206

Telephone communication, 111-112
- managing time by making more, 422

Tenenblat, Leo, EN-16
Tepfenhart, Paul, 414
Terho, Harri, EN-1
Territory management
- buyer's perspective on, 414
- evaluating performance and, 423-426
- goal setting and, 405-409
- resource allocation and, 410-415
- time and, 404

Tescari, Fábio V. C. S., 373, 401
Testimonials, 237
Test results, 237
Text messages, 112-113
Thakkar, Maneesh, 145
Thatcher, Scott, 465-466
Theiss, Jennifer, 123
Third-party-testimony method, 273
Thomas, Stephanie P., EN-11
Thompson, Holly, 55
3-by-3 strategy, 392
Thurasamy, Ramayah, 91
Tickler file, 419
Time
- buyer's perspective on, 414
- negotiation and, 323
- objections related to, 264
- prime selling, 417-418
- strategy for change, 391
- value of, 404

Time-based strategy, 391
Time management
- daily activity planning for, 416-417
- guidelines for, 417-418
- importance of, 415
- making more calls and, 419-422
- for paperwork and reports, 422-423
- planning process for, 418-419
- tips for, 415

Timmons, David, 403
Timonen, Hanna, 123
Title, risk of loss/damage, 45-46
To-do list, 418-419
Tolle, Norman L., EN-16
Toman, Nicholas, EN-7, EN-8
Tomas, G., EN-13
Tombs, Alastair G., 369
Tommi, Laukkanen, EN-6
Toppi, Christopher, 355
Torres, Eduardo, EN-1
Totten, Jeff W., EN-7
Töytäri, Pekka, 197, EN-1, EN-9
Tracy, Brian, 145
Trade fairs, 158
Trade publications, 163
Trade salespeople, 13
Trade secrets, 43
Trade shows, 158
Training
- field sales managers and, 446-447
- relationship development and, 364

Tressler, Andrew D., EN-5
Trial balloon, 336
Trial close, 218, 295-296
Trial offers, 303-304
Trial order, 299
Trimarchi, Michael, EN-11
Trowell, Yusef, 306, EN-10
Trujillo, Derrick, 496
Truong, Yann, EN-8
Trust
- in commitment stage of relationship, 385
- relationships and, 37
- strategic partnerships and, 358

Trust-destroying conflicts, 394
Tsalikis, J., EN-2, EN-12
Tseng, Lu-Ming, 57
Tsoukatos, Evangelos, 91
Tsu-Wei, Yu, 369
Tuleja, Tad, EN-6, EN-8
Tully, Kevin Thomas, 271
Turan, Mehmet, 145
Turcotte, Sally, 90
Turnover (TO), 62, 263
Twain, Mark, 191, 205
24/7 service, 8
Twitter, 114-115, 155-156
Two-way communication process, 94-95. *See also* Communication
Tying agreements, 48-49
Tyler, M., 227

Ueltschy Murfield, Monique L., 145
Ulke, Anne-Kathrin, 227
Unethical requests, 449-450
Uniform Commercial Code (UCC), 45-46
Upgrading, 383
Upselling, 383
Up-to-date pricing information, 277
Urban, Glen L., EN-11
Urbaniak, Anthony J., EN-7, EN-8, EN-9, EN-16
Users, 71
Uzo, Uchenna, EN-10

Valentine, Sean, 57, EN-15
Valenzuela, Leslier, EN-1
Value
- created in sales presentations, 233
- of customers, 346-347
- methods of creating, 6-7
- role of salespeople in creating, 4, 6-7
- selling as creating, 4
- selling to resellers, 249-250
- of time, 404

Value analysis, 76
- cost-benefit analysis and, 246-247

customer value proposition and, 244–246
explanation of, 244
net present value and, 248
opportunity cost and, 248–249
payback period and, 247–248
return on investment (ROI) and, 247
Value proposition. *See* Customer value proposition (CVP)
Valvi, Aikaterini, EN-7
Van Edwards, Vanessa, EN-5
van Knippenberg, Daan, 431
VanMeter, Rebecca, EN-1
van Weele, Arjan J., EN-4
Varela, José A., 57, 497, EN-2, EN-3
Varela-Neira, Concepción, EN-13
Variable call patterns, 420
Vázquez-Casielles, Rodolfo, EN-13
Veeder-Root, Gilbarco, 440, EN-15
Veiga, Ricardo T., EN-13
Vendor analysis, 80
Vendor loyalty, 77
Vendors
outside, 149
supply chain logistics and, 10
trade shows, 158
Venugopali, Pingali, 317, EN-10
Verbal messages, 96–98
Verbal probing, 218
Verbal tools, 233–234
humor, 234
storytelling, 233–234
word pictures, 233–234
Verbeke, Willem, EN-6
Versatility, 139
Vida, Irena, 317, EN-2
Videoconferencing, 189
Vieira, Valter Afonso, EN-5, EN-13
Viljanen, Mika, 255
Virtual sales calls, 189
Visual presenters, 240
Visual tools, 234–240
brochures, 236
catalogs as, 236
charts as, 234–235
graphics as, 234–235
media used to display, 237–240
models, samples, and gifts as, 235–236
photos, illustrations, ads, and maps as, 237
testimonials as, 237
test results as, 237
Vlogs, 155
Voice characteristics, 96–97
Voice mail, 111–112
Voordijk, Hans, 401

Wagner, Janet, 255
Wagner, Marvin, 413
Wahlberg, Olof, 369
Wakefield, Kirk, 57, EN-1
Wakefield, Michael, 27
Walker, Beth A., 462
Walker, Gail, 383
Walsh, Gianfranco, 91
Walton, David, 27
Wang, Guocai, 369, EN-11
Wang, Mo, EN-12
Wang, Wen-Hung, EN-11
Wang, Xifeng, 369, EN-11
Wang, Yichuan, 145
Warranty, 46
Watsabaugh, Doug, 227
Watson IV, George F., 255
Weaver, Trent, 482
Webcasting, 189
Webinars (online seminars), 159
Weilbaker, Dan C., 125, 462
Weinberg, Frankie J., 498, EN-6
Weisfeld-Spolter, Suri, 27, 145, EN-1
Wells, Anna, EN-15
Wentworth, Mary, 375
West, Vicki, 199, 385
West, V. L., EN-3
Whalen, D. Joel, EN-6
Whipple, Judith M., EN-12
White, Lisa, EN-16
White, Steve, 366
Wick, Shawna, 400
Widing, Robert E., 145, EN-8
Widmier, Scott, 57, EN-3, EN-4
Wieseke, Jan, 317
Williams, David, 27
Wilson, Damien, EN-7
Wilson, Hugh N., 255, 462
Win-lose negotiating, 320
browbeating, 335–336
budget limitation tactic, 334
emotional outburst tactic, 334
good-guy-bad-guy routine, 332–333
lowballing, 333–334
red herring, 336
strategies, 332
trial balloon, 336
Win-win negotiating, 320
Win-win not yet negotiating, 338
Win-win relationships, 350
Wirtz, Bernd W., 369, EN-4, EN-5, EN-12
Wise, Jorge, EN-13
Wisker, Zazli Lily, 317, EN-2
Wohlers, Laura, 367
Wolf, Johan, 120
Wong, Lou, 460
Wong, Y. H., EN-11
Word choice, 96
Word-of-mouth information, 77
Word pictures, 97–98, 233–234
World Wide Web. *See* Internet
Worm, Loek, EN-6
Wotruba, Thomas, EN-2
Wouters, Marc, EN-9, EN-10
Wright, Aliah, 452, 471
Written agreements, oral agreements *vs.,* 46
Written proposals, 243–244
Wu, Lei-Yu, EN-11, EN-13
Wu, Yung-De, EN-11

Xu, Xiaowei, EN-5

Yang, Zhiguo, 145
Yeboah Banin, Abena, 145
Yi, Cheng, EN-8
Yi-Ming, Tai, EN-11
Yin, Cheng-Yue, EN-12
Young, Clifford E., 413
Young, Kenneth, 307
Yousaf, Salman, EN-11
Yurova, Yuliya, 27, EN-1
Yu, Ti, EN-16
Yu, Xiaoyu, 172, EN-7
Yu, Yang, 91

Zablah, Alex, EN-10
Zacharias, Nicolas A., EN-1
Zaefarian, Ghasem, EN-5
Zank, G. M., EN-3
Zappulla, Justin, 227
Zboja, James J., 317, EN-13
Zeller, Thomas L., EN-5
Zhang, Annie Liqin, 227
Zhang, Jonathan Z., 255
Zhan, Yujie, EN-16
Zide, Julie, 498
Ziglar, Zig, 147
Zimmerman, R. J., 107, EN-5
Zoltners, Andres, EN-3
Zoning, 420–421